Intellectual Property in Government Contracts
Fifth Edition

Volume 1
Intellectual Property Rights

Ralph C. Nash, Jr.
Leonard Rawicz

The George Washington University
WASHINGTON DC

LAW SCHOOL

CCH INCORPORATED
Chicago

CONTENTS

CHAPTER 1

INTELLECTUAL PROPERTY RIGHTS

I. INTRODUCTION

A. Scope of Text

The Government utilizes the contract process to purchase a wide variety of goods and services. These include existing commercial products and services, the design, development, and manufacture of goods and related services necessary to meet specific Government needs. Additionally, the Government provides financial assistance through grants and cooperative agreements to support research and development by private and public entities, and conducts and collaborates in research and development activities with private sponsors at Government facilities. Through this large expenditure of funds, there is substantial contact with intellectual property.

This material principally deals with the relationship between intellectual property concepts of patent, trade secrets, and copyrights and the Government's procurement and financial assistance processes. It also covers some of the intellectual property aspects of Cooperative Research and Development Agreements (CRADAs) under the Stevenson-Wydler Act at 15 U.S.C. § 3110a et seq. It does not, however, cover the control of intellectual property under the export and security laws or the issuance of secrecy orders under the authority of 35 U.S.C. §§ 181-183, although some cases related to the calculation of compensation for the use of inventions covered by secrecy orders are discussed. Under this statutory authority the Government may delay the processing and disclosure of a patent application, although the Government may itself use and reimburse the inventor for such use.

Although the Government does have some interest in trademarks, as some agencies file and obtain trademark registration, the subject of trademarks is not covered. For a general review of this subject with respect to the Government, see Garret, "Government Trademarks, 20 Idea," J. of Law & Tech. 335-354 (1979).

B. Federal Law

Of the three broadly recognized techniques for dealing with intellectual property, only patents and copyrights stem from the exercise of constitutional power by Congress. Trade secret protection is based on state statutes and the application of common law principles by state courts.

Article I, Section 8, cl. 8. of the Constitution provides that:

> The Congress shall have power ... to promote the Progress of Science and useful Arts, by securing for limited Times to Authors and Inventors the exclusive Rights to their respective Writings and Discoveries.

Under this authority, which has been described as broad authority to legislate, *Diamond v. Chakrabarty*, 447 U.S. 303, 206 U.S.P.Q. 193 (1980), Congress has enacted the Patent Laws, title 35 of the United States Code and the Copyright Laws, title 17 of the United States Code.

1. State Law

The states protect intellectual property under a variety of legal regimes including tort, commercial, and criminal laws. Where the federal law of patents or copyrights apply, state law is generally preempted. The principal protection for intellectual property under state law is for trade secrets under a state's contract law or tort law and in the application of its criminal laws.

2. Trade Secret Law

In the early 1970s, the Supreme Court considered whether the Constitution and patent laws preempted state laws that protected against disclosure or use of trade secrets. In *Kewanee Oil Co. v. Bicron Corp.*, 416 U.S. 470, 181 U.S.P.Q. 673 (1974), the Supreme Court reasoned that the federal patent law did not preempt state trade secret law. The Court concluded that trade secret protection to even clearly patentable inventions does not conflict with the patent policy of disclosure and is not preempted by federal patent law. The Court stated at 493:

> Trade secret law and patent law have coexisted in this country for over one hundred years. Each has its particular role to play, and the operation of one does not take away from the other. Trade secret law encourages the development and exploitation of those items of lesser or different invention than might be accorded protection under the patent laws, but which items still have an important part to play in the technological and scientific advancement of the Nation. Trade secret law promotes the sharing of knowledge, and the efficient operation of industry; it permits the individual inventor to reap the rewards of his labor by contracting with a company large enough to develop and exploit it. Congress, by its silence over these many years, has seen the wisdom of allowing the States to enforce trade secret protection. Until Congress takes affirmative action to the contrary, States should be free to grant protection to trade secrets.

3. Patent Law

In *Bonita Boats, Inc. v. Thunder Craft Boats, Inc.*, 489 U.S. 141, 9 U.S.P.Q. 2d 1847 (1989), the Supreme Court struck down a Florida law that prohibited the use of the process by which boat hulls are made by casting a competitive mold. The Court held that federal patent laws were so pervasive as to make a reasonable inference that Congress left no room for the states to supplement it; the patent laws preempted states from offering substantial protections to utilitarian designs ideas that the patent laws protected.

4. Copyright Law

In *Goldstein v. California,* 412 U.S. 546, 178 U.S.P.Q. 129 (1973), the Supreme Court held that the constitutional grant of power to Congress in the copyright area was not exclusive and that the states were not forbidden from protecting authors if Congress had not preempted the area. However, the federal copyright law was subsequently amended and now contains an explicit statement with regard to its preemption of state laws. 17 U.S.C. § 301 provides for a single federal copyright system for the dual copyright system previously existing in state and federal laws by abolishing the state common law copyright system and preempting any rights, legal or equitable, under state statutes or common law that are equivalent to exclusive rights of the copyright under the federal statute, i.e., to the extent that the exclusive rights are specified by section 106 of title 17, if such works are within the subject matter categories covered by sections 102 and 103 thereof.

II. PATENTS

A. Title 35, United States Code

A patent is a right granted to an inventor by the Government after examination of the patent application to determine whether the invention meets the statutory requirements and the application, the procedural requirements. Title 35 of the U.S. Code created the U. S. Patent and Trademark Office (PTO) in the Department of Commerce, headed by a Commissioner, and establishes the procedure for applying for patents, examining applications and issuing patents. The patent laws provide for remedies including injunctions and damages in the event a patent is infringed.

The basic premise of patent law has been described in two ways: (1) contract theory, and (2) incentives theory.

1. Contract Theory

The patent laws have been described in terms of contract between the inventor and the Government, i.e., the inventor is granted, for a limited term, the right to exclude others from making, using, or selling his invention in consideration for disclosing the invention to the public, Stedman, "Invention and Public Policy," 12 Law & Contemp. Prob. 649, 656 (1947); *John Zink Co. v. National Airoil Burner Co.,* 613 F.2d 547, 205 U.S.P.Q. 494 (5th Cir. 1980).

2. Incentives Theory

The patent laws also have been described in terms of incentives to encourage inventive research, *Diamond v. Chakrabarty,* 447 U.S. 303, 206 U.S.P.Q. 193 (1980) at 307:

> The patent law promote [scientific] progress by offering inventors exclusive rights for a limited period as an incentive for their inventiveness and research efforts. *Kewanee Oil Co. v. Bicron*

Corp., 416 U.S. 470, 480-481, 18t U.S.P.Q. 673, 678 (1974); *Universal Oil Co., v. Globe Co.*, 322 U.S. 471, 484, 61 U.S.P.Q. 382, 388 (1944). The authority of Congress is exercised in the hope that "[t]he productive effort thereby fostered will have a positive effect on society through the introduction of new products and processes of manufacture into the economy, and the emanations by way of increased employment and better lives for our citizens." *Kewanee, supra, at* 480, 181 U.S.P.Q. at 678.

B. Utility Patents

1. Types of Patents

There are three types of patents:

1. Design patents for new, original and ornamental designs for articles of manufacture as covered by 35 U.S.C. § 171-173;

2. Plant patents for asexually reproduced new variety of plants, including cultivated sports, mutants, hybrids, and newly found seedlings other than a tuber propagated plant or a plant found in an uncultivated state, as covered by 35 U.S.C. §§ 161-163 and for sexually reproduced seeds under the Plant Variety Protection Act (7 U.S.C. § 2321 et seq.); and

3. Utility patents as described in section 101 of title 35 of the U.S. Code.

2. Subject Matter/Utility Patents

a. Patentable Subject Matter

35 U.S.C. § 101 describes the subject matter of utility patents as follows:

Whoever invents or discovers any new and useful process, machine, manufacture, or composition of matter, or any new and useful improvement thereof, may obtain a patent therefor, subject to the conditions and requirements of this title.

The term "process," used in section 101, is defined in section 100(b) as follows:

The term "process" means process, art or method, and includes a new use of a known process machine, manufacture, composition of matter, or material.

Section 101 was interpreted by the Supreme Court in *Diamond v. Chakrabarty*, 447 U.S. 303, 206 U.S.P.Q. 193 (1980) as covering "[E]verything under the sun made by man." The Court in finding that microorganisms were a "manufacture" or "composition of matter," held that "in choosing such expansive terms as 'manufacture' and 'composition of matter' modified by comprehensive 'any,' Congress plainly contemplated that the patent laws would be given wide scope."

b. Non-Patentable Subject Matter

While not defined in title 35 of the U.S. Code, the courts have held that mathematical algorithms, mathematical equations, perpetual motion machines, and methods of doing business are not proper subject matter for patents. In *Diamond v. Chakrabarty*, 447 U.S. 303, 206 U.S.P.Q. 193 (1980), the Supreme Court stated at 309:

> This is not to suggest that § 101 has no limits or that it embraces every discovery. The laws of nature, physical phenomena, and abstract ideas have been held not patentable. *See Parker v. Flook*, 437 U.S. 584, 198 U.S.P.Q. 193 (1978); *Gottschalk v. Benson*, 409 U.S. 63, 67, 175 U.S.P.Q. 673, 674-675 (1973); *Fund Brothers Seed Co. v. Kalo Inoculant Co.*, 333 U.S. 127, 130, 76 U.S.P.Q. 280, 281 (1948); *O'Reilly v. Morse*, 15 How. 62, 112-121 (1854); *Le Roy v. Tatham*, 14 How. 156, 175 (1853). Thus, a new mineral discovered in the earth or a new plant found in the wild is not patentable subject matter. Likewise, Einstein could not patent his celebrated law that E =MC; or could Newton have patented the law of gravity. Such discoveries are "manifestations of ... nature, free to all men and reserved exclusively to none." *Fund, supra, at* 130, 76 U.S.P.Q. at 281.

The Supreme Court further distinguished between a patentable process and unpatentable formulas or ideas in several computer program cases. Previously, the Court in *Gottschalk v. Benson*, 409 U.S. 63, 175 U.S.P.Q. 673 (1972) and *Parker v. Flook*, 437 U.S. 584, 198 U.S.P.Q. 193 (1978) held that a program-implemented algorithm was not patentable subject matter within 35 U.S.C. § 101. Subsequently, the Court, by a one vote majority, found that a firmware invention may be patentable, *Diamond v. Diehr*, 450 U.S. 175, 209 U.S.P.Q. 1 (1981) and similarly, in *Diamond v. Bradley*, 450 U.S. 381, 209 U.S.P.Q. 97 (1981), affirmed a C.C.P.A. decision that held that CPU firmware for controlling the CPU in multi-program mode was patentable. Firmware is a microprogram resident in the computer's control memory, or microprograms for multifarious uses so long as the physical mode of the program causes a particular sequence of computer operations to take place, see Moskowitz, "The Patentability of Software Related Inventions After Diehr and Bradley," 63 J. Pat. Off. Soc'y 222 (1981).

In *Diehr* and *Bradley*, the Supreme Court found that the computer program related inventions were within the subject matter categories of 35 U.S.C. § 101 as processes. The invention in *Diehr* was for a computer-implemented method of operating presses to mold and cure rubber. The process comprised the steps of providing a computer with a database for presses, which included parameters of a well-known equation, constantly obtaining the temperature of the mold, calculating the reaction time and opening the presses based on the calculated time and the elapsed time. The Court distinguished *Flook* in that in *Diehr* the applicant did not seek to patent a mathematical formula, but sought to patent a process to cure synthetic rubber, which employed a mathematical equation. Thus, the relevant inquiry appears to be whether the patent sought is simply an abstract mathematical discovery, or instead contains a mathematical formula within a patentable process or structure.

The federal circuit, in a line of cases beginning with *In re Alappat*, 33 F.3d 1526, 31 U.S.P.Q.2d 1545 (Fed. Cir. 1994), has held that claims directed toward a specific machine that used a digital computer program that produced the useful, concrete, and tangible result was patentable subject matter. In *State Street Bank & Trust Co. v. Signature Fin. Group, Inc.*, 149 F.3d 1368, 47 U.S.P.Q. 2d 1596 (Fed. Cir. 1998), *cert. denied*, 119 S. Ct. 851 (1999), the federal circuit considered whether a patent directed to a data processing system for implementing an investment structure for use as an administrator and accounting agent for mutual funds was patentable subject matter. The court held that "the transformation of data, representing discrete dollar amounts, by a machine through a series of mathematical calculations into a final share price, constitutes a practical application of a mathematical algorithm, formula, or calculation, because it produces a useful, concrete and tangible result . . . is patentable subject matter."

More recently, the federal circuit considered a process claim that included a "mathematical algorithm." The district court held the claim to be unpatentable as it fell within the judicially created "mathematical algorithm" exception to patentable subject matter, *AT&T Corp., v. Excel Communications, Inc.*, Federal Circuit 98-1338, April 14, 1999. The federal circuit in overruling the district court stated:

> Since the process of manipulation of numbers is a fundamental part of computer technology, we have had to reexamine the rules that govern the patentability of such technology. The sea-changes in both law and technology stand as a testament to the ability of law to adapt to new and innovative, concepts, while remaining true to basic principles. In an earlier era, the PTO published guidelines essentially rejecting the notion that computer programs were patentable. As the technology progressed, our predecessor court disagreed, and, overturning some of the earlier limiting principles regarding 101, announced more expansive principles formulated with computer technology in mind. In our recent decision in *State Street*, this court discarded the so-called "business method" exception and reassessed the "mathematical algorithm" exception, *see* 149 F.3d at 1373-77, 47 U.S.P.Q. 2d at 1600-04, both judicially-created "exceptions" to the statutory categories of 101. As this brief review suggests, this court (and its predecessor) has struggled to make our understanding of the scope of 101 responsive to the needs of the modem world. . .

As previously noted, we most recently addressed the "mathematical algorithm" exception in *State Street. See* 149 F.3d at 1373-75, 47 U.S.P.Q. 2d at 1600-02. In *State Street*, this court, following the Supreme Court's guidance in *Diehr*, concluded that

"[u]npatentable mathematical algorithms are identifiable by showing they are merely abstract ideas constituting disembodied concepts or truths that are not 'useful' . . . [T]o be patentable an algorithm must be applied in a 'useful' way." *Id.* at 1373, 47 U.S.P.Q. 2d at 1601. In that case, the claimed data processing system for implementing a financial management structure satisfied the 101 inquiry because it constituted a "practical application of a mathematical algorithm... [by] produc[ing] 'a useful, concrete and tangible result.' " *Id.* at 1373, 47 U.S.P.Q. 2d at 1601.

The *State Street* formulation, that a mathematical algorithm may be an integral part of patentable subject matter such as a machine or process if the claimed invention as a whole is applied in a "useful" manner, follows the approach taken by this court en banc in *In re Alappat*, 33 F.3d 1526, 31 U.S.P.Q. 2d 1545 (Fed. Cir. 1994). In *Alappat*, we set out our understanding of the Supreme Court's limitations on the patentability of mathematical subject matter and concluded that:

[The Court] never intended to create an overly broad, fourth category of [mathematical] subject matter excluded from 101. Rather, at the core of the Court's analysis... lies an attempt by the Court to explain a rather straightforward concept, namely, that certain types of mathematical subject matter, standing alone, represent nothing more than abstract ideas until reduced to some type of practical application, and thus that subject matter is not, in and of itself, entitled to patent protection. *Id.* at 1543, 31 U.S.P.Q. 2d at 1556-57 (emphasis added) . . .

. . . Whether stated implicitly or explicitly, we consider the scope of 101 to be the same regardless of the form, machine or process, in which a particular claim is drafted.

See Ogden, "Patentability of Algorithm After Sate Street Bank: The Death of the Physical Requirement," 83 J. Pat. Off. Soc'y 491, July 2001. The net effect is that the federal circuit court no longer will rely on physicality a means of determining whether an algorithm is patentable subject matter. The question will be the traditional patent issue of utility, novelty and unobviousness.

3. *Conditions for Patentability*

a. *Anticipation*

35 U.S.C. § 102 sets forth the basic conditions for patentability:

A person shall be entitled to a patent unless—

(a) the invention was known or used by others in this country, or patented or described in a printed publication in this or a foreign country, before the invention thereof by the applicant for patent, or

(b) the invention was patented or described in a printed publication in this or a foreign country or in a public use or on sale in this country, more than one year prior to the date of the application for patent in the United States, or

(c) he has abandoned the invention, or

(d) the invention was first patented or caused to be patented, or was the subject of an inventor's certificate, by the applicant or his legal representatives or assigns in a foreign country prior to the date of the application for patent in this country on an application for patent or inventor's certificate filed more than twelve months before the filing of the application in the United States, or

(e) the invention was described in a patent granted on an application for patent by another filed in the United States before the invention thereof by the applicant for patent. . . , or

(f) he did not himself invent the subject matter sought to be patented, or

(g) before the applicant's invention thereof the invention was made in this country by another who had not abandoned, suppressed, or concealed it. In determining priority of invention there shall be considered not only the respective dates of conception and reduction to practice of the invention, but also the reasonable diligence of one who was first to conceive and last to reduce to practice, from a time prior to conception by the other.

Under 35 U.S.C. § 102, an invention which is "anticipated" by a prior reference ("prior art") will lack novelty and be unpatentable. Generally, §102(a), § 102(b), and § 102(g) are the relevant sections that describe such patent-defeating "prior art." When a reference is examined, in order for it to have "anticipated" the claimed invention, each and every limitation of the claim must be disclosed in the prior art, *W.L. Gore & Assoc. Inc. v. Garlock, Inc.*, 721 F.2d 1540, 220 U.S.P.Q. 303 (Fed. Cir. 1983), *cert. denied*, 469 U.S. 851 (1984). Further, at least with respect to prior art references arising from a third party, the reference must enable those skilled in the art to make and use the disclosed reference.

b. Prior Publications

Sections 102(a) and 102(b) tend to be used most often in invalidity disputes involving questions of novelty. Both sections allow for printed publications, including patents, to be used for prior art purposes, whether printed in the United States or a foreign country. Generally, a reference will be a "printed publication" when workers skilled in the relevant art are able to gain access to it. Even a single copy of a doctoral thesis in a college library will be sufficient so long as the thesis is meaningfully indexed, *In re Hall*, 781 F.2d 897, 228 U.S.P.Q. 453 (Fed. Cir. 1986). In contrast, see *In re Cronyn*, 890 F.2d 1158, 13 U.S.P.Q.2d 1070 (Fed. Cir. 1989), where the court noted that a thesis shelved in a chemistry library and indexed only according to the author's last name was not "meaningfully" indexed due to the inability to access according to subject matter. As such, reports filed with the Government and available to the public are printed publications for novelty purposes when released. Note that reports filed with a Government agency that are not available under the Freedom of Information Act (FOIA) or through a library will not be considered sufficiently accessible to the public, *Imi-Tech Corp. v. Gagliani*, 691 F. Supp. 214, 6 U.S.P.Q.2d 1241 (S.D. Cal. 1986). See also *Aluminum Co. of Am. v. Reynolds Metals Co.*, 14 U.S.P.Q.2d 1170 (N.D. Ill. 1989), where progress reports given to the Navy and issued under a Government research contract to 33 interested parties did not act as prior art. In *Reynolds*, the court found that there was an implied limitation on access due to the fact that both the Government and the interested parties treated the report as confidential.

In *Pfund v. United States*, 40 Fed. Cl. 313 (1998), the court considered whether a report abstracted in the Department of Commerce publication, *U.S. Government Research Abstracts*, was a section 102(a) "printed publication." The court held that—

> a document is considered a printed publication as of the date on which the document became sufficiently accessible to the public interested in the art. *Constant v. Advanced Micro-Devices, Inc.*, 848 F.2d 1560 (Fed. Cir. 1988); *Carella v. Starlight Archery and Pro Line Co.*, 804 F.2d 135 (Fed. Cir. 1986). If a document became publicly accessible more than one year prior to the filing date of a patent application, then the document constitutes prior art under Section 102(b) regardless of when the patentee conceived of the invention. Where, however, the document became publicly accessible within one year of the filing date of the patent application, the docu-

ment constitutes prior art only if the document was published before the date of the invention. *Mahurkar v. C.R. Bard, Inc.*, 79 F.3d 1572 (Fed. Cir. 1996).

The *U.S. Government Research Abstracts* in which the report in question was listed stated:

> The reports listed in this publication, unless otherwise noted, are available from the Office of Technical Services, U.S. Department of Commerce, at the prices indicated.

> * * *

> This publication is issued twice a month to announce new material available through the Office of Technical Services, which sells copies of Government reports at the cost of reproduction and handling. For additional information and ordering instructions, see inside of front cover.

The inside of the front cover states that the reports listed therein have been "released" by various Government agencies and "may be ordered through any Department of Commerce Field Office." The court held that the report was a printed publication as of the date of the publication of the abstract notwithstanding some minor errors is identifying the author and the number of pages in the report.

In *Pfund* the patentee was a former Government patent attorney, who had prepared a handwritten concept paper on May 3, 1962 of his invention, then prepared and filed a patent application on July 2, 1962. One of the Government's prior art references was a printed publication dated June 5, 1962. The court noted that the date of an invention is presumptively the filing date of the patent application thereon, i.e., a constructive reduction practice. Since this printed publication was prior to the filing date it is a prior art reference unless the inventor establishes an earlier date of invention, 35 U.S.C. § 102(g). If the patentee did not reduce his invention to practice, the patentee is entitled to demonstrate that his invention was prior to the printed publication "by showing (1) conception of the invention prior to the publication date and (2) the exercise of reasonable diligence toward filing his application from a date prior to the publication date up through the filing of the patent application." Here the patentee established at the trial that he conceived the invention before June 5, 1962 and that he was reasonably due diligent between the dates of his conception paper to the filing of the application within a few months.

In *E.I. DuPont De Nemours v. Cetus* (D.C. N.Cal. 1990), 1990 LEXIS 18382, the court considered whether a disclosure in a NSF grant application was a statutory bar under Section 102(b). The district court held that a printed publication is a publication that is sufficiently accessible to the members of the public who are interested in the art through the exercise of reasonable due diligence and that the grant application was so accessible.

Sections 102(a) and 102(b) also allow for a patent-defeating effect to be given when the invention is used publicly in the U.S. Although section 102(a) does not specify that the use must be "public," this limitation has been read into it. As long as the use is not maintained in secret, it will normally be deemed to be "public." There are a few major differences between these two sections. First, section 102(a) does not act to defeat the applicant's own patent when it is his or her own publication or public use at issue. Only section 102(b) can be used when the prior art being used is the applicant's own reference. Further, section 102(b) operates as a statutory bar to obtaining a patent only when the prior art was in existence more than one year prior to the patent application date. Section 102(a) by contrast is keyed to the date of the invention. Thus, although the date of the application is presumed to be the date of invention, if another's publication is printed the day before the application, the applicant can overcome the reference by proving that the invention occurred before the reference. Section 102(b) on the other hand is keyed to the application date and cannot be overcome by demonstrating priority of invention.

c. On Sale

In *Pfaff v. Wells Elecs., Inc.*, 119 S. Ct. 304 (1998), the Supreme Court determined the applicable test for determining an "on-sale" bar under 35 U.S.C. § 102(b). Pfaff had filed an application for a patent for a computer chip socket on April 19, 1982 and for purposes of the on-sale bar any prohibited activity prior to April 19, 1981 would defeat the Pfaff patent. Pfaff commenced work on the socket in November 1980, prepared detailed engineering drawings and sent those drawings to a manufacturer in February or March 1981. Prior to March 17, 1981, Pfaff showed a sketch of his concept to representatives of Texas Instruments. On April 8, 1981, Texas Instruments provided Pfaff with a written conformation of a previously placed oral purchase order for 30,100 sockets for a total price of $91,155. Pfaff did not fill the order until July 1981 and did not make and test a prototype of the socket before offering to sell it in commercial quantities. Pfaff first reduced his invention to practice in the summer of 1981. The socket achieved substantial commercial success before Patent No. 4,491,377 issued to Pfaff on January 1, 1985.

The Supreme Court held that the primary meaning of term "invention" in the Patent Act refers to the inventor's conception rather than to a physical embodiment of that idea and that it was well settled that an invention may be patented before it is reduced to practice. Pfaff could have obtained a patent when he accepted Texas Instruments' order for at that time he had a description and drawings of "sufficient clearness and precision to enable those skilled in the matter" to produce the device. The court held that the "on-sale bar" applies when two conditions are satisfied before the critical date: first, the product must be the subject of a commercial offer for sale and second, the invention must be ready for patenting. Here, the acceptance of the purchase order prior to April 8, 1981, is the offer and there was no question that the sale was commercial. As to the second condition, it may be satisfied in at least two ways, one by proof of a reduction to practice of the invention before the critical date; or by proof that prior to the critical date the inventor had prepared drawings or other descriptions of the invention that were sufficiently specific to enable a person skilled in the art to practice the invention. This condition was satisfied because the drawings sent to the manufacturer before the critical date fully disclosed the invention.

In summary, under *Pfaff* there is an "on-sale" bar under § 102(b) when an invention is: (1) the subject of a commercial offer for sale before the critical date; and (2) ready for patenting before the critical date, *Pfaff*, 525 U.S. at 67, 48 U.S.P.Q.2d at 1646-47.

d. Ready for Patenting

The federal circuit has considered what does "ready for patenting" mean if the invention has not been reduced to practice for an "on-sale" bar under § 102(b). In *Robotic Vision Sys., Inc. v. View Eng'g, Inc.*, 249 F.3d 1307, (Fed. Cir. 2001), at the time of the offer, a computer program required for the invention was not yet written. Was this invention "complete" at the time of the sale before the program was written? The court held that it was completed since the disclosure concerning this program was sufficiently specific at the time of the sale to understand the invention and write the program. The court stated:

> We agree with View that the claimed invention, including the necessary software for implementing the full-tray scanning method, was ready for patenting prior to the critical date. Sometime between March and April of 1991, William Yonescu, a co-inventor of the full-tray scanning method, explained the invention to Daniel Briceno of Robotic and asked him to write the software for full-tray scanning. *Robotic III* at 6. This explanation was sufficiently specific for Briceno to understand the invention and to write the software needed to implement the method. *Id.* Regardless whether or not the software was reduced to practice prior to the critical date, it is undisputed that Briceno ultimately completed the software program pursuant to Yonescu's description of the invention. In *Pfaff*, the Supreme Court, based on the facts of that case, referred to "drawings or other descriptions" as proof that an invention is complete, and hence ready for patenting. In this case, the proof was disclosure to Briceno. Accordingly, because Yonescu's disclosure was sufficiently specific to enable Briceno, a person skilled in the art, to practice the invention, the district court did not err in concluding that the invention was ready for patenting before the critical date.

* * *

. . . . Robotic also argues that the court erred in finding that an "internal" disclosure to a co-worker or subordinate employee "triggered the on-sale bar." Robotic contends that such a result would lead to the logical conclusion that an invention is ready for patenting at the time of conception, thereby obviating the need for a two-prong test for the on-sale bar. We disagree. First, the on-sale bar in this case was not triggered solely by an internal disclosure; rather it was triggered by a prior commercial offer for sale *and* a subsequent enabling disclosure that demonstrated that the invention was ready for patenting prior to the critical date. As we have previously explained, "[c]ompletion of the invention prior to the critical date, pursuant to an offer to sell that invention, would validate what had been theretofore an inchoate, but not yet established bar." *Robotic II* at 1168. Thus, without a commercial offer for sale, the timing of which is entirely within the control of the patentee, *Pfaff*, 525 U.S. at 67, 48 USPQ2d at 1646, an internal disclosure by itself would not satisfy the two-part test for an on-sale bar."

III. COMMERCIAL SALE

In *Group One, Ltd. v. Hallmark Cards, Inc.*, 59 U.S.P.Q.2d 1121 (Fed. Cir. 2001), the federal circuit considered what type of "commercial offer" was necessary for the on-sale bar of § 102(b). The patentee in *Group One* had a number of communications and a meeting with Hallmark Cards regarding their interest in his new machine to curl and shred ribbons. The patentee stated to Hallmark Cards that "[W]e could provide the machine and/or the technology and work on a license/royalty basis." The federal circuit noted that before the *Pfaff* decision by the Supreme Court it had held in *RCA Corp. v. Data Gen. Corp.*, 887 F.2d 1056, 12 U.S.P.Q.2d 1449 (Fed. Cir. 1989), that a proposal submitted in response to a FAA RFP was an on-sale bar for § 102(b) purposes where the proposal was submitted more than one year prior to the patent application date. Even though the FAA contract was a research and development contract, the court in *RCA Corp.* saw the proposal as a definite offer for the sale of the patented invention. It also did not matter that the proposal was not accepted for all that is needed was an offer for sale. Contrast this decision with that in *Envirotech Corp. v. Westech Eng'g Inc.*, 904 F.2d 1571, 15 U.S.P.Q.2d 1230 (Fed. Cir. 1990), where the court held that the patent owner's intent to eventually exploit an invention as a part of its contract for which it bid did not raise the "on-sale" bar. Envirotech submitted proposals for a digester cover for a wastewater treatment plant which met the requested design specifications but which did not disclose the patented invention in its proposal. Unlike in *RCA Corp.*, the bid did not describe the invention that was patented, but merely referenced the necessary specification requirements, and thus no, definite offer to sell the actual invention was found. See, Rooklidge & Hill, "The Law on Unintended Consequences: The On Sale Bar After Pfaff v. Wells Electronics," 82 J. Pat. Off. Soc'y March 2000.

The court in *Group One* rejected its decision in *RCA Corp.* and determined that a different standard was necessary under the *Pfaff* decision, one that relied on the law applicable to commercial transactions to establish what was a "commercial offer." The court stated:

> Furthermore, to the extent it was believed that something less than an offer to sell as understood in general commercial transactions was sufficient to trigger the on-sale bar, it is likely that such belief can no longer be the law. The Supreme Court in *Pfaff v. Wells Electronics, Inc.*, 525 U.S. 55, 48 USPQ2d 1641 (1998), swept away this court's "totality of the circumstances" analysis of the on-sale bar and replaced it with a two-part test: "First, the product must be the subject of a commercial offer for sale. . . . Second, the invention must be ready for patenting." *Id.* at 67, 48 USPQ2d at 1646-47. Though the Court did not elaborate on what was meant by "a commercial offer for sale"—the issue not being directly presented—the language used strongly suggests that the offer must meet the level of an offer for sale in the contract sense, one that would be understood as such in the commercial community. Such a reading leaves no room for "activity which does not rise to the level of a formal 'offer' under contract law principles."

* * *

> In the first place, the court erred in applying the law of Missouri to the question. Because of the importance of having a uniform national rule regarding the on-sale bar, we hold that the question of whether an invention is the subject of a commercial offer for sale is a matter of Federal Circuit law, to be analyzed under the law of contracts as generally understood. . . . As a general proposition, we will look to the Uniform Commercial Code ("UCC") to define whether, as in this case, a communication or series of communications rises to the level of a commercial offer for sale. As this court has previously pointed out, "[t]he UCC has been recognized as the general law governing the sale of goods and is another useful, though not authoritative, source in determining the ordinary commercial meaning of" terms used by the parties. *Enercon GmbH v. Int'l Trade Comm'n*, 151 F.3d 1376, 1382, 47 USPQ2d 1725, 1729 (Fed. Cir. 1998). The Su-

preme Court's formulation of a "commercial offer for sale" in *Pfaff* also supports consulting the UCC. The Supreme Court has also cited the Restatement of Contracts with approval in the commercial contract law context. *See Mobil Oil Co. v. United States*, 530 U.S. 604, __, 120 S. Ct. 2423, 2429-30 (2000).

* * *

Our analysis of the facts leads us to the same conclusion reached by the district court—the correspondence and other interactions between Group One and Hallmark prior to the critical date did not add up to a commercial offer to sell the invention, an offer, for example, which Hallmark could have accepted.

A recent federal circuit decision considered whether a government contract was a sale of an invention triggering the Section 102(b) "on-sale" bar. In *Alexey T. Zacharin v. United States*, (Fed. Cir. No. 99-5086, June 13, 2000) the inventor, Alexey Zacharin a government employee, had no official responsibility for the design of the RAD nevertheless he conceived the invention covered by the '341 patent and reduced it to practice while working as an engineer at the Army. Both parties agree that the test of the t-RAD on December 10, 1978 met every limitation of the claimed invention and that the invention was reduced to practice by that date. Breed was subsequently awarded a cost-plus-incentive-fee Army contract in April 1980, referred to as the 0095 contract, to fabricate 6000 fuse systems and 6000 t-RADs for testing by the Army. Zacharin personally inspected the 6000 t-RAD units that Breed produced under the 0095 contract and accepted them on behalf of the Army. Zacharin subsequently brought an action against the United States under 28 U.S.C. § 1498, seeking compensation from the Government for its use of the patented invention. The court of federal claims found that the invention was "on-sale" more than one year before the application and was therefore invalid. The federal circuit agreed and stated:

> . . . According to Mr. Zacharin, the 0095 contract did not trigger the on-sale bar, because he was working cooperatively with the Army in evaluating the t-RAD for use in the MPSM program and Breed's role in that process was simply to fabricate the test models. Thus, he argues that Breed's acceptance of the 0095 contract was not a commercial offer for sale, but an agreement to support the Army's efforts by fabricating the t-RADs that the Army needed for testing purposes.

We agree with the trial court that the 0095 contract was a commercial offer for sale that invalidated all seven claims of the '341 patent. A sale is "a contract between parties to give and pass rights of property for consideration which the buyer pays or promises to pay the seller for the thing bought or sold." *In re Caveney*, 761 F.2d 671, 676, 226 USPQ 1, 4 (Fed. Cir. 1985). In this case, Breed contracted to fabricate 6000 t-RADs and deliver them to the Army. In fact, Mr. Zacharin inspected and accepted the t-RADs for the Army, implying that he could have rejected any of unacceptable quality. Thus, under the contract Breed manufactured the t-RADs and transferred all its rights in the fabricated t-RADs to the Army in exchange for a payment that guaranteed Breed that its costs would be covered in addition to some amount of profit.

This case is not one in which the inventor took his design to a fabricator "and pa[id] the fabricator for its services in fabricating a few sample products." *See Brasseler, U.S.A. I, L.P. v. Stryker Sales Corp.*, 182 F.3d 888, 891, 51 USPQ2d 1470, 1473 (Fed. Cir. 1999). Rather, Mr.

Zacharin disclosed his invention to a third party, the Army, with the hope and expectation that his t-RAD design would be used in the MPSM program, and the Army entered into a contract for the production of a large number of products embodying the invention. Mr. Zacharin placed no restrictions on the Army's use or disclosure of the design. He cannot now argue that this court should view the 0095 contract as a collaborative offer between him and the Army, after having earlier argued to the PTO in the rights determination that the Army had no rights to the invention of the '341 patent. Moreover, because Mr. Zacharin stipulated that the t-RAD had been reduced to practice before the 0095 contract was entered into, he cannot now argue that the purpose of the 0095 contract was testing of the t-RAD design.

The fact that the sale in question was made in the context of a research and development contract and that there was no fixed price set for the t-RADs does not suffice to avoid the on-sale bar. This court held in *RCA Corp. v. Data General Corp.*, 887 F.2d at 1062-63, 12 USPQ2d at 1454-55, that a cost-plus contract to supply experimental systems incorporating an invention that was reduced to practice constituted an invalidating offer for sale, and that precedent is equally applicable to the contract at issue in this case. Likewise, the fact that the products sold to the Army were to be used for testing rather than as routine production units, is not sufficient to avoid the effect of the on-sale bar, as our predecessor court held in *General Electric Co. v. United States*, 654 F.2d 55, 59 & n.6, 211 USPQ 867, 871 & n.6 (Ct. Cl. 1981). A contract to supply goods is a sales contract, regardless of the means used to calculate payment and regardless of whether the goods are to be used for testing in a laboratory or for deployment in the field.

Finally, under this court's precedents, it is of no consequence that the sale was made by a third party, not by the inventor, *see Abbott Lab. v. Geneva Pharms, Inc.*, 182 F.3d 1315, 1318, 51 USPQ2d 1307, 1309 (Fed. Cir. 1999), or that the product was constructed and the sale made pursuant to the buyer's directions, *see Brasseler*, 182 F.3d at 891, 51 USPQ2d at 1473.

In *Monon Corp. v. Stoughton*, 239 F.3d 1253 (Fed. Cir. 2001), the federal circuit questioned whether a sale was a commercial sale since the agreement provided that after a year the seller could reimburse the sale price to the buyer and obtain return of the vehicle embodying the invention. The case recognizes the concept that a sale of a device embodying the invention will not trigger the on sale bar if the public sale was primarily for experimental purposes.

A. Public Use

In *Baxter Int'l, Inc. v. Cobe Labs., Inc.*, 88 F.3d 1054 (Fed. Cir. 1996), the court determined that the use of a centrifuge in an NIH laboratory, which predated the filing of the plaintiff's patent by more than one year, was a statutory bar under section 102(b). The patentee argued that its use of the patented invention was for experimental purposes and thus not barred by 102(b). The principal case supporting this argument is *City of Elizabeth v. American Nicholson Pavement Co.*, 97 U.S. 126, 134 (1877). There, the Supreme Court that "[t]he use of an invention by the inventor himself, or of any other person under his direction, by way of experiment, and in order to bring the invention to perfection, has never been regarded as [a public] use." The court in *Baxter* found that the use here was public and not experimental. The court stated:

An analysis of experimental use, which is also a question of law, requires consideration of the totality of the circumstances and the policies underlying the public use bar. *E.g., Tone Bros.,* 28 F.3d at 1198, 31 USPQ2d at 1324. Evidentiary factors in determining if a use is experimental include the length of the test period, whether the inventor received payment for the testing, any agreement by the user to maintain the use confidential, any records of testing, whether persons other than the inventor performed the testing, the number of tests, and the length of the test period in relation to tests of similar devices. *TP Lab.,* 724 F.2d at 971-72, 220 USPQ at 582; *see also In re Brigance,* 792 F.2d 1103, 1108, 229 USPQ 988, 991 (Fed. Cir. 1986).

* * *

Suaudeau further testified that others at NIH came into his laboratory and observed the centrifuge in operation, including co-workers, who were under no duty to maintain it as confidential. Nor did Suaudeau make any discernible effort to maintain the centrifuge as confidential. His laboratory was located in a public building, and he testified that he recalled "people coming and looking, people flowing into the lab" before the critical date. He even testified that NIH had an anti-secrecy policy . . . .

The inventor's lack of direction or control over Suaudeau's use of the invention also supports a conclusion that the use was not experimental. One of the policies underlying experimental use as a negation of public use is allowing *an inventor* sufficient time to test an invention before applying for a patent. *Tone Bros.,* 28 F.3d at 1198, 31 U.S.P.Q. 2d at 1324. "The experimental use doctrine operates in the inventor's favor to allow *the inventor* to refine his invention or to assess its value relative to the time and expense of prosecuting a patent application. If it is not the inventor or someone under his control or 'surveillance' who does these things, there appears to us no reason why he should be entitled to rely upon them to avoid the statute." *See In re Hamilton,* 882 F. 2d 1576, 1581, 11 U.S.P.Q. 2d 1890, 1894 (Fed. Cir. 1989) (discussing experimental use in the context of the on-sale bar) (emphasis in original). Providing Cullis, the inventor, with the benefit of Suaudeau's testing is thus contrary to this policy, as Suaudeau was not using or testing the invention for Cullis. *Id.* Accordingly, we hold that public testing before the critical date by a third party for his own unique purposes of an invention previously reduced to practice and ob-mined from someone other than the patentee, when such testing is independent of and not controlled by the patentee, is an invalidating public use, not an experimental use.

B. Non-Obvious Subject Matter

35 U.S.C. § 103(a) contains the basic non-obvious standard for patentability:

(a) A patent may not be obtained though the invention is not identically disclosed or described as set forth in section 102 of this title, if the differences between the subject matter sought to be patented and the prior art are such that the subject matter as a whole would have been obvious at the time the invention was made to a person having ordinary skill in the art to which said subject matter pertains. Patentability shall not be negatived by the manner in which the invention was made.

Although an invention may be patent-eligible and novel, it still must pass the test for non-obviousness. This limitation prevents others from making slight alterations to existing inventions in order to obtain a patent. Although any minute change to the prior art may render the invention novel, it probably will be obvious under section 103 and hence unpatentable.

As section 103 states, if the invention as a whole when compared to all of the prior art would have been obvious at the time the invention was made to a person skilled in the relevant field, the invention is not patentable. The famous case of *Graham v. John Deere Co.*, 383 U.S. 1,148 U.S.P.Q. 459 (1966) restates in-part and clarifies how the courts are to make obvious-ness determinations at 17:

> Under § 103, the scope and content of the prior art are to be determined; differences between prior art and the claims at issue are to be ascertained; and the level of ordinary skill in the per-tinent art resolved. Against this background, the obviousness or nonobviousness of the subject matter is determined. Such secondary considerations as commercial success, long felt but un-solved needs, failure of others, etc., might be utilized to give light to the circumstances sur-rounding the origin of the subject matter sought to be patented. As indicia of obviousness or nonobviousness, these inquiries may have relevancy.

Although in *Graham* the Supreme Court listed some "secondary considerations" which "may have [some] relevancy," the federal circuit has elevated these considerations to manda-tory inquiries which should be factored into the overall obviousness test, see, e.g., *Heidelber-ger Druckmaschinen AG v. Hantscho Commercial Prods., Inc.*, 21 F.3d 1068, 30 U.S.P.Q.2d 1377 (Fed. Cir. 1994); *Continental Can Co. v. Monsanto Co.*, 948 F.2d 1264, 20 U.S.P.Q.2d 1746 (Fed. Cir. 1991). The rational in part is that although an invention may seem obvious in hindsight, these considerations can show whether it would have been obvious at the time of the invention. For instance, if an invention solves a long-felt need that others tried but could not solve, and the invention is in fact successful, it probably was not obvious at the time that it was invented. The argument is that it must not have been obvious at the time since if it was, it can be assumed that one skilled in the art would have come up with the same or similar solution. See *Pfund v. United States*, 40 Fed. Cl. 313 (1998), where the patentee argued as a "secondary consideration" that his patents were placed under secrecy order. The court rejected this argu-ment.

C. Procedure

a. Harmonization Efforts

The International Convention for the Protection of Industrial Property (Paris Convention) initially adopted in 1883 and revised over the years (most recently in 1967, 21 U.S.I.T. 1,853, T.I.A.S No. 6923, 828 U.N.T.S 305) is the basis for international patent laws followed by all developed and many developing countries. The Paris Convention grants the rights of priority and national treatment to the citizens of its member countries. National treatment means that a country may not provide less favorable treatment to foreigners then it does to its citizens. See Donald D. Dems, "Paris Convention Priority," 77 J.P.O.S. 138 (1995). However, there is no minimum standard of protection required for a member country. The right of priority has been implemented by the Patent Cooperation Treaty by providing a one year grace period from the date that a patent application is filed in the citizen's country for filing in another member country.

The World Industrial Property Organization (WIPO), a specialized agency of the United Nations, administers the Paris Convention. The basic requirement of patent systems under the Paris Convention is (1) equal treatment for foreign applications, (2) a 12 month priority period to permit applicants to file in other countries while maintaining their priority date of application, (3) the deferral of penalties for not working a patent for a number of years in a country, and (4) the establishment of special arrangements between member nations to promote cooperation.

One major obstacle to true worldwide harmonization efforts was the United States', Canada's, and the Philippines' use of the first-to-file system. Canada subsequently modified their system in 1989 and adopted a first-to-file system. See Blake R. Wiggs, 73 J.P.O.S. 493 (1991). The result of the difference is that a party first filing for a patent may be able to receive a corresponding patent throughout the world based on its early filing date, but may be challenged in the United States by a party who filed for the same invention after the first party but claimed to be the first inventor based on an early date of invention. Beginning in 1984, WIPO sought to achieve harmonization of the world patent systems in order to encourage manufacturers of patented products to expand their markets abroad and reduce patent infringement costs internationally. In 1986, the United States shifted from seeking greater protection for U.S. intellectual property internationally from WIPO as being more general to specific changes under a General Agreement on Tariff and Trade (GATT) led effort at the Uruguay Round negotiations. The United States even indicated in 1987 that it was willing to consider a first-to-file system if it was part of a balanced harmonization treaty. See Karen M. Caresky, "Internationally Harmonization Through WIPO: An Analysis of the U.S. Proposal to Adopt a First-to-File Patent System," 21 Law and Policy in International Business 289 (1989).

One of the major stumbling blocks to harmonization is the U.S. Governments "first-to-invent" system whereas the rest of the world using a first to invent patent system. The U.S. patent system, as specified by title 35 of the U.S. Code, provides that a patent is awarded to the person who first *made* the invention. This "first-to-invent" system has been used for as long as our nation has had a patent system and is presently embodied in 35 U.S.C. § 102(g), which states:

A person is entitled to a patent unless:

(g) before the applicant's invention thereof the invention was made in this country by another who had not abandoned, suppressed, or concealed it. In determining priority of invention there shall be considered not only the respective dates of conception and reduction to practice of the invention, but also the reasonable diligence of one who was first to conceive and last to reduce to practice, from a time prior to conception by the other.

The argument for this system is that it rewards the "original, true and first inventor," Banner, McDonnell, "First-to-File, Mandatory Reexamination and Mandatory 'Exceptional Circumstances': Ideas for Better? Or Worse," 69 J.P.O.S. 595 (1987). It can also be said that it more closely complies with the constitutional mandate of "securing for limited Times to. . . Inventors the exclusive Rights to their... Discoveries." The rest of the world patent systems are based on the concept that the patent is awarded to the inventor that is the first-to-file a patent application on the invention. Proponents of the first-to-file system argue among other things that under the current system few conflicts exist over who is the first to invent, and when they do occur it is rare that the party trying to overcome the application date prevails. It is further argued that the first-to-file system is more efficient and fairer due to the increased certainty and the fact that patent obstacles such as "secret prior art" will be eliminated, Armitage, Wilder, "Harmonization: Will It Resuscitate a Patent System Suffocating Its Small Entity Users With Cost and Complexity," 1 U. Balt. Intel. Prop. L.J. 116 (1993).

Other elements of patent harmonization are standard terms for patents worldwide and the early publication of patent applications. Most members of the Paris Convention utilize a term of 20 years measured from the filing of the patent application on the invention; publish the filed application within 18 months of filing; and utilize an opposition system where patent applications, after examination, are published for opposition usually to ascertain whether other parties oppose the issuance of a patent on the claimed invention based on prior art or insufficient disclosure. All of these elements should be a member's patent system for true harmonization and the U.S. has changed its patent system over the past 15 years to reflect most of these concepts except with respect to first-to-invent. The following are the changes to the U.S. patent system to reflect harmonization.

b. NAFTA

Upon the approval of the North American Free Trade Agreement (NAFTA), Congress passed the NAFTA Implementation Act, P.L. 103-182, to implement this treaty. Part 6, Chapter 17 of NAFTA provided that each party to the treaty accord nationals of the other parties' treatment no less favorable then it accords to its nationals with regard to intellectual property. NAFTA included protection under copyright for sound recordings, databases, rental rights for computer software and sound recordings, and product and process protection for inventions as well as trade secrets and integrated circuit protection. With respect to patents, P.L. 103-182, § 331 provided for changes to section 104 of title 35 of the U.S. Code to permit applicants to establish a date of invention by reference to acts which occurred in Mexico or Canada.

c. GATT/TRIPs

The General Agreement on Tariff and Trade (GATT), Uruguay Round Agreement was signed in April 1994. The United States implementing legislation, the Uruguay Round Agreement Act, was enacted on December 8, 1994, P.L. 103-465. Under this law the United States agreed to become a member country of the World Trade Organization (WTO) and changed its intellectual property laws as provided for by the Agreement on Trade Related Aspects of Intellectual Property (TRIPs), a Subagreement to GATT. Two TRIPs provisions conflict with U.S. Patent laws: Article 38 provides for a patent term of 20 years form the date of filing; and Article 27 requires that patent rights be available "without discrimination as to the place of invention." Subtitle A of Title V of this implementing Act provides for a number of changes to title 35 of the U.S. Code.

(1) PLACE OF INVENTIONS

TRIPs require that patents be available without discrimination as to place of invention. Therefore, the treatment of inventive activity that has occurred in a WTO member country must be recognized in the United States for the purpose of establishing the date of invention under U.S. patent law. This requirement impacts 35 U.S.C. § 104, which limited such activities to acts that occurred in the United States. This TRIPs requirement was accomplished by modifications to 35 U.S.C. § 104 by P.L. 103-465.

(2) TERM OF PATENT

Effective six months after its enactment (December 8, 1994), the term of patent protection in the United States was modified by P.L. 103-465 from 17 years from the date of issuance of the patent to 20 years from the date of the filing of an application for the patent (or earlier applications claiming priority under another application pursuant to sections 120, 121 or 365(c) of title 35) with extensions for up to five years for delays caused by interference proceedings, secrecy orders, and successful appeals to the Board of Patent Appeals and Interferences or courts. The 20-year term was also the subject of an agreement between the United States and Japan in January of 1994. Japan agreed in exchange to the United States adopting a 20-year patent term to accept English language patent applications for filing in Japan so long as a Japanese translation followed with two months.

(3) INFRINGEMENT

The definition of patent rights, i.e., the right to exclude others from making, using and selling, was expanded by P.L. 103-465 to include the right to exclude others from importing patented inventions into the United States or by offering a patented inventions for sale in the United States, 35 U.S.C. § 271. See Garlepp, "An Analysis of the Patentee's New Exclusive Right to 'Offer to Sell,' " 81 Pat. Off. Soc'y 315, (May 1999).

(4) PROVISIONAL SPECIFICATIONS

The modifications to section 111 of title 35, made by P.L. 103-465 (effective June 8, 1995), establishes a provisional patent application system as a part of the U.S. patent system. This system permits the early filing of a provisional application containing only a specification, drawing, cover which identifies it as a provisional patent application and an appropriate fee ($75 for small business and $150 for large companies) but without an inventor oath and without any patent claims.

d. American Inventors Protection Act of 1999

The American Inventors Protection Act of 1999 was signed into law (P.L. 106-113) on November 29, 1999, as part of the conference report (H. Rept. 106-479) on H.R. 3194, Consolidated Appropriations Act, Fiscal Year 2000. This act contained a number of title that related to the harmonization of the U. S. Patent stem with patent systems of other countries. These included: (1) the Patent Term Guaranty Act of 1999 which extended the term of patents to compensate for certain PTO processing delays and for delays in the prosecution of applications pending more than three years. Extensions are available for delays in issuance of a patent due to interference proceedings, secrecy orders, and appellate review. Diligent applicants are guaranteed a minimum 17-year patent term; (2) the Domestic Publication of Foreign Filed Patent Application Act of 1999 which provides for publication of patent applications 18 months after filing unless the applicant requests otherwise upon filing and certifies that the invention has not and will not be the subject of an application filed in a foreign country. Provisional rights are available to patentees to obtain reasonable royalties if others make, use, sell, or import the invention during the period between publication and grant and provides a prior art effect for published patent applications; and (3) the Optional Inter Partes Reexamination Procedure Act of 1999 which establishes an alternative reexamination procedure that provides for expanded third party participation in the reexamination of patent by the PTO.

e. Patent Law Treaty

The Patent Law Treaty (PLT) was adopted in Geneva in June 2000, as a result of a World Intellectual Property Organization (WIPO) initiative concerned with patent formalities. PLT seeks to harmonize the formal requirements of the signatories patent offices for the granting patents, and to streamline the procedures for obtaining and maintaining a patent. PLT signatories, which includes the U.S., have agreed to a single internationally standard set of formal requirements for national and regional offices, standard forms to be accepted by all patent offices, filing date requirements and mechanisms to avoid unintentional loss of rights as a result of failure to comply with time limits. PLT also provides that a patent may not be revoked or invalidated, without the owner being given the opportunity to make respond on the revocation or invalidity and to make amendments if permitted under applicable law, within a reasonable time limit.

2. Patent Specification

a. Application Requirements

Applications for patents are made in writing by the inventor to the Commissioner of the Patent and Trademark Office (PTO) and are required to include a specification, a drawing, an oath of inventorship, and the prescribed fee. In the alternative, an applicant can file a provisional application containing a drawing, a cover that identifies it as a provisional application, an appropriate fee, and a specification. The provisional application's specification, however, need only comply with the first paragraph of 35 U.S.C. § 112, meaning that a claim is not required to be included. The applicant will then have one year to file a full application. 35 U.S.C. § 111 provides:

(a) In General.

(1) *Written Application.* An application for patent shall be made, or authorized to be made, by the inventor, except as otherwise provided in this title, in writing to the Commissioner.

(2) *Contents.* Such application shall include:

(A) a specification as prescribed by section 112 of this title;

(B) a drawing as prescribed by section 113 of this title; and

(C) an oath by the applicant as prescribed by section 155 of this title.

(3) *Fee and Oath.* The application must be accompanied by the fee required by law. The fee and oath may be submitted after the specification and any required drawing are submitted, within such period and under such conditions, including the payment of a surcharge, as may be prescribed by the Commissioner.

(4) *Failure to Submit.* Upon failure to submit the fee and oath within such prescribed period, the application shall be regarded as abandoned, unless it is shown to the satisfaction of the Commissioner that the delay in submitting the fee and oath was unavoidable or unintentional. The filing date of an application shall be the date on which the specification and any required drawing are received in the Patent and Trademark Office.

b. Contents of Specifications

35 U.S.C. § 112 is the basic requirement for describing the invention and claiming the subject matter, which the applicant regards as its invention specification:

The specification shall contain a written description of the invention, and of the manner and process of making and using it, in such full, clear, concise, and exact terms as to enable any person skilled in the art to which it pertains, or with which it is most nearly connected, to make and use the same, and shall set forth the best mode contemplated by the inventor of carrying out his invention.

The specification shall conclude with one or more claims particularly pointing out and distinctly claiming the subject matter which the applicant regards as his invention.

A claim may be written in independent or, if the nature of the case admits, in dependent or multiple dependent form.

Subject to the following paragraph, a claim in dependent form shall contain a reference to a claim previously set forth and then specify a further limitation of the subject matter claimed. A claim in dependent form shall be construed to incorporate by reference all the limitations of the claim to which it refers.

A claim in multiple dependent form shall contain a reference, in the alternative only, to more than one claim previously set forth and then specify a further limitation of the subject matter claimed. A multiple dependent claim shall not serve as a basis for any other multiple dependent claim. A multiple claim shall be construed to incorporate by reference all the limitations of the particular claim in relation to which it is being considered.

An element in a claim for a combination may be expressed as a means or step for performing a specified function without the recital of structure, material, or acts in support thereof, and such claim shall be construed to cover the corresponding structure, material, or acts described in the specification and equivalents thereof.

The "claims" of the patent describe the scope of the patent itself. Claims are not themselves complex descriptions of the invention, but instead provide the outermost legal limits of protection.

In addition, applicants have a duty to submit information to the PTO that is material to the patentability of the applicant's invention. The PTO has adopted a procedure for the submission of an information disclosure statement by applicants to provide the PTO with information to be considered by the patent examiner during the examination of the application, 37 C.F.R 1.97 and 1.98.

Before the claims setting forth the scope of the invention are presented, however, the first paragraph of section 112 specifies that applicants meet the "written description," "enablement," and "best mode" requirements.

The "written description" requirement is considered to be separate from the enablement requirement. The goal of the written description requirement is to convey the information that the applicant has invented the subject matter claimed in the patent application. This is met if the applicant "convey[s] with reasonable clarity to those skilled in the art that, as of the filing date sought, he or she was in possession" of the claimed subject matter, *Vas-Cath Inc. v. Mahurkar*, 935 F.2d 1555, 19 U.S.P.Q.2d 1111 (Fed. Cir. 1991). Another objective is to put in the public's possession what the applicant claims is his invention and prevent the applicant from claiming subject matter that is not in the application as filed. For example claims may not omit any element of the invention described in the Patent application, *In re Gentry Gallery Inc. v. Berkline Corp.*, 134 F.3d 1473 (Fed. Cir. 1998). See PTO, "Guidelines for Examination of Patent Applications under 35 U.S.C. §112 ¶1, Written Description Requirement," 66 Fed. Reg. 1099, January 5, 2001.

The "enablement" requirement, although similar to the "written description" requirement, has the purpose of enabling one skilled in the art to practice the invention. The applicant will "enable" one skilled in the art when the specification teaches "how to make" and "how to use" the invention. It should be noted that details that would be obvious to one skilled in the relevant art need not be included. In *National Recovery Technologies Inc. v. Magnetic Separation Systems, Inc*, 166 F.3d. 1190 (Fed. Cir. 1999).

The enablement requirement of § 112 demands that the patent specification enable "those skilled in the art to make and use the full scope of the claimed invention without 'undue experimentation.' " *Genentech, Inc. v. Novo Nordisk A/S*, 108 F.3d 1361, 1365, 42 USPQ2d 1001, 1004 (Fed. Cir. 1997) (quoting *In re Wright*, 999 F.2d 1557, 1561, 27 USPQ2d 1510, 1513 (Fed. Cir. 1993)); *see also In re Vaeck*, 947 F.2d 488, 495, 20 USPQ2d 1438, 1444 (Fed. Cir. 1991). The enablement requirement ensures that the public knowledge is enriched by the patent specification to a degree at least commensurate with the scope of the claims.

The final disclosure needed before the claims are set forth is the subjective "best mode" requirement. The applicant must simply include in the application the best mode contemplated for carrying out the invention. The purpose if this requirement is to assure the public obtains a full disclosure of the preferred embodiment in return for the rights given to the patentee, *In re Gay*, 309 F.2d 779, (1962). Two important principles should be noted: (1) the best mode requirement is entirely subjective; and (2) the only point in time that is referenced is the filing date. The enablement requirement serves to require disclosure of the best mode the inventor knew of carrying out the invention at the time of filing, even if she later (after filing the application) finds a better method. See *DANA Corp. v. IPC Ltd*, 860 F.2d 415 (Fed Cir. 1988) ("the best mode is not satisfied by reference to the level of skill in the art, but entails a comparison of the facts known to the inventor at the time the application was filed and the disclosure in the specification." But see *Fonar Corp. v. General Electric Co.*, 107 F.3d 1543 (Fed. Cir. 1997) (best mode requirement is met as long as patent discloses to one skilled in the art the best mode of practicing the claimed invention.).

c. Provisional Patent Applications

In 1995 P.L. 103-465 establishes a provisional patent application a part of the U.S. patent system. A provisional application may be filed containing only a specification, drawing, cover which identifies it as a provisional patent application and an appropriate fee ($75 for small business and $150 for large companies) but without an inventor oath and without any patent claims. The provisional application cannot mature into a patent and it is not examined; nor can it claim priority of an earlier filed application. However, a provisional application is provided the benefits of the Paris Convention priority year and may defeat the patent of another under section 102(e) of title 35 on a patent issuing on a complete application claiming priority from the provisional application. The provisional application is to be maintained in confidence by the PTO. A full patent application is required within 12 months of the filing of the provisional application. The 21-year patent term starts with the filing of the complete applications.

The benefits of the provisional application are: (1) it places domestic applicants on even footing with foreign applicants because the filing of a provisional application does not trigger the start of the 20-year term; (2) it has minimum legal and formal requirements; (3) it is to be relative inexpensive way to establish an early effective filing date in a patent application which establishes a constructive reduction to practice for the invention described in the provisional application; and (4) it provides up to twelve months additional time to develop the invention. In general, provisional applications are to be the equivalent to foreign priority applications under section 119 of title 35.

3. *Confidentiality of Applications/18 Month Publication*

Except for patent applications which are published under the 18 month rule, each patents is published and made available to the public upon the issuance of the patent, 37 C.F.R. § 1.11, as are the assignment records relating to the patent, 37 C.F.R. § 1.12. However, except for the early publication under the eighteen-month rule, prior to issuance, the U. S. PTO maintains patent applications in secret, 35 U.S.C. § 122. This section provides:

> Application for patents shall be kept in confidence by the Patent and Trademark Office and no information concerning the same given without authority of the applicant or owner unless necessary to carry out the provisions of any Act of Congress or in such special circumstances as may be determined by the Commissioner. This requirement is reflected in the rules of practice, 37 C.F.R. 8 1.14(a), and includes abandoned applications, 37 C.F.R. § 1.14(b), and to some extent decisions of the Board of Appeals and Patent Interferences, and the Commissioner of Patents and Trademarks. This statutory requirement is applicable only to the Patent and Trademark Office and nothing in section 122 or the implementing rules restricts the applicant from disclosing the contents of his application.

Section 122 of title 35 of the U.S. Code has been held to permit withholding of agency records from release under the Freedom of Information Act, 5 U.S.C. § 552(b)(3), *Irons & Sears v. Dann*, 606 F.2d 1215, 204 U.S.P.Q. 1 (D.C. Cir.), *cert. denied*, 444 U.S. 1075 (1979); *Irons v. Gottschalk*, 548 F.2d 992, 191 U.S.P.Q. 481 (D.C. Cir. 1976), *cert. denied*, 434 U.S. 965 (1977); *Sears v. Gottschalk*, 502 F.2d 122, 183 U.S.P.Q. 134 (4th Cir. 1974), *cert. denied*, 425 U.S. 904 (1976); *Irons v. Schuyler*, 465 F.2d 608, 174 U.S.P.Q. 289 (D.C. Cir.), *cert. denied*, 409 U.S. 1076 (1972); *Irons v. Diamond*, 670 F.2d 265, 214 U.S.P.Q. 81 (D.C. Cir. 1981). These decisions include abandoned applications, decisions on petitions on abandoned applications, filing dates of patent applications, and patent applications.

As noted above, the American Inventors Protection Act of 1999 provides for the publication of applications for patent, except for applications for design patents and provisional applications, promptly upon the expiration of a period of 18 months after the earliest filing date for which a benefit is sought. However, an applicant may request that its application not be published if the invention disclosed in the application is not the subject of an application filed in another country, or under a multilateral international agreement that requires publication of applications 18 months after filing. If the patent application issues as a patent the patentee is provided provisional rights in Section 154(d) to obtain a reasonable royalty from any person who had actual notice of the publication and had in the period after the publication of the application and issuance of the patent, made, used, offered for sale, sold or imported products made by that process as claimed. Further, publication, unlike publication in some foreign countries, will not trigger opportunities for protests, unless the applicant consents in writing.

4. *Examination and Rejection*

After a patent application is filed, the Commissioner has it examined by the, Patent and Trademark Office employees to determine whether the applicant is entitled to a patent, 35 U.S.C. § 131. If the PTO refuses to grant a patent on the application, i.e., objections are made or if requirements are established, the Commissioner will notify the applicant and set forth his reasons and the prior art references. The applicant, within six months or in such shorter period as may be specified, may seek to modify his application (without introducing new matter into the disclosure of the invention) or may request a further examination, after receiving such notice, the applicant persists in his claim for a patent, with or without amendment, the application is reexamined, 35 U.S.C. § 132. If, however, the Commission determines that the applicant is entitled to a patent under the law for the inventions claimed in its application, the Commissioner will issue a patent therefor, 35 U.S.C. § 131.

5. Issuance of a Patent

If the PTO determines that the applicant is entitled to a patent on the filed application, the PTO issues a notice of allowance and requires the applicant to provide the PTO with the issuance fee within three months, 35 U.S.C. § 151. Upon the payment of this fee, the patent is issued to the applicant or the assignee. If the required fee is not paid, the application is considered to be abandoned, 35 U.S.C. § 151.

6. Appeal

If a claim has been rejected twice by a PTO examiner, the applicant may appeal to the Board of Patent Appeals and Interferences, 35 U.S.C. § 134, and thereafter to the Court of Appeals for the Federal Circuit, 35 U.S.C. § 141, or by civil action against the Commissioner in the United States District Court for the District of Columbia, 35 U.S.C. § 145. Appeals from a district court are also to the federal circuit, 18 U.S.C. § 1295(a)(4)(c).

7. Interferences

Whenever the Commissioner is of the opinion that a pending patent application would interfere with any other pending applications, or with a patent less than one year old, he is to notify the applicant, and establish an interference to determine the question of priority of invention, 35 U.S.C. § 135. In an action instituted under 35 U.S.C. § 135, the question of priority is determined by the Board of Appeals and Patent Interferences. A party dissatisfied with the decision of the Board may appeal to the Court of Appeals for the Federal Circuit, 28 U.S.C. § 1295. Note, however, that the party that prevailed before the Board may elect, under 35 U.S.C. § 141, to have all further proceedings conducted under 35 U.S.C. § 146, which provides for review by civil action in the district courts. Appeals from such district court decisions rest with the federal circuit, 28 U.S.C. § 1295(a)(4)(C). Further, a patentee who suspects that another's patent interferes with his patent may have his patent declared "prior in time," 35 U.S.C. § 291.

Interference-like actions involving the Government often occur when the Government requests rights m a patent application filed by a party who allegedly reduced his invention to practice with federal funds. Such interference actions generally are authorized by agency enabling statutes, see e.g., 42 U.S.C. § 2457 (NASA) and *Williams v. Administrator of NASA,*

463 F.2d 1391 (C.C.P.A. 1972). See also 42 U.S.C. § 2182 (Atomic Energy Commission) and *U.S. Department of Energy v. Szulinski*, 673 F.2d 385,213 U.S.P.Q. 343 (C.C.P.A. 1982). Those statutes provide that the Commission shall forward certain patent applications to agency administrators, and shall issue patents in the name of the administrator upon request, unless the applicant petitions for a hearing before the Board of Interferences. Thus, these statutes avoid the problem of typical 35 U.S.C. § 135 interferences, namely, "determination that there should be an interference is initially a matter of discretion residing solely in the Commissioner," *Tofe v. Winchell*, 645 F.2d 58, 209 U.S.P.Q. 379 (C.C.P.A. 1981). No cases have been found in which the Government was involved in a Title 35 Interference action.

8. Patent Term

The patent term for many years was seventeen years from the date the patent issued. This term has been modified for U.S. patent in 1995 to bring it in line with the internationally accepted patent term, 20 years from the date of the filing of a patent application. The patent 21-year term and the copyright longer term is compared by Waltersheid "The Remarkable—and Irrational Disparity—Between the Patent Term and the Copyright Term", 83 J. Pat. Off. Soc'y 233, April 2001.

Section 154 of Title 35 of the U.S. Code provides for a patent term of 20 years from the date of the filing of an application for the patent (or earlier applications claiming priority under another application pursuant to sections 120, 121 or 365(c) of title 35). When first enacted extensions for up to five years were permitted for delays caused by interference proceedings, secrecy orders, and successful appeals to the Board of Patent Appeals and Interferences or courts. This was modified by the American Inventors Protection Act of 1999, which provides expanded opportunities for extending the patent term by creating new categories of delays that may give rise to a term extension. The patent term extension for a PTO delay is one day for each day after the end of specified periods. For example, this act guarantees that the PTO will either make its rejection, objection, or requirement to a patent application, or issue a written notice of allowance within fourteen months of the filing date of the application. Further, it requires the PTO to respond within four months to a reply to an Office action or to an appeal to the PTO Board. Each of these guarantees is a potential for an increase in the patent term by one day for each day of delay. This Act also states a general limit for patent prosecution of three years from the filing date until issuance, except for examinations under § 132(b), time consumed by an interference, time consumed by an secrecy order, or appellate review by the Board or by a federal court: One day of patent term is added for each day after the end of the three-year period until the patent issues. The term adjustments in Section 154 now provide:

(b) ADJUSTMENT OF PATENT TERM.—

(1) PATENT TERM GUARANTEES.—

(A) GUARANTEE OF PROMPT PATENT AND TRADEMARK OFFICE RESPONSES.— Subject to the limitations under paragraph (2), if the issue of an original patent is delayed due to the failure of the Patent and Trademark Office to—

(i) provide at least one of the notifications under section 132 of this title or a notice of allowance under section 151 of this title not later than 14 months after—

(I) the date on which an application was filed under section 111(a) of this title; or

(II) the date on which an international application fulfilled the requirements of section 371 of this title;

(ii) respond to a reply under section 132, or to an appeal taken under section 134, within 4 months after the date on which the reply was filed or the appeal was taken; 37

(iii) act on an application within 4 months after the date of a decision by the Board of Patent Appeals and Interferences under section 134 or 135 or a decision by a Federal court under section 141, 145, or 146 in a case in which allowable claims remain in the application; or

(iv) issue a patent within 4 months after the date on which the issue fee was paid under section 151 and all outstanding requirements were satisfied, the term of the patent shall be extended 1 day for each day after the end of the period specified in clause (i), (ii), (iii), or (iv), as the case may be, until the action described in such clause is taken.

(B) GUARANTEE OF NO MORE THAN 3-YEAR APPLICATION PENDENCY.— Subject to the limitations under paragraph (2), if the issue of an original patent is delayed due to the failure of the United States Patent and Trademark Office to issue a patent within 3 years after the actual filing date of the application in the United States, not including—

(i) any time consumed by continued examination of the application requested by the applicant under section 132(b);

(ii) any time consumed by a proceeding under section 135(a), any time consumed by the imposition of an order under section 181, or any time consumed by appellate review by the Board of Patent Appeals and Interferences or by a Federal court; or

(iii) any delay in the processing of the application by the United States Patent and Trademark Office requested by the applicant except as permitted by paragraph (3)(C), the term of the patent shall be extended 1 day for each day after the end of that 3-year period until the patent is issued.

(C) GUARANTEE OR ADJUSTMENTS FOR DELAYS DUE TO INTERFERENCES, SECRECY ORDERS, AND APPEALS.—Subject to the limitations under paragraph (2), if the issue of an original patent is delayed due to—

(i) a proceeding under section 135(a);

(ii) the imposition of an order under section 181; or

(iii) appellate review by the Board of Patent Appeals and Interferences or by a Federal court in a case in which the patent was issued under a decision in the review reversing an adverse determination of patentability, the term of the patent shall be extended 1 day for each day of the pendency of the proceeding, order, or review, as the case may be.

(2) LIMITATIONS.—

(A) IN GENERAL.—To the extent that periods of delay attributable to grounds specified in paragraph (1) overlap, the period of any adjustment granted under this subsection shall not exceed the actual number of days the issuance of the patent was delayed.

* * *

(C) REDUCTION OF PERIOD OF ADJUSTMENT.—

(i) The period of adjustment of the term of a patent under paragraph (1) shall be reduced by a period equal to the period of time during which the applicant failed to engage in reasonable efforts to conclude prosecution of the application.

(ii) With respect to adjustments to patent term made under the authority of paragraph (1)(B), an applicant shall be deemed to have failed to engage in reasonable efforts to conclude processing or examination of an application for the cumulative total of any periods of time in excess of 3 months that are taken to respond to a notice from the Office making any rejection, objection, argument, or other request, measuring such 3-month period from the date the notice was given or mailed to the applicant.

(iii) The Director shall prescribe regulations establishing the circumstances that constitute a failure of an applicant to engage in reasonable efforts to conclude processing or examination of an application.

9. *Reexamination and Reissue*

a. *Reexamination*

Sections 301-307 of title 35 provide for a reexamination procedure of a patent in the PTO. Section 301 provides for the public to cite prior art with respect to an issued patent by sending the PTO information and having this information placed in the patent file wrapper. The reexamination procedure permits a more direct challenge in the PTO with respect to the validity of an issued patent. The reexamination procedure has been adopted to permit the correction of errors made by the PTO, to remedy defective governmental action and to remove patents that should never have been granted, *Patlex Corp. v. Mossinghoff*, 758 F.2d 595 (Fed. Cir. 1985). Section 302 permits the patentee, or any other person, to apply for a reexamination of a patent. The reexamination is performed in an ex parte manner based on the art (patents and publications), which the Commissioner, the patentee, or third party have cited against the invention. The patentee has a duty of candor to disclose any patent or printed publication that he is aware of any time during the reexamination 37 C.F.R. § 1.555. If the PTO determines that a reexamination proceeding should take place it notifies the patentee and provides the patentee two months to respond and file any statement on the new issues raised regarding the prior art. The requestor is given two months to reply. An *ex parte* proceeding is then undertaken with the patentee, much like the original examination. The patentee may amend the claims to narrow the invention and clarify it but the broaden of claims is not allowed. The reexamination is conducted with special dispatch. A final rejection of a claim upon reexamination may be appealed by the patentee to the PTO Board of Patent Appeals and Interference and then to the Courts. See Christopher M. Pickett, "The Patent Reexamination Procedure—A Complete Guide Through the Statutes, the Rules and the Caselaw," 75 J.P.O.S. 297 (1993).

b. Reissue

The reissue procedure in section 251 is provided to correct errors made by the applicant without any deceptive intention. Only the patentee may file for the reissue of a patent. Under the reissue procedure the patentee may file a continuation application, amend the patent and ask for a wide consideration of issues, including examination with respect to prior art, sale, or public use as well as the breath of the claims in the patent, but the patentee may enter no new matter into the application for reissue. Otherwise, the provisions of title 35 relating to applications for patent are applicable to reissue applications. No reissued patent may be granted enlarging the scope of the claims of the original patent unless applied for within two years from the grant of the original patent. The rights of persons who made, purchased, or used an invention prior to the reissue may not be abridged by the grant of a reissue patent and such person may continue to use or sell the thing made unless the making, using, or selling of such thing infringes a valid claim of a reissued patent that was in the original patent, 35 U.S.C. § 252.

c. Optional Inter Partes Reexamination Procedure

While the law on reexamination set forth in the law set forth in a. above stays in effect, the American Inventors Protection Act of 1999 provides an optional right in any person to request the reexamination by the PTO of a patent on the basis of prior art cited under section 301. Under the reexamination procedures in a. above, a third party may only request reexamination of the patent but cannot participate in the reexamination process. The third party is provided a copy of office actions and responses but has no right to respond itself. Under the new law the PTO Director is to determine, not later than three months after the filing of a request for reexamination, whether a substantial new question of patentability is raised by the request. If the determination is made for a re-examination, the third party may be involved in the reexamination of the patent for resolution of the question, i.e., the third party has an opportunity to submit a written response to each response filed by the patentee. However, the third party has no right to appeal an adverse decision beyond the PTO Board. The third party is estopped from pursuing a civil action or another reexamination on the same prior art/issues raised, or which could have been raised, before the PTO.

D. Exclusive Rights

1. Right to Exclude

Patents are issued to the applicant or the assignee of record, 35 U.S.C. § 151 and § 152. The issued patent contains the specification and drawings of the application. The patent is granted for a period ending 20 years from the application filing date and provides the patentee with the right to exclude others from making, using, importing, selling, or offering to sell the patented invention. Section 154(a)(1) provides:

> Every patent shall contain a short title of the invention and a grant to the patentee, his heirs or assigns, of the right to exclude others from *making, using, offering for sale, or selling* the invention throughout the United States or *importing* the invention into the United States, and, if the invention is a process, of the right to exclude others from using, offering for sale or selling throughout the United States, or importing into the United States, products made by that process, referring to the specification(m for the particulars thereof. (Emphasis added).

Section 154 embodies an important patent law principle. The patent right granted by the Government to the inventor or his assignee, is the right to exclude others from making, using, or selling the invention patented, *Bloomer v. McQuewan*, 55 U.S. 539 (14 How. 1852). This is not the positive right to make, use, or sell the invention, but instead a grant to the inventor of the constitutional right to exclude others, provided by the Congress under Article 1, Section 8. Hence, the popular saying that upon being granted a patent, all the inventor obtains is the right to sue.

An illustration of this basic exclusive rights principle is as follows: Assume a patent "X" is granted to an inventor for a combination of steps or means for performing a specified function illustrated as means A + B + C. A second patent "Y" is issued subsequently, which provides an improvement over X. The Y patent claim contains the following means A + B + C + D. If the making, using, or selling of items embodying patent Y infringes patent X, the owner of patent X may enjoin the owner or licensee of patent Y from making, using, or selling the Y invention. While patentee Y would own his invention, he could not use his invention without permission from patentee X. In these circumstances, if patentee X desired to license his invention to patentee Y, it would not be logical to grant the licensee the right to make, use or sell the invention, e.g., the right "to practice" the invention. Rather, the license would more correctly contain an agreement by X not to sue Y if he made, used, or sold the Y invention. However see, *Cleveland v. United States*, (121 S. Ct. 365 (2000) where the court misstated this principle as follows: "[T]he Government compares the State's interest in video poker licenses to a patent holder's interest in a patent that she has not yet licensed. Although it is true that both involve the right to exclude, we think the congruence ends there. A patent not only confers the right to exclude others from using an invention, it also protects the holder's right to use, make, or sell the invention herself. 35 U.S.C. 154, 271(d)(1)."

2. Statutory Invention Registration

In 1984 Congress adopted a registration technique for patents, PL. 98-622, § 102(a), November 8, 1984. This provision, section 157 of title 35, permits the filing of a patent application without any claims, much like a provisional application used by a number of foreign countries. The Commissioner, however, is to publish these statutory registrations without examination if the applicant "(1) meets the requirements of section 112 of this title; (2) has complied with the requirements for printing, as set forth in regulations of the Commissioner; (3) waives the right to receive a patent on the invention within such period as may be prescribed by the Commissioner; and (4) pays application, publication, and other processing fees established by the Commissioner." The waiver of (a)(3) takes effect upon publication of the statutory invention registration. Such an application may be considered for a priority claim, i.e., an interference, and publication will be withheld unless priority of invention is finally determined in favor of the applicant. A published statutory invention registration has all of the attributes of a patent except the enforcement rights of section 183 and sections 271 through 289 of title 35 or any of the attributes specified for patents in any other provision of law nor is it considered to be a patented invention for purposes of section 292.

At the time of the passage of section 157 of title 35, it was assumed that the Government would be the principal user of this technique since the Government did not generally seek to enforce its patents against the public. Section 157(d) provided for the Secretary of Commerce to annually report to the Congress on the use of statutory invention registrations including assessment of the degree to which agencies of the Federal Government make use of the statutory invention registration system, the degree to which it aids the management of federally developed technology, and an assessment of the cost savings to the Federal Government of the use of such procedures. However, subsequent changes in the law, particular 35 U.S.C. § 200 et seq. and CRADAs under the Stevenson-Wydler Act (15 U.S.C. § 3710a) have led to much more aggressive patent program by Government agencies and therefore such agencies do not generally file for statutory registrations. See Norman R. Klivans, Comment: "Use of Statutory Invention Registration," 73 J. Pat. Off. Soc'y. 735 (1991).

E. The Inventive Act

1. Making the Invention

Another central patent law concept deals with the making of inventions and the use of the term conception and reduction to practice. These terms are used in most patent rights clauses in Government contracts and grants. However, while derived from patent law concepts, these terms are used differently in the context of Government patent policy.

General patent law principles require both the conception and reduction to practice for the making of an invention, *Eli Lilly & Co. v. Brenner*, 248 F. Supp. 402, 147 U.S.P.Q. 442 (D.D.C. 1965), *rev'd on other grounds*, 375 F.2d 599 (D.C. Cir. 1967). Robinson, The *Law Patents for Useful Inventions* (1890) states at 116:

§ 77. Inventive Act Twofold: Mental and Physical

Every invention contains two elements: (1) An idea conceived by the inventor; (2) An application of that idea to the production of a practical result. Neither of these elements is alone sufficient. An unapplied idea is not an invention. The application of an idea, not original with the person who applies it, is not an invention. Hence, the inventive act in reality consists of two acts; one mental, the conception of an idea; the other manual, the reduction of that idea to practice.

2. Conception

The classic definition of conception was stated in *Mergenthaler v. Scudder*, 11 App. D.C. 264 (1897) at 276:

> The conception of the invention consists in the complete performance of the mental part of the inventive act. All that remains to be accomplished . . . belongs to the department of construction, not invention. It is therefore the formation, in the mind of the inventor, of a definite and permanent idea of the complete and operative invention, as it is thereafter to be applied in practice that constitutes an available conception, within the meaning of the patent law. This definition consists of two elements. First, conception is a "mental" act. Second, this mental act must embody the invention that is actually reduced to practice. Or, to state if differently, the invention that is actually reduced to practice must have been anticipated by the alleged mental act for that act to be deemed the conception of the invention.

Accord, *Mahurkar v. C.R. Bard, Inc.*, 79 F.3d 1572 (Fed. Cir. 1996). (To have conceived of an invention, an inventor must have formed in his or her mind "a definite and permanent idea of the complete and operative invention, as it is hereafter to be applied in practice." *Burroughs Wellcome Co. v. Barr Labs., Inc.*, 40 F.3d 1223, 1228, 32 USPQ2d 1915, 1919 (Fed. Cir. 1994), *cert. denied*, 116 S. Ct. 771 (1996) (citations omitted). The idea must be "so clearly defined in the inventor's mind that only ordinary skill would be necessary to reduce the invention to practice, without extensive research or experimentation." Where it is a joint invention, each joint inventor must generally contribute to the conception of the invention. *Burroughs Wellcome Co. v. Barr Lab., Inc.*, 40 F.3d at 1227-28.

In a Government case, *Technitrol, Inc. v. United States*, 194 Ct. Cl. 596, 440 F.2d 1362, 169 U.S.P.Q. 732 (1971), the Court of Claims, quoting from 1 Walker, *Patents* § 45 (Deller's 2d ed.) at 191-92, defined conception at 609 as:

> [T]he formation in the mind of the inventor of a definite idea of complete and operative invention as it is thereafter to be reduced to practice. . . . The date of conception is the date when the invention idea is crystallized in all of its essential attributes and becomes so clearly defined in the mind of the inventor as to be capable of being converted to reality and reduced to practice by the inventor or by one skilled in the art.

The following conclusions may be drawn from the cases:

> When the inventor, or a person of like skill in the art, continues to work with the basic idea, such work will generally be viewed by the courts as "research," and, therefore, the legal conclusion of "conception" will not be applied to that idea.

> When the inventor turns the idea over to a person of ordinary skill in the art, and that person makes changes in or determines the size, shape, or location of parts that are old in the art, such work will generally be viewed by the courts as not amounting to "research," and, therefore, the legal conclusion of "conceptual" will be applied to the idea.

The significance of the foregoing is that at the moment contemporaneous with the conception, there is no one who can say authoritatively that this occurrence will be accepted as a valid conception of the particular invention, which is actually reduced to practice. Rather, it is only after reduction to practice has occurred that there can be any reasonable conclusion drawn as to whether the preceding mental formation of an idea constituted legal conception. This problem has not drawn much attention despite the fact that in some cases it may make it extremely difficult for a contractor to determine whether he is required to report an idea (invention). Further, since many contract patent provisions allowing contractors the first option to retain title to reported inventions tie the filing of patent applications within a certain time period to the exercise of the option, obvious problems can arise. In particular, it may be premature to file patent applications prior to a reduction to practice. Thus a contractor reporting an invention that has been merely conceptualized might do well to consider carefully the contract requirements for filing.

3. Reduction to Practice

Reduction to practice occurs when an invention has been embodied in some physical form which is used to demonstrate its workability.

a. Physical Embodiment Requirements

The first requirement of reduction to practice, i.e., physical embodiment, presents no real problem. If an invention is mechanical or electrical in nature, in the form of a machine or an article of manufacture, it must be physically constructed. If it is a composition of matter or a process for generating a composition of matter, the composition must have been actually prepared, or the process must have been executed in all of its steps. To meet this requirement, every particular aspect of the invention as claimed in the patent must be found in the physical embodiment. However, it is the claim rather than the physical embodiment that sets the "metes" and "bounds" of the invention.

b. Workability

The second requirement of the reduction to practice definition, i.e., workability, raises a more difficult question. To establish that an invention works, the physical embodiment must be tested. In attempting to rationalize the amount, nature, and extent of testing necessary to establish a legal conclusion of reduction to practice, some courts have sought to characterize the inventions themselves. As a result, a judicially conceived classification of inventions has evolved in cases such as *Sydemann v. Thoma*, 32 App. D.C. 362 (1909) and *Lustig v. Legat*, 154 F.2d 680, 69 U.S.P.Q. 345 (C.C.P.A. 1946). This classification consists of three categories:

(i) Inventions, so "simple" in nature, that no tests are necessary to establish their workability;

(ii) Inventions whose workability can be established in the laboratory; and

(iii) Inventions whose workability can only be shown by testing them in their intended environment.

This attempt to characterize inventions and then to apply a judicially developed standard of testing has been the subject of criticism. Judge Learned Hand, in *Sinko Tool & Mfg. Co. v. Automatic Devices Corp.*, 157 F.2d 974, 71 U.S.P.Q. 199 (2d Cir. 1946), after concluding that this approach tended "too much to proliferate a doctrine which had better remain in a single and supple stem," went on to state at 977:

[a] test under service conditions is necessary in those cases, and in those only, in which the persons qualified in the art would require such a test before they were willing to manufacture and sell the invention as it stands.

The thrust of Judge Hand's argument is that the nature of the invention is immaterial; it is the quality of the testing that is important. Furthermore, the quality of the testing is to be judged, not by a judicial standard, but by a practical standard based upon the needs of the particular art. This position is supported by the fact that satisfactory reduction to practice does not turn on proof of successful commercial use, *Corona Cord Tire Co. v. Dovan Chem. Corp.*, 276 U.S. 358 (1928); *Minnesota Mining & Mfg. Co. v. Van Cleef*, 139 F.2d 550, 60 U.S.P.Q. 115 (7th Cir. 1943), but on tests which successfully prove practical utility for the intended purpose, *Ocumpaugh v. Norton*, 25 App. D.C. 90 (1905); *Van Auken v. Cummings*, 49 F.2d 490, 9 U.S.P.Q. 157 (C.C.P.A. 1931).

In cases where tests on the invention are used to show that it was reduced to practice, the amount of testing required will be determined by the particular facts of each case. Reduction to practice is established when it is shown that the invention is able to perform its intended purpose beyond a probability of failure, *Taylor v. Swingle*, 136 F.2d 914, 58 U.S.P.Q. 468 (C.C.P.A. 1943); *Scott v. Finney*, 34 F.3d 1058, 32 U.S.P.Q.2d 1115 (Fed. Cir. 1994). Thus, tests have been held to establish a reduction to practice when they show actual performance of the intended function with a quality, extent, and character of operation sufficient to indicate that the invention has utility in the environment in which it is to be used, *Layin v. Pierotti*, 129 F.2d 883, 54 U.S.P.Q. 400 (C.C.P.A. 1938). In *Hazeltine Corp. v. United States*, 10 Cl. Ct. 417, 230 U.S.P.Q. 721 (1986), *aff'd*, 820 F.2d 1190, 2 U.S.P.Q. 2d 1744 (Fed. Cir. 1987), a dispute arose over whether an open array antenna system was reduced to practice before or during the course of a contract with the Government. Although the antenna system was tested by the developer before entering the contract, the tests were only laboratory tests not made under actual use or service conditions. The court noted that laboratory tests can be used to prove a reduction to practice if the conditions adequately simulate the conditions of practical use. In this case, however, the court found that no reduction to practice was achieved before the contract since the intended environmental conditions were not adequately simulated, leaving it as mere speculation whether it would operate beyond a probability of failure. See generally, Grauer, "The Legally Complete Invention—A Study of the Requirement of Testing to Establish an Actual Reduction to Practice," 33 Geo. Wash. L. Rev. 740 (1965).

4. Constructive Reduction to Practice

Since the filing of a patent application in the Patent and Trademark Office first requires the completion of an invention, a fiction of a constructive reduction to practice has arisen in the patent laws, *Eli Lilly & Co. v. Brenner*, 248 F. Supp. 402, 147 U.S.P.Q. 442 (D.D.C. 1965); *Dannu Rain v. Carlisle*, 59 U.S.P.Q. 472 (P.O. Bd. of Ex. 1941). This fiction assumes that the filing of the patent application is both the conception and reduction to practice of the invention; that is, the invention was previously conceived and the filing of a patent application completes the inventive act. See *Hyatt v. Boone* (Fed. Cir. No. 96-1514-1515, June 17, 1998; *Yasuko Kawai v. Metlesics*, 480 F.2d 880, 885, 178 USPQ 158, 162 (CCPA 1973) ("[T]he act of filing the United States application has the legal effect of being, constructively at least, a simultaneous conception and reduction to practice of the invention."). This practice, of course, results in many paper patents; patents which pertain to inventions that have never been built or tried. In general, paper patents are to be strictly constructed, Walker, *Patents* § 561 (Deller's 2d ed.).

F. Remedies for Infringement

1. By a Private Party

The making, using, or selling of a patented invention by a person (including any state, any instrumentality thereof, and any officer or employee of a state or instrumentality of a state acting in his official capacity) without authority, and within the United States, during the patent term infringes the patent, 35 U.S.C. § 271(a). Excepted from such infringement actions are medical practitioners' in their performance of medical activities, 35 U.S.C. § 281(c). The terminology regarding infringement has been modified to include the "imports" into the United States and the "offers to sell" a patent invention. Section 271(a) of title 35 now provides:

> Except as otherwise provided in this title, whoever without authority makes, uses, offers to sell, or sells any patented invention, within the United States, or imports into the United States any patented invention during the term of the patent therefor, infringes the patent.

Patent infringement is a tort that includes the active inducement to infringe, 35 U.S.C. § 271(b). Additionally, the sale or offers to sell, or imports of a component of a patented machine, or of a composition, material, or apparatus for use in practicing a patented process, while knowing the same to be made especially for use in an infringement of the patent (and not a stable article or commodity of commerce) is a contributing infringement, 35 U.S.C. § 271(c). See Whale, "The ABCD's of Patent Infringement," 62 J. Pat. Off. Soc'y 136 (1980). The tort implies an invasion of the right of the patentee to exclude others from making, using, and selling the patented invention, Walker, *Patents* § 510 (Deller's 2d ed.).

The remedy for patent infringement is obtained by civil suit in federal district court, 35 U.S.C. § 281. Appeals from the decisions and orders of the various district court, unlike other actions, are exclusively with the jurisdiction of the Court of Appeals for the Federal Circuit. This court has jurisdiction to hear all patent infringement appeals that were previously heard by the various circuit courts of appeal, 28 U.S.C. § 1295(a). The statute of limitations on infringement suits against private parties is six years, 25 U.S.C. § 286.

In all patent suits for infringement the patent is presumed valid, 35 U.S.C. § 282. The burden of establishing invalidity is on the asserting party, 35 U.S.C. § 282. Remedies for infringement by a private party include injunctive relief, 35 U.S.C. § 283, and "damages adequate to compensate for the infringement but in no event less than a reasonable royalty for the use made of the invention by the infringer, together with interest and costs as fixed by the court," 35 U.S.C. § 284. However, to recover damage the patentee needs proof that the infringer was notified of the infringement and continued to infringe thereafter, 35 U.S.C. § 287. Use of a patent notice may serve this function. In any event, the filing of an infringement suit is such notice.

Further, relief is not to be denied for infringement or contributory infringement of a patent or the patentee be deemed guilty of misuse or illegal extension of the patent right by reason of his (1) deriving revenue from acts which if performed by another without his consent would constitute contributory infringement of the patent; (2) licensing or authorizing another to perform acts which if performed without his consent would constitute contributory infringement of the patent; (3) seeking to enforce his patent rights against infringement or contributory infringement; (4) refusing to license or use any rights to the patent; or (5) conditioning the license of any rights to the patent or the sale of the patented product on the acquisition of a license to rights in another patent or purchase of a separate product, unless, in view of the circumstances, the patent owner has market power in the relevant market for the patent or patented product on which the license or sale is conditioned, 35 U.S.C. § 271(d).

In *Warner-Jenkinson Co. v. Hilton Davis Chemical Co.*, 520 U.S. 17 (1997), the Supreme Court upheld the validity of the doctrine of equivalents, that an infringing device did not need to be literally covered by a patent claim for a court to find infringement. However, to apply the doctrine of equivalents in a patent infringement, the court must find an equivalent item for each element of the patent claim. Further, the Court reaffirmed that it was up to the judge to determine the scope of a patent claim not the jury but left open whether a could apply the doctrine of equivalents.

Unique in our patent laws is a new affirmative defense to an action for infringement of patents for methods of doing business contained in the American Inventors Protection Act of 1999 if the defendant, acting in good faith, had actually reduced the subject matter to practice at least one year before the effective filing date of the patent asserted against him or her, and commercially used the subject matter patented before the effective filing date of such patent. "Commercially used" is the use of a method in the United States so long as the use is an internal commercial use or an actual arm's-length sale of a useful end result. Pre-marketing regulatory review is also considered, for purposes of the new law, to constitute commercial use. Limited protection is available to nonprofit research laboratories and other such entities. The affirmative defense protects purchasers of a useful end product from the entity asserting the defense. The infringement defense provided by this Act is limited to the person who performed the actions establishing the defense, and limits the transfer of the right to assert this defense. Also, a patent is not to be deemed invalid under sections 102 or 103 solely because the defense is raised or established.

2. By the Government

A Government infringement of patent rights is characterized as an "unauthorized use" of the patent. The remedies against unauthorized use are limited in comparison to the remedies for private infringement. Thus, no injunction can issue against unauthorized use by the Government, since the patent holder is only entitled to "his reasonable and entire compensation for such use," 28 U.S.C. § 1498(a).

The remedy for unauthorized use is obtained by suit in the United States Court of Federal Claims. The Court of Federal Claims has been vested with jurisdiction over cases previously heard by the Court of Claims, and the U. S. Claims Court under a 28 U.S.C. § 1498. Appellate jurisdiction rests with the Court of Appeals for the Federal Circuit. The statute of limitations for unauthorized use actions is six years and may be extended for six additional years if, prior to the running of the first six years, a claim for compensation was pending before a Government agency having authority to settle such claims, 35 U.S.C. § 286.

IV. TRADE SECRETS

A. Basic Concepts

Trade secrets are generally considered under the topics of torts, equity, and contracts. No protection for the owners of trade secrets is provided for in the Constitution, nor has Congress under other enumerated powers, such as the commerce clause, sought to provide broad protection for trade secrets. State laws have provided protection, however, under a variety of concepts.

In the early 1970s the Supreme Court considered whether the Constitution and patent laws preempted state laws that protected against disclosure or use of trade secrets. The Sixth Circuit Court of Appeals had held that state trade secret laws that protected an inventor of a device, which was an appropriate subject for a patent under the patent laws, were in conflict with the patent laws, *Kewanee Oil Co. v. Bicron Corp.*, 478 F.2d 1074, 178 U.S.P.Q.3 (6th Cir. 1973). The second, fourth, fifth, and ninth circuits had reached an opposite conclusion.

In *Kewanee*, 416 U.S. 470, 181 U.S.P.Q. 673 (1974), the Supreme Court reversed the sixth circuit and reasoned at 475-76:

> The protection accorded the trade secret holder is against the disclosure or unauthorized use of the trade secret by those to whom the secret has been confided under the express or implied restriction of nondisclosure or nonuse. The law also protects the holder of a trade secret against disclosure or use when the knowledge is gained, not by the owner's violation, but by some "improper means," 4 *Restatement of Torts,* § 757(a), which may include theft, wiretapping, or even aerial reconnaissance. A trade secret, however, does not offer protection against discovery by fair and honest means, such as by independent invention, accidental disclosure, or by so-called reverse engineering, that is by starting with the known product and working backward to divine the process which aided in its development or manufacture.

The Court noted that in *Goldstein v. California*, 412 U.S. 546, 178 U.S.P.Q. 129 (1973) it had held that the constitutional grant of power to Congress in the copyright area was not exclusive and that the states were not forbidden from protecting authors if Congress had not preempted the area. Similarly, the Court held that states could regulate the patent area as long as state action did not conflict with federal law. After noting that patent and trade secret laws have different goals and use different techniques of protection to reach the goals, the Court stated at 483:

> Since no patent is available for a discovery, however useful, novel, and nonobvious, unless it falls within one of the express categories of patentable subject matter of 35 U.S.C. § 101, the holder of such a discovery would have no reason to apply for a patent whether trade secret protection existed or not. Abolition of trade secret protection would, therefore, not result in increased disclosure to the public of discoveries in the area of unpatentable subject matter. Also, it is hard to see how the public would be benefited by disclosure of customer lists or advertising campaigns; in fact, keeping such items secret encourages businesses to initiate new and individualized plans of operation, and constructive competition results. This, in turn, leads to a greater variety of business methods than would otherwise be the case if privately developed marketing and other data were passed illicitly among firms involved in the same enterprise.

As to the subject matter within 35 U.S.C. § 101, the Court noted at 484:

> Certainly the patent policy of encouraging invention is not disturbed by the existence of another form of incentive to invention. In this respect the two systems are not and never would be in conflict. Similarly, the policy that matter once in the public domain must remain the public domain is not incompatible with the existence of trade secret protection. By definition a trade secret has not been placed in the public domain.

The Court concluded that trade secret protection even when it clearly covers patentable inventions does not conflict with the patent policy of disclosure and is not preempted by federal patent law. The Court stated at 493:

> Trade secret law and patent law have coexisted in this country for over one hundred years. Each has its particular role to play, and the operation of one does not take away from the other. Trade secret law encourages the development and exploitation of those items of lesser or different invention than might be accorded protection under the patent laws, but which items still

have an important part to play in the technological and scientific advancement of the Nation. Trade secret law promotes the sharing of knowledge, and the efficient operation of industry; it permits the individual inventor to reap the rewards of his labor by contracting with a company large enough to develop and exploit it. Congress, by its silence over these many years, has seen the wisdom of allowing the States to enforce trade secret protection. Until Congress takes affirmative action to the contrary, States should be free to grant protection to trade secrets.

B. Uniform Trade Secrets Act

After ten years of study the National Conference of Commissioners on Uniform State Laws in 1979 approved and recommended for enactment by the states a Uniform Trade Secrets Act (UTSA). The UTSA, with variations, has been adopted in 36 states and the District of Columbia. The UTSA, with the Commission's recommended 1985 Amendments, provides:

§ I [Definitions]

As used in this Act, unless the context requires otherwise:

(1) "Improper means" includes theft, bribery, misrepresentation, breach or inducement of a breach of a duty to maintain secrecy, or espionage through electronic or other means;

(2) "Misappropriation" means:

(i) acquisition of a trade secret of another by a person who knows or has reason to know that the trade secret was acquired by improper means; or

(ii) disclosure or use of a trade secret of another without express or implied consent by a person who

(A) used improper means to acquire knowledge of the trade secret; or

(B) at the time of disclosure or use, knew or had reason to know that his knowledge of the trade secret was

(I) derived from or through a person who had utilized improper means to acquire it;

(II) acquired under circumstances giving rise to a duty to maintain its secrecy or limit its use; or

(III) derived from or through a person who owed a duty to the person seeking relief to maintain its secrecy or limit its use; or

(C) before material change of his position, knew or had reason to know that it was a trade secret and that knowledge of it had been acquired by accident or mistake.

(3) "Person" means a natural person, corporation, business trust, estate, trust, partnership, association, joint venture, government, governmental subdivision or agency, or any other legal or commercial entity.

(4) "Trade secret" means information, including a formula, pattern, compilation, program, device, method, technique, or process, that:

(1) derives independent economic value, actual or potential, from not being generally known to, and not being readily ascertainable by proper means by, other persons who can obtain economic value from its disclosure or use, and

(2) is the subject of efforts that are reasonable under the circumstances to maintain its secrecy.

§ 2 [Injunctive Relief]

(1) Actual or threatened misappropriation may be enjoined. Upon application to the court, an injunction shall be terminated when the trade secret has ceased to exist, but the injunction may be continued for an additional reasonable period of time in order to eliminate commercial advantage that otherwise would be derived from the misappropriation.

(b) ~~If the court determines that it would be unreasonable to prohibit future use~~, In exceptional circumstances, an injunction may condition future use upon payment of a reasonable royalty for no longer than the period of time ~~the~~ for which use could have been prohibited. Exceptional circumstances include, but are not limited to. a material and prejudicial change of position prior to acquiring knowledge or reason to know of misappropriation that renders a prohibitive injunction inequitable.

(c) In appropriate circumstances, affirmative acts to protect a trade secret may be compelled by court order.

§ 3 [Damages]

(a) ~~In addition or in lieu of injunctive relief~~, Except to the extent that a material and prejudicial change of position prior to acquiring knowledge or reason to know of misappropriation renders a monetary recovery inequitable, a complainant ~~may~~ is entitled to recover damages for the ~~actual loss caused by~~ misappropriation. ~~A complainant may also~~ Damage can include both the actual loss caused by the misappropriation and the unjust enrichment caused by misappropriation that is not taken into account in computing damages for actual loss. In lieu of damages measured by any other methods, the damages caused by misappropriation may be measured by imposition of liability for reasonable royalty for a misappropriator's unauthorized disclosure or use of a trade secret.

(b) If willful and malicious misappropriation exists, the court may award exemplary damages in an amount not exceeding twice any award may under subsection (a).

§ 4 [Attorney's Fees]

If (i) a claim of misappropriation is made in bad faith, (ii) a motion to terminate an injunction is made or resisted in bad faith, or (iii) willful and malicious misappropriation exists, the court may award reasonable attorney's fees to the prevailing party.

§ 5 [Preservation of Secrecy]

In an action under this Act, a court shall preserve the secrecy of an alleged trade secret by reasonable means, which may include granting protective orders in connection with discovery proceedings, holding in-camera hearings, sealing the records of the action, and ordering any person involved in the litigation not to disclose an alleged trade secret without prior court approval.

§ 6 [Statute of Limitations]

An action for misappropriation must be brought within 3 years after the misappropriation is discovered or by the exercise of reasonable diligence should have been discovered. For the purposes of this section, a continuing misappropriation constitutes a single claim.

§ 7 [Effect on Other Law]

(a) ~~This~~ Except as provided in subsection (b), this [Act] Act displaces conflicting tort, restitutionary, and other law of this State [pertaining to] providing civil liability remedies for misappropriation of a trade secret.

(b) This Act does not affect:

(1) contractual or other civil liability relief that is remedies, whether or not based upon misappropriation of a trade secret; ~~or~~

(2) ~~criminal liability for~~ other civil remedies that are not based upon misappropriation of a trade secret; or

(3) criminal remedies, whether or not based upon misrepresentation of a trade secret.

§ 8 [Uniformity of Application and Construction]

This Act shall be applied and construed to effectuate its general purpose to make uniform the law with respect to the subject of this Act among states enacting it.

§ 9 [Short Title]

This Act may be cited as the Uniform Trade Secrets Act.

§ 10 [Severability]

If any provision of this Act or its application to any person or circumstances is held invalid, the invalidity does not affect other provisions or applications of the Act which can be given effect without the invalid provision or application, and to this end the provisions of this Act rare severable.

§ 11 [Time of Taking Effect]

This [Act] takes effect on _____, and does not apply to misappropriation occurring prior to the effective date. With respect to a continuing misappropriation that began prior to the effective date, the [Act] also does not apply to the continuing misappropriation that occurs after the effective date.

§ 12 [Repeal]

The following Acts and parts of Acts are repealed: (1), (2), (3)

C. Trade Secret Subject Matter

1. Definition

a. Restatement of Torts

The definition of trade secrets most often followed is contained in the comments to section 757, *Restatement, First, of Torts*. The *Restatement* recognizes that "an exact definition of a trade secret is not possible" but defines a trade secret as—

> any formula, pattern, device or compilation of information which is used in one's business, and which gives him an opportunity to obtain an advantage over competitors who do not know or use it. It may be a formula for a chemical compound, a process of manufacturing, treating or preserving materials, a pattern for a machine or other device, or a list of customers.

Milgrim on Trade Secrets 1977 edition Identifies adoption of the *Restatement, First, of Torts* definition by 25 States, the Supreme Court in *Kewanee*, each of the federal circuit courts, and the Court of Claims, *Milgrim's* § 2.01, Footnote 2. *Milgrim* also cites a number of other trade secret definitions.

The 1979 revision of the *Restatement of Torts ("Restatement, Second, of Torts")* omitted coverage for the torts of interference with business relations on the theory that the influence of tort law has continued to decrease in this area and recovery is more dependent on other general fields of law, *Restatement, Second, of Torts*, (1979). The omitted sections included section 757.

The recently issued *Restatement of the Law Third, Unfair Competition* (1995), defines trade secret as follows:

Section 39. Definition of Trade Secret.

A trade secret is any information that can be used in the operation of a business or other enterprise and that is sufficiently valuable and secret to afford an actual or potential economic advantages over others.

The term "trade secret" is rarely used to denote the mere privacy with which one conducts an ordinary business. Comment b of the *Restatement, First, of Torts,* § 757 notes that a trade secret is not simply information as to single or ephemeral events in the conduct of a business such as the amount of a bid or the date fixed for the introduction of a new product. Comment b goes on to note that:

A trade secret is a process or device for continuous use in the operation of the business. Generally it relates to the production of goods, as, for example, a machine or formula for the production of an article. It may, however, relate to the sale of goods or to other operations in the business, such as a code for determining discounts, rebates or other concessions in a price list or catalogue, or a list of specialized customers, or a method of bookkeeping or other office management.

b. UTSA

The UTSA definition of "trade secret," as set forth above, is somewhat broader than the *Restatement* definition. The Commissioner's Comments on the Act provide the following partial listing of the kinds of activity included in "proper means" as used in the trade secret definition:

Proper means include:

1. Discovery by independent invention;

2. Discovery by "reverse engineering," that is, by starting with the known product and working backward to find the method by which it was developed. The acquisition of the known product must of course, also be by a fair and honest means, such as purchase of the item on the open market for reverse engineering to be lawful;

3. Discovery under a license from the owner of the trade secret

4. Observation of the item in public use or on public display;

5. Obtaining the trade secret from published literature.

The Commissioner's Comments on the UTSA explain its definition of trade secrets as follows:

The definition of "trade secret" contains a reasonable departure from the *Restatement of Torts (First)* definition which required that a trade secret be "continuously used in one's business." The broader definition in the proposed Act extends protection to a plaintiff who has not yet had an opportunity or acquired the means to put a trade secret to use. The definition includes information that has commercial value from a negative viewpoint, for example the results of lengthy and expensive research which proves that a certain process will not work could be of great value to a competitor.

CF. *Telex Corp. v. IBM Corp.*, 510 F.2d 894 (CA 10, 1975) *per curiam, cert. dismissed*, 423 U.S. 802 (1975) (liability imposed for developmental cost savings with respect to product not marketed). Because a trade secret need not be exclusive to confer a competitive advantage, different independent developers can acquire rights in the same trade secret.

The words "method, technique" are intended to include the concept of "know-how."

c. Economic Espionage Act of 1996

The Economic Espionage Act of 1996, P.L. 104-294, defines "trade secrets" in Section 1839(3) as follows:

"trade secret" means all forms and types of financial, business, scientific, technical, economic, or engineering information, including patterns, plans, compilations, program devices, formulas, designs, prototypes, methods, techniques, processes, procedures, programs, or codes, whether tangible or intangible, and whether or how stored, compiled, or memorialized physically, electronically, graphically, photographically, or in writing if-

(A) the owner thereof has taken reasonable measures to keep such information secret; and

(B) the information derives independent economic value, actual or potential, from not being generally known to, and not being readily ascertainable through proper means by, the public; and

The Economic Espionage Act of 1996 now defines two federal crimes, economic espionage and the theft of trade secrets which overlaps state law covering theft of trade secrets.

2. Secrecy

An important element for a trade secret is, of course, secrecy. Comment b to the *Restatement, First, of Torts*, § 757, states that matters of public knowledge or general knowledge in an industry cannot be appropriated by one as his secret and that matters which are completely disclosed by the goods sold cannot be a secret. However, it is not necessary that only the proprietor of the business knows the secret; he may communicate it to others under a pledge of secrecy. In addition, others may know the secret independently, but a substantial element of secrecy must still exist. The *Restatement, First, of Torts*, comment b gives some factors to be considered in determining whether information is a trade secret:

(1) the extent to which the information is known outside of his business; (2) the extent to which it is known by employees and others involved in the business; (3) the extent of the measures taken by him to guard the secrecy of the information; (4) the value of the information to him and his competitors; (5) the amount of effort or money expended by him in developing the information; (6) the ease or difficulty with which the information could be properly acquired or duplicated by others.

An unprotected disclosure of the trade secret destroys its trade secret status, *Milgrim*, § 2.0511]. The secret may also be lost by putting it on display, by disclosing it in trade circulars, technical publications or photographs in annual reports, or by persons in the trade circulating it, *Milgrim,* § 2.0512], although not every sale or display will result in the type of disclosure which terminates the trade secret, *Milgrim,* § 2.05[3]. On the other hand, the secrecy need not be total—depending on the circumstances partial or qualified secrecy will suffice, *Jostens, Inc. v. National Computer Sys., Inc.,* 214 U.S.P.Q. 918 (Minn. 1982); *Milgrim, § 2.04.*

The Commissioner's Comments on the UTSA explain the secrecy requirement in the UTSA (in the definition of trade secrets) as follows:

> Finally, reasonable efforts to maintain secrecy have been held to include advising employees of the existence of a trade secret, limiting access to a trade secret on "need to know basis," and controlling plant access. On the other hand, public disclosure of information through display, trade journal publications, advertising, or other carelessness can preclude protection.

> The efforts required to maintain secrecy are those "reasonable under the circumstances." The courts do not require that extreme and unduly expensive procedures be taken to protect trade secrets against flagrant industrial espionage. See *E. I. du Pont de Nemours & Co., Inc. v. Christopher, supra.* It follows that reasonable use of a trade secret including controlled disclosure to employees and licensees is consistent with the requirement of relative secrecy.

3. Novelty

Novelty or patentability are not requisites for a trade secret, Comment b, *Restatement, First, of Torts,* § 757; *Rivendell Forest Prods., Ltd. v. Georgia-Pacific Corp.,* 28 F.3d 1042, 31 U.S.P.Q.2d 1472 (10th Cir. 1994), although the nature of the secret may be important in determining the appropriate relief against one who obtains the secret by improper means. Some degree of novelty may also be required since that which does not possess novelty is usually known; and secrecy, in the context of a trade secret, implies at least a minimum novelty, Comment, "The Stiffel Doctrine and the Law of Trade Secrets," 62 N.W.L. Rev. 956 (1968); *Kewanee Oil Co. v. Bicron Corp.,* 416 U.S. 470, 181 U.S.P.Q. 673 (1974); *Salsbury Labs., Inc. v. Merieux Lab., Inc.,* 908 F.2d 706, 15 U.S.P.Q.2d 1489 (11th Cir. 1990). Thus, a primary requirement is that the information generally be unknown or not readily ascertained. The courts generally require some uniqueness, although there need not be the degree of novelty required for a patent.

The UTSA definition of trade secret embraces the generally accepted concept of novelty required for a trade secret. It states that the information involved "derives independent economic value, actual or potential from not being generally known to, and not being readily ascertainable by proper means by other person . . . ." The Commissioner's comments explains this novelty concept:

> The language "not being generally known to and not being readily ascertainable by proper means by other persons" does not require that information be generally known to the public for trade secret rights to be lost. If the principal person who can obtain economic benefit from information is aware of it, there is no trade secret. A method of casting metal, for example, may be unknown to the general public but readily known within the foundry industry.

Information is readily ascertainable if it is available in trade journals, reference books, or published materials. Often, the nature of a product lends itself to being readily copies as soon as it is available on the market. On the other hand, if reverse engineering is lengthy and expensive, a person who discovers the trade secret through reverse engineering can have a trade secret in the information obtained from reverse engineering.

D. Trade Secret and Patent Applications

Trade secrets must be included if needed in patent applications to fulfill the 35 U.S.C. § 112 requirement that the specifications "set forth the best mode contemplated by the inventor in carrying out his invention," and that the invention must be described "in such full, clear, concise, and exact terms as to enable any person skilled in the art to make and use the same," *Chemcast Corp. v. Arco Indus. Corp.*, 913 F.2d 923, 16 U.S.P.Q.2d 1033 (Fed. Cir. 1990); *White Consol. Indus. v. Vega Servo-Control, Inc.*, 713 F.2d 788, 218 U.S.P.Q. 961 (Fed. Cir. 1983). Once the patent issues the trade secret contained in the specification it is disclosed to the public, 37 C.F.R. § 1.11; *Plastic & Metal Fabricators Inc. v. Ray*, 303 A.2d 725, 175 U.S.P.Q. 49 (Conn. 1972); *National Welding Equip. Co. v. Hammon Precision Equip. Co.*, 165 F. Supp. 788, 119 U.S.P.Q. 13 (D.C. Cal. 1958). Prior to issuance, the patent application is held secret by the Patent and Trademark Office, and the made secret may still be maintained. If the patent application is abandoned, the right to retain the secrecy in the application continues, 35 U.S.C. § 122; *Sears v. Gottschalk*, 502 F.2d 122, 183 U.S.P.Q. 134, *cert. denied*, 422 U.S. 1056, 186 U.S.P.Q. 161 (1974).

It is clear that any contract concerning the use of the invention may survive the abandonment of the patent application, *Aronson v. Quick Point Pencil Co.*, 440 U.S. 257, 201 U.S.P.Q. 1 (1979). There is a split in the circuit courts as to whether a party must still retain, as a trade secret, information disclosed pursuant to a confidential relationship if the information is published subsequently in an issued patent. The sixth circuit *in A. O. Smith Corp. v. Petroleum Iron Works*, 74 F.2d 934, 25 U.S.P.Q. 29 (6th Cir. 1935) and the seventh circuit in *Shellmar Prods. Co. v. Allen-Qualley Co.*, 87 F.2d 104, 32 U.S.P.Q. 24 (7th Cir. 1936) refused to release the confidential relationship when an injunction had been granted previously to protect the trade secret. The second circuit in *Conmar Prods. Corp. v. Universal Slide Fastener Co.*, 172 F.2d 150, 80 U.S.P.Q. 108 (2d Cir. 1949) rejected this rule, although the court indicated the same results could be achieved by a contract provision stating that nondisclosure of the trade secret would continue after the issuance of a patent.

E. Creation of a Trade Secret Relationship

1. Contracts

Trade secrets may be disclosed pursuant to an express or implied-in-fact contract, written or oral (subject to the state statute of frauds provisions). Contracts are usually used in the employer-employee relationship where the employee agrees not to disclose the employer's trade secrets. Similarly, express contracts are used in technology licensing. *Milgrim* lists a number of advantages and disadvantages of express contracts, *Milgrim* § 3.02.

The advantages include: (a) clarification of the confidential status of information; (b) provision of specific notice and precise identification of the; trade secret; (c) the obtaining of broader protection; (d) the accrual of tax advantages; and (e) the specification of the choice of law applicable.

Disadvantages include: (a) danger that the contract will be held to be an unreasonable restraint on trade; (b) the protection agreed to may be too narrow; (c) the cause of action to protect the trade secret may be limited; and, (d) the contract may have a negative effect on employee relations.

2. Confidential Relationships

Milgrim notes that trade secrets may be protected by the courts by operation of law, *Milgrim*, Chapter 4. This protection is based on quasi-contracts, or contracts implied-in-law, originating in confidential relationships. Under the implied-in-law theory, the court "recognizes that certain relationships carry with them the implied (quasi-contractual) duty of the recipient not to use or disclose them to the prejudice of the discloser." *Milgrim* § 4.02.

A trade secret disclosure may occur in various relationships absent an express or implied-R-fact contract, if a duty, protected by law, nevertheless arises to maintain the secrecy of a trade secret. These confidential relationships include employer-employee; principal-agent; manufacturer-contractor, licensor-licensee; manufacturer-sales agent; and certain buyer-seller activities. These relationships generally arise where confidential information is disclosed in a privileged manner. A violation of the confidence will be protected by the courts. In this regard, the courts generally provide relief against a party who has obtained a trade secret by improper means. But note that one cannot force a confidence on another person. If the receiving party protests that he will not hold the secret in confidence the confidential relationship is not established. Similarly, the confidential relationship does not arise if the receiving party has no notice of the confidential character of the disclosure, *Restatement, First, of Torts*, § 757, comment on clause (b). The question is whether the party receiving the information knew or should have known that the information was a trade secret disclosed m confidence.

The rule with respect to the duty of confidence is stated in section 41 of the *Restatement of the Law Third, Unfair Competition* (1995) as follows:

A person to whom a trade secret has been disclosed owes a duty of confidence to the owner of the trade secret for purposes of the rule stated in section 40 if:

(a) the person made an express promise of confidentiality to the disclosure of the trade secret; or

(b) the trade secret was disclosed to the person under circumstances in which the relationship between the parties to the disclosure or the other facts surrounding the disclosure justify the conclusion that, at the time of the disclosure,

(1) the person knew or had reason to know that the disclosure was intended to in confidence, and

(2) the other party to the disclosure was reasonable in inferring that the person consented to an obligation of confidentiality.

F. Remedies

The owner of a trade secret may have a choice of forums and remedies available if he needs judicial relief. The forums that may be available are state courts in torts or breach of contract actions. Action may be brought in federal courts m diversity cases, or if the trade secret claim is involved with a patent or copyright infringement suit.

1. Legal Theory

The legal theory upon which the relief is sought is important since it may determine the nature and scope of the relief granted. Breach of contract is the major theory used in trade secret cases. A tort action of breach of confidence, or interference with a contractual relationship may also be available to the trade secret owner. Selecting the proper theory may determine the trial procedure, the applicable statute of limitation and the extent of damages.

The *Restatement, First, of Torts*, § 757 defines the following general principles of liability for the disclosure or use of a trade secret:

One who discloses or uses another's trade secret, without a privilege to do so, is liable to the other if

(a) he discovered the secret by improper means, or

(b) his disclosure or use constitutes a breach of confidence reposed in him by the other in disclosing the secret to him, or

(c) he learned the secret from a third person with notice of the facts that it was a secret and that the third person discovered it by improper means or that the third person's disclosure of it was otherwise a breach of his duty to the other, or

(d) he learned the secret with notice of the facts that it was a secret and that its disclosure was made to him by mistake.

Section 40 of the *Restatement of the Law Third, Unfair Competition* (1995), defines the liability for the misappropriation of a trade secret as follows:

One is subject to liability for the appropriation of another's trade secret if:

(a) the actor acquires by means that are improper under the rule stated in section 43 information that the actor knows or has reason to know is the other's trade secret; or

(b) the actor uses or discloses the other's trade secret without the other's consent and, at the time of the use or disclosure,

(1) the actor knows or has reason to know that the information is a trade secret that the actor acquired under circumstances creating a duty of confidence owned by the actor to the other under the rule in section 41; or

(2) the actor knows or has reason to know that the information is a trade secret that the actor acquired by means that are improper under the rule stated in section 43; or

(3) the actor knows or has reason to know that the information is a trade secret that the actor acquired from or through a person who acquired it by means that are improper under the rule stated in section 43 or whose disclosure of the trade secret constituted a breach of a duty of confidence owned to the other under the rule in section 41; or

(4) the actor knows or has reason to know that the information is a trade secret that the actor acquired through an accident or mistake, unless the acquisition was the result of the other's failure to take reasonable precautions to maintain the secrecy of the information.

a. Improper and Proper Means

Except where restrained by a confidential or contractual relationship, one is free to adopt and use another's trade secret if he did not employ improper means in the discovery of the secret. The tort law provides a remedy if one takes another's trade secret by improper means, such as, theft, industrial espionage, wire tapping, fraudulent misrepresentation. For example, in *E.I. DuPont v. Christopher*, 431 F.2d 1012, 166 U.S.P.Q. 421 (5th Cir. 1970), *cert. denied*, 400 U.S. 1024, 168 U.S.P.Q. 385 (1971), the court held that aerial reconnaissance was an improper means for acquiring a trade secret. Reverse engineering or ascertaining a trade secret by independent research is a proper means, *Bonito Boats, Inc. v. Thunder Craft Boats, Inc.*, 489 U.S. 146, 160, 9 U.S.P.Q. 2d 1847 (1989).

The Restatement of the Law Third, Unfair Competition (1995), also defines improper means at section 43 as follows:

Improper means of acquiring another's trade secret under the rule stated in section 40 include theft, fraud, unauthorized interception of communications, inducement of or knowing participation in a breach of confidence, and other means either wrongful in themselves or wrongful under the circumstances of the case. Independent discovery and analysis of publicly available products or information are not improper means of acquisition.

b. Third Parties

Restatement, First, of Torts, § 757 clauses (c) and (d) as well as § 758 deal with the torts related to the disclosure of trade secrets owned by third parties. Section 758 provides:

One who learns another's trade secret from a third person without notice that it is secret and that the third person's disclosure is a breach of his duty to the other, or who learns the secret through a mistake without notice of the secrecy and the mistake,

(a) is not liable to the other for a disclosure or use of the secret prior to receipt of such notice, and

(b) is liable to the other for a disclosure or use of the secret after the receipt of such notice, unless prior thereto he has in good faith paid value for the secret or has so changed his position that to subject him to liability would be inequitable.

Section 2.6 of the UTSA is consistent with this *Restatement* provision, but rejects the *Restatements* absolute immunity of third parties who have paid value, in good faith, for a trade secret misappropriated from another. The UTSA follows *Forrest Labs., Inc. v. Pillsbury*, 452 F.2d 621,171 U.S.P.Q. 731 (7th Cir. 1971). Section 757 of the *Restatement, First, of Torts* deals with situations where there was notice or use of improper means, whereas, section 758, covers instances where one disclosed or used another's trade secret having learned of it without notice or any improper means. For example, in *Curtiss-Wright Corp. v. Edel-Brown Tool & Die Co.*, 407 N.E. 2d 319 (Mass. 1980), the court found that the defendant knew or should have known that the information involved was a trade secret and that the disclosure by a third party to the defendant was a breach of duty, and, therefore, the defendant was liable to the trade secret owner.

2. Relief

a. Injunction

Injunctive relief is usually obtainable in successful trade secret litigation protecting the trade secret owner against the disclosure of the trade secret by the wrongful party or preventing this party from using the trade secret. This may also include injunctive relief against third parties who may have received the trade secret from a party who obtained it using improper means. Equitable relief may also be sought to prevent a breach of contract such as violation by an ex-employee of an agreement not to use a trade secret. Issuance of injunctive relief and restraining orders are within the discretion of the courts and may depend upon the extent the trade secret is beyond the general skill in the art.

Section 2 of the UTSA provides for injunctive relief by a court which is to be terminated when the trade secret ceases to exist, except that the injunction may continue until any commercial advantage (without defining this term) derived from the misappropriation is eliminated. This section also permits, in exceptional circumstances, conditioning future use upon the payment of a reasonable royalty at least for the period that the use could have been prohibited, where the court determines it would be unreasonable to prohibit future use. The Commissioner's comments in 1979 stated that it may be unreasonable to prohibit future use where an overspending public interest exists which requires the denial of a "prohibiting injunction" and cites *Republic Aviation Corp. v. Schenk*, 152 U.S.P.Q. 830 (N.Y. Sup. Ct. 1967), where the court considered that enjoining a misappropriator supplying defense material would have endangered military personnel. Another example of an overriding public interest would be a person's acquisition of a misappropriated trade secret in good faith without reason to know it was misappropriated. The 1985 revisions state that "exceptional circumstances" "include, but are not limited to, a material and prejudicial change of position prior to acquiring knowledge or reason to know of misappropriation that renders a prohibitive injunction inequitable."

Section 44 of the *Restatement of the Law Third, Unfair Competition* (1995), also provides for injunctive relief in the case of the misappropriation of a trade secret, as follows:

(1) If appropriate under the rule stated in Subsection (2), injunctive relief may be awarded to prevent a continuing or threatened appropriation of another's trade secret by one who is subject to liability under the rule stated in section 40.

(2) The appropriateness and scope of injunctive relief depend upon a comparative appraisal of all the factors of the case, including the following factors:

(a) the nature of the interest to be protected;

(b) the nature and extent of the appropriation;

(c) the relative adequacy to the plaintiff of an injunction and of other remedies;

(d) the relative harm likely to result to the legitimate interests of the defendant if an injunction is granted and to the legitimate interests of the plaintiff if an injunction is denied;

(e) the interests of third persons and of the public;

(f) any unreasonable delay by the plaintiff in bringing suit or otherwise asserting its rights;

(g) any related misconduct on the part of the plaintiff; and

(h) the practicality of framing and enforcing the injunction.

(3) The duration of injunctive relief in trade secret actions should be limited to the time necessary to protect the plaintiff from any harm attributable to the appropriation and to deprive the defendant of any economic advantage attributable to the appropriation.

b. Damages

In addition, damages may be sought either along with, or independent of, any request for an injunction. In determining the damages, courts often refer to damages available in the case of a patent infringement. This includes the standard of damages as "reasonable royalties," the defendant's profits or the plaintiff's losses, *Milgrim*, § 7.08[3] and provides for damages for the actual loss caused by the misappropriation in addition to, or, in lieu of, an injunction. Damages under the UTSA may include unjust enrichment not taken into account by the damages for an actual loss, except to the extent that a material and prejudicial change of position occurred by the party prior to such party acquiring knowledge, or reason to know, of the misappropriation and such damages are inequitable.

Exemplary damages, up to twice the damages for actual loss, also are permitted if a willful and malicious misappropriation occurs. Thus, as long as there is no double counting, recovery of both actual losses and the misappropriator's unjust benefit is permitted.

c. Criminal

Most states cover theft of trade secrets under their criminal code. These federal crimes are covered as follows in sections 1831 and 1832 of title 18 of the US Code:

Sec. 1831 Economic espionage. (a) IN GENERAL—Whoever, intending or knowing that the offense will benefit any foreign government, foreign instrumentality, or foreign agent, knowingly—

> (1) steals, or without authorization appropriates, takes, carries away, or conceals, or by fraud, artifice, or deception obtains a trade secret; (2) without authorization copies, duplicates, sketches, draws, photographs, downloads, uploads, alters, destroys, photocopies, replicates, transmits, delivers, sends, mails, communicates, or conveys a trade secret; (3) receives, buys, or possesses a trade secret, knowing the same to have been stolen or appropriated, obtained, or converted without authorization; (4) attempts to commit any offense described in any of paragraphs (1) through (3); or (5) conspires with one or more other persons to commit any offense described in any of paragraphs (1) through (3), and one or more of such persons do any act to effect the object of the conspiracy, shall, except as provided in subsection (b), be fined not more than $500,000 or imprisoned not more than 15 years, or both.

(b)ORGANIZATIONS—Any organization that commits any offense described in subsection (a) shall be fined not more than $10,000,000.

Sec. 1832. Theft of trade secrets. (a) Whoever, with intent to convert a trade secret, that is related to or included in a product that is produced for or placed in interstate or foreign commerce, to the economic benefit of anyone other than the owner thereof, and intending or knowing that the offense will, injure any owner of that trade secret, knowingly—

> (1) steals, or without authorization appropriates, takes, carries away, or conceals, or by fraud, artifice, or deception obtains such information; (2) without authorization copies, duplicates, sketches, draws, photographs, downloads, uploads, alters, destroys, photocopies, replicates, transmits, delivers, sends, mails, communicates, or conveys such information; (3) receives, buys, or possesses such information, knowing the same to have been stolen or appropriated, obtained, or converted without authorization; (4) attempts to commit any offense described in paragraphs (1) through (3); or (5) conspires with one or more other persons to commit any offense described in paragraphs (1) through (3), and one or more of such persons do any act to effect the object of the conspiracy, shall, except as provided in subsection (b), be fined under this title or imprisoned not more than 10 years, or both.

(b) Any organization that commits any offense described in subsection (a) shall be fined not more than $5,000,000.

Sec. 1833. Exceptions to prohibitions. This chapter does not prohibit—(1) any otherwise lawful activity conducted by a governmental entity of the United States, a State, or a political subdivision of a State; or (2) the reporting of a suspected violation of law to any governmental entity of the United States, a State, or a political subdivision of a State, if such entity has lawful authority with respect to that violation.

Sec. 1838. Construction with other laws. This chapter shall not be construed to preempt or displace any other remedies, whether civil or criminal, provided by United States Federal, State, commonwealth, possession, or territory law for the misappropriation of a trade secret, or to affect the otherwise lawful disclosure of information by any Government employee under section 552 of title 5 (commonly known as the Freedom of Information Act).

V. SELECTING THE BEST MODE OF PROTECTION

A. Extent of Protection

Many items are susceptible to protection under various intellectual property rights. Often it is necessary, to select among these various modes of protection over the life of the product, process or technique involved. Other times it may be possible to utilize more than one mode of protection, Noone, "Trade Secrets v. Patent Protection," 31 Res. Mgm't 21 (1978); Mahon, "Trade Secrets and Patents Compared," 50 J. Pat. Off. Soc'y 536 (1968). It may be helpful to review the basic nature of the legal protection provided by the patent law, copyright law, and trade secrets. If one were to rank these forms of protection, patents would be first, followed by trade secrets and then copyrights.

1. Patent Consideration

The patent laws provide the patentee with protection for invention, that is, the inventive idea as expressed in his patent claims. The patentee may exclude others from making, using, or selling his invention even though the other party may have independently developed the invention. Of course, rather than excluding others, the patentee may license other parties and agree to refrain from utilizing his legal right to exclude. Before selecting the patent method, one must be fairly certain that the invention is within the subject matter protected by the patent laws; is of sufficient novelty; is timely filed in the patent office; and that all other procedural matters are adhered to by the inventor. The patent, upon issuance publicly discloses the invention, and is granted for a 20-year period during which the patentee may exclude others from practicing the patented invention, i.e., making, using, or selling.

Remedies, such as injunctive relief and damages, are available in federal courts for patent infringement. It should be stressed that in choosing patent protection, the royalties sought under a patent may not extend beyond the life of the patent, *Brulotte v. Thys Co.*, 379 U.S. 29, 143 U.S.P.Q. 264 (1964), i.e., the monopoly granted under a patent cannot lawfully be used to "negotiate with the leverage of that monopoly" to obtain royalties beyond the life of the patent. In addition, even if one obtains a licensee, the licensee may challenge the validity of the patent and if successful need not pay royalties accrued under the license subsequent to the issuance of the patent.

2. Trade Secret Considerations

Trade secret law covers a broader range of subject matter than the patent laws and protects the basic idea embodied in the trade secret as well as the information that discloses the secret. Owners of trade secrets may not exclude others from practicing the secret unless the other party obtained the trade secret through improper means. Thus, a trade secret is not enforceable against an independent developer. The trade secret may be maintained for as long as the owner desires, requires no procedural step to claim the secret but does require safeguards to maintain the secrecy in disclosing the secret to others. Enforcement is under state law and the degree of protection varies from state to state. In comparing trade secrets and patents, the Supreme Court in *Kewanee Oil Co. v. Bicron Corp.*, 416 U.S. 470, 181 U.S.P.Q. 673 (1974) states at 489-90:

> Trade secret law provides far weaker protection in many respects than the patent law. While trade secret law does not forbid the discovery of the trade secret by fair and honest means, e.g., independent creation or reverse engineering, patent law operates "against the world," forbidding any use of the invention for whatever purpose for a significant length of time. The holder of a trade secret also takes a substantial risk that the secret will be passed on to his competitors, by theft or by breach of a confidential relationship, in a manner not easily susceptible to discovery or proof, *Painton & Co. v. Bourns, Inc., supra*, 442 F.2d, at 224. Where patent law acts as a barrier, trade secret law functions relatively as a sieve. The possibility that an inventor who believes his invention meets the standards of patentability will sit back, rely on trade secret law, and after one year of use forfeit any right to patent protection, 35 U.S.C. § 102(b), is remote indeed.

3. Copyrights

Copyrights protect the expression of authors but not the underlying idea, concept, principle, system, or process. They are available for a broad scope of subject matter. The copyright owner may not prevent anyone from using the copyrighted work since "use" is not one of the exclusive rights set forth in 17 U.S.C. § 106. The owner may prevent others without authority from reproducing the copyrighted work; preparing derivative works; distributing copies to the public by sale or lease; publicly performing the work if it is a literary, musical, dramatic, etc. work; and publicly displaying literary, musical, dramatic, and graphic work. Independent action does not infringe a copyright even if substantially similar to the initial copyrighted work.

4. Contracts

One should also consider the use of a contract, an agreement between the parties in protecting an idea, invention, or trade secret, as the best mode of protection between contracting parties. A case in point is *Aronson v. Quick Point Pencil Co.*, 440 U.S. 257, 201 U.S.P.Q. 12 (1979). Aronson had contracted to provide Quick Point the exclusive right to make and sell a key holder. The agreed upon royalty terms were 5 percent of the selling price which would be reduced to 2-1/2 percent if Aronson's patent application on the key holder was not issued in five years. The patent was never allowed, Quick Point kept selling the key holder and eventually imitators started to obtain a larger share of the sales. The imitators paid Aronson no royalty. A number of years later Quick Point refused to pay any more royalties, claiming the contract was unenforceable on the grounds that the state contract law was preempted by federal patent law. The Supreme Court held that the enforcement of this contract was not inconsistent with federal patent law. The contract did not prevent anyone from copying the key holder but merely required Quick Point to pay the royalty it promised in return for the right to make and sell the key holder (then a novel device) enabling it to preempt the market. The Court held at 264-65:

> No decision of this Court relating to patent justifies relieving Quick Point of its contract obligations. We have held that a state may not forbid the copying of an idea in the public domain which does not meet the requirements for federal patent protection. *Compco Corp. v. Day-Brite Lighting, Inc.,* 376 U.S. 234 (1964); *Sears Roebuck & Co. v. Stiffel Co.,* 376 U.S. 225 (1964). Enforcement of Quick Point's agreement, however, does not prevent anyone from copying the key holder. It merely requires Quick Point to pay the consideration which it promised in return for the use of a novel device which enabled it to preempt the market.

> Enforcement of this royalty agreement is even less offensive to federal patent policies than state law protecting trade secrets. The most commonly accepted definition of trade secrets is restricted to confidential information which is not disclosed in the normal process of exploitation. See *Restatement of Torts* § 757, comment b (1939). Accordingly, the exploitation of trade secrets under state law may not satisfy the federal policy in favor of disclosure, whereas disclosure is inescapable in exploiting a device like the Aronson key holder.

> Enforcement of these contractual obligations, freely undertaken in arm's length negotiation and with no fixed reliance on a patent or a probable patent grant, will:

>> encourage invention in areas where patent law does not reach, and will prompt the independent innovator to proceed with the discovery and exploitation of his invention. Competition is fostered and the public is not deprived of the use of valuable, if not quite patentable invention. [Footnote omitted.] *Id., at* 485.

> The device which is the subject of this contract ceased to have any secrecy as soon as it was first marketed, yet when the contract was negotiated the inventiveness and novelty were sufficiently apparent to induce an experienced novelty manufacturer to agree to pay for the opportunity to be first in the market. Federal patent law is not a barrier to such a contract.

B. Criteria for Selection

A party will usually select the patent, trade secret or copyright route for protecting his technology, or a combination of these modes of protection. Factors to be considered in the selection include:

Use trade secret if—

a. Only limited patent protection can be obtained.

b. Trade secret may not be easily detected by others, i.e., a process which doesn't show up in finished goods, or product is not readily reversed engineered.

c. Patent would be easily designed around.

d. Patent is too expensive to obtain.

e. Rapid obsolescence occurs in the market.

f. Patent licensing is required.

g. Term of patent is too short.

Use patent protection if—

a. Strong claims can be obtained.

b. Others may ascertain technology by reverse engineering or independent invention.

c. There is a problem in protecting the trade secret.

d. Patent will be helpful in licensing.

e. Trade secret may be lost by required disclosure to regulatory body.

Use copyright if—

a. Protection is desired for expression not basic ideas.

b. Market is broad and broad access is needed to fully exploit item.

VI. OTHER TYPES OF INTELLECTUAL PROPERTY

A. Semiconductor Mask Works

Congress created a sui generis method of protecting the intellectual property aspects of the manufacture of semiconductor integrated circuits in 1984, P.L. 98-620, the Semiconductor Chip Protection Act of 1984. This new protection was provided because the existing intellectual property rights did not adequately protect the design layouts used in producing integrated semiconductor chips. The copyright office, for example, had previously refused to register a printed circuit board as being a utilitarian product and not copyrightable. In designing a semiconductor chip, the various semiconductor elements are selected to achieve the necessary electrical elements and electrical interconnections. The elements are configured in three dimensions and are built up in layers by means of a series of masks using photography and depositing and etching techniques to place layers of metallic insulating and semiconductor materials in a desired pattern on a silicon wafer. The design of a chip layout requires extensive efforts and may incur large development costs, but can be copied relatively cheaply by reverse engineering, i.e., removing layers of the semiconductor materials from the chip photographing the results and then using the photographs to produce the masks.

As the sui generis protection provided by the semiconductor chip act to "mask works" falls outside of the patent and copyright system, it is based on Congress' authorities under the Commerce Clause in the Constitution rather than the patent and copyright clause. However, many of the concepts adopted by the semiconductor chip act are similar to the copyright law, and the coverage for semiconductor mask works has been placed in title 17 of the U.S. Code, the copyright section of the U.S. Code, as Chapter 9.

1. Subject Matter

Protection is provided to "mask works," the series of patterns usually produced by photographic means, used to manufacture the semiconductor layers of an integrated circuit chip referred in Chapter 9 as a "semiconductor chip product." 17 U.S.C. § 901(a)(1) defines a "semiconductor chip product" as "the final or intermediate form of any product (A) having two or more layers of metallic, insulating, or semiconductor material, deposited or otherwise placed on, or etched away or otherwise removed from, a piece of semiconductor material in accordance with a predetermined pattern; and (B) intended to perform electronic circuitry functions" A "mask work" is defined in section 901(a)(2)

as a series of related images, however fixed or encoded—

(A) having or representing the predetermined, three-dimensional pattern of metallic, insulating, or semiconductor material present or removed from the layers of a semiconductor chip product; and

(B) in which series the relation of the images to one another is that each image has the pattern of the surface of one form of the semiconductor chip product;

Protection under Chapter 9 is provided to mask works that are "fixed" in a semiconductor chip products. A mask work is "fixed" when its embodiment in the product is sufficiently permanent or stable to permit the mask work to be perceived or reproduced from the product for a period of more than transitory duration, section 901(a)(3) of title 17. However, protection is dependent upon the owner registering the mask work with the Register of Copyright under 17 U.S.C. § 908. Further, a mask work fixed in a semiconductor product under the authority of the owner is eligible for protection, if on the earlier of the date on which the mask work is registered or is first commercially exploited, the owner of the mask work who is either a national or domiciliary of the United States (or of another country providing protection to United States mask works), the mask work is first commercially exploited in the United States, or in a country that is subject to a Presidential proclamation as eligible for protection under Chapter 9. Protection is not available under Chapter 9, if the mask work is not original, consists of a stable commonplace designs (or variations thereof) in a way that is not original. In additions, similar to the copyright laws, protection does not pursuant to 17 U.S.C. § 902(c) extend to—

> any idea, procedure, process, system, method of operation, concept, principle, or discovery, regardless of the form in which it is described, explained, illustrated, or embodied in such work.

2. Exclusive Rights

The owner of a mask work has the exclusive rights under section 905 to do and to authorize any of the following acts:

(1) to reproduce the mask work by optical, electronic, or any other means;

(2) to import or distribute a semiconductor chip product in which the mask work is embodied; and (3) to induce or knowingly to cause another person to do any of the acts described in paragraphs (1) and (2).

3. Limitations on Exclusive Rights

a. Reverse Engineering

The exclusive rights of the owner of mask work is limited (in that it is not an infringement of a mask work protected under this chapter to reverse engineer a chip product). 17 U.S.C. § 906 provides as to reverse engineering:

> (a) Notwithstanding the provisions of section 905, it is not an infringement of the exclusive rights of the owner of a mask work for—

> > (1) a person to reproduce the mask work solely for the purpose of teaching, analyzing, or evaluating the concepts or techniques embodied in the mask work or the circuitry, logic flow, or organization of components used in the mask work; or

> > (2) a person who performs the analysis or evaluation described in paragraph (1) to incorporate the results of such conduct in an original mask work which is made to be distributed.

In *Brooktree Corp. v. Advanced Micro Devices*, 977 F.2d 1555, 24 U.S.P.Q. 2d 1401 (Fed. Cir. 1992), the court held that while it is not an infringement of a protected mask work to reverse engineer a chip and use the knowledge to create an original chip that has a different design layout but which performs the same or equivalent function as an existing chip, it was up to the jury to determine if the reverse engineering had in fact resulted in an original chip or one that was substantially similar to the existing chip.

b. First Sale

Like copyrights, the owner of a semiconductor chip product that was produced under authority of the owner of a mask work "may import or distribute or otherwise dispose of or use, but not reproduce, that particular semiconductor chip product without the authority of the owner of the mask work," 17 U.S.C. § 906(b).

4. Registration of Claims

Unlike copyright requirements, owners of chip products must register their claims within two years after the date on which the mask work is first commercial exploited in the world, 17 U.S.C. § 908. In an action of infringement, the registration by the Register is prima facie evidence of the facts stated in the certificate.

5. Notice

The notice for mask works is an M, an M in a circle, or the word mask force [mask work] and the name of the owner, 17 U.S.C. § 909.

6. Infringement/Enforcement

The owner of a mask work may institute civil action against any person who violates any of the owner's exclusive rights by conduct in or effecting commerce, 17 U.S.C. § 910(a). Civil suit is, however, subject to the requirement that the owner have a certificate of registration. Remedies for infringement include injunctions, the award of actual damages and the profit of the infringer not taken into account in computing the actual damages, and reasonable attorney fees. Minimum statutory damages of $250,000 are also specified.

B. Digital Recording

1. Digital Audio Recording

The concern of owners of audio works that new digital recorders could virtually make an identical copy of CDs led to an effort to restrain the importation of digital recorders into the U.S. based on threats of copyright litigation against the manufacturer of such devices. This resulted in unique coverage in chapter 10 of title 17 for a "digital audio recording device" defined in section 1001 (3) as—

> any machine or device of a type commonly distributed to individuals for use by individuals, whether or not included with or as part of some other machine or device, the digital recording; function of which is designed or marketed for the primary purpose of, and that is capable of, making a digital audio copied recording for private use, except from (A) professional model products, and (B) dictation machines, answering machines, and other audio recording equip-

ment that is designed and marketed primarily for the creation of sound recordings resulting from the fixation of nonmusical sounds.

2. Serial Copy Management

The Act requires each digital audio recording device imported into the U.S. to have the Serial Copy Management System, a system that has the same functional characteristics, or any other system certified by the Secretary of Commerce as prohibiting unauthorized serial copying. Further, the Act prohibits the import, manufacture, or distribution of any device, or offer or perform any service, the primary purpose or effect of which is to avoid, bypass, remove, deactivate, or otherwise circumvent any program or circuit which implements the Serial Copy Management System. The Act also prohibits the encoding of a digital musical recording of a sound recording with inaccurate information relating to the category code, copyright status, or generation status of the source material for the recording.

3. Recording Medium

The Act establishes a royalty payment scheme on digital audio recording devices and on the "digital audio recording medium" used by these machines. The term "digital audio recording medium" is defined in 17 U.S.C. § 1001(4) as:

(A) any material object in a form commonly distributed for use by individuals, that is primarily marketed or most commonly used by consumers for the purpose of making digital audio copied recordings by use of a digital audio recording device.

(B) Such term does not include any material object—

(i) that embodies a sound recording at the time it is first distributed by the importer or manufacturer; or (ii) that is primarily marketed and most commonly used by consumers either for the purpose of making copies of motion pictures or other audiovisual works or for the purpose of making copies of nonmusical literary works, including computer programs or data bases.

4. Royalties

a. Amounts

Each person importing into the U.S. or distributing, or manufacturing and distributing a (i) digital audio recording device or (ii) a digital recording medium must record the notice specified by section 1003 and subsequently deposit the statements of account and applicable royalty payments for such device or medium specified in 17 U.S.C. § 1004. The importer or manufacturer must then file with the Register of Copyright a notice with respect to the device and medium and must file quarterly and annual statements with respect to its distribution.

Royalty payments in the following amounts are then required to be deposited with the Register of Copyright section 1004:

(a) Digital audio recording devices.—

(1) *Amount of payment.*—The royalty payment due under section 1003 for each digital audio recording device imported into and distributed in the United States, or manufactured and distributed in the United States shall be 2 percent of the transfer price. Only the first person to manufacture and distribute or import and distribute such device shall be required to pay the royalty with respect to such device.

(2) *Calculation for devices distributed with other devices.*—With respect to a digital audio recording device first distributed in combination with one or more devices, either as a physically integrated unit or as separate components, the royalty payment shall be calculated as follows:

(A) if the digital audio recording device and such other devices are part of a physically integrated unit, the royalty payment shall be based on the transfer price of the unit, but shall be reduced by any royalty payment made on any digital audio recording device included within the unit that was not first distributed in combination with the unit.

(B) If the digital audio recording device is not part of a physically integrated unit and substantially similar devices have been distributed separately at any time during the preceding 4 calendar quarters, the royalty payment shall be based on the average transfer price of such devices during those 4 quarters.

(C) If the digital audio recording device is not part of a physically integrated unit and substantially similar devices have not been distributed separately at any time during the preceding 4 calendar quarters, the royalty payment shall be based on a constructed price reflecting the proportional value of such device to the combination as a whole.

(3) *Limits on royalties.*—Notwithstanding paragraph (1) or (2), the amount of the royalty payment for each digital audio recording device shall not be less than $1 nor more than the royalty maximum. The royalty maximum shall be $8 per device, except that in the case of a physically integrated unit containing more than 1 digital audio recording device, the royalty maximum for such unit shall be $12. During the 6th year after the effective date of this chapter, and not more than once each year thereafter, any interested copyright party may petition the Librarian of Congress to increase the royalty maximum and, if more than 20 percent of the royalty payments are at the relevant royalty maximum, the Librarian of Congress shall prospectively increase such royalty maximum with the goal of having no more than 10 percent of such payments at the new royalty maximum; however the amount of any such increase as a percentage of the royalty maximum shall in no event exceed the percentage increase in the Consumer Price Index during the period under review.

(b) *Digital audio recording media:* The royalty payment due under section 1003 for each digital audio recording medium imported into and distributed in the United States, or manufactured and distributed in the United States, shall be 3 percent of the transfer price. Only the first person to manufacture and distribute or import and distribute such medium shall be required to pay the royalty with respect to such medium.

b. *Limits on Royalties*

The amount of the royalty payment for each digital audio recording device shall not be less than $1 not more than the royalty maximum. The royalty maximum shall be $8 per device, except that in the case of a physically integrated unit containing more than 1 digital audio recording device, the royalty maximum for such unit shall be $12. During the 6th year after Oct. 28, 1992, and once each year thereafter, any interested copyright party may petition the Librarian of Congress to increase the royalty maximum and, if more than 20 percent of the royalty payments are at the relevant royalty maximum, the Librarian of Congress shall prospectively increase such royalty maximum with the goal of having no more than 10 percent of such payments at the new royalty maximum; however the amount of any such increase as a percentage of the royalty maximum shall in no event exceed the percentage increase in the Consumer Price Index during the period under review.

c. *Payment*

The royalties are then made available to interested copyright parties defined in 17 U.S.C. § 1001 (7) as the owner of the exclusive right under section 106(1) to reproduce a sound recording of a musical work that has been embodied in a digital musical recording or analog musical recording lawfully made under this title that has been distributed; a featured recording artist who performs on a sound recording that has been distributed; or any association or other organization representing persons specified above. Section 1006 provides for the following distribution of royalties to "interested copyright parties "(1) whose musical work or sound recording has been—(A) embodied in a digital musical recording or an analog musical recording lawfully made under this title that has been distributed, and (B) distributed in the form of digital musical recordings or analog musical recordings or disseminated to the public in transmissions, during the period to which such payments pertain; and (2) who has filed a claim under section 1007." The royalty payments shall be divided into 2 funds as follows:

(1) *The sound recordings fund.* 66 2/3 percent of the royalty payments shall be allocated to the Sound Recordings Fund. 2 5/8 percent of the royalty payments allocated to the Sound Recordings Fund shall be placed in an escrow account managed by an independent administrator jointly appointed by the interested copyright parties described in section 1001(7)(A) and the American Federation of Musicians (or any successor entity) to be distributed to non featured musicians (whether or not members of the American Federation of Musicians or any successor entity) who have performed on sound recordings distributed in the United States. 1 3/8 percent of the royalty payments allocated to the Sound Recordings Fund shall be placed in an escrow account managed by an independent administrator jointly appointed by the interested copyright parties described in section 1001 (7)(A) and the American Federation of Television and Radio Artists (or any successor entity) to be distributed to nonfeatured vocalists (whether or not members of the American Federation Television and Radio Artists or any successor entity) who have performed on sound recordings distributed in the United States. 40 percent of the remaining royalty payments in the Sound Recordings Fund shall be distributed to the interested copyright parties described in section 1001(7)(C), and 60 percent of such remaining royalty payments shall be distributed to the interested copyright parties described in section 1001(7)(A).

(2) The *musical works fund.* (A) 33 1/3 percent of the royalty payments shall allocated to the Musical Works Fund for distribution to interested copyright parties described in section 1001(7)(B). (B)(i) Music publishers shall be entitled to 50 percent of the royalty payments allocated to the Musical Works Fund. (ii) Writers shall be entitled to the other 50 percent of the royalty payments allocated to the Musical Works Fund.

5. Infringement

In return for this compulsory royalty payment, section 1008 prohibits infringement actions under title 17 U.S. Code based on the manufacture, importation, or distribution of a digital audio recording device, a digital audio recording medium, an analog recording device, or an analog recording medium, or based on the noncommercial use by a consumer of such a device or medium for making digital musical recordings or analog musical recordings.

6. Civil Remedies

17 U.S.C. § 1009 provides for civil actions by any interested copyright party injured by a violation of sections 1002 or 1003 in an appropriate United States district court and further provides for suit by any person injured by a violation of 17 U.S.C. § 1001 et seq. in an appropriate United States district court for actual damages incurred as a result of such violation, such actions the court may injunctions as it deems reasonable to prevent or restrain such violation and award damages and reasonable attorney's fee to the prevailing party. Statutory damages in the sum of not more than $2,500 per device involved for section 1002, $25 per digital musical recording involved in such violation, and for violations for each transmission or communication that violates section 1002(e), in the sum of not more than $10,000, as the court considers just are also provided. In the case of an innocent violations of section 1002, the court may reduce the total award of damages against a person violating section 1002 to a sum of not less than $250 in any case in which the court finds that the violator was not aware and had no reason to believe that its acts constituted a violation of section 1002.

C. Vessel Hull Design

In response to *Bonita Boat, Inc. v. Thunder Craft Boats, Inc.*, 489 U.S. 149 (1989), holding that the patent laws preempted protection of boat hull designs by the State of Florida, Congress enacted protection for boat hull designs under its interstate commerce authority. The Vessel Hull Design Protection Act, P.L. 105-304, Title V, adds a new chapter 13 to title 17 of the U.S. Code for the protection of original designs of a useful article, which makes the article attractive in appearance to the public. Original designs under the Act are, however, limited to vessel hull, including plugs or molds. A design is "original" if it results from the designer's creative endeavor that provides a distinguishable variation over prior similar articles which is more than merely trivial and has not been copied from another source. A "useful article" is a vessel hull, including a plug or mold, which in normal use has an intrinsic utilitarian function that is not merely to portray the appearance of the article or to convey information. A "hull" is the frame or body of a vessel, including the deck of a vessel, exclusive of masts, sails, yards, and rigging. A "plug" means a device or model used to make a mold for the purpose of exact duplication, regardless of whether the device or model has an intrinsic utilitarian function that is not only to portray the appearance of the product or to convey information. A "mold" means a matrix or form in which a substance for material is used, regardless of whether the matrix or form has an intrinsic utilitarian function that is not only to portray the appearance of the product or to convey information.

> Not protected are designs that are not original; are staple or commonplace, such as a standard geometric figure, a familiar symbol, an emblem, or a motif, or another shape, pattern, or configuration which has become standard, common, prevalent, or ordinary; or different from a design excluded above by only in insignificant details or in elements which are variants commonly used in the relevant trades; are dictated solely by a utilitarian function of the article that embodies it; or are embodied in a useful article that was made public by the designer or owner more than t year before the application for registration.

Protection for a design commences upon the earlier of the date of publication of the registration or the date the design is first made public and continues for a term of 10 years. Design notices are required consisting of the words "Protected Design," the abbreviation "Prot'd Des," or the letter "D" with a circle, or the symbol "*D*," the year of the date on which protection for the design commenced; and the name of the owner, an abbreviation by which the name can be recognized, or a generally accepted alternative designation of the owner.

The owner of a design protected under this Act has the exclusive right to make, have made, or import, for sale or for use in trade, any useful article embodying that design; and sell or distribute for sale or for use in trade any useful article embodying that design. A court having may grant injunctions in accordance to prevent infringement of a protected design and shall award the claimant damages adequate to compensate for an infringement. In addition, the court may increase the damages to such amount, not exceeding $50,000 or $1 per copy, whichever is greater, as the court determines to be just. The damages awarded shall constitute compensation and not a penalty.

The issuance of a design patent under title 35, United States Code, for an original design for an article of manufacture shall terminate any protection of the original design under this chapter. The amendments made by Act remain in effect until the end of the two-year period beginning on such date of enactment.

VII. COPYRIGHT LAW

Copyright is a form of legal protection that protects an author's expression with respect to certain types of original works. Copyright is the exclusive privilege of an author or proprietor to print, copy, publish, or vend copies of the author's literary, artistic, or intellectual productions and to license their production or sale by others, *Ballantine's Law Dictionary* (1969). The purpose of copyright protection is not solely to reward the author but to benefit the public as well. In *Mazer v. Stein*, 347 U.S. 201, 100 U.S.P.Q. 325 (1954), the Supreme Court stated at 219:

The economic philosophy behind the clause empowering Congress to grant patents and copyrights is the conviction that encouragement of individual effort by personal gain is the best way to advance public welfare through the talents of authors and inventors in "Science and useful Arts."

See also *Goldstein v. California*, 412 U.S. 546, 178 U.S.P.Q. 129 (1973); *Twentieth Century Music Corp. v. Aiken*, 422 U.S. 151,186 U.S.P.Q. 65 (1975); and *Sony Corp. of Am. v. Universal City Studios, Inc.*, 464 U.S. 417, 220 U.S.P.Q. 665 (1984). The Supreme Court in *Sony* explained the copyright law as enacted at 429:

The monopoly privileges that Congress may authorize are neither unlimited nor primarily designed to provide a special private benefit. Rather, the limited grant is a means by which an important public purpose may be achieved. It is intended to motivate the creative activity of authors and inventors by the provision of a special reward, and to allow the public access to the products of their genius after the limited period of exclusive control has expired.

A. The Copyright System

1. 1909 Copyright Act/Dual System

a. Federal Protection

Prior to the 1976 Copyright Act, P.L. 94-533, two different systems for the protection of copyrights were recognized in the United States. The basic system was established by federal statute contained in title 17 of the United States Code. Under the law as enacted in 1909, authors were provided with the exclusive rights to their writings for a period of 28 years, renewable for another 28 years. The exclusive rights of title 17 included the right to print, reprint, copy, and vend copyrighted works; to translate; to dramatize nondramatic works; to prepare derivative works such as novels; to deliver or present the work in public for a profit; and to perform the work publicly for a profit. The classes of copyrights included books, periodicals, lectures, dramatic compositions, musical compositions, maps, works of art, reproductions of a work of art, drawings, photographs, prints, and motion pictures, 17 U.S.C. § 5. Protection under this federal law required the publication of the work. Publication terminated any state protection and activated the federal protection.

b. State Protection—Common Law and Statute

At issue over the years was the impact of the federal copyright system on state law, which provided remedies akin to copyright protection under federal law. From the beginning of our nation, it was assumed that a concurrent copyright power, subject to federal preemption, resided in the states. For example, the common law copyright, i.e., the right of the author to first publish his works or to keep it unpublished, was recognized by the Supreme Court in *Wheaton v. Peters*, 33 U.S. 591 (1834) as being protectable under state law.

Further, section 2 of the 1909 Copyright Act specifically provided that the Act would not limit the rights of authors in unpublished works. The Supreme Court also held in *Goldstein v. California*, 412 U.S. 546, 178 U.S.P.Q. 129 (1973) that the states could protect the works of authors as long as the system of protection did not conflict with the federal copyright law. In *Goldstein*, the state law dealt with the unauthorized copying of phonograph records and tapes as a criminal offense. At the time of the *Goldstein* decision, the federal copyright law did not cover phonorecords. Protection under state law theoretically could last in perpetuity since the states were not bound by the restrictions of a "limited time" in the Constitution for protecting the exclusive rights of authors.

2. 1976 Copyright Act

After considering and studying the revision of the 1909 law for about ten years, Congress, in 1976, enacted a new title 17, P.L. 94-553, effective on January 1, 1978, which not only completely revised the 1909 law but also abolished the tort of common law copyright under the state system and included a right in unpublished works in title 17. The congressional reports, which form the basic legislative history, are cited extensively in the following discussion. These are as follows: Conference Report, to accompany S.22; General Revision of the Copyright Law, title 17 of the United States Code, H. Rep. No. 94-1733, 94th Cong., 2d Sess. (1976); S. Rep. No. 94-473, Copyright Law Revision, 94th Cong., 1st Sess. (1975); H. Rep. No. 94-1476, Copyright Law Revision, 94 Cong., 2d Sess. (1976).

The 1976 Copyright Act greatly modified the breadth and coverage of the federal copyright law that was then in existence and specifically provided, in 17 U.S.C. § 301, for the abolishment of state laws that are the equivalent to federal copyright protection under the theory of federal preemption. While this provision clearly abolished the common law copyright, there is still much doubt as to its scope, *M. & D. Nimmer on Copyrights*, § 1.01[B], (hereinafter *"Nimmer")* and § 1:9, Boorstyn, *Copyright Law* (1981).

3. International System

a. Universal Copyright Convention

The United States became a member of the Universal Copyright Convention ("UCC") in 1955. The UCC has 80 member countries and was created as an alternative to the Berne Convention for the Protection of Literary and Artistic Works (hereinafter "Berne") to obtain multilateral protection for countries that refused to adopt the "no formality" regime of the Berne. Basically, the UCC was drafted so that the United States could adhere to this treaty without major change to then existing copyright laws. A published work copyrighted in a national of a state that abided by this treaty and works first published in such a state enjoys copyright protection in the other contracting states to the same extent as works of such other contracting states provides to its own citizens. Similarly, unpublished works would enjoy the same protection in the other contracting states as such states provided to its own nationals.

Formalities required by domestic laws of a contracting state as a condition of copyright protection were regarded as satisfied, for works protected under the UCC that were published outside of a contracting states by an national of another contracting state, if all copies of the woks contained an appropriate copyright notice. Contracting states could adopt other formalities such as registration and deposit of copies as a conditions of copyright protection and with respect to its nationals or works first published in its country could require other formalities.

b. Berne Convention

The "Bern Convention" (defined in section 101 of title 17 of the United States Code as "the Convention for the Protection of Literary and Artistic Works, signed at Berne, Switzerland, on September 9, 1886, and all acts, protocols, and revisions thereto") is the oldest and most important multilateral treaty regarding copyright protection. It was first formalized in 1888 and 80 countries now adhere to the Berne Convention. The United States acceded to the Berne Convention in 1988 and its changes to title 17 of the United States Code to make the changes required by this accession became effective on March 1, 1989 pursuant to the Berne Convention Implementation Act of 1988, P.L. 100-568, enacted October 31, 1988. Copyright protection under Berne is based on "national treatment" and requires signature countries to provide the national of other members of Berne the same protection as it provides to its own citizens. Copyright protection by each member state is to be automatic, without any formalities being required. The rights accorded in the country of origin of the work is governed by the domestic law of that country regardless if the author is a national of that country. The rights accorded by Berne member states are governed exclusive by the laws of the member states where protection is being claimed regardless where similar protection is available in the state of the origin of the work.

Since the United States now belongs to both the UCC and the Berne Convention, the question is how compliance is achieved with both these treaties. The UCC contains provisions to protect the integrity of Berne adherence countries, and provides that states that are parties to both treaties that the terms of Berne will govern.

The United States in order to comply with the requirements of the Berne Convention after it acceded to this treaty modified title 17 to remove the formalities prohibited by Berne for copyright protection. These changes that became effective on March 1, 1989 included:

1. Removal of the copyright notice requirement for works published after March 1, 1989;

2. Extend copyright protection to works originating in other Berne convention states ("Berne works");

3. Modify the deposit requirement to meet the Berne convention standards; and

4. Limit the requirement for the registration of copyright suits to U.S. origin, works and not to Berne works.

c.   NAFTA/GATT and TRIPs

(1) NAFTA

The North American Free Trade Agreement (NAFTA) contained a few copyright provisions that were implemented by the NAFTA Implementation Act (P.L. 103-182). These requirements pertain to the restoration of copyright protect to certain audio visual and motion pictures works that lost protection in the United States because of their publication in Canada or Mexico without proper notice of copyright. Section 334 of P.L. 103-182 adds new section 104A to title 17 to provide for such restoration. To be eligible for restoration, the motion picture work or any work included in the motion picture (1) must have been first fixed in Mexico an entered the public domain in the United States because of first publication anywhere on or after January 1, 1978 and before March 1, 1989 with the required copyright notice; or (2) regardless of where it was fixed must have entered the public domain in the United States because of first publication in Mexico or Canada on or after January 1, 1978 and before March 1, 1989 without the required copyright notice. The NAFTA Implementation Act provides for the filing of a statement of intent to restore copyright protection with the Copyright Office in the United States. This Act also made permanent the record rental provisions of section 109 of title 17.

(2) GATT/TRIPs

The General Agreement on Tariff and Trade (GATT), Uruguay Round, and the Trade Related Aspects of Intellectual Property (TRIPs) Agreement was signed in April 1994 and United States implementing legislation, Uruguay Round Agreement Act was enacted on December 8, 1994, P.L. 103-465. With this law the United States agrees to become a member country of the World Trade Organization and to change its laws to conform to GATT. Title V of this implementing Act, Subtitle A, provides for a number of changes to title 17 of the United States Code. First, the Copyright Software Rental Amendments Act of 1990, that modified section 109 of title 17 by restricting the rental of certain computer programs under the first sale doctrine, was made permanent by section 511 of the implementation Act. Second, the implementation Act, section 512, made it an infringement under sections 502 to 505 of title 17 to fix sounds and/or sounds and images of live musical performances without authority and also makes such an unauthorized act a criminal offense.

The implementation Act also provides for the restoration of copyright protection to works already in existence, and not protected by U.S. federal copyrights but that are subject to copyright protections in a WTO member country that is the source of the work, if such works are covered by the subject matter of section 104(a), and are not in the public domain of the source country through either the expiration of term of protection but is in the public domain in the United States due to the noncompliance with the formalities imposed at any time by United States Copyright Law, including the failure to renew a copyright; the lack of a proper notice; or the failure to comply with any manufacturing requirement; the lack of subject matter protection in the case of sound recordings fixed before February 15, 1972; or the lack of national eligibility; and, at least one author at the time of work was created was a national of an eligible country and had not published in the United States during 30 days following publication in such eligible country. The implementation Act contemplates the filing of a certificate of restoration with the Copyright Office if a party seeks to restore its copyright in the United States.

B. Subject Matter Covered

1. Title 17, Section 102(a)

17 U.S.C. § 102(a) sets forth the subject matter covered by the federal copyright law as follows:

> (a) Copyright protection subsists, in accordance with this title, in original works of authorship fixed in any tangible medium of expression, now known or later developed, from which they can be perceived, reproduced, or otherwise communicated, either directly or with the aid of a machine or device. Works of authorship include the following categories:
>
> (1) literary works;
>
> (2) musical works, including any accompanying words;
>
> (3) dramatic works, including any accompanying music;
>
> (4) pantomimes and choreographic works;
>
> (5) pictorial, graphic, and sculptural works;
>
> (6) motion pictures and other audiovisual works;
>
> (7) sound recordings; and
>
> (8) architectural works.

These categories are not exclusive and are somewhat overlapping. Section 101 utilizes the work "include" to indicate that the listing is illustrative and not a limitation. Therefore, these categories are not necessarily exhaustive, H. Rep. at 53. For example, the Architectural Works Copyright Protection Act of 1990 added the category of "architectural works" to this list. 17 U.S.C. § 101 defines "architectural works" as:

> An "architectural work" is the design of a building as embodied in any tangible medium of expression, including a building, architectural plans, or drawings. The work includes the overall form as well as the arrangement and composition of spaces and elements in the design, but does not include individual standard features.

Architectural work protection under the copyright code is somewhat unique as it provides protection against copying certain elements of an architectural design or drawing by the construction of a three-dimensional building that incorporates the covered designs or drawings.

2. Criteria for Coverage

a. Originality

Congress specifically left undefined the term "original works of authorship," H. Rep. at 51, although it has long been a requirement that a work be original in order to be copyrighted. This is based on the view that inherent in the term "author" is the concept of creating or originating, *Nimmer*, § 2.01[A]; Saidman, "Copyrights: Novelty or Originality?" 55 J. Pat. Off. Soc'y 314 (1973).

Originality in the copyright sense should be distinguished from the concept of novelty, ingenuity, or aesthetic merit. A work can be copyrightable even though it is substantially similar to a work previously produced by others (hence not novel); "Originality means only that the work owes its origin to the author, i.e., is independently created, and not copied from other works," *Nimmer*, § 2.01[A]. As Learned Hand stated in *Sheldon v. Metro-Goldwyn Pictures Corp.*, 81 F.2d 49, 28 U.S.P.Q. 330 (2d Cir. 1936), *aff'd*, 309 U.S. 390, 44 U.S.P.Q. 607 (1940), at 54:

> [I]f by some magic a man who had never known it were to compose anew Keats' Ode On a Grecian Urn, he would be an "author," and, if he copyrighted it, others might not copy that poem, though they might of course copy Keats.

The Supreme Court reviewed whether listings in a telephone directory were of sufficient originality to warrant copyright protection under title 17 of the U.S. Code. In *Feist Pubs., Inc. v. Rural Tel. Serv. Co.*, 499 U.S. 340 (1991), the court, in holding the listings non-copyrightable subject matter, stated:

> The sine qua non of copyright is originality. To qualify for copyright protection, a work must be original to the author. See *Harper & Row, supra,* at 547-549. Original, as the term is used in copyright, means only that the work was independently created by the author (as opposed to copied from other works), and that it possess at least some minimum degree of creativity. 1M. Nimmer & D. Nimmer, *Copyright* §§ 2.01 [A],[B] (1990) (hereinafter Nimmer). To be sure, the requisite level of creativity is extremely low; even a slight amount will suffice. The vast majority of works make that grade quite easily, as they possess some creative spark "no matter how crude, humble or obvious" it might be. *Id.* § 1.08[C][1]. Originality does not signify novelty; a work may be original even though it closely resembles other works so long as the similarity is fortuitous, not the result of copying. To illustrate, assume that two poets, each ignorant of the other, compose identical poems. Neither is novel, yet both are original and, hence, copyrightable. See *Sheldon v. Metro-Goldwyn Pictures,* 81 F.2d 49, 54 (CA 2 1936).

> Originality is a constitutional requirement. The source of Congress' power to enact copyright laws is Article I, § 8, cl. 8 of the Constitution, which authorizes Congress to "secur[e] for limited times to Authors. . . the exclusive Right to their respective writings."

Thus, two authors may copyright essentially similar works so long as each created the work independently, *Sheldon v. Metro-Goldwyn Pictures Corp.*, 81 F.2d 49, 28 U.S.P.Q. 330 (2d Cir. 1936), *aff'd*, 309 U.S. 390, 44 U.S.P.Q. 607 (1946).

b. Writings vs. Works of Authorship

All subject matter covered by copyrights must be a "writing" since this is the constitutional requirement for the Copyright Act. Over the years the courts have held that "writings" or "works" must constitute the fruits of intellectual labor and be in a tangible form, but that only a very slight degree of such labor is needed, *Nimmer,* § 108 [C][1]. However, the constitutional standard of "all the writings of an author" is broader than "original works of authorship," the phrase used in title 17 to establish the general subject matter of copyright. This was done to avoid exhausting the constitutional powers of Congress to legislate in this field, H. Rep. at 51.

c. Fixed in a Tangible Medium

In order to obtain copyright protection under title 17, the work must be "fixed," that is embodied in a copy or a phonorecord. 17 U.S.C. § 101 defines this term:

> A work is "fixed" in a tangible medium of expression when its embodiment in a copy or phonorecord, by or under the authority of the author, is sufficiently permanent or stable to permit it to be perceived, reproduced, or otherwise communicated for a period of more than transitory duration. A work consisting of sounds, images, or both, that are being transmitted, is "fixed" for purposes of this title if a fixation of the work is being made simultaneously with its transmission.

The House Report at 52-53 comments on this requirement:

> This broad language is intended to avoid the artificial and largely unjustifiable distinctions, derived from cases such as *White-Smith Publishing Co. v. Apollo Co.,* 209 U.S. 1 (1908), under which statutory copyrightability in certain cases has been made to depend upon the form or medium in which the work is fixed. Under the bill it makes no difference what the form, manner, or medium of fixation may be—whether it is in words, numbers, notes, sounds, pictures, or any other graphic or symbolic indicia, whether embodied in a physical object in written, primed, photographic, sculptural, punched, magnetic, or any other stable form, and whether it is capable of perception directly or by means of any machine or device "now known or later developed."

>> Under the first sentence of the definition of "fixed" in section 101, a work would be considered "fixed in a tangible medium of expression" if there has been an authorized embodiment in a copy or phonorecord and if that embodiment "is sufficiently permanent or stable" to permit the work "to be perceived, reproduced, or otherwise communicated for a period of more than transitory duration." The second sentence makes clear that, in the case of "a work consisting of sounds, images, or both, that are being transmitted," the work is regarded as "fixed" if a fixation is being made at the same time as the transmission.

d. Created

Copyright protection in a work subsists upon the creation of the work, that is, upon the work being fixed for the first time in a tangible medium of expression. 17 U.S.C. § 101 defines the term "created" with respect to copyrighted works as follows:

A work is "created" when it is fixed in a copy or phonorecord for the first time; where a work is prepared over a period of time, the portion of it that has been fixed at any particular time constitutes the work as of that time, and where the work has been prepared in different versions, each version constitutes a separate work.

e. Works vs. Copies and Phonorecords

A distinction must be made between a "work" covered by the copyright law and copies of the work embodied in "copies" and "phonorecords." These are material objects from which a work can be read or visually perceived either directly or with the aid of a machine. Books, manuscripts, sheet music, film, videotapes, or microfilm are "copies." "Phonorecords" are such items as audiotapes, CDs, or phonograph disks. A "song" is the "work" copyrighted under title 17, and it may be fixed on a magnetic tape, or in sheet music or on a phonograph disk. 17 U.S.C. § 101 defines "copies" and "phonorecords" as:

"Copies" are material objects, other than phonorecords, in which a work is fixed by any method now known or later developed, and from which the work can be perceived, reproduced, or otherwise communicated, either directly or with the aid of a machine or device. The term "copies" includes the material object, other than a phonorecord, in which the work is first fixed.

* * *

"Phonorecords" are material objects in which sounds, other than those accompanying a motion picture or other audiovisual work, are fixed by any method now known or later developed, and from which the sounds can be perceived, reproduced, or otherwise communicated, either directly or with the aid of a machine or device. The term "phonorecords" includes the material, object in which the sounds are first fixed.

The ownership of a copy (material object in which the work is embodied) of a copyrighted work is distinct from the ownership of any of the exclusive rights under a copyright. The transfer of ownership of such material object does not of itself convey any rights in the copyrighted work embodied in the object; nor, in the absence of an agreement, does transfer of ownership of a copyright or of any exclusive rights under a copyright convey property rights in any material object, 17 U.S.C. § 202.

3. Categories of Work

a. Literary Works

The term "literary works," the first category under section 102, is defined in 17 U.S.C. § 101:

"Literary works" are works, other than audiovisual works, expressed in words, numbers, or other verbal or numerical symbols or indicia, regardless of the nature of the material objects, such as books, periodicals, manuscripts, phonorecords, film, tapes, disks, or cards, in which they are embodied.

"Literary works" include the broad category of "books" in the 1909 Copyright Act. The term "literary work" does not connote any criterion of literary merit or qualitative value; it includes catalogs, directories, and similar factual, references, or instructional works and compilations of data, H. Rep. at 54. The category of "literary works" includes computer data bases and computer programs to the extent they incorporate authorship in the program's expression, H. Rep. at 54.

b. Pictorial, Graphic, and Sculptural Works

17 U.S.C. § 101 defines this category of "pictorial, graphic, and sculptural works" as including:

> [T]wo-dimensional and three-dimensional works of fine, graphic, and applied art, photographs, prints and art reproductions, maps, globes, charts, diagrams, models, and technical drawings, including architectural plans. Such works shall include works of artistic craftsmanship insofar as their form but not their mechanical or utilitarian aspects are concerned; the design of a useful article, as defined in this section, shall be considered a pictorial, graphic, or sculptural work only if, and only to the extent that, such design incorporates pictorial, graphic, or sculptural features that can be identified separately from, and are capable of existing independently of, the utilitarian aspects of the article.

Correspondingly, this definition "carries with it no implied criterion of artistic taste, aesthetic value, or intrinsic quality," H. Rep. at 54. It includes works of art, works of graphic arts and illustrations, art reproductions, plans, drawings, photographic works, works for advertising, commerce and applied art, H. Rep. at 54. Scientific or technical drawings are included within this definition and prior to the amendment of the categories architectural drawings and plans were also covered by this category.

Works of applied art encompassing original pictorial, graphic, and sculptural works that are intended to be or have been embodied in useful articles are not covered by this category. The copyright law defines "useful articles" as "an article having an intrinsic utilitarian function that is not merely to portray the appearance of the article or to convey information." An article that is normally a part of a useful article is considered a "useful article," 17 U.S.C. § 101.

With respect to the copyright of "useful articles," the House Report at 54-55, relying on *Mazer v. Stein*, 347 U.S. 201, 100 U.S.P.Q. 325 (1954), noted that:

> The declaration that "pictorial, graphic, and sculptural works" include "works of artistic craftsmanship insofar as their form but not their mechanical or utilitarian aspects are concerned" is classic language; it is drawn from Copyright Office regulations promulgated in the 1940's and expressly endorsed by the Supreme Court in the *Mazer* case.

> The second part of the amendment states that "the design of a useful article. . . , shall be considered a pictorial, graphic, or sculptural work only if, and only to the extent that, such design incorporates pictorial, graphic, or sculptural features that can be identified utilitarian aspects of the article." A "useful article" is defined as "an article having an intrinsic utilitarian function that is not merely to portray the appearance of the article or to convey information." This part

of the amendment is an adaptation of language added to the Copyright Office Regulations in the mid-1950's in an effort to implement the Supreme Court's decision in the *Mazer* case.

In adopting this amendatory language, the Committee is seeking to draw as clear a line as possible between copyrightable works of applied art and uncopyrighted works of industrial design. A two-dimensional panting, drawings, or graphic work is still capable of being identified as such when it is printed on or applied to utilitarian articles such as textile fabrics, wallpaper, containers, and the like. The same is tree when a statute or carving is used to embellish an industrial product or, as in the *Mazer* case, is incorporated into a product without losing its ability to exist independently as a work of art. On the other hand, although the shape of an industrial product may be aesthetically satisfying and valuable, the Committee's intention is not to offer it copyright protection under the bill. Unless the shape of an automobile, airplane, ladies' dress, food processor, television set, or any other industrial product contains some element that, physically or conceptually, can be identified as separable from the utilitarian aspects of that article, the design would not be copyrighted under the bill. The test of separability and independence from the utilitarian aspects of the article does not depend upon the nature of the design—that is, even if the appearance of an article is determined by a esthetic (as opposed to functional) considerations, only elements, if any, which can be identified separately from the useful article as such are copyrightable. And, even if the three-dimensional design contains some such element (for example, a carving on the back of a chair or a floral relief design on silver flatware), copyright protection would extend only to that element, and would not cover the over-all configuration of the utilitarian article as such.

The exclusive rights afforded to owners of "pictorial, graphic and sculptural works" often depend on the extent to which the copyright in such works extends to useful articles. 17 U.S.C. § 113(a) notes that the exclusive right to reproduce a copyrighted pictorial, graphic or sculptural work in copies under section 106 includes the right to reproduce the work in or on any kind of article, whether useful or otherwise. However, sections 113(b) and 113(c) state that the copyright law does not extend to the owner of copyright in a work that portrays a useful article as such, any greater or lesser rights with respect to the making, distribution, or display of the useful article so portrayed than those afforded to such works under the law, whether title 17 or the common law or statutes of a state and does not include any right to prevent the making, distribution, or display of pictures or photographs of such articles in connection with advertisements or commentaries related to the distribution or display of such articles, or in connection with news reports.

c. Motion Pictures and Other Audiovisual Works

The category of "motion pictures and other audiovisual works" includes movies and accompanying sound tracks, video tapes, and discs, *Nimmer*, § 2.09[D] [2]; H. Rep. at 56. The "motion pictures" and "audiovisual works" portion of Category (6) of section 102 are defined by 17 U.S.C. § 101:

> "Motion pictures" are audiovisual works consisting of a series of related images which, when shown in succession, impart an impression of motion, together with accompanying sounds, if any.

"Audiovisual works" are works that consist of a series of related images which are intrinsically intended to be shown by the use of machines or devices such as projectors, viewers, or electronic equipment, together with accompanying sounds, if any, regardless of the nature of the material objects, such as films or tapes, in which the works are embodied.

See generally, Copyright Circular 55, Copyright Registration for Multimedia Works.

d. Sound Recordings

Category (7) of section 102 is defined by 17 U.S.C. § 101:

"Sound recordings" are works that result from the fixation of a series of musical, spoken, or other sounds, but not including the sounds accompanying a motion picture or other audiovisual work, regardless of the nature of the material objects, such as disks, tapes, or other phonorecords, in which they are embodied.

Public Law 92-410 in 1971 was the first instance of federal copyright protection for sound recordings. "The copyrightable work comprises the aggregation of sounds and not the tangible medium of fixation. Thus sound recordings as copyrightable subject matter are distinguished from phonorecords, the latter being physical objects in which the sound is fixed," H. Rep. at 56.

4. Noncopyrightable Subject Matter

a. Factual Works

Not included within copyrightable subject matter are factual works—generally on the basis of the lack of originality and lack of authorship, *Nimmer*, § 2.11 [A], subject to the qualification that copyright protection will be accorded to the literal form of expression if it is original with the copyright claimant, *Nimmer*, § 2.11 [B]. Thus, facts uncovered by a historian while researching a book would not be copyrightable, but the literal expression of the facts—the finished book—would merit copyright protection, Denicola, "Copyright in Collection of Facts: A Theory for the Protection of Nonfiction Literary Works," 81 Col. L. Rev. 516 (1981); Copyright Office Circular 1, Copyright Basics, states that the following works are not protectable:

Works consisting entirely of information that is common property and containing no original authorship. For example, standard calendars, height and weight charts, tape measures and rules, and lists or tables taken from public documents or other common sources.

In *Feist Pubs., Inc. v. Rural Tel Serv. Co.*, 499 U.S. 340, 18 U.S.P.Q. 2d 1275 (1991), the Court stated:

It is the bedrock principle of copyright that mandates the law's seemingly disparate treatment of facts and factual compilations. "No one may claim originality as to facts." *Id.*, § 2.11 [A], p.2-157. This is because facts do not owe their origin to an act of authorship. The distinction is one between creation and discovery: the first person to find and report a particular fact has not created the fact; he or she has merely discovered its existence.

At issue in *Feist* was whether the white pages of a telephone directory was copyrightable. While the Court stated that compilations of facts may possess the requisite degree of originality required for copyright protection, the protection is "thin" because the facts in the compilation are uncopyrighted element of the compilation and thus may be freely copied. The Court stressed that the "sweat of the brow" alone would not substitute for originality under the copyright law and found that the selection coordination and arrangement of the white pages did not satisfy the minimum constitutional standards for copyright protection. See also *Bellsouth Advertising & Pub. Corp. v. Donnelley Info. Pub. Inc.*, 999 F.2d 1436, 28 U.S.P.Q.2d 1001 (11th Cir. 1993), *cert. denied*, 114 S. Ct. 943 (1994), finding "yellow pages" to be validly copyrighted.

b.   Obscene, Seditious, Libelous, Fraudulent, and Immoral Works

Although a work may fall within a protectable category, copyright protection may be denied if the work is considered to be obscene, seditious or libelous, *Nimmer*, § 2.17. Protection may also be denied to fraudulent, immoral, and indecent works, section 1, Latman, The *Copyright Law*, (5th ed. 1979).

c.   Ideas

Copyrightable subject matter does not include ideas, procedures, systems, etc. 17 U.S.C. § 102(b) provides:

> In no case does copyright protection for an original work of authorship extend to any idea, procedure, process, system, method of operation, concept, principle, or discovery, regardless of the form in which it is described, explained, illustrated, or embodied in such work.

This subsection restated the existing law regarding copyright protection, *Nimmer*, § 2.03[D]. A copyright of a particular work does not preclude others from using the ideas or information revealed in the work. Similarly, with regard to computer programs, the copyright does not extend to the methodology or processes adopted by the programmer, rather only to his expression of ideas, H. Rep. at 57. In *American Pental Ass'n v. Delta Pental Plans Ass'n*, 126 F.2d 977 (7th Cir. 1997), the court considered whether a code developed for reporting dental procedures to third party payers was in fact procedures or ideas and therefore uncopyrightable, or expression which is copyrightable. The seventh circuit found the code to be a copyrightable taxonomy classification. The plaintiff could not enjoin the use of forms by the defendant for applying the code but the court would enjoin the copying of the code, or the making of a derivative work based on the code.

d. Title, Names, and Slogans

Also not within copyrightable subject matter are titles, names, short phrases and slogans; familiar symbols or designs; mere variations of typographical ornamentation, lettering, or coloring; and mere listings of ingredients or contents.

5. Compilations and Derivative Works

a. Subject Matter

Copyrightable subject matter includes compilations and derivative works as provided for by 17 U.S.C. § 103:

(a) The subject matter of copyright as specified by section 102 includes compilations and derivative works, but protection for a work employing preexisting material in which copyright subsists does not extend to any part of the work in which such material has been used unlawfully.

(b) The copyright in a compilation or derivative work extends only to the material contributed by the author of such work, as distinguished from the preexisting material employed in the work, and does not imply any exclusive right in the preexisting material. The copyright in such work is independent of, and does not affect or enlarge the scope, duration, ownership, or subsistence of, any copyright protection in the preexisting material.

b. Compilations

Compiled works are defined in 17 U.S.C. § 101:

A "compilation" is a work formed by the collection and assembling of preexisting materials or of data that are selected, coordinated, or arranged in such a way that the resulting work as a whole constitutes an original work of authorship. The term "compilation" includes collective works.

A "collective work" is a work, such as a periodical issue, anthology, or encyclopedia, in which a number of contributions, constituting separate and independent works in themselves, are assembled into a collective whole.

In *Triangle Pubs., Inc. v. New England Newspaper Pub. Co.*, 46 F. Supp. 198 (D. Mass. 1942), the court held valid the copyright in the plaintiff's newspaper's race result charts. The court distinguished between the collecting of discreet statistics, which as independent, isolated facts could not be copyrighted, and the gathering of various race information, which was copyrightable because it involved a new pattern of relationships between facts. A copyright in a compilation protects only this new patterning or relationship, which results from the author's labor of assembling, connecting and categorizing disparate facts.

c. Derivative Works

The protection for derivative works is one of the most important areas of the copyright laws. Derivative works are defined in 17 U.S.C. § 101 as follows:

> A "derivative work" is a work based upon one or more preexisting works, such as a translation, musical arrangement, dramatization, fictionalization, motion picture version, sound recording, art reproduction, abridgment, condensation, or any other form in which a work may be recast, transformed, or adapted. A work consisting of editorial revisions, annotations, elaborations, or other modifications which, as a whole, represent an original work of authorship, is a "derivative work".

This section makes it clear that the copyright in a new version covers only the later added material and has no effect on the copyright or public domain status of the preexisting material.

6. Government Works

a. Prior Acts

Ever since 1895 the copyright laws have specifically treated copyrights with respect to activities of the Federal Government. The initial statutory provision was contained in the Act of June 12, 1895, 28 Stat. 608, and a similar provision was contained in the 1909 Copyright Act. For a general review of the history of this concept, see Price, "Copyright in Government Publications: Historical Background, Judicial Interpretation, and Legislative Clarification," 74 Mil. L. Rev. 19 (1976;); Bargar, Copyright in Government Publications (Study No. 33, 1959) reprinted in 1 Studies on Copyrights 169 (1963).

This law in existence prior to 1978, i.e., the 1909 Copyright Act, provided in 17 U.S.C. § 8:

> No copyright shall subsist in the original text of any work which is in the public domain, or in any work which was published in this country or any foreign country prior to July 1, 1909, and has not been already copyrighted in the United States, or in any publication of the United States Government, or any reprint, in whole or in part, thereof, except that the United States Postal Service may secure copyright on behalf of the United States in the whole or any part of the publications authorized by section 405 of title 39.
>
> The publication or republication by the Government, either separately or in a public document, of any material in which copyright is subsisting shall not be taken to cause any abridgment or annulment of the copyright or to authorize any use or appropriation of such copyright material without the consent of the copyright proprietor.

The lack of a clear definition for the term "publication of the United States Government" caused the greatest problem in understanding the thrust of section 8. For example, works supported by the Government, even if not authored by Government employees could come within the term "publication of the United States Government." Similarly, privately authored works published by the United States Government could conceivably be "publications of the United States Government." See Copyright Law Revision, Report of Register of Copyrights on the General Revision of the U.S. Copyright Laws, House Committee on the Judiciary, 87th Cong., 1st Sess. (1961); and Smith, "Government Documents: Their Copyright and Ownership," ASCAP Copyright L. Symp., No. 22 (1972) at 147. Also questioned was whether section 8 extended to works which were not "publications" whether the prohibition of this section applied to works produced under Government contract or grants, and whether it applied to common law copyrights, Tresansky, "Impact of the Copyright Act of 1976 on the Government," 35 Fed. B.J. 21 (1978). A number of authors have queried whether valid copyright may subsist in Government data, see Andrea Simon, "A Constitutional Analysis of Copyrighting Government Commissioned Work," Nathan Burkan Competition, 1984; Fawkes, "Private Copyrights for Public Agencies," 21 Bull. Copyright Soc'y, 382 (1974); and Metz, "Rights of Federal Personnel Under Copyright Act," 12 Copyright L. Symposium (ASCAP) (1963).

Perhaps the most famous case interpreting section 8 was *Public Affairs Assocs. v. Rickover*, 177 F. Supp. 601, 123 U.S.P.Q. 252 (D.D.C. 1959), *rev'd*, 284 F.2d 262, 127 U.S.P.Q. 231 (D.C. Cir. 1960), *vacated*, 369 U.S. Ill, 132 U.S.P.Q. 535 (1962), *opinion on remand* 268 F. Supp. 444, 153 U.S.P.Q. 598 (D.D.C. 1967). Admiral Rickover prepared a number of speeches on education, only some of which were related to his Navy duties. These speeches were evidently prepared on Rickover's free time but with some Government clerical assistance. The plaintiff claimed that these speeches were in the public domain as publications of the Untied States Government; however, the appeals court found none of these speeches to be a Government publication. This court limited the term "Government publications" to material printed at the cost and direction of the Government and linked to the official duties of the author. The Supreme Court remanded the case for further proceedings relating to the Admiral's official duties and the circumstances of the preparation and delivery of the speeches and the use of Government facilities and personnel. See also *Sherrill v. Grieves*, 57 Wash. L. Reptr. 286, 20 C.O. Bull. 675 (S. Ct. D.C. 1929).

In *Sherrv Universal Match Corp.*, 297 F. Supp. 107, 160 U.S.P.Q. 216 (S.D.N.Y. 1967), *aff'd*, 417 F.2d 497, 164 U.S.P.Q. 225 (2d Cir. 1969), *cert. denied*, 397 U.S. 936, 164 U.S.P.Q. 545 (1970), the court found that a statute designed and created by two soldiers in the U.S. Army during duty hours and with Army equipment was not a "publication of the United States Government" since the term "publication" referred only to printed matter.

As to grant information, the court in *Applied Innovation, Inc. v. Regents of the University of Minn.*, 876 F.2d 626, 11 U.S.P.Q. 2d 1041 (8th Cir. 1989) found that a valid copyright existed in data prepared by a university with the partial support of a grant from the WPA. While the WPA's grant specified that the authors were to publish the results of the research, acknowledge the receipt of Government sponsorship, and make basic research available to the public, it contained no copyright provisions. The WPA had internal regulations that stated their policy not to permit copyrights in works under grants except for scientific periodical or books not devoted primarily to the results of the grant. The court held that since the WPA copyright policy was not published and not otherwise known by the university, the policy was not binding on the university.

b. United States Government Works

The 1976 Copyright Act contains an explicit provision on United States Government works. 17 U.S.C. § 105 states:

> Copyright protection under this title is not available for any work of the United States Government, but the United States Government is not precluded from receiving and holding copyrights transferred to it by assignment, bequest, or otherwise.

17 U.S.C. § 101 defines a "work of the United States Government" as:

> A "work of the United States Government" is a work prepared by an office or employee of the United States Government as part of that person's official duties.

The Conference Report stated at 69-70 that it had adopted the Senate provision on this issue. The Senate Report provides the following insight to this provision at 56-57:

> The basic premise of section 105 of the bill is the same as that of section 8 of the present law—that works produced for the U.S. Government by its officers and employees should not be subject to copyright. The provision applies the principle equally to unpublished and published works.

> A Government official or employee should not be prevented from securing copyright in a work written at his own volition and outside his duties, even though the subject matter involves his Government work or his professional field.

> * * *

> Section 8 of the statute now in effect includes a saving clause intended to make clear that the copyright protection of a private work is not affected if the work is published by the Government. There is no need to restate this principle explicitly in the context of section 105; there is nothing in section 105 that would relieve the Government of its obligation to secure permission in order to publish a copyrighted work, and publication or other use by the Government of a private work could not affect its copyright protection in any way.

For a discussion on Government employee works under section 105, see Tresansky, "Copyright in Government Employee Authored Works," 30 Cath. L. Rev. 605 (1981).

c. Government Contracts and Grants

As to copyrights in works prepared under Government contracts and grants, the general practice has been to permit contractors and grantees to retain copyrights in such works. The legal basis for this practice has been questioned, Price, "Copyright in Government Publications: Historical Background, Judicial Interpretation, and Legislative Clarification," 74 Mil. L. Rev. 19 at 52 (1976). This flexibility was based on the fact that the 1909 Copyright Act was not clear as to its application to Government contracts or grants, Tresansky, "Impact of the Copyright Act of 1976 on the Government," 35 Fed. B.J. 21 (1978). Further, the Government did not promulgate any Government-wide copyright policy with regard to contracts and grants under the 1909 Act, although such a statement was attempted in 1964 by the then Bureau of the Budget. The promulgation of such a policy statement was recommended by the Commission on Government Procurement in 1972, Rep't of Comm. on Gov't Proc., Vol. 4 at 134 (1972). Recommendation 1-16. The development of such a policy statement was undertaken by an interagency group in response to this recommendation, 39 Fed. Reg. 19996 (1974), but was never promulgated. For a general statement on copyright problems in Government contracts under the 1909 Act, see Farmakides & Freudenberg, "Copyright Matters Affecting the Government," 25 Fed. B.J. 86 (1965).

In *Schnapper Affairs Press v. Foley,* 667 F.2d 102, 212 U.S.P.Q. 235 (D.C. Cir. 1981), *cert. denied,* 455 U.S. 948, 215 U.S.P.Q. 96 (1982), the circuit court held that a contractor for the Government, under 17 U.S.C. § 105 or section 8 of the 1909 Copyright Act, may acquire a copyright on a Government commissioned work. The district court previously held that federal funding does not affect the availability of copyright protection, 471 F. Supp. 426, 202 U.S.P.Q. 154 (D.D.C. 1979). See also *Rubin v. Boston Magazine Co.,* 645 F.2d 80, 209 U.S.P.Q. 1073 (lst Cir. 1981), where the court held that a grantee could obtain a copyright in the work supported by an Institute of Mental Health grant.

The court held in *Hart v. Sampley,* 1992 Copyright Law Decisions (D.D.C. 1992), that a statue at the Vietnam Veteran Memorial conveyed to the Department of Interior (with the plaintiff retaining the copyright) was not a commissioned work and was not a work of the United States Government because it was not prepared by an officer or employee of the United States. The defendants claimed that it was a commissioned work. The court held that a commissioned work can be copyrighted. The "Government work" restriction in the copyright law only applies to works of a Government employee and not a commissioned work.

The Senate Report provides the following discussion on the treatment to be accorded to contractor or grantee prepared works at 56-57:

> A more difficult and far-reaching problem is whether the definition should be broadened to prohibit copyright in works prepared under U.S. Government contracts or grants. As the bill is written, the Government agency concerned could determine in each case whether to allow an independent contractor or grantee to secure copyright in works prepared in whole or in part with the use of Government funds. The argument against allowing copyright in this situation is that the public should not be required to pay a "double subsidy," and that it is inconsistent to prohibit copyright in works by Government employees while permitting private copyrights in a growing body of works created by persons who are paid with Government funds.

> * * *

> The bill deliberately avoids making any sort of outright, unqualified prohibition against copyright in works prepared under Government contract or grant. There may well be cases while it would be in the public interest to deny copyright in the writings generated by Government research contracts and the like; it can be assumed that, where a Government agency commissions a work for its own use merely as an alternative to having one of its own employees prepare the work, the right to secure a private copyright would be withheld. However, there are almost cer-

tainly many other cases where the denial of copyright protection would be unfair or would hamper the production and publication of important works. Where, under the particular circumstances, Congress or the agency involved finds that the need to have a work freely available outweighs the need of the private author to secure copyright, the problem can be dealt with by specific legislation, agency regulations, or contractual restrictions.

d. Exception to Copyright Prohibition

There are some exceptions to the broad prohibition of copyrights in Government works. Both Government compilations of standardized scientific and technical reference data under the Standard Reference Data Act, 15 U.S.C. § 290, and publications under 39 U.S.C. § 405 created by the Postal Service under the Postal Reorganization Act of 1970 may be covered by copyright even if the work was prepared by a Government employee. The Senate Report explained this concept at 57:

> The intent of section 105 is to restrict the prohibition against Government copyright to works written by employees of the United States Government within the scope of their official duties. In accordance with the objectives of the Postal Reorganization Act of 1970, this section does not apply to works created by employees of the United States Postal Service. The privilege of securing copyright in its publications does not extend to restrictions on the use of postage-stamps on mail carried by the Postal Service.

e. Foreign Copyrights in Government Works

The Conference Report noted at 69-70 that the National Technical Information Service (NTIS) of the Department of Commerce requested a limited copyright in their Government collection, basically consisting of contract and grant reports, in order to collect royalties for the foreign copying of the NTIS collection. The relief requested by NTIS for limited copyright protection was denied but the following "savings" provision was included in the S. Rep. at 56:

> The prohibition on copyright protection for United States Government works is not intended to have any effect on protection of these works abroad. Works of the governments of most other countries are copyrighted, and there are no valid policy reasons for denying such protection to United States Government works abroad.

C. Exclusive Rights

1. Statutory Rights

The exclusive rights provided to copyright owners are contained in 17 U.S.C. § 106:

Subject to sections 107 through 120, the owner of copyright under this title has the exclusive rights to do and to authorize any of the following:

(1) to reproduce the copyrighted work in copies or phonorecords;

(2) to prepare derivative works based upon the copyrighted work;

(3) to distribute copies or phonorecords of the copyrighted work to the public by sale or other transfer of ownership, or by rental, lease, or lending;

(4) in the case of literary, musical, dramatic, and choreographic works, pantomimes, and motion pictures and other audiovisual works, to perform the copyrighted work publicly; and

(5) in the case of literary, musical, dramatic, and choreographic works, pantomimes, and pictorial, graphic, or sculptural works, including the individual images .of a motion picture or other audiovisual work, to display the copyrighted work publicly.

17 U.S.C. § 101 defines the "copyright owner" with respect to any one of the exclusive rights comprised in a copyright as the owner of that particular right. This recognizes that the five exclusive rights of section 106 are a "bundle of rights," each of which may be subdivided and owned and enforced separately. 17 U.S.C. § 201(d)(2) codifies the concept that any of the exclusive rights that make up a copyright can be transferred and owned separately.

17 U.S.C. §§ 107-120 provide various limitations and exceptions to the broad rights granted by section 106. These include fair use of a copyrighted work, section 107; reproductions by libraries and archives, section 108; effect of a transfer of a copy or phonorecord, section 109; exemption of certain performances and displays, section 110; secondary transmissions, i.e., cable TV, section 111; ephemeral recordings, section 112; computer programs, section 117; noncommercial broadcasting, section 118; and architectural works section 120. Several of the categories of rights and limitations and exceptions are discussed below.

2. Visual Arts

New section 106A of title 17 gives certain moral rights to the author of visual art during the life of the author for including the right of attribution and integrity. Such an author is given the personal right to prevent the use of his or her name as the author of the work, and the right to prevent the use of the author's name in the event of a distortion, mutilation or other modification of the work which would be prejudicial to the author's reputation. Exceptions to these moral rights include modifications resulting from the passage of time or resulting from its conservation.

3. Reproduction Rights

The reproduction right is the right to reproduce copies or phonorecords of the copyrighted work. The House Report comments on the reproduction right at 61-62 state:

Reproduction—Read together with the relevant definitions in section 101, the right "to reproduce the copyrighted work in copies or phonorecords" means the right to produce a material object in which the work is duplicated, transcribed, imitated, or simulated in a fixed form from which it can be "perceived, reproduced, or otherwise communicated, either directly or with the aid of a machine: or device." As under the present law, a copyrighted work would be infringed by reproducing it in whole or in any substantial part, and by duplicating it exactly or by imitation or simulation. Wide departures are variations from the copyrighted works would still be an infringement as long as the author's "expression" rather than merely the author's "ideas" are taken.

"Reproduction" under clause (1) of section 106 is to be distinguished from "display" under clause (5). For a work to be "reproduced," its fixation in tangible form must be "sufficiently permanent or stable to permit it to be perceived, reproduced, or otherwise communicated for a period of more than transitory duration." Thus, the showing of images on a screen or tube would not be a violation of clause (1), although it might come within the scope of clause (5).

Nimmer notes that this provision, by its definition of what constitutes a "copy," overrules *White-Smith Music Pub. Co. v. Apollo Co.*, 209 U.S. 1 (1908). This case held that the unauthorized manufacture and sale of piano music rolls were not infringements of the copyright owner's exclusive right to copy since the rolls were not copies, because a copy must be "a written or printed item in intelligible notation," *Nimmer*, § 8.02[B][3].

4. Preparation of Derivative Works

The second exclusive right "to prepare derivative works" somewhat overlaps the reproduction right. It is broader than that right in the sense that the derivative work need not necessarily be fixed. For example, a ballet may be an infringement of an original work, even though it is not fixed in a tangible medium. The right to prepare a derivative work is described in the H. Rep. at 62:

To be an infringement the "derivative work" must be "based upon the copyrighted work," and the definition in section 101 refers to "a translation, musical arrangement, dramatization, fictionalization, motion picture version, sound recording, art reproduction, abridgement, condensation, or any other form in which a work may be recast, transformed, or adapted." Thus, to constitute a violation of section 106(2), the infringing work must incorporate a portion of the copyrighted work in some form; for example, a detailed commentary on a work or a programmatic musical composition inspired by a novel would not normally constitute infringements under this clause.

5. Public Distribution Rights

The right to publicly distribute copies or phonorecords of a copyrighted work gives the copyright owner the right to control the first public distribution of an authorized copy or phonorecord of his work, H. Rep. at 62. As noted in this report, "the copyright owner's rights under section 106(3) cease with respect to a particular copy or phonorecord once he has parted with ownership of it."

6. Public Performance Right

The exclusive right to perform a literary, musical, or dramatic copyrighted works publicly is further explained by the definitions of "to perform" and "publicly" in 17 U.S.C. § 101:

> To "perform" a work means to recite, render, play, dance, or act it, either directly or by means of any device or process or, in the case of a motion picture or other audiovisual work, to show its images in any sequence or to make the sounds accompanying it audible.

*   *   *

> To perform or display a work "publicly" means—

> (1) to perform or display it at a place open to the public or at any place where a substantial number , of persons outside of a normal circle of a family and its social acquaintances is gathered; or

> (2) to transmit or otherwise communicate a performance or display of the work to a place specified by clause (1) or to the public, by means of any device or process, whether the members of the public capable of receiving the performance or display receive it in the same place or in separate places and at the same time or at different times.

7. Public Display Right

The right of public display is the first explicit statutory recognition in the United States of an exclusive right to show copyrighted works, or an image of copyrighted works to the public, H. Rep. at 63. "To 'display' a work means to show a copy of it, either directly or by means of a film, slide, television image, or any other device or process or, in the case of a motion picture or other audiovisual work, to show individual images nonsequentially," 17 U.S.C. § 101.

D. Limitation on Exclusive Rights

1. Fair Use

a. Judicial Basis

The courts created a limitation on the exclusive rights of the copyright owner under the theory that the rigid application of the copyright statute might stifle the creativity the law was designed to foster. Thus, the doctrine of fair use permits an examination of the facts in each case to see if the "use" is an infringement or if it is in fact a "fair use" of the copyrighted work, *Iowa State Univ. Research Found., Inc. v. American Broadcasting Co.*, 621 F.2d 57, 207 U.S.P.Q. 97 (2d Cir. l080). Four factors have been commonly recognized in fair use cases: (1) the purpose and character of the use; (2) the nature of the copyrighted work; (3) the amount and substantiality of material used in relation to the copyrighted work as a whole; and (4) the effect of the use on the copyright holder's potential market for the work. See *Nimmer*, § 13.05[A] and section 7 II, Latman, *The Copyright Law* (5th ed. 1979).

b. Statutory Basis

In the 1976 Act Congress codified the fair use limitation on the copyright owner's exclusive rights. 17 U.S.C. § 107, as modified, provides:

> Notwithstanding the provisions of sections 106 and 106A, the fair use of a copyrighted work, including such use by reproduction in copies or phonorecords or by any other means specified by that section, for purposes such as criticism, comment, news reporting, teaching (including multiple copies for classroom use), scholarship, or research, is not an infringement of copyright. In determining whether the use made of a work in any particular case is a fair use the factors to be considered shall include—
>
> (1) the purpose and character of the use, including whether such use is of a commercial nature or is for nonprofit educational purposes;
>
> (2) the nature of the copyrighted work;
>
> (3) the amount and substantiality of the portion used in relation to the copyrighted work as a whole; and
>
> (4) the effect of the use upon the potential market for or value of the copyrighted work.
>
> The fact that a work is unpublished shall not itself bar a finding of fair use if such finding is made upon consideration all the above factors.

The courts have made clear that section 107 requires a case-by-case determination whether a particular use is fair, and that fair use is a mixed question of law and fact, *Harper & Row v. Nation Enters.*, 471 U.S. 539, 225 U.S.P.Q. 1073 (1985). See *American Geophysical Union v. Texaco*, 802 F. Supp. 1, 24 U.S.P.Q. 2d 1796 (S.D.N.Y. 1992), *aff'd*, 37 F.3d 881, 32 U.S.P.Q.2d 1545 (2d Cir. 1994), holding that the making of copies of articles from a scientific journal for archival purposes by a Texaco scientist was not a fair use.

c. Classroom Use

The legislative history indicates that this section was intended to restate the judicial doctrine of fair use. Congress specifically considered copying for classroom use as "fair use," and provided the following guidelines which were agreed to by educators, authors and publishers for classroom copying at not-for-profit schools in Conf. Rep. at 670:

> 1. A teacher may make or have made a single copy for scholarly research or use in teaching or preparing to teach a class:

A. A chapter of a book

B. An article from a newspaper or periodical

C. A short story, essay or poem

D. A chart, graph, diagram, drawing, cartoon or picture from a book, paper or periodical.

2. Multiple copies may be made for classroom use provided that copying meets certain spontaneity and cumulative effect requirements and each copy contains a copyright notice.

3. Prohibitions are: copying to create or replace anthologies, compilations or collective works; copying of "consumable" works, or as a substitute for the purchase of books, reports or periodicals; copying directed by higher authorities; and repeated copying of same item from term to term.

d. Unpublished Works

In *Harper & Roe v. Nation Enter.*, 471 U.S. 539, 225 U.S.P.Q. 1073 (1985), the Supreme Court considered the unauthorized publication of excerpts from President Ford's then unpublished memoirs and held that the publication of these excerpts were not a fair use. The Court concluded that the unpublished nature of a work is "[a] key, though not necessarily determinative factor, tending to negate a defense of fair use." The Court stated that the scope of the fair use is narrower than with respect unpublished works and that the author's right of first publication weighs against fair use. In a subsequent case, *Salinger v. Random House, Inc.*, 811 F.2d 90, 1 U.S.P.Q.2d 1673 (2d. Cir.), *cert. denied*, 484 U.S. 890 (1987), the second circuit found that the publication of unpublished letter exceeded the fair use standard interpreting *Harper & Roe as* holding that unpublished works normally enjoy complete protection against copying. See also *New Era Pubs. Int'l v. Henry Holt & Co.*, 873 F.2d 576, I0 U.S.P.Q.2d 1561 (2d Cir.), *reh'g denied*, 884 F.2d 659 (2d Cir. 1989), *cert. denied*, 493 U.S. 1094 (1990). The emphasis that these cases gave to the unpublished nature of a work led the Congress to adopt the following sentence in section 107: "The fact that a work is unpublished shall not itself bar a finding of fair use if such finding is made upon consideration all the above factors."

e. Library Reproduction

A major fair use issue has been the photocopying or duplicating of copyrighted material by libraries, *Williams & Wilkins Co. v. United States*, 203 Ct. Cl. 74, 487 F.2d 1345, 180 U.S.P.Q. 49 (1973), *aff'd per curiam*, 420 U.S. 376, 184 U.S.P.Q. 705 (1975), holding that the copying of medical journals by the National Institute of Health library was fair use and not an infringement. In making its determination, the court stressed the public benefit derived from the use of the copied materials. The 1976 Copyright Act resolved this issue in 17 U.S.C. § 108, which provides in part:

Except as otherwise provided in this title and notwithstanding the provisions of section 106, it is not an infringement of copyright for a library or archives, or any of its employees acting within the scope of their employment, to reproduce no more than one copy or phonorecord of a work, or to distribute such copy or phonorecord, under the conditions specified by this section, if—

(1) the reproduction or distribution is made without any purpose of direct or indirect commercial advantage;

(2) the collections of the library or archives are (i) open to the; public, or (ii) available not only to researchers affiliated with the library or archives or with the institution of which it is a part, but also to other persons doing research in a specialized field; and

(3) the reproduction or distribution of the work includes a notice of copyright that appears on the copy or phonorecord that is reproduced under the provisions of this section, or includes a legend stating that the work may be protected by copyright if no such notice can be found on the copy or phonorecord that is reproduced under the provisions of this section.

* * *

(g) The rights of reproduction and distribution under this section extend to the isolated and unrelated reproduction or distribution of a single copy or phonorecord of the same material cm separate occasions, but do not extend to cases where the library or archives, or its employee—

(1) is aware or has substantial reason to believe that it is engaging in the related or concerted reproduction or distribution of multiple copies or phonorecords of the same material, whether made on one occasion or over a period of time, and whether intended for aggregate use; by one or more individuals or for separate use by individual members of a group; or

(2) engages in the systematic reproduction or distribution of single or multiple copies or phonorecords of material described in subsection (d): Provided, That nothing in this clause prevents a library or archives from participating in interlibrary arrangements that do not have, as their purpose or effect, that the library or archives receiving such copies or phonorecords for distribution does so in such aggregate quantities as to substitute for a subscription to or purchase of such work.

From the length of the provisions it can be recognized that this was one of the hardest-fought provisions of the Copyright Law revision. The exemption of section 108, applicable basically to literary and dramatic works, is available to libraries and their employees, rather than to individuals who use the library's equipment or who obtain a copy of a work from a library, *Nimmer,* § 8.03[A]. In making a reproduction, the library must do so without any direct or indirect commercial advantage; its collection must be open (not restricted to library staff); and the reproduction must include a copyright notice. The library will not be liable for infringing copies made by individual library users, so long as a notice warning against possible copyright infringement is posted on any copying machines available for public use. For a general overview of this provision, see excerpts from Library Photocopying and the U.S. Copyright Law of 1976, "An Overview for Librarians and Their Counsel," 367 P.T.C.J. Appendix D (1978).

Section 108(b) states that the rights to reproduce and distribute under section 108 apply to published and unpublished works solely for security, preservation, or deposit for research in another library. Section 108(c) permits a library to copy a published work which is unattainable at a fair price to replace their copy, if stolen, lost or deteriorating. Section 108(d) specifies that the rights of reproduction are limited to a single copy of an article or other contribution of a copyrighted collection when the library has no notice that the copy would be used for any private purpose other than private study, scholarship, or research. Also, a copyright warning notice must be prominently displayed in accordance with regulations prescribed by the Register of Copyrights. An entire work may be copied under conditions similar to those in section 108(d) if it is unavailable at a fair price, section 108(e). Regulations on this matter have been issued, 37 C.F.R. § 201.14.

The following Display Warning of Copyright must be displayed in libraries at the place where orders are accepted for copies:

NOTICE WARNING CONCERNING COPYRIGHT RESTRICTIONS

The copyright law of the United States (Title 17, United States Code) governs the making of photocopies or other reproductions of copyrighted material.

Under certain conditions specified in the law, libraries and archives are authorized to furnish a photocopy or other reproduction. One of these specified conditions is that the photocopy or re-production is not to be "used for any purpose other than private study, scholarship, or re-search." If a user makes a request for, or later uses, a photocopy or reproduction for purposes in excess of fair use, that user may be liable for copyright infringement.

This institution reserves the right to refuse to accept a copying order if, in its judgment, fulfill-ment of the order would involve violation of copyright law.

2. *First Sale Doctrine*

a. *Legal Ownership of a Copy*

17 U.S.C. § 109 deals with the right of the legal owner (as distinguished from a lessee) of a copy of a copyrighted work legally made to transfer, by sale or otherwise, and to display to viewers present, his or her copy or phonorecord of the work without obtaining permission from the owner of the exclusive rights. Section 109 provides:

(a) Notwithstanding the provisions of section 106(3), the owner of particular copy or phonore-cord lawfully made under this title, or any person authorized by such owner, is entitled, without the authority of the copyright owner, to sell or otherwise dispose of the possession of that copy or phonorecord. Notwithstanding the preceding sentence, copies or phonorecords of works sub-ject to restored copyright under section 104A that are manufactured before the date of restora-tion of copyright or, with respect to reliance parties, before publication or service of notice un-der section 104A(e), may be sold or otherwise disposed of without the authorization of the owner of the restored copyright for purposes of direct or indirect commercial advantage only during the 12-month period beginning on—(1) the date of the publication in the Federal Register of the notice of intent filed with the Copyright Office under section 104A(d)(2)(A), or (2) the date of the receipt of actual notice served under section 104A(d)(2)(B), whichever occurs first.

* * *

(c) Notwithstanding the provisions of section 106(5), the owner of a particular copy lawfully made under this title, or any person authorized by such owner, is entitled, without the authority of the copyright owner, to display that copy publicly, either directly or by the projection of no more than one image at a time, to viewers present at the place where the copy is located.

(d) The privileges prescribed by subsections (a) and (c) do not, unless authorized by the copyright owner, extend to any person who has acquired possession of the copy or phonorecord from the copyright owner, by rental, lease, loan, or otherwise, without acquiring ownership of it.

Under this provision, referred to as the first sale doctrine, the owner of a copy of a copyrighted work (other than a phonorecord or a computer program, as noted below) obtained from the owner of the copyright is entitled to dispose of it by sale, rental, or other means. Thus, a purchaser of a copy of a copyrighted book may resell it without control of its price by the copyright owner, unless a prior contract was established by the parties, *Independent News Co. v. Williams*, 293 F.2d 510, 129 U.S.P.Q. 377 (3d Cir. 1961). However, the owner of the book cannot reproduce or perform the copyrighted work publicly without the copyright owner's consent, H. Rep. at 79. Similarly, the owner of a copyrighted painting may publicly display the work (subject to certain rights of the artist) without the consent of the copyright owner, unless the parties have a contract that provides otherwise.

b. Compact Disks and Computer Software Programs

The right to lease and display has been modified with respect to certain copyrighted works, notably phonorecords (such as audio tapes, CDs and vinyl records) and computer programs. First in 1984 (P.L. 98-104, § 4) with respect to audio recordings and then in 1990 (P.L. 101-650, § 802) with respect to computer software, the first sale doctrine was drastically modified. Section 109 provides:

(b)(1)(A) Notwithstanding the provisions of subsection (a), unless authorized by the owners of copyright in the sound recording or the owner of copyright in a computer program (including any tape, disk, or other medium embodying such program), and in the case of a sound recording in the musical works embodied therein, neither the owner of a particular phonorecord nor any person in possession of a particular copy of a computer program (including any tape, disk, or other medium embodying such program), may, for the purposes of direct or indirect commercial advantage, dispose of, or authorize the disposal of, the possession of that phonorecord or computer program (including any tape, disk, or other medium embodying such program) by rental, lease, or lending, or by any other act or practice in the nature of rental, lease, or lending. Nothing in the preceding sentence shall apply to the rental, lease, or lending of a phonorecord for nonprofit purposes by a nonprofit library or nonprofit-educational institution. The transfer of possession of a lawfully made copy of a computer program by a nonprofit educational institution to another nonprofit educational institution or to faculty, staff, and students does not constitute rental, lease, or lending for direct or indirect commercial purposes under this subsection.

(B) This subsection does not apply to—

(i) a computer program which is embodied in a machine or product and which cannot be copied during the ordinary operation or use of the machine or product; or

(ii) a computer program embodied in or used in conjunction with a limited purpose computer that is designed for playing video games and may be designed for other purposes.

(C) Nothing in this subsection affects any provision of chapter 9 of this title.

(2) (A) Nothing in this subsection shall apply to the lending of a computer program for nonprofit purposes by a nonprofit library, if each copy of a computer program which is lent by such library has affixed to the packaging containing the program a warning of copyright in accordance with requirements that the Register of Copyrights shall prescribe by regulation.

(B) Not later than three years after the date of the enactment of the Computer Software Rental Amendments Act of 1990 [Dec. 1, 1990], and at such times thereafter as the Register of Copyright considers appropriate, the Register of Copyrights, after consultation with representatives of copy-right owners and librarians, shall submit to the Congress a report stating whether this paragraph has achieved its intended purpose of maintaining the integrity of the copyright system while providing nonprofit libraries the capability to fulfill their function. Such report shall advise the Congress as to any information or recommendations that the Register of Copyrights considers necessary to carry out the purposes of this subsection.

(3) Nothing in this subsection shall affect any provision of the antitrust laws. For purposes of the preceding sentence, "antitrust laws" has the meaning given that term in the first section of the Clayton Act [15 U.S.C. § 12] and includes section 5 of the Federal Trade Commission Act [15 U.S.C. § 45] to the extent that section relates to unfair methods of competition.

(4) Any person who distributes a phonorecord or a copy of a computer program (including any tape, disk, or other medium embodying such program) in violation of paragraph (1) is an infringer of copyright under section 501 of this title and is subject to the remedies set forth in sections 502, 503, 504, 505, and 509. Such violation shall not be a criminal offense under section 506 or cause such person to be subject to the criminal penalties set forth in section 2319 of title 18.

(e) Notwithstanding the provisions of sections 106(4) and 106(5), in the case of an electronic audiovisual game intended for use in coin-operated equipment, the owner of a particular copy of such a game lawfully made under this title, is entitled, without the authority of the copyright owner of the game, to publicly perform or display that game in coin-operated equipment, except that this subsection shall not apply to any work of authorship embodied in the audiovisual game if the copyright owner of the electronic audiovisual game is not also the copyright owner of the work of authorship.

3. *Computer Programs*

Section 117 of the 1976 Copyright Act provided that the Act did not afford the copyright owner of a computer program any exclusive rights that were not present under the 1909 Act. The National Commission on New Technology Uses of Copyrighted Works (CONTU), established by P.L. 93-573, was authorized to conduct a study of copyright protection associated with computer systems. Since CONTU had not finished their work at the time the 1976 Copyright Act was considered by the Congress, section 117 retained the prior law as it applied to such systems.

Congress, in 1980, in amending the Patent Laws adopted the thrust of CONTU's recommendations regarding the copyright of computer programs and amended the, copyright law as follows, P.L. 96-517. Public Law 96-517 added a definition of computer programs to 17 U.S.C. § 101:

A "computer program" is a set of statements or instructions to be used directly or indirectly in a computer in order to bring about a certain result.

17 U.S.C. § 117 also was amended by P.L. 96-517 and further in 1998 to provide:

(a) *Making of additional copy or adaptation by owner of copy.* Notwithstanding the provisions of section 106, it is not an infringement for the owner of a copy of a computer program to make or authorize the making of another copy or adaptation of that computer program provided:

(1) that such a new copy or adaptation is created as an essential step in the utilization of the computer program in conjunction with a machine and that it is used in no other manner, or

(2) that such new copy or adaptation is for archival purposes only and that all archival copies are destroyed in the event that continued possession of the computer program should cease to be rightful.

(b) *Lease, sale, or other transfer of additional copy or adaptation.* Any exact copies prepared in accordance with the provisions of this section may be leased, sold, or otherwise transferred, along with the copy from which such copies were prepared, only as part of the lease, sale, or other transfer of all rights in the program. Adaptations so prepared may be transferred only with the authorization of the copyright owner.

(c) *Machine maintenance or repair.* Notwithstanding the provisions of section 106, it is not an infringement for the owner or lessee of a machine to make or authorize the making of a copy of a computer program if such copy is made solely by virtue of the activation of a machine that lawfully contains an authorized copy of the computer program, for purposes only of maintenance or repair of that machine, if—

(1) such new copy is used in no other manner and is destroyed immediately after the maintenance or repair is completed; and

(2) with respect to any computer program or part thereof that is not necessary for that machine to be activated, such program or part thereof is not accessed or used other than to make such new copy by virtue of the activation of the machine.

(d) *Definitions.* For purposes of this section

(1) the "maintenance" of a machine is the servicing of the machine in order to make it work in accordance with its original specifications and any changes to those specifications authorized for that machine; and (2) the "repair" of a machine is the restoring of the machine to the state of working in accordance with its original specifications and any changes to those specifications authorized for that machine.

The purpose of this section was to make it clear that a computer program was copyrightable as a "literary work," and that the 1976 Copyright Act overruled the *White-Smith v. Apollo* piano roll case. The only problem with obtaining broad copyright protection for computer programs was the existing section 117, which, in effect, said that the 1976 changes were not available for computer programs. By deleting section 117, broad copyright protection would be available for computer programs, but, in doing this, it would be necessary to provide the owner of a copy of program with certain minimum rights. While such rights could be implied, CONTU suggested that these rights be expressed and flow to the rightful possessor of the program. This concept was adopted by congress, but the "possessor" of the program, the language suggested by CONTU, was changed to the "owner" of a copy.

E. Unpublished Works

1. Publication

Publication is no longer the key to obtaining a copyright as it was under the 1909 Act. Publication is defined in 17 U.S.C. § 101:

"Publication" is the distribution of copies or phonorecords of a work to the public by sale or other transfer of ownership, or by rental, lease, or lending. The offering to distribute copies or phonorecords to a Soup of persons for purposes of further distribution, public performance, or public display, constitutes publication. A public performance or display of a work does not of itself constitute publication.

A work is published if one or more copies or phonorecords embodying the work are distributed to the public—that is distributed to persons under no explicit or implicit restrictions with regard to the disclosure of the contents, H. Rep. at 138. Any form or dissemination in which the material object does not change hands, for example, displays on television, is not a publication no matter how many people are exposed to the work. Publication is still important under the 1976 Act since, upon publication, a work must bear a copyright notice and publication may effect the duration of the copyright.

2. *Protection for Unpublished Works*

The coverage for unpublished works and the abolition of the common law copyright system is contained in 17 U.S.C. §§ 104 and 301:

> (a) Unpublished works. The works specified by sections 102 and 103, while unpublished, are subject to protection under this title without regard to the nationality or domicile of the author.

3. *Preemption*

17 U.S.C.§ 301 substitutes a single federal system for the dual copyright system previously existing in state and federal laws by abolishing the state common law copyright system. A work under section 104 automatically obtains statutory protection when it is "created." A work is "created" pursuant to the definition of section 101 "when it is fixed in a copy or phonorecord for the first time; where the work is prepared over a period of time, the portion of it that has been fixed at any particular time constitutes the work as of that time; and where the work has been prepared in different versions, each version constitutes a separate work." 17 U.S.C. § 301 preempts any rights, legal or equitable, under state statutes or common law that are equivalent to exclusive rights of the copyright under the federal statute, i.e., to the extent that the exclusive rights are specified by section 106, if such works are within the subject matter categories covered by sections 102 and 103. Preemption occurs "regardless of when the work was created and whether it is published or unpublished, disseminated, or undisseminated in the public domain or copyrighted under the federal statute," H. Rep. at 130-31. Of course, works which have not been fixed in any tangible medium of expression would not be covered by late preemption provision of section 301 and state law protection is still possible. Section 301 now provides:

> (1) On and after January 1, 1978, all legal or equitable rights that are equivalent to any of the exclusive rights within the general scope of copyright as specified by section 106 in works of authorship that are fixed in a tangible medium of expression and come within the subject matter of copyright as specified by sections 102 and 103, whether created before or after that date and whether published or unpublished, are governed exclusively by this title. Thereafter, no person is entitled to any such right or equivalent right in any such work under the common law or statutes of any State.
>
> (2) Nothing in this title annuls or limits any rights or remedies under the common law or statutes of any State with respect to—
>
> > (1) subject matter that does not come within the subject matter of copyright as specified by sections 102 and 103, including works of authorship not fixed in any tangible medium of expression; or
> >
> > (2) any cause of action arising from undertakings commenced before January 1, 1978;
> >
> > (3) activities violating legal or equitable rights that are not equivalent to any of the exclusive rights within the general scope of copyright as specified by section 106; or

(4) State and local landmarks, historic preservation, zoning, or building codes,, relating to architectural works protected under section 102(a)(8).

(e) The scope of Federal preemption under this section is not affected by the adherence of the United States to the Berne Convention or the satisfaction of obligations of the United States thereunder.

(f)(1) On or after the effective date set forth in section 610(a) of the Visual Artists Rights Act of 1990 [17 U.S.C. § 106A note], all legal or equitable rights that are equivalent to any of the rights conferred by section 106A with respect to works of visual art to which the rights conferred by section 106A apply are governed exclusively by section 106A and section 113(d) and the provisions of this title relating to such sections. Thereafter, no person is entitled to any such right or equivalent right in any work of visual art under the common law or statutes of any State.

(2) Nothing in paragraph (1) annuls or limits any rights or remedies under the common law or statutes of any State with respect to—

(A) any cause of action from undertakings commenced before the effective date set forth in section 610(a) of the Visual Artists Rights Act of 1990 [17 U.S.C. § 106A note];

(B) activities violating legal or equitable rights that are not equivalent to any of the rights conferred by section 106A with respect to works of visual art; or

(C) activities violating legal or equitable rights which extend beyond the life of the author.

The House Report on section 301 as originally adopted explains the impact of section 301 (b) at 131-33:

In a general way subsection (b) of section 301 represents the obverse of subsection (a). It sets out, in broad terms and without necessarily being exhaustive, some of the principal areas of protection that preemption would not prevent the states from protecting. Its purpose is to make clear, consistent with the 1964 Supreme Court decisions in *Sears, Roebuck & Co. v. Stiffel Co.*, 376 U.S. 225, and *Compco Corp. v. Day-brite Lighting, Inc.*, 376 U.S. 234, that preemption does not extend to causes of action, or subject matter outside the scope of the revised Federal copyright statute.

The numbered clauses of subsection (b) list three general areas left unaffected by the preemption: (1) subject matter that does not come within the subject matter of copyright; (2) causes of action arising under State law before the effective date of the statute; and (3) violations of rights that are not equivalent to any of the exclusive rights under copyright.

The examples in clause (3), while not exhaustive, are intended to illustrate rights and remedies that are different in nature from the rights comprised in a copyright and that may continue to be protected under State common law or statute. The evolving common law rights of "privacy," "publicity," and trade secrets, and the general laws of defamation and fraud, would remain unaffected as long as the causes of action contain elements, such as an invasion of personal rights or a breach of trust or confidentiality that are different in kind from copyright infringement. Nothing in the bill derogates from the rights of parties to contract with each other and to sue for breaches of contract; however, to the extent that the unfair competition concept known as "interference with contract relations" is merely the equivalent of copyright protection, it would be preempted.

The application of this section has raised questions concerning the viability of trade secret law to certain works. In *Avco Corp. v. Precision Air Parts, Inc.*, 210 U.S.P.Q. 894 (M.D. Ala. 1981), *aff'd on other grounds*, 676 F.2d 494, 216 U.S.P.Q. 1086 (11th Cir.), *cert. denied*, 459 U.S. 1037 (1982), the district court held that claims of misappropriation of trade secrets based on copying plans and making derivative works were preempted. The district court in *Warrington Assocs., Inc. v. Real-Time Eng'g Sys., Inc.*, 522 F. Supp. 367, 316 U.S.P.Q. 1024 (N.D. IL 1981) held that trade secret claims were not preempted by section 301. See also *Technicon Medical Info. Sys. Corp. v. Green Bay Packaging, Inc.*, 211 U.S.P.Q. 343 (E.D. Wisc. 1980), where a copyright notice on a work did not in itself defeat a trade secret; *M. Bryce & Assocs., Inc. v. Gladstone*, 319 N.W. 2d 907, 215 U.S.P.Q. 81 (1982), which held that trade secrets were not preempted despite a general publication of a technical manual with a copyright notice. Generally, state trade secret law will not be preempted by the Federal Copyright Act because a violation of a trade secret requires elements which form no part of a copyright infringement claim, see *Data Gen. Corp. v. Grumman Sys. Support Corp.*, 36 F.3d 1147, 32 U.S.P.Q.2d 1385 (lst Cir. 1994); *Computer Assocs. Int'l., Inc. v. Altai, Inc.*, 982 F.2d 693 (2d Cir. 1992); *Avtec Sys., Inc. v. Peiffer*, 21 F.3d 568, 30 U.S.P.Q. 2d 1365 (4th Cir. 1994). Thus, if a state's trade secret law requires some sort of action other than the copying or reproduction of the work such as a breach of trust or confidentiality via the use of the work, the state law will not be preempted. But where a trade secret claim under state law based precisely upon the same elements as the plaintiff's copyright claim was preempted by the copyright law. See *Foresight Resources Corp. v. Larry Pfortmiller*, 719 F. Supp. 1006, 13 U.S.P.Q. 2d 1721 (D.D.K. 1989).

F. Copyright Term

The copyright term of 28 years, renewable for an additional 28-year term, in the 1909 Copyright law has been significantly changed by the new copyright system. Since the 28 + 28 period was changed periodically during 1965 to 1976 to extend the copyright period for a year at a time until Congress could consider a new copyright law, copyrights renewed under the 1909 Act never expired. Subsequently, the new Copyright Act extended those copyrights, if in their renewal period, for the duration provided in that law, 17 U.S.C. § 304(b), or for an additional period of years if in their first term, 17 U.S.C. § 304(a).

The term for copyrights created after January 1, 1978, under the 1976 law is the life of the author plus 50 years after the author's death, 17 U.S.C. § 302(a). The date of expiration is measured by the end of the calendar year, 17 U.S.C. § 305. In the case of a joint work, the copyright endures for a term of the life of the last surviving author plus 50 years, 17 U.S.C. § 302(b). Works for hire and anonymous works under this law subsist for 75 years from the date of first publication or 100 years from their creation whichever expires first, 17 U.S.C. § 302(c).

There is a presumption that the author's death has occurred 75 years from the date of first publication or 100 years from the date of the work's creation, whichever expires first. However, to obtain the benefit of this presumption, one must obtain a certificate from the Copyright Office stating that its records do not disclose that the author is alive or that he has been dead for less than 50 years. Reliance upon this presumption is a defense to any infringement action.

The Sonny Bono Copyright Term Extension Act, P.L. 105-298, changed the above noted copyright term by adding 20 years to the term specified in the 1976 law as noted in the following table.

	1909 COPYRIGHT ACT*	1976 COPYRIGHT ACT	1998 SONNY BONO ACT
ORIGINAL WORKS			
Author—sole	28 years plus renewal for 28 years	Life plus 50 years	Life plus 70 years
Author—joint	28 years plus renewal for 28 years	Life plus 50 years of last surviving author	Life plus 70 years of last surviving author
Author—anonymous/work for hire	28 years plus renew for 28 years	Earlier of 75 years from date of first publication or 100 years from creation	Earlier of 95 years from date of first publication or 120 years from creation
EXISTING WORKS			
Extension of copyright terrain(author-sole)		If in first term under 1909 Act, copyright extended for 47 years	If in first term under 1909 Act, copyright extended for 67 years
Extension of copyright terms(Author-joint)		If in first term under 1909 Act, copyright extended but in no event after 12/31/2027	If in first term under 1909 Act, copyright extended but in no event after 12/31/2047
Works created prior to 1978 but not published or in public domain	No time period for unpublished works	Same term as for original works but if work is published before 1/2003 then is expires after 12/31/2027	Same term as for original works but if work is published before 1/2003 then it expires after 12/31/2047
Works created prior to 1978 in their initial term	28 year renewal period	Remainder of 28 year initial period plus a renewal of 47 years	Remainder of 28 year initial period plus a renewal of 67 years
Works created pr/or to 1978 but are in their renewal term	28 year renewal term	75 years from date copyright initially obtained	75 years from date copyright initially obtained

*The term was extended while Congress considered the revision of the copyright laws until 1978 and in effect copyrights under the 1909 Act, if renewed, have a 75-year term.

The Act includes provisions for the use of copyrights works during this 20-year extension for libraries, archives and non-profit organizations. But before they may use this right, a determination must be made concerning factors such as whether the work is subject to normal commercial exploitation. A copyright owner may provide notice to this effect to the Register of Copyrights. There is also a sense of Congress provision regarding voluntary negotiations over the benefits of this additional 20-year period.

G. Copyright Ownership

1. Initial Ownership

a. Individual and Joint Works

Copyrights initially vest in the author or authors of the work. 17 U.S.C. § 201(a) provides that the initial ownership of the copyright in a work vests in the author or authors of the work. The authors of a joint work are co-owners of copyright in the entire work. That is, each author may use or license the work without the other's consent but may be required to account for any profits made to the other owner, *Oddo v. Reis*, 743 F.2d 630, 222 U.S.P.Q. 799 (9th Cir. 1984); *Weisman v. Freeman*, 868 F.2d 1313 (2d Cir. 1989). A joint work is defined by 17 U.S.C. § 101 as a work prepared by two or more authors with the intention that their contributions be merged into inseparable or interdependent parts as unitary whole. See, for example, *Sheshadri v. Kasraian*, 130 F.3d 798 (7th Cir. 1997) for a review of joint authorship.

b. Works for Hire

As to "works for hire," deemed as "the employer or other person for whom the work was prepared is considered the author for purposes of this title, and, unless the parties have expressly agreed otherwise in a written instrument signed by them, owns all of the rights comprised in the copyright," 17 U.S.C. § 201 (b). This is an important concept since it includes most works prepared by Government contractors and grantees at least as to the rights of the contractor or the grantee employees. A "work for hire" is defined in 17 U.S.C. § 101 as:

(1) a work prepared by an employee within the scope of his or her employment; or

(2) a work specially ordered or commissioned for use as a contribution to a collective work, as a part of a motion picture or other audiovisual work, as a translation, as a supplementary work, as a compilation, as an instructional text, as a test, as answer material for a test, or an atlas, if the parties expressly agree in a written instrument signed by them that the work shall be considered a work made for hire. For the purpose of the foregoing sentence, a "supplementary work" is a work prepared for publication as a secondary adjunct to a work by another author for the purpose of introducing, concluding, illustrating, explaining, revising, commenting upon, or assisting in the use of the other work, such as forewords, afterwards, pictorial illustrations, maps, charts, tables, editorial notes, musical arrangements, answer material for tests, bibliographies, appendixes, and indexes, and an "instructional text" is a literary, pictorial, or graphic work prepared for publication and with the purpose of use in systematic instructional activities.

The copyright code does not define the term "employee." The courts initially adopted inconsistent standards as to who was an employee under the work for hire doctrine. For example, in *Aldon Accessories Ltd. v. Spiegel*, 738 F.2d 548, 222 U.S.P.Q. 951 (2d Cir.), *cert. denied*, 469 U.S. 982 (1984), the court adopted a "supervision and control test." In *Dumas v. Goremerman*, 865 F.2d 1093, 9 U.S.P.Q.2d 1701 (9th Cir. 1989), however, the court adopted a "formal salaried employee test." The Supreme Court in *Community for Creative Non-Violence v. Reid*, 490 U.S. 730, 10 U.S.P.Q.2d 1985 (1989) considered whether an independent contractor was an employee to whom the work for hire doctrine applied. The Court set out the following nonexclusive factors to be considered to determine whether an independent contractor was an employee under the general common law: the hiring parties right to control the manner and means by which the work is accomplished; the skills required; the source of the instrumentalities and tools; the location of the work; the duration of the relationship between the parties; whether the hiring party has the right to assign additional work; the extent of the hired party's discretion over when and how long to work; the method of payment; the hired party's role in hiring and paying assistants; whether the work is a part of the regular business of the hiring party; whether the hiring party is in business; the provision of employee benefits; and the tax treatment of the hired party. For application of this rule, see *Graham v. James*, 144 F.3d 229 (2d 1998), holding that a computer software programmer was not an employee as the hiring party had little control over the programmer, provided no benefits, and did not have the right to assign other projects to the programmer; and *Macro v. Accent Pub. Co.*, 969 F.2d 1547 (3d Cir. 1992), finding that a freelance photographer was not an employee of a magazine publisher.

c. Collective Works

As to collective works (i.e., a work, such as a periodical issue, anthology, or encyclopedia, in which a number of contributions, constituting separate and independent works in themselves, are assembled into a collective whole), copyright in each separate contribution to a collective work is distinct from copyright in the collective work as a whole, and vests initially in the author of the contribution, 17 U.S.C. § 201(c). In the absence of an express transfer of the copyright or of any rights under it, the owner of copyright in the collective work is presumed to have acquired only the privilege of reproducing and distributing the contribution as part of that particular collective work, any revision of that collective work, and any later collective work in the same series, 17 U.S.C. § 201(c).

In *New York Times Co. v. Tasini*, __ U.S. __, (Supreme Court No. 00-201, June 25, 2001) a group of freelance authors who acted as independent contractors writing articles for the defendant publications sued the publishers and electronic database owners (e.g., LEXIS/NEXIS) for placing the authors' articles into an electronic database, in text only format, without their consent In placing these works into the electronic database to permit word for word searching. When an article was identified by the search, the original publication source was noted but each article appeared in isolation from the rest of the publication in which the article first appeared. In response to the authors' complaint, the publishers raised the privilege accorded collective works" copyright owners by §201(c) of the Copyright Act, which reads:

> Copyright in each separate contribution to a collective work is distinct from copyright in the collective work as a whole, and vests initially in the author of the contribution. In the absence

of an express transfer of the copyright or of any rights under it, the owner of copyright in the collective work is presumed to have acquired only the privilege of reproducing and distributing the contribution as part of that particular collective work, any revision of that collective work, and any later collective work in the same series.

The defendants argued that the authors' permission to initially publish their works in the defendants' publications, which under copyright law was a collective work, was covered by §201(c) as a "revision" of that collective work. The court disagreed and held that the electronic databases reproduced and distributed articles standing alone and not in context, not "as part of. . . any revision" thereof, or "as part of . . . any later collective work in the same series."

2. Transfer of Interests in Copyrights

a. Conveyance Requirements

Transfer of ownership of a copyright is specified by 17 U.S.C. § 201(d) and (e):

(d) *Transfer of ownership.*

> (1) The ownership of a copyright may be transferred in whole or in part by any means of conveyance or by operation of law, and may be bequeathed by will or pass as personal property by the applicable laws of interstate succession.

> (2) Any of the exclusive rights comprised in a copyright, including any subdivision of any of the rights specified by section 106, may be transferred as provided by clause (I) and owned separately. The owner of any particular exclusive right is entitled, to the extent of that right, to all of the protection and remedies accorded to the copyright owner by this title.

Subsection (d)(2) explicitly recognizes the principle of divisibility of the exclusive rights of a copyright. The last sentence makes it clear that the owner of one of the exclusive rights of the copyright may sue an infringer in his own name, H. Rep. at 123. As to formalities of a transfer of any of the exclusive rights, 17 U.S.C. § 204(a) provides that:

> A transfer of copyright ownership, other than by operation of law, is not valid unless an instrument of conveyance, or a note or memorandum of the transfer, is in writing and signed by the owner of the rights conveyed or such owner's duly authorized agent.

Note that the transfer of any exclusive rights (other than by operation of law) must be in writing and must be signed by the owner of the exclusive rights or by the owner's agent. The owner of any exclusive right may register his claim in copyright. Transfer of a right on a nonexclusive basis does not require a writing. In *Magnuson v. Video Yesteryear*, 85 F.3d 1424 (9th Cir. 1996), the court held that an oral transfer confirmed in writing later can transfer ownership of a copyright where the parties to the transfer do not dispute the facts.

b. Transfer of a Copyright

Under 17 U.S.C. § 202, the purchase of an original manuscript or photographic negative does not transfer the copyright. Nor does the transfer of the copyright convey the rights in the material object. Ownership of a copyright is separate and distinct from ownership of the tangible object in which the copyright is embodied. Transfer of the ownership of either the copyright or the object does not transfer ownership of the other. This changes the common law doctrine, which presumed that artists or authors transferred their common law rights when they sold their work of art or manuscript, *Pushman v. New York Graphics Soc'y, Inc.*, 287 N.Y. 302, 52 U.S.P.Q. 273, 39 N.E. 2d 249 (1942). 17 U.S.C. § 202 provides:

> Ownership of a copyright, or of any of the exclusive rights under a copyright, is distinct from ownership of any material object in which the work is embodied. Transfer of ownership of any material object, including the copy or phonorecord in which the work is first fixed, does not of itself convey a copyrighted work embodied in the object; nor, in the absence of an agreement, does transfer of any rights in the ownership of a copyright or of any exclusive rights under a copyright convey property rights in any material object.

H. Copyright Notice

1. Form of Notice for Published Works

To obtain a copyright in a published work it is no longer necessary for the copyright owner to place a notice on all publicly distributed copies. In 1989 in order to conform Title 17 to the requirements of the Berne Convention, changes were made to the mandatory notice requirements of 17 U.S.C. § 401. The prior copyright laws of the United States all required notice of copyright on certain works as a condition of copyright protection under the code. Now such a copyright notice is not required but is permissible but if a notice of copyright in proper form and position appears on the published copy or copies of a work to which a defendant in a copyright infringement suit had access, then the court is to give no weight to a defendant's defense based on innocent infringement, except as provided in the last sentence of section 504(c)(2). The form of the notice and its position is specified by 17 U.S.C. § 401 below:

> (a) *General provisions.* Whenever a work protected under this title is published in the United States or elsewhere by authority of the copyright owner, a notice of copyright as provided by this section may be placed on publicly distributed copies from which the work can be visually perceived, either directly or with the aid of a machine or device.

> (b) *Form of notice.* If a notice appears on the copies, it shall consist of the following three elements:

>> (1) the symbol (c) (the letter C in a circle), or the word "Copyright", or the abbreviation "Copr."; and

>> (2) the year of first publication of the work; in the case of compilations or derivative works incorporating previously published material, the year date of first publication of the compi-

lation or derivative work is sufficient. The year date may be omitted where a pictorial, graphic, or sculptural work, with accompanying text matter, if any, is reproduced in or on greeting cards, postcards, stationery, jewelry, dolls, toys, or any useful articles; and

(3) the name of the owner of copyright in the work, or an abbreviation by which the name can be recognized, or a generally known alternative designation of the owner.

(c) *Position of notice. The* notice shall be affixed to the copies in such manner and location as to give reasonable notice of the claim of copyright. The Register of Copyrights shall prescribe by regulation, as examples, specific methods of affixation and positions of the notice on various types of works that will satisfy this requirement, but these specifications shall not be considered exhaustive.

(d) *Evidentiary weight of notice.* If a notice of copyright in the form and position specified by this section appears on the published copy or copies to which a defendant in a copyright infringement suit had access, then no weight shall be given to such a defendant's interposition of a defense based on innocent infringement in mitigation of actual or statutory damages, except as provided in the last sentence of section 504(c)(2).

A similar notice with the letter P in a circle, the date of first year publication and the owner's name is also provided for phonorecords, 17 U.S.C. § 402. As to collective works each separate work may bear its own notice of copyright, however, a single notice applicable to the work as a whole is sufficient for sections 401(d) and 402(d) purposes, 17 U.S.C. § 403. While a copyright notice is not required for works first published after March 1, 1989, the Copyright Office highly recommends the use of a notice because it informs the public that the work is protected by copyright, identifies the owner, and shows the year of first publication. "Furthermore, in the event a work is infringed, if the work carries a proper notice, the court will not allow a defendant to claim 'innocent infringement'—that is, that he or she did not realize that the work was protect," Copyright Office Circular 1, Copyright Basics.

2. Lack of Notice

a. Prior to Berne Convention

Under the 1909 copyright law a copyright notice was required on all published works. The lack of such a notice rendered the copyright invalid. The 1976 Copyright Act, while still requiring a copyright notice on published works, liberalized the impact of omitting such notice or in correcting errors as to the name or date used on copies of a copyrighted work publicly distributed by the authority of the copyright owner. 17 U.S.C. § 405(a) provides, for works published after January 1, 1978, that such omissions do not invalidate the copyright in a work if—

(1) the notice has been omitted from no more than a relatively small number of copies or phonorecords distributed to the public; or

2) registration for the work has been made before or is made within five years after the publication without notice, and a reasonable effort is made to add notice to all copies or phonorecords that are distributed to the public in the United States after the omission has been discovered; or

(3) the notice has been omitted in violation of an express requirement in writing that, as a condition of the copyright owner's authorization of the public distribution of copies or phonorecords, they bear the prescribed notice.

b. Berne Convention Changes

The notice requirement was changed for works created after March 1, 1989 by the Berne Convention Implementation Act of 1988, P.L. 100-568. This Act was passed to provide for the adherence of the United States to the Berne Convention, i.e., the Convention for the Protection of Literary and Artistic Works, signed at Berne, Switzerland, on September 9, 1986, and all acts, protocols, and revisions thereto. The changed requirements with respect to omissions essentially preserves the prior copyright acts' notice requirements for works created or published as applicable under such acts. New section 405 provides:

(a) Effect of omission on copyright. With respect to copies and phonorecords publicly distributed by authority of the copyright owner before the effective date of the Berne Convention Implementation Act of 1988, the omission of the copyright notice described in sections 401 through 403 from copies or phonorecords publicly distributed by authority of the copyright owner does not invalidate the copyright in a work if—

(1) the notice has been omitted from no more than a relatively small number of copies or phonorecords distributed to the public; or

(2) registration for the work has been made before or is made within five years after the publication without notice, and a reasonable effort is made to add notice to all copies or phonorecords that are distributed to the public in the United States after the omission has been discovered; or

(3) the notice has been omitted in violation of an express requirement in writing that, as a condition of the copyright owner's authorization of the public distribution of copies or phonorecords, they bear the prescribed notice.

(b) *Effect of omission on innocent infringers.* Any person who innocently infringes a copyright, in reliance upon an authorized copy or phonorecord from which the copyright notice has been omitted and which was publicly distributed by authority of the copyright owner before the effective date of the Berne Convention Implementation Act of 1988, incurs no liability for actual or statutory damages under section 504 for any infringing acts committed before receiving actual notice that registration for the work has been made under section 408, if such person proves that he or she was misled by the omission of notice. In a suit for infringement in such a case the court may allow or disallow recovery of troy of the infringer's profits attributable to the infringement, and may enjoin the continuation of the infringing undertaking or may require, as a condition or permitting the continuation of the infringing undertaking, that the infringer pay the copyright owner a reasonable license fee in an amount and on terms fixed by the court.

(c) *Removal of notice*. Protection under this title is not affected by the removal, destruction, or obliteration of the notice, without the authorization of the copyright owner, from any publicly distributed copies or phonorecords.

c. Effect of Notice Errors

Prior to March 1, 1989, if an error on copyright notice occurred, or if copies or phonorecords were publicly distributed by the owner of the copyright and contained the wrong name of the owner, the copyright would not be invalidated. However, an innocent infringer had a defense if such person proves they were misled by the notice and began their undertaking in good faith under a license from the person named in the copyright notice, unless such work was registered in the name of the rightful owner or such ownership interest was recorded in the copyright office, 17 U.S.C. § 406(a). If an error is in the date of a copyrighted work distributed prior to Mach 31, 1989 by authority of the copyright owner, and such date is earlier than the year of the first publication, then the term of the copyright is to be computed from the year on the notice. If, however, the year is later than the more than one year from which the first publication occurred or the date is missing, the work is considered as being published without notice, 17 U.S.C. § 406(b).

An innocent infringer, who, before March 1, 1989, relied on and was misled by the omission of the copyright notice, incurred no actual or statutory damages for infringing acts prior to receipt of actual notice, 17 U.S.C. § 405(b). The courts, however, could allow recovery of the infringer's profits, enjoin future infringement, and require the infringer to pay a royalty for continued use of the exclusive rights infringed. If the copyright notice was removed from publicly distributed copies without the authorization of the copyright owner, the owner's exclusive rights and remedies are unaffected, 17 U.S.C. § 405(c).

3. Works Incorporating Government Works

A special notice is required by section 403 on publications incorporating works of the United States Government:

> Sections 401(d) and 402(d) shall not apply to a work published in copies or phonorecords consisting predominantly of one or more works of the United States Government unless the notice of copyright appearing on the published copies or phonorecords to which a defendant in the copyright infringement suit had access includes a statement identifying, either affirmatively or negatively, those portions of the copies of phonorecords embodying any work or works protected under this title.

This provision is an attempt by Congress to inform the public where a publisher reprints a Government work with some new matter. In the past, such work contained a copyright notice in the name of the publisher without informing the public that a major portion of the work was in the public domain.

4. Deposit Requirements

17 U.S.C. § 407(a) provides for the owner of either the copyright or any exclusive rights in the work to register its claim and deposit copies of the work or a phonorecord, with an application form, and the fee prescribed by the copyright office pursuant to 17 U.S.C. § 708. Works deposited in the Copyright Office are available for use by the Library of Congress, 17 U.S.C. § 407(b). Pursuant to section 407(c), the Register of Copyright may exempt categories of works from the deposit requirement. However, neither registration of a claim of copyright or the deposit of a work is a condition of copyright. Where a work has not been deposited, the Register may make a written demand for the required deposit of a work on any person obligated to make a deposit under section 407, 17 U.S.C. § 407(d).

5. Registration

Registration of a claim of copyright pursuant to 17 U.S.C. § 409 is to be made on the forms prescribed by the Register and includes the name and address of the copyright claimant; in the case of a work other than an anonymous or pseudonymous work, the name and nationality or domicile of the author or authors, and, if one or more of the authors is dead, the dates of their deaths; if the work is anonymous or pseudonymous, the nationality or domicile of the author or authors; in the case of a work made for hire, a statement to this effect; if the copyright claimant is not the author, a brief statement of how the claimant obtained ownership of the copyright; the title of the work, together with any previous or alternative titles under which the work can be identified; the year in which creation of the work was completed; if the work has been published, the date and nation of its first publication; in the case of a compilation or derivative work, an identification of any preexisting work or works that it is based on or incorporates, and a brief, general statement of the additional material covered by the copyright claim being registered; in the case of a published work containing material of which copies are required by section 601 to be manufactured in the United States, the names of the persons or organizations who performed the processes specified by subsection (c) of section 601 with respect to that material, and the places where those processes were performed; and any other information regarded by the Register of Copyrights as bearing upon the preparation or identification of the work or the existence, ownership, or duration of the copyright.

6. Issuance of Certificate

17 U.S.C. § 410 provides for an examination of the registration claim by the Register of Copyrights to determine if the material deposited constitutes copyrightable subject matter and that the other legal and formal requirements of this title have been met. If so, the Register registers the claim and issues the applicant a certificate of registration under the seal of the Copyright Office. If the Register determines that the material deposited does not constitute copyrightable subject matter or that the claim is invalid for any other reason, the Register is to refuse registration and notify the applicant in writing of the reasons for such refusal. A registration made before, or within five years after, first publication of the work is prima facie evidence of the validity of the copyright and of the facts stated in the copyright certificate in judicial proceedings. Except for Berne Convention works (other than U.S. works) registration is a

prerequisite for brining a copyright infringement claim in the district courts, 17 U.S.C. § 411(a). See *International Trade Management v. United States,* 553 F. Supp. 402 (1982) for the need to register before brining a copyright claim against the U.S. under 28 U.S.C. § 1498(b).

I. Remedies

1. Berne Convention—United States Works

Prior to instituting an action for infringement, statutory damages or attorney fees, a copyright originating in the United States must be registered, 17 U.S.C. § 411 (a). For purposes of section 411, a work is a "United States work" only if—

(1) in the case of a published work, the work is first published—

(A) in the United States;

(B) simultaneously in the United States and another treaty party or parties, whose law grants a term of copyright protection that is the same as or longer than the term provided in the United States;

(C) simultaneously in the United States and a foreign nation that is not a treaty party; or

(D) in a foreign nation that is not a treaty party, and all of the authors of the work are nationals, domiciliaries, or habitual residents of, or in the case of an audiovisual work legal entities with headquarters in, the United States;

(2) in the case of an unpublished work, all the authors of the work are nationals, domiciliaries, or habitual residents of the United States, or, in the case of an unpublished audiovisual work, all the authors are legal entities with headquarters in, the United States; or

(3) in the case of a pictorial, graphic, or sculptural work incorporated in a building or structure, the building or structure is located in the United States.

2. Berne Convention Works

In order to comply with the requirements of the Berne Convention, a different rule was provided for Berne Convention works. 17 U.S.C. § 101 defined such a work as follows:

A work is a "Berne Convention work" if—

(1) in the case of an unpublished work, one or more of the authors is a national of a nation adhering to the Berne Convention, or in the case of a published work, one or more of the authors is a national of a nation adhering to the Berne Convention on the date of first publication;

(2) the work was first published in a nation adhering to the Berne Convention, or was simultaneously first published in a nation adhering to the Berne Convention and in a foreign nation that does not adhere to the Berne Convention;

(3) in the case of an audiovisual work—

(A) if one or more of the authors is a legal entity, that author has its headquarters in a nation adhering to the Berne Convention; or

(B) if one or more of the authors is an individual, that author is domiciled, or has his or her habitual residence in, a nation adhering to the Berne Convention; or

(4) in the case of a pictorial, graphic, or sculptural work that is incorporated in a building or other structure, the building or structure is located in a nation adhering to the Berne Convention; or

(5) in the case of an architectural work embodied in a building, such building is erected in a country adhering to the Berne Convention.

For purposes of paragraph (1), an author who is domiciled in or has his or her habitual residence in, a nation adhering to the Berne Convention is considered to be a national of that nation. For purposes of paragraph (2), a work is considered to have been simultaneously published in two or more nations if its dates of publication are within 30 days of one another.

Any one who violates the exclusive rights of the copyright owner infringes the copyright, 17 U.S.C. § 501. The owner of the exclusive rights may institute suits in any district court for an injunction, 17 U.S.C. § 502; and for actual damages suffered as a result of the infringement, as well as for any profit attributed to the infringement which was not considered in computing actual damages, 17 U.S.C.§ 504. Damages may be actual or statutory damages, 17 U.S.C. § 504(c). Statutory damages, as set by the court, generally, between $500 and $20,000, can be obtained only if the work was registered with the copyright office before a particular infringing act occurred, 17 U.S.C. § 504(c). The court may increase the judgment to not more than $100,000 if the infringement was willful, 17 U.S.C. § 504(c)(2). The statutory damages may be reduced to $200 if the infringer had no reason to believe that his acts constituted an infringement, 17 U.S.C. § 504(c)(2). If the infringement was willful and for the purpose of commercial advantage or private financial gain, a court may impose a fine or imprisonment for up to one year, or both, 17 U.S.C. § 506(a). It is also a criminal offense to fraudulently place a copyright notice on any article knowing the notice to be false, or to publicly distribute any article bearing a false notice, 17 U.S.C. § 506(d), (e).

3. No Electronic Theft (NET) Act

The No Electronic Theft (NET) Act, P.L. 105-147, reverses *United States v. LaMacchia*, 871 F. Supp. 535 (D. Mass. 1994), which held that electronic piracy of copyrighted works may not be prosecuted under the federal wire fraud statute; and that criminal sanctions available under titles 17 and 18 of the U.S. Code for copyright infringement do not apply in instances where the defendant does not realize any commercial advantage or private financial gain.

LaMacchia was a MIT graduate student. He ran a bulletin board that encouraged purchasers of copyrighted computer games and software to upload these works. He then made the works available to other persons with access to a password for downloading for personal use without license from copyright owners. LaMacchia did not benefit financially. The district court ruled that Congress never envisioned protecting copyrights under the wire fraud statute and noted that criminal copyright infringement law required proof that the defendant acted willfully and for commercial advantage or private financial gain.

The No Electronic Theft Act criminalizes computer theft of copyrighted works, whether or not the defendant derives a direct financial benefit from the misappropriation. The Act defines "financial gain" as including receipts, or expectation of receipt, of any thing of value, including the receipt of copyrighted works. Under section 506(a) any person who infringes a copyright willfully either (1) for purposes of commercial advantage or private financial gain; or (2) by the reproduction or distribution, including by electronic means, during any 180-day period, of one or more copies or phonorecords of one or more copyrighted works with a total retail value of more than $1,000, shall be punished as provided under section 2319 of Title 18. The Act does not punish de minimus infringement. However, the Department of Justice, in its discretion, may use the newly-defined misdemeanor standard to extract plea bargains from infringers who would otherwise be prosecuted under the felony threshold (10 copies with a total retail value of $2,500 or more). Taken together, the changes set forth in the Act will result in the following criminal penalties governing willful infringement under section 2319 of Title 18:

(1) For purposes of commercial advantage or private financial gain::

(a) imprisonment of not more than five years, or fines of not more than $250,000 per individual ($500,000 per organization), or both, if the offense consists of the reproduction or distribution, including by electronic means, in any 180-day period, of at least 10 copies or phonorecords of one or more copyrighted works with a total retail value of $2,500;

(b) imprisonment of not more than 10 years, or fines of not more than $250,000 per individual ($500,000 per organization), or both, if the offense is a second or subsequent offense under (a); (c) imprisonment of not more than one year, or fines of not more than $ 100,000, or both, in every other case.

(2) For reproduction or distribution, including by electronic means, during any 180-day period, of one or more copies or phonorecords of one or more copyrighted works, which have a total retail value of more than $1,000: (a) imprisonment of not more than three years, or fines of not more than $250,000 per individual ($500,000 per organization), or both, in a case involving a total retail value of $2,500 or more; (b) imprisonment of not more than six years, or fines of not more than $250,000 per individual ($500,000 per organization), or both, if the offense is a second or subsequent offense under (a); and (c) imprisonment of not more than one year, or fines of not more than $100,000, or both, in a case involving a total retail value of $1,000.

J. Anti-Circumvention

1. Digital Millennium Copyright Act of 1998

Title I of the Digital Millennium Copyright Act of 1998 (Pub. L. No. 105-304, Oct. 28, 1998) ("DMCA") implements the World Intellectual Property Organization treaties ("WIPO") negotiated in December 1996. The WIPO Copyright Treaty ("WCT") and the WIPO Performances and Phonograms Treaty ("WPPT"). These treaties contains virtually identical language obligating member states to prevent circumvention of technological measures used to protect copyrighted works, and to prevent tampering with the integrity of copyright management information. In addition to making certain technical amendments to U.S. law, Title I of the DMCA implements the WCT and the WPPT by creating two new prohibitions in a new Chapter 12 of Title 17 of the US Code; Section 1201, on the circumvention of technological measures used by copyright owners to protect their works and Section 1202, on tampering with copyright management information.

2. Black Box Control

Section 1201 responds to the ease in which programmers are able to break or crack the protection adopted by software proprietors who broadly distributed their software and who then made the cracking program available commercially. Section 1201 of the DMCA prohibits both the use of methods and tools and the manufacture, distribution and offering to the public of the tools or services to perform the "circumvention" but only if such tools or services are either (i) primarily designed for such purpose, or (ii) have only limited commercial purpose beyond such circumvention or (iii) are marketed for the prohibited purpose. Because of the controversial nature of this "black box" provision, the prohibition on "circumvention" did not take effect for two years after the effective date of the DMCA, but the ban on the manufacture, distribution and offering to the public of tools or services was effective immediately. Section 1201(a)(2) provides:

> No person shall manufacture, import, offer to the public, provide, or otherwise traffic in any technology, product, service, device, component, or part thereof, that—(A) is primarily designed or produced for the purpose of circumventing a technological measure that effectively controls access to a work protected under this title: (B) has only limited commercially significant purpose or use other than to circumvent a technological measure that effectively controls access to a work protected under this title; or (C) is marketed by that person or another acting in concert with that person with that person's knowledge for use in circumventing a technological measure that effectively controls access to a work protected under this title.

Section 1201 provides exceptions to the above noted anti-circumvention measures to various groups as well as exemptions of less general application. These are for (1) nonprofit library, archive and educational institution, the prohibition on circumvention of access control measures is subject to an exception that permits these entities to circumvent solely for the purpose of making a good faith determination whether they wish to obtain authorized access to the work; (2) reverse engineering, the exception permits circumvention, and the development of technological means for such circumvention, by a person who has lawfully obtained a right to use a copy of a computer program for the sole purpose of identifying and analyzing elements of the program necessary to achieve interoperability with other programs, to the extent that such acts are permitted under copyright law; (3) encryption research, the exception permits circumvention of access control measures, and the development of the technological means to do so, in order to identify flaws and vulnerabilities of encryption technologies; (4) protection of minors, the exception allows a court applying the prohibition to a component or part to consider the necessity for its incorporation in technology that prevents access of minors to material on the Internet; (5) personal privacy, the exception permits circumvention when the technological measure, or the work it protects, is capable of collecting or disseminating personally identifying information about the online activities of a natural person; (6) security testing, this exception permits circumvention of access control measures, and the development of technological means for such circumvention, for the purpose of testing the security of a computer, computer system or computer network, with the authorization of its owner or operator.

a. Integrity of Copyright Management Information

The other part of the framework is the prohibition on removing, changing or altering "copyright management information" ("CMI"). CMI is defined in Section 1202(c) as identifying information about the work, the author, the copyright owner, and in certain cases, the performer, writer or director of the work, as well as the terms and conditions for use of the work, and such other information as the Register of Copyrights may prescribe by regulation. Information concerning users of works is explicitly excluded. CMI is used to assist in the automated licensing of digital works. For example, the music industry is making songs available digitally for use in commercials from one of the major music publishers.

Section 1202 implements the obligation to protect the integrity of copyright management information (CMI). Section 1202 deals with false CMI and with the removal or alteration of CMI. Section 1202(a) prohibits the knowing provision or distribution of false CMI, if done with the intent to induce, enable, facilitate or conceal infringement. Section 1202(b) bars the intentional removal or alteration of CMI without authority, as well as the dissemination of CMI or copies of works, knowing that the CMI has been removed or altered without authority. Liability under subsection (b) requires that the act be done with knowledge or, with respect to civil remedies, with reasonable grounds to know that it will induce, enable, facilitate or conceal an infringement.

b. Remedies

Section 1203(a) provides that any person injured by a violation of section 1201 or 1202 may bring a civil action in Federal court. Section 1203(b) gives courts the power to grant a range of equitable and monetary remedies similar to those available under the Copyright Act, including statutory damages. The court has discretion to reduce or remit damages in cases of innocent violations, where the violator proves that it was not aware and had no reason to believe its acts constituted a violation. (Section 1203(c)(5)(A)). In addition, it is a criminal offense to violate section 1201 or 1202 wilfully and for purposes of commercial advantage or private financial gain. Under section 1204 penalties range up to a $500,000 fine or up to five years imprisonment for a first offense, and up to a $1,000,000 fine or up to 10 years imprisonment for subsequent offenses. Nonprofit libraries, archives and educational institutions are entirely exempted from criminal liability. (Section 1204(b)).

CHAPTER 2

COOPERATIVE RESEARCH AND DEVELOPMENT AGREEMENTS AND OTHER TRANSACTIONS

I. GENERAL

The Cooperative Research And Development Agreement or CRADA was created by the Federal Technology Transfer Act (FTTA) of 1986 (P.L. 98462), which amended the Stevenson-Wydler Technology Innovation Act of 1980 (P.L. 96-480). Initially, the use of CRADAs was limited by the FTTA to federal laboratories that were operated by federal employees, i.e., *Government-owned, Government-operated* (GOGO) laboratories. The FTTA was broadened in 1989 by the National Competitiveness Technology Transfer Act (National Defense Authorization Act for FYs 1990, 1991, section 3131-3133, P.L. 101-189) by authorizing the use of CRADAs by *Government-owned, Contractor-operated* (GOCO) laboratories, subject to the approval by the applicable federal agency. In 1996, a further change was made to the Government's CRADA authority by the; Technology Transfer Improvements Act of 1995, P.L. 104-113, March 7, 1996. This latter Act provides the CRADA participant with either the right to pre-negotiate an exclusive license in a field-of-use to inventions made under the CRADA or to receive an assignment of title to such inventions. The literature often refers to the legislative authority for CRADAs as the "Stevenson-Wydler Act" or the "Federal Technology Transfer Act." In as much as the Federal Technology Transfer Act of 1986 (as well as the National Competitiveness Technology Transfer Act, Technology Transfer Improvements Act of 1995) are amendments to the Stevenson-Wydler Act, this chapter will refer to this authority as the "Stevenson-Wydler Act" as meaning this Act as well as all its amendments.

A CRADA is an agreement (or in other words, a contract) between a federal agency, as represented by a Government-owned laboratory (either Government or contractor operated), and another party, usually a private-sector organization. The private-sector organization is often referred to as the *collaborator*.

CRADA authority under the Stevenson-Wydler Act is Government-wide, available to all federal agencies operating R&D laboratories. In addition, a number of congressionally authorized programs contain special CRADA authority for carrying out the program which may provide the applicable agency additional authority for their CRADAs. For example, ARPA and the Secretary of each of the military departments are authorized by 10 U.S.C. § 2371a to permit the directors of any federally funded research and development center to—

enter into cooperative research and development agreements with any person, any agency or instrumentality of the United States, any unit of State or local government, and any other entity under the authority granted by section 12 of the Stevenson-Wydler Technology Innovation Act of 1980 (15 U.S.C. § 3710a). Technology may be transferred to a non-Federal party to such an agreement consistent with the provisions of sections 11 and 12 of such Act (15 U.S.C. §§ 3710, 3710a).

A "cooperative research and development agreement" or CRADA under the Stevenson-Wydler Act is defined by 15 U.S.C. § 3710a(d)(1) as—

> any agreement between one or more Federal laboratories and one or more non-Federal parties under which the Government, through its laboratories, provides personnel, services, facilities, equipment, intellectual property, or other resources with or without reimbursement (but not funds to non-Federal parties) and the non-Federal parties provide funds, personnel, services, facilities, equipment, intellectual property, or other resources toward the conduct of specified research or development efforts which are consistent with the missions of the laboratory; except that such term does not include a procurement contract or cooperative agreement as those terms are used in sections 6303, 6304, and 6305 of title 31, United States Code;

The thrust of a CRADA is that the Government laboratory undertakes the performance of a task or the loan of its equipment or facilities to a non-federal entity in order to further utilize the laboratory's technology and know-how in a setting that will encourage the transfer of this technology and know-how to commercial products or processes by the non-federal party. In return, the Government benefits in advancing its research and development mission. For a general review of the Government's use of CRADA authority and a finding that CRADAs are a valuable asset to the Government's portfolio of technology transfer programs, see U.S. General Accounting Office, Technology Transfers, Benefits of Cooperative R&D Agreements (GAO/RCED 95-52), December 1994. The CRADA mechanism furthers the federal technology transfer goals by allowing private enterprise easy access to Government technology and intellectual property.

A CRADA may require the collaborator to deliver existing proprietary information to the Government laboratory and often includes work performed by the collaborator either at its own facilities or at the Government laboratory's facilities at the same time the Government laboratory is performing the CRADA work. Of course, much of the technology involved already exists, but the goal is usually to further develop or enhance existing technology using the Government laboratory's know-how, personnel, facilities or intellectual property. The CRADA must, therefore, cover the rights in preexisting intellectual property belonging to the collaborator or the Government and the rights of the Government and the collaborator in the technology developed under the CRADA.

A. Funds-in/Funds-out

1. Funds-out Agreements

Most Government activities are either carried out by the Government itself or under funds-out agreements with other parties, that is, agreements between a Government agency and another party where the agency finances the activity to be performed by the other party for the agency. Funds-out agreements are of three general types: *procurement contracts, grants, and cooperative agreements* (not to be confused with CRADAs). Agency use of procurement contracts, grants, and cooperative agreements is specified by the Federal Grant and Cooperative Agreements Act of 1977 (P.L. 97-258, Sept. 13, 1982, 96 Stat. 1004), codified in 31 U.S.C. §§ 6301-6308, as follows—

Sec. 6303. Using procurement contracts. An executive agency shall use a procurement contract as the legal instrument reflecting a relationship between the United States Government and a State, a local government, or other recipient when—

(1) the principal purpose of the instrument is to acquire (by purchase, lease, or barter) property or services for the direct benefit or use of the United States Government; or (2) the agency decides in a specific instance that the use of a procurement contract is appropriate.

Sec. 6304. Using grant agreements. An executive agency shall use a grant agreement as the legal instrument reflecting a relationship between the United States Government and a State, a local government, or other recipient when—

(1) the principal purpose of the relationship is to transfer a thing of value to the State or local government or other recipient to carry out a public purpose of support or stimulation authorized by a law of the United States instead of acquiring (by purchase, lease, or barter) property or services for the direct benefit or use of the United States Government; and (2) substantial involvement is not expected between the executive agency and the State, local government, or other recipient when carrying out the activity contemplated in the agreement.

Sec. 6305. Using cooperative agreements. An executive agency shall use a cooperative agreement as the legal instrument reflecting a relationship between the United States Government and a State, a local government, or other recipient when—

(1) the principal purpose of the relationship is to transfer a thing of value to the State, local government, or other recipient to carry out a public purpose of support or stimulation authorized by a law of the United States instead of acquiring (by purchase, lease, or barter) property or services for the direct benefit or use of the United States Government; and

(2) substantial involvement is expected between the executive agency and the State, local government, or other recipient when carrying out the activity contemplated in the agreement.

This listing of funds-out agreements is not exclusive. From the federal agency's standpoint funds-out agreements include grants, cooperative agreements, leases of equipment or facilities, price guarantees and loan agreements, or interagency procurements under the Economy Act of 1932 (31 U.S.C. § 1535) (wherein one federal agency performs work for another federal agency), work performed for state and local governments under the Intergovernmental Cooperation Act of 1968, or work performed for another government entity under a specific statute. Nevertheless, the above listings are the general broad categories of funds-out agreements. Most funds-out instruments are subject to substantial regulatory control. Procurement contracts awarded by most agencies are subject to the FAR system requirements and a number of statutory requirements, such as 10 U.S.C. Chapter 137, for DOD, the Federal Property and

Administrative Services Act of 1949 and the Office of Federal Procurement Policy Act for non-military agencies. Grants and Cooperative Agreements are subject to OMB Circulars and OFPP Directives. On the other hand CRADAs are subject to few such regulatory requirements.

2. Funds-in Agreements

Funds-in agreements provide a mechanism for federal agencies to undertake work for private parties or to permit non-Government entities to use Government-owned facilities for non-Governmental purposes for a fee. Where the use of federal facilities is on an incidental or a nonexclusive basis, the Government has taken the view that special statutory authority is not required for such use and the on-site federal official in charge of the facility has the authority to permit such use, subject to a user's charge. See OMB Circular A-25, User Charges, 58 Fed. Reg. 38142, July 15, 1993, issued under the authority of 31 U.S.C. § 9701.

Use of federal facilities, equipment or staff on a more extensive basis generally has been viewed as requiring special statutory authority. Few federal agencies had such authority, or if such authority existed few adopted the practice of making their facilities available to the public unless such a program was a part of the agency's mission. For example, "work for others" contained in section 33 of the Atomic Energy Act of 1954, as amended, 42 U.S.C. § 2053 (1994) provides authority for the Department of Energy (DOE) to undertake activities and studies for other parties where private facilities are inadequate for such activities. While the Atomic Energy Commission, and its successor agencies, the Energy Research and Development Administration and the DOE, undertook some activities for others they did so sparingly. Another example is the Unitary Wind Tunnel Plan Act of 1949 (50 U.S.C. § 511 et seq.), which provided the Administrator of NASA with the authority to operate certain wind tunnels and to make such facilities available to the industry "primarily to industry for testing experimental models in connection with the development of aircraft and missiles."

a. Cooperative Research and Development Agreements

(1) FEDERAL LABORATORIES

CRADA authority under the Stevenson-Wydler Act, flows to all federal, Government-owned laboratories that are operated with either Government personnel ("GOGO" laboratories) or contractor-personnel ("GOCO" laboratories). The term "laboratory" is defined in Stevenson-Wydler Act, 15 U.S.C. § 3710a(d)(2), as under a specific statute for another—

(A) a facility or group of facilities owned, leased, or otherwise used by a Federal agency, a substantial purpose of which is the performance of research, development, or engineering by employees of the Federal Government;

(B) a group of Government-owned, contractor-operated facilities (including a weapon production facility of the Department of Energy) under a common contract, when a substantial purpose of the contract is the performance of research and development, or the production, maintenance, testing, or dismantlement of a nuclear weapon or its components, for the Federal Government; and

(C) a Government-owned, contractor-operated facility (including a weapon production facility of the Department of Energy) that is not under a common contract described in subparagraph (B), and the primary purpose of which is the performance of research and development, or the production, maintenance, testing, or dismantlement of a nuclear weapon or its components, for the Federal Government, but such term does not include any facility covered by Executive Order No. 12344 42 USCS § 7158 note], dated February 1, 1982, pertaining to the naval nuclear propulsion program;

The term "weapon production facility" of the DOE is further defined in the Stevenson-Wydler Act, 15 U.S.C. § 3710a(d)(4), as "a facility under the control or jurisdiction of the Secretary of Energy that is operated for national security purposes and is engaged in the production, maintenance, testing, or dismantlement of a nuclear weapon or its components."

(2) DIRECTOR'S AUTHORITY

The authority of the director of federal laboratories that are either GOGO and GOCO, to enter into CRADAs is specified by the Stevenson-Wydler Act in 15 U.S.C. § 3710a(a) as follows—

(a) *General authority.* Each Federal agency may permit the director of any of its Government-operated Federal laboratories, and, to the extent provided in an agency-approved joint work statement or, if permitted by the agency, in an agency-approved annual strategic plan, the director of any of its Government-owned, contractor-operated laboratories—

(1) to enter into cooperative research and development agreements on behalf of such agency (subject to subsection (c) of this section) with other Federal agencies; units of State or local government; industrial organizations (including corporations, partnerships, and limited partnerships, and industrial development organizations); public and private foundations; nonprofit organizations (including universities); or other persons (including licensees of inventions owned by the Federal agency); and

(2) to negotiate licensing agreements under section 207 of title 35, United States Code, or under other authorities (in the case of a Government-owned, contractor-operated laboratory, subject to subsection (c) of this section) for inventions made or other intellectual property developed at the laboratory and other inventions or other intellectual property that may be voluntarily assigned to the Government.

(3) ENUMERATED CRADA AUTHORITIES

The Stevenson-Wydler Act provides authority under CRADAs for a laboratory director to accept property, services, personnel and funds from a collaborator and to provide personnel, services and property, but not funds, to the collaborator. It also includes patent licensing and the allocation of ownership rights in inventions made under CRADAs, the determination of rights in other intellectual property developed under a CRADA, and the authority to permit laboratory inventors to participate in the commercialization of their inventions, subject to certain conflicts requirements. Specifically, CRADA authority in the Stevenson-Wydler Act, 15 U.S.C. § 3710a(3), includes authority in a laboratory—

(A) accept, retain, and use funds, personnel, services, and property from a collaborating party and provide personnel, services, and property to a collaborating party;

(B) use funds received from a collaborating party in accordance with subparagraph (A) to hire personnel to carry out the agreement who will not be subject to full-time-equivalent restrictions of the agency;

(C) to the extent consistent with any applicable agency requirements or standards of conduct, permit an employee or former employee of the laboratory to participate in an effort to commercialize an invention made by the employee or former employee while in the employment or service of the Government; and

(D) waive, subject to reservation by the Government of a nonexclusive, irrevocable, paid-up license to practice the invention or have the invention practiced throughout the world by or on behalf of the Government, in advance, in whole or in part, any right of ownership which the Federal Government may have to any subject invention made under the agreement by a collaborating party or employee of a collaborating party.

A few programs have been authorized by Congress that go beyond the Stevenson-Wydler Act and permit agencies to use CRADAs for carrying out the program authorized by the Act and to provide funds to the collaborator. For example, the Intermodal Surface Transportation Efficiency Act of 1991, (P.L. 102-240) authorizes the Secretary of Transportation to perform research, development and technology transfer activities with respect to motor carrier transportation and all phases of highway planning and development (including construction, operation, modernization, development, design, maintenance, safety, financing, and traffic conditions) and the effect thereon of state laws and to test, develop, or assist in the testing and developing any material, invention, patented article. The Department of Transportation may use CRADAs for these activities and fund up to 50 percent of the cost of such research, or higher, if, there is a substantial public interest or benefit, 23 U.S.C. § 307. Similarly, the Water Resources Development Act of 1988 (P.L. 100-676) authorized Corps of Engineers laboratories to enter into CRADAs and fund up to 50 percent of the costs of such projects, 10 U.S.C. § 2313. In addition, DOD has authority to conduct research under 10 U.S.C. § 2371 and may fund up to 50 percent of the cost of such research and use a CRADA as the transactional instrument therefore, 10 U.S.C. § 2371. DOE has similar authority under 42 U.S.C. § 13541 to undertake joint ventures for energy research and to use CRADAs for such joint ventures. Presumably such joint ventures may include DOE funding.

(4) GOCOs

Where a federal laboratory is operated under a Government contract (i.e., a GOCO laboratory) CRADAs awarded by the laboratory must be within its approved joint work statement. This term is defined in the Stevenson-Wydler Act, 15 U.S.C. § 3710(a)(d)(3), as a proposal prepared by the director of a GOCO laboratory describing the purpose and scope of a proposed

CRADA, which assigns rights and responsibilities among the agency, the laboratory, and the other party or parties to the proposed CRADA. The Stevenson-Wydler Act, 15 U.S.C. § 3710a(c)(5)(C), contains detailed procedures for the approval and modification of joint work statements by the contracting federal agency and provides for specified time periods for their consideration by the agency. This section provides—

(i) Any non-Federal entity that operates a laboratory pursuant to a contract with a Federal agency shall submit to the agency any cooperative research and development agreement that the entity proposes to enter into and the joint work statement if required with respect to that agreement.

(ii) A Federal agency that receives a proposed agreement and joint work statement under clause (i) shall review and approve, request specific modifications to, or disapprove the proposed agreement and joint work statement within 30 days after such submission. No agreement may be entered into by a Government-owned, contractor-operated laboratory under this section before both approval of the agreement and approval of a joint work statement under this clause.

(iii) In any case in which an agency which has contracted with an entity referred to in clause (i) disapproves or requests the modification of a cooperative research and development agreement or joint work statement submitted under that clause, the agency shall transmit a written explanation of such disapproval or modification to the head of the laboratory concerned.

(iv) Any agency that has contracted with a non-Federal entity to operate a laboratory may develop and provide to such laboratory one or more model cooperative research and development agreements for purposes of standardizing practices and procedures, resolving common legal issues, and enabling review of cooperative research and development agreements to be carried out in a routine and prompt manner.

(v) A Federal agency may waive the requirements of clause (i) or (ii) under such circumstances as the agency considers appropriate.

(5) Limitations

CRADA authority is to be used by non-federal entities operating a Government-owned laboratory only if—

(1) The implementation shall advance program missions at the laboratory, including any national security mission. (2) Classified information and unclassified sensitive information protected by law, regulation, or Executive order shall be appropriately safeguarded, 15 U.S.C. § 3710a(g).

Further, CRADA authority does not limit the existing authority of an agency to accept other funds-in type of work based on other statutory authority. In this regard the Stevenson-Wydler Act, 15 U.S.C. § 3710a(f), states that, "[N]othing in this section is intended to limit or diminish existing authorities of any agency."

(6) APPROVAL PROCEDURES

The agency contracting for the operation of its laboratories may establish a procedure for reviewing proposed CRADAs and determine whether a proposed CRADA should be awarded. The CRADA review procedure is constrained as to time (i.e., a 30-day period) by the Stevenson-Wydler Act and the agency must provide for a written explanation in the event a proposed CRADA is disapproved, 15 U.S.C. § 3710a(c)(5). If the agency fails to complete its review within 30-days, the agency is to submit a report to Congress within 10 days after the end of the 30-day period on the reasons for such failure and shall, at the end of each successive 30-day period thereafter during which such failure continues, submit to the Congress another report on the reasons for the continuing failure, 15 U.S.C. § 3710a(c)(5)(v).

(7) CRADA MODELS

Agencies are to provide the contractor-operator with model CRADAs "for the purposes of standardizing practices and procedures, resolving common legal issues, and enabling review of cooperative research and development agreements to be carried out in a routine and prompt manner," 15 U.S.C. § 3710a(c)(5)(C)(iii). See section IV of this Chapter for a list of agency model CRADA agreements available on the Internet.

(8) EXECUTIVE ORDER 12591

Federal agencies have been given directions by the President by Executive Order No. 12591, Facilitating Access to Science and Technology, Apr. 10, 1987, 52 Fed. Reg. 13414, to utilize their CRADA authority. See Appendix 1 to this Chapter. This Executive Order provides that—

in order to ensure that Federal agencies and laboratories assist universities and the private sector in broadening our technology base by moving new knowledge from the research laboratory into the development of new products and processes, it is hereby ordered as follows:

Section I. Transfer of Federally Funded Technology.

(a) The head of each Executive department and agency, to the extent permitted by law, shall encourage and facilitate collaboration among Federal laboratories, State and local governments, universities, and the private sector, particularly small business, in order to assist in the transfer of technology to the marketplace.

(b) The head of each Executive department and agency shall, within overall funding allocations and to the extent permitted by law:

(1) delegate authority to its Government-owned, Government-operated Federal laboratories:

(A) to enter into cooperative research and development agreements with other Federal laboratories, State and local governments, universities, and the private sector; and

(B) to license, assign, or waive rights to intellectual property developed by the laboratory either under such cooperative research or development agreements and from within individual laboratories.

(2) identify and encourage persons to act as conduits between and among Federal laboratories, universities, and the private sector for the transfer of technology developed from federally funded research and development efforts;

(3) ensure that State and local governments, universities, and the private sector are provided with information on the technology, expertise, and facilities available in Federal laboratories;

b. Space Act Agreements

NASA does not generally enter into CRADAs since it views its authority under the National Aeronautics and Space Act of 1958, 42 U.S.C. § 2451 et seq., to enter into contracts, leases, cooperative agreements or other transactions (i.e., Space Act Agreements) as similar to but broader than CRADA authority. See, Carl L. Vacketta et al "Technology Transfer" Briefing Papers No. 94-12, November 1994, Federal Publications, Inc. NASA Space Act Agreement authority is contained in 42 U.S.C. § 2473(c), as follows—

(5) without regard to section 3324(a) and (b) of title 31, to enter into and perform such contracts, leases, cooperative agreements, or other transactions as may be necessary in the conduct of its work and on such terms as it may deem appropriate, with any agency or instrumentality of the United States, or with any State, Territory, or possession, or with any political subdivision thereof, or with any person, firm, association, corporation, or educational institution. To the maximum extent practicable and consistent with the accomplishment of the purpose of this chapter, such contracts, leases, agreements, and other transactions shall be allocated by the Administrator in a manner, which will enable small-business concerns to participate equitably and proportionately in the conduct of the work of the Administration.

One area of flexibility in the use of Space Act Agreements over CRADAs is the allocation of intellectual property rights. NASA views the requirements of the Stevenson-Wydler Act with respect to invention rights as being more limited then the Space Act patent requirements.

c. DOE Work for Others

Section 33 of the Atomic Energy Act of 1954, as amended, (42 U.S.C. § 2053) provides DOE with the authority to undertake *work for others* in a broad range of energy areas. This authority has been used over the years in special situations but has not led to the scope of activities that DOE has undertaken with CRADAs under the Stevenson-Wydler Technology Act. This section states:

Where the [DOE] finds private facilities or laboratories are inadequate for the purpose, it is authorized to conduct for other persons, through its own facilities, such of those activities and studies of the types specified in section 31 [42 U.S.C. § 2051*] as it deems appropriate to the development of energy. To the extent the [DOE] determines that private facilities or laboratories are inadequate for the purpose, and that the [DOE's] facilities, or scientific or technical resources have the potential of lending significant assistance to other persons in the fields of protection of public health and safety, the [DOE] may also assist other persons in these fields by conducting for such persons, through the [DOE's] own facilities, research and development or training activities and studies. The [DOE] is authorized to determine and make such charges as in its discretion may be desirable for the conduct of the activities and studies referred to in this section.

*. . . includes the conduct of research and development activities relating to—(1) nuclear processes; (2) the theory and production of atomic energy, including processes, materials, and devices related to such production; (3) utilization of special nuclear material and radioactive material for medical, biological, agricultural, health, or military purposes; (4) utilization of special nuclear material, atomic energy, and radioactive material and processes entailed in the utilization or production of atomic energy or such material for all other purposes, including industrial or commercial uses, the generation of usable energy, and the demonstration of advances in the commercial or industrial application of atomic energy; (5) the protection of health and the promotion of safety during research and production activities; and (6) the preservation and enhancement of a viable environment by developing more efficient methods to meet the Nation's energy needs.

DOE has implemented this authority, as well as its authority to award CRADAs in DOE Order 481.1 Non-Department of Energy Funded Work (Work for Others). This Order requires the applicable DOE officer to certify that the work to be performed is consistent with or complementary to the DOE mission and the mission of the facility doing the work, that the work would not adversely impact DOE's work at the facility, would not place the facility in direct competition with the domestic private sector, and would not create a detrimental future burden on DOE resources.

3. Mixed Funding

a. DOD Transactions

(1) GENERAL AUTHORITY

The Federal Acquisition Streamlining Act (FASA) of 1994, P.L. 103-355, § 1301(b) broadened the provisions in title 10 of the U.S. Code that authorizes DOD agencies to enter into a new forms of research and development transactions, generally referred to by DOD as *flexible cooperative agreements and other transactions* under 10 U.S.C. § 2371. The Final Report of the Integrated Product Team on "The Services' Use of 10 U.S.C. § 2371 'Other Transactions' and 845 Prototype Authorities," DOD, 18 March 1996-10 June 1996, (IPT Report) page 4, defines *other transactions* as transaction other than contracts, grants, or cooperative agreements and notes that other transactions are not subject to statutes and regulations that apply to "contracts, grants, and cooperatives agreements." The IPT Report notes that other transactions are of two types: (1) other transactions for research under 10 U.S.C. § 2371; and (2) other transactions under section 845 for the acquisition of prototype projects relevant to weapon systems. Based on DDR&E issued guidance, *flexible cooperative agreements are* cooperative agreements with commercial organization used for research projects to stimulate development of dual use technology, IPT Report, page 8-9. See also Interim-Guidance Draft of DOD 3210.6R, February 4, 1994, DOD Grant and Agreement Regulatory System (DGARS), Part 37, Cooperative Agreement Under 10 U.S.C. § 2371.

The principal advantages of these instruments is that they give DOD agencies the ability to depart from many of the requirements of the procurement laws, such as, the Truth in Negotiations Act, the Cost Accounting Standards, and the complex requirements of the FAR and DFARS. Thus, DOD may adopt commercial practices and more flexible arrangements under this authority.

The authority for *other transactions* was originally enacted in 1989 as a part of the Defense Authorization Act for FY 1990 and 1991, P.L. 101-189, section 251 as two-year test authority in DARPA. This authority was subsequently broadened and made permanent. For a detailed background, see GAO Report to Congressional Committees, "DOD Research, Acquiring Research by Nontraditional Means," March 29, 1995, GAO/NSIAD-96-11. Section 2371 grants to the Secretary of Defense and Secretary of each military department the authority, in carrying out advance research, to—

> enter into transactions *(other than contracts, cooperative agreements, and grants)* under the authority of this subsection in carrying out basic, applied, and advanced research projects. The authority under this subsection is in addition to the authority provided in section 2358 of this title to use contracts, cooperative agreements, and grants in carrying out such projects. (Emphasis added.)

It is not clear what form other transactions and flexible cooperative agreements will take, since they are not defined in sections 2371 and 2358. Under § 2371(e)(1) and (3) use of other transactions and flexible cooperative agreements is only to be undertaken "when the use of a standard contract, grant, or cooperative agreement for such project is not feasible or appropriate," and "to the extent the Secretary determines practicable, the funds provided by the Government under the cooperative agreement or other transaction do not exceed the total amount provided by other parties to the cooperative agreement or other transaction," i.e., 50 percent cost sharing. There appears to be some confusion over the use of the term contract in this legislation since surely other transactions, grants and cooperative agreements are contracts. Evidently, in the use of the term standard contract in section 2371, the Congress meant to use the term procurement contract, as this term is defined in 31 U.S.C. § 6303. Section 2371(e) states—

> (1) The Secretary of Defense shall ensure that—
>
> > (A) to the maximum extent practicable, no cooperative agreement containing a clause under subsection (d) and no transaction entered into under subsection
> >
> > (a) provides for research that duplicates research being conducted under existing programs carried out by the Department of Defense; and

(B) to the extent that the Secretary determines practicable, the funds provided by the Government under a cooperative agreement containing a clause

under subsection (d) or a transaction authorized by subsection (a) do not exceed the total amount provided by other parties to the cooperative agreement or other transaction.

(2) A cooperative agreement containing a clause under subsection (d) or a transaction authorized by subsection (a) may be used for a research project when the use of a standard contract, grant, or cooperative agreement for such project is not feasible or appropriate.

10 U.S.C. § 2371(g) requires DOD to issue regulations to carry out this section. DOD has established a DOD Grant and Agreement Regulation System, DOD 3210.6R (Feb. 27, 1995). DOD issued proposed regulations grants and cooperative agreement rules, 61 Fed Reg. 43867, August 26, 1996. While these proposed rules cover awards to commercial organizations, the proposed rules note that DOD intends to adopt additional rules for selected research agreements with commercial organizations. This new provision is intended to be more flexible with respect to administrative requirements than those contained in the proposed grant and cooperative agreement rules. "The greater flexibility would be available for a certain class of research agreements that is designated to help integrate the defense and non-defense portions of the U.S. technology and industrial base," 61 Fed Reg. 43868, August 26, 1996. DOD issued its final grant rule in 63 Fed. Reg. 12151, March 12, 1998.

ARPA (and its predecessor DARPA) have used "cooperative agreements and other transactions" for consortia research and dual-use projects. Over 100 other transactions have been entered into by ARPA between 1989 and 1995, including ARPA's implementation of the Technology Reinvestment Program, IPT Report at page 16. While the various military services also have been granted authority for other transactions under section 2371, they principally have used flexible cooperative agreements, unless the Bayh-Dole or other such factor required the instrument to be an other transaction, IPT Report at page 16-19.

Further, *other transactions* authority may involve a unique funding arrangement. Funds advanced by the private collaborator may be placed into an account at the Treasury Department, 10 U.S.C. § 2371(d). This account can contain funds from various unrelated Section 2371 collaborators.

(2) OTHER AUTHORITY

DOD has general authority under 10 U.S.C. § 2358 to undertake basic, advanced and applied research and development projects. This section was amended in 1993 by P.L. 103-160 to provide that DOD could enter into contracts, cooperative agreements and grants with private business as well as with educational or research institutions in conducting its research (basic, applied, and advanced) and development projects. Under section 2371, DOD may use its cooperative agreement authority in much the same manner as its other transaction authority.

In addition to the authority to use *other transactions* and flexible cooperative agreements for research and to some extent development projects, section 845 of the DOD Authorization

Act of 1994, provided DARPA with the authority to use cooperative agreements and other transactions on a trial basis for prototype weapons projects. Section 845 waives the requirements in section 2371(e)(2) and (3) that the recipient cost match and that DOD determine that the, use of "standard contract, grant, or cooperative agreement" for the project "is not feasible or appropriate" before it uses this prototyping authority. The argument for this authority is that it permits the agency to adopt commercial contracting practices, eliminate the need for an audit and review of contractor records, contain only a minimum of socioeconomic clauses, and permit the activities to proceed on a cooperative basis.

(3) INTELLECTUAL PROPERTY

DOD takes the position that 35 U.S.C. § 200 et seq. (the Bayh-Dole Act) does not apply to other transactions but that such law applies to flexible cooperative agreements, Richard N. Kuyath "The Untapped Potential of the Department of Defense's 'Other transaction' Authority," Vol. 24, No. 4, Pub. Cont. L.J, Pages 521-577 (Sum. 1995), at 536-537. The Conference Report on the National Defense Authorization Act for Fiscal Year 1992 (S. Rep. No. 311,102 Cong. 676 (1991)) and the House Armed Services Committee Report on the FY 95 authorization bill (H.R. Rep. No. 499, 103d. Cong. 2d Sess. 385) supports the position that 35 U.S.C. § 200 et seq. does not apply to other transactions. The 1992 report stated—

> The conferees also recognize that the regulations applicable to the allocation of patent and data rights under the procurement statutes may not he appropriate to partnership arrangements in certain cases. The conferees believe that the option to support partnerships pursuant to section 2371 of title 10, United States Code, provides adequate flexibility for the Defense Department and other partnership participants to agree to allocations of intellectual property rights in a manner that will meet the needs of all parties involved in a transaction.

With respect to intellectual property the ARPA Draft Guidance for Use of Other Transactions (February 1995) with multi-parties (i.e., a consortium) states—

> *Article VII, "Patent Rights"* describes the allocation of patent rights in inventions conceived or first reduced to practice under the Agreement. ARPA initially requires that a standard patent rights clause, based on the Bayh-Dole Act, be included in all agreements. The full text of this clause is set forth below. However, individual situations may warrant exceptions to the standard allocation of rights. Any such exceptions are open to negotiation by the parties upon a detailed explanation of need by the Consortium. As a matter of form, the language of the standard clause should not be altered; instead, any exceptions to the provisions of the clause should be added to the end of the clause or set out in a side agreement.

> In general, the Bayh-Dole Act (and ARPA's standard Agreement provisions) allow the Consortium to retain title to patentable inventions subject to a so-called "Government-purpose license"—a non-exclusive, non-transferable, irrevocable, paid-up license to ARPA to practice the invention or have it practiced on behalf of the United States throughout the world--and to "march-in rights" that allow the Government to require an invention to be made available to a third party if the inventor does not reduce it to practical application in a reasonable time. A Consortium may request limitations on these rights. However, ARPA will not agree to any limitation unless the Consortium can present a compelling business justification, in the specific

context contemplated by the Agreement and in terms of the goals of the specific project, for the necessity of the requested limitation of the Government's rights. Typical ARPA concessions that may be granted based on such a compelling justification have included delaying the effective date of the Government purpose license and specifically defining what are the reasonable efforts toward practical application that will preclude exercise of march-in rights.)

The patent rights clause used by ARPA in its model other transaction agreement for consortiums replaces the term "Government" with ARPA in a number of instances which has the effect of narrowing the rights acquired by the Government under this clause. Further, this clause does not automatically apply to subcontractors, which in effect permits the "contractor" to obtain title to subcontractor inventions. This model also takes the view that the Government authorization and consent clause regarding patent infringement does not apply since the work being performed under the other transaction is not being performed for the Government, see Richard N. Kuyath "The Untapped Potential of the Department of Defense's 'Other transaction' Authority," Vol. 24, No. 4, Pub. Cont. L.J, at pages 552-554 (Summer 1995) and *Hughes Aircraft Co. v. United States,* 534 F. 2d 889 (1976), which held that a cooperative agreement was sufficient authority to be under the authorization or consent provisions of 28 U.S.C. § 1498(a). Reliance on Committee Report for the conclusion that the Bayh-Dole Act does not apply to other transactions is suspect in view of 35 U.S.C. § 210 (a part of the Bayh-Dole Act), which states, as least with respect to the rights to inventions in contracts with small business and nonprofit organizations, that—

The Act creating this chapter shall be construed to take precedence over any future Act unless that Act specifically cites this Act and provides that it shall take precedence over this Act.

As to data rights, the ARPA guidance provide for a data rights provision but because of the mixed funding rights similar to the DFARS Government purposes rights are normally to be acquired by ARPA in Subject Data, i.e., the right to use the data for Government purposes only. However, these rights are negotiable. The ARPA guidance states—

Article VIII, "Data Rights," addresses the allocation between the parties of intellectual property rights other than patent rights in "Data" (defined in the Article as "recorded information, regardless of form or method of recording, which includes but is not limited to, technical data, software, trade secrets, and mask works") generated under the Agreement. The rights granted to or retained by the Government in this provision are negotiable between ARPA and the Consortium and will vary greatly depending upon the type of Data anticipated and the requirements of the parties. At a minimum, the Government will retain the rights to all Data generated under the Agreement that are minimally necessary to make meaningful the patent rights allocated to the Government in Article VII. In most cases, the Government's rights in Data will include rights to use, duplicate, or disclose Data, in whole or in part and in any manner, for Government Act unless that Act specifically cites this Act and provides that it shall take precedence over this Act.

The data rights guidance given in DOD's Interim-Guidance Draft of DOD 3210.6-R Attachment 2—February 4, 1994, Attachment 2—February 4, 1994, 37-8 with respect to flexible cooperative agreements states—

(h) *Rights in technical data and computer software.* Given that "cooperative agreements under 10 U.S.C. § 2371" entail substantial cost sharing by recipients, grants officers must exercise discretion in negotiating Government rights to technical data and computer software resulting from advanced research under the agreements. The following considerations are intended to serve as guidelines, within which grants officers necessarily have considerable latitude to negotiate provisions appropriate to any of a wide variety of circumstances that may arise:

(1) A goal of the Department of Defense is to encourage recipients to commercially develop technologies resulting from DoD-sponsored research. That will enable increased DoD reliance in the future on the commercial technology and industrial base as a source of readily available, reliable, and affordable components, subsystems, computer software, manufacturing processes, and other technological products for military systems.

(2) Grants officers should generally seek to obtain for the Department of Defense an irrevocable, world-wide license to use, modify, reproduce, release, or disclose for governmental purposes technical data or computer software generated under cooperative agreements. A governmental purpose is any activity in which the United States Government is a party, but a license for governmental purposes does not include the right to use, or have or permit others to use, modify, reproduce, release, or disclose technical data or computer software for commercial purposes.

(3) Licenses of different scope may be negotiated when necessary to accomplish program objectives or to protect the Government's interests. Consult with counsel before negotiating a license of different scope.

(4) To protect the recipient's interests in licenses, technical data, or computer software, cooperative agreements should require the recipient to mark the data or software whose disclosure they desire to protect with a legend identifying the data or software as licensed data/software subject to use, release, or disclosure Restrictions. Prior to releasing or disclosing data or software marked with a restrictive legend to third parties, grants officers should require such persons to agree in writing to use the data or software only for governmental purposes and to make no further release or disclosure of the data or software without the permission of the licensor (i.e., the recipient).

b. Nonnuclear Research

DOE also has authority to enter into a variety of arrangements with private parties to perform research and development and demonstration activities. As an example of DOE's broad authority, the Energy Policy Act of 1992 (P.L. 102-486) (EPAct) provides that in the development of a number of nonnuclear technologies DOE has the authority to use novel arrangements with parties developing such technology including CRADAs and "joint ventures." See 42 U.S.C. § 13541. The use of this authority is specified by EPAct as including DOE's coal research, development, demonstration, and commercial applications, for enhanced oil recovery, oil shale, natural gas supply, natural gas end-use technologies, general transportation, advanced automotive fuel economy, alternative fuel vehicle program, biofuels user facility, renewable hydrogen energy, advanced diesel emissions program, general improved energy efficiency, natural gas and electric heating and cooling technologies, natural gas and electric heating and cooling technologies, advanced buildings for 2005, electric drives, improving efficiency in energy-intensive industries, renewable energy, high efficiency heat engines, fusion energy, high-temperature superconductivity program, national advanced materials program, and the National Advanced Manufacturing Technologies Program, 42 U.S.C. § 13331 et seq. DOE, however, proposed to use this authority for a broader range of research and development activities that were within the Department's mission before the enactment of EPAct, see 60 Fed. Reg. 10295, Feb. 23, 1995.

DOE entered into over 1,100 CRADAs by the end of 1994, see Inside Energy/Federal Lands, Page 1, December 5, 1994. A number of these CRADAs, have been announced as joint funding initiatives. While the Stevenson-Wydler Act limits the use of Government funds in a CRADA, DOE's CRADAs are also based on its other statutory sources permitting joint funding. Further, DOE originally planned to expand it partnerships with industry while cutting back on CRADAs with individual partners based on the amount of leveraging obtained by the Government through partnering arrangements, Inside Energy/Federal Lands, Page 1, December 5, 1994. This was based on the proposed notice in 60 Fed. Reg. 10295, Feb. 23, 1995, Part 10 C.F.R. Part 600, Financial Assistance Rules, which states that DOE intends to use its partnering authority outside of the areas specifically mentioned by EPAct. 42 U.S.C. § 13541 authority provides—

(a) *Research, development, and demonstration.* (1) Except as otherwise provided in this Act, research, development, and demonstration activities under this Act may be carried out under the procedures of the Federal Nonnuclear Research and Development Act of 1974 (42 U.S.C. §§ 5901-5920), the Atomic Energy Act of 1954 (42 U.S.C. §§ 2011 et seq.), or any other Act under which the Secretary is authorized to carry out such activities, but only to the extent the Secretary is authorized to carry out such activities under each such Act. An objective of any demonstration program under this Act shall be to determine the technical and commercial feasibility of energy technologies.

(2) Except as otherwise provided in this Act, in carrying out research, development, and demonstration programs and activities under this Act, the Secretary may use, to the extent authorized under applicable provisions of law, contracts, cooperative agreements, cooperative research and development agreements under the Stevenson-Wydler Technology Innovation Act of 1980 (15 U.S.C. § 3701 et seq.), grants, joint ventures, and any other form of agreement available to the Secretary.

(b) *Commercial application.* Except as otherwise provided in this Act, in carrying out commercial application programs and commercial application activities under this Act, the Secretary may use, to the extent authorized under applicable provisions of law, contracts, cooperative agreements, cooperative research and development agreements under the Stevenson-Wydler Technology Innovation Act of 1980 (15 U.S.C. §§ 3701 et seq.), grants, joint ventures, and any other form of agreement available to the Secretary. An objective of any commercial application program under this Act shall be to accelerate the transition of technologies from the research and development stage.

(c) *"Joint venture" defined.* For purposes of this section, the term "joint venture" has the meaning given the term "joint research and development venture" under section 4301(a)(6) and

(b) of title 15, except that such term may apply under this section to research, development, demonstration, and commercial application joint ventures.

(e) *Guidelines and procedures.* The Secretary shall provide guidelines and procedures for the transition, where appropriate of energy technologies from research through development and demonstration under subsection (a) of this section to commercial application under subsection (b) of this section. Nothing in this section shall preclude the Secretary from—(1) entering into a contract, cooperative agreement, cooperative research and development agreement under the Stevenson-Wydler Technology Innovation Act of 1980 (15 U.S.C. §§ 3701 et seq.), grant, joint venture, or any other form of agreement available to the Secretary under this section that relates to research, development, demonstration, and commercial application; or (2) extending a contract, cooperative agreement, cooperative research and development agreement under the Stevenson-Wydler Technology Innovation Act of 1980, grant, joint venture, or any other form of agreement available to the Secretary that relates to research, development, and demonstration to cover commercial application.

c. Advanced Technology Program

The Department of Commerce issued amendments to the implementing regulations, 63 Fed Reg. 64411, November 29, 1998, covering this program to provide that title to invention arising from the assistance provided by this program must vest in a company incorporated in the United States. The U.S. Government reserves a nonexclusive, nontransferable, irrevocable paid-up license to practice or have practiced for or on its behalf any such "intellectual property." The patent provision adopted follows:

Sec. 295.8 Intellectual property rights; Publication of research results.

(a)(1) *Patent Rights.* Title to inventions arising from assistance provided by the Program must vest in a company or companies incorporated in the United States. Joint ventures shall provide to NIST a copy of their written agreement which defines the disposition of ownership rights among the members of the joint venture, and their contractors and subcontractors as appropriate, that complies with the first sentence of this paragraph. The United States will reserve a nonexclusive, nontransferable, irrevocable, paid-up license to practice or have practiced for or on behalf of the United States any such intellectual property, but shall not, in the exercise of such license, publicly disclose proprietary information related to the license. Title to any such intellectual property shall not be transferred or passed, except to a company incorporated in the United States, until the expiration of the first patent obtained in connection with such intellectual property. Nothing in this paragraph shall be construed to prohibit the licensing to any company of intellectual property rights arising from assistance provided under this section.

(2) *Patent Procedures.* Each award by the Program shall include provisions assuring the retention of a governmental use license in each disclosed invention, and the government's retention of march-in rights. In addition, each award by the Program will contain procedures regarding reporting of subject inventions by the funding Recipient to the Program, including the subject inventions of members of the joint venture (if applicable) in which the funding Recipient is a participant, contractors and subcontractors of the funding Recipient. The funding Recipient shall disclose such subject inventions to the Program within two months after the inventor discloses it in writing to the Recipient's designated representative responsible for patent matters.

The disclosure shall consist of a detailed, written report which provides the Program with the following the title of the present invention; the names of all inventors; the name and address of the assignee (if any); an acknowledgment that the United States has rights in the subject invention; the filing date of the present invention, or in the alternative, a statement identifying that the Recipient determined that filing was not feasible; an abstract of the disclosure; a description or summary of the present invention; the background of the present invention or the prior art; a description of the preferred embodiments; and what matter is claimed. Upon issuance of the patent, the funding Recipient or Recipients must notify the Program accordingly, providing it with the Serial Number of the patent as issued, the date of issuance, a copy of the disclosure as issued, and if appropriate, the name, address, and telephone number(s) of an assignee.

II. ENTITLES RESPONSIBLE FOR TECHNOLOGY TRANSFER

Technology transfer is decentralized in the United States Government. It is administered by various executive agencies with some overview by Congress. Except in areas where the Government has a broader welfare role, like health, environmental pollution, agriculture, energy conservation, etc., or a mission unrelated to commercial activities such as with respect to military equipment, the Government primarily funds basic and applied research, allowing commercial firms to pursue development and commercialization of the technology and information that it discovers or develops. Nevertheless, it appears "that university and Government research is finding its way to most major industries," in areas such as computer, chemical and pharmaceutical with companies related to these industries being the most prominent beneficiaries of Government licensing; see Daniel M. McGavock et al., "Licensing Practices, Business Strategy, and Factors Affecting Royalty Rates: Results of a Survey," 13 Licensing L. & Bus. Rep. 205, 215 (March-April 1991).

A number of agencies have specific statutory missions to transfer technology developed by the program to the public and operate technology transfer programs in this regard. Perhaps the most famous of which is the NASA Technology Utilization Program. Other agencies have been authorized to undertake a technology transfer mission in hopes of saving the technology developed by the Government or the laboratory that developed the technology by having commercial sources fund the further development of the technology for commercial purposes. For example, DOD was directed by the Defense Conversion, Reinvestment, and Transition Assistance Act (P.L. 102-484, §§ 4001-4501 (1992)) to "encourage, to the extent consistent with national security objectives, the transfer of technology between laboratories and research centers of the Department of Defense and other Federal agencies, State and local governments, colleges and universities, and private persons in cases that are likely to result in accomplishing the objectives set forth in section 2501(a) of this title" (i.e., maintaining an advanced research capability, further the national security objectives through programs of reinvestment, diversification, and conversion of defense resources that promote economic growth in high-wage, high-technology industries and preserve the industrial and technical skill base; promoting economic growth through further reduction of the federal budget deficit that, by reducing the public sector demand for capital, increases the amount of capital available for private investment and job creation in the civilian sector; and bolstering the national technology base, including support and exploitation of critical technologies with both military and civilian application).

The Stevenson-Wydler Act made it clear for the first time that all federal laboratories have a technology transfer mission. Section 3710 provides—

(a) *Policy.* (1) It is the continuing responsibility of the Federal Government to ensure the full use of the results of the Nation's Federal investment in research and development. To this end the Federal Government shall strive where appropriate to transfer federally owned or originated technology to State and local governments and to the private sector.

(2) Technology transfer, consistent with mission responsibilities, is a responsibility of each laboratory science and engineering professional.

(3) Each laboratory director shall ensure that efforts to transfer technology are considered positively in laboratory job descriptions, employee promotion policies, and evaluation of the job performance of scientists and engineers in the laboratory.

(f) *Agency reporting.* Each Federal agency which operates or directs one or more Federal laboratories shall report annually to the Congress, as part of the agency's annual budget submission, on the activities performed by that agency and its Federal laboratories pursuant to the provisions of this section. The report shall be transmitted to the Center for the Utilization of Federal Technology by November 1 of each year in which it is due.

This requirement was buttressed by Executive Order. No. 12591, Facilitating Access to Science and Technology, April 10, 1987. This Order provides:

(a) The head of each Executive department and agency, to the extent permitted by taw, shall encourage and facilitate collaboration among Federal laboratories, State and local governments, universities, and the private sector, particularly small business, in order to assist in the transfer of technology to the marketplace.

A. Offices of Research and Technology Applications

Pursuant to 15 U.S.C. § 3710(b) below, every federal laboratory must have an Office of Research and Technology Applications (ORTA). In laboratories with over 200 employees, there must be at least one full-time ORTA staffer. The ORTA is to identify and assess the commercial applicability and value of laboratory technologies, know-how and ideas, and to disseminate them where and when appropriate. Under section 3710(c), the ORTA also coordinates with the Federal Laboratory Consortium and the NTIS in technology transfer, and facilitates technology transfer in the laboratory's locale. Originally, ORTAs were to be funded with 0.5 percent of a lab's annual R&D budget. However, this provision was optional, and was "universally waived during the Act's 9-year history," H. Rep. on the National Competitiveness Technology Transfer Act, H. Conf. Rep. No. 331, 101st Cong., 1st Sess. 761 (1989). For this reason, the National Competitiveness Technology Transfer Act, P.L. 101-189, repealed the 0.5 percent spending target. Now, section 3710(b)(2) only requires that a "Federal agency which operates or directs one or more Federal laboratories shall make available sufficient funding." In addition to the laboratory ORTAs, many agencies (like NIH) have an overarching Office of Technology Transfer.

(b) *Establishment of Research and Technology Applications Offices.* Each Federal laboratory shall establish an Office of Research and Technology Applications. Laboratories having existing organizational structures which perform the functions of this section may elect to combine the Office of Research and Technology Applications within the existing organization. The staffing and funding levels for these offices shall be determined between each Federal laboratory and the Federal agency operating or directing the laboratory, except that:

(1) each laboratory having 200 or more full-time equivalent scientific, engineering, and related technical positions shall provide one or more full-time equivalent positions as staff for its Office of Research and Technology Applications, and

(2) each Federal agency which operates or directs one or more Federal laboratories shall make available sufficient funding, either as a separate line item or from the agency's research and development budget, to support the technology transfer function at the agency and at its laboratories, including support of the Offices of Research and Technology Applications.

Furthermore, individuals filling positions in an Office of Research and Technology Applications shall be included in the overall laboratory/agency management development program so as to ensure that highly competent technical managers are full participants in the technology transfer process. The agency head shall submit to Congress at the time the President submits the budget to Congress an explanation of the agency's technology transfer program for the preceding year and the agency's plans for conducting its technology transfer function for the upcoming year, including plans for securing intellectual property rights in laboratory innovations with commercial promise and plans for managing such innovations so as to benefit the competitiveness of United States industry.

(c) *Functions of Research and Technology Applications Offices.* It shall be the function of each Office of Research and Technology Applications—

(1) to prepare application assessments for selected research and development projects in which that laboratory is engaged and which in the opinion of the laboratory may have potential commercial applications;

(2) to provide and disseminate information on federally owned or originated products, processes, and services having potential application to State and local governments and to private industry;

(3) to cooperate with and assist the National Technical Information Service, the Federal Laboratory Consortium for Technology Transfer, and other organizations which link the research and development resources of that laboratory and the Federal Government as a whole to potential users in State and local government and private industry;

(4) to provide technical assistance to State and local government officials; and

(5) to participate, where feasible, in regional, State, and local programs designed to facilitate or stimulate the transfer of technology for the benefit of the region, State, or local jurisdiction in which the Federal laboratory is located.

Agencies which have established organizational structures outside their Federal laboratories, which have as their principal purpose the transfer of federally owned or originated technology to state and local government and to the private sector may elect to perform the functions of this subsection in such organizational structures. No Office of Research and Technology Applications or other organizational structures performing the functions of this subsection shall substantially compete with similar services available in the private sector.

B. Federal Laboratory Consortium for Technology Transfer

The Federal Laboratory Consortium for Technology Transfer (FLC) was organized in 1974 to facilitate technology transfer between the Department of Defense and state and local governments. In 1986 the FLC was formally charted by the Federal Technology Transfer Act of 1986 with the mission to promote and facilitate the transfer of federal laboratory technology to the US economy. All federal laboratories with staffing of 200 or more full-time equivalent scientific, engineering, and related technical positions where required to become part of the FLC, 15 U.S.C. § 3710(e)(2). Today, roughly 600 Federal labs participate in FLC. For information of the FLC see website http://www. zyn.com/flc/theflc.htm and, Barbara A. Duncombe, "Federal Technology Transfer: A Look at the Benefits and Pitfalls of One of the Country's Best Kept Secrets," 37 Fed. Bar News & J. 608, 609 (1990); see also Staff of the Senate Committee on Commerce, Science and Transportation, Commercialization of Federally-Funded R&D: A Guide to Technology Transfer from Federal Laboratories, S. Print 130, 100th Cong., 1st Sess. 6 (Comm. Print 1988). The Federal Technology Transfer Act of 1986 made membership in FLC mandatory. Section 3 of Stevenson-Wydler Act, 15 U.S.C. § 3710(e), conferred on the Federal Laboratory Consortium the formal mission to promote and strengthen technology transfer across the federal research system. ORTA officers in each laboratory also serves as that laboratory's representative in the Consortium. FLC is essentially a network of Government laboratories; it has no main office or full-time employees. Section 3710(e) provides:

Establishment of Federal Laboratory Consortium for Technology Transfer.

(1) There is hereby established the Federal Laboratory Consortium for Technology Transfer (hereinafter referred to as the "Consortium") which, in cooperation with Federal Laboratories and the private sector, shall—

  (A) develop and (with the consent of the Federal laboratory concerned) administer techniques, training courses, and materials concerning technology transfer to increase the awareness of Federal laboratory employees regarding the commercial potential of laboratory technology and innovations;

  (B) furnish advice and assistance requested by Federal agencies and laboratories for use in their technology transfer programs (including the planning of seminars for small business and other industry);

  (C) provide a clearinghouse for requests, received at the laboratory level, for technical assistance from States and units of local governments, businesses, industrial development organizations, not-for-profit organizations including universities, Federal agencies and laboratories, and other persons, and—

(i) to the extent that such requests can be responded to with published information available to the National Technical Information Service, refer such requests to that service, and

(ii) otherwise refer these requests to the appropriate Federal laboratories and agencies;

(D) facilitate communication and coordination between Offices of Research and Technology Applications of Federal laboratories;

(E) utilize (with the consent of the agency involved) the expertise and services of the National Science Foundation, the Department of Commerce, the National Aeronautics and Space Administration, and other Federal agencies, as necessary;

(F) with the consent of any Federal laboratory, facilitate the use by such laboratory of appropriate technology transfer mechanisms such as personnel exchanges and computer-based systems;

(G) with the consent of any Federal laboratory, assist such laboratory to establish programs using technical volunteers to provide technical assistance to communities related to such laboratory;

(H) facilitate communication and cooperation between Offices of Research and Technology Applications of Federal laboratories and regional, State, and local technology transfer organizations;

(I) when requested, assist colleges or universities, businesses, nonprofit organizations, State or local governments, or regional organizations to establish programs to stimulate research and to encourage technology transfer in such areas as technology program development, curriculum design, long-term research planning, personnel needs projections, and productivity assessments;

(J) seek advice in each Federal laboratory consortium re, on from representatives of State and local governments, large and small business, universities, and other appropriate persons on the effectiveness of the program (and any such advice shall be provided at no expense to the Government); and

(K) work with the Director of the National Institute on Disability and Rehabilitation Research to compile a compendium of current and projected Federal Laboratory technologies and projects that have or will have an intended or recognized impact on the available range of assisted technology for individuals with disabilities (as defined in section 3 of the Assistive Technology Act of 1998 [29 U.S.C. § 3002], including technologies and projects that incorporate the principles of universal design (as defined in section 3 of such Act [29 U.S.C. § 3002]), as appropriate.

(2) The membership of the Consortium shall consist of the Federal laboratories described in clause (1) of subsection (b) and such other laboratories as may choose to join the Consortium.

The representatives to the Consortium shall include a senior staff member of each Federal laboratory which is a member of the Consortium and a senior representative appointed from each Federal agency with one or more member laboratories.

(3) The representatives to the Consortium shall elect a Chairman of the Consortium.

(4) The Director of the National Institute of Standards and Technology shall provide the Consortium, on a reimbursable basis, with administrative services, such as office space, personnel, and support services of the Institute, as requested by the Consortium and approved by such Director.

(5) Each Federal laboratory or agency shall transfer technology directly to users or representatives of users, and shall not transfer technology directly to the Consortium. Each Federal laboratory shall conduct and transfer technology only in accordance with the practices and policies of the Federal agency which owns, leases, or otherwise uses such Federal laboratory.

(6) Not later than one year after the date of the enactment of this subsection [enacted Oct. 20, 1986], and every year thereafter, the Chairman of the Consortium shall submit a report to the President, to the appropriate authorization and appropriation committees of both Houses of the Congress, and to each agency with respect to which a transfer of funding is made (for the fiscal year or years involved) under paragraph (7), concerning the activities of the Consortium and the expenditures made by it under this subsection during the year for which the report is made. Such report shall include an annual independent audit of the financial statements of the Consortium, conducted in accordance with generally accepted accounting principles.

(7) (A) Subject to subparagraph (B), an amount equal to 0.008 percent of the budget of each Federal agency from any Federal source, including related overhead, that is to be utilized by or on behalf of the laboratories of such agency for a fiscal year referred to in subparagraph (B)(ii) shall be transferred by such agency to the National Institute of Standards and Technology at the beginning of the fiscal year involved. Amounts so transferred shall be provided by the Institute to the Consortium for the purpose of carrying out activities of the Consortium under this subsection.

   (B) A transfer shall be made by any Federal agency under subparagraph (A), for any fiscal year, only if the amount so transferred by that agency (as determined under such subparagraph) would exceed $10,000.

   (C) The heads of Federal agencies and their designees, and the directors of Federal laboratories, may provide such additional support for operations of the Consortium as they deem appropriate.

C. Agencies

1. Department of Commerce

a. General Oversight Role

The Department of Commerce was instrumental in seeking the enactment of CRADA authority for federal laboratories and plays a central role in promoting the use of CRADAs. This role is explained in 15 U.S.C. § 3710(g) as follows:

Functions of the Secretary.

(1) The Secretary, through the Under Secretary, and in consultation with other Federal agencies, may—

(A) make available to interested agencies the expertise of the Department of Commerce regarding the commercial potential of inventions and methods and options for commercialization which are available to the Federal laboratories, including research and development limited partnerships;

(B) develop and disseminate to appropriate agency and laboratory personnel model provisions for use on a voluntary basis in cooperative research and development arrangements; and

(C) furnish advice and assistance, upon request, to Federal agencies concerning their cooperative research and development programs and projects.

(2) Two years after the date of the enactment of this subsection [enacted Oct. 20, 1986] and every two years thereafter, the Secretary shall submit a summary report to the President and the Congress on the use by the agencies and the Secretary of the authorities specified in this Act [15 U.S.C. §§ 3701 et seq.]. Other Federal agencies shall cooperate in the report's preparation.

(3) Not later than one year after the date of the enactment of the Federal Technology Transfer Act of 1986 [enacted Oct. 20, 1986], the Secretary shall submit to the President and the Congress a report regarding—

(A) any copyright provisions or other types of barriers which tend to restrict or limit the transfer of federally funded computer software to the private sector and to State and local governments, and agencies of such State and local governments; and

(B) the feasibility and cost of compiling and maintaining a current and comprehensive inventory of all federally funded training software.

b. National Institute for Standards and Technology

The National Institute for Standards and Technology (NIST) is the major laboratory in the Department of Commerce. NIST specializes in metrology, the science of measurement.

Metrology has applications in computer chip mask design, image resolution and other fields of current interest. NIST also has a strong basic sciences division, and is a frequent CRADA participant. Once the Bureau of Standards, NIST was transformed and expanded by the Omnibus Trade and Competitiveness Act of 1988. NIST operates technology transfer programs like the Regional Clusters for the Transfer of Manufacturing Technology. NIST is expected to work closely with FLC.

Within Commerce, NIST runs the Advanced Technology Program (ATP). The ATP was authorized by the Omnibus Trade and Competitiveness Act of 1988 (P.L. 100-418) to focus on fostering economic growth by developing high risk enabling technologies. ATP sponsors a limited number of joint venture research and development efforts in vanguard technologies with the private entity paying at least half of the project costs. The private joint venture firm has the option of retaining commercial patent rights to the invention made by the joint venture with the Government receiving a royalty free license and a share in royalties proportionately equal to its contribution to the joint venture. See 15 C.F.R. § 295.2(d) (1994). As to copyrights, the ATP joint venturer may retain the copyright in the work created under the joint venture with the Government receiving a broad royalty free license. This license is limited somewhat in the case of software copyrights where the Government's license to distribute software is limited to users in the United States, 15 C.F.R. § 295.5 (1994).

NIST also provides assistance and information to those seeking to take advantage of federal technology transfer policies. Types of available assistance include: (1) free technical assistance, on-site or via telephone; (2) access to nonclassified federal research, whether completed or in progress; (3) use of federal lab facilities or equipment on a cost basis; (4) access to patented federal inventions for purposes of licensing; (5) participation in CRADAs; and (6) access to Government publications and databases.

Section 3710. Utilization of Federal technology

(d) *Center for the Utilization of Federal Technology.* The National Technical Information Service shall:

(1) serve as a central clearinghouse for the collection, dissemination and transfer of information on federally owned or originated technologies having potential application to State and local governments and to private industry;

(2) utilize the expertise and services of the National Science Foundation and the Federal Laboratory Consortium for Technology Transfer; particularly in dealing with State and local governments;

(3) receive requests for technical assistance from State and local governments, respond to such requests with published information available to the Service, and refer such requests to the Federal Laboratory Consortium for Technology Transfer to the extent that such requests require a response involving more than the published information available to the Service;

(4) provide funding, at the discretion of the Secretary, for Federal laboratories to provide the assistance specified in subsection (c)(3);

(5) use appropriate technology transfer mechanisms such as personnel exchanges and computer based systems; and

(6) maintain a permanent archival repository and clearinghouse for the collection and dissemination of nonclassified scientific, technical, and engineering information.

c. National Technology Information Service

The National Technology Information Service (NTIS) of the Department of Commerce is an archive and clearinghouse for "federally owned or originated technologies having potential application to State and local governments and to private industry," 15 U.S.C. § 3710(d)(1). NTIS also serves as a coordinating body for the Federal Laboratory Consortium and the National Science Foundation, and, "at the discretion of the Secretary," § 3710(d)(4) provides funding for federal laboratories in order that those laboratories may meet their obligation to disseminate information under § 3710(c)(3).

2. Department of Defense

DOD was given a technology transfer mission as part of the Defense Conversion, Reinvestment, and Transition Assistance Act of 1992, Pub L. 102-484, § 4202 (1992), 10 U.S.C. § 2514. This Act also established the Office of Technology Transition 10 U.S.C. § 2515 to ensure that technology developed for DOD is integrated into the private sector in order to enhance national technology and industrial base, reinvestment, and conversion activities consistent with the objectives set forth in 10 U.S.C. § 2501(a), Defense Conversion, Reinvestment, and Transition Assistance Act of 1992, Pub L. 102-484. This office is to monitor the research and development activities carried out by or for DOD; identify research and development activities that use technologies, or result in technological advancements, having potential nondefense commercial applications; serve as a clearinghouse for the transition of such technologies and technological advancements from DOD to the private sector; conduct activities in consultation and coordination with the Department of Energy and the Department of Commerce; and provide private firms with assistance to resolve problems associated with security clearances, proprietary rights, and other legal considerations involved in such a transition of technology.

DOD has implemented its domestic technology transfer program (T2) as an integral part of DOD's national security mission. See DOD Directive No. 5535.5, DOD Domestic Technology Transfer (T2) Program, May 19, 1999 and DOD Instruction 5535.8, DOD Technology Transfer Program Procedures, May 14, 1999. This program has been assigned to the Director, Defense Research and Engineering and requires the Secretaries of the Military Departments and heads of other DOD Components to ensure that domestic T2 receives a high priority. This directive specifies DOD's policy for supporting technology transfers as follows:

4. POLICY. It is DoD policy that:

4.1. Consistent with national security objectives under 10 U.S.C. 2501 (reference (e)), domestic T2 activities are integral elements of DoD pursuit of the DoD national security mission and concurrently improve the economic, environmental, and social well-being of U.S. citizens (Section 3702 of reference (d)). Concurrently, T2 supports a strong industrial base that the Department of Defense may utilize to supply DoD needs. Those activities must have a high-priority role in all DoD acquisition programs and are recognized as a key activity of the DoD laboratories and all other DoD activities (such as test, logistics, and product centers and depots and arsenals) that may make use of or contribute to domestic T2.

4.2. Domestic T2 programs, including spin-off, dual use, and spin-on activities, make the best possible use of national scientific and technical capabilities to enhance the effectiveness of DoD forces and systems.

4.3. It is further DoD policy to:

4.3.1. Promote domestic T2 through a variety of activities, such as CRADAs, cooperative agreements, other transactions, education partnerships, State and local government partnerships, exchange of personnel, presentation of technical papers, and other ongoing DoD activities.

4.3.2. Promote domestic T2 through U.S. and foreign patenting, patent licensing, and protecting other intellectual property rights. DoD inventions applicable for licensing shall be publicized to accelerate transfer of technology to the domestic economy. T2 is of the greatest benefit when the patented invention is commercialized (35 U.S.C. 200 and 207, reference (h)).

4.3.3. Allow non-Federal entities to use independent research and development funding as a part of their contributions to domestic T2 activities, including CRADAS, cooperative arrangements, and other transactions (Subpart 31.205-18(e) of the FAR, reference (i)).

4.3.4. Include domestic T2 as a duty and responsibility in position descriptions for applicable scientific, engineering, management, and executive positions.

4.3.5. Allow CRADAs between a DoD Component and DoD contractors, in accordance with DoD conflict of interest roles (DoD Directive 5500.7, reference (j)) and export control laws and regulations.

4.3.6. Ensure that domestic transfers of technology are accomplished without actual or apparent personal or organizational conflicts of interest or violations of ethics standards.

4.3.7. Allow conduct of T2 activity with foreign persons, industrial organizations, or government R&D activities, in accordance with export control laws, regulations, and policies and laws, regulations and policies governing foreign military sales (FMS). Consideration should be given to whether or not the government of such persons or industrial organization allows similar relationships and whether such activities benefit the U.S. industrial base and are consistent with the U.S. export control and FMS frameworks (E.O. 12591, reference (k)).

4.3.8. Encourage domestic T2 by giving preference to U.S. small business firms, consortia involving U.S. small business firms, and firms located in the United States.

3. NIH

The lead technology transfer agency for the Public Health Service (PHS) research laboratories is the National Institutes of Health (NIH). The NIH Office of Technology Transfer (OTT) provides direction for the implementation of the Stevenson-Wydler Act for a broad range of heath related programs. The PHS has prepared a Technology Transfer Manual which specifies the PHS patent and licensing policies for the PHS laboratories and its CRADA policy. A number of model forms for CRADAs, materials transfer CRADAs, Material Transfer Agreements, confidential disclosures, and license agreements are available from the OTT web site, see http://www.nih.gov/od/ott.htm.

III. AWARD OF CRADAS

A. Statutory Award Requirements

The authority to enter into a CRADA is reposed in federal laboratory directors under 15 U.S.C. §§ 3710a (a) and (b). A director can negotiate licensing agreements, receive funds, accept or provide personnel and services, enter into intellectual property agreements, grant presumptive rights to inventions, and waive all Government rights to an invention except for a Government-purposes license. There are no Government-wide standard clauses or regulations for CRADAs. Each agency however may issue suitable procedures to implement this requirement. As a consequence of the decentralization of CRADA authority, agreements vary by agency. All CRADAs have a few elements in common, however, and certain other elements that might be preferable if applied Government-wide. The only requirement in the Stevenson-Wydler Act with regard to the selection of CRADA collaborators is in 15 U.S.C. § 3710a(c)(4), which states—

> The laboratory director in deciding what cooperative research and development agreements to enter into shall:
>
> (1) give special consideration to small business firms, and consortia involving small business firms; and
>
> (B) give preference to business units located in the United States which agree that products embodying inventions made under the cooperative research and development agreement or produced through the use of such inventions will be manufactured substantially in the United States and, in the case of any industrial organization or other person subject to the control of a foreign company or government, as appropriate, take into consideration whether or not such foreign government permits United States agencies, organizations, or other persons to enter into cooperative research and development agreements and licensing agreements.

If the federal laboratory awarding the CRADA is operated by a GOCO, the agency in approving the CRADA to be entered into by the laboratory director is to guided by the purposes of the Stevenson-Wydler Technology Innovation Act of 1980 and the laboratory must obtain the applicable agency's consent to the award of the CRADA, 15 U.S.C. § 3710a(c)(5)(A) and (D).

B. Agency Award Practices

A CRADA is not a procurement contract, and thus is not subject to the Competition In Contracting Act (CICA), 41 U.S.C. § 251 (1984). For example, see Military-Civilian Technology Transfer, Army Regulation 70-57 ¶ 2-6 (1991), which observes that "[c]ompetitive procedures normally associated with awards of procurement contracts need not be applied to CRADAs." The CRADA is distinguished from procurement contract in that the Government is usually the contract performer rather than being a purchaser. Though the Government identifies transferable technologies, solicits CRADA offers and actively recruits CRADA partners, its fundamental role in a cooperative agreement is (or has been) suppletive of the collaborator. The Government supplies facilities, personnel, and often the germ of a commercial idea awaiting development. However, the collaborator provides funds, and generally controls the direction of research. This is appropriate, considering the larger objectives of the CRADA system. A private-sector collaborator is by hypothesis better at bringing products to market than is the Government.

Government agencies have adopted differing policies as to announcing the availability of CRADA opportunities and the award of CRADAs. NIST, for example, may use an Announcement of Opportunity for CRADAs in the *Federal Register*. Similarly, various Department of Health and Human Services (HHS) organizations announce the availability CRADA opportunities in the *Federal Register*, as does the Geological Survey of the Department of Interior. Some departments announce the proposed grant of an exclusive license and possibility of working a CRADA with the licensee regarding the noticed invention, or that an exclusive license is available and may involve a CRADA with respect to the invention being licensed for commercialization purposes. Some agency also provide notice in the *Federal Register* if they intend to negotiate a CRADA with a particular collaborator, others announce their CRADA opportunities in the *Commerce Business Daily* (CBD).

PHS "fair access" to CRADA opportunities' policy is probably the most detailed statement in this regard.

PHS's CRADA Policy states—

In compliance with the intent of the FTTA and PHS Manual Chapter No. 402, PHS Policy for Promoting Fair Access to CRADA Opportunities, the PHS shall ensure that outside organizations have fair access to collaborative opportunities, the licensing of federal technology, and PHS scientific expertise, giving special consideration to small business and preference to those that are located in the U.S. and agree to manufacture in the U.S. products developed under the CRADA. Fair Access to CRADAs is not to be considered as synonymous with the term "open competition," as defined for contracts and small purchases. Evidence of fair access or discussion of unique resource requirements should be maintained as part of the official ICD CRADA file. U.S. Public Health Service, Technology Transfer Manual, Chapter No. 400, Paragraph C. 7. As a part of its review of proposed CRADAs, the PHS policy provides for the principal investigator to complete a "Conflict of Interest and Fair Access Survey" form which documents information about the availability of the CRADA opportunity to others. This documentation is then reviewed as a part of the CRADA process by the PHS scientist ethics officer. See Paragraph D.3, Internal review Process Chapter No. 401, PHS Technology Transfer manual. Also see, U.S. Public Health Service Manual, Technology Transfer Manual, Chapter No. 400, CRADA Policy (July 27, 1995); and Chapter 401, PHS Policy for Promoting Fair Access to CRADA Opportunities, (Jan. 29, 1996), http://www.nih.gov/od/ott/ 401new.htm. Chapter 401, which contain guidelines for achieving fair access to CRADA opportunities. These guidelines note that there are many way of achieving fair access. One of the most important ways is restricting the scope of CRADAs so as to provide increased opportunities to other parties, others are to make compilations of CRADA opportunities available to the public, presentations at meeting, advertising request for CRADA partners for the development of specific technologies, such as, *Federal Register* notices, trade publications, association publications, press releases, and scientific professional journal.

C. Chem Service, Inc. v. Environmental Monitoring Systems Laboratory

The CRADA is a flexible form of agreement, with the potential to be used in place of a procurement contract. Such a substitution would permit both parties to circumvent some of the more onerous requirements of the federal procurement system. This "loophole" in the procurement regulations was resolved in *Chem Serv., Inc. v. Environmental Monitoring Sys. Lab.*, 12 F.3d 1256 (3d Cir. 1993). In that case the Environmental Protection Agency entered into CRADAs with a number of parties, the result of which was to be a rating system, for use by EPA in evaluating research materials. Chem Service, a publisher of research materials, challenged the award of the CRADA on various grounds. One complaint alleged that the deal was a procurement contract in all essential features. As a de facto procurement contract, the award should have been made competitively, pursuant to the Competition in Contracting Act of 1984. The third circuit agreed, applying CICA to all agreements (including CRADAs) having the "essential features" of a procurement contract, or duplicative of the functions of a procurement contract. CICA governs agreements, which mirror procurement contracts, even if not formally referred to as such. The fact that a procurement contract by definition involves the use of federal funds while a CRADA by definition does not permit the use of federal funds is not addressed in the opinion.

In *Chem Service*, the third circuit court restricted its holding to cases where the CRADA mechanism is used to circumvent procurement law. Though the third circuit held that CRADAs are not subject to CICA per se, there is evidence to suggest that norms of competition are being quietly incorporated into the CRADA system. The impetus of the holding has made most CRADA-granting agencies incorporate competitive procedures. Proof that a CRADA was awarded competitively is helpful when an agreement comes under attack as improper or not in the public interest. For instance, the fact that the CRADA involved was advertised and awarded using competitive procedures was relied upon by NIH when the National Cancer Institute's development agreement with Bristol-Myers Squibb to develop taxol for commercial use was subjected to Congressional scrutiny. See, Exclusive Agreements Between Federal Agencies and Bristol-Myers Squibb Co. for Drug Development: Is the Public Interest Protected?: Hearing Before the Subcommittee on Regulation, Business Opportunities, and Energy of the Committee on Small Business, House of Representatives, 102d Cong., 1st Sess. 18 (1991) (Testimony of Bruce Crabner, Director, Division of Cancer Treatment, National Cancer Institute).

D. Standing to Challenge CRADAs

Chem Service strengthened earlier holdings on another CRADA-related issue. The third circuit held that a party affected by the CRADA subject matter or by its granting has standing to sue provided that the general criteria of standing to a particular injury, fairly traceable to the action at issue, and likely to be alleviated by the remedy sought—are met. The fact that a CRADA was granted where a competitive procurement should have been employed suffices to establish a legally cognizable injury to those (a) affected by the CRADA itself, as was Chem Service, or (b) unfairly locked out of the CRADA "bidding" process. *Chem Service* confirmed a series of Comptroller General decisions holding that a party has standing to challenge a CRADA if he can prove that it was used to avoid procurement contract rules or if a conflict of interest was involved, *Management Dev. Group*, 64 Comp. Gen. 669 (B-219245), 85-2 CPD ¶ 134 (proof of conflict of interest or avoidance of contracting requirements confers standing to challenge CRADA); *Resource Dev. Program & Servs., Inc.,* Comp. Gen. Dec. B-235331, 89-1 CPD ¶ 471 (proof that CRADA was used to avoid procurement law requirements confers standing); 94-2 CPD ¶ 257 (in finding that a protest was untimely filed the Comptroller General noted that CRADAs under the Stevenson-Wydler Act may only be used where the purpose of the agreement for technology transfer from a federal laboratory to a non-federal entity for the purpose of conducting specific R&D work or in collaboration with the nonfederal entity; and if the agency action was impermissible under the Stevenson-Wydler Act, GAO would object to its use.) For a similar decision with respect to DOD's "other transaction" authority, see *Energy Conversion Devices, Inc.,* B-260514, 1995 U.S. Comp. Gen. LEXIS 399 (June 16, 1995).

IV. TERMS AND CONDITIONS OF CRADAS

The Federal Technology Transfer Act of 1986 provides the basic authority for Government laboratories to do work for the private sector. CRADAs "allow for shared costs, shared risks and shared expertise," Barbara A. Duncombe, "Federal Technology Transfer: A Look at the Benefits and Pitfalls of One of the Country's Best Kept Secrets," 37 Fed. Bar News & J. 608, 610 (1990). As to the terms of a CRADA, 10 U.S.C. § 3710a(c) provides that the "Federal agency may issue regulations on suitable procedures for implementing the provisions of this section." However, with few exceptions, no such regulatory guidance has been issued. For some agency guidance see, PHS Cooperative Research and Development Agreement Policy, Technology Transfer Manual, Chapter No. 400; PHS Policy for Promoting Fair Access to Cooperative Research and Development Agreement Opportunities, Chapter 401; and PHS CRADA Procedures, Chapter 402.

While there is no standard CRADA for use by all agencies the Commerce model CRADA comes closest to being a Governmental standard. "Most agencies have recast the Commerce model to fit their own needs," Robert H. Swennes II, "Commercializing Government Inventions: Utilizing the Federal Technology Transfer Act of 1986," 20 Pub. Cont. L.J. 365, 371 (Spr. 1991). This Materials agreement seems to be a mechanism for transferring proprietary materials to or from a federal laboratory rather than a research and development agreement. However, trade secrets and patent rights are covered by this agreement.

DOE also has some model CRADAs, for example, the DOE Small Business CRADA sample has been published, 59 Fed. Reg. 13317, March 21, 1994. As a consequence of the decentralization of CRADA authority, agreements vary by agency. For some additional model CRADAs see the following Internet sites.

1. **Air Force** http://web-tech.robins.af, mil.Aechxfer/sample.htm

2. **Navy** http://infonext.nrl.navy.mil/-techtmn/cradas.htm

3. **DOE** http://www.gc.doe.gov/gc-02/crada\toc.htm and http://www.doe.gov/techtranJ cradama.html

4. **PHS Model Agreements and Forms** http://www.nih.gov/od/ott

A. Intellectual Property Rights

1. Preexisting Data Rights

a. Collaborator's Preexisting Information

The protection of a collaborator's preexisting data rights under a CRADA are generally covered by the treatment accorded to the collaborator's preexisting trade secrets and copyrights. Generally, copyrights in the collaborator preexisting data are important only where the CRADA relates to things that rely on copyright protection, such as computer software. Since the Government is subject to infringement actions in the event its use of the copyrighted work exceeds any direct or implied right it may have in a private copyright, the CRADA should expressly grant the laboratory (Government) the right to use the collaborator's copyright works in order to accomplish the laboratory's activities under the CRADA, or if such an express grant is missing from the CRADA, such a right may be implied from the nature of the CRADA itself.

Usually the more important issues with regard to a collaborator's preexisting data has been the extent that the laboratory will protect the collaborator's trade secret private data that has been delivered to the laboratory as a part of the CRADA work. While it is believed that laboratories will normally attempt to protect a collaborator's trade secret information, the issue of protection may involve a request for information under the Freedom of Information Act (FOIA). If the laboratory is operated by federal employees then the FOIA standards and not the only the terms of the CRADA will determine whether the collaborator's data will be released. Similarly, if the laboratory is operated by a contractor, the terms of the contract term between the operator and the Government with respect to treatment to be accorded private data and whether the agency applies the FOIA to the data in the hands of its contractor-operator must be taken into consideration. This is evidently so notwithstanding the general view that FOIA release requirements do not reach data in the hands of a contractor.

The Stevenson-Wydler Act, 15 U.S.C. § 3710a(c)(7), provides broad protection for a collaborator's private data under the FOIA as follows—

(7)(A) No trade secrets or commercial or financial information that is privileged or confidential, under the meaning of section 552(b)(4) of title 5, United States Code, which is obtained in the conduct of research or as a result of activities under this Act [15 U.S.C. §§ 3701 et seq.] from a non-Federal party participating in a cooperative research and development agreement shall be disclosed.

Similarly, NASA may protect private information obtained under their Space Act Agreements. 42 U.S.C. § 2454 provides—

(a) Information obtained or developed by the Administrator in the performance of his functions under this chapter shall be made available for public inspection, except (A) information authorized or required by Federal statute to be withheld, (B) information classified to protect the national security, and (C) information described in subsection (b) of this section: Provided, That nothing in this chapter shall authorize the withholding of information by the Administrator from the; duly authorized committees of the Congress.

The legal problem that has not been answered with respect to the language in 15 U.S.C. § 3710a(c)(7) and 42 U.S.C. § 2454(a) is whether such language qualifies under 5 U.S.C. § 552(b)(3) of FOIA, which allows an agency to withhold information from release:

(3) specifically exempted from disclosure by statute (other than section 552b of this title), provided that such statute (A) requires that the matters be withheld from the public in such a manner as to leave no discretion on the issue, or (B) establishes particular criteria for withholding or refers to particular types of matters to be withheld;

In the only decision on this portion of the Stevenson-Wydler Act the court in *Delorme Pub. Co. v. NOAA*, 917 F. Supp. 867, (D.C.D. Me 1996) noted that it would normally have examined the Stevenson-Wydler Act withholding requirements of § 3710a(c)(7) of title 15 under this FOIA standard in resolving whether an decision of an agency to withhold a contractor's preexisting data, requested by a third party under FOIA, was proper. However, as the plaintiff never raised this issue the court, other than noting that a problem may exist under this section of the Stevenson-Wydler Act, held that the plaintiff waived this argument.

b. Government Preexisting Information

As noted elsewhere in this text, the Government may not claim a copyright in Government works, i.e., works prepared by its employees as a part of their official duties. Similarly, the Government has difficulty in protecting technology developed in-house as a trade secret principally for the reason that the FOIA has no clear exemption for trade secrets developed in-house by the Government. Where preexisting information is developed by a Government laboratory operated by a contractor, the contract between these parties must be examined to determine the Government's and the contractor's rights this information. In addition of course, the terms of the CRADA must also be examined closely to ascertain the rights of the Government or the operator in the technical information generated by the laboratory's preexisting work.

2. Technology Developed Under CRADAs

The collaborator may desire to own the technical information developed under a CRADA, especially if the collaborator is funding the work and expects to commercialize the results. The Stevenson-Wydler Act provides that the work resulting from a CRADA may be protected from release under the FOIA for a period of five years of it meets if the information meets the "trade secret or commercial or financial information that is privileged or confidential" FOIA test, 15 U.S.C. § 3710a(c)(7). However, as noted above, copyright protection cannot be provided if the work is prepared by a Government employee. The Space Act in 42 U.S.C. § 2454(b) and DOE in 42 U.S.C. § 13541(d) have similar provisions. These provisions state—

Section 3710 a. Cooperative research and development agreements

(c) *Contract considerations.*

> (7)(B) The director, or in the case of a contractor-operated laboratory, the agency, for a period of up to 5 years after development of information that results from research and development activities conducted under this Act [15 U.S.C. § 3701 et seq.] and that would be a trade secret or commercial or financial information that is privileged or confidential if the information had been obtained from a non-Federal party participating in a cooperative research and development agreement, may provide appropriate protections against the dissemination of such information, including exemption from subchapter II of chapter 5 of title 5, United States Code.

42 U.S.C.§ 2454. Access to information

(b) The Administrator, for a period of up to 5 years after the development of information that results from activities conducted under an agreement entered into under section 2473(c)(5) and (6) of this title, and that would be a trade secret or commercial or financial information that is privileged or confidential under the meaning of section 552(b)(4) of title 5 if the information had been obtained from a non-Federal party participating in such an agreement, may provide appropriate protections against the dissemination of such information, including exemption from subchapter II of chapter 5 of title 5.

42 U.S.C. §13541. Research, development, demonstration, and commercial application activities

(d) *Protection of information.* Section 12(c)(7) of the Stevenson-Wydler Technology Innovation Act of 1980 (15 U.S.C. § 3710a(c)(7)), relating to the protection of information, shall apply to research, development, demonstration, and commercial application programs and activities under this Act.

Therefore, the statutory authority exists for up to five years of trade secret like protection for technology developed under a CRADA by a federal laboratory but of course the CRADAs itself must provide for such protection since the statutory authority is discretionary with the agency or laboratory. In this regard it should be noted that many laboratories have a broad publication and dissemination policy which overlays the CRADA work. For example, Paragraph C. 4, of CRADA Policy, Chapter No. 400 of the PHS Technology Transfer Manual states—

> It is fundamental to the mission of PHS that research results be published and discussed at public forum. Further, PHS scientists must operate within an atmosphere of scientific collegiality. Reasonable confidentiality requirements and brief delays in dissemination of research results are permitted under a CRADA, as necessary, in order to protect proprietary materials and intellectual property rights. CRADAs which in any way attempt to unreasonable restrict or constrain scientific interaction or the dissemination of research information will not be approve. In considering any proposed CRADA, consideration must be given to the possibility that the level of confidentiality associated with that CRADA project might, on balance, inappropriately impair the degree of openness necessary to maintain effective scientific communication and to serve the public interest.

In *Delorme Pub. Co. v. NOAA*, 917 F. Supp. 867, (D.C.D. Me 1996), Delorme brought suit under the Freedom of Information Act (FOIA) seeking the release of documents in electronic form of certain NOAA nautical charts created in anticipation of and during CRADA activities. NOAA claimed that the Stevenson-Wydler Act exempted this information from disclosure for five years citing 15 U.S.C. § 3710a(c)(7)(B). The district court held that this information, created in anticipation of a CRADA, was "conducted under" the Stevenson-Wydler Act and would qualify as "commercial" and "confidential" if obtained from the private partner. Since NOAA found that the release of this information would result in competitive harm and impair the Government's ability to obtain CRADA partners, the court permitted this information to be withheld from release under FOIA. As to information created during the CRADA the court also held that this information could be withheld from release for five years under the terms of the Stevenson-Wydler Act.

3. *Other Means of Protecting Proprietary Information*

NIH uses a "Materials Cooperative research and Development Agreement" or "Materials CRADA" for the transfer of proprietary information when no further interaction between the parties is contemplated. Essentially, the MTA/CRADA is a contract that permits the parties to use the transferred material and "to the extent permitted by law" protect the proprietary aspect of the information or materials. The MTA/CRADA delineates the circumstances under which the information or materials in question may be used—only for research, and not on human subjects—and provides limited intellectual property protection for a recipient. Under the MTA/CRADA model, section 3, proprietary information marked "confidential" will be protected for three years from the date of disclosure. Under section 4, the PHS recipient agrees retain control over the material or information and not transfer it to others not under his direct supervision without written approval of the collaborator. The PHS recipient also agrees to destroy all confidential information when the research project for which the information was needed is completed, upon termination of the MTA/CRADA, or after one year, whichever is sooner.

If an invention is made, i.e., conceived or first actually reduced to practice in the performance of the PHS research plan during the term of the MTA/CRADA (unless the invention was conceived prior to the effective date of this CRADA but reduced to practice during its term) solely by a PHS employee or jointly by a PHS employee and an employee of the collaborator, the MTA/CRADA grants the collaborator an "exclusive or nonexclusive license, which is substantially in the form of the model PHS license agreement." The commercial terms of this license are to be negotiated by the parties after the invention is made "to fairly reflect the nature of the invention, the relative contributions of the Parties to the invention and the CRADA, the risks incurred by the collaborator and the costs of subsequent research and development needed to bring the invention to the marketplace. The field of use of the license will be commensurate with the scope of the research plan."

Section 6 of the MTA/CRADA requires the prompt report by PHS to the collaborator of each subject invention reported by a PHS employee and each patent application filed by PHS. The collaborator then has three months after the patent application is filed on the invention to make its license election and must complete its negotiation within nine months. If PHS has not responded to the collaborator's license proposal within nine month, a one-month extension is granted commencing upon the date that PHS responds thereto. If proposal is rejected, and the collaborator is seeking an exclusive license, than the collaborator has a right of first refusal for a six-month period if PHS makes an offer to others on more favorable terms than it offered the collaborator. If an exclusive license is granted it is subject to the "march-in rights" specified by the Stevenson-Wydler Act.

For biotechnology, NIH employs a Uniform Biological Material Transfer Agreement (UBMTA) having the essential features of the MTA. However, the UBMTA is designed to facilitate the transfer of study objects (cell lines, et cetera) between nonprofit institutions, rather than between the Government and the private sector. See URL http://www/nih.gov/od/ott/ubmmta.htm and 59 Fed. Reg. 32000 (1994).

Based on the structure of the MTA/CRADA, it appears possible that a collaborator could insist on a separate agreement governing proprietary information, setting liquidated damages figures and disclosure procedures independent of the CRADA. The separate agreement has the advantage of not being governed by CRADA liability provisions, which sharply limit recoveries from the Government.

4. Record of Technology Transfer Activities

Some agencies maintain restricted-access records of patent and technology, transfer activities under the Privacy Act of 1974. The Corps of Engineers retains a record of all technology transfer and patent activities, including royalty information. The Corps also maintains files on individuals involved in patents or technology transfer. Technology transfer is rarely the subject of litigation, so the decision to retain these files would appear to be largely administrative. See

Privacy Act notice in 59 Fed. Reg. 47843-03 (1994). The Stevenson-Wydler Act requires each agency to maintain a record of all CRADAs entered into under this authority, 15 U.S.C. § 3710a(c)(6).

B. Invention Rights Under CRADAs

Invention rights under CRADA generally concern the rights to inventions made by laboratory employees performing CRADA activities, the inventions made by the collaborator's employees and joint invention, i.e., made by employees of both the laboratory and the collaborator during the CRADA activities. CRADAs of course often relate to invention previously made by laboratory employees so rights in such inventions may also be the subject of a CRADA. As to laboratory made inventions, in 1996, the Technology Transfer Improvements Act of 1995, P.L. 104-113 (March 7, 1996) modified the Stevenson-Wydler Act to provide that the collaborator is either to acquire the right to pre-negotiate an exclusive license in a field-of-use to inventions made under the CRADA or receive an assignment of title to such inventions, subject to a non-exclusive license in the Government.

1. Laboratory Inventions

a. CRADA Activities

Federal agencies have historically provided some rights in the inventions made during the collaboration activities under a CRADA to the collaborator. This policy is now mandatory. Pub L. 104-113, March 7, 1996, amended section 3701a(b) of title 15 (Stevenson-Wydler Act) to provide for an option in the collaborator either to obtain an exclusive license in a pre-negotiated field of use or an assignment of patent rights to CRADA inventions. Where such rights are in the form of an exclusive license, 15 U.S.C. § 3710a(b)(4) provides that the collaborating party "shall have the right of enforcement under chapter 29 of title 35 of the U.S. Code." This settles the question of whether the Government's exclusive licensee may bring an infringement action on the licensed patent. The collaborator's rights in CRADA inventions set forth above are to be established by the terms of the CRADA. If the collaborator retains title to the CRADA inventions made by laboratory employees or an exclusive license therein pursuant to 15 U.S.C. § 3710a(b), the laboratory is to receive a "nonexclusive, nontransferable, irrevocable, paid-up license from the collaborating party to the laboratory to practice the invention or have the invention practiced throughout the world by or on behalf of the Government." This license flows to the laboratory for the benefit of the Government rather than directly to the Government itself, which is somewhat awkward if the laboratory is a GOCO operation.

The scope of the collaborator's rights in CRADA inventions rights is now specified by 15 U.S.C. § 3710a(b) as follows—

Enumerated Authority.—(1) Under an agreement entered into pursuant to subsection (a)(1), the laboratory may grant, or agree to grant in advance, to a collaborating party patent licenses or assignments, or options thereto, in any invention made in whole or in part by a laboratory employee under the agreement, for reasonable compensation when appropriate. The laboratory shall ensure, through such agreement, that the collaborating party has the option to choose an exclusive license for a pre-negotiated field of use for any such invention under the agreement or, if there is more than one collaborating party, that the collaborating parties are offered the option to hold licensing rights that collectively encompass the rights that would be held under such an exclusive license by one party . . .

* * * *

(4) A collaborating party in an exclusive license in any invention made under an agreement entered into pursuant to subsection (a)(1) shall have the right of enforcement under chapter 29 of title 35, United States Code.

(5) A Government-owned, contractor-operated laboratory that enters into a cooperative research and development agreement pursuant to subsection (a)(1) may use or obligate royalties or other income accruing to the laboratory under such agreement with respect to any invention only—

(A) for payments to inventors;

(B) for purposes described in clauses (i), (ii), (iii), and (iv) of section 14(a)(1)(B); and

(C) for scientific research and development consistent with the research mad development missions and objectives of the laboratory.

These provisions authorize the laboratory to permit the collaborator to acquire title to inventions that would normally reside in the Government based on its "agreement" with its employees or the contractor's employees (under the contract for operating the laboratory). Thus, the underlying Government policies on acquiring invention rights from its employees and contractors impacts the collaborator's right under a CRADA. The collaborator's invention rights are subject to a nonexclusive, nontransferable, irrevocable, paid-up license to the laboratory "to practice the invention or have the invention practiced throughout the world by or on behalf of the Government" (15 U.S.C. § 3710a(b)(1)(A)).

In addition, the laboratory is to provide for "march-in rights" in the CRADA, i.e., the right to require the collaborator to grant licenses to responsible applicants on reasonable terms, if the Government finds that the exercise of such rights is necessary to meet health and safety needs; or for is for public use specified by Government regulations and such needs or public use are not being reasonably satisfied by the collaborator, or the collaborator has failed to comply with the agreement described in subsection (c)(4)(B) of 3710a relating to providing preference to domestic businesses in tire manufacturing of the product covered by the invention. The collaborator may challenge the Government's decision to exercise its "march-in rights" under the roles set out under the Bayh-Dolc Act, 35 U.S.C. § 203(2). These "march-in rights" are contained in 15 U.S.C. § 3710a(b)(1) as follows—

In consideration for the Government's contribution under the agreement, grants under this paragraph shall be subject to the following explicit conditions:

(A) A nonexclusive, nontransferable, irrevocable, paid-up license from the collaborating party to the laboratory to practice the invention or have the invention practiced throughout the world by or on behalf of the Government. In the exercise of such license, the Government shall not publicly disclose trade secrets or commercial or financial information that is privileged or confidential within the meaning of section 552C0)(4) of title 5, United States Code, or which would be considered as such if it had been obtained from a non-Federal party.

(B) If a laboratory assigns title or grants an exclusive license to such an invention, the Government shall retain the right—

(i) to require the collaborating party to grant to a responsible applicant a nonexclusive, partially exclusive, or exclusive license to use the invention in the applicant's licensed field of use, on terms that are reasonable under the circumstances; or

(ii) if the collaborating party fails to grant such a license, to grant the license itself.

(C) The Government may exercise its right retained under subparagraph (B) only in exceptional circumstances and only if the Government determines that—

(i) the action is necessary to meet health or safety needs that are not reasonably satisfied by the collaborating party;

(ii) the action is necessary to meet requirements for public use specified by Federal regulations, and such requirements are not reasonably satisfied by the collaborating party; or

(iii) the collaborating party has failed to comply with an agreement containing provisions described in subsection (c)(4)(B).

This determination is subject to administrative appeal and judicial review under section 203(2) of title 35, United States Code.

The thrust of this section was explained in the Congressional Record, 104th Cong. 2nd Sess., H1264, February 27, 1996, as follows—

Section 4. Title to intellectual property arising from cooperative research and development agreements guarantees an industrial partner to a joint Cooperative Research and Development Agreement (CRADA) the option to choose, at minimum, an exclusive license for a pre-negotiated field of use to the resulting invention. Reiterates Government's right to use the invention for its legitimate needs, but requires the obligation to protect from public disclosure any information classified as privileged or confidential under Exemption 4 of the Freedom of Information Act (FOIA).

In exceptional circumstances, provides that when the laboratory assigns ownership or an exclusive license to the industry partner, licensing to others may be required if needed to satisfy compelling public health, safety or regulatory concerns. In such rare circumstances, the industry partner would have administrative appeal and judicial review, similar to the Bayh-Dole Act. (P.L. 96-517). Also, clarifies current law defining the contributions laboratories can make in the CRADA. Permits agencies to use royalties in hiring temporary personnel to assist in the CRADA or related projects. Enumerates how a Government-owned, Government-operated (GOGO) laboratory and a Government-owned, contractor-operated (GOCO) laboratory may use resulting royalties.

Another "march-in" type right was adopted by NIH based on a "reasonable pricing" requirement. This policy was standard in all NIH CRADAs and exclusive licenses beginning in 1989. This policy required that a requirement be included in each CRADA and exclusive license that there be a reasonable relationship between the pricing of NIH licensed products, the public investment in such products, and the health and safety needs of the public. It was long argued that this policy had a chilling effect on prospective licensees as they could not determine what would be considered to be "reasonable pricing" for their products by the NIH. The adoption of this policy is believed to be an outgrowth of NIH's experience with the drug AZT used by AIDs patients. The high price of AZT and the belief that NIH employees deserved to be named as the co-inventors of the patents covering this drug or at least that the price should reflect the fact that NIH subsidized the clinical trials for this drug, generated the view that NIH needed to protect the public interest by adopting a reasonable pricing policy in the transfer of NIH technology. This view held that unless NIH adopted a reasonable pricing requirement in their CRADAs and exclusive licenses the public would not have reasonable access to NIH technology funded with public money. The contention of co-inventorship of AZT proved to be wrong, see *Burroughs Wellcome Co. v. BarrLabs., Inc.*, 40 F.3d 1223, 32 U.S.P.Q. 2D 1915 (Fed. Cir. 1994) In 1995 NIH abandoned its reasonable pricing requirements as it had a detrimental effect and lessened the opportunity for NIH to transfer NIH developed technology to U.S. industry.

In *Johns Hopkins University v. CellPro*, 152 F.3d (Fed. Cir. 1998), the district court for the District of Delaware found that CellPro infringed two patents owned by John's Hopkins University that were licensed to Baxter Healthcare ordered CellPro to pay damages to punish CellPro's "bad-faith infringement" of the Hopkins patents and enjoined CellPro from further infringement which was partially stayed to permit CellPro to continue clinical trials pending FDA approval of stem cell concentration system licensed under the patent. A few months after CellPro requested HHS to invoke the Government's "march-in rights" in the Hopkins patents. NIH after examining the petition and the many letters from the research community and the congress determined that the exercise of its "march-in rights" was not warranted but carefully noting that the stem cells covered by the patents were available to patients either as a licensed product or under clinical research protocols. On September 1998 CellPro announced that it was selling all its assets, that it would appoint Baxter Healthcare as its distributor of its stem cell system and sell all remaining issues with John Hopkins for payments totaling $15.6 million.

b. Preexisting Laboratory Inventions

CRADAs often used in conjunction with preexisting inventions that were made by the laboratory employees (and which are owned by the Government) as a mechanism to further fund the development of the inventions. In such cases, the collaborator is often offered rights in the inventions as an inducement to fund its further development. The Stevenson-Wydler Act provides that the laboratory may negotiate a patent license with the collaborator in preexisting Government-owned inventions under the Government's licensing authority (e.g., 35 U.S.C. § 207) stemming from the work of the laboratory as well as other inventions that may be assigned to the Government (15 U.S.C. § 3710a(a)(2)).

2. Collaborator's Inventions

The collaborator also may hold rights to preexisting inventions that relate to the CRADA technology, may perform some of the CRADA work itself at its own facilities, or may assign its own employees to the work at the laboratory as a part of the CRADA activities. The collaborator's preexisting rights very seldom is the subject of the CRADA and the Government will not under normal fact patterns related to CRADA's lay claim to such inventions. However, with respect to inventions made by the collaborator's employee's as part of the CRADA activities the CRADA invention provision will be directed to such inventions since they usually cover all inventions made under the CRADA activities.

The normal CRADA coverage is to provide for ownership of such inventions in the collaborator with a license reserved in the Government. This is now required by the 1996 amendments to the Stevenson-Wydler Act, 15 U.S.C. § 3710a(b)(2), which now provides:

> Under agreements entered into pursuant to subsection (a)(1), the laboratory shall ensure that a collaborating party may retain title to any invention made solely by its employee in exchange for normally granting the Government a nonexclusive, nontransferable, irrevocable, paid-up license to practice the invention or have the invention practiced throughout the world by or on behalf of the Government for research or other Government purposes.

3. Joint Inventions

Inventions are often made by collaborating workers and in such case these inventions are owned jointly by the inventors (or their employer if such invention has been assigned to such employers). In CRADA situations, inventions made jointly by laboratory and collaborator employees would be owned jointly by the Government and the collaborator. The Government will usually waive its rights, based on its employee/inventor, to a jointly-held invention to the collaborator, possibly in exchange for royalty payments. The authority to waive such rights are contained in the Bayh-Dole Act, 35 U.S.C. § 202(e).

If the collaborator declines to pursue the intellectual property rights in a CRADA invention, the rights must be offered to the inventor. An agency laboratory will usually take title to an invention produced by the agency's employees, concede title to an invention produced by private employees, and take joint title to a jointly produced invention.

V. EMPLOYEE RIGHTS

A. Allocation of Rights

Unlike most employers, the Government does not require its employees to execute an agreement to assign all the inventions that may be made by the employee during the course of the employment to the Government. Instead the Government relies on the terms of E.O. 9865 (foreign rights) and E.O. 10096 (domestic rights). These Executive Orders have been incorporated into the Department of Commerce rules at 37 C.F.R. § 501. See Appendix 4, E.O. 10096, which was issued in 1950 after an extensive study by the Department of Justice. While this Executive Order was said to apply the common law rules regarding the ownership of invention rights by employers and employees, it actual adopted what is the more modern American practice of employers acquiring ownership rights to most of the inventions made by their employees during the course of the employment. Common law provides that in the absence of a agreement to the contrary the employer owns all rights in inventions made by employees who have been hired to invent and a "shop right" license in all other employee inventions. A shop right is the right of the employer to use his employee's invention in-house. In the customary American practice this common law rule is overcome with an agreement signed by each employee upon his/her employment agreeing to assign all invention rights during the employment to the employer.

The Government's policy/agreement with its employees is somewhat more liberal than that adopted by most employee but still provides the Government with rights to most of the inventions made by employees within the course of their employment. For example, where the Government has the right to acquire title to an invention but does not desire to file for a patent, the employee may obtain the ownership of such inventions, subject to a Government license (see section l(d) of E.O. 10096). Section 1 of Executive Order 10096, provides the following policy for all Government employees with respect to domestic patent rights—

(a) The Government shall obtain the entire right, title, and interest in and to all inventions made by any Government employee (1) during working hours, or (2) with a contribution by the Government of facilities, equipment, materials, funds, or information, or of time or services of other Government employees on official duty, or (3) which bear a direct relation to or are made in consequence of the official duties of the inventor.

(b) In any case where the contribution of the Government, as measured by any one or more of the criteria set forth in paragraph (a) last above, to the invention, is insufficient equitably to justify a requirement of assignment to the Government of the entire right, title and interest to such invention, or in any case where the Government has insufficient interest in an invention to obtain entire right, title and interest therein (although the Government could obtain some under paragraph (a), above), the Government agency concerned, subject to the approval of the Chairman of the Government Patents Board (now Secretary of Commerce. See Ex. Ord. No. 10930 set out as a note below) (provided for in paragraph 3 of this order and hereinafter referred to as the Chairman), shall leave title to such invention in the employee, subject, however, to the reservation to the Government of a nonexclusive, irrevocable, royalty-free license in the invention with power to grant licenses for all governmental purposes, such reservation, in the terms thereof, to appear, where practicable, in any patent, domestic or Foreign, which may issue on such invention.

(c) In applying the provisions of paragraphs (a) and (b), above, to the facts and circumstances relating to the making of any particular invention, it shall be presumed that an invention made by an employee who is employed or assigned (i) to invent or improve or perfect any art, machine, manufacture, or composition of matter, (ii) to conduct or perform research, development work, or both, (iii) to supervise, direct, coordinate, or review Government financed or conducted research, development work, or both, or (iv) to act in a liaison capacity among governmental or nongovernmental agencies or individuals engaged in such work, or made by an employee included within any other category of employees specified by regulations issued pursuant to section 4(b) hereof, falls within the provisions of paragraph (a), above, and it shall be presumed that any invention made by any other employee fails within the provisions of paragraph (b), above. Either presumption may be rebutted by the facts or circumstances attendant upon the conditions under which any particular invention is made and, notwithstanding the foregoing, shall not preclude a determination that the invention falls within the provisions of paragraph (d) next below.

(d) In any case wherein the Government neither (1) pursuant to the provisions of paragraph (a) above, obtains entire right, title and interest in and to an invention nor (2) pursuant to the provisions of paragraph (b) above, reserves a nonexclusive, irrevocable, royalty-free license in the invention with power to grant licenses for all governmental purposes, the Government shall leave the entire right, title and interest in and to the invention in the Government employee, subject to law.

B. Stevenson-Wydler

Under 15 U.S.C. § 3710d, like E.O. 10096, the Government should allow the employee who conceives an invention to take title to it, if the Government chooses not to pursue the filing of a patent or the commercialization of the invention. In such cases the Government retains a "nonexclusive, nontransferable, irrevocable, paid-up license to practice the invention or have the invention practiced throughout the world by or on behalf of the Government." Section 3710d provides—

(a) *In general.* If a Federal agency which has the ownership of or the right of ownership to an invention made by a Federal employee [15 U.S.C. §§ 3701 et seq.] does not intend to file for a patent application or otherwise to promote commercialization of such invention, the agency shall allow the inventor, if the inventor is a Government employee or former employee who made the invention during the course of employment with the Government, to obtain or retain title to the invention (subject to reservation by the Government of a nonexclusive, nontransferable, irrevocable, paid-up license to practice the invention or have the invention practiced throughout the world by or on behalf of the Government). In addition, the agency may condition the inventor's right to title on the timely filing of a patent application in cases when the Government determines that it has or may have a need to practice the invention.

(b) *Definition.* For purposes of this section, Federal employees include special Government employees as defined in section 202 of title 18, United States Code.

(c) *Relationship to other laws.* Nothing in this section is intended to limit or diminish existing authorities of any agency.

This provision was recently modified to clarify the congressional intent that rights to inventions should be offered to employees when the agency is not pursuing them. This section as changed permits a federal scientists, or a former laboratory employee, in the event that the Federal Government chooses not to pursue the right of ownership to his or her invention or otherwise promote its commercialization, to obtain or retain title to the invention for the purposes of commercialization. Where an employees invention is unrelated to the employees assigned duties, the Government obtains no rights. *See Aerojet-General Corp.,* ASBCA 47206, 97-1 BCA ¶ 28,889; and *Zachavin v. United States,* No. 96-5076, slip op. at 8-10 (Fed. Cir. 1997).

C. Role of PTO

The procedures governing the allocation of invention rights to employees are left to the head of each agency. The U.S. Patent and Trademark Office (PTO) in the Department of Commerce serves as an arbiter for inventor protests; see the uniform patent policy with respect to rights in inventions made by Government employees, 37 C.F.R. § 501.

D. NIH

The allocation of invention rights regarding the human genome has caused a serious problem at NIH. As a consequence of the ongoing Human Genome Project, NIH possesses a large library of cDNA sequences. Gene sequences can be patented so long as the traditional standards (novelty, nonobviousness, enablement) are met. Pursuant to Article 7.6 of the NIH/ADAMHA model CRADA, "if NIH decides not to pursue patent rights on its own behalf, current regulations of the Department of Health and Human Services require that it allow employees. . . , to pursue such rights on their own," Rebecca S. Eisenberg, "Genes, Patents, and Product Development," 257 Science 903, 904 (August 1992). In 1992, responding to dual concerns that some sequences might be published, and that inventors might exercise their right to patent their discoveries privately in the absence of agency action, NIH filed for patents on a number of the sequences in its cDNA library. NIH believed that Bayh-Dole compelled it to pursue the commercialization of any available intellectual property, and securing patent rights was seen as the first step in this process. Some argue that NIH "sought patent protection for [the cDNA sequences] as an interim measure. This action protected options, fostered public discussion, and forced no outcome or policy decisions," Reid G. Adler, "Genome Research: Fulfilling the Public's Expectations for Knowledge and Commercialization," 257 Science 908 (August 1992).

In 1993, NIH abandoned the attempt to patent its DNA library in the face of international opprobrium. NIH decided that the aggressive patenting policy was "at odds with [the] international harmony required for a concerted human genome mapping and sequencing project," G. Kenneth Smith and Denise M. Kettelberger, "Patents and the Human Genome Project," 22

AIPLA Q.J. 27, 63 (1994). The tension between inventor rights and the agency mission at NIH (and elsewhere) remains unresolved.

E. "Property" and Licenses Under CRADAs

The Government is required by law to publicly announce any licensing activities, 37 C.F.R. Part 404.7. An interpretation of the CRADA enabling legislation suggests an issue regarding the licensing of Government intellectual property. 15 U.S.C. § 3710a(b)(1) lists "personnel, services, and property" as the commodities that may be provided by the federal partner in a CRADA. Broadly construed, "property" encompasses intellectual property. The American Technology Preeminence Act of 1991 confirmed that intellectual property is included in section 3710a. The amended section 3710d(1) lists "personnel, services, facilities, equipment, intellectual property, or other resources as available from the collaborator." In effect, this allows a Government laboratory to license preexisting intellectual property to a CRADA partner without an explicit licensing agreement, and without public announcement. However, such an interpretation seems to interfere with the requirement that there be public disclosure prior to the granting of a license by the Government. Federal licensing rules, 37 C.F.R. Part 404.7, state that a Government invention cannot be licensed until three months after notice of its availability has been published in the *Federal Register*. Since the statutory language is explicit—"property" includes intellectual property, and the federal laboratory can provide property to the collaborator in a CRADA—it appears that the CRADA allows contracting parties to circumvent the licensing disclosure requirement.

VI. CONFLICT OF INTEREST

A. Statutory Requirements

A major legal problem inherent in the development of potentially useful commercial goods by Government employees is the possibility of a conflict of interest. A conflict of interest exists when a Government employee's personal stake in a matter is in tension with the Government's desired outcome. The conflicts of interest requirements in the Stevenson-Wydler Technology Innovation Act of 1980 is specified by 15 U.S.C. § 3710a(c), as follows—

Contract considerations.

(3)(A) Any agency using the authority given it under subsection (a) shall review standards of conduct for its employees for resolving potential conflicts of interest to make sure they adequately establish guidelines for situations likely to arise through the use of this authority, including but not limited to cases where present or former employees or their partners negotiate licenses or assignments of titles to inventions or negotiate cooperative research and development agreements with Federal agencies (including the agency with which the employee involved is or was formerly employed).

(B) If, in implementing subparagraph (A), an agency is unable to resolve potential conflicts of interest within its current statutory framework, it shall propose necessary statutory changes to be forwarded to its authorizing committees in Congress.

B. Employee Conflict of Interest

Government laboratory employees are subject to a variety of ethics laws. Each federal department and agency has conflict-of-interest guidelines and ethics officers. Generally, employees who interface with the private sector are considered more susceptible to conflicts of interest, and are often given special guidance. The guidance provided the Designated Representative of the Authorized Departmental Officer in a Department of Agriculture CRADA is typical:

a. You and your blood relatives that are members of your household may not have any financial interest that may be directly affected by the Cooperator without Agency approval. Financial interests are instruments of financial debt, for example, stocks, or bonds.

b. You and your blood relatives that are members of your household may not be actually employed by or receive promises of employment from the Cooperator.

c. You and your blood relatives that are members of your household may not have nonofficial work-related connections with the Cooperator that have or may have had a real or potential personal financial benefit without Agency's approval.

d. Should you have any questions concerning conflict of interest, feel free to contact your Ethics Officer.

The Public Heath Service Policy, Chapter 402 of the Technology Transfer Manual, provides for the completion of a conflicts of interest and fair access form by the principal investigator to assure that all proposed collaborations are free from real and apparent conflicts of interest. This form is reviewed by the applicable agency ethics officer for compliance with all laws, regulations and agency policy, and by team that reviews all CRADA awards. See, Sharon Smith Holson, "Contact with the FDA—Ground Rules for Industry and Constraints for Agency Personnel when Interacting with Industry," 48 Food & Drug L.J. 35 (1993). This serves to underscore the gravity of the conflicts-of-interest problem: the CRADA is meant to be negotiated and entered into at the laboratory level precisely to avoid a lengthy formal review process.

1. Improper Use of Government Intellectual Property

Conflicts of interest may arise in the course of employment. Often this involves negotiations and the award of contracts. Parties negotiating a contract may have financial incentives that are conflict with the interests of the Government. For instance, a laboratory employee who developed an invention might be in charge of negotiating license fees for the use of the invention. In the process, the employee would be negotiating his own royalty rate and the natural desire to maximize royalties might conflict with the Government's desire to commercialize the invention as efficiently as possible. In such a situation, the Government wants a fair return on its research investment, but it is not looking to maximize profits, as the inventor might be.

The Stevenson-Wydler Act created another potential conflict of interest. Under these laws, technology transfer efforts are considered in employee evaluations. A laboratory director may try to "force" a technology transfer, entering into imprudent agreements to bolster the laboratory's CRADA award record.

2. Improper Business Contracts

An improper business contact between a federal laboratory and a private sector entity is the other major problem suggested by the technology transfer system. These are usually cases in which a laboratory employee is in some way promoting a private business derived from the employee's Government research. Such conflicts can take the form of "the use of Government resources, interference with [Government] duties, the transfer of proprietary data, and [a greater financial interest in his spin-off business than in his job," Sharon Smith Holson, "Contact with the FDA—Ground Rules for Industry and Constraints for Agency Personnel when Interacting: with Industry," 48 Food & Drag L.J. 35 (1993). An employee might use laboratory facilities to develop business products, or even use ideas developed at the lab to drive a sideline business venture. Alternatively, a laboratory employee (or a relative) might funnel work from the research facility to the business.

3. Government Patent Licensing

The Bayh-Dole Act provides explicit authority for the Government to license patents owned by the Government. Most of these patents resulted from inventions made by Government employees although the Government may also obtain patents on inventions made by its contractors, but for the most part since contractors have a prior right to retain the ownership of these inventions the Government only obtains the ownership rights in inventions that have been rejected by the contractor. These inventions seldom are of commercial value, except for inventions made by contractors' operating Government-owned laboratories where the Government has a greater opportunity to obtain ownership rights in inventions.

Sections 206, 208 and 209 of the title 35 of the U.S. Code provide for the issuance of regulations by the Department of Commerce for the patenting and licensing of Government-owned inventions. These licensing requirements have been implemented by the Department of Commerce (DOC) (37 C.F.R. § 404, Licensing of Government Owned Inventions, Appendix 4). These DOC regulations provide for the grant of non-exclusive, exclusive and partially exclusive licenses in Government-owned patents or patent applications by the agency having custody of the invention. Prior publication of availability in the *Federal Register* is required before an exclusive and partially exclusive license may be granted. In addition, a few agencies have published their own licensing regulations. See 32 C.F.R. § 746 (Navy), 14 C.F.R. § 1425.200 (NASA), and 10 C.F.R. § 781 (DOE).

The General Accounting Office (GAO) has studied the results of six agencies' invention licensing activities (NIH, NASA, Army, USAF, Navy and DOE) during fiscal years 1996, 1997 and 1998 and has reported the following information:

The total royalties received by these agencies over 3 years amounted to $107.5 million with NIH accounting for 95% of these royalties.

The number of new licenses issued by these agencies have remained constant 279 in fiscal year 1996, 292 in fiscal year 1997 and 295 in fiscal year 1998.

NIH had 71.1% of the total 1,391 active licenses granted by these agencies.

73.2% of the 634 licenses granted during these three fiscal years were non-exclusive.

Most licenses, 59.8% of those granted during these three fiscal years, were granted to small businesses.

See Technology Transfer, Number and Characteristics of Inventions Licensed by Six Federal Agencies, General Accounting Office, June 1999, GAO-99-173.

4. Royalty Sharing

As to sharing royalties with inventors, the Government's basic royalty-sharing requirements are found at 15 U.S.C. § 3710c. Pertinent portions read:

(a) *In general.*

(1) Except as provided in paragraphs (2) and (4), any royalties or other payments received by a Federal agency from the licensing and assignment of inventions under agreements entered into by Federal laboratories under section 12 [15 U.S.C. § 3710a], and from the licensing of inventions of Federal laboratories under section 207 of title 35, United States Code, or under any other provision of law, shall be retained by the laboratory which produced the invention and shall be disposed of as follows:

(A)(i)The head of the agency or laboratory, or such individual's designee, shall pay each year the first $2,000, and thereafter at least 15 percent, of the royalties or other payments to the inventor or co-inventors.

(ii) An agency or laboratory may provide appropriate incentives, from royalties, or other payments, to laboratory employees who are not an inventor of such inventions but who substantially increased the technical value of such inventions.

(iii) The agency or laboratory shall retain the royalties and other payments received from an invention until the agency or laboratory makes payments to employees of a laboratory under clause (i) or (ii).

(B) The balance of the royalties or other payments shall be transferred by the agency to its laboratories, with the majority share of the royalties or other payments from any invention going to the laboratory where the invention occurred. The royalties or other payments so transferred to any laboratory may be used or obligated by that laboratory during the fiscal year in which they are received or during the succeeding fiscal year—

(i) to reward scientific, engineering, and technical employees of the laboratory, including developers of sensitive or classified technology, regardless of whether the technology has commercial applications;

(ii) to further scientific exchange among the laboratories of the agency;

(iii) for education and training of employees consistent with the research and development missions and objectives of the agency or laboratory, and for other activities that increase the potential for transfer of the technology of the laboratories of the agency;

(iv) for payment of expenses incidental to the administration and licensing of intellectual property by the agency or laboratory with respect to inventions made at that laboratory, including the fees or other costs for the services of other agencies, persons, or organizations for intellectual property management and licensing services; or

(v) for scientific research and development consistent with the research and development missions and objectives of the laboratory.

(C) All royalties or other payments retained by the agency or laboratory after payments have been made pursuant to subparagraphs (A) and (B) that is unobligated and unexpended at the end of the second fiscal year succeeding the fiscal year in which the royalties and other payments were received shall be paid into the Treasury.

(2) If, after payments to inventors under paragraph (1), the royalties or other payments received by an agency in any fiscal year exceed 5 percent of the budget of the Government-operated laboratories of the agency for that year, 75 percent of such excess shall be paid to the Treasury of the United States and the remaining 25 percent may be used or obligated under paragraph (1)(B). Any funds not so used shall be paid into the Treasury of the United States.

(3) Any payment made to an employee under this section shall be in addition 'to the regular pay of the employee and to any other awards made to the employee, and shall not affect the entitlement of the employee to any regular pay, annuity, or award to which he is otherwise entitled or for which he is otherwise eligible or limit the amount thereof. Any payment made to an inventor as such shall continue after the inventor leaves the laboratory or agency. Payments made under this section shall not exceed $150,000 per year to any one person, unless the President approves a larger award (with the excess over $150,000 being treated as a Presidential award under section 4504 of title 5, United States Code).

(4) A Federal agency receiving royalties or other payment a result of invention management services performed for another Federal agency or laboratory under section 207 of title 35, United States Code, may retain such royalties or payment to the extent required to offset the payment to inventors under clause (iv) of paragraph (1)(A), costs and expenses incurred under clause (i) of paragraph (1)(B), and the cost of foreign patenting and maintenance for any invention of the other agency. All royalties and other payment remaining af-

ter offsetting the payments to inventors, costs, and expenses described in the preceding sentence shall be transferred to the agency fix which the services were performed, for distribution in accordance with of paragraph (1)(B).

(b) *Certain assignments.* If the invention involved was one assigned to the Federal agency—(1) by a contractor, grantee, or participant, or an employee of a contractor, grantee, or participant, in an agreement or other arrangement with the agency, or (2) by an employee of the agency who was not working in the laboratory at the time the invention was made, the agency unit that was involved in such assignment shall be considered to be a laboratory for purposes of this section.

15 U.S.C. § 3710c promises a share of the profits to inventing employees. However, under the current statutory scheme royalties are not a very compelling incentive. Individual laboratories are permitted to set up royalty-sharing agreements of various sorts. In any arrangement, under the changes to the Stevenson-Wydler Act in 1996 the inventors must receive at least the first $2,000 of the royalties received by the Government during each year, and thereafter at least 15 percent of all income arising from the invention. Government royalty payments now top out at $150,000 per year. While this is a substantial figure, it vastly undervalues the commercial potential of some inventions.

This change in 1996 was described to the House (National Technology Transfer and Advancement Act of 1995, House of Representatives, Congressional Record, 104th Cong., 2nd Sess., Page H1264, February 27, 1996) as follows—

Section 5. Distribution of income from intellectual property received by Federal laboratories. Requires that agencies must pay federal inventors each year the first $2,000 and thereafter at least 15% of the royalties received by the agency for the inventions made by the employee. Increases an inventor's maximum royalty award to S 150,000 per year. Allows for rewarding other laboratory personnel involved in the project, permits agencies to pay for related administrative and legal costs, and provides a significant new incentive by allowing the laboratory to use royalties for related research in the laboratory. Provides for federal laboratories to return all unobligated and unexpended royalty revenue to the Treasury after the end of the second fiscal year after the year which the royalties were earned. No trade secrets or commercial or financial information that is privileged or confidential, under the meaning of section 552(b)(4) of title 5, United States Code, which is obtained in the conduct of research or as a result of activities under this Act [15 U.S.C. §§ 3701 et seq.] from a non-Federal party participating in a cooperative research and development agreement shall be disclosed.

Royalties are not the only financial incentive employed by the Government to promote technology transfer. 15 U.S.C. § 3710b requires laboratories with over $50,000,000 in R&D funds to set up award programs (1) for successful or useful inventions, and (2) for technology transfer efforts. Though these awards are probably not all that substantial compared to potential patent royalty payments, the law does address the GAO finding that scientists are often motivated by recognition and accolades as much as by the promise of financial rewards.

Section 3710b. Rewards for scientific, engineering, and technical personnel of federal agencies.

The head of each Federal agency that is making expenditures at a rate of more than $50,000,000 per fiscal year for research and development in its Government-operated laboratories shall use the appropriate statutory authority to develop and implement a cash awards program to reward its scientific, engineering, and technical personnel for—

(1) inventions, innovations, computer software, or other outstanding scientific or technological contributions of value to the United States due to commercial application or due to contributions to missions of the Federal agency or the Federal Government, or

(2) exemplary activities that promote the domestic transfer of science and technology development within the Federal Government and result in utilization of such science and technology by American industry or business, universities, State or local governments, or other non-Federal parties.

The Gallo AIDS blood test made royalties of $25.2 million for NIH between 1987 and 1991, U.S. GAO Technology Transfer: Barriers Limit Royalty Sharing's Effectiveness, GAO/RCED-93-6 30 (December 1992). The test's inventor received $100,000 per year during this period—less than 2 percent of the revenues collected by NIH. NIH is the most successful of all the agencies in obtaining royalties on their inventions.

The Government is searching for ways to administer royalties without creating conflicts of interest, to reconcile the profit motive with conflict-of-interest law. In keeping with the underlying philosophy that guides technology transfer law, it is assumed that some financial incentive is necessary to motivate technology transfer. This is because technology transfer is a function unrelated to the scientific pursuits of scientists and laboratory managers. Scientists have generally reported that their incentives to perform research derive from publication, recognition and other forms of prestige award. The profit motive plays a secondary role. However, a financial incentive is appropriate, because the ultimate result of a successful transfer will be a profitable new device or product. The problem is that the receipt of money from outside sources may distort basic working incentives, perhaps leading Government scientists to hold out on new research ideas, to engage in unsound scientific practices in order to receive royalty rewards, or to shift research avenues towards subjects with a high profit potential but little scientific merit.

One conflict of interest question revolved around the requirements of 18 U.S.C. § 208, which makes it a criminal act for an employee of the Government to take part in matters in which he has a financial interest. If a Government employee-inventor assigned his invention rights to the Government which in mm licensed the invention to a third party for royalties, could the employee continue to work on the invention without violating section 208? In an opinion of the Department of Justice, Office of Legal Counsel (OLC), 1993 OLC LEXIS 3, September 1993, OLC held that royalty payments to federal employees was considered to be federal compensation received directly from the Government and not from the licensee and, therefore, was not a "financial interest" under section 208. Therefore, the employee-inventors could continue to work on their invention including the commercialization of their inventions and working on such invention under a CRADA. Where the employee-inventors have assigned the domestic rights in their invention to the Government but have obtained the foreign rights thereto and have licensed a third party under the foreign rights, they are barred from working on a CRADA with such third party by section 208.

5. GOCO Conflicts

The problem can be cast in terms of agency theory. Principal-agent theory focuses on situations in which a principal (here, a Government agency) uses an agent (a laboratory contractor-director) to accomplish the Government's (i.e., the principal) goal of technology transfer. In a principal-agent relationship, parties often have divergent interests and asymmetrical access to information. These dichotomies give rise to conflicts of interest, situations in which the agent has preferences that do not match those of the principal.

Conflict of interest is of special concern in laboratory facilities owned by the Government but operated by private contractors. The temptation to favor one's business allies and disfavor competing firms is manifest. In an attempt to remedy this problem, the National Competitiveness; Technology Transfer Act required an additional term in all GOCO management-and-operation contracts, clarifying the conflict-of-interest standard to which contractor employees should be held in a CRADA. The language of this clause is left to the federal agency involved.

The National Competitiveness Technology Transfer Act (Section 3133(d) of P.L. 101-189, as amended by P.L. 101-510, div. A, title VIII, Sec. 828(a), Nov. 5, 1990, 104 Stat. 1607, provided that:

(1) Not later than 150 days after the date of enactment of this Act (Nov. 29, 1989), each agency which has contracted with a non-Federal entity to operate a Government-owned laboratory shall propose for inclusion in that laboratory's operating contract, to the extent not already included and subject to paragraph (6), appropriate contract provisions that—

a. establish technology transfer, including cooperative research and development agreements, as a mission for the laboratory under section 11 (a)(1) of the Stevenson-Wydler Technology Innovation Act of 1980 (15 U.S.C. § 3710(a)(1));

(B) describe the respective obligations and responsibilities of the agency and the laboratory with respect to this part (part C (Sec. 3131-3133) of title XXXI of div. C of Pub. L. 101-189, see Short Title of 1989 Amendment note under section 3701 of this title) and section 12 of the Stevenson-Wydler Technology Innovation Act of 1980 (15 U.S.C. § 3710a);

(C) require that, except as provided in paragraph (2), no employee of the laboratory shall have a substantial role (including an advisory role) in the preparation, negotiation, or approval of a cooperative research and development agreement if, to such employee's knowledge—

(i) such employee, or the spouse, child, parent, sibling, or partner of such employee, or an organization (other than the laboratory) in which such employee serves as an officer, director, trustee, partner, or employee—(I) holds a financial interest in any entity, other than the laboratory, that has a substantial interest in the preparation, negotiation, or approval of the cooperative research and development agreement; or (II) receives a gift or gratuity from any entity, other than the laboratory, that has a substantial interest in the preparation, negotiation, or approval of the cooperative research and development agreement; or

(ii) a financial interest in any entity, other than the laboratory, that has a substantial interest in the preparation, negotiation, or approval of the cooperative research and development agreement, is held by any person or organization with whom such employee is negotiating or has any arrangement concerning prospective employment;

(D) require that each employee of the laboratory who negotiates or approves a cooperative research and development agreement shall certify to the agency that the circumstances described in subparagraph (C)(i) and (ii) do not apply to such employee;

(E) require the laboratory to widely disseminate information on opportunities to participate with the laboratory in technology transfer, including cooperative research and development agreements; and

(F) provides for an accounting of all royalty or other income received under cooperative research and development agreements.

(2) The requirements described in paragraph (1)(C) and (D) shall not apply in a case where the negotiating or approving employee advises the agency that reviewed the applicable joint work statement under section 12(c)(5)(C)(i) of the Stevenson-Wydler Technology Innovation Act of 1980 (15 U.S.C. § 3710a(c)(5)(C)(i)) in advance of the matter in which he is to participate and the nature of any financial interest described in paragraph (1)(C), and where the agency employee determines that such financial interest is not so substantial as to be considered likely to affect the integrity of the laboratory employee's service in that matter.

(3) Not later than 180 days after the date of enactment of this Act (Nov. 29, 1989), each agency which has contracted with a non-Federal entity to operate a Government-owned laboratory shall submit a report to the Congress which includes a copy of each contract provision amended pursuant to this subsection.

(4) No Government-owned, contractor-operated laboratory may enter into a cooperative research and development agreement under section 12 of the Stevenson-Wydler Technology Innovation Act of 1980 (15 U.S.C. § 3710a) unless—

(A) that laboratory's operating contract contains the provisions described in paragraph (1)(A) through (F); or

(B) such laboratory agrees in a separate writing to be bound by the provisions described in paragraph (1)(A)through (F).

(5) Any contract for a Government-owned, contractor-operated laboratory entered into after the expiration of 150 days after the date of enactment of this Act (Nov. 29, 1989) shall contain the provisions described in paragraph (1)(A) through (F).

(6) Contract provisions referred to in paragraph (1) shall include only such provisions as are necessary to carry out paragraphs (1) and (2) of this subsection.

Under DOE's GOCO conflict-of-interest clause, the contractor is required to "develop implementing procedures that seek to avoid employee and organizational conflict of interest, in the conduct of its technology transfer activities." These procedures must include provisions which:

1. Ensure employee competency, conduct and integrity, in connection with the CRADA activity;

2. Review and approve employee activities so as to avoid conflicts of interest arising from commercial utilization activities relating to Contractor-developed Intellectual Property;

3. Conduct work performed using royalties so as to avoid interference with or adverse effects on ongoing DOE projects and programs;

4. Conduct activities relating to commercial utilization of Contractor-developed Intellectual Property so as to avoid interference with or adverse effects on user facility or WFO [reimbursed Work For Others] activities of the Contractor;

5. Conduct DOE funded projects and programs so as to avoid the: appearance of conflicts of interest or actual conflicts of interest with non-Government funded work;

6. Notify the Contracting Officer with respect to any new work to be performed under the Contract for the Department or other Federal agencies where the new work or proposal involves Intellectual Property in which the Contractor has obtained or intends to request or elect title;

7. Except as provided elsewhere in this Contract, obtain the approval of the Contracting Officer for any licensing of or assignment of title to Intellectual Property rights by the Contractor to any business or corporate affiliate of the Contractor;

8. Obtain the approval of the Contracting Officer prior to any assignment, exclusive: licensing, or option for exclusive licensing, of Intellectual Property to any current of former Laboratory employee or consultant;

9. Notify non-Federal sponsors of WFO activities, or non-Federal users of user facilities, of any relevant Intellectual Property interest of the Contractor prior to execution of WFOs or user agreements.

a.   Section 800 Panel Proposals

The 1992-1993 DOD Acquisition Law Advisory Panel (Section 800 of the 1992 National Defense Authorization Act, P.L. 102-585) proposed two changes in the current law. First, it proposed to erect a firewall between negotiators and those with a financial stake in the negotiation. At least from the Government's side, those researchers who may stand to profit from a CRADA or licensing agreement are permitted to involve themselves in the negotiation of those agreements only in limited circumstances. However, the panel draws a distinction between negotiation and commercialization. The panel's second recommendation is—

> that section 3710a of the Federal Technology Transfer Act be amended to provide that employees or former employees may assist contractors in commercializing inventions, notwithstanding that such employees may have received, or may subsequently be entitled to receive, royalties: pursuant to section 3710c. This will clarify that such royalties, in and of themselves, do not constitute a conflict of interest. Recognizing that there are some situations where royalties should be considered a conflict of interest, the proposed amendment includes a limiting proviso that royalties may be considered a financial interest if the inventor or author participated in the selection of the collaborating party to the cooperative research and development agreement or in the negotiation of the licensing agreement.

Acquisition Law Advisory Panel (Section 800 Panel), "Streamlining Defense Acquisition Laws: Report of the Acquisition Law Advisory Panel to the United States Congress," Chapter 5: Intellectual Property 8 (January 1993). The Panel's major concern is improper use of Government intellectual property: conflicts of interest regarding the development of inventions and associated agreements. Improper business contacts are involved only in that the mere existence of a business contact does not imply a conflict of interest.

b. GAO Proposals

In a report to Congress, GAO suggests a Government-wide uniform royalty formula, modeled on a system successfully practiced by the DOD and NASA. The system gives the inventor a lump sum, the first $1000 or more in revenues resulting from his invention. The inventor then receives a royalty on later sales (on the order of 30 percent), to a statutory maximum of $100,000 per year. It is believed that such a system both increases inventive incentives and decreases conflict-of-interest problems, the latter by eliminating the need for individual royalty negotiations, U.S. GAO, Technology Transfer: Barriers Limit Royalty Sharing's Effectiveness, GAO/RCED-93-6 63 (December 1992). The DOD royalty policy, as described in Army Regulation 70-57 ¶ 2-5 and ¶ 2-9 (1991), awards employee inventors the first $1000 in invention revenues, and 20 percent of all royalties received by the Government thereafter, to the statutory maximum of $100,000. See also Army Regulation 672-20.

C. Former Employee Conflict of Interest

Conflict of interest can also occur after an employee has ceased to work for the Government. In this case, agency theory ceases to apply, since the Government and the employee no longer have a principal-agent relationship. It is likely that the employee still has to the Government, especially in the case of employee scientists, contract officials and military personnel.

A major category of possible malfeasance mirrors the "improper business contacts" discussed above for current employees. Situations might involve a former employee using contacts at a laboratory to secure favorable business or development deals.

The n-CHIP controversy—a case of improper business contacts—is a good example of the problems inherent in holding contractors to Government ethics standards. It also highlights the conflicts that arise at the juncture between academia and the market.

In 1988, Lawrence Livermore National Laboratories (LLNL) (a DOE laboratory operated for DOE under a contract with the University of California) attempted to license a microprocessor technology with the potential to produce supercomputers the size of cigarette packages. An unknown computer concern called n-CHIP, comprising three former LLNL scientists, landed the exclusive rights to the new technology. Another computer company, Quadrant, protested the award. Quadrant argued that the ties between n-CHIP and LLNL, coupled with the lack of public notice, constituted a "conspiracy" between the two principals. LLNL was also accused of not informing the DOE of Quadrant's interest in the technology before allowing DOE to sign off on the patent waiver. Quadrant argued that there was a conflict of interest involved in the licensing proceedings between LLNL and n-CHIP. The DOE Inspector General eventually agreed.

The case is not wholly one-sided. At heart, Quadrant was arguing that a nonexclusive licensing of the technology would be more effective in ensuring that the technology reached the marketplace. Although the Inspector General sided with Quadrant on the conflict-of-interest issue, the question of the most efficient way to bring the product to market is not addressed. As with antitrust law, it is possible that an overzealous adherence to formalistic definitions of suspect categories (i.e., "conflict of interest") may work at cross purposes to the overarching intentions of technology transfer law (that is, to ensure the widest possible dissemination of Government technology into the private sector). See Jeff Barber & Dave Kramer, "Company Charges Conspiracy at Livermore," Inside Energy/With Fed. Lands, September 18, 1989; David Kramer, "IG Finds Labs Failed to Follow it: [sic] Own Policies in Licensing n-CHIP," Inside Energy/With Fed. Lands, October 25, 1993.

APPENDIX 1

EXECUTIVE ORDER NO. 12591
FACILITATING ACCESS TO SCIENCE AND TECHNOLOGY

Source: The provisions of Executive Order 12591 of Apr. 10, 1987, appear at 52 FR 13414, 3 CFR, 1987 Comp., p. 220, unless otherwise noted.

By the authority vested in me as President by the Constitution and laws of the United States of America, including the Federal Technology Transfer Act of 1986 (Public Law 99-502), the Trademark Clarification Act of 1984 (Public Law 98-620), and the University and Small Business Patent Procedure Act of 1980 (Public Law 96-517), and in order to ensure that Federal agencies and laboratories assist universities and the private sector in broadening our technology base by moving new knowledge from the research laboratory into the development of new products and processes, it is hereby ordered as follows:

Sec. 1. *Transfer of Federally Funded Technology.*

(a) The head of each Executive department and agency, to the extent permitted by law, shall encourage and facilitate collaboration among Federal laboratories, State and local governments, universities, and the private sector, particularly small business, in order to assist in the transfer of technology to the marketplace.

(b) The head of each Executive department and agency shall, within overall funding allocations and to the extent permitted by law:

(1) delegate authority to its government-owned, government-operated Federal laboratories:

(A) to enter into cooperative research and development agreements with other Federal laboratories, State and local governments, universities, and the private sector; and

(B) to license, assign, or waive rights to intellectual property developed by the laboratory either under such cooperative research or development agreements and from within individual laboratories.

(2) identify and encourage persons to act as conduits between and among Federal laboratories, universities, and the private sector for the transfer of technology developed from federally funded research and development efforts;

(3) ensure that State and local governments, universities, and the private sector are provided with information on the technology, expertise, and facilities available in Federal laboratories;

169

(4) promote the commercialization, in accord with my Memorandum to the Heads of Executive Departments and Agencies of February 18, 1983, of patentable results of federally funded research by granting to all contractors, regardless of size, the title to patents made in whole or in part with Federal funds, in exchange for royalty-free use by or on behalf of the government;

(5) implement, as expeditiously as practicable, royalty-sharing programs with inventors who were employees of the agency at the time their inventions were made and cash award programs; and

(6) cooperate, under policy guidance provided by the Office of Federal Procurement Policy, with the heads of other affected departments and agencies in the development of a uniform policy permitting Federal contractors to retain rights to software, engineering drawings, and other technical data generated by Federal grants and contracts, in exchange for royalty-free use by or on behalf of the government.

Sec. 2. *Establishment of the Technology Share Program.* The Secretaries of Agriculture, Commerce, Energy, and Health and Human Services and the Administrator of the National Aeronautics and Space Administration shall select one or more of their Federal laboratories to participate in the Technology Share Program. Consistent with its mission and policies and within its overall funding allocation in any year, each Federal laboratory so selected shall:

(a) Identify areas of research and technology of potential importance to long-term national economic competitiveness and in which the laboratory possesses special competence and/or unique facilities;

(b) Establish a mechanism through which the laboratory performs research in areas identified in Section 2(a) as a participant of a consortium composed of United States industries and universities. All consortia so established shall have, at a minimum, three individual companies that conduct the majority of their business in the United States; and

(c) Limit its participation in any consortium so established to the use of laboratory personnel and facilities. However, each laboratory may also provide financial support generally not to exceed 25 percent of the total budget for the activities of the consortium. Such financial support by any laboratory in all such consortia shall be limited to a maximum of $5 million per annum.

Sec. 3. *Technology Exchange—Scientists and Engineers.* The Executive Director of the President's Commission on Executive Exchange shall assist Federal agencies, where appropriate, by developing and implementing an exchange program whereby scientists and engineers in the private sector may take temporary assignments in Federal laboratories, and scientists and engineers in Federal laboratories may take temporary assignments in the private sector.

Sec. 4. *International Science and Technology.* In order to ensure that the United States benefits from and fully exploits scientific research and technology developed abroad,

(a) The head of each Executive department and agency, when negotiating or entering into cooperative research and development agreements and licensing arrangements with foreign persons or industrial organizations (where these entities are directly or indirectly controlled by a foreign company or government), shall, in consultation with the United States Trade Representative, give appropriate consideration:

(1) to whether such foreign companies or governments permit and encourage United States agencies, organizations, or persons to enter into cooperative research and development agreements and licensing arrangements on a comparable basis;

(2) to whether those foreign governments have policies to protect the United States intellectual property rights; and

(3) where cooperative research will involve data, technologies, or products subject to national security export controls under the laws of the United States, to whether those foreign governments have adopted adequate measures to prevent the transfer of strategic technology to destinations prohibited under such national security export controls, either through participation in the Coordinating Committee for Multilateral Export Controls (COCOM) or through other international agreements to which the United States and such foreign governments are signatories.

(b) The Secretary of State shall develop a recruitment policy that encourages scientists and engineers from other Federal agencies, academic institutions, and industry to apply for assignments in embassies of the United States; and

(c) The Secretaries of State and Commerce and the Director of the National Science Foundation shall develop a central mechanism for the prompt and efficient dissemination of science and technology information developed abroad to users in Federal laboratories, academic institutions, and the private sector on a fee-for-service basis.

Sec. 5. *Technology Transfer from the Department of Defense.* Within 6 months of the date of this Order, the Secretary of Defense shall identify a list of funded technologies that would be potentially useful to United States industries and universities. The Secretary shall then accelerate efforts to make these technologies more readily available to United States industries and universities.

Sec. 6. *Basic Science and Technology Centers.* The head of each Executive department and agency shall examine the potential for including the establishment of university research centers in engineering, science, or technology in the strategy and planning for any future research and development programs. Such university centers shall be jointly funded by the Federal Government, the private sector, and, where appropriate, the States and shall focus on areas of fundamental research and technology that are both scientifically promising and have the potential to contribute to the Nation's long-term economic competitiveness.

Sec. 7. *Reporting Requirements.* (a) Within 1 year from the date of this Order, the Director of the Office of Science and Technology Policy shall convene an interagency task force comprised of the heads of representative agencies and the directors of representative Federal laboratories, or their designees, in order to identify and disseminate creative approaches to technology transfer from Federal laboratories. The task force will report to the President on the progress of and problems with technology transfer from Federal laboratories.

(b) Specifically, the report shall include:

(1) a listing of current technology transfer programs and an assessment of the effectiveness of these programs;

(2) identification of new or creative approaches to technology transfer that might serve as model programs for Federal laboratories;

(3) criteria to assess the effectiveness and impact on the Nation's economy of planned or future technology transfer efforts; and

(4) a compilation and assessment of the Technology Share Program established in Section 2 and, where appropriate, related cooperative research and development venture programs.

Sec. 8. *Relation to Existing Law.* Nothing in this Order shall affect the continued applicability of any existing laws or regulations relating to the transfer of United States technology to other nations. The head of any Executive department or agency may exclude from consideration, under this Order, any technology that would be, if transferred, detrimental to the interests of national security.

TITLE 15—COMMERCE AND TRADE
CHAPTER 63—TECHNOLOGY INNOVATION

Sec. 3710a. Cooperative research and development agreements

(a) *General authority*

Each Federal agency may permit the director of any of its Government-operated Federal laboratories, and, to the extent provided in an agency-approved joint work statement, the director of any of its Government-owned, contractor-operated laboratories—

(1) to enter into cooperative research and development agreements on behalf of such agency (subject to subsection (c) of this section) with other Federal agencies; units of State or local government; industrial organizations (including corporations, partnerships, and limited partnerships, and industrial development organizations); public and private foundations; nonprofit organizations (including universities); or other persons (including licensees of inventions owned by the Federal agency); and

(2) to negotiate licensing agreements under section 207 of title 35, or under other authorities (in the case of a Government-owned, contractor-operated laboratory, subject to subsection (c) of this section) for inventions made or other intellectual property developed at the laboratory and other inventions or other intellectual property that may be voluntarily assigned to the Government.

(b) *Enumerated authority*

(1) Under an agreement entered into pursuant to subsection (a)(1) of this section, the laboratory may grant, or agree to grant in advance, to a collaborating party patent licenses or assignments, or options thereto, in any invention made in whole or in part by a laboratory employee under the agreement, for reasonable compensation when appropriate. The laboratory shall ensure, through such agreement, that the collaborating party has the option to choose an exclusive license for a pre-negotiated field of use for any such invention under the agreement or, if there is more than one collaborating party, that the collaborating parties are offered the option to hold licensing rights that collectively encompass the rights that would be held under such an exclusive license by one party. In consideration for the Government's contribution under the agreement, grants under this paragraph shall be subject to the following explicit conditions:

(A) A nonexclusive, nontransferable, irrevocable, paid-up license from the collaborating party to the laboratory to practice the invention or have the invention practiced throughout the world by or on behalf of the Government. In the exercise of such license, the Government shall not publicly disclose trade secrets or commercial or financial information that is privileged or confidential within the meaning of section 552(b)(4) of title 5 or which would be considered as such if it had been obtained from a non-Federal party.

(B) If a laboratory assigns title or grants an exclusive license to such an invention, the Government shall retain the right—

(i) to require the collaborating party to grant to a responsible applicant a nonexclusive, partially exclusive, or exclusive license to use the invention in the applicant's licensed field of use, on terms that are reasonable under the circumstances; or

(ii) if the collaborating party fails to grant such a license, to grant the license itself.

(C) The Government may exercise its right retained under subparagraph (B) only in exceptional circumstances and only if the Government determines that—

(i) the action is necessary to meet health or safety needs that are not reasonably satisfied by the collaborating party;

(ii) the action is necessary to meet requirements for public use specified by Federal regulations, and such requirements are not reasonably satisfied by the collaborating party; or

(iii) the collaborating party has failed to comply with an agreement containing provisions described in subsection (c)(4)(B) of this section.

This determination is subject to administrative appeal and judicial review under section 203(2) of title 35.

(2) Under agreements entered into pursuant to subsection (a)(1) of this section, the laboratory shall ensure that a collaborating party may retain title to any invention made solely by its employee in exchange for normally granting the Government a nonexclusive, nontransferable, irrevocable, paid-up license to practice the invention or have the invention practiced throughout the world by or on behalf of the Government for research or other Government purposes.

(3) Under an agreement entered into pursuant to subsection (a)(1) of this section, a laboratory may—

(A) accept, retain, and use funds, personnel, services, and property from a collaborating party and provide personnel, services, and property to a collaborating party;

(B) use funds received from a collaborating party in accordance with subparagraph (A) to hire personnel to carry out the agreement who will not be subject to full-time-equivalent restrictions of the agency;

(C) to the extent consistent with any applicable agency requirements or standards of conduct, permit an employee or former employee of the laboratory to participate in an effort to commercialize an invention made by the employee or former employee while in the employment or service of the Government; and

      (D) waive, subject to reservation by the Government of a nonexclusive, irrevocable, paid-up license to practice the invention or have the invention practiced throughout the world by or on behalf of the Government, in advance, in whole or in part, any right of ownership which the Federal Government may have to any subject invention made under the agreement by a collaborating party or employee of a collaborating party.

      (4) A collaborating party in an exclusive license in any invention made under an agreement entered into pursuant to subsection (a)(1) of this section shall have the right of enforcement under chapter 29 of title 35.

      (5) A Government-owned, contractor-operated laboratory that enters into a cooperative research and development agreement pursuant to subsection (a)(1) of this section may use or obligate royalties or other income accruing to the laboratory under such agreement with respect to any invention only—

      (A) for payments to inventors;

      (B) for purposes described in clauses (i), (ii), (iii), and (iv) of section 3710c(a)(1)(B) of this title; and

      (C) for scientific research and development consistent with the research and development missions and objectives of the laboratory.

    (c) *Contract considerations*

      (1) A Federal agency may issue regulations on suitable procedures for implementing the provisions of this section; however, implementation of this section shall not be delayed until issuance of such regulations.

      (2) The agency in permitting a Federal laboratory to enter into agreements under this section shall be guided by the purposes of this chapter.

      (3)(A) Any agency using the authority given it under subsection (a) of this section shall review standards of conduct for its employees for resolving potential conflicts of interest to make sure they adequately establish guidelines for situations likely to arise through the use of this authority, including but not limited to cases where present or former employees or their partners negotiate licenses or assignments of titles to inventions or negotiate cooperative research and development agreements with Federal agencies (including the agency with which the employee involved is or was formerly employed).

      (B) If, in implementing subparagraph (A), an agency is unable to resolve potential conflicts of interest within its current statutory framework, it shall propose necessary statutory changes to be forwarded to its authorizing committees in Congress.

      (4) The laboratory director in deciding what cooperative research and development agreements to enter into shall—

(A) give special consideration to small business firms, and consortia involving small business firms; and

(B) give preference to business units located in the United States which agree that products embodying inventions made under the cooperative research and development agreement or produced through the use of such inventions will be manufactured substantially in the United States and, in the case of any industrial organization or other person subject to the control of a foreign company or government, as appropriate, take into consideration whether or not such foreign government permits United States agencies, organizations, or other persons to enter into cooperative research and development agreements and licensing agreements.

(5)(A) If the head of the agency or his designee desires an opportunity to disapprove or require the modification of any such agreement presented by the director of a Government-operated laboratory, the agreement shall provide a 30-day period within which such action must be taken beginning on the date the agreement is presented to him or her by the head of the laboratory concerned.

(B) In any case in which the head of an agency or his designee disapproves or requires the modification of an agreement presented by the director of a Government-operated laboratory under this section, the head of the agency or such designee shall transmit a written explanation of such disapproval or modification to the head of the laboratory concerned.

(C)(i) Except as provided in subparagraph (D), any agency which has contracted with a non-Federal entity to operate a laboratory shall review and approve, request specific modifications to, or disapprove a joint work statement that is submitted by the director of such laboratory within 90 days after such submission. In any case where an agency has requested specific modifications to a joint work statement, the agency shall approve or disapprove any resubmission of such joint work statement within 30 days after such resubmission, or 90 days after the original submission, whichever occurs later. No agreement may be entered into by a Government-owned, contractor-operated laboratory under this section before both approval of the agreement under clause (iv) and approval under this clause of a joint work statement.

(ii) In any case in which an agency which has contracted with a non-Federal entity to operate a laboratory disapproves or requests the modification of a joint work statement submitted under this section, the agency shall promptly transmit a written explanation of such disapproval or modification to the director of the laboratory concerned.

(iii) Any agency which has contracted with a non-Federal entity to operate a laboratory or laboratories shall develop and provide to such laboratory or laboratories one or more model cooperative research and development agreements, for the purposes of standardizing practices and procedures, resolving common legal issues, and enabling review of cooperative research and development agreements to be carried out in a routine and prompt manner.

(iv) An agency which has contracted with a non-Federal entity to operate a laboratory shall review each agreement under this section. Within 30 days after the presentation, by the director of the laboratory, of such agreement, the agency shall, on the basis of such review, approve or request specific modification to such agreement. Such agreement shall not take effect before approval under this clause.

(v) If an agency fails to complete a review under clause (iv) within the 30-day period specified therein, the agency shall submit to the Congress, within 10 days after the end of that 30-day period, a report on the reasons for such failure. The agency shall, at the end of each successive 30-day period thereafter during which such failure continues, submit to the Congress another report on the reasons for the continuing failure. Nothing in this clause relieves the agency of the requirement to complete a review under clause (iv).

(vi) In any case in which an agency which has contracted with a non-Federal entity to operate a laboratory requests the modification of an agreement presented under this section, the agency shall promptly transmit a written explanation of such modification to the director of the laboratory concerned.

(D)(i) Any non-Federal entity that operates a laboratory pursuant to a contract with a Federal agency shall submit to the agency any cooperative research and development agreement that the entity proposes to enter into with a small business firm and the joint work statement required with respect to that agreement.

(ii) A Federal agency that receives a proposed agreement and joint work statement under clause (i) shall review and approve, request specific modifications to, or disapprove the proposed agreement and joint work statement within 30 days after such submission. No agreement may be entered into by a Government-owned, contractor-operated laboratory under this section before both approval of the agreement and approval of a joint work statement under this clause.

(iii) In any case in which an agency which has contracted with an entity referred to in clause (i) disapproves or requests the modification of a cooperative research and development agreement or joint work statement submitted under that clause, the agency shall transmit a written explanation of such disapproval or modification to the head of the laboratory concerned.

(6) Each agency shall maintain a record of all agreements entered into under this section.

(7)(A) No trade secrets or commercial or financial information that is privileged or confidential, under the meaning of section 552(b)(4) of title 5, which is obtained in the conduct of research or as a result of activities under this chapter from a non-Federal party participating in a cooperative research and development agreement shall be disclosed.

(B) The director, or in the case of a contractor-operated laboratory, the agency, for a period of up to 5 years after development of information that results from research and development activities conducted under this chapter and that would be a trade secret or commercial or financial information that is privileged or confidential if the information had been obtained from a non-Federal party participating in a cooperative research and development agreement, may provide appropriate protections against the dissemination of such information, including exemption from subchapter II of chapter 5 of title 5.

(d) *Definitions*

As used in this section—

(1) the term "cooperative research and development agreement" means any agreement between one or more Federal laboratories and one or more non-Federal parties under which the Government, through its laboratories, provides personnel, services, facilities, equipment, intellectual property, or other resources with or without reimbursement (but not funds to non-Federal parties) and the non-Federal parties provide funds, personnel, services, facilities, equipment, intellectual property, or other resources toward the conduct of specified research or development efforts which are consistent with the missions of the laboratory; except that such term does not include a procurement contract or cooperative agreement as those terms are used in sections 6303, 6304, and 6305 of title 31;

(2) the term "laboratory" means—

(A) a facility or group of facilities owned, leased, or otherwise used by a Federal agency, a substantial purpose of which is the performance of research, development, or engineering by employees of the Federal Government;

(B) a group of Government-owned, contractor-operated facilities (including a weapon production facility of the Department of Energy) under a common contract, when a substantial purpose of the contract is the performance of research and development, or the production, maintenance, testing, or dismantlement of a nuclear weapon or its components, for the Federal Government; and

(C) a Government-owned, contractor-operated facility (including a weapon production facility of the Department of Energy) that is not under a common contract described in subparagraph (B), and the primary purpose of which is the performance of research and development, or the production, maintenance, testing, or dismantlement of a nuclear weapon or its components, for the Federal Government, but such term does not include any facility covered by Executive Order No. 12344, dated February 1, 1982, pertaining to the naval nuclear propulsion program;

(3) the term "joint work statement" means a proposal prepared for a Federal agency by the director of a Government-owned, contractor-operated laboratory describing the purpose and scope of a proposed cooperative research and development agreement, and assigning rights and responsibilities among the agency, the laboratory, and any other party or parties to the proposed agreement; and

(4) the term "weapon production facility of the Department of Energy" means a facility under the control or jurisdiction of the Secretary of Energy that is operated for national security purposes and is engaged in the production, maintenance, testing, or

dismantlement of a nuclear weapon or its components.

(e) *Determination of laboratory missions*

For purposes of this section, an agency shall make separate determinations of the mission or missions of each of its laboratories.

(f) *Relationship to other laws*

Nothing in this section is intended to limit or diminish existing authorities of any agency.

(g) *Principles*

In implementing this section, each agency which has contracted with a non-Federal entity to operate a laboratory shall be guided by the following principles:

(1) The implementation shall advance program missions at the laboratory, including any national security mission.

(2) Classified information and unclassified sensitive information protected by law, regulation, or Executive order shall be appropriately safeguarded.

DEPARTMENT OF DEFENSE
DIRECTIVE NO. 5535.3

May 21, 1999

DDR&E

SUBJECT: DoD Domestic Technology Transfer (T2) Program

References: (a) DoD Directive 5535.3, "Licensing of Government-Owned Inventions by the Department of Defense," November 2, 1973 (hereby canceled)

(b) Secretary of Defense Memorandum, "DoD Domestic Technology Transfer/Dual Use Technology Development," June 2, 1995 (hereby canceled)

(c) DoD 3200.12-R-4, "Domestic Technology Transfer Program Regulation," December 1988, authorized by DoD Directive 3200.12, February 11, 1983 (hereby canceled)

(d) Sections 3702, 3703, 3705, 3706, 3710, 3712, 3715 of title 15, United States Code

(e) through (k), see enclosure 1

1. REISSUANCE AND PURPOSE

This Directive:

1.1. Reissues reference (a) and supersedes references (b) and (c).

1.2. Implements, establishes policy, and assigns responsibility for DoD domestic T2 activities under reference (d), as they apply to the Department of Defense, and under 10 U.S.C. (reference (e)), as they apply to the T2 activities of the Department of Defense.

2. APPLICABILITY

This Directive applies to the Office of the Secretary of Defense (OSD), the Military Departments, the Defense Agencies, and the DoD Field Activities (hereafter referred to collectively as "the DoD Components").

3. DEFINITIONS

The following terms, used in this Directive, are defined in DoD Instruction 5535.8 (reference (f)):

3.1. Cooperative Research and Development Agreement (CRADA).

3.2. Laboratory (as broadly defined in 15 U.S.C. 3710a(d)(2)(A), reference (d), for this Directive).

3.3. Nonprofit institution (Sections 3703 and 3710(i) of reference (d) and E.O. 12999 (reference (g)) for this Directive).

3.3. Technical assistance.

3.4. T2.

4. POLICY

It is DoD policy that:

4.1. Consistent with national security objectives under 10 U.S.C. 2501 (reference (e)), domestic T2 activities are integral elements of DoD pursuit of the DoD national security mission and concurrently improve the economic, environmental, and social well-being of U.S. citizens (Section 3702 of reference (d)). Concurrently, T2 supports a strong industrial base that the Department of Defense may utilize to supply DoD needs. Those activities must have a high-priority role in all DoD acquisition programs and are recognized as a key activity of the DoD laboratories and all other DoD activities (such as test, logistics, and product centers and depots and arsenals) that may make use of or contribute to domestic T2.

4.2. Domestic T2 programs, including spin-off, dual use, and spin-on activities, make the best possible use of national scientific and technical capabilities to enhance the effectiveness of DoD forces and systems.

4.3. It is further DoD policy to:

4.3.1. Promote domestic T2 through a variety of activities, such as CRADAs, cooperative agreements, other transactions, education partnerships, State and local government partnerships, exchange of personnel, presentation of technical papers, and other ongoing DoD activities.

4.3.2. Promote domestic T2 through U.S. and foreign patenting, patent licensing, and protecting other intellectual property rights. DoD inventions applicable for licensing shall be publicized to accelerate transfer of technology to the domestic economy. T2 is of the greatest benefit when the patented invention is commercialized (35 U.S.C. 200 and 207, reference (h)).

4.3.3. Allow non-Federal entities to use independent research and development funding as a part of their contributions to domestic T2 activities, including CRADAs, cooperative arrangements, and other transactions (Subpart 31.205-18(e) of the FAR, reference (i)).

4.3.4. Include domestic T2 as a duty and responsibility in position descriptions for applicable scientific, engineering, management, and executive positions.

4.3.5. Allow CRADAs between a DoD Component and DoD contractors, in accordance with DoD conflict of interest rules (DoD Directive 5500.7, reference (j)) and export control laws and regulations.

4.3.6. Ensure that domestic transfers of technology are accomplished without actual or apparent personal or organizational conflicts of interest or violations of ethics standards.

4.3.7. Allow conduct of T2 activity with foreign persons, industrial organizations, or government R&D activities, in accordance with export control laws, regulations, and policies and laws, regulations and policies governing foreign military sales (FMS). Consideration should be given to whether or not the government of such persons or industrial organization allows similar relationships and whether such activities benefit the U.S. industrial base and are consistent with the U.S. export control and FMS frameworks (E.O. 12591, reference (k)).

4.3.8. Encourage domestic T2 by giving preference to U.S. small business firms, consortia involving U.S. small business firms, and firms located in the United States.

5. RESPONSIBILITIES

5.1. The Under Secretary of Defense for Acquisition and Technology shall ensure that the Director, Defense Research and Engineering, shall:

5.1.1. Implement 10 U.S.C. 2515 (reference (e)) to monitor all DoD R&D activities; identify DoD R&D activities using technologies and technology advancements that have potential non-DoD commercial application; serve as a clearinghouse for, coordinate, and otherwise help the transfer of technology to the U.S. private sector; assist private firms to resolve policy issues involved with the transfer of technology from the Department of Defense; and consult and coordinate with other Federal Departments on matters involving T2.

5.1.2. Serve as oversight authority for execution of all domestic T2 science and technology (S&T) matters and coordination with, as applicable, other DoD officials for matters under their oversight. As part of that oversight, the Director, Defense Research and Engineering, (DDR&E) shall define core domestic T2 S&T mechanisms and provide policy guidance for DoD Component investments in such mechanisms.

5.1.3. Develop policy for DoD Component participation in, and support of, Federal S&T domestic T2 programs.

5.1.4. Develop guidance for implementation of domestic T2 policy, to include coordination with other DoD officials for matters under their cognizance.

5.1.5. Coordinate input from the DoD Components and prepare reports to the Congress, as required by 15 U.S.C. (reference (d)) and reference (e), the Office of Management and

Budget, and others, as may be imposed by higher authority.

5.1.6. Ensure that the DoD Components establish T2 awards programs and make applicable T2 awards.

5.1.7. Ensure that the Administrator, Defense Technical Information Center (DTIC), maintains and provides development support for T2 databases useful to the Office of the DDR&E (ODDR&E) and the DoD Components.

5.2. The Secretaries of the Military Departments and the Heads of the other DoD Components , including the Directors of the Defense Agencies, under the OSD Principal Staff Assistants, shall:

5.2.1. Ensure that domestic T2 is a high priority in their organizations. That includes establishing processes to promote T2 and developing plans for improving T2 for matters under their oversight, to include specific objectives and milestones.

5.2.2. Provide inputs for reports, as required by the ODDR&E, including T2 transaction and program investment data to DTIC.

5.2.3. Develop personnel policies for R&D executives, managers, laboratory directors, scientists, and engineers that make domestic T2 a critical factor for consideration in promotions, a critical element in performance appraisals, and a duty and responsibility in position descriptions where applicable. Those policies also shall ensure that members of the Office of Research and Technology Applications (ORTA) staff are included in the overall laboratory and/or Agency and/or DoD Field Activity management development programs.

5.2.4. Execute a T2 education and training program for scientists and engineers and other personnel who may be involved in domestic T2.

5.2.5. Establish an awards program, including cash awards, to recognize domestic T2 accomplishments.

5.2.6. Institute policies for protecting inventions and other intellectual property arising from Federally supported R&D. That includes policies for patenting inventions, licensing the patented inventions, and maintaining the patents with commercial potential. Costs and expenses to acquire and maintain those patents shall be funded by the DoD Components. That shall not preclude collaborating parties from paying costs and expenses associated with protecting intellectual property rights.

5.2.7. Institute policies under which laboratories may be authorized to license, assign, or waive rights to intellectual property and distribute royalties and other payments, in accordance with DoD Instruction 5535.8 (reference (f)).

5.2.8. Implement marketing and outreach programs.

5.2.9. Provide support of mission-related domestic T2 activities with mission program element funds and ensure that domestic T2 programs have adequate staff and resources, giving particular attention to payment of salaries and travel expenses of scientific, engineering, legal, and ORTA personnel involved in T2. That includes costs and expenses associated with initiation and/or negotiation of CRADAs and other agreements.

5.2.10. Ensure implementation of all T2 functions, as required in 15 U.S.C. 3710(c) (reference (d)), by the ORTA or other domestic T2 focal points.

5.2.11. Allow use of partnership intermediaries to obtain domestic T2 support. Approval authority may be redelegated to the heads of the DoD laboratories.

5.2.12. Ensure that the directors and/or the commanders of laboratories make domestic T2 a high-priority element of their S&T programs by plan, budget, and execution.

5.2.13. Ensure that laboratories and other activities prepare applications assessments for selected R&D projects that may have commercial applications.

5.2.14. Encourage laboratories to provide technical assistance services, including help by technical volunteers, to State and local governments, school systems, and other organizations, where applicable.

5.3. The Heads of the DoD Components (other than the Secretaries of the Military Departments), including the Directors of the Defense Agencies, under the OSD Principal Staff Assistants, are delegated the authority of the Secretary of Defense to:

5.3.1. Loan, lease, or give research equipment or educationally useful Federal equipment, consistent with export control laws and regulations, which is excess to the needs of the laboratory to an educational institution or nonprofit institution for the conduct of technical and scientific education and research activities (Section 3710(i) of reference (d), and E.O. 12999 and 10 U.S.C. 2194, references (g) and (e)). That authority may be further delegated.

5.3.2. Enter into CRADAs with entities other than foreign governmental entities (Section 3710a of reference (d)). That authority may be further delegated.

6. INFORMATION REQUIREMENTS

The Secretaries of the Military Departments and the Heads of the other DoD Components shall provide inputs for reports, as required by the ODDR&E in paragraph 5.2.2., above, including T2 transaction and program investment data to the DTIC under Reports Control Symbol DDA&T(A)2020.

7. EFFECTIVE DATE

This Directive is effective immediately.

Enclosures - 1

E1. References, continued

E1. ENCLOSURE 1

REFERENCES, continued

(e) Sections 2501, 2506, 2514-2516, 2358, 2371, 2194, 2195 of title 10, United States Code

(f) DoD Instruction 5535.8, "DoD Technology Transfer Program Procedures," May 14, 1999

(g) Executive Order 12999, "Educational Technology: Ensuring Opportunity for All Children in the Next Century," April 17, 1996

(h) Sections 200 and 207-209 of title 35, United States Code

(i) Federal Acquisition Regulation, Subpart 31.205-18(e), "Independent Research and Development and Bid and Proposal Costs," current edition

(j) DoD Directive 5500.7, "Standards of Conduct," August 30, 1993

(k) Executive Order 12591, "Facilitating Access to Science and Technology," April 10 1987

TITLE 37—PATENTS, TRADEMARKS, AND COPYRIGHTS
CHAPTER IV—ASSISTANT SECRETARY FOR TECHNOLOGY POLICY,
DEPARTMENT OF COMMERCE PART 404—
LICENSING OF GOVERNMENT OWNED INVENTIONS
37 C.F.R. 404.1

---

37 C.F.R. § 404.1 Scope of part.

This part prescribes the terms, conditions, and procedures upon which a federally owned invention, other than an invention in the custody of the Tennessee Valley Authority, may be licensed. It supersedes the regulations at 41 CFR Subpart 101-4.1. This part does not affect licenses which (a) were in effect prior to July 1, 1981; (b) may exist at the time of the Government's acquisition of title to the invention, including those resulting from the allocation of rights to inventions made under Government research and development contracts; (c) are the result of an authorized exchange of rights in the settlement of patent disputes; or (d) are otherwise authorized by law or treaty.

37 C.F.R. § 404.2 Policy and objective.

It is the policy and objective of this subpart to use the patent system to promote the utilization of inventions arising from federally supported research or development.

37 C.F.R. § 404.3 Definitions.

(a) Federally owned invention means an invention, plant, or design which is covered by a patent, or patent application in the United States, or a patent, patent application, plant variety protection, or other form of protection, in a foreign country, title to which has been assigned to or otherwise vested in the United States Government.

(b) Federal agency means an executive department, military department, Government corporation, or independent establishment, except the Tennessee Valley Authority, which has custody of a federally owned invention.

(c) Small business firm means a small business concern as defined in section 2 of Pub. L. 85-536 *(15 U.S.C. 632)* and implementing regulations of the Administrator of the Small Business Administration.

(d) Practical application means to manufacture in the case of a composition or product, to practice in the case of a process or method, or to operate in the case of a machine or system; and, in each case, under such conditions as to establish that the invention is being utilized and that its benefits are to the extent permitted by law or Government regulations available to the public on reasonable terms.

(e) United States means the United States of America, its territories and possessions, the District of Columbia, and the Commonwealth of Puerto Rico.

37 C.F.R. § 404.4 Authority to grant licenses.

Federally owned inventions shall be made available for licensing as deemed appropriate in the public interest. Federal agencies having custody of federally owned inventions may grant nonexclusive, partially exclusive, or exclusive licenses thereto under this part.

37 C.F.R. § 404.5 Restrictions and conditions on all licenses granted under this part.

(a)(1) A license may be granted only if the applicant has supplied the Federal agency with a satifactory plan for development or marketing of the invention, or both, and with information about the applicant's capability to fulfill the plan.

(2) A license granting rights to use or sell under a federally owned invention in the United States shall normally be granted only to a licensee who agrees that any products embodying the invention or produced through the use of the invention will be manufactured substantially in the United States.

(b) Licenses shall contain such terms and conditions as the Federal agency determines are appropriate for the protection of the interests of the Federal Government and the public and are not in conflict with law or this part. The following terms and conditions apply to any license:

(1) The duration of the license shall be for a period specified in the license agreement, unless sooner terminated in accordance with this part.

(2) The license may be granted for all or less than all fields of use of the invention or in specified geographical areas, or both.

(3) The license may extend to subsidiaries of the licensee or other parties if provided for in the license but shall be nonassignable without approval of the Federal agency, except to the successor of that part of the licensee's business to which the invention pertains.

(4) The licensee may provide the license the right to grant sublicenses under the license, subject to the approval of the Federal agency. Each sublicense shall make reference to the license, including the rights retained by the Government, and a copy of such sublicense shall be furnished to the Federal agency.

(5) The license shall require the licensee to carry out the plan for development or marketing of the invention, or both, to bring the invention to practical application within a period specified in the license, and to continue to make the benefits of the invention reasonably accessible to the public.

(6) The license shall require the licensee to report periodically on the utilization or efforts at obtaining utilization that are being made by the licensee, with particular reference to the plan submitted.

(7) Licenses may be royalty-free or for royalties or other consideration.

(8) Where an agreement is obtained pursuant to § 404.5(a)(2) that any products embodying the invention or produced through use of the invention will be manufactured substantially in the United States, the license shall recite such agreement.

(9) The license shall provide for the right of the Federal agency to terminate the license, in whole or in part, if:

(i) The Federal agency determines that the licensee is not executing the plan submitted with its request for a license and the licensee cannot otherwise demonstrate to the satisfaction of the Federal agency that it has taken or can be expected to take within a reasonable time effective steps to achieve practical application of the invention;

(ii) The Federal agency determines that such action is necessary to meet requirements for public use specified by Federal regulations issued after the date of the license and such requirements are not reasonably satisfied by the licensee;

(iii) The licensee has willfully made a false statement of or willfully omitted a material fact in the license application or in any report required by the license agreement; or

(iv) The licensee commits a substantial breach of a covenant or agreement contained in the license.

(10) The license may be modified or terminated, consistent with this part, upon mutual agreement of the Federal agency and the licensee.

(11) Nothing relating to the grant of a license, nor the grant itself, shall be construed to confer upon any person any immunity from or defenses under the antitrust laws or from a charge of patent misuse, and the acquisition and use of rights pursuant to this part shall not be immunized from the operation of state or Federal law by reason of the source of the grant.

37 C.F.R. § 404.6 Nonexclusive licenses.

(a) Nonexclusive licenses may be granted under federally owned inventions without publication of availability or notice of a prospective license.

(b) In addition to the provisions of § 404.5, the nonexclusive license may also provide that, after termination of a period specified in the license agreement, the Federal agency may restrict the license to the fields of use or geographic areas, or both, in which the licensee has brought the invention to practical application and continues to make the benefits of the invention reasonably accessible to the public. However, such restriction shall be made only in order to grant an exclusive or partially exclusive license in accordance with this subpart.

37 C.F.R. § 404.7 Exclusive and partially exclusive licenses.

(a)(1) Exclusive or partially exclusive domestic licenses may be granted on federally owned inventions three months after notice of the invention's availability has been announced in the FEDERAL REGISTER, or without such notice where the Federal agency determines that expeditious granting of such a license will best serve the interest of the Federal Government and the public; and in either situation, only if;

(i) Notice of a prospective license, identifying the invention and the prospective licensee, has been published in the Federal Register, providing opportunity for written objections within at least a 15-day period;

(ii) After expiration of the period in § 404.7(a)(1)(i) and consideration of any written objections received during the period, the Federal agency has determined that;

(A) The interests of the Federal Government and the public will best be served by the proposed license, in view of the applicant's intentions, plans, and ability to bring the invention to practical application or otherwise promote the invention's utilization by the public;

(B) The desired practical application has not been achieved, or is not likely expeditiously to be achieved, under any nonexclusive license which has been granted, or which may be granted, on the invention;

(C) Exclusive or partially exclusive licensing is a reasonable and necessary incentive to call forth the investment of risk capital and expenditures to bring the invention to practical application or otherwise promote the invention's utilization by the public; and

(D) The proposed terms and scope of exclusivity are not greater than reasonably necessary to provide the incentive for bringing the invention to practical application or otherwise promote the invention's utilization by the public;

(iii) The Federal agency has not determined that the grant of such license will tend substantially to lessen competition or result in undue concentration in any section of the country in any line of commerce to which the technology to be licensed relates, or to create or maintain other situations inconsistent with the antitrust laws; and

(iv) The Federal agency has given first preference to any small business firms submitting plans that are determined by the agency to be within the capabilities of the firms and as equally likely, if executed, to bring the invention to practical application as any plans submitted by applicants that are not small business firms.

(2) In addition to the provisions of § 404.5, the following terms and conditions apply to domestic exclusive and partially exclusive licenses;

(i) The license shall be subject to the irrevocable, royalty-free right of the Government of the United States to practice and have practiced the invention on behalf of the

United States and on behalf of any foreign government or international organization pursuant to any existing or future treaty or agreement with the United States.

(ii) The license shall reserve to the Federal agency the right to require the licensee to grant sublicenses to responsible applicants, on reasonable terms, when necessary to fulfill health or safety needs.

(iii) The license shall be subject to any licenses in force at the time of the grant of the exclusive or partially exclusive license.

(iv) The license may grant the licensee the right of enforcement of the licensed patent pursuant to the provisions of Chapter 29 of Title 35, United States Code, or other statutes, as determined appropriate in the public interest.

(b)(1) Exclusive or partially exclusive licenses may be granted on a federally owned invention covered by a foreign patent, patent application, or other form of protection, provided that;

(i) Notice of a prospective license, identifying the invention and the prospective licensee, has been published in the Federal Register, providing opportunity for written objections within at least a 15-day period and following consideration of such written objections received during the period.

(ii) The agency has considered whether the interests of the Federal Government or United States industry in foreign commerce will be enhanced; and

(iii) The Federal agency has not determined that the grant of such license will tend substantially to lessen competition or result in undue concentration in any section of the United States in any line of commerce to which the technology to be licensed relates, or to create or maintain other situations inconsistent with antitrust laws.

(2) In addition to the provisions of § 404.5 the following terms and conditions apply to foreign exclusive and partially exclusive licenses:

(i) The license shall be subject to the irrevocable, royalty-free right of the Government of the United States to practice and have practiced the invention on behalf of the United States and on behalf of any foreign government or international organization pursuant to any existing or future treaty or agreement with the United States.

(ii) The license shall be subject to any licenses in force at the time of the grant of the exclusive or partially exclusive license.

(iii) The license may grant the licensee the right to take any suitable and necessary actions to protect the licensed property, on behalf of the Federal Government.

(c) Federal agencies shall maintain a record of determinations to grant exclusive or partially exclusive licenses.

37 C.F.R. § 404.8 Application for a license.

An application for a license should be addressed to the Federal agency having custody of the invention and shall normally include:

(a) Identification of the invention for which the license is desired including the patent application serial number or patent number, title, and date, if known;

(b) Identification of the type of license for which the application is submitted;

(c) Name and address of the person, company, or organization applying for the license and the citizenship or place of incorporation of the applicant;

(d) Name, address, and telephone number of the representative of the applicant to whom correspondence should be sent;

(e) Nature and type of applicant's business, identifying products or services which the applicant has successfully commercialized, and approximate number of applicant's employees;

(f) Source of information concerning the availability of a license on the invention;

(g) A statement indicating whether the applicant is a small business firm as defined in § 404.3(c)

(h) A detailed description of applicant's plan for development or marketing of the invention, or both, which should include:

(1) A statement of the time, nature and amount of anticipated investment of capital and other resources which applicant believes will be required to bring the invention to practical application;

(2) A statement as to applicant's capability and intention to fulfill the plan, including information regarding manufacuturing, marketing, financial, and technical resources;

(3) A statement of the fields of use for which applicant intends to practice the invention; and

(4) A statement of the geographic areas in which applicant intends to manufacture any products embodying the invention and geographic areas where applicant intends to use or sell the invention, or both;

(i) Identification of licenses previously granted to applicant under federally owned inventions;

(j) A statement containing applicant's best knowledge of the extent to which the invention is being practiced by private industry or Government, or both, or is otherwise available commercially; and

(k) Any other information which applicant believes will support a determination to grant the license to applicant.

37 C.F.R. § 404.9 Notice to Attorney General.

A copy of the notice provided for in § 404.7 (a)(1)(i) and (b)(1)(i) will be sent to the Attorney General.

37 C.F.R. § 404.10 Modification and termination of licenses.

Before modifying or terminating a license, other than by mutual agreement, the Federal agency shall furnish the licensee and any sublicensee of record a written notice of intention to modify or terminate the license, and the licensee and any sublicensee shall be allowed 30 days after such notice to remedy any breach of the license or show cause why the license shall not be modified or terminated.

37 C.F.R. § 404.11 Appeals.

In accordance with procedures prescribed by the Federal agency, the following parties may appeal to the agency head or designee any decision or determination concerning the grant, denial, interpretation, modification, or termination of a license:

(a) A person whose application for a license has been denied.

(b) A licensee whose license has been modified or terminated, in whole or in part; or

(c) A person who timely filed a written objection in response to the notice required by § 404.7(a)(1)(i) or § 404.7(b)(1)(i) and who can demonstrate to the satisfaction of the Federal agency that such person may be damaged by the agency action.

37 C.F.R. § 404.12 Protection and administration of inventions.

A Federal agency may take any suitable and necessary steps to protect and administer rights to federally owner inventions, either directly or through contract.

37 C.F.R. § 404.13 Transfer of custody.

A Federal agency having custody of a federally owned invention may transfer custody and administration, in whole or in part, to another Federal agency, of the right, title, or interest in such invention.

37 C.F.R. § 404.14 Confidentiality of information.

Title 35, United States Code, section 209, provides that any plan submitted pursuant to § 404.8(h) and any report required by § 404.5(b)(6) may be treated by the Federal agency as commercial and financial information obtained from a person and privileged and confidential and not subject to disclosure under section 552 of Title 5 of the United States Code.

APPENDIX 5

SAMPLE FEDERAL NOTICES FOR CRADAS

Commerce Business Daily

[Posted in CBDNet on July 27, 2001]

[Printed Issue Date: July 31, 2001]

From the Commerce Business Daily Online via GPO Access [cbdnet.access.gpo.gov]

PART: U.S. GOVERNMENT PROCUREMENTS

SUBPART: SERVICES

CLASSCOD: A—Research and Development

OFFADD: National Technology Transfer Center, Wheeling Jesuit

University, 316 Washington Ave., Wheeling, WV 26003-6295

SUBJECT: A—RESEARCH & DEVELOPMENT—THE VA HAS DISCOVERED AND CHARACTERIZED A NEW AND DISTINCT PATHWAY DRIVING INFLAMMATION IN JOINTS AFFLICTED BY RHEUMATOID ARTHRITIS (RA) AND/OR OTHER INFLAMMATORY DISEASES, WHICH MAY LEAD TO THE DESIGN AND DEVELOPMENT OF EFFECTIVE DISEASE-MODIFYING ANTIRHEUMATIC DRUGS SOL 00-045

DUE 083101

POC Mr. William Chard - 800-678-6882 or 304-243-2039

DESC: The Department of Veterans Affairs (VA), through the Robert C. Byrd National Technology Transfer Center (NTTC), is seeking a commercial partner to license and/or further develop this technology through a Cooperative Research and Development Agreement (**CRADA**) in order to expedite bringing the technology to market.

--- The VA has discovered and characterized a new and distinct pathway driving inflammation in joints afflicted by rheumatoid arthritis (RA) and/or other inflammatory diseases, which may lead to the design and development of effective disease-modifying antirheumatic drugs (DMARDs) for RA. The subject technology DMARD action is based on the hypothesized relationship between fibrin sequences and the promotion or inhibition of inflammation on fibroblastic cells.

195

--- The current stage of development of the invention is basic research. This research, however, has a clear path to applied research and potential product development. The subject technology appears to have potential applications in combating inflammation in synovial joints, such as RA, and may occur in systemic lupus crythcmatosus and other rheumatic conditions. The VA has submitted an application for international patent protection under the Patent Cooperation Treaty (PCT).

EMAILADD: wchard@nttc.edu

EMAILDESC: e-mail

CITE: (W-208 SN50T1P8)

Commerce Business Daily

[Posted in CBDNet on August 1, 2001] [Printed Issue Date: August 6, 2001]

From the Commerce Business Daily Online via GPO Access [cbdnet.access.gpo.gov]

PART: U.S. GOVERNMENT PROCUREMENTS

SUBPART: SERVICES

CLASSCOD: B—Special Studies and Analyses - Not R&D—Potential Sources Sought

OFFADD: Commander, Naval Air Warfare Center, Weapons Division, Code 210000D, 1 Administration Circle, China Lake, CA 93555-6100

SUBJECT: B—GLOBAL POSITIONING SYSTEM (GPS)/INERTIAL MEASUREMENT UNIT (IMU) TIME SPACE POSITION INDICATOR (TSPI) UNIT COOPERATIVE RESEARCH AND DEVELOPMENT AGREEMENT OPPORTUNITY & LICENSING OPPORTUNITY

SOL 001

DUE 083101

POC Martha H. Harrington, Code 4T1100D, (760) 939-1814; harringtonmh@ navair.navy.mil

DESC: The Naval Air Warfare Center Weapons Division is developing a GPS/IMU based TSPI unit under the Joint Advanced Missile Instrumentation (JAMI) Program that will provide tracking for high dynamic missiles and targets. The unit under development is called the JAMI TSPI Unit (JTU). We are now looking for an industrial partner for a Cooperative Research and Development Agreement (**CRADA**) to conduct joint research and development and to expedite technology transfer of Naval Air Warfare Center Weapons Division innovations. The JAMI Team has conducted extensive investigations into fast acquisition GPS tracking technology and into on board IMU processing to allow the system to continue to provide precision track during telemetry or GPS dropouts. The Government anticipates as part of a cooperative research and development effort to provide electrical and software designs and critical components already under development such as the Inertial Sensor Package and GPS sensor. We desire an industrial partner to provide mechanical packaging design support and producability analysis of the overall design. The Government may grant an exclusive or a partially exclusive license on federally owned inventions developed under a Cooperative Research and Development Agreement. Interested parties must submit a two to three page white paper describing the cooperative arrangement envisioned. This paper must include the industrial partner's plan for commercial exploitation, what technologies and data they are willing to share with the Government as well as physical and financial assets they bring to the partnership. The white paper must be received by 31 August 2001, by the Technology Transfer Office, Code 4T1100D, China Lake, CA (see address below). The objectives of Navy domestic technology transfer are: (1) to disseminate technology originally developed in support of military applications for production in the private sectors; (2) to provide joint cooperative development programs that address problems of critical concern to the Navy and other agencies or organizations; and (3) to leverage research and development opportunities of mutual interest to the Navy and industrial organizations. In pursuit of these objectives the Navy transfers technology to other Federal Government agencies, state and local governments, small and large United States businesses, non-profit organizations and such public service organizations as schools, hospitals and foundations. Under the Navy Domestic Technology Transfer Program, the Government is permitted to receive funds from a non-Federal party. However, the Government is not permitted to fund a non-Federal party.

For more information contact Martha H. Harrington, phone number (760) 939-1814. Send the white papers to Commander, Naval Air Warfare Center Weapons Division, Technology Transfer Office, 4T1100D, Attn: Martha H. Harrington, 1 Administration Circle, CHINA LAKE, CA 93555-6100. This synopsis is for information and planning purposes only and does not constitute an RFB or RFP; it is not a commitment by the Government, and does not guarantee any future contracts to be let by the Government.

Participation in this **CRADA** is strictly voluntary and does not in any way suggest, imply, or impose a U.S. Government obligation or guarantee for future contractual related services, agreements, or other considerations with regards to the Joint Advanced Missile Instrumentation (JAMI) Program or any other CTEIP funded programs.

CITE: (W-213 SN50T7B2)

Federal Register

June 21, 2001 (Volume 66, Number 120)][Notices]

[Page 33255-33256]

From the Federal Register Online via GPO Access [wais.access.gpo.gov]

DEPARTMENT OF HEALTH AND HUMAN SERVICES

Centers for Disease Control and Prevention,

Cooperative Research and Development Agreement (**CRADA**)

AGENCY: Centers for Disease Control and Prevention (CDC), HHS.

ACTION: Notice.

SUMMARY: The Centers for Disease Control and Prevention (CDC) is seeking a **CRADA** partner for collaboration to examine the use of anti-substance P antibodies and/or anti-substance P F(ab)2 antibody fragments to prevent and/or treat an inflammatory response mediated by substance P associated with respiratory viral infection (particularly respiratory syncytial virus [RSV]). Anti-substance P antibody treatment would be used in combination with agents for anti-viral treatment (e.g., Ribavirin, palivizumab, and RSV fusion inhibitors) to ameliorate substance P-mediated inflammation and disease pathogenesis.

Because CRADAs are designed to facilitate the development of scientific and technologic knowledge into useful, marketable products, a great deal of freedom is given to Federal agencies in implementing collaborative research. CDC may accept staff, facilities, equipment, supplies, and money from the other participants in a **CRADA**; CDC may provide staff, facilities, equipment, and supplies to the project. There is a single restriction in this exchange: CDC MAY NOT PROVIDE FUNDS to the other participants in a **CRADA**.

DATES: This opportunity is available until July 23, 2001. Respondents may be provided a longer period of time to furnish additional information if CDC finds this necessary.

ADDRESSES: The responses must be made to: Lisa Blake-DiSpigna, Technology Transfer Coordinator, National Center for Infectious Diseases, Centers for Disease Control and Prevention, 1600 Clifton Rd. NE., Mailstop C-19, Atlanta, GA 30333.

FOR FURTHER INFORMATION CONTACT:

Technical: Ralph A. Tripp, Ph.D., Respiratory and Enteric Viruses, Division of Viral and Rickettsial Diseases, National Center for Infectious Diseases, Centers for Disease Control and Prevention, 1600 Clifton Rd. NE., Mailstop G-09, Atlanta, GA 30333, telephone (404) 639-3427.

Business: Lisa Blake-DiSpigna, Technology Transfer Coordinator, National Center for Infectious Diseases, Centers for Disease Control and Prevention, 1600 Clifton Rd. NE., Mailstop C-19, Atlanta, GA 30333, telephone (404) 639-3227.

SUPPLEMENTARY INFORMATION: The goal of this **CRADA** is to seek a partner for collaboration to examine the development and use of anti-substance P antibodies and/or anti-SP F(ab)'2 antibody fragments to prevent and/or treat an inflammatory response mediated by substance P that is associated with respiratory viral infection (particularly RSV). The methods comprise the administration to the subject of a pharmaceutically effective amount of anti-SP antibodies or anti-SP F(ab)'2 antibody fragments to inhibit the activity of endogenous SP in the subject. Anti-SP antibody or anti-SP F(ab)'2 antibody treatment will be used in combination with anti-viral drugs and anti-viral reagents to inhibit the activity of endogenous SP in the subject so as to reduce the level of cytokine/chemokine-based inflammation and pulmonary cell infiltration and alter the disease course.

Respondents should provide evidence of expertise in the development and evaluation of anti-viral drugs and anti-viral reagents, evidence of experience in animal models systems including non-human primate models, commercialization of anti-viral drugs and anti-viral reagents, and supporting data (e.g., publications, proficiency testing, certifications, resumes, etc.) of qualifications for the principle investigator who would be involved in the **CRADA**. The respondent will develop the final research plan in collaboration with CDC.

Applicant submissions will be judged according to the following criteria:

    1. Expertise in development and evaluation of anti-viral drugs and anti-viral reagents;

    2. Expertise in evaluation of anti-viral drugs, reagents and anti-viral treatments in animal model systems including non-human primates;

    3. Evidence of scientific credibility. The company has the capability of bringing the product to fruition, in part determined by past accomplishments with similar products, and/or that the company has published related studies in peer-reviewed journals;

    4. Evidence of commitment and ability to develop anti-substance P monoclonal antibodies for use with anti-viral drugs, anti-viral reagents or antiviral treatments; and

    5. Evidence of an existing infrastructure to commercialize successful technologies.

This **CRADA** is proposed and implemented under the 1986 Federal Technology Transfer Act: Public Law 99-502.

Dated: June 14, 2001.

Thena M. Durham,

Director, Executive Secretariat, Office of the Director, Centers for

Disease Control and Prevention (CDC).

Federal Register

July 23, 2001 (Volume 66, Number 141)][Notices]

[Page 38294-38295]

From the Federal Register Online via GPO Access [wais.access.gpo.gov]

[DOCID:fr23jy01-85]

DEPARTMENT OF HEALTH AND HUMAN SERVICES

National Institutes of Health

National Cancer Institute (NCI); Development of Therapeutic Antibodies and Vaccines From Tumor Associated Antigens in Human Lymphoma

AGENCY: National Cancer Institute, National Institutes of Health, PHS, DHHS.

ACTION: Notice of an opportunity for Cooperative Research and Development Agreement (**CRADA**).

An opportunity for a Cooperative Research and Development Agreement (**CRADA**) is available for collaboration with the NCI intramural Center for Cancer Research (CCR) to develop therapeutic antibodies and vaccines from novel tumor associated antigens in human lymphoma. This collaboration specifically excludes idiotype as the lymphoma antigen. Collaborative projects will focus upon cancer and/or areas of high public health significance and high national and international priority.

SUMMARY: Pursuant to the Federal Technology Transfer Act of 1986 (FTTA, 15 U.S.C. 3710 as amended; and Executive Order 12591 of April 10, 1987, the National Cancer Institute (NCI) of the National Institutes of Health (NIH) of the Public Health Service (PHS) of the Department of Health and Human Services (DHHS) seeks one Cooperative Research and Development Agreement (**CRADA**) with a pharmaceutical or biotechnology company to develop therapeutic antibodies and vaccines from tumor associated antigens in human lymphoma. The **CRADA** would have an expected duration of one (1) to five (5) years. The goals of the **CRADA** include the rapid publication of research results and timely commercialization of products, and/or methods of treatment or prevention that may result from the research. The **CRADA** Collaborator will have an option to negotiate the terms of an exclusive or non-exclusive commercialization license to subject inventions arising under the **CRADA** and which are the subject of the **CRADA** Research Plan.

ADDRESSES: Proposals and questions about this **CRADA** opportunity may be addressed to Jeffrey W. Thomas, Ph.D., Technology Transfer Branch, National Cancer Institute, Fairview

Center, Room 502, Frederick, MD 21701 (phone: 301-846-5465; fax: 301-846-6820; email: jeffreyt@mail.nih.gov). Scientific inquires should be submitted to Larry W. Kwak, M.D., Ph.D., CCR, National Cancer Institute, Bldg. 567, Room 205, Frederick MD, 21702-1201 (phone: 301-846-1607; Fax: 301-846-6107; e-mail kwak@mail.ncifcfr.gov).

EFFECTIVE DATE: Inquiries regarding **CRADA** proposals and scientific matters may be forwarded at any time. Confidential, preliminary **CRADA** proposals, preferably two pages or less, must be submitted to the NCI on or before August 22, 2001. Guidelines for preparing final **CRADA** proposals will be communicated shortly thereafter to all respondents with whom initial confidential discussions will have established sufficient mutual interest. **CRADA** proposals may be accepted after the initial 30 day period if a **CRADA** Collaborator is not identified from the initial pool of respondents.

SUPPLEMENTARY INFORMATION:

Technology Available

The intramural CCR NCI is seeking a collaborative partner to develop therapeutic antibodies and vaccines from novel tumor associated antigens (TAAs) in human lymphoma. Identification of novel TAA proteins differentially expressed in human lymphoma samples may be useful targets for the development of such therapeutic antibodies and vaccines. This collaboration specifically excludes idiotype as the lymphoma antigen. The CCR has experience with collection and characterization of primary human lymphomas, understanding of basic lymphoma immunobiology, and unique reagents generated from patients who have undergone immunotherapy. As part of the proposed collaboration, the CCR will utilize its expertise to collect and characterize human lymphoma samples prior to protein and genetic analysis. Also, clinical data from well-characterized vaccinated patients will be available for clinical correlation. CCR is seeking a collaborative partner with experience in proteomics to identify TAAs differentially expressed in lymphoma samples that may have potential as therapeutic or diagnostic targets. For example, the partner may have expertise in liquid chromatography and mass spectrometry to identify proteins differentially expressed in lymphomas, compared to normal B lymphocytes. Additionally, the use of gene expression techniques to confirm the proteomics results is envisioned. Genetic analysis of the identified TAAs will be essential in the development of effective immunotherapies; thus, the collaborative partner must have a strong background in genetic analysis to understand the effects of variations (e.g. polymorphisms) and to recognize genetic components that could be used to develop effect vaccines and therapeutic antibodies. Thus, the potential collaborator must be a leader in proteomics, bioinformatics and genomics and have a demonstrated interest, expertise, or ability in the development of cancer vaccines.

NCI and Collaborator Responsibilities

The role of the National Cancer Institute in this **CRADA** will include, but not be limited to:

1. Providing intellectual, scientific, and technical expertise and experience to the research project.

2. Providing the Collaborator with human lymphoma samples suitable for proteomic and genomic analysis.

3. Planning research studies and interpreting research results.

4. Publishing research results.

The role of the **CRADA** Collaborator may include, but not be limited to:

1. Providing significant intellectual, scientific, and technical expertise or experience to the research project.

2. Providing essential research materials, such as enzymes or other reagents, extracts, compounds, hardware, software and access to databases.

3. Planning research studies and interpreting research results.

4. Providing technical expertise and/or financial support (e.g. facilities, personnel and expertise) for **CRADA**-related research as outlined in the **CRADA** Research Plan.

5. Publishing research results.

Selection criteria for choosing the **CRADA** Collaborator may include, but not be limited to:

1. The ability to collaborate with NCI on research and development of this technology involving the development of lymphoma vaccines. This ability can be demonstrated through experience, expertise, and the ability to contribute intellectually in this or related areas.

2. The demonstration of adequate resources to perform the research, development and commercialization of this technology (e.g. facilities, personnel and expertise) and accomplish objectives according to an appropriate timetable to be outlined in the **CRADA** Collaborator's proposal.

3. The willingness to commit best effort and demonstrated resources to the research, development and commercialization of this technology as defined above.

4. The demonstration of expertise in the commercial development, production, marketing and sales of antitumor products.

5. The willingness to cooperate with the National Cancer Institute in the timely publication of research results.

6. The agreement to be bound by the appropriate DHHS regulations relating to human subjects, PHS policies relating to the use and care of laboratory animals, and the dissemination of research tools according to NIH policy.

7. The willingness to accept the legal provisions and language of the **CRADA** with only minor modifications, if any. These provisions govern the equitable distribution of patent

rights to **CRADA** inventions.

Generally, the rights of ownership are retained by the organization that is the employer of the inventor, with (1) the grant of a license for research and other Government purposes to the Government when the **CRADA** Collaborator's employee is the sole inventor, or (2) the grant of an option to elect an exclusive or non-exclusive license to the **CRADA** Collaborator when the Government employee is the sole inventor.

Dated: July 11, 2001.

Kathleen Sybert, Chief, Technology Transfer Branch, National Cancer Institute, National Institutes of Health.

Federal Register

May 1, 2001 (Volume 66, Number 84)][Notices]

[Page 21778]

From the Federal Register Online via GPO Access [wais.access.gpo.gov]

[DOCID:fr01my01-101]

DEPARTMENT OF THE INTERIOR

Geological Survey Technology Transfer Act of 1986; Chevron Research and Technology Co.

AGENCY: Geological Survey, Interior.

ACTION: Notice of Proposed Cooperative Research & Development Agreement

(**CRADA**) Negotiations.

SUMMARY: The United States Geological Survey (USGS) is contemplating entering into a Cooperative Research and Development Agreement (**CRADA**) with the Chevron Research and Technology Company, a division of Chevron U.S.A. Inc. for the purpose of evaluating hyperspectral remote sensing technology that permits the rapid assessment of vegetation type.

INQUIRIES: If any other parties are interested in similar activities with the USGS, please contact Delores Richardson, Administrative Officer, USGS National Wetlands Research Center, 700 Cajundome Blvd., Lafayette, LA 70506, phone (337) 266-8515.

SUPPLEMENTARY INFORMATION: This notice is submitted to meet the USGS requirements stipulated in Survey Manual Chapter 500.20.

Susan Haseltine, Chief Scientist for Biology.

Federal Register

July 5, 2001 (Volume 66, Number 129)][Notices]

[Page 35443-35444]

From the Federal Register Online via GPO Access [wais.access.gpo.gov]

[DOCID:fr05jy01-56]

DEPARTMENT OF HEALTH AND HUMAN SERVICES

National Institutes of Health National Cancer Institute: Opportunity for License(s) and/or Cooperative Research and Development Agreement(s) (CRADAs) for the Development of Geldanamycin Analogs for Clinical Use

AGENCY: National Institutes of Health, PHS, DHHS.

ACTION: Notice.

SUMMARY: The National Cancer Institute (NCI) seeks Licensee(s) and/or Cooperative Research and Development Agreement **(CRADA)** Collaborator(s) for the development of geldanamycin analogs for clinical use in three areas. The three areas are: (1) A unique clinical formulation of 17-allylaminogeldanamycin (17-AAG). (2) A suite of geldanamycin analogs (other than 17-AAG) modified at the 11 and/or 17 positions, several of which have improved solubility and reduced toxicity in comparison to geldanamycin. (3) A coupled met kinase-uPA kinase assay, as described in Cancer Research 60 (2): 342-9, and data and expertise regarding geldanamycin analog activity as measured by that assay. The invention for item (1) is claimed in PCT Patent Application PCT/US99/30631 entitled "Water-Insoluble Drug Delivery System"; the inventions for item (2) are claimed in U.S. Patent Application 60/246,258, entitled "Geldanamycin Derivatives having Selective Affinity for HSP-90 and Methods of Using Same," U.S. Patent Application 60/280,016, entitled "Geldanamycin Derivatives Having Selective Affinity for HSP90 over GRP94 and Method of Using Same," and U.S. Patent Application 60/280,078, entitled "Geldanamycin Derivatives and Method of Treating Cancer Using Same"; the technology for item (3) is described in Cancer Research 60 (2): 342-9, "The Geldanamycins Are Potent Inhibitors of the Hepatocyte Growth Factor/Scatter Factor-Met-Urokinase Plasminogen Activator-Plasmin Proteolytic Network."

DATES: Respondees interested in licensing the invention(s) will be required to submit an "Application for License to Public Health Service Inventions" no later than sixty (60) days from the date of this announcement. Applications submitted thereafter may be considered if a suitable Licensee is not selected from among the timely responses.

Interested **CRADA** applicants must submit to the NCI Technology Transfer Branch (TTB) a confidential proposal summary no later than sixty (60) days from the date of this announcement for consideration. **CRADA** proposal summaries submitted thereafter may be considered if a suitable **CRADA** Collaborator is not selected from among the timely responses. Guidelines for preparing full **CRADA** proposals will be communicated shortly thereafter to all respondents with whom initial confidential discussions will have established sufficient mutual interest.

ADDRESSES: Inquiries directed to obtaining license(s) for the technology should be addressed to Kai Chen, Ph.D., M.B.A., Supervisory Technology Licensing Specialist, Office of Technology Transfer, National Institutes of Health, 6011 Executive Blvd., Suite 325, Rockville, MD 20852, (Tel. 301-496-7056, extension 247; FAX 301-402-0220).

CRADA inquiries and proposals regarding this opportunity should be addressed to Robert Wagner, M.S., M. Phil., Technology Transfer Specialist (Tel. 301-496-0477, FAX 301-402-2117), Technology Transfer Branch, National Cancer Institute, 6120 Executive Blvd., Suite 450, Rockville, MD 20852.

SUPPLEMENTARY INFORMATION: Respondees interested in licensing the technology will be required to submit an Application for License to Public Health Service Inventions. Inventions described in the patent applications are available for either exclusive or non-exclusive licensing in accordance with 35 U.S.C. 207 and 37 CFR Part 404. Information about patent application(s) and pertinent information not yet publicly described can be obtained under the terms of a Confidential Disclosure Agreement.

A Cooperative Research and Development Agreement (**CRADA**) is the anticipated joint agreement to be entered into with NCI pursuant to the Federal Technology Transfer Act of 1986 and Executive Order 12591 of April 10, 1987, as amended. A **CRADA** is an agreement designed to enable certain collaborations between Government laboratories and non-Government laboratories. It is not a grant, and it is not a contract for the procurement of goods/services. The NCI is prohibited from transferring funds to a **CRADA** collaborator. Under a **CRADA**, NCI can contribute facilities, staff, materials, and expertise. The **CRADA** Collaborator will have an option to negotiate the terms of an exclusive or nonexclusive commercialization license to subject inventions arising under the **CRADA**. **CRADA** applicants should be aware that a license to the above mentioned patent rights may be necessary in order to commercialize products arising from a **CRADA**. The expected duration of the **CRADA**(s) would be for up to five (5) years. The goals of CRADAs include the rapid publication of research results and timely commercialization of products, diagnostics, and treatments that result from the research.

The NCI Seeks Licensee(s) and/or **CRADA** Collaborator(s) in One or More of the Following Areas for the Development of Geldanamycin Analogs for Clinical Use

1. Clinical Development of 17-AAG: Patent protection for the formulation of 17-allylaminogeldanamycin (17-AAG) for clinical use is pending. NCI is actively engaged in the clinical development of this agent and is seeking a **CRADA** collaborator whose role would include production of the drug for clinical trials. **CRADA** applicants should be aware that a license to the related patent rights may be necessary in order to commercialize products

arising from the **CRADA**. 17-AAG is currently in Phase 1 clinical trials under an NCI-sponsored Investigational New Drug Application (IND). The data contained in this IND, along with the data that will emerge from NCI's ongoing clinical trials, would be available to the **CRADA** Collaborator.

2. Optimization of Compounds for Cytotoxic Endpoints: A suite of geldanamycin analogs (other than 17-AAG) modified at the 11 and/or 17 positions, several of which have improved solubility and altered toxicity in comparison to geldanamycin, are described in several pending NCI patent applications. NCI is seeking a licensee(s) and/or **CRADA** Collaborator(s) interested in continued optimization of compound pharmacology for selection of a compound to enter the clinic. Criteria for selection of a compound would include cytotoxic endpoints and regression of model tumors. Such a resulting compound(s) would be expected to have a different spectrum of activity or formulation as that for 17-AAG as described in (1) above.

3. Optimization of Compounds for Anti-Metastatic Endpoint: The technology for the coupled met kinase—uPA Kinase assay is described in Cancer Research 60 (2): 342-9. NCI research has defined this assay as generating lead compounds for anti-metastatic use. While encompassing some compounds from (2) above, lead compounds will have a very distinct set of development endpoints demonstrating suitability for long term chronic oral dosing, and will show evidence of activity in anti-metastasis and/or anti-angiogenesis assays without necessarily having evidence of activity in classical cytotoxic models. NCI is seeking a **CRADA** Collaborator(s) interested in using this assay to optimize compounds related to geldanamycin for use as anti-metastatic agents.

Party Contributions to CRADAS

The Role of the NCI in Each of the CRADAs May Include, but Not Be Limited to

1. Providing intellectual, scientific, and technical expertise and experience to the research project.

2. Providing the **CRADA** Collaborator with information and data relating to the **CRADA** technology.

3. Planning research studies and interpreting research results.

4. Carrying out research pursuant to the planned collaboration, including, but not limited to:

(a). Screening, pharmacology and in vivo model studies for compounds pertinent to cytotoxic endpoints;

(b). Assays to optimize compounds with desired pharmacology for chronic use;

(c). Pharmacology and determination of in vivo activity of anti-metastatic compounds;

(d). Production of precursors and prodrugs from fermentation sources; and

(e). Possible sponsorship of clinical trials of promising compounds.

5. Publishing research results.

The Role of the **CRADA** Collaborator May Include, but Not Be Limited to

1. Providing significant intellectual, scientific, and technical expertise or experience to the research project, including, but not limited to:

(a). Structure-based design of geldanamycin analogs with suitable properties;

(b). Chemical modification of fermented lead structures;

(c). Pharmacology, toxicology, and formulation;

(d). Support for clinical trials in the form of drug and funding.

2. Planning research studies and interpreting research results.

3. Providing technical and/or financial support to facilitate scientific goals and to further design applications of the technology outlined in the agreement.

4. Publishing research results.

Selection Criteria for Choosing the **CRADA** Collaborator May Include, but Not Be Limited to

1. A demonstrated background and expertise in the preclinical and clinical development of antineoplastic agents, structure-based design, and the conduct of in vivo animal model studies pertaining to metastasis or tumor regression.

2. A demonstrated record of success in pre-clinical lead selection and optimization and/or successful clinical trials of antineoplastic therapeutics leading to a commercial product.

3. The demonstration of the necessary resources to produce sufficient drug for all clinical trials in a timely manner.

4. The ability to collaborate with NCI on further research and development of the technology. This ability will be demonstrated through experience and expertise in this or related areas of technology indicating the ability to contribute intellectually to ongoing research and development.

5. The demonstration of adequate resources to perform the research and development of the technology (e.g. facilities, personnel and expertise) and to accomplish the objectives according to an appropriate timetable to be outlined in the **CRADA** Collaborator's proposal.

6. The willingness to commit best effort and demonstrated resources to the research and development of this technology, as outlined in the **CRADA** Collaborator's proposal.

7. The demonstration of expertise in the commercial development and production of products related to this area of technology.

8. The ability to provide financial support for **CRADA**-related Government activities.

9. The willingness to cooperate with the National Cancer Institute in the timely publication of research results.

10. The agreement to be bound by the appropriate DHHS regulations relating to human subjects, and all PHS policies relating to the use and care of laboratory animals.

11. The willingness to accept the legal provisions and language of the **CRADA** with only minor modifications, if any. These legal provisions govern the distribution of future patent rights to **CRADA** inventions.

Generally, the rights of ownership are retained by the organization that is the employer of the inventor, with (1) the grant of a license for research and other Government purposes to the Government when the **CRADA** Collaborator's employee is the sole inventor, or (2) the grant of an option to elect an exclusive or nonexclusive license to the **CRADA** Collaborator when the Government employee is the sole inventor.

Dated: June 25, 2001.

Kathleen Sybert,Chief, Technology Transfer Branch, National Cancer Institute, National Institutes of Health.

Dated: June 27, 2001.

Jack Spiegel, Director, Division of Technology Transfer and Development, Office of Technology Transfer, National Institutes of Health.

SAMPLE CRADA

MODEL PUBLIC HEALTH SERVICE CRADA

Revised May 27, 1999

COOPERATIVE RESEARCH AND DEVELOPMENT AGREEMENT

This Cooperative Research and Development Agreement, hereinafter referred to as the "CRADA," consists of this Cover Page, an attached Agreement, and various Appendices referenced in the Agreement. This Cover Page serves to identify the Parties to this CRADA:

(1) the following Bureau(s), Institute(s), Center(s) or Division(s) of the National Institutes of Health ("NIH"), the Food and Drug Administration ("FDA"), and the Centers for Disease Control and Prevention ("CDC"): _____, hereinafter singly or collectively referred to as the Public Health Service ("PHS"); and (2) _____, which has offices at _____, hereinafter referred to as the "Collaborator."

COOPERATIVE RESEARCH AND DEVELOPMENT AGREEMENT

Article 1. Introduction

This Cooperative Research and Development Agreement (CRADA) between PHS and the Collaborator will be effective when signed by all Parties. The research and development activities which will be undertaken by each of the Parties in the course of this CRADA are detailed in the Research Plan (RP) which is attached as Appendix A. The funding and staffing commitments of the Parties are set forth in Appendix B. Any exceptions or changes to the CRADA are set forth in Appendix C. This CRADA is made under the authority of the Federal Technology Transfer Act, 15 U.S.C. §3710a and is governed by its terms.

Article 2. Definitions

As used in this CRADA, the following terms shall have the indicated meanings:

2.1 **"Affiliate"** means any corporation or other business entity controlled by, controlling, or under common control with Collaborator. For this purpose, A "control" means direct or indirect beneficial ownership of at least fifty (50) percent of the voting stock or at least fifty (50) percent interest in the income of such corporation or other business.

2.2 "**Cooperative Research and Development Agreement**" or "**CRADA**" means this Agreement, entered into by PHS pursuant to the Federal Technology Transfer Act of 1986, as amended, 15 U.S.C. 3710a et seq. and Executive Order 12591 of October 10, 1987.

211

2.3 "**Government**" means the Government of the United States as represented through the PHS agency that is a Party to this agreement.

2.4 "**IP**" means intellectual property.

2.5 "**Invention**" means any invention or discovery which is or may be patentable or otherwise protected under title 35, United States Code, or any novel variety or plant which is or may be protectable under the Plant Variety Protection Act (7 U.S.C. 2321 et seq.).

2.6 "**Principal Investigator(s)**" or "**Pis**" means the persons designated respectively by the Parties to this CRADA who will be responsible for the scientific and technical conduct of the RP.

2.7 "**Proprietary/Confidential Information**" means confidential scientific, business, or financial information provided that such information does not include:

2.7.1 information that is publicly known or available from other sources who are not under a confidentiality obligation to the source of the information;

2.7.2 information which has been made available by its owners to others without a confidentiality obligation;

2.7.3 information which is already known by or available to the receiving Party without a confidentiality obligation; or

2.7.4 information which relates to potential hazards or cautionary warnings associated with the production, handling or use of the subject matter of the Research Plan of this CRADA.

2.8 "**Research Materials**" means all tangible materials other than Subject Data first produced in the performance of this CRADA.

2.9 "**Research Plan**" or "**RP**" means the statement in Appendix A of the respective research and development commitments of the Parties to this CRADA.

2.10 "**Subject Invention**" means any Invention of the Parties, conceived or first actually reduced to practice in the performance of the Research Plan of this CRADA.

2.11 "**Subject Data**" means all recorded information first produced in the performance of this CRADA by the Parties.

Article 3. Cooperative Research

3.1 **Principal Investigators.** PHS research work under this CRADA will be performed by the PHS laboratory identified in the RP, and the PHS Principal Investigator (PI) designated in the RP will be responsible for the scientific and technical conduct of this project on behalf of PHS. Also designated in the RP is the Collaborator PI who will be responsible for the scientific and technical conduct of this project on behalf of the Collaborator.

3.2 **Research Plan Change.** The RP may be modified by mutual written consent of the Principal Investigators. Substantial changes in the scope of the RP will be treated as amendments under Article 13.6.

Article 4. Reports

4.1 **Interim Reports.** The Parties shall exchange formal written interim progress reports on a schedule agreed to by the PIs, but at least within twelve (12) months after this CRADA becomes effective and at least within every twelve (12) months thereafter. Such reports shall set forth the technical progress made, identifying such problems as may have been encountered and establishing goals and objectives requiring further effort, any modifications to the Research Plan pursuant to Article 3.2, and identify Subject Inventions pursuant to Article 6.1.

4.2 **Final Reports.** The Parties shall exchange final reports of their results within four (4) months after completing the projects described in the RP or after the expiration or termination of this CRADA.

Article 5. Financial and Staffing Obligations

5.1 **PHS and Collaborator Contributions.** The contributions of the Parties, including payment schedules, if applicable, are set forth in Appendix B. PHS shall not be obligated to perform any of the research specified herein or to take any other action required by this CRADA if the funding is not provided as set forth in Appendix B. PHS shall return excess funds to the Collaborator when it sends its final fiscal report pursuant to Article 5.2, except for staffing support pursuant to Article 10.3. Collaborator acknowledges that the U.S. Government will have the authority to retain and expend any excess funds for up to one (1) year subsequent to the expiration or termination of the CRADA to cover any costs incurred during the term of the CRADA in undertaking the work set forth in the RP. Model PHS

5.2 **Accounting Records.** PHS shall maintain separate and distinct current accounts, records, and other evidence supporting all its obligations under this CRADA, and shall provide the Collaborator a final fiscal report pursuant to Article 4.2.

5.3 **Capital Equipment.** Equipment purchased by PHS with funds provided by the Collaborator shall be the property of PHS. All capital equipment provided under this CRADA by one party for the use of another Party remains the property of the providing Party unless other disposition is mutually agreed upon by in writing by the Parties. If title to this equipment remains with the providing Party, that Party is responsible for maintenance of the equipment and the costs of its transportation to and from the site where it will be used.

Article 6. Patent Applications

6.1 **Reporting.** The Parties shall promptly report to each other in writing each Subject Invention and any patent applications filed thereon resulting from the research conducted under this CRADA that is reported to them by their respective employees. Each Party shall report all Subject Inventions to the other Party in sufficient detail to determine inventorship.

Such reports shall be treated as Proprietary/Confidential Information in accordance with Article 8.4.

6.2 **Filing of Patent Applications.** Each party shall be responsible for filing patent or other IP applications in a timely manner and at its own expense and after consultation with the other Party. The Parties will consult and mutually determine a filing strategy for jointly-owned subject inventions.

6.3 **Patent Expenses.** The expenses attendant to the filing of patent or other IP applications generally shall be paid by the Party filing such application. If an exclusive license to any Subject Invention is granted to the Collaborator, the Collaborator shall be responsible for all past and future out-of-pocket expenses in connection with the preparation, filing, prosecution and maintenance of any applications claiming such exclusively-licensed inventions and any patents or other IP grants that may issue on such applications.

The Collaborator may waive its exclusive license rights on any application, patent or other IP grant at any time, and incur no subsequent compensation obligation for that application, patent or IP grant.

6.4 **Prosecution of Intellectual Property Applications.** Within one month of receipt or filing, each Party shall provide the other Party with copies of the applications and all documents received from or filed with the relevant patent or other IP office in connection with the prosecution of such applications. Each Party shall also provide the other Party with the power to inspect and make copies of all documents retained in the patent or other IP application files by the applicable patent or other IP office. Where licensing is contemplated by Collaborator, the Parties agree to consult with each other with respect to the prosecution of applications for PHS Subject Inventions described in Article 6.3 and joint Subject Inventions described in Article 6.4. If the Collaborator elects to file and prosecute IP applications on joint Subject Inventions pursuant to Article 6.4, PHS will be granted an associate power of attorney (or its equivalent) on such IP applications.

Article 7. Licensing

7.1 **Option for Commercialization License.** With respect to Government IP rights to any Subject Invention not made solely by the Collaborator's employees for which a patent or other IP application is filed, PHS hereby grants to the Collaborator an *exclusive* option to elect an exclusive or nonexclusive commercialization license, which is substantially in the form of the appropriate model PHS license agreement. This option does not apply to Subject Inventions conceived prior to the effective date of this CRADA that are reduced to practice under this CRADA, if prior to that reduction to practice, PHS has filed a patent application on the invention and has licensed it or offered to license it to a third party. The terms of the license will fairly reflect the nature of the invention, the relative contributions of the Parties to the invention and the CRADA, the risks incurred by the Collaborator and the costs of subsequent research and development needed to bring the invention to the marketplace. The field of use of the license will be commensurate with the scope of the RP.

7.2 **Exercise of License Option.** The option of Article 7.1 must be exercised by written notice mailed within three (3) months after either (I) Collaborator receives written notice from PHS that the patent or other IP application has been filed; or (ii) the date Collaborator files such IP application. Exercise of this option by the Collaborator initiates a negotiation period that expires nine (9) months after the exercise of the option. If the last proposal by the Collaborator has not been responded to in writing by PHS within this nine (9) month period, the negotiation period shall be extended to expire one (1) month after PHS so responds, during which month the Collaborator may accept in writing the final license proposal of PHS. In the absence of such acceptance, or an extension of the time limits by PHS, PHS will be free to license such IP rights to others. In the event that the Collaborator elects the option for an exclusive license, but no such license is executed during the negotiation period, PHS agrees not to make an offer for an exclusive license on more favorable terms to a third party for a period of six (6) months without first offering Collaborator those more favorable terms. These times may be extended at the sole discretion of PHS upon good cause shown in writing by the Collaborator.

7.3 **License for PHS Employee Inventions and Joint Inventions.** Pursuant to 15 U.S.C. § 3710a(b)(1)(A), for Subject Inventions made under this CRADA by a PHS employee(s) or jointly by such employee(s) and employees of the Collaborator pursuant to Articles 6.3 and 6.4 and licensed pursuant to the option of Article 7.1, the Collaborator grants to the Government a nonexclusive, nontransferable, irrevocable, paid-up license to practice the invention or have the invention practiced throughout the world by or on behalf of the Government. In the exercise of such license, the Government shall not publicly disclose trade secrets or commercial or financial information that is privileged or confidential within the meaning of 5 U.S.C. 552(b)(4) or which would be considered as such if it had been obtained from a non-Federal party.

7.4 **License in Collaborator Inventions.** Pursuant to 15 U.S.C. § 3710a(b)(2), for inventions made solely by Collaborator employees under this CRADA pursuant to Article 6.2, the Collaborator grants to the Government a nonexclusive, nontransferable, irrevocable, paid-up license to practice the invention or have the invention practiced throughout the world by or on behalf of the Government for research or other Government purposes.

7.5 **Third Party License.** Pursuant to 15 U.S.C. § 3710a(b)(1)(B), if PHS grants an exclusive license to a Subject Invention made wholly by PHS employees or jointly with a Collaborator under this CRADA, pursuant to Articles 6.3 and 6.4, the Government shall retain the right to require the Collaborator to grant to a responsible applicant a nonexclusive, partially exclusive, or exclusive sublicense to use the invention in Collaborator's licensed field of use on terms that are reasonable under the circumstances; or if the Collaborator fails to grant such a license, to grant the license itself. The exercise of such rights by the Government shall only be in exceptional circumstances and only if the Government determines (I) the action is necessary to meet health or safety needs that are not reasonably satisfied by Collaborator, (ii) the action is necessary to meet requirements for public use specified by Federal regulations, and such requirements are not reasonably satisfied by the Collaborator; or (iii) the Collaborator has failed to comply with an agreement containing provisions described in 15 U.S.C. 3710a(c)(4)(B). The determination made by the Government under this Article is subject to administrative appeal and judicial review under

35 U.S.C. 203(2).

7.6 **Joint Inventions Not Exclusively Licensed.** In the event that the Collaborator does not acquire an exclusive commercialization license to IP rights in all fields in joint Subject Inventions described in Article 6.4, then each Party shall have the right to use the joint Subject Invention and to license its use to others in all fields not exclusively licensed to Collaborator. The Parties may agree to a joint licensing approach for such IP rights.

Article 8. Proprietary Rights and Publication

8.1 **Right of Access.** PHS and the Collaborator agree to exchange all Subject Data produced in the course of research under this CRADA. Research Materials will be shared equally by the Parties to the CRADA unless other disposition is agreed to by the Parties. All Parties to this CRADA will be free to utilize Subject Data and Research Materials for their own purposes, consistent with their obligations under this CRADA.

8.2 **Ownership of Subject Data and Research Materials.** Subject to the sharing requirements of Paragraph 8.1 and the regulatory filing requirements of Paragraph 8.3, the producing Party will retain ownership of and title to all Subject Inventions, all Subject Data and all Research Materials produced solely by their investigators. Jointly developed Subject Inventions, Subject Data and Research Materials will be jointly owned.

8.3 **Dissemination of Subject Data and Research Materials.** To the extent permitted by law, the Collaborator and PHS agree to use reasonable efforts to keep Subject Data and Research Materials confidential until published or until corresponding patent applications are filed. Any information that would identify human subjects of research or patients will always be maintained confidentially. To the extent permitted by law, the Collaborator shall have the exclusive right to use any and all CRADA Subject Data in and for any regulatory filing by or on behalf of Collaborator, except that PHS shall have the exclusive right to use Subject Data for that purpose, and authorize others to do so, if the CRADA is terminated or if Collaborator abandons its commercialization efforts. Collaborator acknowledges the basic research mission of the PHS, and agrees that after publication, PHS may make unpatented research materials arising out of this CRADA available to third parties for further research.

8.4 **Proprietary/Confidential Information.** Each Party agrees to limit its disclosure of Proprietary/Confidential Information to the amount necessary to carry out the Research Plan of this CRADA, and shall place a confidentiality notice on all such information. Confidential oral communications shall be reduced to writing within 30 days by the disclosing Party. Each Party receiving Proprietary/Confidential Information agrees that any information so designated shall be used by it only for the purposes described in the attached Research Plan. Any Party may object to the designation of information as Proprietary/Confidential Information by another Party. Subject Data and Research Materials developed solely by the Collaborator may be designated as Proprietary/Confidential Information when they are wholly separable from the Subject Data and Research Materials developed jointly with PHS investigators, and advance designation of such data and material categories is set forth in the RP. The exchange of other confidential information, e.g., patient-identifying data, should be similarly limited and treated. Jointly developed Subject Data and Research Material derived from the Research Plan may be disclosed by Collaborator to a third party under a confidentiality agreement for the purpose of possible sublicensing pursuant to the Licensing Agreement and subject to Article 8.7.

8.5 **Protection of Proprietary/Confidential Information.** Proprietary/Confidential Information shall not be disclosed, copied, reproduced or otherwise made available to any other person or entity without the consent of the owning Party except as required under court order or the Freedom of Information Act (5 U.S.C. §552). Each Party agrees to use its best efforts to maintain the confidentiality of Proprietary/Confidential Information. Each Party agrees that the other Party is not liable for the disclosure of Proprietary/Confidential Information which, after notice to and consultation with the concerned Party, the other Party in possession of the Proprietary/Confidential Information determines may not be lawfully withheld, provided the concerned Party has been given an opportunity to seek a court order to enjoin disclosure.

8.6 **Duration of Confidentiality Obligation.** The obligation to maintain the confidentiality of Proprietary/Confidential Information shall expire at the earlier of the date when the information is no longer Proprietary Information as defined in Article 2.7 or three (3) years after the expiration or termination date of this CRADA. The Collaborator may request an extension to this term when necessary to protect Proprietary/Confidential Information relating to products not yet commercialized.

8.7 **Publication.** The Parties are encouraged to make publicly available the results of their research. Before either Party submits a paper or abstract for publication or otherwise intends to publicly disclose information about a Subject Invention, Subject Data or Research Materials, the other Party shall be provided thirty (30) days to review the proposed publication or disclosure to assure that Proprietary/Confidential Information is protected. The publication or other disclosure shall be delayed for up to thirty (30) additional days upon written request by any Party as necessary to preserve U.S. or foreign patent or other IP rights.

Article 9. Representations and Warranties

9.1 **Representations and Warranties of PHS.** PHS hereby represents and warrants to the Collaborator that the official signing this CRADA has authority to do so.

9.2 **Representations and Warranties of the Collaborator.**

The Collaborator hereby represents and warrants to PHS that the Collaborator has the requisite power and authority to enter into this CRADA and to perform according to its terms, and that the Collaborator's official signing this CRADA has authority to do so. The Collaborator further represents that it is financially able to satisfy any funding commitments made in Appendix B.

The Collaborator certifies that the statements herein are true, complete, and accurate to the best of its knowledge. The Collaborator is aware that any false, fictitious, or fraudulent statements or claims may subject it to criminal, civil, or administrative penalties.

Article 10. Termination

10.1 **Termination By Mutual Consent.** PHS and the Collaborator may terminate this CRADA, or portions thereof, at any time by mutual written consent. In such event the Parties shall specify the disposition of all property, inventions, patent or other IP applications and other results of work accomplished or in progress, arising from or performed under this CRADA, all in accordance with the rights granted to the Parties under the terms of this Agreement.

10.2 **Unilateral Termination.** Either PHS or the Collaborator may unilaterally terminate this entire CRADA at any time by giving written notice at least thirty (30) days prior to the desired termination date, and any rights accrued in property, patents or other IP rights shall be disposed of as provided in paragraph 10.1, except that PHS may, at its option, retain funds transferred to PHS prior to unilateral termination by Collaborator for use in completing the Research Plan solely or with another partner.

10.3 **Staffing.** If this CRADA is mutually or unilaterally terminated prior to its expiration, funds will nevertheless remain available to PHS for continuing any staffing commitment made by the Collaborator pursuant to Article 5.1 above and Appendix B, if applicable, for a period of six (6) months after such termination. If there are insufficient funds to cover this expense, the Collaborator agrees to pay the difference.

10.4 **New Commitments.** No Party shall make new commitments related to this CRADA after a mutual termination or notice of a unilateral termination and shall, to the extent feasible, cancel all outstanding commitments and contracts by the termination date.

10.5 **Termination Costs.** Concurrently with the exchange of final reports pursuant to Articles 4.2 and 5.2, PHS shall submit to the Collaborator for payment a statement of all costs incurred prior to the date of termination and for all reasonable termination costs including the cost of returning Collaborator property or removal of abandoned property, for which Collaborator shall be responsible.

Article 11. Disputes

11.1 **Settlement.** Any dispute arising under this CRADA which is not disposed of by agreement of the Principal Investigators shall be submitted jointly to the signatories of this CRADA. If the signatories are unable to jointly resolve the dispute within thirty (30) days after notification thereof, the Assistant Secretary for Health (or his/her designee or successor) shall propose a resolution. Nothing in this Article shall prevent any Party from pursuing any additional administrative remedies that may be available and, after exhaustion of such administrative remedies, pursuing all available judicial remedies.

11.2 **Continuation of Work.** Pending the resolution of any dispute or claim pursuant to this Article, the Parties agree that performance of all obligations shall be pursued diligently in accordance with the direction of the PHS signatory.

Article 12. Liability

12.1 **Property.** The U.S. Government shall not be responsible for damages to any Collaborator property provided to PHS, where Collaborator retains title to the property, or any property acquired by Collaborator for its own use pursuant to this CRADA.

12.2 **NO WARRANTIES.** EXCEPT AS SPECIFICALLY STATED IN ARTICLE 9, THE PARTIES MAKE NO EXPRESS OR IMPLIED WARRANTY AS TO ANY MATTER WHATSOEVER, INCLUDING THE CONDITIONS OF THE RESEARCH OR ANY INVENTION OR PRODUCT, WHETHER TANGIBLE OR INTANGIBLE, MADE, OR DEVELOPED UNDER THIS CRADA, OR THE OWNERSHIP, MERCHANTABILITY, OR FITNESS FOR A PARTICULAR PURPOSE OF THE RESEARCH OR ANY INVENTION OR PRODUCT.

12.3 **Indemnification.** The Collaborator agrees to hold the U.S. Government harmless and to indemnify the Government for all liabilities, demands, damages, expenses and losses arising out of the use by the Collaborator for any purpose of the Subject Data, Research Materials and/or Subject Inventions produced in whole or part by PHS employees under this CRADA, unless due to the negligence or willful misconduct of PHS, its employees, or agents. The Collaborator shall be liable for any claims or damages it incurs in connection with this CRADA. PHS has no authority to indemnify the Collaborator.

12.4 **Force Majeure.** Neither Party shall be liable for any unforeseeable event beyond its reasonable control not caused by the fault or negligence of such Party, which causes such Party to be unable to perform its obligations under this CRADA, and which it has been unable to overcome by the exercise of due diligence. In the event of the occurrence of such a *force majeure* event, the Party unable to perform shall promptly notify the other Party. It shall further use its best efforts to resume performance as quickly as possible and shall suspend performance only for such period of time as is necessary as a result of the *force majeure* event.

Article 13. Miscellaneous

13.1 **Governing Law.** The construction, validity, performance and effect of this CRADA shall be governed by Federal law, as applied by the Federal Courts in the District of Columbia. Federal law and regulations will preempt any conflicting or inconsistent provisions in this CRADA.

13.2 **Entire Agreement.** This CRADA constitutes the entire agreement between the Parties concerning the subject matter of this CRADA and supersedes any prior understanding or written or oral agreement.

13.3 **Headings.** Titles and headings of the articles and subarticles of this CRADA are for convenient reference only, do not form a part of this CRADA, and shall in no way affect its interpretation. The PHS component that is the Party for all purposes of this CRADA is the Bureau(s), Institute(s), Center(s) or Division(s) listed on the Cover Page herein.

13.4 **Waivers.** None of the provisions of this CRADA shall be considered waived by any Party unless such waiver is given in writing to the other Party. The failure of a Party to insist upon strict performance of any of the terms and conditions hereof, or failure or delay to exercise any rights provided herein or by law, shall not be deemed a waiver of any rights of any Party.

13.5 **Severability.** The illegality or invalidity of any provisions of this CRADA shall not impair, affect, or invalidate the other provisions of this CRADA.

13.6 **Amendments.** If either Party desires a modification to this CRADA, the Parties shall, upon reasonable notice of the proposed modification or extension by the Party desiring the change, confer in good faith to determine the desirability of such modification or extension. Such modification shall not be effective until a written amendment is signed by the signatories to this CRADA or by their representatives duly authorized to execute such amendment.

13.7 **Assignment.** Neither this CRADA nor any rights or obligations of any Party hereunder shall be assigned or otherwise transferred by either Party without the prior written consent of the other Party.

13.8 **Notices.** All notices pertaining to or required by this CRADA shall be in writing and shall be signed by an authorized representative and shall be delivered by hand or sent by certified mail, return receipt requested, with postage prepaid, to the addresses indicated on the signature page for each Party. Notices regarding the exercise of license options shall be made pursuant to Article 7.2. Any Party may change such address by notice given to the other Party in the manner set forth above.

13.9 **Independent Contractors.** The relationship of the Parties to this CRADA is that of independent contractors and not agents of each other or joint venturers or partners. Each Party shall maintain sole and exclusive control over its personnel and operations. Collaborator employees who will be working at PHS facilities may be asked to sign a Guest Researcher or Special Volunteer Agreement appropriately modified in view of the terms of this CRADA.

13.10 **Use of Name or Endorsements.** By entering into this CRADA, PHS does not directly or indirectly endorse any product or service provided, or to be provided, whether directly or indirectly related to either this CRADA or to any patent or other IP license or agreement which implements this CRADA by its successors, assignees, or licensees. The Collaborator shall not in any way state or imply that this CRADA is an endorsement of any such product or service by the U.S. Government or any of its organizational units or employees. Collaborator issued press releases that reference or rely upon the work of PHS under this CRADA shall be made available to PHS at least 7 days prior to publication for review and comment.

13.11 **Exceptions to this CRADA.** Any exceptions or modifications to this CRADA that are agreed to by the Parties prior to their execution of this CRADA are set forth in Appendix C.

13.12 **Reasonable Consent.** Whenever a Party's consent or permission is required under this CRADA, such consent or permission shall not be unreasonably withheld.

Article 14. Duration of Agreement

14.1 **Duration.** It is mutually recognized that the duration of this project cannot be rigidly defined in advance, and that the contemplated time periods for various phases of the RP are only good faith guidelines subject to adjustment by mutual agreement to fit circumstances as the RP proceeds. In no case will the term of this CRADA extend beyond the term indicated in the RP unless it is revised in accordance with Article 13.6.

14.2 **Survivability.** The provisions of Articles 4.2, 5-8, 10.3-10.5, 11.1, 12.2-12.4, 13.1, 13.10 and 14.2 shall survive the termination of this CRADA.

SIGNATURES BEGIN ON THE NEXT PAGE

FOR PHS:

_____ _____

Date

_____

Mailing Address for Notices:

_____

_____

_____

_____

_____

FOR THE COLLABORATOR:

_____ _____

Date

_____

Mailing Address for Notices:

_____

_____

_____

_____

APPENDIX A

RESEARCH PLAN

TITLE   OF
CRADA:_____

PHS   PRINCIPAL
INVESTIGATOR:_____

his/her
Laboratory:_____

COLLABORATOR   PRINCIPAL
INVESTIGATOR:_____

TERM OF CRADA:_____ (___) years.

The Research Plan which follows this page should be concise but of sufficient detail to permit reviewers of this CRADA to evaluate the scientific merit of the proposed collaboration. The RP should explain the scientific importance of the collaboration and the research goals of PHS and the Collaborator. The respective contributions in terms of expertise and/or research materials of PHS and Collaborator should be summarized. Initial and subsequent projects contemplated under the RP, and the time periods estimated for their completion, should be described and pertinent methodological considerations summarized. Pertinent literature references may be cited and additional relevant information included.

APPENDIX B

FINANCIAL AND STAFFING CONTRIBUTIONS OF THE PARTIES

APPENDIX C

EXCEPTIONS OR MODIFICATIONS TO THIS CRADA

APPENDIX 7

INVENTION RIGHTS

GOVERNMENT EMPLOYEE INVENTION RIGHTS

EX. ORD. NO. 9424. ESTABLISHMENT OF A REGISTER OF GOVERNMENT INTERESTS IN PATENTS Ex. Ord. No. 9424, Feb. 18, 1944, 9 Fed. Reg. 1959, provided:

1. The Secretary of Commerce shall cause to be established in the United States Patent Office (now Patent and Trademark Office) a separate register for the recording of all rights and interests of the Government in or under patents and applications for patents.

2. The several departments and other executive agencies of the Government, including Government-owned or Government-controlled corporations, shall forward promptly to the Commissioner of Patents (now Patents and Trademarks) for recording in the separate register provided for in paragraph 1 hereof all licenses, assignments, or other interests of the Government in or under patents or applications for patents, in accordance with such rules and regulations as may be prescribed pursuant to paragraph 4 hereof; but the lack of recordation in such register of any right or interest of the Government in or under any patent or application therefor shall not prejudice in any way the assertion of such right or interest by the Government.

3. The register shall be open to inspection except as to such entries or documents which, in the opinion of the department or agency submitting them for recording, should be maintained in secrecy: Provided, however, That the right of inspection may be restricted to authorized representatives of the Government pending the final report to the President by the National Patent Planning Commission under Executive Order No. 8977 of December 12, 1941, and action thereon by the President.

4. The Commissioner of Patents (now Patents and Trademarks), with the approval of the Secretary of Commerce, shall prescribe such rules and regulations as he may deem necessary to effectuate the purposes of this order.

EX. ORD. NO. 9865. PATENT PROTECTION ABROAD OF INVENTIONS RESULTING FROM RESEARCH FINANCED BY THE GOVERNMENT Ex. Ord. No. 9865, June 14, 1947, 12 Fed. Reg. 3907, as amended by Ex. Ord. No. 10096, Jan. 23, 1950, 15 Fed. Reg. 389, provided:

1. All Government departments and agencies shall, whenever practicable, acquire the right to file foreign patent applications on inventions resulting from research conducted or financed by the Government.

2. All Government departments and agencies which have or may hereafter acquire title to inventions or the right to file patent applications abroad thereon, shall fully and continuously

223

inform the Chairman of Government Patents Board (now Secretary of Commerce. See Ex. Ord. No. 10930 set out as a note below) concerning such inventions, except as provided in section 6 hereof, and shall make recommendations to the Chairman of Government Patents Board (now Secretary of Commerce) as to which of such inventions should receive patent protection by the United States abroad and the foreign jurisdictions in which such patent protection should be sought. The recommendations of such departments and agencies shall indicate the immediate or future industrial, commercial or other value of the invention concerned, including its value to public health.

3. The Chairman of Government Patents Board (now Secretary of Commerce) shall determine whether, and in what foreign jurisdictions, the United States should seek patents for such inventions, and, to the extent of appropriations available therefor, shall procure patent protection for such inventions, taking all action, consistent with existing law, necessary to acquire and maintain patent rights abroad. Such determinations of the said Department shall be made after full consultation with United States industry and commerce, with the Department of State, and with other Government agencies familiar with the technical, scientific, industrial, commercial or other economic or social factors affecting the invention involved, and after consideration of the availability of valid patent protection in the countries determined to be immediate or potential markets for, or producers of, products, processes, or services covered by or relating to the invention.

4. The Chairman of Government Patents Board (now Secretary of Commerce) shall administer foreign patents acquired by the United States under the terms of this order and shall issue licenses thereunder in accordance with law under such rules and regulations as he shall prescribe. Nationals of the United States shall be granted licenses on a nonexclusive royalty free basis except in such cases as he shall determine and proclaim it to be inconsistent with the public interest to issue such licenses on a nonexclusive royalty free basis.

5. The Department of State, in consultation with the Chairman of Government Patents Board (now Secretary of Commerce), shall negotiate arrangements among governments under which each government and its nationals shall have access to the foreign patents of the other participating governments. Patents relating to matters of public health may be licensed by the Chairman of Government Patents Board (now Secretary of Commerce), with the approval of the Secretary of State, to any country or its nationals upon such terms and conditions as are in accordance with law and as the Chairman of Government Patents Board (now Secretary of Commerce) determines to be appropriate, regardless of whether such country is a party to the arrangements provided for in this section.

6. There shall be exempted from the provisions of this order (a) all inventions within the jurisdiction of the Atomic Energy Commission except in such cases as the said Commission specifically authorizes the inclusion of an invention under the terms of this order; and (b) all other inventions officially classified as secret or confidential for reasons of the national security. Nothing in this order shall supersede the declassification policies and procedures established by Executive Orders Nos. 9568 of June 8, 1945, 9604 of August 25, 1945, and 9809 of December 12, 1946.

TRANSFER OF FUNCTIONS. Atomic Energy Commission abolished and all functions transferred to Administrator of Energy Research and Development Administration (unless otherwise specifically provided) by section 5814 of Title 42, The Public Health and Welfare. Energy Research and Development Administration terminated and functions vested by law in Administrator thereof transferred to Secretary of Energy (unless otherwise specifically provided) by sections 7151(a) and 7293 of Title 42.

EX. ORD. NO. 10096. UNIFORM GOVERNMENT PATENT POLICY FOR INVEN- TIONS BY GOVERNMENT EMPLOYEES Ex. Ord. No. 10096, Jan. 23, 1950, 15 Fed. Reg. 389, as amended by Ex. Ord. No. 10695, Jan. 16, 1957, 22 Fed. Reg. 365; Ex. Ord. No. 10930, Mar. 24, 1961, 26 Fed. Reg. 2583, provided:

NOW, THEREFORE, by virtue of the authority vested in me by the Constitution and statutes, and as President of the United States and Commander in Chief of the armed forces of the United States, in the interest of the establishment and operation of a uniform patent policy for the Government with respect to inventions made by

Government employees, it is hereby ordered as follows:

1. The following basic policy is established for all Government agencies with respect to inventions hereafter made by any Government employee:

   (a) The Government shall obtain the entire right, title, and interest in and to all inventions made by any Government employee (1) during working hours, or (2) with a contribution by the Government of facilities, equipment, materials, funds, or information, or of time or services of other Government employees on official duty, or (3) which bear a direct relation to or are made in consequence of the official duties of the inventor.

   (b) In any case where the contribution of the Government, as measured by any one or more of the criteria set forth in paragraph (a) last above, to the invention, is insufficient equitably to justify a requirement of assignment to the Government of the entire right, title and interest to such invention, or in any case where the Government has insufficient interest in an invention to obtain entire right, title and interest therein (although the Government could obtain some under paragraph (a), above), the Government agency concerned, subject to the approval of the Chairman of the Government Patents Board (now Secretary of Commerce. See Ex. Ord. No. 10930 set out as a note below) (provided for in paragraph 3 of this order and hereinafter referred to as the Chairman), shall leave title to such invention in the employee, subject, however, to the reservation to the Government of a nonexclusive, irrevocable, royalty-free license in the invention with power to grant licenses for all governmental purposes, such reservation, in the terms thereof, to appear, where practicable, in any patent, domestic or Foreign, which may issue on such invention.

   (c) In applying the provisions of paragraphs (a) and (b), above, to the facts and circumstances relating to the making of any particular invention, it shall be presumed that an invention made by an employee who is employed or assigned (i) to invent or improve or perfect any art, machine, manufacture, or composition of matter, (ii) to conduct or perform research, development work, or both, (iii) to supervise, direct, coordinate, or review

Government financed or conducted research, development work, or both, or (iv) to act in a liaison capacity among governmental or nongovernmental agencies or individuals engaged in such work, or made by an employee included within any other category of employees specified by regulations issued pursuant to section 4(b) hereof, falls within the provisions of paragraph (a), above, and it shall be presumed that any invention made by any other employee falls within the provisions of paragraph (b), above. Either presumption may be rebutted by the facts or circumstances attendant upon the conditions under which any particular invention is made and, notwithstanding the foregoing, shall not preclude a determination that the invention falls within the provisions of paragraph (d) next below.

(d) In any case wherein the Government neither (1) pursuant to the provisions of paragraph (a) above, obtains entire right, title and interest in and to an invention nor (2) pursuant to the provisions of paragraph (b) above, reserves a nonexclusive, irrevocable, royalty-free license in the invention with power to grant licenses for all governmental purposes, the Government shall leave the entire right, title and interest in and to the invention in the Government employee, subject to law.

(e) Actions taken, and rights acquired, under the foregoing provisions of this section, shall be reported to the Chairman (now Secretary of Commerce) in accordance with procedures established by him.

2. Subject to considerations of national security, or public health, safety, or welfare, the following basic policy is established for the collection, and dissemination to the public, of information concerning inventions resulting from Government research and development activities:

(a) When an invention is made under circumstances defined in paragraph 1(a) of this order giving the United States the right to title thereto, the Government agency concerned shall either prepare and file an application for patent therefor in the United States Patent Office (now Patent and Trademark Office) or make a full disclosure of the invention promptly to the Chairman (now Secretary of Commerce), who may, if he determines the Government interest so requires, cause application for patent to be filed or cause the invention to be fully disclosed by publication thereof: Provided, however, That, consistent with present practice of the Department of Agriculture, no application for patent shall, without the approval of the Secretary of Agriculture, be filed in respect of any variety of plant invented by any employee of that Department.

(b) (Revoked. Ex. Ord. No. 10695, Jan. 16, 1957, 22 Fed. Reg. 365)

3. (a) (Revoked. Ex. Ord. No. 10930, Mar. 24, 1961, 26 Fed. Reg. 2583)

(b) The Government Patents Board shall advise and confer with the Chairman concerning the operation of those aspects of the Government's patent policy which are affected by the provisions of this order or of Executive Order No. 9865, and suggest modifications or improvements where necessary.

(c) (Revoked. Ex. Ord. No. 10930, Mar. 24, 1961, 26 Fed. Reg. 2583)

(d) The Chairman shall establish such committees and other working groups as may be required to advise or assist him in the performance of any of his functions.

(e) The Chairman of the Government Patents Board (now Secretary of Commerce) and the Chairman of the Interdepartmental Committee on Scientific Research and Development (provided for by Executive Order No. 9912 of December 24, 1947), shall establish and maintain such mutual consultation as will effect the proper coordination of affairs of common concern.

4. With a view to obtaining uniform application of the policies set out in this order and uniform operations thereunder, the Chairman (now Secretary of Commerce) is authorized and directed:

(a) To consult and advise with Government agencies concerning the application and operation of the policies outlined herein;

(b) After consultation with the Government Patents Board, to formulate and submit to the President for approval such proposed rules and regulations as may be necessary or desirable to implement and effectuate the aforesaid policies, together with the recommendations of the Government Patents Board thereon;

(c) To submit annually a report to the President concerning the operation of such policies, and from time to time such recommendations for modification thereof as may be deemed desirable;

(d) To determine with finality any controversies or disputes between any Government agency and its employees, to the extent submitted by any party to the dispute, concerning the ownership of inventions made by such employees or rights therein; and

(e) To perform such other or further functions or duties as may from time to time be prescribed by the President or by statute.

5. The functions and duties of the Secretary of Commerce and the Department of Commerce under the provisions of Executive Order No. 9865 of June 14, 1947 are hereby transferred to the Chairman and the whole or any part of such functions and duties may be delegated by him to any Government agency or officer: Provided, That said Executive Order No. 9865 shall not be deemed to be amended or affected by any provision of this Executive order other than this paragraph 5.

6. Each Government agency shall take all steps appropriate to effectuate this order, including the promulgation of necessary regulations which shall not be inconsistent with this order or with regulations issued pursuant to paragraph 4(b) hereof.

7. As used in this Executive order, the next stated terms, in singular and plural, are defined as follows for the purposes hereof:

(a) "Government agency" includes any executive department and any independent commission, board, office, agency, authority, or other establishment of the Executive Branch of the Government of the United States (including any such independent regulatory commission or board, any such wholly-owned corporation, and the Smithsonian Institution), but excludes the Atomic Energy Commission.

(b) "Government employee" includes any officer or employee, civilian or military, of any Government agency, except such part-time consultants or employees as may be excluded by regulations promulgated pursuant to paragraph 4(b) hereof.

(c) "Invention" includes any art, machine, manufacture, design, or composition of matter, or any new and useful improvement thereof, or any variety of plant, which is or may be patentable under the patent laws of the United States.

EX. ORD. NO. 10695. TRANSFER OF RECORDS TO DEPARTMENT OF COMMERCE
Section 2 of Ex. Ord. 10695, Jan. 16, 1957, 22 Fed. Reg. 365, provided that:

"The Chairman of the Government Patents Board is hereby authorized to transfer to the Department of Commerce any or all of the records heretofore prepared by the Board pursuant to paragraph 2(b) of Executive Order No. 10096."

EX. ORD. NO. 10930. ABOLITION OF GOVERNMENT PATENTS BOARD Ex. Ord. No. 10930, Mar. 24, 1961, 26 Fed. Reg. 2583, provided:

By virtue of the authority vested in me as President of the United States, it is ordered as follows:

Sec. 1. The Government Patents Board, established by section 3(a) of Executive Order No. 10096 of January 23, 1950 (set out above), and all positions established thereunder or pursuant thereto are hereby abolished.

Sec. 2. All functions of the Government Patents Board and of the Chairman thereof under the said Executive Order No. 10096, except the functions of conference and consultation between the Board and the Chairman, are hereby transferred to the Secretary of Commerce, who may provide for the performance of such transferred functions by such officer, employee, or agency of the Department of Commerce as he may designate.

Sec. 3. The Secretary of Commerce shall make such provision as may be necessary and consonant with law for the disposition or transfer of property, personnel, records, and funds of the Government Patents Board.

Sec. 4. Except to the extent that they may be inconsistent with this order, all determinations, regulations, rules, rulings, orders, and other actions made or issued by the Government Patents Board, or by any Government agency with respect to any function transferred by this order, shall continue in full force and effect until amended, modified, or revoked by appropriate authority.

Sec. 5. Subsections (a) and (c) of section 3 of Executive Order No. 10096 are hereby revoked, and all other provisions of that order are hereby amended to the extent that they are inconsistent with the provisions of this order.

John F. Kennedy.

APPENDIX 8

THE UNDER SECRETARY OF DEFENSE
ACQUISITION, TECHNOLOGY
AND LOGISTICS

---

21 Dec 2000

MEMORANDUM FOR SECRETARIES OF THE MILITARY DEPARTMENTS

DIRECTORS OF DEFENSE AGENCIES

SUBJECT: "Other Transaction" Authority (OTA) for Prototype Projects

Reference: DoD Directive 5134.1, "Under Secretary of Defense for Acquisition and Technology (USD(A&T))," September 17, 1999

This directive-type memorandum assigns responsibilities and prescribes procedures for implementation and use of OTA for certain prototype projects directly relevant to weapons or weapon systems proposed to be acquired or developed by the Department of Defense.

For DoD, "other transactions" is a term commonly used to refer to the 10 U.S.C. 2371 authority to enter into transactions other than contracts, grants or cooperative agreements. OTA provides tremendous flexibility since instruments for prototype projects, awarded pursuant to this authority, generally are not subject to federal laws and regulations limited in applicability to procurement contracts.

It is DoD policy, under the above reference, to establish policies and programs that improve, streamline and strengthen DoD Component technology access and development programs, encourage open-market competition and technology-driven prototype efforts that offer increased military capabilities at lower total ownership costs and faster fielding times, and exploit the cost-reduction potential of accessing innovative or commercially developed technologies. OTA for prototype projects is a vital tool that will help the Department achieve these objectives. This authority should be used wisely, when it is appropriate.

Agreements Officers and Project Managers are encouraged to pursue competitively awarded prototype projects that can be adequately defined to establish a fixed-price type of agreement and attract nontraditional defense contractors participating to a significant extent.

Agreements Officers should take the lead in encouraging business process innovations and ensuring that business decisions are sound. The OT Guide (attached) is intended to provide a framework for the government team to consider and apply, as appropriate, when using OTA for prototype projects.

However, there are some mandatory requirements included in the Guide that are evident by the prescriptive language used.

The Director, Defense Procurement shall monitor compliance with this memorandum and update the OT Guide, as needed. The Secretaries of the Military Departments and the Directors of the Defense Agencies shall establish agency procedures necessary to implement the OT Guide. Any delegation of authority to use this OTA will be to officials whose level of responsibility, business acumen, and judgment enable them to operate in this relatively unstructured environment.

The guide must be considered for solicitations issued after January 5, 2001. The new reporting requirements are applicable to any prototype projects awarded after 1 October 2000.

s/ J.S. Gansler

Attachment

As stated

"OTHER TRANSACTIONS" (OT) GUIDE FOR PROTOTYPE PROJECTS

UNDER SECRETARY OF DEFENSE FOR ACQUISITION, TECHNOLOGY AND LOGISTICS

C2.3 INTELLECTUAL PROPERTY

C2.3.1. <u>General</u>.

C2.3.1.1. As certain intellectual property requirements normally imposed by the Bayh-Dole Act (35 U.S.C. 202-204) and 10 U.S.C. 2320-21 do not apply to Other Transactions, Agreements Officers can negotiate terms and conditions different from those typically used in procurement contracts. However, in negotiating these clauses, the Agreements Officer must consider other laws that affect the government's use and handling of intellectual property, such as the Trade Secrets Act (18 U.S.C. 1905); the Economic Espionage Act (18 U.S.C. 1831-39); the Freedom of Information Act (5 U.S.C. 552); 10 U.S.C. 130; 28 U.S.C. 1498; 35 U.S.C. 205 and 207-209; and the Lanham Act, partially codified at 15 U.S.C. 1114 and 1122. C2.3.1.2. Intellectual property collectively refers to rights governed by a variety of different laws, such as patent, copyright, trademark, and trade secret laws. Due to the complexity of intellectual property law and the critical role of intellectual property created under prototype projects, Agreements Officers, in conjunction with the Program Manager, should obtain the assistance of Intellectual Property Counsel as early as possible in the acquisition process.

C2.3.1.3. The Agreements Officer should assess the impact of intellectual property rights on the government's total life cycle cost of the technology, both in costs attributable to royalties from required licenses, and in costs associated with the inability to obtain competition for the future production, maintenance, upgrade, and modification of prototype technology. In addition, insufficient intellectual property rights hinder the government's ability to adapt the developed technology for use outside the initial scope of the prototype project. Conversely, where the government overestimates the intellectual property rights it will need, the government might pay for unused rights and dissuade new business units from entering into an Agreement. Bearing this in mind, the Agreements Officer should carefully assess the intellectual property needs of the government.

C2.3.1.4. In general, the Agreements Officer should seek to obtain intellectual property rights consistent with the Bayh-Dole Act (35 U.S.C. 201-204) for patents and 10 U.S.C. 2320-21 for technical data, but may negotiate rights of a different scope when necessary to accomplish program objectives and foster government interests. The negotiated intellectual property clauses should facilitate the acquisition strategy, including any likely production and follow-on support of the prototyped item, and balance the relative investments and risks borne by the parties both in past development of the technology and in future development and maintenance of the technology. Due to the complex nature of intellectual property clauses, the clauses should be incorporated in full text. Also, the Agreements Officer should consider the effect of other forms of intellectual property *(e.g.,* trademarks, registered vessel hulls, etc.), that may impact the acquisition strategy for the technology.

C2.3.1.5. The Agreements Officer should ensure that the disputes clause included in the agreement can accommodate specialized disputes arising under the intellectual property clauses, such as the exercise of intellectual property march-in rights or the validation of restrictions on technical data or computer software.

C2.3.1.6. The Agreements Officer should consider how the intellectual property clauses applicable to the awardee flow down to others, including whether to allow others to submit any applicable intellectual property licenses directly to the government.

C2.3.1.7. Where the acquisition strategy relies on the commercial marketplace to produce, maintain, modify, or upgrade the technology, there may be a reduced need for rights in intellectual property for those purposes. However, since the government tends to use technology well past the norm in the commercial marketplace, the Agreements Officer should plan for maintenance and support of fielded prototype technology when the technology is no longer supported by the commercial market and consider obtaining at no additional cost a paid-up unlimited license to the technology.

C2.3.1.8. The Agreements Officer should consider restricting awardees from licensing technology developed under the Agreement to domestic or foreign firms under circumstances that would hinder potential domestic manufacture or use of the technology. The Agreements Officer must also be aware that export restrictions prohibit awardees from disclosing or licensing certain technology to foreign firms.

C2.3.1.9. Additional Matters. The Agreements Officer should consider including in the intellectual property clauses any additional rights available to the government in the case of inability or refusal of the private party or consortium to continue to perform the Agreement. It may also be appropriate to consider negotiating time periods after which the government will automatically obtain greater rights (for example, if the original negotiated rights limited government's rights for a specified period of time to permit commercialization of the technology).

C2.3.2. Rights in Inventions and Patents.

C2.3.2.1. The Agreements Officer should negotiate a patents rights clause necessary to accomplish program objectives and foster the government's interest. In determining what represents a reasonable arrangement under the circumstances, the Agreements Officer should consider the government's needs for patents and patent rights to use the developed technology, or what other intellectual property rights will be needed should the agreement provide for trade secret protection instead of patent protection.

C2.3.2.2. The agreement should address the following issues:

C2.3.2.2.1. Definitions. It is important to define all essential terms in the patent rights clauses, and the Agreements Officer should consider defining a subject invention to include those inventions conceived or first actually reduced to practice under the Agreement.

C2.3.2.2.2. Allocation of Rights. The Agreements Officer should consider allowing the participant to retain ownership of the subject invention while reserving, for the government, a nonexclusive, nontransferable, irrevocable, paid-up license to practice or have practiced for or on behalf of the United States the subject invention throughout the world. In addition, the agreement should address the government's rights in background inventions (e.g., inventions created prior to or outside the agreement) that are incorporated into the prototype design and may therefore affect the government's life cycle cost for the technology.

C2.3.2.2.3. March-in Rights. The Agreements Officer should consider negotiating government march-in rights in order to encourage further commercialization of the technology. While the march-in rights outlined in the Bayh-Dole Act may be modified to best meet the needs of the program, only in rare circumstances should the march-in rights be entirely removed.

C2.3.2.2.4. Disclosure/Tracking Procedures. The Agreements Officer may consider changing the timing of submission of the disclosures, elections of title, and patent applications.

C2.3.2.2.5. Option for Trade Secret Protection. The Agreements Officer may consider allowing subject inventions to remain trade secrets as long as the government's interest in the continued use of the technology is protected. In making this evaluation, the Agreements Officer should consider whether allowing the technology to remain a trade secret creates an unacceptable risk of a third party patenting the same technology, the government's right to utilize this technology with third parties, and whether there are available means to mitigate these risks outside of requiring patent protection.

C2.3.2.2.6. Additional Considerations. The Agreement Officer should consider whether it is appropriate to include clauses that address Authorization and Consent, Indemnity, and Notice and Assistance:

C2.3.2.2.6.1. Authorization and Consent. Authorization and consent policies provide that work by an awardee under an agreement may not be enjoined by reason of patent infringement and shifts liability for such infringement to the government (see 28 U.S.C. 1498). The government's liability for damages in any such suit may, however, ultimately be borne by the awardee in accordance with the terms of a patent indemnity clause (see 2.3.2.2.6.3). The agreement should not include an authorization and consent clause when both complete performance and delivery are outside the United States, its possessions, and Puerto Rico.

C2.3.2.2.6.2. Notice and Assistance. Notice policy requires the awardee to notify the Agreements Officer of all claims of infringement that come to the awardee's attention in connection with performing the agreement. Assistance policy requires the awardee, when requested, to assist the government with any evidence and information in its possession in connection with any suit against the government, or any claims against the government made before suit has been instituted that alleges patent or copyright infringement arising out of performance under the agreement.

C2.3.2.2.6.3. Indemnity. Indemnity clauses mitigate the government's risk of cost increases caused by infringement of a third-party owned patent. Such a clause may be appropriate if the supplies or services used in the prototype technology developed under the agreement normally are or have been sold or offered for sale to the public in the commercial open market, either with or without modifications. In addition, where trade secret protection is allowed in lieu of patent protection for patentable subject inventions, a perpetual patent indemnity clause might be considered as a mechanism for mitigating the risks described in C2.3.2.2.5 above. The agreement should not include a clause whereby the government expressly agrees to indemnify the awardee against liability for infringement.

C2.3.3. Rights in Technical Data and Computer Software

C2.3.3.1. As used in this section, "Computer software" means computer programs, source code, source code listings, object code listings, design details, algorithms, processes, flow charts, formulae and related material that would enable the software to be reproduced, recreated, or recompiled. Computer software does not include computer data bases or computer software documentation. "Computer software documentation" means owner's manuals, user's manuals, installation instructions, operating instructions, and other similar items, regardless of storage medium, that explain the capabilities of the computer software or provide instructions for using the software. "Technical data" means recorded information, regardless of the form or method of the recording, of a scientific or technical nature (including computer software documentation). The term does not include computer software or data incidental to contract administration, such as financial and/or management information.

C2.3.3.2. Technical Data Rights and Computer Software Rights refer to a combined copyright, know-how, and/or trade secret license that defines the government's ability to use, reproduce, modify, release, and disclose technical data and computer software. The focus of license negotiations often centers around the government's ability to release or disclose outside the government. In addition, computer software licenses require additional consideration because restrictions may impact the government's use, maintenance, and upgrade of computer software used as an operational element of the prototype technology.

C2.3.3.3. The Agreement should address the following issues:

C2.3.3.3.1. Definitions. The Agreements Officer should ensure that all essential terms are defined, including all classes of technical data and computer software, and all categories of applicable license rights. Where the terms "technical data," "computer software," "computer software documentation," or other standard terms used in the DFARS are used in the agreement, and this prototype technology is likely to be produced, maintained, or upgraded using traditional procurement instruments, these terms must be defined the same as used in the DFARS in order to prevent confusion.

C2.3.3.3.2. Allocation of Rights. The agreement must explicitly address the government's rights to use, modify, reproduce, release, and disclose the relevant technical data and computer software. The government should receive rights in all technical data and computer software that is developed under the agreement, regardless of whether it is delivered, and should receive rights in all delivered technical data and computer software, regardless of whether it was developed under the agreement.

C2.3.3.3.3. Delivery Requirements. While not required to secure the government's rights in the technical data and computer software, if delivery of technical data, computer software, or computer software documentation is necessary, the Agreements Officer should consider the delivery medium, and for computer software, whether that includes both executable and source code. In addition, the Agreements Officer should consider including an identification list detailing what technical data and computer software is being delivered with restrictions.

C2.3.3.3.4. Restrictive Legends. The Agreements Officer should ensure that the Agreement requires descriptive restrictive markings to be placed on delivered technical data and computer software for which the government is granted less than unlimited rights. The agreement should address the content and placement of the legends, with special care to avoid confusion between the classes of data defined by the agreement and the standard markings prescribed by the DFARS. In addition, the agreement should presume that all technical data and computer software delivered without these legends is delivered with unlimited rights.

C2.3.3.3.5. Special Circumstances. The agreement should account for certain emergency or special circumstances in which the government may need additional rights, such as the need to disclose technical data or computer software for emergency repair or overhaul.

C2.3.3.3.6. The Agreements Officer should also account for commercial technical data and commercial computer software incorporated into the prototype. As compared to non-commercial technical data and computer software, the government typically does not require as extensive rights in commercial technical data and software. However, depending on the acquisition strategy, the government may need to negotiate for greater rights in order to utilize the developed technology.

CHAPTER 3

I. DETERMINING OWNERSHIP OF PATENTS

Although the various contract Patent Rights clauses or statutory provisions vest different rights in the Government, they apply only to inventions made in the performance of the contract. Thus, if the contractor can demonstrate that an invention falls outside of contract performance, the Government will get no rights. This section discusses this crucial issue.

For the purpose of analysis, it is useful to divide the problem into two questions. First, what aspect of the inventive process must occur under the contract in order to make either the contract clause or the required statutory patent provisions apply? In this regard most of the statutes or Patent Rights clauses apply if either conception or actual reduction to practice of the invention occurs during contract performance. Thus, the answer to this question requires knowledge of the meaning of these terms. Second, how closely related must these legal events be to the contract itself? The language used to describe this relationship varies but generally is stated in a somewhat imprecise term: "in the course of or under" the contract, or "in the performance of work under" the contract. The relationships between inventors and the work performed on Government contracts must be investigated in order to answer this question.

A. Making of the Invention

1. *Basic Principles*

a. *Terminology*

(1) MADE

The 1963 and 1971 Presidential Policy Statements of Government Patent Policy use the term "made" to describe the inventive act. This term is defined in section 4(f) of the 1971 Presidential Policy Statement (3 C.F.R. § 1075, 1080) as "the conception or first actual reduction to practice" of such inventions. This definition of "made," which refers to conception or reduction to practice in the alternative, is also found in 35 U.S.C. § 201(g), the patent policy for small businesses and nonprofit organizations; the National Aeronautics and Space Act of 1958, 42 U.S.C. § 2457(j)(3); and the Federal Nonnuclear Energy Research and Development Act of 1974, 42 U.S.C. § 5908(m)(3). The Atomic Energy Act of 1954, as amended, is not as clear. The Act states that it covers any invention "made or conceived" under the contract (omitting the term "reduction to practice"), 42 U.S.C. § 2182. However, since the term "made" was used in conjunction with "conceived" both in the Act and in the implementing AEC regulations and clauses, it is not unreasonable to conclude that it meant "first actually reduced to practice." The Federal Nonnuclear Energy Research and Development Act of 1974, 42 U.S.C. § 5908, also uses the term "made or conceived." However, in other subsections the term "made" is used alone.

Thus, the Government obtains rights under the applicable contract Patent Rights clause or statutory provision if *either* of two events in the inventive process, *conception or actual reduction to practice*, occurs during contract performance. Further, each of these events is generally thought to describe an occurrence that happens at a demonstrable instant in time.

(2) PATENT LAW BASIS

The terms *conception* and *actual reduction to practice* are terms of art which have a long history in various facets of patent law. The patent cases have defined these terms primarily in interference proceedings (i.e., proceedings in which adverse parties attempt to prove priority of invention so that one will be entitled to patent therein) or patent infringement litigation (i.e., litigation by which a patentee attempts to prove that he invented the patented subject matter prior to the alleged "prior art" offered by the infringer as anticipating that subject matter). See, for example, *Standard Mfg. Co. v. United States*, 25 Cl. Ct. 1 (1991). The date of invention is also an issue in certain situations. For example, a patent applicant may overcome a cited patent or publication during the prosecution of his application in the U.S. Patent and Trademark Office by claiming the completion of the invention before the date of the publication or the filing date of the patent. See Rule 131 of the U.S. Patent and Trademark Office, Rules of Practice, 37 C.F.R. § 1.131. See *Hazeltine Corp. v. United States*, 10 Cl. Ct. 417, 445 (1986), where the court states that there is "no principled justification for not turning to 'other' reduction to practice cases for guidance" in a Government contract case regarding the making of an invention.

In interferences and Rule 131 practice, the inventor tries vigorously to establish an early date of conception or reduction to practice, or both, to convince the Patent Office or the court that such date or dates preceded those established by the adverse party for the cited patent or publication. Also, the inventor is almost always attempting to prove his own acts. A rare exception occurs in infringement cases where the defense that the patent alleged to be infringed was "on sale" more than one year prior to its filing date is supported by a claim that the invention was "reduced to practice" prior to the alleged sale, *Gould Inc. v. United States*, 217 Ct. Cl. 167, 579 F.2d 571, 198 U.S.P.Q. 156 (1978). Similarly, where the acts constituting reduction to practice which would invalidate the plaintiff's patent have been performed by a third party, the court has placed the burden of establishing the reduction to practice on the defendant, *General Elec. Co. v. United States*, 228 Ct. Cl. 192, 654 F.2d 55, 211 U.S.P.Q. 867 (1981).

When the issue is the Government's right in a patent or patentable subject matter related to a Government contract, the nature of the inquiry is altered. There is no question of priority of invention or of prior art. Rather, the issue is the date on which either conception or reduction to practice occurred so that it may be ascertained whether either of these acts occurred during the contractual period. Yet patent law methodology tends to be used in interpreting the meaning of the terms, *conception* and *first actual reduction to practice.*

(3) EVENTS-ORIENTED TEST

The Government has adopted an *events-oriented* test to determine which inventions are subject to the contract. This test is the result of defining the making of inventions in terms of conception or reduction to practice in relation to contractual activity. Usually the issue is whether the particular acts alleged to be either the conception of the invention or its reduction to practice occurred in the performance of under, or in the course of or under, the contract.

Determining whether an invention is or is not subject to a Government contract is not based on equitable consideration, i.e., which party expended greater funds. It is quite possible under this definition for the invention to be subject to the contract even though the Government expends little in its conception while the contractor pays entirely for its practical development including its reduction to practice. Similarly, it often occurs that the Government funds the development of an invention described in an unsolicited proposal (i.e., the invention is already conceived) but does not complete funding through the reduction to practice and thus obtains no rights in the invention.

b. Application of Rule

Applying the basic rule of ownership of inventions to Government contracts will result, in many cases, in the parties to the contract contesting when the two critical events, i.e., conception or reduction to practice, have occurred in relationship to the scope of or the timing of the contract. If the invention in question was both conceived and reduced to practice before the contract, it will not be "subject" to the Patent Rights clause typically used in Government contracts. For example, in *Alford v. United States*, 179 Ct. Cl. 938, 151 U.S.P.Q. 416 (1967), the Government alleged that the invention was made under a Government contract and, therefore, that the Government had acquired a royalty-free license in the invention. The court found that the inventor had conceived, constructed and successfully tested the invention before the contract, and that the invention was therefore reduced to practice *before* the contract. For similar fact situations, see *Eastern Rotorcraft Corp. v. United States*, 181 Ct. Cl. 299, 384 F.2d 429, 155 U.S.P.Q. 729 (1967); *Bendix Corp. v. United States*, 220 Ct. Cl. 507, 600 F.2d 1364, 204 U.S.P.Q. 617 (1979); and *Gould Inc. v. United States*, 217 Ct. Cl. 167, 579 F.2d 571, 198 U.S.P.Q. 156 (1978).

An invention conceived before award and reduced to practice after the completion of the contract is not subject to the typical Government contract patent rights clause, and thus the Government will obtain no rights in the invention. This sequence of events is rarely reported in the caselaw. In *Eastern Rotocraft Corp. v. United States*, 184 Ct. Cl. 709, 397 F.2d 978, 158 U.S.P.Q. 294 (1968), however, the court found such a chain of events and ruled that the Government was not entitled to patent rights.

If the invention was conceived before the contract and never reduced to practice, the Government will not obtain any rights based on its contract, *Ormsby v. NASA*, 847 OG. 337 (Bd. Pat. Int. 1968). Of course, an invention either conceived or reduced to practice during the period of the contract will be subject to the contract Patent Rights clause if it is otherwise related to the contract work, *Technical Dev. Corp. v. United States*, 220 Ct. Cl. 128, 597 F.2d 733, (1979); *Leesona Corp. v. United States*, 208 Ct. Cl. 871, 530 F.2d 896, 192 U.S.P.Q. 672 (1976), *cert. denied*, 444 U.S. 991 (1979); *Rosen v. NASA*, 152 U.S.P.Q. 757 (Bd. Pat. Int. 1966). Similarly, an invention conceived *prior to* the contract but first actually reduced to practice *under* the contract becomes subject to the Patent Rights clause. This is true even if the invention is filed as a patent application in the U.S. Patent and Trademark Office (i.e. a constructive reduction to practice) prior to the contract, *McDonnell Douglas Corp. v. United States*, 229 Ct. Cl. 323, 670 F.2d 156 214 U.S.P.Q. 857 (1982). See Prahinski, "Interpretation of Term, 'First Actual Reduction to Practice' Used in Patent Rights Clauses of Government Contracts," 55 J. Pat. Off. Soc'y 107 (1973).

c. *Contract Period*

(1) INITIATION AND COMPLETION OF CONTRACT

The precise dates of the initiation and completion of a Government contract, which defines the contract period and thus the critical time frame for consideration of the making of inventions, would seem, at first blush, to be easily ascertainable. However, questions arise over these dates.

The *completion date* of the contract is the most troublesome since contracts technically remain "open" for a number of years after the completion of the contract work. While the Patent Rights clauses do not explicitly state that they are limited to the time the R&D work actually is performed, logic would seem to so limit these clauses. For example, in *Eastern Rotorcraft Corp. v. United States*, 184 Ct. Cl. 709, 397 F.2d 978, 158 U.S.P.Q. 294 (1968), the invention was reduced to practice after all design work was completed under the contract but during the period in which the contract was still open. Since the Patent Rights clauses in the contract required the invention to be made during "the performance of the experimental, developmental or research work called for under the contract," the court found that the invention was not subject to the clause. Whether the result would have been the same without this language is not as clear, though logically it should be.

The contract *initiation date* is somewhat less ambiguous but it is not necessarily the date of contract execution. The contract may extend back in time and may include work performed previously by a precontract cost agreement. In such cases, the contract Patent Rights clause would be applicable to any earlier work.

(2) STATUTORY RELATED DECISIONS

The issue of whether the inventive act is within the contract period may be resolved differently when a statute controls the patent rights disposition. In *Hummer v. NASA*, 500 F.2d 1383,

183 U.S.P.Q. 45 (C.C.P.A. 1974), the Court of Customs and Patent Appeals held that the Government was entitled to the issuance of the patent on an invention that had not been conceived prior thereto, and that was not reduced to practice until after the completion of the contract. The court based its decision on its view of the legislative history of 42 U.S.C. § 2457(a). The court stated at 1388:

> Appellants' is an unacceptably strained interpretation of § 305. To accept it would be to restrict the statute in a way which would defeat the intent of Congress. We have no doubt that there are many instances when NASA will contract for the development of hardware under circumstances where the contractor's obligation will end with the delivery of the item to NASA. In at least some of those instances, the reduction to practice of this hardware would be carried out by NASA itself or by other persons not in privity with the inventor. We think that § 305 should be construed to extend to those situations.
>
> We are satisfied that this construction of the statute is in accord with Congressional intent as indicated in the legislative history to the National Aeronautics and Space Act. In the House Report, submitted by the Select Committee on Astronautics and Space Exploration, the following appears:
>
>> Subsection (a) [of § 305] provides that title to inventions and discoveries made pursuant to or as the result of contracts with the Administration shall become the property of the United States. . . .
>
> It is our view, therefore, that when an invention is developed under contract with NASA and subsequently reduced to practice outside the contract, the invention can be considered to have been made as the result of the contract. (Footnote omitted.)

This holding apparently lacks general applicability, however, because it is based on a specific statute.

Particular statutory language may bring conception or reduction to practice occurring prior to actual contract execution within the ambit of the Government's rights. For example, the Space Act, 42 U.S.C. § 2457(j)(2) defines "contract" as "any actual or proposed contract, agreement, understanding, or other arrangement, and includes any assignment, substitution of parties, or subcontract executed or entered into thereunder." While NASA generally has decided that "a proposed contract" or "other arrangement" does not include inventions made during the proposal preparation period, a DOE case raises doubts concerning this interpretation. The Court of Customs and Patent Appeals (now incorporated into the Federal Circuit Court of Appeals) held in interpreting the Atomic Energy Act of 1954, as amended, 42 U.S.C. § 2182, which applies to "inventions . . . made or conceived in the course of or under any contract, subcontract, or arrangement . . . regardless of whether the contract, subcontract, or arrangement involved the expenditure of funds," that an invention made while responding to a purchase order of an AEC contractor may satisfy the "arrangement" requirements of the Atomic Energy Act, *Department of Energy v. White*, 653 F.2d 479, 210 U.S.P.Q. 425 (C.C.P.A. 1981), *cert. denied*, 454 U.S. 1144 (1982). The CCPA also held, in effect, that it was not necessary for a patent clause to be in the contract for this section to apply.

NASA has always viewed the Space Act to apply to inventions made under its contract whether or not a patent clause was included in the contract. In fact, the New Technology clause in the NASA FAR Supplement at 18-52.227-70 (48 C.F.R. § 1852.227-70) does not allocate patent rights, but rather states that the Space Act applies and establishes certain presumptions based on the reporting of an invention. See 60 Fed. Reg. 40508, 40521, Aug. 9, 1995. Allocation of rights to other than small businesses or non-profit organizations are handled by the NASA patent waiver regulations 14 C.F.R. § 1245.100. This treatment is different than the DOE approach. The DOE Acquisition Regulations (DEAR) clearly allocate patent with respect to invention made by large businesses based on the contract terms and conditions, DEAR 952.227-13 (48 C.F.R. § 952.227-13, see 60 Fed. Reg. 11812, March 2, 1995).

2. Reduction to Practice

The patent law views the making of an invention as a two step process involving a mental element and physical acts. Although conception, the mental element, is usually thought to occur before the physical act of reduction to practice, this discussion will cover reduction to practice first. Reduction to practice occurs when an invention has been embodied in some physical form which is used to demonstrate its workability, *Eastern Rotorcraft Corp. v. United States*, 181 Ct. Cl. 299, 384 F.2d 429, 155 U.S.P.Q. 729 (1967).

a. Physical Embodiment

The embodiment of the invention in a physical form generally presents little difficulty even though some inventions, especially those operating in space in the absence of a gravity field, may be difficult to construct and operate as claimed, *Williams v. NASA*, 463 F.2d 1391, 175 U.S.P.Q. 5 (C.C.P.A. 1972), *cert. denied*, 412 U.S. 950 (1973); *Hummer v. NASA*, 500 F.2d 1383, 183 U.S.P.Q. 45 (C.C.P.A. 1974). If an invention is mechanical or electrical in nature, in the form of a machine or an article of manufacture, the apparatus must be a physically constructed, operative embodiment of the invention, *Rosen v. NASA*, 152 U.S.P.Q. 757 (Bd. Pat. Int. 1966); *Hazeltine Corp. v. United States*, 10 Cl. Ct. 417, 230 U.S.P.Q. 721 (1986), *aff'd*, 820 F.2d 1190 (Fed. Cir. 1987) (The test of the structure for a reduction to practice must include every essential element.). If it is a composition of matter or a process for generating a composition of matter, the composition must have been actually prepared, or the process must have been executed in all of its steps. In patent law, the invention is embodied in a physical form sufficient to meet the requirements of reduction to practice when every particular of the invention, as claimed in the patent, is found in the physical embodiment. Thus, at least a functioning model is necessary, *Birmingham v. Randall*, 171 F.2d 957, 80 U.S.P.Q. 371 (C.C.P.A. 1976); *Physics Technology Lab., Inc.*, ASBCA 17979, 77-1 BCA ¶ 12,301; *U.M.C. Elecs. Co. v. U.S.*, 816 F.2d 647 (Fed. Cir. 1987), *cert. denied*, 484 U.S. 1025 (1988); *Standard Mfg. Co. v. United States*, 25 Cl. Ct. 1 (1991). But it is the patent claims, rather than the physical embodiment in question, that are the "metes" and "bounds" of the invention.

b. Workability

The second requirement, workability, raises a more difficult question. To establish that an invention works, the physical embodiment must be tested. In this regard, the authorities frequently cite the following quotation from *Robinson on Patents* (1890), § 127:

> Moreover, the law demands, for the completion of the inventive act, that the art shall be so practiced, or the article of manufacture be so tested, that its efficacy and utility are fully demonstrated. "Reduction to practice" means "reduction to successful practice." Experiments in the direction of the desired result are not such reduction, no matter how nearly they approximate that end. The work of the inventor must be finished, physically as well as mentally.

(1) TESTING REQUIREMENT

In attempting to rationalize the amount, nature, and extent of testing necessary to establish a legal conclusion of reduction to practice, cases such as *Sydeman v. Thoma*, 32 App. D.C. 362 (D.C. Cir. 1909) and *Lustig v. Legat*, 154 F.2d 680, 69 U.S.P.Q. 345 (C.C.P.A. 1946), have sought to characterize the inventions themselves. As a result, a judicially conceived classification of inventions has evolved, consisting of three categories:

(1) Inventions, so "simple" in nature, that no tests are necessary to establish their workability;

(2) Inventions whose workability can be established in the laboratory; and

(3) Inventions whose workability can only be shown by testing them under conditions that are comparable to their intended environment.

This attempt to characterize inventions and to apply a judicially developed standard of testing has been subject to criticism. Judge Learned Hand, in *Sinko Tool & Mfg. Co. v. Automatic Devices Corp.*, 157 F.2d 974, 71 U.S.P.Q. 199 (2d Cir. 1946), after concluding that this approach tended "too much to proliferate a doctrine which had better remain in a single and supple stem," stated at 977:

> [A] test under service conditions is necessary in those cases, and in those only, in which persons qualified in the art would require such a test before they were willing to manufacture and sell the invention, as it stands.

Judge Hand argued that the quality of the testing should be judged, and that it is important for it to be judged by a practical standard, not a judicial standard, based upon the needs of the particular art. This position is supported by the fact that satisfactory reduction to practice does not turn on proof of successful commercial use, *Corona Cord Tire Co. v. Dovan Chem. Corp.*, 276 U.S. 358 (1928); *Minnesota Mining & Mfg. Co. v. Van Cleef*, 139 F.2d 550, 60 U.S.P.Q. 115 (7th Cir. 1943), but on tests which successfully prove practical utility for the intended purpose, *Ocumpaugh v. Norton*, 25 App. D.C. 90 (D.C. Cir. 1905); *Van Auken v. Cummings*, 49 F.2d 490 9 U.S.P.Q. 157 (C.C.P.A. 1931); *Williams v. NASA*, 463 F.2d 1391, 175 U.S.P.Q. 5 (C.C.P.A. 1972), *cert. denied*, 412 U.S. 950 (1973); *Alford v. United States*, 179 Ct. Cl. 938, 151 U.S.P.Q. 416 (1967). Therefore, reduction to practice is established when it is shown that the invention is able to perform its intended purpose beyond a probability of failure, *Taylor v. Swingle*, 136 F.2d 914, 58 U.S.P.Q. 468 (C.C.P.A. 1943).

Tests have been held to establish a reduction to practice when they show actual performance of the invention's intended function. Actual performance is proven when the operation of the invention is of such a quality, extent, and character that the utility of the invention in its intended environment is established, *Lavin v. Pierotti*, 129 F.2d 883, 54 U.S.P.Q. 400 (C.C.P.A. 1942); *Steenstrup v. Heath*, 95 F.2d 514, 37 U.S.P.Q. 205 (C.C.P.A. 1938).

It has been argued that if the particular art has not been developed to the extent that adequate experience or standard test procedures exist, testing which establishes the feasibility of a concept may be insufficient to establish a reduction to practice even though it may be sufficient to win a contract award, Kempf, "Reduction to Practice of Space Inventions," 50 J. Pat. Off. Soc'y 105 (1968), citing *Bell Aerosystems Co.*, ASBCA 9005, 67-1 BCA ¶ 6203 and *Rosen v. NASA*, 152 U.S.P.Q. 757 (Bd. Pat. Int. 1966). But see *Williams v. NASA*, 463 F.2d 1391, 175 U.S.P.Q. 5 (C.C.P.A. 1972) (NASA took financial risk by entering into contract for invention and this satisfied reduction in practice test).

There are no preconceived standards under which inventions must be tested for a court to find a reduction to practice. Each case must be determined upon its particular facts. This analytical framework has been enunciated and has been used by the Court of Claims. See, e.g., *Eastern Rotorcraft Corp. v. United States*, 181 Ct. Cl. 299, 384 F.2d 429, 155 U.S.P.Q. 729 (1967). The Armed Services Board of Contract Appeals also enunciated this approach in *General Dynamics Corp.*, ASBCA 14466, 73-1 BCA ¶ 9960, 177 U.S.P.Q. 773 (1973). See also *Couch v. Barnett*, 23 App. D.C. 446 (D.C. Cir. 1904).

(2) SIMPLE INVENTIONS

The result of this rationale is that "simple" inventions may require little or no testing to demonstrate workability. This situation was recognized in *Mason v. Hepburn*, 13 App. D.C. 86 (D.C. Cir. 1898), where the court stated at 89:

> [S]ome devices are so simple, and their purpose and efficacy so obvious, that the complete construction of one of a size and form intended for and capable of practical use might well be regarded as a sufficient reduction to practice, without actual use or test in an effort to demonstrate their complete success or probable commercial value.

The *Mason* case involved the invention of a "magazine clip." Other devices considered to have been simple (i.e., whose workability was obvious) were a fuse box, *Sachs v. Wadsworth*, 48 F.2d 928, 9 U.S.P.Q. 252, (C.C.P.A. 1931); an electric circuit protector, *Rolfe v. Hoffman*, 26 App. D.C. 336 (D.C. Cir. 1905); a means for mounting an outlet box, *Buchanan v. Lademann*, 54 F.2d 425, 12 U.S.P.Q. 28 (C.C.P.A. 1932); a horse collar, *Couch v. Barnett*, 23 App. D.C. 446 (D.C. Cir. 1904); a snap hook, *Schartow v. Schleicher*, 35 App. D.C. 347 (D.C. Cir. 1910); a clamp for holding a razor blade in position, *Gaisman v. Gillette*, 36 App. D.C. 440 (D.C. Cir. 1911); and a lock washer, *Olson v. Thompson*, 77 F.2d 104, 25 U.S.P.Q. 388 (C.C.P.A. 1935).

A careful reading of these cases establishes that all the inventions were "tested," but, because of their nature, the only testing needed to show suitability for performing the intended function was visual examination. While it could be argued that this factor is not determinative, it should be considered in light of Judge Hand's statement in *Sinko*, that "testing under service conditions is necessary. . . [only when] persons qualified in the art would require such a test before they were willing to manufacture and sell the invention, as it stands." Here, Judge Hand was comparing laboratory testing, rather than mere visual testing, with actual testing. However, he analyzed all three concepts. See Grauer, "The Legally Complete Invention," 33 Geo. Wash. L. Rev. 740 (1965) at 747, for citations to several cases that discuss the need for testing simple inventions. It should be recognized that the cases stating that "simple" inventions need not be tested turned not on the simplicity of the invention, but on the fact that the workability of the invention was obvious.

(3) Laboratory Testing vs. Testing in Actual

A more difficult issue arises when the invention's workability is not obvious, such that the invention requires some physical testing (beyond mere visual observation) to establish its utility in the intended environment. In the following discussion of cases concerning the validity of "laboratory" vs. "actual" testing a distinct pattern evolves.

In more recent cases the courts, while discussing the historical classifications, have determined whether tests conducted in the particular instance were sufficient to establish workability. The court in *Elmore v. Schmitt*, 278 F.2d 510, 125 U.S.P.Q. 653 (C.C.P.A. 1960) noted that to prove reduction to practice one must show that the invention "worked as intended in its practical contemplated use," citing *Gaiser v. Linder*, 253 F.2d 433, 117 U.S.P.Q. 209 (C.C.P.A. 1958). See also *Kruger v. Resnick*, 197 F.2d 348, 94 U.S.P.Q. 65 (C.C.P.A. 1952). In *Elmore*, the court stated at 513 that when tests are conducted under laboratory rather than actual service conditions, the sufficiency of those tests "necessarily depend[s] on the circumstances of the particular case under consideration including, inter alia, the simplicity or complexity of the device involved and the nature and character of the laboratory tests, as well as the conditions to which the device is subjected when in practical use." In other words, the court must be convinced that the particular laboratory tests reasonably reflect the way the invention will operate when in commercial use.

The invention in *Elmore* was a magnetic core digital binary counter for a computer system. The inventor's tests consisted of applying a variety of pulses to the counter with a pulse generator and of using a resistor to simulate the load. The resulting wave forms were examined by an oscilloscope. The court recognized that oscilloscopes were used in the art to evaluate wave forms and that such testing may provide, in some cases, a more complete indication of the invention's characteristics than could be obtained from observing the invention in a practical system. The court found that the laboratory tests conducted on the counter did not adequately establish a reduction to practice because, although it was intended to function in a system, it was never so tested. The court added, at 514, that the party relying on laboratory tests must establish that those "tests duplicated the essential conditions of some practical use" of the invention. The court, in regard to the other tests actually conducted, said that the "record fails . . . to show that [they] . . . accurately reproduced the operating conditions which would be encountered in any practical use of the invention." The import of the underlined phrase is that even if the laboratory tests were insufficient to establish a reduction to practice of the counter for use in a computer system, had they shown that the counter would operate satisfactorily in regard to some other practical use, a reduction to practice would have been established. For other cases following a similar standard, see *White v. Lemmerman*, 341 F.2d 110, 144 U.S.P.Q. 409 (C.C.P.A. 1965); *Knowles v. Tibbetts*, 347 F.2d 591, 146 U.S.P.Q. 59 (C.C.P.A. 1965), *cert. denied*, 383 U.S. 927 (1966); and *Koval v. Bodenschatz*, 463 F.2d 442, 174 U.S.P.Q. 451 (C.C.P.A. 1972).

Paivinen v. Sands, 339 F.2d 217, 144 U.S.P.Q. 1 (C.C.P.A. 1964), also involved a magnetic core logic circuit invention which was laboratory tested. The court found that the tests had sufficiently simulated actual commercial conditions and were valid proof upon which to establish a reduction to practice. The court distinguished *Elmore* on the grounds that the tests therein were insufficient to establish a reduction to practice because "it was not shown that the test arrangement was designed to simulate any practical application of the invention." The court then stated in *Elmore* at 226-27:

> [W]e did not hold that laboratory testing is unacceptable as a means of proving a reduction to practice, but rather that, for such tests to be acceptable proof of such reduction to practice, a relationship must be established which relate the test conditions to the intended functional setting of the invention.

In Grauer, "The Legally Complete Invention," 33 Geo. Wash. L. Rev. 740 (1965), the author notes that although the record in *Paivinen* provided ample evidence of the relationship of the circuit parameters lacking in *Elmore*, the court did not discuss the issue of whether "the tests accurately reproduced the conditions of temperature, vibration, or sustained operation which would usually be encountered in a specific use" as required by *Elmore*. It would seem that under the rationale of the *Elmore* case, as long as the invention's workability for some practical use is established, there is no need to inquire any further, i.e., to determine if the device would work under environmental conditions inherent in some other possible use. In this regard, see *Harding v. Steingiser*, 318 F.2d 748, 138 U.S.P.Q. 32 (C.C.P.A. 1963), involving the invention of a stabilized polyethylene composition.

In *Hazeltine Corp. v. United States*, 10 Cl. Ct. 417, 451 (1986), the court considered whether the plaintiff's laboratory tests were sufficient to constitute a reduction to practice. The court stated that the question was whether the test would convince a person of ordinary skill in the art that the device would work beyond a probability of failure and whether the device would be operable in the environment of its practical contemplated use.

(A) THE AIRCRAFT CASES

The courts in a number of cases involving aircraft inventions have held that because of the multitude of natural phenomena that may affect the performance of the invention in its intended use, the laboratory tests conducted were inadequate to establish a reduction to practice. In *Gaiser v. Linder*, 253 F.2d 433, 117 U.S.P.Q. 209 (C.C.P.A. 1958), an ice preventive coating invention for aircraft windshields was tested but no flight tests were made and no coated windshields were ever installed in any aircraft. Tests had been conducted in a laboratory involving the application of an electric current to the film, which had uneven electric resistance, to determine whether uniform heat distribution could be obtained on a glass surface; but the court noted that the uniform heat distribution was intended to occur under flight conditions rather than in the laboratory. The court, relying heavily upon the fact that aircraft windshields are subject to various environmental conditions (e.g., sun, wind, precipitation, vibration, and pressure) and are normally subjected to deflection and pressure tests before being used commercially, stated at 436:

> [A]ssuming . . . that the invention here is of such a nature that it could be reduced to practice without flight tests, we agree . . . that the minimum testing required would involve conditions simulating those of actual use.

The rationale offered by the court for this position was that:

> Unless laboratory tests accurately duplicate flight conditions, there is a definite possibility that some factor not present in the laboratory may cause failure in actual use.

For other "aircraft" cases, see Grauer, "The Legally Complete Invention," 33 Geo. Wash. L. Rev. 740 (1965) at 750, n. 55.

The Court of Claims has not, in recent times, recognized that "aircraft cases" represent a special class of reduction to practice cases. For example, both *Technical Dev. Corp. v. United States*, 202 Ct. Cl. 237, 179 U.S.P.Q. 180 (1973), *cert. denied*, 416 U.S. 983 (1974) and *Bendix Corp. v. United States*, 220 Ct. Cl. 507, 600 F.2d 1364, 204 U.S.P.Q. 617 (1979) involved jet engine controls but the court found a reduction to practice occurred through laboratory tests without duplicating the multitude of natural phenomena which would be encountered by these inventions when incorporated into an aircraft. In *Bendix*, the court rejected the Government's argument that the "aircraft cases" require flight testing before a jet engine fuel control invention may be reduced to practice, and found that bench tests performed by plaintiff before its contract with the Government were sufficient for a reduction to practice. The court recognized that it was impossible in 1946 for a private corporation to flight test a jet engine airplane invention since all such aircraft belonged to the Government. The Government, after the plaintiff's bench tests, had enough confidence to immediately install the invention in the aircraft and to allow its test pilots to fly it for over an hour.

(B) FARRAND OPTICAL

Farrand Optical Co. v. United States, 325 F.2d 328, 139 U.S.P.Q. 249 (2d Cir. 1963) is a decision of particular interest. There, the invention was a telescopic optical system for scanning a full hemisphere. The inventor tested the invention by placing a box containing the optical system mounted on a window sill with one end outside the building. The observations made therefrom established that a viewer could, in fact, scan a full hemisphere. It was later offered to the Government for incorporation into aircraft gun sights but was never flight tested before supplied to the Government. The court, after reviewing the aircraft cases, stated at 333:

But it does not follow that any invention which is to become a part of a device to be used in an airplane cannot be reduced to practice by means other than actual flight testing. The essential inquiry here is whether the advance in the art represented by the invention . . . was embodied in a workable device that demonstrated that it could do what it was claimed capable of doing.

The court then found at 333-34 that the advance in the art:

lay not in overcoming peculiar optical problems encountered in flight; rather it was construction of a device that would, in effect, put the viewer's eye immediately outside the structure that he occupied.

The court further concluded that "the tests under actual condition" rule cannot be an absolute requirement. "Its applicability must depend on the nature of the device, the circumstances of its intended use, and the state of the art." Since the laboratory tests had established the workability of the invention for the purpose of putting the "viewer's eye immediately outside the structure that he occupied" and the problems remaining in adapting the invention to aircraft use were within the state of the existing art, the court held that the tests were sufficient proof of a reduction to practice. The court reasoned that only the advance in the art had to be demonstrated as workable, and that once this was done, adapting a gun sight for practical installation could be accomplished by persons of ordinary skill using known techniques.

This testing approach requires the examination of prior art in determining the advance relied upon in the claimed invention. A reading of the claims involved in the case shows that the invention claimed was limited to an optical system and that this invention would not be effected by environmental conditions of flight. The question of whether the claimed invention could in fact be adapted to a particular commercial or military use was, in the court's analysis, irrelevant to the basic inquiry. See also Nemerovski, "Reduction to Practice: The Farrand Optical Illusion," 43 J. Pat. Off. Soc'y 99 (1961); and *Kearfott Div. of Gen. Precision, Inc.*, ASBCA 5551, 61-2 BCA ¶ 3241.

(C) SPACE INVENTIONS

Space inventions, where it is almost impossible to duplicate the lack of gravity in a laboratory environment, have raised unique reduction to practice issues. For a general discussion of the reduction to practice of space inventions, see Kempf, "Reduction to Practice of Space Inventions," 50 J. Pat. Off. Soc'y 105 (1968). Perhaps the most important decision regarding space inventions is the Court of Customs and Patent Appeals decision in *Williams v. NASA*, 463 F.2d 1391, 175 U.S.P.Q. 5 (C.C.P.A. 1972), *cert. denied*, 412 U.S. 950 (1973), where a contractor's laboratory test prior to the contract was held to constitute a reduction to practice. The invention in dispute was on apparatus for controlling the attitude or orientation of the spin axis of a spinning body (i.e., a satellite) by applying a processing torque to the body via a rocket jet at a position spaced from the spin axis of the satellite. The rocket jet was controlled from a remote location. The Board of Patent Interferences had found that every element of the claimed invention was incorporated in the laboratory test but that the tests were insufficient since they did not simulate the essential conditions of any contemplated functional setting of the invention, 175 U.S.P.Q. 9. Hughes Aircraft Company attempted to establish that the invention, while described in a spacecraft setting, was applicable to gyroscopes and that therefore the laboratory testing was sufficient. On appeal, the court did not consider the use of the invention on gyroscopes since it found that the laboratory tests prior to the NASA contract proved substantial utility of the invention. The court did consider whether the laboratory tests simulated any functional setting of the invention. In discussing whether the tests duplicated any contemplated functional setting of the invention the court stated at 1399:

> [T]he tests of the dynamic wheel were limited to tests in an environment of typical laboratory temperature, an estimated 70 degrees with average humidity and an atmospheric pressure incidental to an estimated 100 feet of altitude. There were no other tests, such as vibration on the dynamic wheel. No quantitative measurements were made of the degrees of precession of the spin axis on the wheel that were obtained. There was control of the orientation of the spin axis of the body only in the sense that the precession of that axis, as mechanically restricted by the ball joint supporting the wheel, occurred in the direction that was sought by the operator through the application of the jet forces directly on the rotating wheel itself at preselected instantaneous spin angle positions of the wheel and in synchronism with the wheel rotation.

> We find nothing in the record which would indicate that the factors referred to by the board were such as to raise any significant doubts that the processing system proved out in the dynamic wheel tests would be operative with a spinning body used as described in the application. Nor did the board advance any reasoning to support such doubts.[6] In their petition for reconsideration, in particular, appellants pointed out that some target seeking vehicles operate near the earth, where temperature, humidity and pressure conditions approximate those in the laboratory where the dynamic wheel was tested. They also pointed out that space is a benign environment and that a satellite in orbit is not normally subjected to shock and vibration. No reason is apparent from the record why a *free* spinning body would not be expected to precess in response to pulses from the jet nozzle in the manner demonstrated on the dynamic wheel tests or why there would be a limitation on the degree of precession obtainable.

>> 6 We note that, with the exception of humidity, the environmental tests the board thought should have been made closely parallel the tests run on the components of the Comsat prototype discussed *supra*. However, those tests appear to have been primarily in the nature of design work directed to commercialization of the product in which the attitude control system was regarded as already proven out by the dynamic wheel tests. It is well established that suitability for commercial use is not a requirement for reduction to practice. *Hradel v. Griffith*, 54 CCPA 911, 367 F.2d 851 (1966). The board advanced no reason why any aspect of the attitude control system would be adversely effected by a lack of humidity, and none is apparent to us.

The court indicated that the fact that the Government risked millions of dollars on the project, based on laboratory tests performed by the contractor before the contract, established the sufficiency of the test. The court stated at 1399-1400:

> A significant, and often controlling, consideration in determining the sufficiency of tests for reduction to practice lies in whether the tests show that the invention will serve the purpose for which it is intended so conclusively that practical men, men skilled in the art, would take the risk of putting it into commercial use. *Larsen v. Marzall*, 90 U.S. App. D.C. 260, 195 F.2d 200, 92 U.S.P.Q. 306 (D.C. Cir. 1952): *Farrand Optical Co. v. United States*, 325 F.2d 328

(2d Cir. 1963); *Goodrich v. Harmsen*, 58 C.C.P.A. 1144, 442 F.2d 377 (1971). Viewed in light of the impression made on those skilled in the art, appellants' tests unquestionably met the requirements for actual reduction to practice. Hughes' experts promptly adapted the present attitude control system in place of a different system originally planned for its Comsat program, which it was offering to government agencies and others. NASA, obviously as the result of consideration by its technical staff and advisors of the program and the Hughes activities under it, including the dynamic wheel test, entered into the 1961 contract for the Syncom program at the risk of millions of dollars.

In an early decision on the same tests for a related invention, the Board of Patent Interferences held that the tests in question did not demonstrate the functions of the invention claimed, *Rosen v. NASA*, 152 U.S.P.Q. 757 (Bd. Pat. Int. 1966).

The CCPA considered the reduction to practice of a second space invention in *Hummer v. NASA*, 500 F.2d 1383, 183 U.S.P.Q. 45 (C.C.P.A. 1974), and found no reduction to practice in the laboratory testing of a space-related invention. The Patent and Trademark Office Board of Patent Interferences had held that NASA owned an invention described as a spinscan camera which was placed on a synchronous satellite to photograph the earth, 183 U.S.P.Q. 47 (1972). The inventors, Hummer and Upton, worked for Santa Barbara Research Center (SBRC), a wholly-owned subsidiary of Hughes Aircraft Company. Prior to its Government contracts, SBRC built a laboratory version of the spin-scan camera and took photographs, but instead of rotating the camera as it would rotate to provide the necessary scan, the laboratory model used a rotating mirror for generating the scan. The board held that this test was not a reduction to practice of the claimed invention, although it may have been a reduction to practice of a functionally equivalent device. After the tests, SBRC contracted with the University of Wisconsin under a Weather Bureau grant and a NASA contract to construct a prototype and a flight model of the camera. Hughes had a NASA contract to construct the ATS satellite, which included the incorporation of the camera into the satellite. The board held that there was no reduction to practice under either the Weather Bureau grant or the NASA contract since neither the prototype nor the flight model was mounted on a rotating body. The first actual reduction to practice was found to occur after the ATS-1 satellite was in orbit. Nevertheless, the board held that NASA was entitled to the invention as discussed previously.

On appeal the CCPA agreed with this PTO Board decision. On the issue of reduction to practice by the early SBRC demonstration it stated at 1387-88:

> To constitute an actual reduction to practice, the device demonstrated must include every limitation of the claim. See *Fredkin v. Irasek*, 55 C.C.P.A. 1302, 397 F.2d 342 (1968). In the instant case, the device tested at SBRC failed to satisfy all the limitations of the claims in question. We believe the facts of this case distinguish it from Dean and agree with the board's conclusion that the claimed invention includes a rotating body. Had it been appellants' intent to indicate otherwise, it would have been simple enough to do so.

* * *

Apart from the tests with the non-rotating prototype, appellants do not allege any other pre-contractual reduction to practice. In view of the fact that we find ourselves in agreement with the board on the inadequacy of the tests done on the prototype, we hold that the first reduction to practice of the claimed invention came when the ATS-1 satellite was successfully orbited and transmitted electronic signals to earth from which photographs were made.

See also *Erhardt v. NASA*, 171 U.S.P.Q. 295 (Bd. Pat. Int. 1969).

(4) COMPUTER SIMULATION

In *McDonnell Douglas Corp. v. United States*, 229 Ct. Cl. 323, 670 F.2d 156, 214 U.S.P.Q. 857 (1982), McDonnell argued that the invention was reduced to practice by computer simulation, i.e., while no embodiment was actually constructed the computer simulation of the invention was its reduction to practice. The court ruled that it did not need to reach this argument since actual physical testing under the contract established that the prior computer simulation was inadequate to prove workability of the invention. Actual testing revealed significant flaws in the plaintiff's design, making the device incapable of meeting important elements of the claim. One problem noted by the court was that the system would not work under a high humidity environment. The court noted:

Tests which fail to simulate the varying and multiple conditions of the invention's intended environment will not serve to prove the operability, stability and reliability of the invention for practical use. *Technical Development Corp. v. United States*, 202 Ct. Cl. 237, 308-10 (1973), *cert. denied*, 416 U.S. 983, 94 S. Ct. 2384, 40 L. Ed. 2d 759 (1974); see *Leesona Corp. v. United States*, 208 Ct. Cl. 871, 895, 530 F.2d 896, 910 (1976). McDonnell's precontract tests did not test the guidance system under high humidity conditions (hardly an improbable circumstance in the conditions for use of a missile designed to be launched against a tank or comparable moving target) and must be considered inadequate when the physical tests revealed nonoperability under those conditions.

See *Hazeltine Corp. v. United States*, 10 Cl. Ct. 417, 448 (1986), *aff'd*, 820 F.2d 1190 (Fed. Cir. 1987) ("The Court of Customs and Patent Appeals long held that reduction of an 'equivalent' was insufficient to constitute a reduction to practice of a claimed invention in the context of an interference proceeding." The Claims Court found that an infringement claim against the Government was more akin to an interference proceeding than a prior reference case.) See also Colaianni, "Patent Licenses—The Court of Claims Search for Equity," 64 J. Pat. Off. Soc'y 164 (1982).

c. Location of Reduction to Practice

Another interesting facet of reduction to practice of space and certain other inventions is 35 U.S.C. § 104, which at that time limited the proof of an invention date to activities in the United States except for persons domiciled in the United States serving in a foreign country on behalf of the United States. (See changes in this section based on NAFTA and GATT.) Where the invention is reduced to practice in a spacecraft in outer space, may such operation be relied upon to establish the reduction to practice of the invention? Successful operation in space was relied upon in *Rosen v. NASA*, 152 U.S.P.Q. 757 (Bd. Pat. Int. 1966), which viewed the operation of the spacecraft and its control point in the United States as an integrated instrumentality not removed from the United States even though the spacecraft was in equatorial orbit during the testing. It also has been suggested that since the Treaty on Outer Space and the U.N. Resolution of 1962 provide that "states on whose registry an object launched into space is carried shall retain jurisdiction and control over such objects and any personnel thereon while in outer space," any activity on a spacecraft orbited from the United States is within the jurisdiction of the United States, and any reduction to practice in such a craft is within the United States, Kempf, "Reduction to Practice of Space Inventions," 50 J. Pat. Off. Soc'y 105 (1968).

3. Conception

The invention process must include both conception and reduction to practice. Although conception almost always precedes reduction to practice, the inventor will never know with certainty whether a legally sufficient conception has occurred until reduction to practice has been demonstrated. Noting this limitation on the independent nature of the concept of conception, the case law in this area can be considered.

The classic definition of conception was stated in *Mergenthaler v. Scudder*, 11 App. D.C. 264 (D.C. Cir. 1897), where the court stated at 276:

> The conception of the invention consists in the complete performance of the mental part of the inventive act. All that remains to be accomplished . . . belongs to the department of construction, not invention. It is therefore the formation, in the mind of the inventor, *of a definite and permanent idea of the complete and operative invention, as it is thereafter to be applied in practice* that constitutes an available conception, within the meaning of the patent law.

The Court of Claims in *Technitrol, Inc. v. United States*, 194 Ct. Cl. 596, 440 F.2d 1362, 169 U.S.P.Q. 732 (1971), quoting from I Walker, *Patents* ☐ 45 (Deller's 2d ed.) at 191-92, defined conception at 609 as:

> [T]he formation in the mind of the inventor of a definite idea of a complete and operative invention as it is thereafter to be reduced to practice . . . . The date of conception is the date when the inventive idea is crystallized in all of its essential attributes and becomes so clearly defined in the mind of the inventor as to be capable of being converted to reality and reduced to practice by the inventor or by one skilled in the art.

See *Technitrol, Inc. v. United States*, 194 Ct. Cl. 596, 440 F.2d 1362, 169 U.S.P.Q. 732 (1969). See also *Amax Fly Ash Corp. v. United States*, 206 Ct. Cl. 756, 514 F.2d 1041, 185 U.S.P.Q. 437 (1975); *Rosen v. NASA*, 152 U.S.P.Q. 757 (Bd. Pat. Int. 1966); *Gould Inc. v. United States*, 217 Ct. Cl. 167, 579 F.2d 571, 198 U.S.P.Q. 156 (1978); *FilmTec Corp. v. Hydranautics*, 982 F.2d 1546, 25 U.S.P.Q.2d 1283 (Fed. Cir. 1992), *cert. denied*, 114 S. Ct. 85 (1993).

4. Burden of Proof

The burden of proof to establish the making of the invention in contests over patent rights under a Government contract has been divided by the courts. This split burden was established in *Williams v. NASA*, 463 F.2d 1391, 175 U.S.P.Q. 5 (C.C.P.A. 1972), *cert. denied*, 412 U.S. 950 (1973) and was adopted by the ASBCA in a contract dispute over the reduction to practice of certain inventions under DOD contracts, *General Dynamics Corp.*, ASBCA 14466, 73-1 BCA ¶ 9960, 177 U.S.P.Q. 773 (1973). The board stated at 46,755:

The sole issue for decision is whether any or all of the five inventions involved in this dispute were reduced to practice prior to the time appellant commenced work under NObsr-77628, which was on or about 1 July 1959. The parties are initially in dispute over which side has the overall burden of proof. Appellant says that since the Government is claiming licenses to practice these inventions, the Government has the burden of establishing that the reductions to practice took place after performance under the contract commenced. The Government, on the other hand, contends that appellant has the burden of establishing that the reductions to practice occurred prior to the outset of performance.

In disposing of this question we consider persuasive the opinion of the Court of Customs and Patent Appeals in *Williams et al. v. Administrator of the National Aeronautics and Space Administration (NASA)*, 463 F.2d 1391 (C.C.P.A. 1972). In that case the Government was claiming title to an invention on the ground that it had been reduced to practice in the course of the contractor's performance of a NASA contract. Although that case involved 42 U.S.C. § 2457, which vested title to such patents in the United States, and not the Patent Rights clause, the issues relating to reduction to practice were very similar to the issues raised in this appeal. In *Williams*, the Court resorted to basic tenets of the law of evidence. It held that the general burden of persuasion was on the Government to establish the validity of its allegation that the inventions were reduced to practice under the contract. However, it further held (at p. 1401) that:

"This case was concerned with what happened prior to and outside of the contract-events occurring under the control of the inventor, the facts surrounding which he is in a position to know and NASA is not in a position to know. We feel that acts such as those shown—here, should be treated as affirmative defenses, and the burden of proof must be placed on the inventor."

We consider this division of the burden of proof applicable to the resolution of the present dispute.

In the absence of any evidence as to events which transpired prior to the award of NObsr-77628, the Government would prevail on the basis of the evidence establishing that work involving the patented inventions was performed under the contract, and the dates on which the inventor's drafts were prepared. However, the Patent Rights clause speaks in terms of actual conception and reduction to practice. The dates on which the inventor's drafts were prepared are relevant to the question of when the inventions were reduced to practice, but they are not conclusive. Judicial authorities do not support the proposition that an actual reduction to practice is dependent upon such formalities as the preparation of inventor's drafts or the filing of patent applications. See *Eastern Rotorcraft Corporation v. United States*, 181 Ct. Cl. 299, 384 F.2d 429 (1967). Moreover, as our findings of fact indicate, a considerable amount of evidence has been presented concerning the design and testing of modules embodying the patented inventions prior to the award of the contract. Whether or not that work satisfied the standards for reduction to practice is the dispositive question.

The Court of Claims has adopted the same burden of proof standard. In *Technical Dev. Corp. v. United States*, 220 Ct. Cl. 128, 597 F.2d 733 (1979), the Government's defense was that it was licensed based on a conception or reduction to practice under its contract. The court stated at 151-52:

> The defendant bears the burden of proof on the license defense and must establish by a preponderance of the evidence that a conception or a first actual reduction to practice occurred in the performance of a Government contract. Cf. *Mine Safety Appliances Co. v. United States*, 176 Ct. Cl. 777, 364 F.2d 385, 150 U.S.P.Q. 453 (1966).
>
> * * *
>
> If the defendant proves that the invention was reduced to practice in the performance of such a Government contract, then the burden shifts to the plaintiff to prove that a first reduction to practice of the invention occurred prior to the award of the contract. The proof of conception and/or reduction to practice is a heavy one for either party and requires more than self-serving testimony or uncorroborated records and documents. If the defendant succeeds in proving by a preponderance of the evidence that conception has occurred in the performance of a Government contract, then the Government is entitled to a license.

The Court of Claims has also considered the burden of proof issue where the invention was clearly conceived prior to the contract but the plaintiff also claimed that first actual reduction to practice occurred prior to the contract. The court in *McDonnell Douglas Corp. v. United States*, 229 Ct. Cl. 323, 670 F.2d 156, 214 U.S.P.Q. 857 (1982), stated at 161:

> McDonnell, both because it is the plaintiff and because it is the party asserting the prior reduction to practice, has the burden of showing that the device had been reduced to practice before that critical date. See *Lockheed Aircraft Corp. v. United States*, 213 Ct. Cl. 395, 405, 553 F.2d 69, 74 (1977); cf., *Coffin v. Ogden*, 85 U.S. (18 Wall.) 120, 124 (1873) (burden of proof rests on party asserting earlier invention); *Perry v. United States*, 112 Ct. Cl. 1, 33-34, 76 F. Supp. 503, 507 (1948) (plaintiff asserting reduction prior to an anticipatory disclosure shoulders strict burden).

See also *Hazeltine Corp. v. United States*, 10 Cl. Ct. 417 (1986), *aff'd*, 820 F.2d 1190 (Fed. Cir. 1987), where the patent clause in the contract stated that it was a prima facie presumption that an invention was first actually reduced to practice during the contract if the invention was constructively reduced to practice during the contract.

B. Inventor-Contractor Relationship

1. Reduction to Practice By Other Than Inventor

A general rule of patent law is that only the inventor is entitled to a patent on the invention. The inventor may employ or assist him in completing his invention (i.e., reducing it to practice) and if such persons in the course of the experiments make valuable additions ancillary to the plan and preconceived design of the inventor (not amounting to a new invention) such suggestions are generally regarded as the inventor's property and are embodied in his patent as a part of his invention, *Agawam Co. v. Jordan*, 74 U.S. 583 (1868); *Pointer v. Six Wheel Corp.*, 177 F.2d 153 (9th Cir. 1949); *Walker on Patents* § 37 (2d ed. Deller). Conversely, if the suggestions contain inventive concepts, the person making the suggestions is entitled to the patent even if he is an employee. This principle was stated by the Court in *Agawam* at 603:

> But where the suggestions go to make up a complete and perfect machine, embracing the substance of all that is embodied in the patent subsequently issued to the party to whom the suggestions were made, the patent is invalid, because the real invention or discovery belonged to another.

Thus, a party reducing to practice an invention that is based on someone else's conception is not entitled to a patent on the invention. This principle also applies to independent contractors who complete another party's invention, *Polaroid Corp. v. Horner*, 197 F. Supp. 950, 131 U.S.P.Q. 102 (D.D.C. 1961). In this case, Polaroid was awarded a Navy contract to develop a radiation dosimeter. During the early part of the contract Polaroid exchanged ideas with the Government program personnel and later produced a dosimeter. Both the Government and Polaroid filed patent applications and claimed the Polaroid-developed dosimeter as their reduction to practice. The Board of Patent Interference determined that Navy employees conceived the invention and incorporated it into their specifications with little supplied beyond mechanical details in constructing the invention. Polaroid's Navy contract placed Polaroid in the role of a skilled helper and assistant (i.e., employee in the context of Agawam) for which it was paid. The board ruled that an independent contractor was within the employee-employer relation stated in *Agawam*. The court adopted the board's view and stated further at 956:

> Limiting this decision to the peculiar facts of this case and rendering no decision as to the interpretation of Government research and development contracts generally, the Court agrees with the conclusion of the Board and is of the opinion that the rule of patent law stated in *Agawam Woolen Company v. Jordan, supra*, is applicable. See also *Milton v. Kinglsey*, 1896, 7 App-D.C. 531. As was stated in *Gedge v. Cromwell*, 1902, 19 App. D.C. 192:

> "By virtue of this contract, . . . Cromwell . . . undertook, and engaged himself to the appellant, technically for the benefit of the appellant . . . . It is difficult to conceive a situation in which the principle of the decision of the Supreme Court of the United States in the case of *Agawam [Woolen] Company v. Jordan* . . . would be more appropriate than in that which is here disclosed."

The Court continued, referring to its decision in *Milton v. Kinglsey, supra*:

> "The question is not one of partnership or of general fiduciary relationship—for there may be partnership and fiduciary relationship for one purpose and not for another; but it is one of fiduciary employment in the special subject-matter of invention. The rule is that one, who, by way of partnership or contract, or in any other, empowers another person to make experiments upon his own conception for the purpose of perfecting it in its details, is entitled to the ownership of such improvements in the conception as may be suggested by such other person.

"Under the circumstances of this case . . . if [Cromwell] . . . originated and devised the alleged improvements made by him upon the conception of the appellant . . . his improvements, under what we must regard as the settled principle of the law, must be held to inure to the benefit of the appellant."

2. Research and Development Employees

a. Space Act

Both Section 305(a) of the Space Act, 42 U.S.C. § 2457(a), and § 9(a) of the Federal Non-nuclear Energy Research and Development Act of 1974, 42 U.S.C. § 5908(a), contain detailed language defining the relationship of the inventor to the applicable contract work which must exist for rights to vest in the Government. For example, the Space Act states:

Sec. 2457(a) Whenever any invention is made in performance of any work under any contract of the Administration, and the Administrator determines that—

(1) the person who made the invention was employed or assigned to perform research, development, or exploration work and the invention is related to the work he was employed or assigned to perform, or that it was within the scope of his employment duties, whether or not it was made during working hours, or with a contribution by the Government of the use of Government facilities, equipment, materials, allocated funds, information proprietary to the Government, or services of Government employees during working hours; or

(2) the person who made the invention was not employed or assigned to perform research, development, or exploration work but the invention is nevertheless related to the contract, or to the work or duties he was employed or assigned to perform, and was made during working hours, or with a contribution from the Government of the sort referred to in clause (1).

Such invention shall be the exclusive property of the United States, and if such invention is patentable a patent therefor shall be issued to the United States upon application made by the Administrator.

In order to effectuate this provision with respect to large businesses, paragraph (b)(1) of the NASA New Technology clause (April 1988), NASA FAR Supplement 18.52.227-70, establishes a presumption that subject inventions have been made in the manner specified in paragraphs (1) and (2) of Section 305(a) and that this presumption is conclusive unless, at the time of reporting, the contractor overcomes the presumption in writing with supporting detail that the invention was not made in the manner specified by paragraphs (1) and (2). The NASA Administrator then makes the determination of whether the invention falls within these two paragraphs. The Act requires this determination before vesting any rights in the Government; Johnson, "Rights to Inventions under NASA Contracts," 21 Fed. B.J. 37, (1961). For an account of the legislative history of this provision, see Maltby, "The National Aeronautics and Space Act of 1958 Patent Provisions," 27 Geo. Wash. L. Rev. 49 (1958); and O'Brien and Parker, "Property Rights in Inventions Under the National Aeronautics and Space Act of

1958," 19 Fed. B.J. 255 (1959), for a discussion of paragraphs (1) and (2) of Section 305(a) and a comparison of this provision with the common law.

While the language of 42 U.S.C. § 5908(a)(1) and (2) is similar to the Space Act language, DOE's patent rights clause for use with large businesses in DEAR 952.227-13 does not contain the presumption procedure used by NASA in its New Technology clause but rather follows the allocation of rights language of FAR 52.227-13.

b. Contractual Restrictions

At one time the Department of Defense procurement regulations, the Armed Services Procurement Regulations (ASPR) limited the Government's royalty-free rights to subject inventions under its Patent Rights clause to subject inventions made by technical personnel, ASPR 9-107.1(c) (Rev. 23 Dec. 1955). The Government obtained a royalty-free right in subject inventions made by other than technical personnel only to the extent that the contractor could grant such a right without incurring an obligation to pay compensation to others on account of such grant. The term "technical personnel" was defined as—

> any person employed by or working under contract with the Contractor (other than a subcontractor) . . . by reason of the nature of his duties in connection with the performance of this contract, would reasonably be expected to make inventions.

Thus, in order to claim its royalty-free license the Defense agencies not only had to establish the making of the invention under contract, but also that the inventor was within the definition of technical personnel, *Rel-Reeves, Inc. v. United States*, 209 Ct. Cl. 595, 534 F.2d 274, 198 U.S.P.Q. 384 (1976).

3. Of the Contractor

The definition of "subject invention" of 35 U.S.C. § 201(e) is "any invention *of the contractor* conceived or first actually reduced to practice in the performance of work under a funding agreement" (emphasis added). This, of course, is the same language that is incorporated into the Patent Rights clauses of the FAR 52.227.11 to 13. It attempts to make clear that reduction to practice must relate to the contractor's invention. Therefore, a contractor employed to reduce to practice someone else's invention would not report this reduction to practice under the contractor's Patent Rights clause since it would not be an invention of the contractor.

4. Inventions By Other Than Contractor Employees

Inventions may be made under the contract, or in performance thereof, by someone other than contractor's employee. The inventor may be a consultant rather than an employee of the contractor, or the inventor may have licensed the invention to the contractor. In these situations there may be questions of whether either the conception or the reduction to practice of an invention is reportable to the Government, and whether the inventor, by agreement with the contractor, may exclude the Government from obtaining any rights in the invention. The decisions on these points are inconsistent. In *Hobbs v. United States*, 376 F.2d 488, 153 U.S.P.Q. 378 (5th Cir. 1967), Hobbs was a consultant to an AEC contractor but refused to assign his inventions to the contractor. The invention was made during the consultancy period and the consultant was paid by the contractor with Government funds. The Government claimed a "shop right." The court held that the Government obtained no rights. This invention was made during the period of the 1946 Atomic Energy Act, which had no statutory policy regarding rights to contractor's inventions, although the AEC's contract had a Patent Rights clause which provided that the Government contracting officer could determine the ownership of patent rights to inventions made under the contract.

A somewhat contrary result was obtained in *Technical Dev. Corp. v. United States*, 202 Ct. Cl. 237, 179 U.S.P.Q. 180 (1973), *cert. denied*, 416 U.S. 983 (1974), where the court found that an invention made by a party who did not have a direct contract or subcontract with the Government was nevertheless a subject invention. The court found that the Government's subcontractor and the inventor were joint adventurers by operation of law. This determination was based on the conduct of the parties, where the parties (subcontractor and inventor) had agreed to share in the proceeds paid to the subcontractor regarding the development of a jet engine fuel control system pursuant to a Government subcontract, and where these parties cooperated as joint entrepreneurs in developing the system and a community of interest existed. Since the subcontractor was bound by the Party Rights clause, the inventor was likewise bound. The court relied on *Wood v. Western Beef Factory, Inc.*, 378 F.2d 96 (10th Cir. 1967); *Lentz v. United States*, 171 Ct. Cl. 537, 346 F.2d 570 (1965); *Bushman Constr. Co. v. Air Force Academy Housing, Inc.*, 327 F.2d 481 (10th Cir. 1964) and 2 Rowley on Partnership §§ 52.8-12 and 52.56-57 for the joint venture portion of this decision. As an alternative, the trial judge, relying on *Mine Safety Appliances Co. v. United States*, 176 Ct. Cl. 777, 364 F.2d 385, 150 U.S.P.Q. 453 (1966) found that the Government had an implied license irrespective of the precise nature of the relationship between the parties. The court adopted both defenses (i.e., implied license and joint venture) but indicated its preference for the implied license defense.

II. RELATING THE INVENTION TO THE CONTRACT

Although an invention, either conception or actual reduction to practice, may be made during the contract period, the Government will obtain rights only in the invention if the necessary relationship of the inventors and the invention to the contract exists, i.e., if the invention is subject to the contract and hence a "subject invention." It is clear that an invention made by a contractor's employee working directly on research or development work called for by the contract would be a subject invention. Also, an invention made by an employee working on a commercial project unrelated to any Government contract of his employer would not be a subject invention. Between these two extremes, the rights of the Government are less clear.

The required relationship between the invention and the contract is described by various terms and phrases in the statutes, regulations, and applicable contract clauses. In some instances the words used are dispositive. In other cases, the courts appear to look to broader principles to determine whether the Government should obtain rights to an invention.

A. Statutory and Contractual Terminology

1. Space Act

Specific statutory language is found in the National Aeronautics and Space Act of 1958, 42 U.S.C. § 2457(a), which states that it deals with inventions "made in the performance of any work under any contract of the Administration." Although this language appeared to apply to all NASA contracts, it was interpreted to relate only to contracts "involving the performance of work of the research type," O'Brien & Parker, "Property Rights in Inventions Under the National Aeronautics and Space Act of 1958," 19 Fed. B.J. 255, 258 (1959).

The NASA Acquisition Regulations require its New Technology clause to be inserted in contracts or subcontracts, with other than small business firms and nonprofit organizations, only when such contracts have as a purpose "the performance of experimental, developmental design or engineering work," NASA FAR Supplement 18-27.373(b). This contract clause gives the NASA rights to "Reportable Items-any invention, discovery, improvement or innovation, whether or not the same is susceptible of protection under the United States patent laws, which is made in the performance of work under this contract." This language seems to preclude Government rights in inventions that are not related to the work called for by the contract or not paid for with contract funds. See *Erardt v. NASA*, 171 U.S.P.Q. 295 (Bd. of Pat. Inter. 1969), holding that the Space Act requires that to be subject to this section work must be done pursuant to some provision of the contract to be subject to this section— that is, "work which the contract requires or authorizes."

2. Nonnuclear

Slightly different language is contained in § 9(a) of the Federal Nonnuclear Energy Research and Development Act of 1974, 42 U.S.C. § 5908(a), specifying Government rights—

whenever any invention is made or conceived in the course of or under any contract of the Administration, other than nuclear energy research, development and demonstration pursuant to the Atomic Energy Act of 1954.

42 U.S.C. § 5908(m) defines contract as follows:

contract, grant, agreement, understanding or other arrangement which includes research development or demonstration work.

On the question of whether a demonstration performed under an ERDA (a predecessor agency to DOE) loan guarantee was within the provision, ERDA determined that such guarantees did not include "work" within this definition. See Memorandum of the ERDA Deputy General Counsel, Oct. 29, 1975, incorporated in the Conference Report accompanying H.R. 3474, H.R. Rep. 696, 94th Cong., 1st Sess. (1971).

3. *Atomic Energy Act of 1954*

Section 152 of the Atomic Energy Act of 1954, 42 U.S.C. § 2182, is quite different and provides:

> Any invention or discovery, useful in the production or utilization of special nuclear material or atomic energy, made or conceived in the course of or under any contract, subcontract, or arrangement entered into with or for the benefit of the Commission, regardless of whether the contract, subcontract, or arrangement involved the expenditure of funds by the Commission, shall be vested in, and be the property of, the Commission.

This language gives the Government rights in inventions in the specified fields if they were made "in the course of or under" the type of agreements listed. This statement appears to be somewhat broader than the Space Act language since it is not keyed to the work called for by the contract. In addition, the disclaimer of a necessary relationship between the invention and Government funds seems to broaden the Government's rights, *Department of Energy v. White*, 653 F.2d 479, 210 U.S.P.Q. 425 (C.C.P.A. 1981).

Section 152 also requires that the invention be "useful in the production or utilization of special nuclear material or atomic energy" before this section is applicable. This requirement has been tested in a number of cases where the Government, seeking to obtain title to an invention, has met with the objection that the subject matter of the invention did not meet the statutory test as it was not "useful in" producing or using atomic energy or special nuclear energy.

In *Piper v. Atomic Energy Commission*, 502 F.2d 1393, 183 U.S.P.Q. 235 (C.C.P.A. 1974), the court held that certain chemical compounds useful as anti-radiation medicine invented under an Army contract, which was for the AEC's benefit, were not "useful in" the production or utilization of special nuclear material or atomic energy. Evidently the Army contract provided the Government with title to resulting inventions if 42 U.S.C. § 2182 was applicable-otherwise the Government obtained a license. The court, relying on the legislative history, held that the congressional intent in enacting this section was to liberalize the Atomic Energy Act and to expand the private ownership of patents in nuclear energy which would be accomplished by giving "useful in" a narrow meaning, accord, *Department of Energy v. Westland*, 565 F.2d 685 196 U.S.P.Q. 3 (C.C.P.A. 1977). This reasoning was subsequently rejected by the same court, *Department of Energy v. White*, 653 F.2d 479, 210 U.S.P.Q. 425 (C.C.P.A. 1981). The court reexamined the legislative history of the Atomic Energy Act of 1954 and determined that an improved ion radiation detector is useful in the production or utilization of special nuclear material or atomic energy under the Act. Absent express congressional intent, the court held that it should not go beyond the plain meaning of the words "useful in" and stated at 489:

> Certainly, an invention which is essential to the production of atomic energy is encompassed by the term "useful in," and therefore, may be subject to a direction proceeding. Likewise, an invention having only an incidental use in atomic energy production is plainly outside the term

"useful in," and therefore not subject to the direction proceeding. Between these limits, however, lies the gray area in which the present invention resides.

We approach this twilight zone guided by a "rule of reason." Is the subject invention reasonably related to a use in the production of special nuclear material or atomic energy? Each case must turn on its own facts.

4. Presidential Statement

The 1963 Presidential Policy Statement adopted the same language as the Atomic Energy Act of 1954 in relating an invention to a Government contract. Thus, it required that inventions be made "in the course of under the contract" for the policy statement to be applicable. Following the issuance of the 1963 Presidential Statement, the Department of Defense altered its clauses to incorporate the same language. This appears to have been a broadening of the Defense Department clause which had previously given the Government rights only in inventions made "in the performance of the experimental, developmental or research worked for or required under this contract." Most Government R&D contracts, except where a statute provides otherwise, now use the operative language of "in the performance of work under" in relating a subject invention to the contract work.

5. 35 U.S.C. § 200 et seq.

The revisions to the patent act in 35 U.S.C. § 200 et seq., applicable to small businesses and nonprofit organizations, adopted the Space Act language "in the performance of work under" in defining "subject inventions," 35 U.S.C. § 201(e).

B. "License" Theory

A number of judicial and administrative interpretations of the varying language dealing with the relationship of the invention to the contract have evolved. In most cases, the specific words of the Patent Rights clause or statute do not appear to have played a key role in determining the Government rights, but the courts and boards have sometimes reached a decision that the equities favor granting the Government the contractual royalty-fee license in the patent. Nevertheless, it would seem clear that the Government will obtain such a license only if the contractor's invention is related in some way to the work performed under the contract. Thus, if an engineer, improperly assigned to a contract, conceived an invention that was completely unrelated to the work being done under the contract, the Government should obtain no rights to such an invention. For example, in *Erhardt v. NASA*, 171 U.S.P.Q. 295 (Bd. of Pat. Inter. 1969), an invention was made during the performance of work which had been specifically deleted from the contract work statement. Although NASA claimed that it nevertheless paid for the work and that it should be entitled to the patent rights, the board ruled for the contractor stating that, if this was the case, NASA should seek a refund of its funds but was not entitled to the patent. See also *Fitch & Baum v. AEC*, 491 F.2d 1392, 181 U.S.P.Q. 41 (C.C.P.A. 1974), which held that the Atomic Energy Act did not cover an invention outside of the work called for by the contract work statement. However, in *Department of Energy v. White*, 653 F.2d

479, 210 U.S.P.Q. 425 (C.C.P.A. 1981), the court found that work done under a purchase order with an AEC contractor was related to an "arrangement" with the Atomic Energy Commission because the subcontractor knew the AEC was working, in the field.

1. Invention Related to Supply Activities

In supply contracts it is less likely to contract for inventive work and, hence, less likely that a relationship between an invention and the contract will be found. In *Erie Resistor Corp. v. United States*, 150 Ct. Cl. 490, 279 F.2d 231, 125 U.S.P.Q. 658 (1960), the contractor sued the United States for patent infringement. The infringing device was a transducer, or electrical to mechanical converter, using barium titanate which was clearly the subject of, and claimed in, the patent. The contractor undertook a plant expansion program, which was financed partly through loans by the Government. In addition, the Government paid a substantial amount for test work by the contractor to investigate certain properties of barium titanate to be used as an insulator for electrical capacitors or condensers delivered under a supply contract. The barium titanate transducers, however, were entirely different electrical devices than the condensers. The court held that, although the invention of the transducer was made in the contractor's plant during the time of the condenser supply contract, the Government did not obtain a royalty free license therein. The court relied heavily upon findings that (1) the contract called for the production of condensers in accordance with Government specifications, and (2) the contract was a supply contract, which contained a standard patent clause but never required or paid for any research and development in the transducer field.

2. Research Contracts

a. Mine Safety Appliance

When research work is contracted for, invention is clearly a contemplated outcome of contract performance, and the contract usually contains a broad statement of the work. As a result, the necessary relationship is easier to find. The key case in this area is *Mine Safety Appliances Co. v. United States*, 176 Ct. Cl. 777, 364 F.2d 385, 150 U.S.P.Q. 453 (1966). The inventors working on an aviation medicine contract had developed a patentable item, a crash helmet, during the time they were working on a Government contract calling for research on the effects of acceleration on the human body. They claimed that the invention was beyond the scope of the contract. The contract provided that:

> (1) The Contractor shall, in accordance with any instructions issued by the Director of the Planning Division, Office of Research and Inventions, furnish the necessary personnel and facilities and shall conduct research, using a human centrifuge, on the physiological, biochemical and anatomical effects of acceleration on the body, relative to pilot position in high speed aircraft, and shall investigate and study: (a) Physiological Effects: The mechanisms operating in the pooling of blood; dynamics of circulation within the skull and the laws governing intracranial pressure; the load on the heart and its capacity to operate under high acceleration; and the vasomotor reflexes. (b) Biochemical Effects: The changes in the blood in its passage through the brain under conditions of reduced flow incident to acceleration. (c) Anatomical Effects: The

capacity of the tissues to withstand high acceleration without-tearing, rupturing, or bruising, and the displacement of organs in the body under high acceleration.

The Government's patent rights under the contracts were as follows:

> (a)Where used in this Section, and not elsewhere in this contract, the expression, "Subject Invention" means each invention, improvement and discovery conceived or first actually reduced to practice (i) in the performance of this contract, . . . or (ii) in the performance of any research or development work relating to the subject matter hereof which was done upon the understanding that this contract or any subcontract hereunder would be awarded . . . (b) Contractor agrees to and does hereby grant to the Government an irrevocable, non-exclusive, non-transferable and royalty-free license to practice, and cause to be practiced for the Government, throughout the world, each Subject Invention in the manufacture, use and disposition according to law of any article or material, and the use of any method.

The court held that the Government did not have to prove that the invention occurred directly in the performance of the contract stating at 787-88:

> That provision, in granting the United States a royalty-free nonexclusive license to practice "each invention, improvement and discovery . . . conceived or first actually reduced to practice (i) in the performance of this contract," does not mean that, before a license can ensue each and every component of the invention must be found to have occurred or been discovered as an integral part of the contract performance. Nor does the grant mean that the contractor must have been engaged to make the whole of the particular discovery or to study all aspects of the problem. At least in those instances in which the invention was conceived or practiced during the existence of the contract, it is enough that an important factor in the invention was itself within the contractual scope, or resulted directly from the course of contract performance. That is the import, as we understood it, of the general phrase "in the performance of this contract." It is immaterial, therefore, whether or not the practical development of impact head gear was, in and of itself, within the Navy agreement. That was only one aspect, though an important one of the invention. The physiological, biochemical, and anatomical research on impactacceleration and the study of energy-absorbing materials-which had to precede or accompany the practical headgear applications-were also necessary and important components; and such research was an integral part of the contract. Without these contract-covered inquiries, the final invention would not have been made.

In this case, the salary of one of the inventors was "almost entirely" paid by the Government at the time of the invention. However, after the Government had rejected the contractor's request to develop a crash helmet under the contract, the helmet work was treated as a separate project by the contractor. Private facilities and funds were used to do the fabrication and testing of the helmet. Nevertheless, the court found the necessary relationship to the Government's research contract to hold that the Government was entitled to a license to the patent.

It is clear that the Court of Claims arrived at a different result from *Erie Resistor* primarily because a different approach was used in analyzing the problem. In *Erie Resistor*, the court confined its attention to the language of the contract through which the Government claimed an interest in the invention while in *Mine Safety*, the court did not confine itself to the strict terms of the contract. Rather, the court appears to be saying that a license will be implied for the

Government to use any invention, the conception or reduction to practice of which was aided or benefited by a Government funded research project, even though the invention is not strictly a part of the project. The court said at 788:

> The impact-acceleration research carried on by the inventors and their associates necessarily came under the Navy program. The Government desired and paid for a royalty-free nonexclusive license resulting from that type of research (among others), and neither U.S.C. nor the inventors could avoid that Federal right by unilateral action. Such a license is wholly appropriate because Lombard and Roth, in conceiving and first practicing the invention, undoubtedly benefited from this research. We also infer, secondarily, that they probably gained from their knowledge of and proximity to the kind of acceleration research-whole body acceleration experienced in flight-which plaintiffs admit to be under the contract.

To accommodate this result the court adopted a liberal interpretation of the license-grant clause in the contract. The court said, "it is fitting to read the license-grant of Section 17 liberally, as we do, and not to confine it severely within a narrow compass." Apparently the court believed that its interpretation was merely a restatement of a general consensus that the Government is entitled to at least a "royalty-free non-exclusive license for practice of inventions made under or in the course of a federal contract."

b. Technitrol

The courts and boards of contract appeals have had an opportunity to consider other cases in which the relationship of the invention to the contract was at issue and the approach used in *Mine Safety* has generally been followed where broad research goals were stated in the contract. Perhaps the major case in this series is *Technitrol, Inc. v. United States*, 194 Ct. Cl. 596, 440 F.2d 1362, 169 U.S.P.Q. 732 (1971). There, the Court of Claims found that the Government had a license under the patent at issue. In so doing the court stated at 612-17:

> We now come to consider whether the components of the Sharpless conception-again, excluding the automatic reset feature may still fail to have been conceived "in the performance of" the EDVAC contract, although temporally developed before Sharpless separated from the Moore School. It is possible, of course, for an invention to lie outside the performance of the government contract, even though crystallized during the period of that project, because its subject matter is distinct from the government work. We have stated, in large part, the principles which govern construction of government license clauses, depending on conception "in the performance of [the] contract," in *Mine Safety Appliances Company v. United States, supra,* 176 Ct. Cl. 777, 364 F.2d 285 (1966).

* * *

What *Mine Safety* teaches is that the issue of license vel non should be approached liberally by asking what the United States (acting for its taxpayers) can fairly be said to have purchased through its sponsorship of the contract project. The Federal Government has the right to use, royalty-free, those ideas, improvements, discoveries, and inventions crystallized during performance of the federal contract which have a "close and umbilical relationship" to the work and research funded by the United States. Having borne the expense of that effort, the public is entitled to enjoy the fruits without further charge. Accordingly, as we said in *Mine Safety*, "[i]t is fitting to read the license grant of Section 17 [which is the same as the license clause of the EDVAC contract] liberally . . . and not to confine it severely within a narrow compass." 176 Ct. Cl. at 789, 364 F.2d at 392.

The record therefore fully supports the conclusion that a magnetic information storage device-the system used in the Sharpless patent-was well within the scope of the EDVAC contract. Plaintiff contends otherwise, and the trial commissioner agreed, on the ground that the EDVAC machine actually built employed an acoustic mercury delay line device. But the ENIAC and EDVAG contracts were for research and development and their scope cannot fairly be limited to the features embodied in the machines physically produced. The Government spent nearly $900,000 on the ENIAC and EDVAC contracts; it was paying not merely or even primarily for specific machines but for the advancement of knowledge in computer technology produced by the research. Indeed, the ENIAC machine was obsolete before it was even completed-the knowledge gained in producing it gave engineers at the Moore School the ability, which they recognized, to create a much more useful computer, the EDVAC. There was a continuous line of research running from the ENIAC project through the EDVAC contract, devoted to increasing human understanding, as well as the actual performance, of high speed computers. The particular machines built under the two interrelated programs were not the sole aim of the contracts, nor the only results for which the Government paid. It paid, too, for the exploration of the field and the acquisition of new knowledge, and it is entitled to the crystallized ideas, improvements, and inventions emerging from that process of ongoing study, inquiry, and creation. Scientific research is not a straight and narrow journey, with blinders, along a single path to a known destination. In the process of discovery and invention under a research and development program many roads are uncovered; some are pursued immediately and some must wait for another day. One "product" of the research is the overall accretion in knowledge, and this encompasses the untraveled ways sketched out, as well as the trodden ones. The possible use of a magnetic memory system was revealed by the ENIAC-EDVAC research and was well within the scope of the EDVAC contract.

The sum of it is that we find the Mine Safety requirement of a "close and umbilical connection" between the government-sponsored research and the "private" invention to have been fully satisfied in this instance: the ENIAC spawned the EDVAC which in turn revealed the concept of a magnetic data storage system in an unbroken chain of descent. All of the Sharpless invention (leaving aside the automatic reset feature) was therefore conceived during and in the performance of the EDVAC contract. We are not saying this is so merely because Sharpless happened to use some knowledge or idea gained through this work on that project. We are saying, rather, that the discrete "invention, improvement and discovery" which Sharless conceived before he left the project—his conception of a magnetic storage data system, embodied in the patent in suit—had a very close and integral connection, as a whole, with the government-financed project. His "invention, improvement and discovery" was not separate from, or independent of, the ongoing EDVAC program; on the contrary, it was inseparable from it. Accordingly, we hold that the United States is licensed as to all elements of the Sharpless invention (excluding, for the time being, the automatic reset feature).

Also important is the court's view of the relationship of the Patent Rights clause in the contract to the terminology and concepts of the patent laws. The court stated at 608:

> Moreover, it is unnecessary to delimit fully the scope of the patent claims in order to move toward resolution of the license issue. The contractual provision does not tie the Government's license to the patent laws; any invention, improvement or discovery conceived in the course of performance of the EDVAC contract, whether or not patentable, is licensed to the Government.

The logic of *Technitrol* was followed by the Federal Circuit in *FilmTec Corp. v. Hydranautics*, 982 F.2d 1546 (Fed. Cir. 1992). Here, the invention was found to be made during the performance of a contract with the Office of Water Research and Technology of the Department of Interior. The applicable statute to this work adopted the patent policy of the Federal Non-Nuclear Research and Development Act that relates to non-nuclear work of the Department of Energy. This Act vests title to inventions made under a contract in the Government unless a waiver of such title is provided by the Government. The court in a collateral attack on the ownership of the invention made by an alleged infringer held that the invention was conceived under the contract and that the government had title to the invention pursuant to the terms of the Act.

c. Rutgers v. United States

In *Rutgers v. United States*, No. 96-399C (COFC, September 16, 1998), after the ONR contracting officer issued a final decision finding that the Government was entitled to a nonexclusive license in Rutgers patented invention based on an ONR contract with Rutgers, Rutgers filed suit in the COFC seeking a declaration that the Government had no rights in its patent. The Rutgers inventors submitted a number of proposal to ONR and DARPA for piezoelectric films research. In 1980 they were awarded a contract by ONR. Two patents were awarded to the inventors related to this contract work and Rutgers granted the Government a license in these inventions. In 1988 they submitted a proposal to extend this contract, instead a short form contract incorporating this proposal by reference was awarded to Rutgers.

In response to an inquiry by a DARPA employee in October 1989 the Rutgers' inventors conceived another related invention which they ultimately patented, receiving 30 claims— three of which were independent claims. In April 1990 they reduced to practice the independent claims of this patented invention. In August 1990 they submitted a proposal to modify their ONR contract and direct their research into the area of the invention. ONR agreed to the modification on December 19, 1990, effective as of November 15, 1990. Rutgers admitted that it used $95,000 of the contract money to purchase test equipment used on the invention. The disclosure report on the invention stated that the invention was funded by ONR/DARPA. A patent application on this invention was filed on December 14, 1990 as a continuation of the earlier patent applications filed by the inventors In June 1991 Rutgers sent ONR a letter with a copy of the patent application indicating that they would comply with the patent rights clause of the contract. This patent application was then abandoned by Rutgers and a new application filed. This new patent application matured into the patent and is the subject of this suit. The Government seeks a license in this patent.

The court noted that a license defense is an affirmative defense which imposes the burden of proving the existence of a license on the defendant, here the Government. Whether the

Government is entitled to a license is to be resolved by determining whether the invention was either conceived or first reduced to practice in performing the ONR contract.

The contract incorporated the April 1984 version of the Federal Acquisition Regulations Patent Rights Clause (patent rights clause) which states that "[w]ith respect to any subject invention in which the Contractor retains title, the Federal Government shall have a nonexclusive, nontransferable, irrevocable, paid-up license to practice or have practiced for or on behalf of the United States the subject invention throughout the world." The court noted that "[T]he phrase 'in the performance of' has long been construed liberally by the courts." In *Mine Safe Appliances Co. v. United States*, 364 F.2d 385 (Ct. Cl. 1966), the Court of Claims quoted the following with approval:

> Inventions made under a Government contract are the product of expenditures from the public treasury in the course of a governmental function; the public, having in a sense ordered and paid for the invention through its representatives, should not again be taxed for its use, nor excluded from its use nor permitted to use it upon restrictive conditions advantageous to no one but the patent owner. *Id.* at 392 (quoting Investigation of Government Patent Practices and Policies, Report and Recommendations of the Attorney General to the President, Vol. I, pp. 88-89 (1947)). The court expounded upon that language, stating:

>> Under such a liberal construction. . . [t]he Government has the right to use, royalty-free, those inventions which have a "close and umbilical relationship" to the work and research funded by the United States and were crystallized during performance of the federal contract. If the invention is so tied to the work to be done under the contract as to contribute significantly to the results anticipated by that agreement, the Government is entitled to a license. *Technical Development Corp.*, 597 F. 2d at 745-46 (citations omitted).

The court first examined the scope of the ONR contract as originally awarded and found that it did not cover the subject matter of the patent. However, the modification of the contract in December of 1990 incorporating Rutgers proposal as the work statement significantly expanded the scope of the research covered by the contract to encompass the technology of the patent. Then the court determined when the independent claims of the patent were conceived and reduced to practice.

As to conception the court found that:

> An invention is conceived "when a definite and permanent idea of an operative; invention, including, every feature of the subject matter sought to be patented, is known." *Pfund v. United States*, 40 Fed. Cl. 313, 334 (1998) (quoting *Sewell v. Walters*, 21 F. 3d 411,415 (Fed. Cir. 1994)). The parties agree that the "April 20, 1990 disclosure is *the first complete* written description of the invention claimed by the *independent claims* of the '979 patent. . . ." The court finds that the parties' agreement satisfies the requirements of a conception, and the court further finds that the independent claims of patent '979 were conceived by April 20, 1990.

This conception occurred during the time period of the original ONR contract. As the scope of the original contract did not include the subject matter of the patent conception did not occur in the performance of the original contract. Similarly, the court found that the reduction to practice of the independent claims occurred prior to November 15, 1990, the date the original contract was modified. As to the dependent claims, the court found that the Government did not meet its burden of proof to show that these inventions claims were conceived in the performance of the modified contract or that they were reduced to practice under the modified contract.

d. ASBCA Cases

The Armed Service Board of Contract Appeals has also considered this issue. The ASBCA in New York University, ASBCA 14779, 71-1 BCA ¶ 8774, upheld the Government's claim to a license in an invention conceived under a study contract with a university, in spite of the university's claim that the invention was outside the scope of the study, because the contract did not require the university to arrive at any specific solution to the matter under investigation. The board found that the grant of a royalty-free license in the Patent Rights-License clause should be liberally construed and that Mine Safety applied. The contract did not prohibit the contractor from conceiving inventions, which would aid the Government in attaining the goal it sought. The contract was for broad research efforts and the contractor originally had reported the work as being related to the contract.

The contractor in *American Nucleonics Corp.*, ASBCA 15370, 73-1 BCA ¶ 10,025, claimed to have both conceived and reduced to practice an invention during a funding hiatus. The contract had a "best efforts" performance-type work statement with a DOD Patent Rights-License clause. The contract funding expired and while the contractor was negotiating for additional funding he continued to work on the project. The contractor then claimed that the invention was made during the funding hiatus. The contractor eventually received additional funds but independently paid for the work during the funding hiatus. However, the board ruled that the contractor could have claimed such costs under the contract after the extensions were agreed upon. The board, relying on either Mine Safety or Technitrol, found that the invention was "made" "in the course of or under" the contract as provided by the Patent Rights clause. The term in the Patent Rights clause "in the course of or under this contract" was viewed by the board to be an even broader term than the term in the Mine Safety contract, "in the performance of" the contract. See also *Area Therm Co.*, ASBCA 25607, 85-2 BCA ¶ 18,166.

3. Development Contracts

a. Benefits Derived From Private Effort

In development contracts, work statements are usually more definitive than in research contracts, with the result that the court can determine more easily whether the necessary relationship exists. As a result, the *Mine Safety* doctrine is less likely to apply. For example, in *Rel-Reeves, Inc. v. United States*, 209 Ct. Cl. 595, 534 F.2d 274, 198 U.S.P.Q. 384 (1976), the Government claimed that it had an express license in the patent in question based on the work statement in the contract and the fact that the inventor was within the term "Technical Personnel" as defined in the Patent Rights clause in the contract, even though he was not working on the contract at the time he made the invention. The court held that this case was not like *Mine*

Safety or *Technitrol* since the Government received the benefits of the contractor's private work, rather than the reverse. Further, it was not clear that the Government work was R&D in designation. The invention was made by a technical person not working on the contract and knowledge of the invention was not derived from Government work. Even though the Government alluded to various "connections" between its contracts and the inventor, the Government did not supply hard facts to support its allegations. The court, at 628, noted a number of factors that played a significant role in *Mine Safety,* which were not present here:

(1) USC's (the contractor) acquiescence that the research relating to the development of the crash helmet (the invention at issue in that case) was covered by its Navy contract;

(2) The fact that both the Navy and USC anticipated and foresaw that protective gear would result from the knowledge gained from the contract; and

(3) The fact that work on the patented crash helmet was carried out by the co-patentees in close physical proximity (cheek-by jowl) to the work under the Navy contract.

Moreover, the fact that the co-patentees in *Mine Safety* would not have been able to make their invention but for the knowledge gained from their work under the Navy contract also appears to have played an important part in the *Mine Safety* case.

b. Mutuality of Effort

In *Leesona Corp. v. United States,* 208 Ct. Cl. 871, 530 F.2d 986, 192 U.S.P.Q. 672 (1976), the Government claimed a license based on the "close umbilical connection" doctrine of *Mine Safety* in that the whole history of dealings between the parties showed a mutual effort that led to the creation of the devices. The court found that, in fact, the reverse of *Mine Safety* had occurred. In *Mine Safety,* the contractor's allegedly separate project was obtaining benefits from the Government project being carried on at the same time, while here the benefits flowed the other way. The Government contributed no money at all to the plaintiff's developments and received the benefits on its contracts.

The Government attempted to rely on *Mine Safety* and *Technitrol* to establish an express license in the patent alleged to be infringed by the Government in *Lockheed Aircraft Corp. v. United States,* 213 Ct. Cl. 395, 553 F.2d 69, 193 U.S.P.Q. 449 (1977). The court found that the Government had not established a sufficient connection to utilize the *Mine Safety* doctrine. The Court identified a number of distinguishing factors. First, it was not shown that the inventor performed design work on the subject matter of the invention which was reimbursed under the contract, or that he relied on the knowledge derived from the Government work to make his invention. Further, the Government file contained a signed statement that the patent requirements of the contract had been complied with by the plaintiff. This gave some credence to the argument that the invention was not part of the contract since the project officer also had independent constructive notice of the contractor's invention. The court found that the Government had not established the presence of such a "close and umbilical connection" between the contract work and the invention to reach the conclusion of *Mine Safety* and *Technitrol.*

c. Joint Venturer

In contrast, the trial commissioner in *Technical Dev. Corp. v. United States*, 202 Ct. Cl. 237, 179 U.S.P.Q. 180 (1973), *cert. denied*, 416 U.S. 983 (1974), found that the Government was entitled to a license in an invention reduced to practice during performance of a development contract because the inventor had presented the invention to the contractor and had taken contract funds during the development work. The commissioner relied on *Mine Safety* or *Ordnance Eng'g Corp. v. United States*, 68 Ct. Cl. 301 (1929). The court adopted the view that the Government had an implied license rather than a direct license as under *Mine Safety*. Plaintiff's petition for certiorari to the Supreme Court argued that the Court of Claims, beginning with *Mine Safety*, and subsequently in *Technitrol*, had gone too far in accepting the Government's license defenses. Here, according to the plaintiff, the court found that even privity of contract was unimportant. In a second decision, *Technical Dev. Corp. v. United States*, 220 Ct. Cl. 128, 597 F.2d 733 (1979), three different inventions for electronically controlling jet engine fuel flow were considered. The contract tests were held to be a reduction to practice and the prior testing by the plaintiff was found to be inconclusive. The court found, relying on *Mine Safety* and *Technitrol*, that these inventions were either conceived or reduced to practice in the performance of the plaintiff's Government contract. For general discussions of cases that have developed from Mine Safety, see Raubitschek, "The Vesting of Government Rights in DOD-Financed Inventions," 31 Fed. B. J. 237 (1972) and Davis, "Patent Licenses Under Government Contracts: New Judicial Scrutiny," 55 J. Pat. Off. Soc'y 503 (1973). For an argument that these decisions of the Court of Claims are based on equitable considerations, see Colianni, "Patent Licenses—The Court of Claims Search for Equity," 64 J. Pat. Off. Soc'y 164 (1982).

C. Situations Where Statute Calls for Title

1. Atomic Energy Act

Whether an approach as favorable to the Government would be used where the Government was claiming title to a patent rather than a license is an open issue. See *FilmTec Corp. v. Hydranautics*, 982 F.2d 1546 (Fed. Cir. 1992), where the Federal Circuit held that the Government held title to an invention based on the conception of the invention on a Government contract and federal statute even though the invention was never reported to the government. The court permitted a collateral attack on the ownership of the patent that resulted in the defeat of an infringement claim brought by the ostensible owner of the patent.

In this context the Court of Customs and Patent Appeals rejection of the AEC's claim to title in *Fitch & Baum v. AEC*, 491 F.2d 1392, 181 U.S.P.Q. 41 (C.C.P.A. 1974) should be reviewed. The AEC claimed that the contractor's invention was related to AEC subcontract AT-143 and AEC contract AT-2884 and, therefore, requested that the patent issue to the AEC under the Atomic Energy Act. The evidence established that the invention was clearly within the scope of AT-143 but that this contract had been completed before the invention was conceived. Further, the Board of Patent Interferences found that the contractor used some material produced under AT-143 and/or AT-2884 to make the invention and that a complete conception of the invention should be considered to have been made in the course of or under contract AT-2884. Since contract AT-2884 was in existence at the time the invention was made, the issue presented to the court was whether the invention was within the scope of the work under AT-2884. AEC claimed that the invention was conceived "in the course" of AT-2884 even though the actual inventive work did not fall within its exact contract terms. The AEC urged that the requisite nexus between the contract and the invention was present since contract AT-143 indicated AEC's interest in the subject matter of the invention and AT-2884 continued some facet of the work encompassed within the broader scope at AT-143. The court, in holding that AEC had no rights in the invention, seems to have adopted a narrow construction on the phrase "in the course of or under" the contract. The court stated at 1395:

Whether or not the AEC had a continuing "interest" in the invention and whether that interest was known to Grace and, presumably to many others is equally irrelevant. The question is not one of AEC's "interest." The AEC was presumably capable of incorporating that interest in AT-2884 if it did in fact have such interest and a desire that Grace should seek to satisfy it. The sole question is one of AEC's rights stemming from contractual obligations of Grace which existed at the time the invention was made or conceived. In deciding the issue under 42 U.S.C. § 2182, the only relevant interests are those the satisfaction of which is sought or encompassed in a contract viable at the time an invention is made or conceived.

We agree with the board that whether the claimed microspheres were or were not made from sols left over from work done under the expired contract AT-143 should not influence the decision herein. Similarly, the admitted occasional errors in record keeping, leading to the board's reference to some commingling of AEC and Grace "work" and an "unresolved" question of whether AEC funds were used for Grace "projects" cannot be decisive factors. We are unable, as was the board, to determine on the evidence of record that the AEC has established commingling of a nature which might require that the work so done be considered to be encompassed by the AEC contract.

Appellee's argument regarding AT-2884 resolves into an insistence that "in the course of" must be interpreted as "during the life of" a contract. To so hold would, of course, destroy the very raison d'etre of contracts, the very purpose of which is to spell out, as closely as possible, the work to be done, the goals to be sought and the rights and obligations of the parties. Reasonable men of affairs would have no difficulty in drafting a contract calling for assignment of "all inventions made or conceived during the life of this contract." That was not done here.

The rule of statutory interpretation requires that the phrase "in the course of" and word "under" mean different things. In our view, an invention made or conceived in performing, or as a result of performing, the work required by a contract is made or conceived "in the course of" that contract. That would be true even though the invention was not specifically sought in the terms of the contract. An invention is made or conceived "under" a contract when it is made or conceived during the life of the contract and the invention is, in whole or in part, specifically provided for by that contract. Neither of these fact situations applies here.

A similar decision was also reached by the Board of Patent Interferences in another contest between AEC and the W.R. Grace Company over the same two contracts. In *Smith & Fitch v. AEC*, 175 U.S.P.Q. 617 (Bd. Pat. Inter. 1972), the board held that the invention in question was not "made or conceived in the course of or under" contract AT-2884 or subcontract

AT-143 in that the invention was directed to an item different from that contemplated by these contracts. The board found that the work required by these contracts was far different from the invention in issue.

Department of Energy v. Szulinski, 673 F.2d 385, 213 U.S.P.Q. 345, (C.C.P.A. 1982) gives some guidance regarding overlapping contract situations. Here, ARHCO (Atlantic-Richfield Hanford Company) was the Government's on-site operator/contractor for AEC's (DOE's) chemical processing operations in Richland, Washington, and was responsible for "waste management (including crude fission products recovery) and long term storage for all high level waste." In addition, ARHCO, under a separate AEC "Private Contract" was to investigate the potential for civilian oriented nuclear business, including reprocessing of civilian reactor fuels, for the Richland area. The results of the Private Contract would be the sole property of ARHCO. Szulinski, an ARHCO employee, made an invention that was directed to a system for the storage of radioactive material. The inventor, Szulinski, worked in ARHCO's Commercial Nuclear studies group for both the AEC Operating Contract and on the private contract. The invention was conceived during the period of both contracts but was never reduced to practice. The Board of Patent Interferences, concluding that the invention dealt only with spent civilian reactor fuel rods and relying on *Fitch & Baum v. AEC*, 491 F.2d 132, 181 U.S.P.Q. 41 (C.C.P.A. 1974), held that the conception had not occurred "under" the Operating Contract because the contract made no specific provision for such an invention; nor was the invention made "in performing, or as a result of performing, the work required" by the Operating Contract and was thus not conceived "in the course of" the operating contract under the Fitch test since that contract related only to waste management and the spent fuel rods were not waste. The CCPA reversed, holding that the invention was not limited to spent fuel rod storage but covered the storage of radioactive material generally and, therefore, was conceived in ARHCO's performing, or as a result of its performing, a service associated with its waste management Operating Contract. In response to ARHCO's claim that the invention arose out of its endeavors on the private contract, the court noted that no clear division existed between the inventor's work on behalf of ARHCO's private contract and his work on the Operating Contract. The court stated at 387:

> [T]he record does not substantiate Szulinskils allegation that a clear division existed between his efforts on behalf of ARHCO's private sector development and those benefiting DOE pursuant to the Operating Contract. There is testimony suggesting that ARHCO's management was alerted to the problem of separating the company's commercial development costs from its disbursements under government contracts. Nevertheless, Szulinski presents no convincing evidence that his work under the Operating Contract was, in fact, substantially disentangled from work performed specifically for ARHCO's project to develop commercial reprocessing of spent fuel elements. (Footnotes omitted)

Further, the inventor testified he knew of no restriction on the flow of information between the private and the operating contracts.

2. *Space Act*

The CCPA considered the relationship of an invention to a NASA contract in which the R&D was essentially completed before the invention was reduced to practice. This case required the court to interpret the statutory term "in the performance of work under a contract" contained in the Space Act at 42 U.S.C. § 2457(a). The court in *Hummer v. NASA*, 500 F.2d 1383, 183 U.S.P.Q. 45 (C.C.P.A. 1974) determined whether this invention would still be considered to fall under the contract. The court held that a narrow reading of the Space Act excluding this invention would not be in keeping with Congressional intent. The court stated at 1388:

> Appellants' principal argument urging that we hold that NASA is not entitled to the patent which will issue from their application is based upon an interpretation of § 305(a), where it indicates that an invention shall be the property of the United States if ". . . made in the performance of any work under any contract of the administration . . . ." They argue that the effect of this language in the total context of § 305(a) means that the event of a first actual reduction to practice creates a right in the United States to title to the invention only if the reduction to practice is accomplished during the life of a contract with NASA by efforts of the inventors themselves or persons acting on their behalf.

> To factually support their legal argument, appellants point out that the SBRC subcontract under the University of Wisconsin's prime contract with NASA terminated when the camera arrangement was delivered. Furthermore, the NASA contract with Hughes called only for the fabrication of ATS spacecraft. Hughes personnel did not participate in the launch or operation of those spacecraft under any contract with NASA. They also point out that there is nothing in the record to indicate that NASA had a contract with anyone to launch or operate the ATS-1. It would follow from these facts that no right in the United States arose under § 305 because the reduction to practice was not one ". . . made in the performance of any work under any contract of the Administration . . . ."

> Appellants' is an unacceptably strained interpretation of § 305. To accept it would be to restrict the statute in a way which would defeat the intent of Congress. We have no doubt that there are many instances when NASA will contract for the development of hardware under circumstances where the contractor's obligation will end with the delivery of the item to NASA. In at least some of those instances, the reduction to practice of this hardware would be carried out by NASA itself or by other persons not in privity with the inventor. We think that § 305 should be construed to extend to those situations. We are satisfied that this construction of the statute is in accord with Congressional intent as indicated in the legislative history to the National Aeronautics and Space Act. In the House Report, submitted by the Select Committee on Astronautics and Space Exploration, the following appears:

> Subsection (a) [of § 305] provides that title to inventions and discoveries made pursuant to or as the result of contracts with the Administration shall become the property of the United States . . . . [Emphasis ours.]

> It is our view, therefore, that when an invention is developed under contract with NASA and subsequently reduced to practice outside the contract, the invention can be considered to have been made as the result of the contract.

Appellants make one other argument of substance disputing NASA's right to title to the invention. Briefly stated, that argument is that NASA did not contract or pay for any "inventing" under the subcontract between SBRC and the University of Wisconsin. AU it paid for was the mere manufacture of an already designed camera. In appellants' words, "NASA merely purchased a copy of an already existing device, a device so thoroughly tested it had the reliability of an off the shelf item."

The substance of this argument lies in the nature of the subcontract. That contract was to be performed in two parts. SBRC was to be paid by the University of Wisconsin for work under each part from two different funds. Work under the first part was paid for with funds from a Weather Bureau Grant, whereas NASA was the source of the funds for the second part.

The scope of work to be performed by SBRC was set forth in a document entitled "Statement of Work and Performance Schedule for Spin-Scan Cloud Camera Program," which was drawn up prior to, but incorporated by reference into, the subcontract. According to the statement of work, SBRC is required in the first part to 11 . . . design, fabricate, assemble and functionally test one spin-scan cloud camera. Part two, however, requires SBRC to 11 . . . fabricate, assemble and functionally test one flight model spin-scan camera identical to the prototype fabricated under Part I . . . .

It is appellants' contention that any "inventing" under their contract with the University of Wisconsin would have come under Part 1, which speaks of "design" work. Thus, if they are not entitled to the patent, it should go the University of Wisconsin or the Weather Bureau, who paid for the design, rather than to NASA. However, we are not persuaded by this argument since the claimed invention is not the camera arrangement alone. As we have already indicated, the claims require the camera arrangement in combination with a rotating body.

Insofar as the record reveals, the only use of the Weather Bureau camera was to install it on a prototype satellite that was never launched. The contract between SBRC and the University Of Wisconsin requires that SBRC report to the Weather Bureau only those inventions conceived or first reduced to practice under Part 1. Neither of those conditions was met. Furthermore, the only reduction to practice of the invention came as a result of a risk taken by NASA by including the camera arrangement in a satellite launched by it. Despite the fact that non-space uses of the claim invention are alluded to in the record, no practical use of the camera or the camera arrangement as claimed, other than the use by NASA, has been demonstrated.

3. *Special Procedures*

Section 152 of the Atomic Energy Act of 1954, 42 U.S.C. § 2182, and § 305 (c) of the Space Act, 42 U.S.C. § 2457(c), provide special procedures for ascertaining the ownership of inventions which may have been "made" during the contractual activities of AEC (now DOE) and NASA. These provisions require the submission of statements by the inventor, under oath, setting forth the full facts concerning the making of the invention to any contract or other arrangement of DOE (atomic energy only) or NASA. The applicable statements and the patent applications are shown to these agencies, and if the agency considers the invention, which has not been previously reported, to have been made under its contract, the agency may request title to any patent issuing on the application. The applicant may contest this request before the Patent Office Board of Patent Interference. Appeal from this Board is to the Court of Appeals for the Federal Circuit, *UMC Indus., Inc. v. Seaborg*, 439 F.2d 953, 169 U.S.P.Q. 325 (9th Cir. 1971). A review of the requirements of this statement was contained in the Official Gazette, U.S. Patent and Trademark Office, Vol. 914, No. 1, Page 2, Sept. 4, 1973. The pertinent parts are:

> The "full facts" involved in the conception and making of an invention should include those which are unique to that invention. The use of form paragraphs or printed forms which set forth only broad generalized statements of fact is not ordinarily regarded as meeting the requirements of these statutes.

> This office has construed the word "applicant" in both of these statutes to mean the inventor or joint inventors in person. Accordingly, in the ordinary situation, the statements must be signed by the inventor or joint inventors, if available. This construction is consistent with the fact that no other person could normally be more knowledgeable of the "full facts concerning the circumstances under which such invention was made," (42 U.S.C. § 2457) or, "full facts surrounding the making or conception of the invention or discovery" (42 U.S.C. § 2182).

> In instances where an applicant does not have first-hand knowledge whether the invention involved work under any contract, subcontract, or arrangement with or for the benefit of the Atomic Energy Commission, or had any relationship to any work under any contract of the National Aeronautics and Space Administration, and includes in his statement information of this nature derived from others, his statement should identify the source of his information. Alternatively, the statement by the applicant could be accompanied by a supplemental declaration or oath, as to the contractual matters, by the assignee or other person, e.g., an employee thereof, who has the requisite knowledge.

A number of cases under these statutory provisions have been discussed in earlier parts of this chapter. For an early discussion on this requirement, see Rosenblum, "Practice Before the Patent Office under Section 152 of the Atomic Energy Act and Section 305 of the National Aeronautics and Space Act," 25 Fed. B.J. 74 (1965).

D. Parallel Research Problems

Companies performing in-house research and development which parallel the research and development activities they conduct under Government contract have a major problem in assuring that the Government does not claim invention rights in the fruits of a company's independent research and development activities. In concept, where one contracts to perform research and development for pay and then undertakes to perform similar activities for oneself, the presumption that an invention which is covered by both activities falls under the Government funded work is proper in view of the conflicts of interests that may be involved. The contractor, therefore, should take precautions to overcome this presumption. These may include: (a) physically segregating the private from the Government work; (b) segregating the employees and information resulting from the Government and private work; (c) specifically defining the Government work so that the contract statement will not overlap with the private activities; (d) specifically eliminating from the contract work statement any requirement for work being done in the private area; (e) keeping separate and distinct financial records for each product so that no Government money or supplies are used in the private area; (f) disclosing the private work to the Government and obtaining an acknowledgment that such work is not to be funded by the Government.

In this regard, see *Pacific Technica Corp. v. United States*, 11 Ct. Cl. 393 (1986), *aff'd in part*, 835 F.2d 871 (1987).

The only evidence that plaintiff offered to disprove this was its log sheets that indicate the expenditures made by plaintiff during the projectile contract. Plaintiff maintained that all expenditures relating to the projectile contract were made under its internal account no. 37 and that all expenditures made for plaintiff's allegedly independent spin-stabilized sabot project were made under account no. 34. Plaintiff asserts that it made a conscious effort to segregate all of its costs and to charge pertinent costs to the respective job number. Plaintiff's assertion that the periodic and final audits by defendant auditors of plaintiff's records and accounting procedures confirms the legal independence of its fin-stabilized sabot and spin-stabilized sabot projects. However, plaintiff has not refuted the defendant's clear showing that plaintiff's personnel performed significant development and refinement of spin-stabilized sabot design while charging the work hours to the account set aside for fin-stabilized sabot work. This court recognizes that plaintiff's records, kept in the ordinary course of business, are reliable because the company relies upon them for their day-to-day business. Fed. Rule of Evidence 802(6). Yet, the court also recognizes the insufficiency of plaintiff's records to refute doing spin-stabilized sabot work and charging it to the projectile contract. This does not overcome defendant's showing that many spin-stabilized sabot work hours went unreported when spin-stabilized sabot work was documented, while only fin-stabilized sabot hours under the projectile contract were billed. If spin-stabilized sabot hours were worked, they should have been reported. Thus, under the same reliability of Rule 802(6), the failure of a record to mention a matter which would normally be mentioned is sufficient evidence of its nonoccurrence. Fed. R. Evid. 802(7). Any contention by plaintiff that such hours were not ordinarily recorded would show a lack of conscious effort to keep plaintiff's accounts separate.

Plaintiff's performance of spin-stabilized sabot work under the projectile contract led to reduction to practice of the sabot patent. The court finds that government funds were used in the development and significant improvement of sabot art applicable to the defendant's use of spin-stabilized sabot technology. The court agrees with *Technical Development Corp. v. United States*, 220 Ct. Cl. 128, 597 F.2d 733 (1979) that "it is enough that a significant feature of the invention was itself, within the contractual scope, or resulted directly from the course of the contract performance." *Id.*, 220 Ct. Cl. at 149, 597 F.2d at 745 (citing *Mine Safety Appliances Co. v. United States*, 176 Ct. Cl. 777, 787-88, 364 F.2d 385, 381 (1966)). Significant and essential features from the sabot design of the sabot patent were first actually reduced to practice under the projectile contract. The defendant has the right to use, royalty-free those inventions which have a "close and umbilical relationship" to the work and research funded by the United States and crystallized during performance of a federal contract. *Technical Development*, 220 Ct. Cl. at 150, 597 F.2d at 745. As a contributor to the advancement of the art, defendant has title to the sabot invention. However, this title would be strictly limited to the 20mm spin-stabilized sabot that is compatible with the Phalanx system if the sabot patent were not invalidated.

E. Patentability Standard

The term "subject invention" as it is used in the Patent Rights clauses is broad in that the 1971 Presidential Statement Policy standard for this term is an invention "which is or may be patentable" under U.S. Patent Law or patent laws of any foreign country. Therefore, if an invention is not patentable under Title 35 of the U.S. Code but is patentable under a foreign patent system it falls under this definition. If applied literally, contractors would need an understanding of the patent system in each foreign country before deciding whether a particular item was reportable under the FPR and DAR Patent Rights clauses for large businesses, Fuscher, "A Study of How the Government Obtains Patent Rights Under the DAR and FPR Patent Rights Clauses," 10 Pub. Ct. L.J. 296 (1978).

A more practical definition has been used with regard to small business firms and non-profit organizations where "inventions" are defined as inventions or discoveries which are or may be patentable or otherwise protectable under the patent laws of the United States, 35 U.S.C. § 201(d) although it is not known what "otherwise protectable" means under the patent laws.

The definition of "subject invention" utilized in prior ASPR Patent Rights clauses was even broader. They applied to "inventions, improvements, or discoveries (whether or not patentable)" and this has been characterized as defining an "idea," *AMP, Inc. v. United States*, 182 Ct. Cl. 86, 389 F.2d 448, 156 U.S.P.Q. 647 (1968), *cert. denied*, 391 U.S. 964 (1969). This concept was a part of the ASPR until 1975 when ASPR was revised to be consistent with the FPR patent language of the Presidential Policy Statement.

III. IMPLIED RIGHTS IN BACKGROUND INVENTIONS

The discussion thus far has centered on determining whether an invention may be considered a foreground or a subject invention under a contract. However, under the Court of Claims decision in *AMP, Inc. v. United States*, 182 Ct. Cl. 86, 389 F.2d 448, 156 U.S.P.Q. 647, *cert. denied*, 391 U.S. 964 (1968), the question of whether the Government's rights in a subject invention also entitles it to an implied license in a dominating background invention has come to the fore.

A. Implied License Theory

1. *Eastern Rotocraft Corporation*

In an earlier case, *Eastern Rotorcraft Corp. v. United States*, 181 Ct. CL 299, 384 F.2d 429, 155 U.S.P.Q. 729 (1967), the Court of Claims had rejected the Government's argument that it had an implied license in a dominating patent that pre-existed the contract under which it obtained rights to a subject invention. The Government contended that the express license to use a subject invention also gave it an implied license to use the contractor's dominant patent upon which the suit was based. Otherwise, the Government contended, its license to use the subject invention would be valueless. This position was rejected at 304:

> Factually, this contention is not true because when the patent in suit expires, defendant will be able to freely make nets using both patents. And contractually, it is not sound inasmuch as the contract states that the Government will not obtain a license either "directly or by implication" to inventions made outside the contract.

See also *Leesona Corp. v. United States*, 208 Ct. Cl. 871, 530 F.2d 896, 192 U.S.P.Q. 672, *cert. denied*, 444 U.S. 991 (1976).

2. AMP, Inc.

In *AMP, Inc. v. United States*, 182 Ct. CL 86, 389 F.2d 448, 156 U.S.P.Q. 647, *cert. denied*, 391 U.S. 964 (1968), the Government was held to have rights to a dominating patent which the contractor purchased after the completion of the contract. AMP developed a crimping tool on a Government contract, which contained the usual Patent Rights clause granting the Government a royalty-free license in subject inventions, and further stated, "Nothing contained in this paragraph shall be deemed to grant any license under any invention other than a subject invention." The contract also had a reproduction rights clause in which AMP agreed to grant a license to the Government in all patents it owned prior to completion of the contract, to the extent it had the right to do so, in the event the Government desired to reproduce the tool developed under the contract. An invention covering the tool was made under the contract (the Byrem Patent) and the Government was given a royalty-free license to practice this invention. Later AMP learned about a dominating patent, bought the patent, and brought suit against the Government on the dominating patent.

The court found that the law of implied license applied to after-acquired patents and was applicable to invention rights the Government acquired in its R&D contract, stating at 90-95:

> This principle of law has been stated to be that when a person sells a patent which employs an invention which infringes a prior patent, the person selling is estopped from bringing an action against his grantee for that infringement, even though the earlier patent is acquired after the sale of the later patent. *United Printing Machinery Co. v. Cross Paper Feeder Co.*, 220 F.2d 322 (D.Ct. Mass. 1915); 4 Deller's Walker on Patents, § 395, p. 565 (2d ed. 1965). The same principle applies to the grant of a patent right by license as well as assignment. *Steam Stone Cutter Co. v. Shortsleeves*, 22 Fed. Cases, 1168 (C.C.Vt. 1879).

> One argument made by plaintiff should be dealt with first because it introduces a distortion into the theory of implied license, and adds an unnecessary complexity to the case at bar. Plaintiff has argued that all cases cited by defendant are distinguishable from the instant case because they rest on a finding of estoppel. . . . An analysis of the cases, however, demonstrates that the form of estoppel used in these cases to support an implied license has not been estoppel in pais. The cases do not require a showing of false representation.

> This estoppel is actually in the nature of a legal estoppel. The essence of legal estoppel that can be found in the estoppel of the implied license doctrine involves the fact that the licensor (or

assignor) has licensed (or assigned) a definable property right for valuable consideration and then has attempted to derogate or detract from that right. The grantor is estopped from taking back in any extent that for which he has already received consideration.

It is not enough, however, to demonstrate that estoppel in pais is not a prerequisite for implying a license by law. It is also necessary to define the property right granted to defendant by plaintiff, and also to show how plaintiff is attempting to derogate or detract from that right.

In the case before us, plaintiff granted to the Government "an irrevocable, nonexclusive, non-transferable and royalty-free license to practice, and cause to be practiced for the Government throughout the world each Subject Invention in the manufacture, use, and disposition according to law, of any article or material, and in the use of any method; . . ." (Art. 38(b) of contract). Article 38(a)(i) of the contract defines specifically the nature of a Subject Invention: "The term 'Subject Invention' means any invention, improvement or discovery (whether or not patentable) . . ."

The facet of this licensing agreement which is of crucial importance and which plaintiff ignores is that it licenses the Government to use an idea and not just the Byrem Patent itself. The Subject Invention may be practiced by or for the Government throughout the world "whether or not patentable." Art. 38(a)(i). Thus the license was to practice or cause to be practiced an idea regardless of its patentability. It is the idea embodied by the Byrem tool, which also happens to be patented that was licensed to the Government. Relying on this license, the Government caused to be practiced this invention conceived of by plaintiff's employee, G.H. Byrem. The tools which allegedly infringe the patent in suit were identical in structure to the Byrem tool. The Government only did what it was licensed to do, no more and no less. Consequently, plaintiff is estopped from denying the Government the use of this tool. Plaintiff cannot negate the license it granted, and for which it received valuable consideration. Whatever rights third parties may have had against the Government are irrelevant to plaintiff's case since plaintiff licensed its rights to defendant, whereas other parties did not.

Plaintiff is also wrong in stating that the consideration paid is only for the research and development of the Byrem tool. This argument, in effect, asks us to overlook one part of the contract. It is elementary that money paid by one party pursuant to a contract is consideration for performance of all the terms of the contract, and not just some of the terms.

This case signaled the court's adoption of a broader view. Judge Davis, in a concurring opinion, stated that he would have decided the issue based on the express license granted by the contractor to the Government to practice the invention. This concept was later adopted in *Technitrol, Inc. v. United States*, 194 Ct. Cl. 596, 440 F.2d 1362, 169 U.S.P.Q. 732 (1971). The Court of Appeals in the Seventh Circuit also applied the estoppel theory to a patent acquired by the plaintiff after granting the defendant a license in a subservient patent in the settlement of an interference, *Minnesota Mining & Mfg. Co. v. E.I. Dupont De Nemours & Co.*, 448 F.2d 54, 171 U.S.P.Q. 11 (7th Cir. 1971).

B. Effect of Negating Language

The *AMP* case also established that the negating statement in the Patent Rights clause was not inconsistent with the Government obtaining rights in a contractor's after-acquired patent. The Court stated at 95-96:

> We must next consider the argument so strenuously urged by plaintiff, viz., that the contract precludes an implied license by its very terms. Plaintiff specifically points to the language of Article 38(b), which states:
>
>> Nothing contained in this paragraph shall be deemed to grant any license under any invention other than a Subject Invention.
>
>> Plaintiff argues that after-acquired patents (i.e., patents acquired after termination of the contract) are the only patents which fall into this clause. Unless the clause is so construed, it has no meaning whatsoever.
>
> *   *   *
>
> The language of Article 38(b) relied on by plaintiff does not preclude such a result since it refers only to inventions other than the Subject Invention. It is only intended to exclude subject matter of substantially different nature. Cf., *Green et al v. Aerosol Research Co.*, 374 F.2d 791, 152 U.S.P.Q 657 (7th Cir. 1967). Thus the language does have meaning, and it does harmonize with the whole of Article 38.

The negating language in *AMP* differed from the negating language in *Eastern Rotorcraft*. In *Eastern Rotorcraft*, the negating language actually came from the portion of the old ASPR Patent Rights clause that dealt with data. Upon the ASPR revision of December 1955 where the data provision was established as a separate clause entitled Reproduction and use of Technical Data the negating language was included in this clause, i.e.:

> Provided, however, that nothing contained in this paragraph shall be deemed, directly or by implication, to grant any license under any patent now or hereafter issued or to grant any right to reproduce anything else called for by this contract.

A negating sentence was, however, incorporated into the Patent Rights clause of ASPR 9-107(c). The clause, by the revision of 23 December 1955, stated in subparagraph (b)(2):

> Nothing contained in this Patent Rights clause shall be deemed to grant any license under any invention other than a Subject Invention.

The Patent Rights clause of DAR 7-302.23 and FPR 19.107-5 promulgated in 1975, contained the following negating language in paragraph (c), Minimum rights acquired by the Government:

> Nothing contained in this paragraph (c) shall be deemed to grant to the Government any rights with respect to any invention other than a Subject Invention.

Now FAR 52.227-12, the patent rights clause used primarily with large business states in paragraph (m):

> Other inventions: Nothing contained in this clause shall be deemed to grant the Government any rights with respect to any invention other than a subject invention.

There is no corresponding provision in the patent rights clause of FAR 52.227-11 that is applicable to small businesses and nonprofit organizations.

It has been argued that the negating language in the Patent Rights clause of AMP was drafted expressly to exclude the results in *AMP*. The trial judge in *Lockheed Aircraft Co. v. United States*, 190 U.S.P.Q. 134 (1976), noted that the testimony on the development of the DOD Patent Rights clause established that the term "performance of experimental, development or research work called for" used in prior DOD clauses and the negating language in the clause, "nothing contained in this paragraph shall be deemed to grant any license under any invention other than a subject invention," was added to prevent the Government from obtaining a license on a background or dominant patent and concluded that this "reflects a conscious attempt by the Government drafters to reserve for the Government license rights to only those inventions made in the research and development work expressly called for by the contract terms." The court, however, omitted this part of the trial judge's opinion without comment, *Lockheed Aircraft Co. v. United States*, 213 Ct. Cl. 395, 553 F.2d 69, 193 U.S.P.Q. 449 (1977).

C. Basis for Implied License

1. Data Rights

The cases, however, indicate that the Government's claim to an implied license in background patents has been interpreted narrowly. In *Ordnance Eng'g Corp. v. United States*, 68 Ct. Cl. 301 (1929), the Court of Claims held that Government contract that contained no patent rights clause but was made at Government expense upon Government suggestion in collaboration with and under a contractual relationship with the plaintiff. In *Tripp v. United States*, 186 Ct. Cl. 872, 406 F.2d 1066, 157 U.S.P.Q. 90 (1969), the contract gave the Government the right to use various notes, designs, drawings, memoranda, and other technical data without further compensation. The court found that the Government had reasonable notice about the contractor's patent and that it was unreasonable to assume that the parties intended a patent license to pass along with the data rights.

2. Failure to Disclose Patent Rights

Failure, by a contractor, to disclose the existence of a patent will not result in an implied license in favor of the Government. In *Alford v. United States*, 179 Ct. Cl. 938, 151 U.S.P.Q. 416 (1966), the Government urged that the inventor should be estopped from asserting a patent against the Government because it was pending while he was working under a Government contract. The court rejected this defense holding that the inventor had no duty or contractual obligation to tell the Government about background rights. Similarly, the Government claimed in *Rel-Reeves Inc. v. United States*, 209 Ct. Cl. 595, 534 F.2d 274, 186 U.S.P.Q. 21 (1976), that the plaintiff should be equitably estopped by false representations and concealment of material facts from denying an implied license in the Government. The court, in rejecting these defenses, held that four elements must be present to establish this defense: (1) the party to be estopped must know the facts; (2) he must intend that his conduct shall be acted on or must so act that the party asserting the estoppel has a right to believe it is so intended; (3) the latter must be ignorant of the facts; and (4) he must rely on the former's conduct to his injury, relying on *United States v. Georgia Pacific Co.*, 421 F.2d 92, 96 (9th Cir. 1970). Here, the Government claimed that the plaintiff did not specify that the patented feature was proprietary when specifically requested by the Government to identify all proprietary information that the plaintiff in another procurement had stated that the invention in question had been filed as a patent application when, in fact, it had not been so filed; and that, based on such allegations, the Patent Rights clause was removed from the contract. The court rejected this defense on the basis that the invention in question was only a conception when the Government asked for an identification of proprietary items and, as such, could be construed as only an idea and not proprietary. Further, it does not appear that the Government detrimentally relied on any of the plaintiff's statements.

3. *Relationship of the Parties*

In *Leesona Corp. v. United States*, 208 Ct. Cl. 871, 530 F.2d 896, 192 U.S.P.Q. 672, *cert. denied*, 44 U.S. 991 (1976), the Government argued for an implied license based on the mere existence of a related Government contract at the time the invention was made; the history of the mutual dealings of the parties that led to the creation of the subject devices; and, finally, because it was expressly licensed under certain subject inventions. As to the last item, the court in rejecting the Government's claim, relied on the negating language in the Patent Rights clause that the Government shall not obtain a license, "by implication or otherwise" to any invention other than those expressly licensed. Generally, the court found that the Government had not supported its allegations.

4. *Problem Identification*

Perhaps a more pertinent factual situation relates to contractors who perform private in-house research with the Government as a customer in mind but without a specific contract to do so. This fact situation was considered in *Breese Inc. v. United States*, 140 Ct. Cl. 9, 115 U.S.P.Q. 179 (1957). The Government had asked Breese Burner to develop a conversion package for a stove but entered into no contract and paid Breese no funds. Impliedly, there was an understanding that if Breese succeeded, the Army would buy from Breese and, in fact, it did so initially. Later, the Government bought infringing units and in response to Bressels suit claimed a "general license." The court rejected this argument noting that the Government did not contribute any funds to the development of the invention.

5. *Aid in Reduction to Practice*

The Government has also preferred an implied license defense where it has assisted the inventor in reducing the invention to practice. In *Amax Fly Ash Corp. v. United States*, 206 Ct. Cl. 756, 514 F.2d 1041, 185 U.S.P.Q. 437 (1975), the court rejected the Government's argument that it was entitled to a royalty-free license based on its contribution of personnel and facilities during a demonstration of the invention. The court found neither a "close and umbilical connection" between the invention and any contract work for the Government nor a joint venture created by the demonstration. Further, all expenses, except for some minor fittings, were borne by the plaintiff.

CHAPTER 4

STATUTORY AND REGULATORY
PROVISIONS ON PATENTS

CHAPTER 18—PATENT RIGHTS IN INVENTIONS
MADE WITH FEDERAL ASSISTANCE

35 U.S.C. §§ 200-212

Sec. 200. POLICY AND OBJECTIVE (35 USC § 200)

It is the policy and objective of the Congress to use the patent system to promote the utilization of inventions arising from federally supported research or development; to encourage maximum participation of small business firms in federally supported research and development efforts; to promote collaboration between commercial concerns and nonprofit organizations, including universities; to ensure that inventions made by nonprofit organizations and small business firms are used in a manner to promote free competition and enterprise; to promote the commercialization and public availability of inventions made in the United States by United States industry and labor; to ensure that the Government obtains sufficient rights in federally supported inventions to meet the needs of the Government and protect the public against nonuse or unreasonable use of inventions; and to minimize the costs of administering policies in this area.

Sec. 201. DEFINITIONS (35 USC § 201)

§ 201. Definitions

As used in this chapter [*35 USCS §§ 200* et seq.]—

(a) The term "Federal agency" means any executive agency as defined in section 105 of title 5, United States Code, and the military departments as defined by section 102 of title 5, United States Code.

(b) The term "funding agreement" means any contract, grant, or cooperative agreement entered into between any Federal agency, other than the Tennessee Valley Authority, and any contractor for the performance of experimental, developmental, or research work funded in whole or in part by the Federal Government. Such term includes any assignment, substitution of parties, or subcontract of any type entered into for the performance of experimental, developmental, or research work under a funding agreement as herein defined.

(c) The term "contractor" means any person, small business firm, or nonprofit organization that is a party to a funding agreement.

(d) The term "invention" means any invention or discovery which is or may be patentable or otherwise protectable under this title [*35 USCS §§ 1* et seq.] or any novel variety of plant which is or may be protectable under the Plant Variety Protection Act *(7 U.S.C 2321* et seq.).

(e) The term "subject invention" means any invention of the contractor conceived or first actually reduced to practice in the performance of work under a funding agreement: Provided, That in the case of a variety of plant, the date of determination (as defined in section 41(d) of the Plant Variety Protection Act *(7 U.S.C. 2401*(d))) must also occur during the period of contract performance.

(f) The term "practical application" means to manufacture in the case of a composition or product, to practice in the case of a process or method, or to operate in the case of a machine or system; and, in each case, under such conditions as to establish that the invention is being utilized and that its benefits are to the extent permitted by law or Government regulations available to the public on reasonable terms.

(g) The term "made" when used in relation to any invention means the conception or first actual reduction to practice of such invention.

(h) The term "small business firm" means a small business concern as defined at section 2 of Public Law 85-536 *(15 U.S.C. 632)* and implementing regulations of the Administrator of the Small Business Administration.

(i) The term "nonprofit organization" means universities and other institutions of higher education or an organization of the type described in section 501(c)(3) of the Internal Revenue Code of 1954 *(26 U.S.C. 501*(c)) and exempt from taxation under section 501(a) of the Internal Revenue Code *(26 U.S.C. 501*(a)) or any nonprofit scientific or educational organization qualified under a State nonprofit organization statute.

Sec. 202. DISPOSITION OF RIGHTS (35 USC § 202)

§ 202. Disposition of rights

(a) Each nonprofit organization or small business firm may, within a reasonable time after disclosure as required by paragraph (c)(1) of this section, elect to retain title to any subject invention: Provided, however, That a funding agreement may provide otherwise (i) when the contractor is not located in the United States or does not have a place of business located in the United States or is subject to the control of a foreign government, (ii) in exceptional circumstances when it is determined by the agency that restriction or elimination of the right to retain title to any subject invention will better promote the policy and objectives of this chapter[,] (iii) when it is determined by a Government authority which is authorized by statute or Executive order to conduct foreign intelligence or counter-intelligence activities that the restriction or elimination of the right to retain title to any subject invention is necessary to protect the security of such activities or, (iv) when the funding agreement includes the operation of a Government-owned, contractor-operated facility of the Department of Energy primarily dedicated to that Department's naval nuclear propulsion or weapons related programs and all funding agreement limitations under this subparagraph on the contractor's right to elect title to a subject invention are limited to inventions occurring under the above two programs of the Department of Energy. The rights of the nonprofit organization or small business firm shall be subject to the provisions of paragraph (c) of this section and the other provisions of this chapter [*35 USCS §§ 200* et seq.].

(b)(1) The rights of the Government under subsection (a) shall not be exercised by a Federal agency unless it first determines that at least one of the conditions identified in clauses (i) through (iv) of subsection (a) exists. Except in the case of subsection (a)(iii), the agency shall file with the Secretary of Commerce, within thirty days after the award of the applicable funding agreement, a copy of such determination. In the case of a determination under subsection (a)(ii), the statement shall include an analysis justifying the determination. In the case of determinations applicable to funding agreements with small business firms, copies shall also be sent to the Chief Counsel for Advocacy of the Small Business Administration. If the Secretary of Commerce believes that any individual determination or pattern of determinations is contrary to the policies and objectives of this chapter or otherwise not in conformance with this chapter, the Secretary shall so advise the head of the agency concerned and the Administrator of the Office of Federal Procurement Policy, and recommend corrective actions.

(2) Whenever the Administrator of the Office of Federal Procurement Policy has determined that one or more Federal agencies are utilizing the authority of clause (i) or (ii) of subsection (a) of this section in a manner that is contrary to the policies and objectives of this chapter, the Administrator is authorized to issue regulations describing classes of situations in which agencies may not exercise the authorities of those clauses.

(3) At least once every five years, the Comptroller General shall transmit a report to the Committees on the Judiciary of the Senate and House of Representatives on the manner in which this chapter [*35 USCS §§ 200* et seq.] is being implemented by the agencies and on such other aspects of Government patent policies and practices with respect to federally funded inventions as the Comptroller General believes appropriate.

(4) If the contractor believes that a determination is contrary to the policies and objectives of this chapter or constitutes an abuse of discretion by the agency, the determination shall be subject to the last paragraph of section 203(2).

(c) Each funding agreement with a small business firm or nonprofit organization shall contain appropriate provisions to effectuate the following:

(1) That the contractor disclose each subject invention to the Federal agency within a reasonable time after it becomes known to contractor personnel responsible for the administration of patent matters, and that the Federal Government may receive title to any subject invention not disclosed to it within such time.

(2) That the contractor make a written election within two years after disclosure to the Federal agency (or such additional time as may be approved by the Federal agency) whether the contractor will retain title to a subject invention: Provided, That in any case

where publication, on sale, or public use, has initiated the one year statutory period in which valid patent protection can still be obtained in the United States, the period for election may be shortened by the Federal agency to a date that is not more than sixty days prior to the end of the statutory period: And provided further, That the Federal Government may receive title to any subject invention in which the contractor does not elect to retain rights or fails to elect rights within such times.

(3) That a contractor electing rights in a subject invention agrees to file a patent application prior to any statutory bar date that may occur under this title [*35 USCS §§ 1* et seq.] due to publication, on sale, or public use, and shall thereafter file corresponding patent applications in other countries in which it wishes to retain title within reasonable times, and that the Federal Government may receive title to any subject inventions in the United States or other countries in which the contractor has not filed patent applications on the subject invention within such times.

(4) With respect to any invention in which the contractor elects rights, the Federal agency shall have a nonexclusive, nontransferrable, irrevocable, paid-up license to practice or have practiced for or on behalf of the United States any subject invention throughout the world: Provided, That the funding agreement may provide for such additional rights;[,] including the right to assign or have assigned foreign patent rights in the subject invention, as are determined by the agency as necessary for meeting the obligations of the United States under any treaty, international agreement, arrangement of cooperation, memorandum of understanding, or similar arrangement, including military agreement relating to weapons development and production.

(5) The right of the Federal agency to require periodic reporting on the utilization or efforts at obtaining utilization that are being made by the contractor or his licensees or assignees: Provided, That any such information as well as any information on utilization or efforts at obtaining utilization obtained as part of a proceeding under section 203 of this chapter shall be treated by the Federal agency as commercial and financial information obtained from a person and privileged and confidential and not subject to disclosure under section 552 of title 5 of the United States Code.

(6) An obligation on the part of the contractor, in the event a United States patent application is filed by or on its behalf or by any assignee of the contractor, to include within the specification of such application and any patent issuing thereon, a statement specifying that the invention was made with Government support and that the Government has certain rights in the invention.

(7) In the case of a nonprofit organization, (A) a prohibition upon the assignment of rights to a subject invention in the United States without the approval of the Federal agency, except where such assignment is made to an organization which has as one of its primary functions the management of inventions (provided that such assignee shall be subject to the same provisions as the contractor); (B) a requirement that the contractor share royalties with the inventor; (C) except with respect to a funding agreement for the operation of a Government-owned-contractor-operated facility, a requirement that the balance of any royalties or income earned by the contractor with respect to subject inventions, after payment

of expenses (including payments to inventors) incidental to the administration of subject inventions, be utilized for the support of scientific research or education; (D) a requirement that, except where it proves infeasible after a reasonable inquiry, in the licensing of subject inventions shall be given to small business firms; and (E) with respect to a funding agreement for the operation of a Government-owned-contractor-operated facility, requirements (i) that after payment of patenting costs, licensing costs, payments to inventors, and other expenses incidental to the administration of subject inventions, 100 percent of the balance of any royalties or income earned and retained by the contractor during any fiscal year up to an amount equal to 5 percent of the annual budget of the facility, shall be used by the contractor for scientific research, development, and education consistent with the research and development mission and objectives of the facility, including activities that increase the licensing potential of other inventions of the facility; provided that if said balance exceeds 5 percent of the annual budget of the facility, that 75 percent of such excess shall be paid to the Treasury of the United States and the remaining 25 percent shall be used for the same purposes as described above in this clause (D); and (ii) that, to the extent it provides the most effective technology transfer, the licensing of subject inventions shall be administered by contractor employees on location at the facility.

(8) The requirements of sections 203 and 204 of this chapter [*35 USCS §§ 203, 204*].

(d) If a contractor does not elect to retain title to a subject invention in cases subject to this section, the Federal agency may consider and after consultation with the contractor grant requests for retention of rights by the inventor subject to the provisions of this Act and regulations promulgated hereunder.

(e) In any case when a Federal employee is a coinventor of any invention made with a nonprofit organization, a small business firm, or a non-Federal inventor, the Federal agency employing such coinventor may, for the purpose of consolidating rights in the invention and if it finds that it would expedite the development of the invention—

(1) license or assign whatever rights it may acquire in the subject invention to the nonprofit organization, small business firm, or non-Federal inventor in accordance with the provisions of this chapter [*35 USCS §§ 200* et seq.]; or

(2) acquire any rights in the subject invention from the nonprofit organization, small business firm, or non-Federal inventor, but only to the extent the party from whom the rights are acquired voluntarily enters into the transaction and no other transaction under this chapter [*35 USCS §§ 200* et seq.] is conditioned on such acquisition.

(f)(1) No funding agreement with a small business firm or nonprofit organization shall contain a provision allowing a Federal agency to require the licensing to third parties of inventions owned by the contractor that are not subject inventions unless such provision has been approved by the head of the agency and a written justification has been signed by the head of the agency. Any such provision shall clearly state whether the licensing may be required in connection with the practice of a subject invention, a specifically identified work object, or both. The head of the agency may not delegate the authority to approve provisions or sign justifications required by this paragraph.

(2) A Federal agency shall not require the licensing of third parties under any such provision unless the head of the agency determines that the use of the invention by others is necessary for the practice of a subject invention or for the use of a work object of the funding agreement and that such action is necessary to achieve the practical application of the subject invention or work object. Any such determination shall be on the record after an opportunity for an agency hearing. Any action commenced for judicial review of such determination shall be brought within sixty days after notification of such determination.

Sec. 203. MARCH-IN RIGHTS (35 USC § 203)

(1.[(1)] With respect to any subject invention in which a small business firm or non-profit organization has acquired title under this chapter [*35 USCS §§ 200* et seq.], the Federal agency under whose funding agreement the subject invention was made shall have the right, in accordance with such procedures as are provided in regulations promulgated hereunder to require the contractor, an assignee or exclusive licensee of a subject invention to grant a nonexclusive, partially exclusive, or exclusive license in any field of use to a responsible applicant or applicants, upon terms that are reasonable under the circumstances, and if the contractor, assignee, or exclusive licensee refuses such request, to grant such a license itself, if the Federal agency determines that such—

(a) action is necessary because the contractor or assignee has not taken, or is not expected to take within a reasonable time, effective steps to achieve practical application of the subject invention in such field of use;

(b) action is necessary to alleviate health or safety needs which are not reasonably satisfied by the contractor, assignee, or their licensees;

(c) action is necessary to meet requirements for public use specified by Federal regulations and such requirements are not reasonably satisfied by the contractor, assignee, or licensees; or

(d) action is necessary because the agreement required by section 204 has not been obtained or waived or because a licensee of the exclusive right to use or sell any subject invention in the United States is in breach of its agreement obtained pursuant to section 204.

(2) A determination pursuant to this section or section 202(b)(4) shall not be subject to the Contract Disputes Act *(41 U.S.C. § 601* et seq.). An administrative appeals procedure shall be established by regulations promulgated in accordance with section 206. Additionally, any contractor, inventor, assignee, or exclusive licensee adversely affected by a determination under this section may, at any time within sixty days after the determination is issued, file a petition in the United States Claims Court [United States Court of Federal Claims], which shall have jurisdiction to determine the appeal on the record and to affirm, reverse, remand or modify, [",] as appropriate, the determination of the Federal agency. In cases described in

paragraphs (a) and (c), the agency's determination shall be held in abeyance pending the exhaustion of appeals or petitions filed under the preceding sentence.

Sec. 204. PREFERENCE FOR UNITED STATES INDUSTRY (35 USC § 204)

Notwithstanding any other provision of this chapter, no small business firm or non-profit organization which receives title to any subject invention and no assignee of any such small business firm or nonprofit organization shall grant to any person the exclusive right to use or sell any subject invention in the United States unless such person agrees that any products embodying the subject invention or produced through the use of the subject invention will be manufactured substantially in the United States. However, in individual cases, the requirement for such an agreement may be waived by the Federal agency under whose funding agreement the invention was made upon a showing by the small business firm, nonprofit organization, or assignee that reasonable but unsuccessful efforts have been made to grant licenses on similar terms to potential licensees that would be likely to manufacture substantially in the United States or that under the circumstances domestic manufacture is not commercially feasible.

Sec. 205. CONFIDENTIALITY (35 USC § 205)

Federal agencies are authorized to withhold from disclosure to the public information disclosing any invention in which the Federal Government owns or may own a right, title, or interest (including a nonexclusive license) for a reasonable time in order for a patent application to be filed. Furthermore, Federal agencies shall not be required to release copies of any document which is part of an application for patent filed with the United States Patent and Trademark Office or with any foreign patent office.

Sec. 206. UNIFORM CLAUSES AND REGULATIONS (35 USC § 206)

The Secretary of Commerce may issue regulations which may be made applicable to Federal agencies implementing the provisions of sections 202 through 204 of this chapter [*35 USCS §§ 202*-204] and shall establish standard funding agreement provisions required under this chapter [*35 USCS §§ 200* et seq.]. The regulations and the standard funding agreement shall be subject to public comment before their issuance.

Sec. 207. DOMESTIC AND FOREIGN PROTECTION OF FEDERALLY OWNED INVENTIONS (35 USC § 207)

(a) Each Federal agency is authorized to—

(1) apply for, obtain, and maintain patents or other forms of protection in the United States and in foreign countries on inventions in which the Federal Government owns a right, title, or interest;

(2) grant nonexclusive, exclusive, or partially exclusive licenses under federally owned inventions, royalty-free or for royalties or other consideration, and on such terms and conditions, including the grant to the licensee of the right of enforcement pursuant to the

provisions of chapter 29 of this title [*35 USCS §§ 281* et seq.] as determined appropriate in the public interest;

(3) undertake all other suitable and necessary steps to protect and administer rights to federally owned inventions on behalf of the Federal Government either directly or through contract, including acquiring rights for and administering royalties to the Federal Government in any invention, but only to the extent the party from whom the rights are acquired voluntarily enters into the transaction, to facilitate the licensing of a federally owned invention; and

(4) transfer custody and administration, in whole or in part, to another Federal agency, of the right, title or interest in any federally owned invention.

(b) For the purpose of assuring the effective management of Government-owned inventions, the Secretary of Commerce is authorized to—

(1) assist Federal agency efforts to promote the licensing and utilization of Government-owned inventions;

(2) assist Federal agencies in seeking protection and maintaining inventions in foreign countries, including the payment of fees and costs connected therewith; and

(3) consult with and advise Federal agencies as to areas of science and technology research and development with potential for commercial utilization.

Sec. 208. REGULATIONS GOVERNING FEDERAL LICENSING (35 USC § 208)

The Secretary of Commerce is authorized to promulgate regulations specifying the terms and conditions upon which any federally owned invention, other than inventions owned by the Tennessee Valley Authority, may be licensed on a nonexclusive, partially exclusive, or exclusive basis.

Sec. 209. RESTRICTIONS ON LICENSING OF FEDERALLY OWNED INVENTIONS (35 USC § 209)

(a) No Federal agency shall grant any license under a patent or patent application on a federally owned invention unless the person requesting the license has supplied the agency with a plan for development and/or marketing of the invention, except that any such plan may be treated by the Federal agency as commercial and financial information obtained from a person and privileged and confidential and not subject to disclosure under section 552 of title 5 of the United States Code.

(b) A Federal agency shall normally grant the right to use or sell any federally owned invention in the United States only to a licensee that agrees that any products embodying the invention or produced through the use of the invention will be manufactured substantially in the United States.

(c)(1) Each Federal agency may grant exclusive or partially exclusive licenses in any invention covered by a federally owned domestic patent or patent application only if, after public notice and opportunity for filing written objections, it is determined that—

(A) the interests of the Federal Government and the public will best be served by the proposed license, in view of the applicant's intentions, plans, and ability to bring the invention to practical application or otherwise promote the invention's utilization by the public;

(B) the desired practical application has not been achieved, or is not likely expeditiously to be achieved, under any nonexclusive license which has been granted, or which may be granted, on the invention;

(C) exclusive or partially exclusive licensing is a reasonable and necessary incentive to call forth the investment of risk capital and expenditures to bring the invention to practical application or otherwise promote the invention's utilization by the public; and

(D) the proposed terms and scope of exclusivity are not greater than reasonably necessary to provide the incentive for bringing the invention to practical application or otherwise promote the invention's utilization by the public.

(2) A Federal agency shall not grant such exclusive or partially exclusive license under paragraph (1) of this subsection if it determines that the grant of such license will tend substantially to lessen competition or result in undue concentration in any section of the country in any line of commerce to which the technology to be licensed relates, or to create or maintain other situations inconsistent with the antitrust laws.

(3) First preference in the exclusive or partially exclusive licensing of federally owned inventions shall go to small business firms submitting plans that are determined by the agency to be within the capabilities of the firms and equally likely, if executed, to bring the invention to practical application as any plans submitted by applicants that are not small business firms.

(d) After consideration of whether the interests of the Federal Government or United States industry in foreign commerce will be enhanced, any Federal agency may grant exclusive or partially exclusive licenses in any invention covered by a foreign patent application or patent, after public notice and opportunity for filing written objections, except that a Federal agency shall not grant such exclusive or partially exclusive license if it determines that the grant of such license will tend substantially to lessen competition or result in undue concentration in any section of the United States in any line of commerce to which the technology to be licensed relates, or to create or maintain other situations inconsistent with antitrust laws.

(e) The Federal agency shall maintain a record of determinations to grant exclusive or partially exclusive licenses.

(f) Any grant of a license shall contain such terms and conditions as the Federal agency determines appropriate for the protection of the interests of the Federal Government and the public, including provisions for the following:

(1) periodic reporting on the utilization or efforts at obtaining utilization that are being made by the licensee with particular reference to the plan submitted: Provided, That any such information may be treated by the Federal agency as commercial and financial information obtained from a person and privileged and confidential and not subject to disclosure under section 552 of title 5 of the United States Code;

(2) the right of the Federal agency to terminate such license in whole or in part if it determines that the licensee is not executing the plan submitted with its request for a license and the licensee cannot otherwise demonstrate to the satisfaction of the Federal agency that it has taken or can be expected to take within a reasonable time, effective steps to achieve practical application of the invention;

(3) the right of the Federal agency to terminate such license in whole or in part if the licensee is in breach of an agreement obtained pursuant to paragraph (b) of this section; and

(4) the right of the Federal agency to terminate the license in whole or in part if the agency determines that such action is necessary to meet requirements for public use specified by Federal regulations issued after the date of the license and such requirements are not reasonably satisfied by the licensee.

Sec. 210. PRECEDENCE OF CHAPTER (35 USC § 210)

(a) This chapter shall take precedence over any other Act which would require a disposition of rights in subject inventions of small business firms or nonprofit organizations contractors in a manner that is inconsistent with this chapter, including but not necessarily limited to the following:

(1) section 10(a) of the Act of June 29, 1935, as added by title I of the Act of August 14, 1946 (7 U.S.C. 427i(a); 60 Stat. 1085);

(2) section 205(a) of the Act of August 14, 1946 (7 U.S.C. 1624(a); 60 Stat. 1090);

(3) section 501(c) of the Federal Mine Safety and Health Act of 1977 (30 U.S.C. 951(c); 83 Stat. 742);

(4) section 30168(e) of title 49;

(5) section 12 of the National Science Foundation Act of 1950 (42 U.S.C. 1871(a); 82 Stat. 360);

(6) section 152 of the Atomic Energy Act of 1954 (42 U.S.C. 2182; 68 Stat. 943);

(7) section 305 of the National Aeronautics and Space Act of 1958 (42 U.S.C. 2457);

(8) section 6 of the Coal Research Development Act of 1960 (30 U.S.C. 666; 74 Stat. 337);

(9) section 4 of the Helium Act Amendments of 1960 (50 U.S.C. 167b; 74 Stat. 920);

(10) section 32 of the Arms Control and Disarmament Act of 1961 (22 U.S.C. 2572; 75 Stat. 634);

(11) section 9 of the Federal Nonnuclear Energy Research and Development Act of 1974 (42 U.S.C. 5901; 88 Stat. 1878);

(12) section 5(d) of the Consumer Product Safety Act (15 U.S.C. 2054(d); 86 Stat. 1211);

(13) section 3 of the Act of April 5, 1944 (30 U.S.C. 323; 58 Stat. 191);

(14) section 8001(c)(3) of the Solid Waste Disposal Act (42 U.S.C. 6981(c); 90 Stat. 2829);

(15) section 219 of the Foreign Assistance Act of 1961 (22 U.S.C. 2179; 83 Stat. 806);

(16) section 427(b) of the Federal Mine Health and Safety Act of 1977 (30 U.S.C. 937(b); 86 Stat. 155);

(17) section 306(d) of the Surface Mining and Reclamation Act of 1977 (30 U.S.C. 1226(d); 91 Stat. 455);

(18) section 21(d) of the Federal Fire Prevention and Control Act of 1974 (15 U.S.C. 2218(d); 88 Stat. 1548);

(19) section 6(b) of the Solar Photovoltaic Energy Research Development and Demonstration Act of 1978 (42 U.S.C. 5585(b); 92 Stat. 2516);

(20) section 12 of the Native Latex Commercialization and Economic Development Act of 1978 (7 U.S.C. 178(j); 92 Stat. 2533); and

(21) section 408 of the Water Resources and Development Act of 1978 (42 U.S.C. 7879; 92 Stat. 1360).

The Act creating this chapter shall be construed to take precedence over any future Act unless that Act specifically cites this Act and provides that it shall take precedence over this Act.

(b) Nothing in this chapter is intended to alter the effect of the laws cited in paragraph (a) of this section or any other laws with respect to the disposition of rights in inventions made in the performance of funding agreements with persons other than nonprofit organizations or small business firms.

(c) Nothing in this chapter is intended to limit the authority of agencies to agree to the disposition of rights in inventions made in the performance of work under funding agreements with persons other than nonprofit organizations or small business firms in accordance with the Statement of Government Patent Policy issued on February 18, 1983, agency regulations, or other applicable regulations or to otherwise limit the authority of agencies to allow such persons to retain ownership of inventions except that all funding agreements, including those with other than small business firms and nonprofit organizations, shall include the requirements established in paragraph 202(c)(4) and section 203 of this title. Any disposition of rights in inventions made in accordance with the Statement or implementing regulations, including any disposition occurring before enactment of this section, are hereby authorized.

(d) Nothing in this chapter shall be construed to require the disclosure of intelligence sources or methods or to otherwise affect the authority granted to the Director of Central Intelligence by statute or Executive order for the protection of intelligence sources or methods.

(e) The provisions of the Stevenson-Wydler Technology Innovation Act of 1980 shall take precedence over the provisions of this chapter to the extent that they permit or require a disposition of rights in subject inventions which is inconsistent with this chapter.

Sec. 211. RELATIONSHIP TO ANTITRUST LAWS (35 USC § 211)

Nothing in this chapter shall be deemed to convey to any person immunity from civil or criminal liability, or to create any defenses to actions, under any antitrust law.

Sec. 212. DISPOSITION OF RIGHTS IN EDUCATIONAL AWARDS (35 USC § 212)

No scholarship, fellowship, training grant, or other funding agreement made by a Federal agency primarily to an awardee for educational purposes will contain any provision giving the Federal agency any rights to inventions made by the awardee.

Memorandum to the Heads of Executive Departments and Agencies

Subject: Government Patent Policy

To the extent permitted by law, agency policy with respect to the disposition of any invention in the performance of a federally-funded research and development contract, grant or cooperative agreement award shall be the same or substantially the same as applied to small business firms and nonprofit organizations under Chapter 38 of Title 35 of the United States Code.

In awards not subject to Chapter 38 of Title 35 of the United States Code, any of the rights of the Government or obligations of the performer described in 35 U.S.C. 202-204 may be waived or omitted if the agency determines (1) that the interests of the United States and the general public will be better served thereby as, for example, where this is necessary to obtain a uniquely or highly qualified performer; or (2) that the award involves co-sponsored, cost-sharing, or joint venture research and development, and the performer, cosponsor or joint venturer is making substantial contribution of funds, facilities or equipment to the work performed under the award.

In addition, agencies should protect the confidentiality of invention disclosure, patent applications and utilization reports required in performance or in consequence of awards to the extent permitted by 35 U.S.C. 205 or other applicable laws.

Ronald Reagan

DEPARTMENT OF COMMERCE

PART 401

RIGHTS TO INVENTIONS MADE BY NONPROFIT ORGANIZATIONS AND SMALL BUSINESS FIRMS UNDER GOVERNMENT GRANTS, CONTRACTS, AND COOPERATIVE AGREEMENTS
37 C.F.R. 401
(CURRENT AUG. 2001)

37 C.F.R. § 401.1 Scope.

(a) Traditionally there have been no conditions imposed by the government on research performers while using private facilities which would preclude them from accepting research funding from other sources to expand, to aid in completing or to conduct separate investigations closely related to research activities sponsored by the government. Notwithstanding the right of research organizations to accept supplemental funding from other sources for the purpose of expediting or more comprehensively accomplishing the research objectives of the government sponsored project, it is clear that the ownership provisions of these regulations would remain applicable in any invention "conceived or first actually reduced to practice in performance" of the project. Separate accounting for the two funds used to support the project in this case is not a determining factor. These regulations would remain applicable in any invention "conceived or first actually reduced to practice in performance" of the project. Separate accounting for the two funds used to support the project in this case is not a determining factor.

(1) To the extent that a non-government sponsor established a project which, although closely related, falls outside the planned and committed activities of a government-funded project and does not diminish or distract from the performance of such activities, inventions made in performance of the non-government sponsored project would not be subject to the conditions of these regulations. An example of such related but separate projects would be a government sponsored project having research objectives to expand scientific understanding in a field and a closely related industry sponsored project having as its objectives the application of such new knowledge to develop usable new technology. The time relationship in conducting the two projects and the use of new fundamental knowledge from one in the performance of the other are not important determinants since most inventions rest on a knowledge base built up by numerous independent research efforts extending over many years. Should such an invention be claimed by the performing organization to be the product of non-government sponsored research and be challenged by the sponsoring agency as being reportable to the government as a "subject invention", the challenge is appealable as described in § 401.11(d).

(2) An invention which is made outside of the research activities of a government-funded project is not viewed as a "subject invention" since it cannot be shown to have been "conceived or first actually reduced to practice" in performance of the project. An obvious example of this is a situation where an instrument purchased with government funds is later used, without interference with or cost to the government-funded project, in making an invention all expenses of which involve only non-government funds.

(b) This part implements 35 U.S.C. 202 through 204 and is applicable to all Federal agencies. It applies to all funding agreements with small business firms and nonprofit organizations executed after the effective date of this part, except for a funding agreement made primarily for educational purposes. Certain sections also provide guidance for the administration of funding agreements which predate the effective date of this part. In accordance with 35 U.S.C. 212, no scholarship, fellowship, training grant, or other funding agreement made by a Federal agency primarily to an awardee for educational purposes will contain any provision giving the Federal agency any rights to inventions made by the awardee.

(c) The march-in and appeals procedures in §§ 401.6 and 401.11 shall apply to any march-in or appeal proceeding under a funding agreement subject to Chapter 18 of Title 35, U.S.C., initiated after the effective date of this part even if the funding agreement was executed prior to that date.

(d) At the request of the contractor, a funding agreement for the operation of a government-owned facility which is in effect on the effective date of this part shall be promptly amended to include the provisions required by §§ 401.3(a) unless the agency determines that one of the exceptions at 35 U.S.C. 202(a)(i) through (iv) § 401.3(a)(8) through (iv) of this part) is applicable and will be applied. If the exception at § 401.3(a)(iv) is determined to be applicable, the funding agreement will be promptly amended to include the provisions required by § 401.3(c).

(e) This regulation supersedes OMB Circular A-124 and shall take precedence over any regulations dealing with ownership of inventions made by small businesses and nonprofit organizations which are inconsistent with it. This regulation will be followed by all agencies pending amendment of agency regulations to conform to this part and amended Chapter 18 of Title 35. Only deviations requested by a contractor and not inconsistent with Chapter 18 of Title 35, United States Code, may be made without approval of the Secretary. Modifications or tailoring of clauses as authorized by § 401.5 or § 401.3, when alternative provisions are used under § 401.3(a)(1) through (4), are not considered deviations requiring the Secretary's approval. Three copies of proposed and final agency regulations supplementing this part shall be submitted to the Secretary at the office set out in § 401.16 for approval for consistency with this part before they are submitted to the Office of Management and Budget (OMB) for review under Executive Order 12291 or, if no submission is required to be made to OMB, before their submission to the FEDERAL REGISTER for publication.

(f) In the event an agency has outstanding prime funding agreements that do not contain patent flow-down provisions consistent with this part or earlier Office of Federal Procurement Policy regulations (OMB Circular A-124 or OMB Bulletin 81-22), the agency shall take appropriate action to ensure that small business firms or nonprofit organizations that are subcontractors under any such agreements and that received their subcontracts after July 1, 1981, receive rights in their subject inventions that are consistent with Chapter 18 and this part.

(g) This part is not intended to apply to arrangements under which nonprofit organizations, small business firms, or others are allowed to use government-owned research facilities and normal technical assistance provided to users of those facilities, whether on a reimbursable or nonreimbursable basis.

This part is also not intended to apply to arrangements under which sponsors reimburse the government or facility contractor for the contractor employee's time in performing work for the sponsor. Such arrangements are not considered "funding agreements" as defined at 35 U.S.C. 201(b) and § 401.2(a) of this part.

37 C.F.R. § 401.2 Definitions.

As used in this part—

(a) The term funding agreement means any contract, grant, or cooperative agreement entered into between any Federal agency, other than the Tennessee Valley Authority, and any contractor for the performance of experimental, developmental, or research work funded in whole or in part by the Federal government. This term also includes any assignment, substitution of parties, or subcontract of any type entered into for the performance of experimental, developmental, or research work under a funding agreement as defined in the first sentence of this paragraph.

(b) The term contractor means any person, small business firm or nonprofit organization which is a party to a funding agreement.

(c) The term invention means any invention or discovery which is or may be patentable or otherwise protectable under Title 35 of the United States Code, or any novel variety of plant which is or may be protectable under the Plant Variety Protection Act (7 U.S.C. 2321 et seq.).

(d) The term subject invention means any invention of a contractor conceived or first actually reduced to practice in the performance of work under a funding agreement; provided that in the case of a variety of plant, the date of determination (as defined in section 41(d) of the Plant Variety Protection Act, 7 U.S.C. 2401(d)) must also occur during the period of contract performance.

(e) The term practical application means to manufacture in the case of a composition of product, to practice in the case of a process or method, or to operate in the case of a machine or system; and, in each case, under such conditions as to establish that the invention is being utilized and that its benefits are, to the extent permitted by law or government regulations, available to the public on reasonable terms.

(f) The term made when used in relation to any invention means the conception or first actual reduction to practice of such invention.

(g) The term small business firm means a small business concern as defined at section 2 of Pub. L. 85-536 (15 U.S.C. 632) and implementing regulations of the Administrator of the Small Business Administration. For the purpose of this part, the size standards for small business concerns involved in government procurement and subcontracting at 13 CFR 121.5 will be used.

(h) The term nonprofit organization means universities and other institutions of higher education or an organization of the type described in section 501(c)(3) of the Internal Revenue Code of 1954 (26 U.S.C. 501(c) and exempt from taxation under section 501(a) of the Internal Revenue Code (26 U.S.C. 501(a)) or any nonprofit scientific or educational organization qualified under a state nonprofit organization statute.

(i) The term Chapter 18 means Chapter 18 of Title 35 of the United States Code.

(j) The term "Secretary" means the Assistant Secretary of Commerce for Technology Policy.

(k) The term electronically filed means any submission of information transmitted by an electronic or optical-electronic system.

(l) The term electronic or optical-electronic system means a software-based system approved by the agency for the transmission of information.

(m) The term patent application or "application for patent" includes a provisional or nonprovisional U.S. national application for patent as defined in 37 CFR 1.9 (a)(2) and (a)(3), respectively, or an application for patent in a foreign country or in an international patent office.

(n) The term initial patent application means a nonprovisional U.S. national application for patent as defined in 37 CFR 1.9(a)(3).

37 C.F.R. § 401.3 Use of the standard clauses at § 401.14.

(a) Each funding agreement awarded to a small business firm or nonprofit organization (except those subject to 35 U.S.C. 212) shall contain the clause found in § 401.14(a) with such modifications and tailoring as authorized or required elsewhere in this part. However, a funding agreement may contain alternative provisions—

(1) When the contractor is not located in the United States or does not have a place of business located in the United States or is subject to the control of a foreign government; or

(2) In exceptional circumstances when it is determined by the agency that restriction or elimination of the right to retain title to any subject invention will better promote the policy and objectives of Chapter 18 of Title 35 of the United States Code; or

(3) When it is determined by a government authority which is authorized by statute or executive order to conduct foreign intelligence or counterintelligence activities that the

restriction or elimination of the right to retain title to any subject invention is necessary to protect the security to such activities; or

(4) When the funding agreement includes the operation of the government-owned, contractor-operated facility of the Department of Energy primarily dedicated to that Department's naval nuclear propulsion or weapons related programs and all funding agreement limitations under this subparagraph on the contractor's right to elect title to a subject invention are limited to inventions occurring under the above two programs.

(b) When an agency exercises the exceptions at § 401.3(a)(2) or (3), it shall use the standard clause at § 401.14(a) with only such modifications as are necessary to address the exceptional circumstances or concerns which led to the use of the exception. For example, if the justification relates to a particular field of use or market, the clause might be modified along lines similar to those described in § 401.14(b). In any event, the clause should provide the contractor with an opportunity to receive greater rights in accordance with the procedures at § 401.15. When an agency justifies and exercises the exception at § 401.3(a)(2) and uses an alternative provision in the funding agreement on the basis of national security, the provision shall provide the contractor with the right to elect ownership to any invention made under such funding agreement as provided by the Standard Patent Rights Clause found at § 401.14(a) if the invention is not classified by the agency within six months of the date it is reported to the agency, or within the same time period the Department of Energy does not, as authorized by regulation, law or Executive order or implementing regulations thereto, prohibit unauthorized dissemination of the invention. Contracts in support of DOE's naval nuclear propulsion program are exempted from this paragraph.

(c) When the Department of Energy exercises the exception at § 401.3(a)(4), it shall use the clause prescribed at § 401.14(b) or substitute thereto with such modification and tailoring as authorized or required elsewhere in this part.

(d) When a funding agreement involves a series of separate task orders, an agency may apply the exceptions at § 401.3(a)(2) or (3) to individual task orders, and it may structure the contract so that modified patent rights provisions will apply to the task order even though the clauses at either § 401.14(a) or (b) are applicable to the remainder of the work. Agencies are authorized to negotiate such modified provisions with respect to task orders added to a funding agreement after its initial award.

(e) Before utilizing any of the exceptions in 401.3(a) of this section, the agency shall prepare a written determination, including a statement of facts supporting the determination, that the conditions identified in the exception exist. A separate statement of facts shall be prepared for each exceptional circumstances determination, except that in appropriate cases a single determination may apply to both a funding agreement and any subcontracts issued under it or to any funding agreement to which such an exception is applicable. In cases when § 401.3(a)(2) is used, the determination shall also include an analysis justifying the determination. This analysis should address with specificity how the alternate provisions will better achieve the objectives set forth in 35 U.S.C. 200. A copy of each determination, statement of facts, and, if applicable, analysis shall be promptly provided to the contractor or prospective contractor along with a notification to the contractor or prospective contractor of its rights to appeal the determination of the exception under 35 U.S.C. 202(b)(4) and § 401.4 of this part.

(f) Except for determinations under § 401.3(a)(3), the agency shall also provide copies of each determination, statement of fact, and analysis to the Secretary. These shall be sent within 30 days after the award of the funding agreement to which they pertain. Copies shall also be sent to the Chief Counsel for Advocacy of the Small Business Administration if the funding agreement is with a small business firm. If the Secretary of Commerce believes that any individual determination or pattern of determinations is contrary to the policies and objectives of this chapter or otherwise not in conformance with this chapter, the Secretary shall so advise the head of the agency concerned and the Administrator of the Office of Federal Procurement Policy and recommend corrective actions.

(g) To assist the Comptroller General of the United States to accomplish his or her responsibilities under 35 U.S.C. 202, each Federal agency that enters into any funding agreements with nonprofit organizations or small business firms shall accumulate and, at the request of the Comptroller General, provide the Comptroller General or his or her duly authorized representative the total number of prime agreements entered into with small business firms or nonprofit organizations that contain the patent rights clause in this part or under OMB Circular A-124 for each fiscal year beginning with October 1, 1982.

(h) To qualify for the standard clause, a prospective contractor may be required by an agency to certify that it is either a small business firm or a nonprofit organization. If the agency has reason to question the status of the prospective contractor as a small business firm, it may file a protest in accordance with 13 CFR 121.9. If it questions nonprofit status, it may require the prospective contractor to furnish evidence to establish its status as a nonprofit organization.

37 C.F.R. § 401.4 Contractor appeals of exceptions.

(a) In accordance with 35 U.S.C. 202(b)(4) a contractor has the right to an administrative review of a determination to use one of the exceptions at § 401.3(a) (1) through (4) if the contractor believes that a determination is either contrary to the policies and objectives of this chapter or constitutes an abuse of discretion by the agency. Paragraph (b) of this section specifies the procedures to be followed by contractors and agencies in such cases. The assertion of such a claim by the contractor shall not be used as a basis for withholding or delaying the award of a funding agreement or for suspending performance under an award. Pending final resolution of the claim the contract may be issued with the patent rights provision proposed by the agency; however, should the final decision be in favor of the contractor, the funding agreement will be amended accordingly and the amendment made retroactive to the effective date of the funding agreement.

(b)(1) A contractor may appeal a determination by providing written notice to the agency within 30 working days from the time it receives a copy of the agency's determination, or within such longer time as an agency may specify in its regulations. The contractor's notice should specifically identify the basis for the appeal.

(2) The appeal shall be decided by the head of the agency or by his/her designee who is at a level above the person who made the determination. If the notice raises a genuine dispute over the material facts, the head of the agency or the designee shall undertake, or refer the matter for, fact-finding.

(3) Fact-finding shall be conducted in accordance with procedures established by the agency. Such procedures shall be as informal as practicable and be consistent with principles of fundamental fairness. The procedures should afford the contractor the opportunity to appear with counsel, submit documentary evidence, present witnesses and confront such persons as the agency may rely upon. A transcribed record shall be made and shall be available at cost to the contractor upon request. The requirement for a transcribed record may be waived by mutual agreement of the contractor and the agency.

(4) The official conducting the fact-finding shall prepare or adopt written findings of fact and transmit them to the head of the agency or designee promptly after the conclusion of the fact-finding proceeding along with a recommended decision. A copy of the findings of fact and recommended decision shall be sent to the contractor by registered or certified mail.

(5) Fact-finding should be completed within 45 working days from the date the agency receives the contractor's written notice.

(6) When fact-finding has been conducted, the head of the agency or designee shall base his or her decision on the facts found, together with any argument submitted by the contractor, agency officials or any other information in the administrative record. In cases referred for fact-finding, the agency head or the designee may reject only those facts that have been found to be clearly erroneous, but must explicitly state the rejection and indicate the basis for the contrary finding. The agency head or the designee may hear oral arguments after fact-finding provided that the contractor or contractor's attorney or representative is present and given an opportunity to make arguments and rebuttal. The decision of the agency head or the designee shall be in writing and, if it is unfavorable to the contractor shall include an explanation of the basis of the decision. The decision of the agency or designee shall be made within 30 working days after fact-finding or, if there was no fact-finding, within 45 working days from the date the agency received the contractor's written notice. A contractor adversely affected by a determination under this section may, at any time within sixty days after the determination is issued, file a petition in the United States Claims Court, which shall have jurisdiction to determine the appeal on the record and to affirm, reverse, remand, or modify as appropriate, the determination of the Federal agency.

37 C.F.R. § 401.5 Modification and tailoring of clauses.

(a) Agencies should complete the blank in paragraph (g)(2) of the clauses at § 401.14 in accordance with their own or applicable government-wide regulations such as the Federal Acquisition Regulation. In grants and cooperative agreements (and in contracts, if not inconsistent with the Federal Acquisition Regulation) agencies wishing to apply the same clause to all subcontractors as is applied to the contractor may delete paragraph (g)(2) of the clause and delete the words "to be performed by a small business firm or domestic nonprofit organization" from paragraph (g)(1). Also, if the funding agreement is a grant or cooperative agreement, paragraph (g)(3) may be deleted. When either paragraph (g)(2) or paragraphs (g) ment, paragraph (g)(3) may be deleted. When either paragraph (g)(2) or paragraphs (g) (2) and (3) are deleted, the remaining paragraph or paragraphs should be renumbered appropriately.

(b) Agencies should complete paragraph (l), "Communications", at the end of the clauses at § 401.14 by designating a central point of contact for communications on matters relating to the clause. Additional instructions on communications may also be included in paragraph (l).

(c) Agencies may replace the italicized words and phrases in the clauses at § 401.14 with those appropriate to the particular funding agreement. For example, "contracts" could be replaced by "grant," "contractor" by "grantee," and "contracting officer" by "grants officer." Depending on its use, "Federal agency" can be replaced either by the identification of the agency or by the specification of the particular office or official within the agency.

(d) When the agency head or duly authorized designee determines at the time of contracting with a small business firm or nonprofit organization that it would be in the national interest to acquire the right to sublicense foreign governments or international organizations pursuant to any existing treaty or international agreement, a sentence may be added at the end of paragraph (b) of the clause at § 401.14 as follows:

> This license will include the right of the government to sublicense foreign governments, their nationals, and international organizations, pursuant to the following treaties or international agreements.

The blank above should be completed with the names of applicable existing treaties or international agreements, agreements of cooperation, memoranda of understanding, or similar arrangements, including military agreements relating to weapons development and production. The above language is not intended to apply to treaties or other agreements that are in effect on the date of the award but which are not listed. Alternatively, agencies may use substantially similar language relating the government's rights to specific treaties or other agreements identified elsewhere in the funding agreement. The language may also be modified to make clear that the rights granted to the foreign government, and its nationals or an international organization may be for additional rights beyond a license or sublicense if so required by the applicable treaty or international agreement. For example, in some exclusive licenses or even the assignment of title in the foreign country involved might be required. Agencies may also modify the language above to provide for the direct licensing by the contractor of the foreign government or international organization.

(e) If the funding agreement involves performance over an extended period of time, such as the typical funding agreement for the operation of a government-owned facility, the following language may also be added:

> The agency reserves the right to unilaterally amend this funding agreement to identify specific treaties or international agreements entered into or to be entered into by the government after the effective date of this funding agreement and effectuate those license or other rights which are necessary for the government to meet its obligations to

foreign governments, their nationals and international organizations under such treaties or international agreements with respect to subject inventions made after the date of the amendment.

(f) Agencies may add additional subparagraphs to paragraph (f) of the clauses at § 401.14 to require the contractor to do one or more of the following:

(1) Provide a report prior to the close-out of a funding agreement listing all subject inventions or stating that there were none.

(2) Provide, upon request, the filing date, patent application number and title; a copy of the patent application; and patent number and issue date for any subject invention in any country in which the contractor has applied for a patent.

(3) Provide periodic (but no more frequently than annual) listings of all subject inventions which were disclosed to the agency during the period covered by the report.

(g) If the contract is with a nonprofit organization and is for the operation of a government-owned, contractor-operated facility, the following will be substituted for paragraph (k)(3) of the clause at § 401.14(a):

(3) After payment of patenting costs, licensing costs, payments to inventors, and other expenses incidental to the administration of subject inventions, the balance of any royalties or income earned and retained by the contractor during any fiscal year on subject inventions under this or any successor contract containing the same requirement, up to any amount equal to five percent of the budget of the facility for that fiscal year, shall be used by the contractor for scientific research, development, and education consistent with the research and development mission and objectives of the facility, including activities that increase the licensing potential of other inventions of the facility. If the balance exceeds five percent, 75 percent of the excess above five percent shall be paid by the contractor to the Treasury of the United States and the remaining 25 percent shall be used by the contractor only for the same purposes as described above. To the extent it provides the most effective technology transfer, the licensing of subject inventions shall be administered by contractor employees on location at the facility.

(h) If the contract is for the operation of a government-owned facility, agencies may add the following at the end of paragraph (f) of the clause at § 401.14(a):

(5) The contractor shall establish and maintain active and effective procedures to ensure that subject inventions are promptly identified and timely disclosed and shall submit a description of the procedures to the contracting officer so that the contracting officer may evaluate and determine their effectiveness.

37 C.F.R. § 401.6 Exercise of march-in rights.

(a) The following procedures shall govern the exercise of the march-in rights of the agencies set forth in 35 U.S.C. 203 and paragraph (j) of the clause at § 401.14.

(b) Whenever an agency receives information that it believes might warrant the exercise of march-in rights, before initiating any march-in proceeding, it shall notify the contractor in writing of the information and request informal written or oral comments from the contractor as well as information relevant to the matter. In the absence of any comments from the contractor within 30 days, the agency may, at its discretion, proceed with the procedures below. If a comment is received within 30 days, or later if the agency has not initiated the procedures below, then the agency shall, within 60 days after it receives the comment, either initiate the procedures below or notify the contractor, in writing, that it will not pursue march-in rights on the basis of the available information.

(c) A march-in proceeding shall be initiated by the issuance of a written notice by the agency to the contractor and its assignee or exclusive licensee, as applicable and if known to the agency, stating that the agency is considering the exercise of march-in rights. The notice shall state the reasons for the proposed march-in in terms sufficient to put the contractor on notice of the facts upon which the action would be based and shall specify the field or fields of use in which the agency is considering requiring licensing. The notice shall advise the contractor (assignee or exclusive licensee) of its rights, as set forth in this section and in any supplemental agency regulations. The determination to exercise march-in rights shall be made by the head of the agency or his or her designee.

(d) Within 30 days after the receipt of the written notice of march-in, the contractor (assignee or exclusive licensee) may submit in person, in writing, or through a representative, information or argument in opposition to the proposed march-in, including any additional specific information which raises a genuine dispute over the material facts upon which the march-in is based. If the information presented raises a genuine dispute over the material facts, the head of the agency or designee shall undertake or refer the matter to another official for fact-finding.

(e) Fact-finding shall be conducted in accordance with the procedures established by the agency. Such procedures shall be as informal as practicable and be consistent with principles of fundamental fairness. The procedures should afford the contractor the opportunity to appear with counsel, submit documentary evidence, present witnesses and confront such persons as the agency may present. A transcribed record shall be made and shall be available at cost to the contractor upon request. The requirement for a transcribed record may be waived by mutual agreement of the contractor and the agency. Any portion of the march-in proceeding, including a fact-finding hearing that involves testimony or evidence relating to the utilization or efforts at obtaining utilization that are being made by the contractor, its assignee, or licensees shall be closed to the public, including potential licensees. In accordance with 35 U.S.C. 202(c)(5), agencies shall not disclose any such information obtained during a march-in proceeding to persons outside the government except when such release is authorized by the contractor (assignee or licensee).

(f) The official conducting the fact-finding shall prepare or adopt written findings of fact and transmit them to the head of the agency or designee promptly after the conclusion of the fact-finding proceeding along with a recommended determination. A copy of the findings of fact shall be sent to the contractor (assignee or exclusive licensee) by registered or certified mail. The contractor (assignee or exclusive licensee) and agency representatives will be given

30 days to submit written arguments to the head of the agency or designee; and, upon request by the contractor oral arguments will be held before the agency head or designee that will make the final determination.

(g) In cases in which fact-finding has been conducted, the head of the agency or designee shall base his or her determination on the facts found, together with any other information and written or oral arguments submitted by the contractor (assignee or exclusive licensee) and agency representatives, and any other information in the administrative record. The consistency of the exercise of march-in rights with the policy and objectives of 35 U.S.C. 200 shall also be considered. In cases referred for fact-finding, the head of the agency or designee may reject only those facts that have been found to be clearly erroneous, but must explicitly state the rejection and indicate the basis for the contrary finding. Written notice of the determination whether march-in rights will be exercised shall be made by the head of the agency or designee and sent to the contractor (assignee of exclusive licensee) by certified or registered mail within 90 days after the completion of fact-finding or 90 days after oral arguments, whichever is later, or the proceedings will be deemed to have been terminated and thereafter no march-in based on the facts and reasons upon which the proceeding was initiated may be exercised.

(h) An agency may, at any time, terminate a march-in proceeding if it is satisfied that it does not wish to exercise march-in rights.

(i) The procedures of this part shall also apply to the exercise of march-in rights against inventors receiving title to subject inventions under 35 U.S.C. 202(d) and, for that purpose, the term "contractor" as used in this section shall be deemed to include the inventor.

(j) An agency determination unfavorable to the contractor (assignee or exclusive licensee) shall be held in abeyance pending the exhaustion of appeals or petitions filed under 35 U.S.C. 203(2).

(k) For purposes of this section the term exclusive licensee includes a partially exclusive licensee.

(l) Agencies are authorized to issue supplemental procedures not inconsistent with this part for the conduct of march-in proceedings.

37 C.F.R. § 401.7 Small business preference.

(a) Paragraph (k)(4) of the clauses at § 401.14 Implements the small business preference requirement of 35 U.S.C. 202(c)(7)(D). Contractors are expected to use efforts that are reasonable under the circumstances to attract small business licensees. They are also expected to give small business firms that meet the standard outlined in the clause a preference over other applicants for licenses. What constitutes reasonable efforts to attract small business licensees will vary with the circumstances and the nature, duration, and expense of efforts needed to bring the invention to the market. Paragraph (k)(4) is not intended, for example, to prevent nonprofit organizations from providing larger firms with a right of first refusal or other options in inventions that relate to research being supported under long-term or other arrangements with larger companies. Under such circumstances it would not be reasonable to seek and to give a preference to small business licensees.

(b) Small business firms that believe a nonprofit organization is not meeting its obligations under the clause may report their concerns to the Secretary. To the extent deemed appropriate, the Secretary will undertake informal investigation of the concern, and, if appropriate, enter into discussions or negotiations with the nonprofit organization to the end of improving its efforts in meeting its obligations under the clause. However, in no event will the Secretary intervene in ongoing negotiations or contractor decisions concerning the licensing of a specific subject invention. All the above investigations, discussions, and negotiations of the Secretary will be in coordination with other interested agencies, including the Small Business Administration; and in the case of a contract for the operation of a government-owned, contractor operated research or production facility, the Secretary will coordinate with the agency responsible for the facility prior to any discussions or negotiations with the contractor.

37 C.F.R. § 401.8 Reporting on utilization of subject inventions.

(a) Paragraph (h) of the clauses at § 401.14 and its counterpart in the clause at Attachment A to OMB Circular A-124 provides that agencies have the right to receive periodic reports from the contractor on utilization of inventions. Agencies exercising this right should accept such information, to the extent feasible, in the format that the contractor normally prepares it for its own internal purposes. The prescription of forms should be avoided. However, any forms or standard questionnaires that are adopted by an agency for this purpose must comply with the requirements of the Paperwork Reduction Act. Copies shall be sent to the Secretary.

(b) In accordance with 35 U.S.C. 202(c) (5) and the terms of the clauses at § 401.14, agencies shall not disclose such information to persons outside the government. Contractors will continue to provide confidential markings to help prevent inadvertent release outside the agency.

37 C.F.R. § 401.9 Retention of rights by contractor employee inventor.

Agencies which allow an employee/inventor of the contractor to retain rights to a subject invention made under a funding agreement with a small business firm or nonprofit organization contractor, as authorized by 35 U.S.C. 202(d), will impose upon the inventor at least those conditions that would apply to a small business firm contractor under paragraphs (d)(1) and (3); (f)(4); (h); (i); and (j) of the clause at § 401.14(a).

37 C.F.R. § 401.10 Government assignment to contractor of rights in invention of government Employee.

In any case when a Federal employee is a co-inventor of any invention made under a funding agreement with a small business firm or nonprofit organization and the Federal agency employing such co-inventor transfers or reassigns the right it has acquired in the subject invention from its employee to the contractor as authorized by 35 U.S.C. 202(e), the assignment will be made subject to the same conditions as apply to the contractor under the patent rights clause of its funding agreement. Agencies may add additional conditions as long as they are consistent with 35 U.S.C. 201-206.

37 C.F.R. § 401.11 Appeals.

(a) As used in this section, the term standard clause means the clause at § 401.14 of this part and the clauses previously prescribed by either OMB Circular A-124 or OMB Bulletin 81-22.

(b) The agency official initially authorized to take any of the following actions shall provide the contractor with a written statement of the basis for his or her action at the time the action is taken, including any relevant facts that were relied upon in taking the action.

(1) A refusal to grant an extension under paragraph (c)(4) of the standard clauses.

(2) A request for a conveyance of title under paragraph (d) of the standard clauses.

(3) A refusal to grant a waiver under paragraph (i) of the standard clauses.

(4) A refusal to approve an assignment under paragraph (k)(1) of the standard clauses.

(5) A refusal to grant an extension of the exclusive license period under paragraph (k)(2) of the clauses prescribed by either OMB Circular A-124 or OMB Bulletin 81-22.

(c) Each agency shall establish and publish procedures under which any of the agency actions listed in paragraph (b) of this section may be appealed to the head of the agency or designee. Review at this level shall consider both the factual and legal basis for the actions and its consistency with the policy and objectives of 35 U.S.C. 200-206.

(d) Appeals procedures established under paragraph (c) of this section shall include administrative due process procedures and standards for fact-finding at least comparable to those set forth in § 401.6 (e) through (g) whenever there is a dispute as to the factual basis for an agency request for a conveyance of title under paragraph (d) of the standard clause, including any dispute as to whether or not an invention is a subject invention.

(e) To the extent that any of the actions described in paragraph (b) of this section are subject to appeal under the Contract Dispute Act, the procedures under the Act will satisfy the requirements of paragraphs (c) and (d) of this section.

37 C.F.R. § 401.12 Licensing of background patent rights to third parties.

(a) A funding agreement with a small business firm or a domestic nonprofit organization will not contain a provision allowing a Federal agency to require the licensing to third parties of inventions owned by the contractor that are not subject inventions unless such provision has been approved by the agency head and a written justification has been signed by the agency head. Any such provision will clearly state whether the licensing may be required in connection with the practice of a subject invention, a specifically identified work object, or both. The agency head may not delegate the authority to approve such provisions or to sign the justification required for such provisions.

(b) A Federal agency will not require the licensing of third parties under any such provision unless the agency head determines that the use of the invention by others is necessary for the practice of a subject invention or for the use of a work object of the funding agreement and that such action is necessary to achieve practical application of the subject invention or work object. Any such determination will be on the record after an opportunity for an agency hearing. The contractor shall be given prompt notification of the determination by certified or registered mail. Any action commenced for judicial review of such determination shall be brought within sixty days after notification of such determination.

37 C.F.R. § 401.13 Administration of patent rights clauses.

(a) In the event a subject invention is made under funding agreements of more than one agency, at the request of the contractor or on their own initiative the agencies shall designate one agency as responsible for administration of the rights of the government in the invention.

(b) Agencies shall promptly grant, unless there is a significant reason not to, a request by a nonprofit organization under paragraph (k)(2) of the clauses prescribed by either OMB Circular A-124 or OMB Bulletin 81-22 inasmuch as 35 U.S.C. 202(c)(7) has since been amended to eliminate the limitation on the duration of exclusive licenses. Similarly, unless there is a significant reason not to, agencies shall promptly approve an assignment by a nonprofit organization to an organization which has as one of its primary functions the management of inventions when a request for approval has been necessitated under paragraph (k)(1) of the clauses prescribed by either OMB Circular A-124 or OMB Bulletin 81-22 because the patent management organization is engaged in or holds a substantial interest in other organizations engaged in the manufacture or sale of products or the use of processes that might utilize the invention or be in competition with embodiments of the invention. As amended, 35 U.S.C. 202(c)(7) no longer contains this limitation. The policy of this subsection should also be followed in connection with similar approvals that may be required under Institutional Patent Agreements, other patent rights clauses, or waivers that predate Chapter 18 of Title 35, United States Code.

(c) The President's Patent Policy Memorandum of February 18, 1983, states that agencies should protect the confidentiality of invention disclosure, patent applications, and utilization reports required in performance or in consequence of awards to the extent permitted by 35 U.S.C. 205 or other applicable laws. The following requirements should be followed for funding agreements covered by and predating this part 401.

(1) To the extent authorized by 35 U.S.C. 205, agencies shall not disclose to third parties pursuant to requests under the Freedom of Information Act (FOIA) any information disclosing a subject invention for a reasonable time in order for a patent application to be filed. With respect to subject inventions of contractors that are small business firms or nonprofit organizations, a reasonable time shall be the time during which an initial patent

application may be filed under paragraph (c) of the standard clause found at § 401.14(a) or such other clause may be used in the funding agreement. However, an agency may disclose such subject inventions under the FOIA, at its discretion, after a contractor has elected not to retain title or after the time in which the contractor is required to make an election if the contractor has not made an election within that time. Similarly, an agency may honor a FOIA request at its discretion if it finds that the same information has previously been published by the inventor, contractor, or otherwise. If the agency plans to file itself when the contractor has not elected title, it may, of course, continue to avail itself of the authority of 35 U.S.C. 205.

(2) In accordance with 35 U.S.C. 205, agencies shall not disclose or release for a period of 18 months from the filing date of the patent application to third parties pursuant to requests under the Freedom of Information Act, or otherwise, copies of any document which the agency obtained under this clause which is part of an application for patent with the U.S. Patent and Trademark Office or any foreign patent office filed by the contractor (or its assignees, licensees, or employees) on a subject invention to which the contractor has elected to retain title. This prohibition does not extend to disclosure to other government agencies or contractors of government agencies under an obligation to maintain such information in confidence.

(3) A number of agencies have policies to encourage public dissemination of the results of work supported by the agency through publication in government or other publications of technical reports of contractors or others. In recognition of the fact that such publication, if it included descriptions of a subject invention could create bars to obtaining patent protection, it is the policy of the executive branch that agencies will not include in such publication programs copies of disclosures of inventions submitted by small business firms or nonprofit organizations, pursuant to paragraph (c) of the standard clause found at § 401.14(a), except that under the same circumstances under which agencies are authorized to release such information pursuant to FOIA requests under paragraph (c)(1) of this section, agencies may publish such disclosures.

(4) Nothing in this paragraph is intended to preclude agencies from including in the publication activities described in the first sentence of paragraph (c)(3), the publication of materials describing a subject invention to the extent such materials were provided as part of a technical report or other submission of the contractor which were submitted independently of the requirements of the patent rights provisions of the contract. However, if a small business firm or nonprofit organization notifies the agency that a particular report or other submission contains a disclosure of a subject invention to which it has elected title or may elect title, the agency shall use reasonable efforts to restrict its publication of the material for six months from date of its receipt of the report or submission or, if earlier, until the contractor has filed an initial patent application. Agencies, of course, retain the discretion to delay publication for additional periods of time.

(5) Nothing in this paragraph is intended to limit the authority of agencies provided in 35 U.S.C. 205 in circumstances not specifically described in this paragraph.

37 C.F.R. § 401.14 Standard patent rights clauses.

(a) The following is the standard patent rights clause to be used as specified in § 401.3(a).

Patent Rights (Small Business Firms and Nonprofit Organizations)

(a) Definitions

(1) Invention means any invention or discovery which is or may be patentable or otherwise protectable under Title 35 of the United States Code, or any novel variety of plant which is or may be protected under the Plant Variety Protection Act (7 U.S.C. 2321 et seq.).

(2) Subject invention means any invention of the contractor conceived or first actually reduced to practice in the performance of work under this contract, provided that in the case of a variety of plant, the date of determination (as defined in section 41(d) of the Plant Variety Protection Act, 7 U.S.C. 2401(d)) must also occur during the period of contract performance.

(3) Practical Application means to manufacture in the case of a composition or product, to practice in the case of a process or method, or to operate in the case of a machine or system; and, in each case, under such conditions as to establish that the invention is being utilized and that its benefits are, to the extent permitted by law or government regulations, available to the public on reasonable terms.

(4) Made when used in relation to any invention means the conception or first actual reduction to practice of such invention.

(5) Small Business Firm means a small business concern as defined at section 2 of Pub. L. 85-536 (15 U.S.C. 632) and implementing regulations of the Administrator of the Small Business Administration. For the purpose of this clause, the size standards for small business concerns involved in government procurement and subcontracting at 13 CFR 121.3-8 and 13 CFR 121.3-12, respectively, will be used.

(6) Nonprofit Organization means a university or other institution of higher education or an organization of the type described in section 501(c)(3) of the Internal Revenue Code of 1954 (26 U.S.C. 501(c) and exempt from taxation under section 501(a) of the Internal Revenue Code (25 U.S.C. 501(a)) or any nonprofit scientific or educational organization qualified under a state nonprofit organization statute.

(b) Allocation of Principal Rights

The Contractor may retain the entire right, title, and interest throughout the world to each subject invention subject to the provisions of this clause and 35 U.S.C. 203. With respect to any subject invention in which the Contractor retains title, the Federal government shall have a nonexclusive, nontransferable, irrevocable, paid-up license to practice or have practiced for or on behalf of the United States the subject invention throughout the world.

(c) Invention Disclosure, Election of Title and Filing of Patent Application by Contractor

(1) The contractor will disclose each subject invention to the Federal Agency within two months after the inventor discloses it in writing to contractor personnel responsible for patent matters. The disclosure to the agency shall be in the form of a written report and shall identify the contract under which the invention was made and the inventor(s). It shall be sufficiently complete in technical detail to convey a clear understanding to the extent known at the time of the disclosure, of the nature, purpose, operation, and the physical, chemical, biological or electrical characteristics of the invention. The disclosure shall also identify any publication, on sale or public use of the invention and whether a manuscript describing the invention has been submitted for publication and, if so, whether it has been accepted for publication at the time of disclosure. In addition, after disclosure to the agency, the Contractor will promptly notify the agency of the acceptance of any manuscript describing the invention for publication or of any on sale or public use planned by the contractor.

(2) The Contractor will elect in writing whether or not to retain title to any such invention by notifying the Federal agency within two years of disclosure to the Federal agency. However, in any case where publication, on sale or public use has initiated the one year statutory period wherein valid patent protection can still be obtained in the United States, the period for election of title may be shortened by the agency to a date that is no more than 60 days prior to the end of the statutory period.

(3) The contractor will file its initial patent application on a subject invention to which it elects to retain title within one year after election of title or, if earlier, prior to the end of any statutory period wherein valid patent protection can be obtained in the United States after a publication, on sale, or public use. The contractor will file patent applications in additional countries or international patent offices within either ten months of the corresponding initial patent application or six months from the date permission is granted by the Commissioner of Patents and Trademarks to file foreign patent applications where such filing has been prohibited by a Secrecy Order.

(4) Requests for extension of the time for disclosure, election, and filing under subparagraphs (1), (2), and (3) may, at the discretion of the agency, be granted.

(d) Conditions When the Government May Obtain Title

The contractor will convey to the Federal agency, upon written request, title to any subject invention—

(1) If the contractor fails to disclose or elect title to the subject invention within the times specified in (c), above, or elects not to retain title; provided that the agency may only request title within 60 days after learning of the failure of the contractor to disclose or elect within the specified times.

(2) In those countries in which the contractor fails to file patent applications within the times specified in (c) above; provided, however, that if the contractor has filed a patent application in a country after the times specified in (c) above, but prior to its receipt of

the written request of the Federal agency, the contractor shall continue to retain title in that country.

(3) In any country in which the contractor decides not to continue the prosecution of any application for, to pay the maintenance fees on, or defend in reexamination or opposition proceeding on, a patent on a subject invention.

(e) Minimum Rights to Contractor and Protection of the Contractor Right to File

(1) The contractor will retain a nonexclusive royalty-free license throughout the world in each subject invention to which the Government obtains title, except if the contractor fails to disclose the invention within the times specified in (c), above. The contractor's license extends to its domestic subsidiary and affiliates, if any, within the corporate structure of which the contractor is a party and includes the right to grant sublicenses of the same scope to the extent the contractor was legally obligated to do so at the time the contract was awarded. The license is transferable only with the approval of the Federal agency except when transferred to the successor of that party of the contractor's business to which the invention pertains.

(2) The contractor's domestic license may be revoked or modified by the funding Federal agency to the extent necessary to achieve expeditious practical application of the subject invention pursuant to an application for an exclusive license submitted in accordance with applicable provisions at 37 CFR part 404 and agency licensing regulations (if any). This license will not be revoked in that field of use or the geographical areas in which the contractor has achieved practical application and continues to make the benefits of the invention reasonably accessible to the public. The license in any foreign country may be revoked or modified at the discretion of the funding Federal agency to the extent the contractor, its licensees, or the domestic subsidiaries or affiliates have failed to achieve practical application in that foreign country.

(3) Before revocation or modification of the license, the funding Federal agency will furnish the contractor a written notice of its intention to revoke or modify the license, and the contractor will be allowed thirty days (or such other time as may be authorized by the funding Federal agency for good cause shown by the contractor) after the notice to show cause why the license should not be revoked or modified. The contractor has the right to appeal, in accordance with applicable regulations in 37 CFR part 404 and agency regulations (if any) concerning the licensing of Government-owned inventions, any decision concerning the revocation or modification of the license.

(f) Contractor Action to Protect the Government's Interest

(1) The contractor agrees to execute or to have executed and promptly deliver to the Federal agency all instruments necessary to (i) establish or confirm the rights the Government has throughout the world in those subject inventions to which the contractor elects to retain title, and (ii) convey title to the Federal agency when requested under paragraph (d) above and to enable the government to obtain patent protection throughout the world in that subject invention.

(2) The contractor agrees to require, by written agreement, its employees, other than clerical and nontechnical employees, to disclose promptly in writing to personnel identified as responsible for the administration of patent matters and in a format suggested by the contractor each subject invention made under contract in order that the contractor can comply with the disclosure provisions of paragraph (c), above, and to execute all papers necessary to file patent applications on subject inventions and to establish the government's rights in the subject inventions. This disclosure format should require, as a minimum, the information required by (c)(1), above. The contractor shall instruct such employees through employee agreements or other suitable educational programs on the importance of reporting inventions in sufficient time to permit the filing of patent applications prior to U.S. or foreign statutory bars.

(3) The contractor will notify the Federal agency of any decisions not to continue the prosecution of a patent application, pay maintenance fees, or defend in a reexamination or opposition proceeding on a patent, in any country, not less than thirty days before the expiration of the response period required by the relevant patent office.

(4) The contractor agrees to include, within the specification of any United States patent applications and any patent issuing thereon covering a subject invention, the following statement, "This invention was made with government support under (identify the contract) awarded by (identify the Federal agency). The government has certain rights in the invention."

(g) Subcontracts

(1) The contractor will include this clause, suitably modified to identify the parties, in all subcontracts, regardless of tier, for experimental, developmental or research work to be performed by a small business firm or domestic nonprofit organization. The subcontractor will retain all rights provided for the contractor in this clause, and the contractor will not, as part of the consideration for awarding the subcontract, obtain rights in the subcontractor's subject inventions.

(2) The contractor will include in all other subcontracts, regardless of tier, for experimental developmental or research work the patent rights clause required by (cite section of agency implementing regulations or FAR).

(3) In the case of subcontracts, at any tier, when the prime award with the Federal agency was a contract (but not a grant or cooperative agreement), the agency, subcontractor, and the contractor agree that the mutual obligations of the parties created by this clause constitute a contract between the subcontractor and the Federal agency with respect to the matters covered by the clause; provided, however, that nothing in this paragraph is intended to confer any jurisdiction under the Contract Disputes Act in connection with proceedings under paragraph (j) of this clause.

(h) Reporting on Utilization of Subject Inventions

The Contractor agrees to submit on request periodic reports no more frequently than annually on the utilization of a subject invention or on efforts at obtaining such utilization that are being made by the contractor or its licensees or assignees. Such reports shall include information regarding the status of development, date of first commercial sale or use, gross royalties received by the contractor, and such other data and information as the agency may reasonably specify. The contractor also agrees to provide additional reports as may be requested by the agency in connection with any march-in proceeding undertaken by the agency in accordance with paragraph (j) of this clause. As required by 35 U.S.C. 202(c)(5), the agency agrees it will not disclose such information to persons outside the government without permission of the contractor.

(i) Preference for United States Industry

Notwithstanding any other provision of this clause, the contractor agrees that neither it nor any assignee will grant to any person the exclusive right to use or sell any subject inventions in the United States unless such person agrees that any products embodying the subject invention or produced through the use of the subject invention will be manufactured substantially in the United States. However, in individual cases, the requirement for such an agreement may be waived by the Federal agency upon a showing by the contractor or its assignee that reasonable but unsuccessful efforts have been made to grant licenses on similar terms to potential licensees that would be likely to manufacture substantially in the United States or that under the circumstances domestic manufacture is not commercially feasible.

(j) March-in Rights

The contractor agrees that with respect to any subject invention in which it has acquired title, the Federal agency has the right in accordance with the procedures in 37 CFR 401.6 and any supplemental regulations of the agency to require the contractor, an assignee or exclusive licensee of a subject invention to grant a nonexclusive, partially exclusive, or exclusive license in any field of use to a responsible applicant or applicants, upon terms that are reasonable under the circumstances, and if the contractor, assignee, or exclusive licensee refuses such a request the Federal agency has the right to grant such a license itself if the Federal agency determines that:

(1) Such action is necessary because the contractor or assignee has not taken, or is not expected to take within a reasonable time, effective steps to achieve practical application of the subject invention in such field of use.

(2) Such action is necessary to alleviate health or safety needs which are not reasonably satisfied by the contractor, assignee or their licensees;

(3) Such action is necessary to meet requirements for public use specified by Federal regulations and such requirements are not reasonably satisfied by the contractor, assignee or licensees; or

(4) Such action is necessary because the agreement required by paragraph (i) of this clause has not been obtained or waived or because a licensee of the exclusive right to use or sell any subject invention in the United States is in breach of such agreement.

(k) Special Provisions for Contracts with Nonprofit Organizations

If the contractor is a nonprofit organization, it agrees that:

(1) Rights to a subject invention in the United States may not be assigned without the approval of the Federal agency, except where such assignment is made to an organization which has as one of its primary functions the management of inventions, provided that such assignee will be subject to the same provisions as the contractor;

(2) The contractor will share royalties collected on a subject invention with the inventor, including Federal employee co-inventors (when the agency deems it appropriate) when the subject invention is assigned in accordance with 35 U.S.C. 202(e) and 37 CFR 401.10;

(3) The balance of any royalties or income earned by the contractor with respect to subject inventions, after payment of expenses (including payments to inventors) incidential incidental to the administration of subject inventions, will be utilized for the support of scientific research or education; and

(4) It will make efforts that are reasonable under the circumstances to attract licensees of subject invention that are small business firms and that it will give a preference to a small business firm when licensing a subject invention if the contractor determines that the small business firm has a plan or proposal for marketing the invention which, if executed, is equally as likely to bring the invention to practical application as any plans or proposals from applicants that are not small business firms; provided, that the contractor is also satisfied that the small business firm has the capability and resources to carry out its plan or proposal. The decision whether to give a preference in any specific case will be at the discretion of the contractor. However, the contractor agrees that the Secretary may review the contractor's licensing program and decisions regarding small business applicants, and the contractor will negotiate changes to its licensing policies, procedures, or practices with the Secretary when the Secretary's review discloses that the contractor could take reasonable steps to implement more effectively the requirements of this paragraph (k)(4).

(l) Communication

(Complete According to Instructions at 401.5(b))

(b) When the Department of Energy (DOE) determines to use alternative provisions under § 401.3(a)(4), the standard clause at § 401.14(a), of this section, shall be used with the following modifications unless a substitute clause is drafted by DOE:

(1) The title of the clause shall be changed to read as follows: Patent Rights to Nonprofit DOE Facility Operators.

(2) Add an "(A)" after "(1)" in paragraph (c)(1) and add subparagraphs (B) and (C) to paragraph (c)(1) as follows:

(B) If the subject invention occurred under activities funded by the naval nuclear propulsion or weapons related programs of DOE, then the provisions of this subparagraph (c)(1)(B) will apply in lieu of paragraphs (c)(2) and (3). In such cases the contractor agrees to assign the government the entire right, title, and interest thereto throughout the world in and to the subject invention except to the extent that rights are retained by the contractor through a greater rights determination or under paragraph (e), below. The contractor, or an employee-inventor, with authorization of the contractor, may submit a request for greater rights at the time the invention is disclosed or within a reasonable time thereafter. DOE will process such a request in accordance with procedures at 37 CFR 401.15. Each determination of greater rights will be subject to paragraphs (h)-(k) of this clause and such additional conditions, if any, deemed to be appropriate by the Department of Energy.

(C) At the time an invention is disclosed in accordance with (c)(1)(A) above, or within 90 days thereafter, the contractor will submit a written statement as to whether or not the invention occurred under a naval nuclear propulsion or weapons-related program of the Department of Energy. If this statement is not filed within this time, subparagraph (c)(1)(B) will apply in lieu of paragraphs (c)(2) and (3). The contractor statement will be deemed conclusive unless, within 60 days thereafter, the Contracting Officer disagrees in writing, in which case the determination of the Contracting Officer will be deemed conclusive unless the contractor files a claim under the Contract Disputes Act within 60 days after the Contracting Officer's determination. Pending resolution of the matter, the invention will be subject to subparagraph (c)(1)(B).

(3) Paragraph (k)(3) of the clause will be modified as prescribed at § 401.5(g).

37 C.F.R. § 401.15 Deferred determinations.

(a) This section applies to requests for greater rights in subject inventions made by contractors when deferred determination provisions were included in the funding agreement because one of the exceptions at § 401.3(a) was applied, except that the Department of Energy is authorized to process deferred determinations either in accordance with its waiver regulations or this section. A contractor requesting greater rights should include with its request information on its plans and intentions to bring the invention to practical application. Within 90 days after receiving a request and supporting information, or sooner if a statutory bar to patenting is imminent, the agency should seek to make a determination. In any event, if a bar to patenting is imminent, unless the agency plans to file on its own, it shall authorize the contractor to file a patent application pending a determination by the agency. Such a filing shall normally be at the contractor's own risk and expense. However, if the agency subsequently refuses to allow the contractor to retain title and elects to proceed with the patent application under government ownership, it shall reimburse the contractor for the cost of preparing and filing the patent application.

(b) If the circumstances of concerns which originally led the agency to invoke an exception under § 401.3(a) are not applicable to the actual subject invention or are no longer valid because of subsequent events, the agency should allow the contractor to retain title to the invention on the same conditions as would have applied if the standard clause at § 401.14(a) had been used originally, unless it has been licensed.

(c) If paragraph (b) is not applicable the agency shall make its determination based on an assessment whether its own plans regarding the invention will better promote the policies and objectives of 35 U.S.C. 200 than will contractor ownership of the invention. Moreover, if the agency is concerned only about specific uses or applications of the invention, it shall consider leaving title in the contractor with additional conditions imposed upon the contractor's use of the invention for such applications or with expanded government license rights in such applications.

(d) A determination not to allow the contractor to retain title to a subject invention or to restrict or condition its title with conditions differing from those in the clause at § 401.14(a), unless made by the head of the agency, shall be appealable by the contractor to an agency official at a level above the person who made the determination. This appeal shall be subject to the procedures applicable to appeals under § 401.11 of this part.

37 C.F.R. § 401.16 Electronic filing.

Unless otherwise requested or directed by the agency,

(a) the written report required in (c)(1) of the standard clause in § 401.14(a) may be electronically filed;

(b) the written election required in (c)(2) of the standard clause in § 401.14(a) may be electronically filed; and

(c) the close-out report in (f)(1) and the information identified in (f)(2) and (f)(3) of § 401.5 may be electronically filed.

37 C.F.R. 37 C.F.R. § 401.17 Submissions and inquiries.

All submissions or inquiries should be directed to Director, Technology Competitiveness Staff, Office of Technology Policy, Technology Administration, telephone number 202-482-2100, Room H4418, U.S. Department of Commerce, Washington, D.C. 20230.

PATENTS

FAR SUBPART 27.1—27.3

FAR 52.227-1—FAR 52.227-13

FAR 27.101 Applicability.

The policies, procedures, and clauses prescribed by this Part 27 are applicable to all agencies. Agencies are authorized to adopt alternate policies, procedures, and clauses, but only to the extent determined necessary to meet the specific requirements of laws, executive orders, treaties, or international agreements. Any agency action adopting such alternate policies, procedures, and clauses shall be covered in published agency regulations.

FAR 27.102 [Reserved]

FAR 27.103 Policy.

The policies pertaining to patents, data, and copyrights are set forth in this Part 27 and the related clauses in Part 52.

FAR 27.104 General guidance.

(a) The Government encourages the maximum practical commercial use of inventions made while performing Government contracts.

(b) Generally, the Government will not refuse to award a contract on the grounds that the prospective contractor may infringe a patent.

(c) Generally, the Government encourages the use of inventions in performing contracts and, by appropriate contract clauses, authorizes and consents to such use, even though the inventions may be covered by U.S. patents and indemnification against infringement may be appropriate.

(d) Generally, the Government should be indemnified against the infringement of U.S. patents resulting from performing contracts when the supplies or services acquired under the contracts normally are or have been sold or offered for sale by any supplier to the public in the commercial open market or are the same as such supplies or services with relatively minor modifications.

(e) The Government acquires supplies or services on a competitive basis in accordance with Part 6, but it is important that the efforts directed toward full and open competition not improperly demand or use data relating to private developments.

(f) The Government honors the rights in data resulting from private developments and limits its demands for such rights to those essential for Government purposes.

(g) The Government honors rights in patents, data, and copyrights, and complies with the stipulations of law in using or acquiring such rights.

(h) Generally, the Government requires that contractors obtain permission from copyright owners before including privately owned copyrighted works in data required to be delivered under Government contracts.

FAR 27.200 Scope of subpart.

This subpart prescribes policy with respect to—

(a) Patent infringement liability resulting from work performed by or for the Government;

(b) Royalties payable in connection with performing Government contracts; and

(c) Security requirements covering patent applications containing classified subject matter filed by contractors.

FAR 27.201 Authorization and consent.

FAR 27.201-1 General.

(a) In those cases where the Government has authorized or consented to the manufacture or use of an invention described in and covered by a patent of the United States, any suit for infringement of the patent based on the manufacture or use of the invention by or for the United States by a contractor (including a subcontractor at any tier) can be maintained only against the Government in the U.S. Claims Court and not against the contractor or subcontractor (28 U.S.C. 1498). To ensure that work by a contractor or subcontractor under a Government contract may not be enjoined by reason of patent infringement, the Government shall give authorization and consent in accordance with this regulation. The liability of the Government for damages in any such suit against it may, however, ultimately be borne by the contractor or subcontractor in accordance with the terms of any patent indemnity clause also included in the contract, and an authorization and consent clause does not detract from any patent indemnification commitment by the contractor or subcontractor. Therefore, both a patent indemnity clause and an authorization and consent clause may be included in the same contract.

(b) The contracting officer shall not include in any solicitation or contract—

(1) Any clause whereby the Government expressly agrees to indemnify the contractor against liability for patent infringement; or

(2) Any authorization and consent clause when both complete performance and delivery are outside the United States, its possessions, and Puerto Rico.

FAR 27.201-2 Clauses on authorization and consent.

(a) The contracting officer shall insert the clause at 52.227-1, Authorization and Consent, in solicitations and contracts (including those for construction; architect-engineer services; dismantling, demolition, or removal of improvements; and noncommon carrier communication services), except when using simplified acquisition procedures or both complete performance and delivery are outside the United States, its possessions, and Puerto Rico. Although the clause is not required when simplified acquisition procedures are used, it may be used with them.

(b) The contracting officer shall insert the clause with its Alternate I in all R&D solicitations and contracts (including those for construction and architect-engineer services calling exclusively for R&D work or exclusively for experimental work), unless both complete performance and delivery are outside the United States, its possessions, and Puerto Rico. When a proposed contract involves both R&D work and supplies or services, and the R&D work is the primary purpose of the contract, the contracting officer shall use this alternate. In all other proposed contracts involving both R&D work and supplies or services, the contracting officer shall use the basic clause. Also, when a proposed contract involves either R&D or supplies and materials, in addition to construction or architect-engineer work, the contracting officer shall use the basic clause.

(c) If the solicitation or contract is for communication services with a common carrier and the services are unregulated and not priced by a tariff schedule set by a regulatory body, the contracting officer shall use the clause with its Alternate II.

FAR 27.202 Notice and assistance.

FAR 27.202-1 General.

The contractor is required to notify the contracting officer of all claims of infringement that come to the contractor's attention in connection with performing a Government contract. The contractor is also required, when requested, to assist the Government with any evidence and information in its possession in connection with any suit against the Government, or any claims against the Government made before suit has been instituted, on account of any alleged patent or copyright infringement arising out of or resulting from the contract performance.

FAR 27.202-2 Clause on notice and assistance.

The contracting officer shall insert the clause at 52.227-2, Notice and Assistance Regarding Patent and Copyright Infringement, in supply, service, or research and development solicitations and contracts (including construction and architect-engineer contracts) which anticipate a contract value above the simplified acquisition threshold, except when complete performance and delivery are outside the United States, its possessions, and Puerto Rico, unless the contracts indicate that the supplies or other deliverables are ultimately to be shipped into one of those areas.

FAR 27.203 Patent indemnification of Government by contractor.

FAR 27.203-1 General.

(a) To the extent set forth in this section, the Government requires reimbursement for liability for patent infringement arising out of or resulting from performing construction contracts or contracts for supplies or services that normally are or have been sold or offered for sale by any supplier to the public in the commercial open market or that are the same as such supplies or services with relatively minor modifications. Appropriate clauses for indemnification of the Government are prescribed in the following subsections.

(b) A patent indemnity clause shall not be used in the following situations:

(1) When the clause at 52.227-1, Authorization and Consent, with its Alternate I, is included in the contract, except that in contracts calling also for supplies of the kind described in paragraph (a) above, a patent indemnity clause may be used solely with respect to such supplies.

(2) When the contract is for supplies or services (or such items with relatively minor modifications) that clearly are not or have not been sold or offered for sale by any supplier to the public in the commercial open market. However, a patent indemnity clause may be included in—

(i) sealed bid contracts to obtain an indemnity regarding specific components, spare parts, or services so sold or offered for sale (see 27.203-2(b) below), and—

(ii) contracts to be awarded (either by sealed bidding or negotiation) if a patent owner contends that the acquisition would result in patent infringement and the prospective contractor, after responding to a solicitation that did not contain an indemnity clause, is willing to indemnify the Government against such infringement either—

(A) Without increase in price on the basis that the patent is invalid or not infringed, or

(B) For other good reasons.

(3) When both performance and delivery are to be outside the United States, its possessions, and Puerto Rico, unless the contract indicates that the supplies or other deliverables are ultimately to be shipped into one of those areas.

(4) When the contract is awarded using simplified acquisition procedures.

(5) When the contract is solely for architect-engineer work (see Part 36).

FAR 27.203-2 Clauses for sealed bid contracts (excluding construction).

(a) Except when prohibited by 27.203-1(b) above, the contracting officer shall insert the clause at 52.227-3, Patent Indemnity, in sealed bid contracts for supplies or services (excluding construction and dismantling, demolition, and removal of improvements), if the contracting officer determines that the supplies or services (or such items with relatively minor modifications) normally are or have been sold or offered for sale by any supplier to the public in the commercial open market. Also, the clause may be included as authorized in 27.203-1(b)(2)(i).

(b) In solicitations and contracts (excluding those for construction) that call in part for specific components, spare parts, or services (or such items with relatively minor modifications) that normally are or have been sold or offered for sale by any supplier to the public in the commercial open market, the contracting officer may use the clause with its Alternate I or II, as appropriate. The choice between Alternate I (identification of excluded items) and Alternate II (identification of included items) should be based upon simplicity, Government administrative convenience and ease of identification of the items.

(c) In solicitations and contracts for communication services and facilities where performance is by a common carrier, and the services are unregulated and are not priced by a tariff schedule set by a regulatory body, use the basic clause with its Alternate III.

FAR 27.203-3 Negotiated contracts (excluding construction).

A patent indemnity clause is not required in negotiated contracts (except construction contracts covered at 27.203-5), but may be used as discussed in 27.203-4 below. A decision to omit a patent indemnity clause in a negotiated fixed-price contract described in this subsection should be based on a price consideration to the Government for forgoing the indemnification rights normally received by commercial purchasers of the same supplies or services.

FAR 27.203-4 Clauses for negotiated contracts (excluding construction).

(a) The contracting officer may insert the clause at 52.227-3, Patent Indemnity—

(1) As authorized in 27.203-1(b)(2)(ii); and

(2) Except as prohibited by 27.203-1(b), in solicitations anticipating negotiated contracts (and such contracts) for supplies or services (excluding construction and dismantling, demolition, and removal of improvements), if the contracting officer determines that the supplies or services (or such items with relatively minor modifications) normally are or have been sold or offered for sale by any supplier to the public in the commercial open market. Ordinarily, the contracting officer, in consultation with the prospective contractor, should be able to determine whether the supplies or services being purchased normally are or have been sold or offered for sale by any supplier to the public in the commercial open market. (For negotiated construction contracts, see 27.203-5.)

(b) In solicitations and contracts that call in part for specific components, spare parts, or services (or such items with relatively minor modifications) that normally are or have been sold or offered for sale by any supplier to the public in the commercial open market, the contracting officer may use the clause with its Alternate I or II, as appropriate. The choice between Alternate I (identification of excluded items) and Alternate II (identification of included items) should be based upon simplicity, Government administrative convenience, and the ease of identification of the items.

(c) In solicitations and contracts for communication services and facilities where performance is by a common carrier, and the services are unregulated and are not priced by a tariff schedule set by a regulatory body, the clause shall be used with its Alternate III.

FAR 27.203-5 Clause for construction contracts and for dismantling, demolition, and removal of improvements contracts.

Except as prohibited by 27.203-1(b), the contracting officer shall insert the clause at 52.227-4, Patent Indemnity—Construction Contracts, in solicitations and contracts for construction or that are fixed-price for dismantling, demolition, or removal of improvements. If it is determined that the construction will necessarily involve the use of structures, products, materials, equipment, processes, or methods that are nonstandard, noncommercial, or special, the contracting officer may expressly exclude them from the patent indemnification by using the basic clause with its Alternate I.

FAR 27.203-6 Clause for Government waiver of indemnity.

If, in the Government's interest, it is appropriate to exempt one or more specific United States patents from the patent indemnity clause, the contracting officer shall obtain written approval from the agency head or designee and shall insert the clause at 52.227-5, Waiver of Indemnity, in solicitations and contracts in addition to the appropriate patent indemnity clause. The contracting officer shall document the contract file with a copy of the written approval.

FAR 27.204 Reporting of royalties—anticipated or paid.

FAR 27.204-1 General.

(a)(1) To determine whether royalties anticipated or actually paid under Government contracts are excessive, improper, or inconsistent with any Government rights in particular inventions, patents, or patent applications, contracting officers shall require prospective contractors to furnish certain royalty information and shall require contractors to furnish certain royalty reports. Contracting officers shall take appropriate action to reduce or eliminate excessive or improper royalties.

(2) Royalty information shall not be required (except for information under 27.204-3) in sealed bid contracts unless the need for such information is approved at a level above that of the contracting officer as being necessary for proper protection of the Government's interest.

(b) Any solicitation that may result in a negotiated contract for which royalty information is desired or for which cost or pricing data is obtained (see 15.403) should contain a provision requesting information relating to any proposed charge for royalties. If the response to a solicitation includes a charge for royalties, the contracting officer shall, before award of the contract, forward the information relating to the proposed payments of royalties to the office having cognizance of patent matters for the contracting activity concerned. The cognizant office shall promptly advise the contracting officer of appropriate action. Before award, the contracting officer shall take action to protect the Government's interest with respect to such royalties, giving due regard to all pertinent factors relating to the proposed contract and the advice of the cognizant office.

(c) The contracting officer, when considering the approval of a subcontract, shall require and obtain the same royalty information and take the same action with respect to such subcontracts in relation to royalties as required for prime contracts under paragraph (b) of this subsection. However, consent need not be withheld pending receipt of advice in regard to such royalties from the office having cognizance of patent matters.

(d) The contracting officer shall forward the royalty information and/or royalty reports received to the office having cognizance of patent matters for the contracting activity concerned for advice as to appropriate action.

FAR 27.204-2 Solicitation provision for royalty information.

The contracting officer shall insert a solicitation provision substantially as shown in 52.227-6, Royalty Information, in any solicitation that may result in a negotiated contract for which royalty information is desired or for which cost or pricing data is obtained under 15.403. If the solicitation is for communication services and facilities by a common carrier, use the provision with its *Alternate I.*

FAR 27.204-3 Patents—notice of Government as a licensee.

(a) When the Government is obligated to pay a royalty on a patent because of a license agreement between the Government and a patent owner and the contracting officer knows (or has reason to believe) that the licensed patent will be applicable to a prospective contract, the Government should furnish information relating to the royalty to prospective offerors since it serves the interest of both the Government and the offerors. In such situations, the contracting officer should include in the solicitation a notice of the license, the number of the patent, and the royalty rate recited in the license.

(b) When the Government is obligated to pay such a royalty, the solicitation should also require offerors to furnish information indicating whether or not each offeror is a licensee under the patent or the patent owner. This information is necessary so that the Government may either—

(1) Evaluate an offeror's price by adding an amount equal to the royalty; or

(2) Negotiate a price reduction with an offeror-licensee when the offeror is licensed under the same patent at a lower royalty rate.

(c) If the Government is obligated to pay a royalty on a patent involved in the prospective contract, the contracting officer shall insert in the solicitation, substantially as shown, the provision at 52.227-7, Patents—Notice of Government Licensee.

FAR 27.205 Adjustment of royalties.

(a) If at any time the contracting officer has reason to believe that any royalties paid, or to be paid, under an existing or prospective contract or subcontract arc inconsistent with Government rights, excessive, or otherwise improper, the facts shall be promptly reported to the office having cognizance of patent matters for the contracting activity concerned. The cognizant office shall review the royalties thus reported and such royalties as are reported under 27.204 and 27.206 and, in accordance with agency procedures, shall either recommend appropriate action to the contracting officer or, if authorized, shall take appropriate action.

(b) In coordination with the cognizant office, the contracting officer shall promptly act to protect the Government against payment of royalties on supplies or services—

(1) With respect to which the Government has a royalty-free license;

(2) At a rate in excess of the rate at which the Government is licensed; or

(3) When the royalties in whole or in part otherwise constitute an improper charge.

(c) In appropriate cases, the contracting officer in coordination with the cognizant office shall obtain a refund pursuant to any refund of royalties clause in the contract (see 27.206) or negotiate for a reduction of royalties.

(d) For guidance in evaluating information furnished pursuant to 27.204 and 27.205(a) above, see 31.205-37 and 31.311-34. See also 31.109 regarding advance understandings on particular cost items, including royalties.

FAR 27.206 Refund of royalties.

FAR 27.206-1 General.

When a fixed-price contract is negotiated under circumstances that make it questionable whether or not substantial amounts of royalties will have to be paid by the contractor or a subcontractor, such royalties may be included in the target or contract price, provided the contract specifies that the Government will be reimbursed the amount of such royalties if they are not paid. Such circumstances might include, for example, either a pending Government anti-trust action or prospective litigation on the validity of a patent or patents or on the enforceability of an agreement (upon which the contractor or subcontractor bases the asserted obligation) to pay the royalties to be included in the target or contract price.

FAR 27.206-2 Clause for refund of royalties.

The contracting officer shall insert the clause at 52.227-9, Refund of Royalties, in negotiated fixed-price contracts and solicitations contemplating such contracts if the contracting officer determines that circumstances make it questionable whether or not substantial amounts of royalties will have to be paid by the contractor or a subcontractor at any tier.

FAR 27.207 Classified contracts.

FAR 27.207-1 General.

(a) Unauthorized disclosure of classified subject matter, whether in patent applications or resulting from the issuance of a patent, may be a violation of 18 U.S.C. 792 *et seq.* (Espionage and Censorship), and related statutes, and may be contrary to the interests of national security.

(b) Upon receipt from the contractor of a patent application, not yet filed, that has been submitted by the contractor in compliance with paragraph (a) or (b) of the clause at 52.227-10, Filing of Patent Applications—Classified Subject Matter, the contracting officer shall ascertain the proper security classification of the patent application. Upon a determination that the application contains classified subject matter, the contracting officer shall inform the contractor of any instructions deemed necessary or advisable relating to transmittal of the application to the United States Patent Office in accordance with procedures in the National Industrial Security Program Operating Manual. If the material is classified "Secret" or higher, the contracting officer shall make every effort to notify the contractor of the determination within 30 days, pursuant to paragraph (a) of the clause.

(c) In the case of all applications filed under the provisions of this section 27.207, the contracting officer, upon receiving the application serial number, the filing date, and the information furnished by the contractor under paragraph (d) of the clause at 52.227-10, Filing of Patent Applications—Classified Subject Matter, shall promptly submit that information to personnel having cognizance of patent matters in order that the steps necessary to ensure the security of the application may be taken.

(d) A request for the approval referred to in paragraph (c) of the clause at 52.227-10, Filing of Patent Applications—Classified Subject Matter, must be considered and acted upon promptly by the contracting officer in order to avoid the loss of valuable patent rights of the Government or the contractor.

FAR 27.207-2 Clause for classified contracts.

The contracting officer shall insert the clause at 52.227-10, Filing of Patent Applications—Classified Subject Matter, in all classified solicitations and contracts and in all solicitations and contracts where the nature of the work or classified subject matter involved in the work reasonably might be expected to result in a patent application containing classified subject matter.

FAR 27.208 Use of patented technology under the North American Free Trade Agreement.

(a) The requirements of this section apply to the use of technology covered by a valid patent when the patent holder is from a country that is a party to the North American Free Trade Agreement (NAFTA).

(b) Article 1709(10) of NAFTA generally requires a user of technology covered by a valid patent to make a reasonable effort to obtain authorization prior to use of the patented technology. However, NAFTA provides that this requirement for authorization may be waived in situations of national emergency or other circumstances of extreme urgency, or public noncommercial use.

(c) Section 6 of Executive Order 12889 of December 27, 1993, waives the requirement to obtain advance authorization for—

(1) An invention used or manufactured by or for the Federal Government, except that the patent owner must be notified whenever the agency or its contractor, without making a patent search, knows or has demonstrable reasonable grounds to know that an invention described in and covered by a valid U.S. patent is or will be used or manufactured without a license; and

(2) The existence of a national emergency or other circumstances of extreme urgency, except that the patent owner must be notified as soon as it is reasonably practicable to do so.

(d) Section 6(c) of Executive Order 12889 provides that the notice to the patent owner does not constitute an admission of infringement of a valid privately owned patent.

(e) When addressing issues regarding compensation for the use of patented technology, Government personnel should be advised that NAFTA uses the term "adequate remuneration." Executive Order 12889 equates "remuneration" to "reasonable and entire compensation" as used in 28 U.S.C. 1498, the statute which gives jurisdiction to the U.S. Court of Federal Claims to hear patent and copyright cases involving infringement by the U.S. Government.

(f) Depending on agency procedures, either the technical/requiring activity or the contracting officer shall ensure compliance with the notice requirements of NAFTA Article 1709(10). A contract award should not be suspended pending notification to the right holder.

(g) When questions arise regarding the notice requirements or other matters relating to this section, the contracting officer should consult with legal counsel.

FAR 27.209 Use of patented technology under the General Agreement on Tariffs and Trade (GATT).

(a) Article 31 of Annex 1C, Agreement on Trade-Related Aspects of Intellectual Property Rights, to GATT (Uruguay Round) addresses situations where the law of a member country allows for use of a patent without authorization from the patent holder, including use by the Government.

(b) The contracting officer should consult with legal counsel regarding questions under this section.

FAR 27.300 Scope of subpart.

This subpart prescribes policies, procedures, and contract clauses with respect to inventions made in the performance of work under a Government contract or subcontract thereunder if a purpose of the contract or subcontract is the conduct of experimental, developmental, or research work, except to the extent statutory requirements necessitate different agency policies, procedures, and clauses as specified in agency supplemental regulations.

FAR 27.301 Definitions.

As used in this subpart—

"Invention" means any invention or discovery that is or may be patentable or otherwise protectable under title 35 of the U.S. Code or any novel variety of plant that is or may be protectable under the Plant Variety Protection Act (7 U.S.C. 2321, *et seq.*).

"Made" when used in relation to any invention, means the conception or first actual reduction to practice of such invention.

"Nonprofit organization" means a university or other institution of higher education or an organization of the type described in section 501(c)(3) of the Internal Revenue Code of 1954 (26 U.S.C. 501(c)) and exempt from taxation under section 501(a) of the Internal Revenue Code (26 U.S.C. 501(a)), or any nonprofit scientific or educational organization qualified under a State nonprofit organization statute.

"Practical application" means to manufacture, in the case of a composition or product; to practice, in the case of a process or method; or to operate, in the case of a machine or system; and, in each case, under such conditions as to establish that the invention is being utilized and that its benefits are, to the extent permitted by law or Government regulations, available to the public on reasonable terms.

"Small business firm" means a small business concern as defined at 15 U.S.C. 632 and implementing regulations of the Administrator of the Small Business Administration. (For the purpose of this definition, the size standard contained in 13 CFR 121.3-8 for small business contractors and in 13 CFR 121.3-12 for small business subcontractors will be used. See FAR Part 19).

"Subject invention" means any invention of the contractor conceived or first actually reduced to practice in the performance of work under a Government contract; provided, that in the case of a variety of plant, the date of determination defined in section 41(d) of the Plant Variety Protection Act, 7 U.S.C. 2401(d), must also occur during the period of contract performance.

FAR 27.302 Policy.

(a) *Introduction.* The policy of this section is based on Chapter 18 of title 35, U.S.C. (Pub. L. 95-517, Pub. L. 98-620, 37 CFR Part 401), the Presidential Memorandum on Government Patent Policy to the Heads of Executive Departments and Agencies dated

February 18, 1983, and Executive Order 12591, which provides that, to the extent permitted by law, the head of each Executive Department and agency shall promote the commercialization, in accord with the Presidential Memorandum, of patentable results of federally funded research by granting to all contractors, regardless of size, the title to patents made in whole or in part with Federal funds, in exchange for royalty-free use by or on behalf of the Government. The objectives of this policy are to use the patent system to promote the utilization of inventions arising from federally supported research or development; to encourage maximum participation of industry in federally supported research and development efforts; to ensure that these inventions are used in a manner to promote free competition and enterprise; to promote the commercialization and public availability of the inventions made in the United States by United States industry and labor; to ensure that the Government obtains sufficient rights in federally supported inventions to meet the needs of the Government and protect the public against nonuse or unreasonable use of inventions; and, to minimize the costs of administering policies in this area.

(b) *Contractor right to elect title.* Under the policy set forth in paragraph (a) of this section, each contractor may, after disclosure to the Government as required by the patent rights clause included in the contract, elect to retain title to any invention made in the performance of work under the contract. To the extent an agency's statutory requirements necessitate a different policy, or different procedures and/or contract clauses to effectuate the policy set forth in paragraph (a) of this section, such policy, procedures, and clauses shall be contained in or expressly referred to in that agency's supplement to this subpart. In addition, a contract may provide otherwise—

(1) When the contractor is not located in the United States or does not have a place of business located in the United States or is subject to the control of a foreign-government (see 27.303(c));

(2) In exceptional circumstances when it is determined by the agency that restriction or elimination of the right to retain title in any subject invention will better promote the policy and objectives of Chapter 18 of title 35, U.S.C. and the Presidential Memorandum;

(3) When it is determined by a Government authority which is authorized by statute or Executive Order to conduct foreign intelligence or counterintelligence activities that the restriction or elimination of the right to retain title to any subject invention is necessary to protect the security of such activities; or

(4) When the contract includes the operation of a Government-owned, contractor-operated facility of the Department of Energy primarily dedicated to the Department's naval nuclear propulsion or weapons related programs and all funding agreement limitations under 35 U.S.C. 202(a)(iv) for agreements with small business firms and nonprofit organizations are limited to inventions occurring under the above two programs.

In the case of small business firms and nonprofit organizations, when an agency justifies and exercises the exception at subparagraph (b)(2) of this section on the basis of national security, the contract shall provide the contractor with the right to elect ownership to any invention made under such contract as provided by the clause at 52.227-11, Patent Rights—

Retention by the Contractor (Short Form), if the invention is not classified by the agency within 6 months of the date it is reported to the agency, or within the same time period the Department of Energy (DOE) does not, as authorized by regulation, law or Executive Order or implementing regulations thereto, prohibit unauthorized dissemination of the invention. Contracts in support of DOE's naval nuclear propulsion program are exempted from this paragraph. When a contract involves a series of separate task orders, an agency may apply the exceptions at subparagraph (b)(2) or (3) of this section to individual task orders, and it may structure the contract so that modified patent rights clauses will apply to the task order even though the clause at 52.227-11 is applicable to the remainder of the work. In those instances when the Government has the right to acquire title at the time of contracting, the contractor may, nevertheless, request greater rights to an identified invention (see 27.304-1(a)). The right of the contractor to retain title shall, in any event, be subject to the provisions of paragraphs (c) through (g) of this section.

(c) *Government license.* The Government shall have at least a nonexclusive, nontransferable, irrevocable, paid-up license to practice, or have practiced for or on behalf of the United States, any subject invention throughout the world; and may, if provided in the contract (see Alternate I of the applicable patent rights clause), have additional rights to sublicense any foreign government or international organization pursuant to existing treaties or agreements identified in the contract, or to otherwise effectuate such treaties or agreements. In the case of long term contracts, the contract may also provide (see Alternate II) such rights with respect to treaties or agreements to be entered into by the Government after the award of the contract.

(d) *Government right to receive title.* (1) The Government has the right to receive title to any invention if the contract so provides pursuant to a determination made in accordance with subparagraph (b)(1), (2), (3), or (4) of this section. In addition, to the extent provided in the patent rights clause, the Government has the right to receive title to an invention—

(i) If the contractor has not disclosed the invention within the time specified in the clause;

(ii) In any country where the contractor does not elect to retain rights or fails to elect to retain rights to the invention within the time specified in the clause;

(iii) In any country where the contractor has not filed a patent application within the time specified in the clause;

(iv) In any country where the contractor decides not to continue prosecution of a patent application, pay maintenance fees, or defend in a reexamination or opposition proceeding on the patent; and/or

(v) In any country where the contractor no longer desires to retain title.

(2) For the purposes of this paragraph, election or filing in a European Patent Office Region or under the Patent Cooperation Treaty constitutes election or filing in any country covered therein to meet the times specified in the clause, provided that the Govern-

ment has the right to receive title in those countries not subsequently designated by the contractor.

(e) *Utilization reports.* The Government shall have the right to require periodic reporting on the utilization or efforts at obtaining utilization that are being made by the contractor or its licensees or assignees. Such reporting by small business firms and nonprofit organizations may be required in accordance with instructions as may be issued by the Department of Commerce. Agencies should protect the confidentiality of utilization reports which are marked with restrictions to the extent permitted by 35 U.S.C. 205 or other applicable laws and 37 CFR Part 401. Agencies shall not disclose such utilization reports to persons outside the Government without permission of the contractor. Contractors will continue to provide confidential markings to help prevent inadvertent release outside the agency.

(f) *March-in rights.* (1) With respect to any subject invention in which a contractor has acquired title, contracts provide that the agency shall have the right (unless provided otherwise in accordance with 27.304-1(f)) to require the contractor, an assignee, or exclusive licensee of a subject invention to grant a nonexclusive, partially exclusive, or exclusive license in any field of use to a responsible applicant or applicants, upon terms that are reasonable under the circumstances, and if the contractor, assignee, or exclusive licensee refuses such request, to grant such a license itself, if the agency determines that such action is necessary—

(i) Because the contractor or assignee has not taken, or is not expected to take within a reasonable time, effective steps to achieve practical application of the subject invention in such field of use;

(ii) To alleviate health or safety needs which are not reasonably satisfied by the contractor, assignee, or their licensees;

(iii) To meet requirements for public use specified by Federal regulations and such requirements are not reasonably satisfied by the contractor, assignee, or licensees; or

(iv) Because the agreement required by paragraph (g) below has neither been obtained nor waived, or because a licensee of the exclusive right to use or sell any subject invention in the United States is in breach of its agreement obtained pursuant to paragraph (g) below.

(2) This right of the agency shall be exercised only after the contractor has been provided a reasonable time to present facts and show cause why the proposed agency action should not be taken, and afforded an opportunity to take appropriate action if the contractor wishes to dispute or appeal the proposed action, in accordance with 27.304-1(g).

(g) *Preference for United States industry.* Unless provided otherwise in accordance with 27.304-1(f), contracts provide that no contractor which receives title to any subject invention and no assignee of any such contractor shall grant to any person the exclusive right to use or sell any subject invention in the United States unless such person agrees that any products embodying the subject invention or produced through the use of the subject invention will be manufactured substantially in the United States. However, in individual cases, the requirement for such an agreement may be waived by the agency upon a showing by the contractor or assignee that reasonable but unsuccessful efforts have been made to grant licenses on similar terms to potential licensees that would be likely to manufacture substantially in the United States or that under the circumstances domestic manufacture is not commercially feasible.

(h) *Small business preference.* (1) Nonprofit organization contractors are expected to use efforts that are reasonable under the circumstances to attract small business licensees. They are also expected to give small business firms that meet the standard outlined in the clause at 52.227-11, Patent Rights—Retention by the Contractor (Short Form), a preference over other applicants for licenses. What constitutes reasonable efforts to attract small business licensees will vary with the circumstances and the nature, duration, and expense of efforts needed to bring the invention to the market. Subparagraph (k)(4) of the clause is not intended, for example, to prevent nonprofit organizations from providing larger firms with a right of first refusal or other options in inventions that relate to research being supported under long-term or other arrangements with larger companies. Under such circumstances, it would not be reasonable to seek and to give a preference to small business licensees.

(2) Small business firms that believe a nonprofit organization is not meeting its obligations under the clause may report their concerns to the Secretary of Commerce. To the extent deemed appropriate, the Secretary of Commerce will undertake informal investigation of the concern, and, if appropriate, enter into discussions or negotiations with the nonprofit organization to the end of improving its efforts in meeting its obligations under the clause. However, in no event will the Secretary of Commerce intervene in ongoing negotiations or contractor decisions concerning the licensing of a specific subject invention. All the above investigations, discussions, and negotiations of the Secretary of Commerce will be in coordination with other interested agencies, including the Small Business Administration; and in the case of a contract for the operation of a Government-owned, contractor-operated research or production facility, the Secretary of Commerce will coordinate with the agency responsible for the facility prior to any discussions or negotiations with the contractor.

(i) *Minimum rights to contractor.* (1) When the Government acquires title to a subject invention, the contractor is normally granted a revocable, nonexclusive, royalty-free license to that invention throughout the world. The contractor's license extends to its domestic subsidiaries and affiliates, if any, within the corporate structure of which the contractor is a part and includes the right to grant sublicenses of the same scope to the extent the contractor was legally obligated to do so at the time the contract was awarded. The license is transferable only with the approval of the contracting officer except when transferred to the successor of that part of the contractor's business to which the invention pertains.

(2) The contractor's domestic license may be revoked or modified to the extent necessary to achieve expeditious practical application of the subject invention pursuant to an application for an exclusive license submitted in accordance with the applicable provisions in the Federal Property Management Regulations and agency licensing regulations. This license will not be revoked in that field of use or the geographical areas in which the contractor has achieved practical application and continues to make the benefits of the invention reasonably accessible to the public. The license in any foreign country may be revoked or modified to the

extent the contractor, its licensees, or its domestic subsidiaries or affiliates have failed to achieve practical application in that country. See the procedures at 27.304-1(e).

(j) *Confidentiality of inventions.* The publication of information disclosing an invention by any party before the filing of a patent application may create a bar to a valid patent. Accordingly, 35 U.S.C. 205 and 37 CFR Part 40 provide that Federal agencies are authorized to withhold from disclosure to the public information disclosing any invention in which the Federal Government owns or may own a right, title, or interest (including a nonexclusive license) for a reasonable time in order for a patent application to be filed. Furthermore, Federal agencies shall not be required to release copies of any document which is part of an application for patent filed with the United States Patent and Trademark Office or with any foreign patent office. The Presidential Memorandum on Government Patent Policy specifies that agencies should protect the confidentiality of invention disclosures and patent applications required in performance or in consequence of awards to the extent permitted by 35 U.S.C. 205 or other applicable laws.

FAR 27.303 Contract clauses.

In contracts (and solicitations therefor) for experimental, developmental, or research work (but see 27.304-3 regarding contracts for construction work or architect-engineer services), a patent rights clause shall be inserted as follows:

(a)(1) The contracting officer shall insert the clause at 52.227-11, Patent Rights—Retention by the Contractor (Short Form), if all the following conditions apply:

(i) The contractor is a small business concern or nonprofit organization as defined in 27.301 or, except for contracts of the Department of Defense (DOD), the Department of Energy (DOE), or the National Aeronautics and Space Administration (NASA), any other type of contractor.

(ii) No alternative patent rights clause is used in accordance with paragraphs (c) or (d) of this section or 27.304-2.

(2) To the extent the information is not required elsewhere in the contract, and unless otherwise specified by agency supplemental regulations, the contracting officer may modify 52.227-11 (f) to require the contractor to do one or more of the following:

(i) Provide periodic (but not more frequently than annually) listings of all subject inventions required to be disclosed during the period covered by the report.

(ii) Provide a report prior to the closeout of the contract listing all subject inventions or stating that there were none.

(iii) Provide, upon request, the filing date, serial number and title, a copy of the patent application, and patent number and issue date for any subject invention in any country in which the contractor has applied for patents.

(iv) Furnish the Government an irrevocable power to inspect and make copies of the patent application file when a Federal Government employee is a coinventor.

(3) If the acquisition of patent rights for the benefit of a foreign government is required under a treaty or executive agreement, or if the agency head or a designee determines at the time of contracting that it would be in the national interest to acquire the right to sublicense foreign governments or international organizations pursuant to any existing or future treaty or agreement, the contracting officer shall use the clause at 52.227-11, with its Alternate I. If other rights are necessary to effectuate the treaty or agreement, Alternate I may be appropriately modified. In long term contracts, Alternate II shall be added if necessary to effectuate treaties or agreements to be entered into.

(4) If the contracting officer includes the clause at 52.227-11, Patent Rights— Retention by the Contractor (Short Form), in a contract with a nonprofit organization for the operation of a Government-owned facility, the contracting officer will include Alternate III in lieu of subparagraph (k)(3) of the clause.

(5) If the contract is for the operation of a Government-owned facility, the contracting officer may include Alternate IV with the clause at 52.227-11.

(b)(1) The contracting officer shall insert the clause at 52.227-12, Patent Rights— Retention by the Contractor (Long Form), if all the following conditions apply:

(i) The contractor is other than a small business firm or nonprofit organization.

(ii) No alternative clause is used in accordance with paragraph (c) or (d) of this section or 27.304-2.

(iii) The contracting agency is one of those excepted under subdivision (a)(1)(i) of this section.

(2) If the acquistion of patent rights for the benefit of a foreign government is required under a treaty or executive agreement or if the agency head or a designee determines at the time of contracting that it would be in the national interest to acquire the right to sublicense foreign governments or international organizations pursuant to any existing or future treaty or agreement, the contracting officer shall use the clause at 52.227-12, with its Alternate I. If other rights are necessary to effectuate the treaty or agreement, Alternate I may be appropriately modified. In long term contracts, Alternate II shall be added if necessary to effectuate treaties or agreements to be entered into.

(c)(1) The contracting officer shall insert the clause at 52.227-13, Patent Rights— Acquisition by the Government, if any of the following conditions apply:

(i) No alternative clause is used in accordance with subparagraphs (c)(2) and (4) or paragraph (d) of this section or 27.304-2.

(ii) The work is to be performed outside the United States, its possessions, and Puerto Rico by contractors that are not small business firms, nonprofit organizations as defined in 27.301, or domestic firms. For purposes of this subparagraph, the contracting officer may presume that a contractor is not a domestic firm unless it is known that the firm is not foreign owned, controlled, or influenced. (See 27.304-4(a) regarding subcontracts with U.S. firms.)

(2) Pursuant to their statutory requirements, DOE and NASA may specify in their supplemental regulations use of a modified version of the clause at 52.227-13 in contracts with other than small business concerns or nonprofit organizations.

(3) If the acquisition of patent rights for the benefit of a foreign government is required under a treaty or executive agreement or if the agency head or a designee determines at the time of contracting that it would be in the national interest to acquire the right to sublicense foreign governments or international organizations pursuant to any existing or future treaty or agreement, the contracting officer shall use the clause with its Alternate I. If other rights are necessary to effectuate the treaty or agreement, Alternate I may be appropriately modified. In long term contracts, Alternate II shall be added if necessary to effectuate treaties or agreements to be entered into.

(4) Section 401 of title 37 of the Code of Federal Regulations provides that in contracts with small business firms and nonprofit organizations, when an agency exercises the exceptions at 27.302(b)(2) or (3) it shall use the clause 52.227-11, with such modifications as are necessary to address the exceptional circumstances or concerns which led to the use of the exception. The greater rights determinations provision of 52.227-13(b)(2) shall be included in the modified clause.

(d)(1) If one of the following applies, the contracting officer may insert the clause prescribed in paragraph (a) or (b) of this section as otherwise applicable, agency supplemental regulations may provide another clause and specify its use, or the contracting officer shall insert the clause prescribed in paragraph (c) of this section:

(i) The contractor is not located in the United States or does not have a place of business located in the United States or is subject to the control of a foreign government.

(ii) There are exceptional circumstances and the agency head determines that restriction or elimination of the right to retain title to any subject invention will better promote the policy and objectives of Chapter 18 of title 35 of the United States Code.

(iii) It is determined by a Government authority which is authorized by statute or executive order to conduct foreign intelligence or counterintelligence activities that restriction or elimination of the right to retain any subject invention is necessary to protect the security of such activities.

(iv) The contract includes the operation of a Government-owned, contractor-operated facility of the Department of Energy primarily dedicated to that Department's naval nuclear propulsion or weapons related programs.

(2) Before using any of the exceptions under subparagraph (d)(1) of this section in a contract with a small business firm or a nonprofit organization and before using the exception of subdivision (d)(1)(ii) of this section for any contractor, the agency shall prepare a written determination, including a statement of facts supporting the determination, that the conditions identified in the exception exist. A separate statement of facts shall be prepared for each exceptional circumstances determination, except that in appropriate cases a single determination may apply to both a contract and any subcontracts issued under it, or to any contract to which an exception is applicable. In cases when subdivision (d)(1)(ii) of this section is used, the determination shall also include an analysis justifying the determination. This analysis should address, with specificity, how the alternate provisions will better achieve the objectives set forth in 35 U.S.C. 200. For contracts with small business firms and non-profit organizations, a copy of each determination, statement of facts, and, if applicable, analysis shall be promptly provided to the contractor or offeror along with a notification of its appeal rights under 35 U.S.C. 202(b)(4) in accordance with 27.304-1(a). In the case of small business and nonprofit contractors, except for determination under subdivision (d)(1)(iii) of this section, the agency shall, within 30 days after award of a contract, also provide copies of each determination, statement of fact, and analysis to the Secretary of Commerce. These shall be sent within 30 days after the award of the contract to which they pertain. In the case of contracts with small business concerns, copies will also be sent to the Chief Counsel for Advocacy of the Small Business Administration.

(e) For those agencies excepted under paragraph (a)(1)(i) of this section, only small business firms or non-profit organizations qualify for the clause at 52.227-11. If one of these agencies has reason to question the status of the prospective contractor, the agency may file a protest in accordance with 13 CFR 121.3-5 if small business firm status is questioned, or require the prospective contractor to furnish evidence of its status as a nonprofit organization.

(f) Alternates I and II to the clauses at 52.227-11, 52.227-12, and 52.227-13, as applicable, may be modified to make clear that the rights granted to the foreign government or international organization may be for additional rights beyond a license or sublicense if so required by the applicable treaty or international agreement. For example, in some cases exclusive licenses or even assignment of title in the foreign country involved might be required. In addition, the Alternate may be modified to provide for direct licensing by the contractor of the foreign government or international organization.

FAR 27.304 Procedures.

FAR 27.304-1 General.

(a) *Contractor appeals of exceptions.* (1) In accordance with 35 U.S.C. 202(b)(4), a small business firm or nonprofit organization contractor has the right to an administrative review of a determination to use one of the exceptions at 27.303(d)(1)(i)-(iv) if the contractor believes that a determination is either (i) contrary to the policies and objectives of this subsection or (ii) constitutes an abuse of discretion by the agency. Subparagraphs (a)(2) through (7) of this subsection specify the procedures to be followed by contractors and agencies in such cases. The assertion of such a claim by the contractor shall not be used as a basis for withholding or delaying the award of a contract or for suspending performance under an award.

However, pending final resolution of the claim, the contract may be issued with the patent rights provision proposed by the agency; but should the final decision be in favor of the contractor, the contract will be amended accordingly and the amendment made retroactive to the effective date of the contract.

(2) A contractor may appeal a determination by providing written notice to the agency within 30 working days from the time it receives a copy of the agency's determination, or within such longer time as an agency may specify in its regulations. The contractor's notice should specifically identify the basis for the appeal.

(3) The appeal shall be decided by the head of the agency or designee who is at a level above the person who made the determination. If the notice raises a genuine dispute over the material facts, the head of the agency or designee shall undertake or refer the matter for fact-finding.

(4) Fact-finding shall be conducted in accordance with procedures established by the agency. Such procedures shall be as informal as practicable and be consistent with principles of fundamental fairness. The procedures should afford the contractor the opportunity to appear with counsel, submit documentary evidence, present witnesses, and confront such persons as the agency may rely upon. A transcribed record shall be made and shall be available at cost to the contractor upon request. The requirement for a transcribed record may be waived by mutual agreement of the contractor and the agency.

(5) The official conducting the fact-finding shall prepare or adopt written findings of fact and transmit them to the head of the agency or designee promptly after the conclusion of the fact-finding proceeding along with a recommended decision. A copy of the findings of fact and recommended decision shall be sent to the contractor by registered or certified mail.

(6) Fact-finding should be completed within 45 working days from the date the agency receives the contractor's written notice.

(7) When fact-finding has been conducted, the head of the agency or designee shall base his or her decision on the facts found, together with any argument submitted by the contractor, agency officials, or any other information in the administrative record. In cases referred for fact-finding, the agency head or designee may reject only those facts that have been found to be clearly erroneous, but must explicitly state the rejection and indicate the basis for the contrary finding. The agency head or designee may hear oral arguments after fact-finding provided that the contractor or contractor's attorney or representative is present and given an opportunity to make arguments and rebuttal. The decision of the agency head or designee shall be in writing and if it is unfavorable to the contractor, include an explanation of the basis of the decision. The decision of the agency or designee shall be made within 30 working days after fact-finding or, if there was no fact-finding, within 45 working days from the date the agency received the contractor's written notice. In accordance with 35 U.S.C. 203, a small business firm or a nonprofit organization contractor adversely affected by a determination under this section may, at any time within 60 days after the determination is issued, file a petition in the United States Claims Court, which shall have jurisdiction to

determine the appeal on the record and to affirm, reverse, remand, or modify, as appropriate, the determination of the Federal agency.

(b) *Greater rights determinations.* Whenever the contract contains the clause at 52.227-13, Patent Rights—Acquisition by the Government, the contractor (or an employee-inventor of the contractor after consultation with the contractor) may request greater rights to an identified invention within the period specified in such clause. Requests for greater rights may be granted if the agency head or designee determines that the interests of the United States and the general public will be better served thereby. In making such determinations, the agency head or designee shall consider at least the following objectives:

(1) Promoting the utilization of inventions arising from federally-supported research and development.

(2) Ensuring that inventions are used in a manner to promote full and open competition and free enterprise.

(3) Promoting public availability of inventions made in the United States by United States industry and labor.

(4) Ensuring that the Government obtains sufficient rights in federally-supported inventions to meet the needs of the Government and protect the public against nonuse or unreasonable use of inventions.

(c) *Retention of rights by inventor.* If the contractor does not elect to retain title to a subject invention, the agency may consider and, after consultation with the contractor, grant requests for retention of rights by the inventor. Retention of rights by the inventor will be subject to the conditions in paragraph (d) (except subparagraphs (d)(1), (f)(4), and paragraphs (h), (i), and (j) of the applicable Patent Rights—Retention by the Contractor clause).

(d) *Government assignment to contractor of rights in Government employees' inventions.* When a Government employee is a coinventor of an invention made under a contract with a small business firm or nonprofit organization, the agency employing the coinventor may transfer or reassign whatever right it may acquire in the subject invention from its employee to the contractor, subject at least to the conditions of 35 U.S.C. 202-204.

(e) *Additional requirements.* (1) If it is desired to have the right to require any of the following, when using the clause at 52.227-11, Patent Rights—Retention by the Contractor (Short Form), the contract shall be modified to require the contractor to do one or more of the following:

(i) Provide periodic (but not more frequently than annually) listings of all subject inventions required to be disclosed during the period covered by the report.

(ii) Provide a report prior to the closeout of the contract listing all subject inventions or stating that there were none.

(iii) Provide, upon request, the filing date, serial number, and title; a copy of the patent application; and patent number and issue date for any subject invention in any country in which the contractor has applied for patents.

(iv) Furnish the Government an irrevocable power to inspect and make copies of the patent application file when a Federal Government employee is a coinventor.

(2) To the extent provided by such modification (and automatically under the terms of the clauses at 52.227-12, Patent Rights—Retention by the Contractor (Long Form), and 52.227-13, Patent Rights—Acquisition by the Government, the contracting officer may require the contractor to—

(i) Furnish a copy of each subcontract containing a patent rights clause (but if a copy of a subcontract is furnished under another clause, a duplicate shall not be requested under the patent rights clause);

(ii) Submit interim and final invention reports listing subject inventions and notifying the contracting officer of all subcontracts awarded for experimental, developmental, or research work;

(iii) Submit information regarding the filing date, serial number and title, and, upon request, a copy of the patent application, and patent number and issue date for any subject invention in any country for which the contractor has retained title; and

(iv) Submit periodic reports on the utilization of a subject invention or on efforts at obtaining utilization that are being made by the contractor or its licensees or assignees.

(3) The contractor is required to deliver to the contracting officer an instrument confirmatory of all rights to which the Government is entitled and to furnish the Government an irrevocable power to inspect and make copies of the patent application file. Such delivery should normally be made within 6 months after filing each patent application, or within 6 months after submitting the invention disclosure if the application has been previously filed.

(f) *Revocation or modification of contractor's minimum rights.* Before revocation or modification of the contractor's license in accordance with 27.302(i)(2), the contracting officer will furnish the contractor a written notice of intention to revoke or modify the license, and the contractor will be allowed 30 days (or such other time as may be authorized by the contracting officer for good cause shown by the contractor) after the notice to show cause why the license should not be revoked or modified. The contractor has the right to appeal, in accordance with applicable regulations in 37 CFR Part 404 and agency licensing regulations, any decisions concerning the revocation or modification.

(g) *Exercise of march-in rights.* The following procedures shall govern the exercise of the march-in rights set forth in 35 U.S.C. 203, paragraph (j) of the Patent Rights—Retention by the Contractor clauses, and subdivision (c)(1)(ii) of the Patent Rights—Acquisition by the Government clause:

(1) When the agency receives information that it believes might warrant the exercise of march-in rights, before initiating any march-in proceeding in accordance with the procedures of subparagraph (g)(2) of this section, it shall notify the contractor in writing of the information and request informal written or oral comments from the contractor. In the absence of any comments from the contractor within 30 days the agency may, at its discretion, initiate the procedures below. If a comment is received, whether or not within 30 days, then the agency shall, within 60 days after it receives the comment, either initiate the procedures below or notify the contractor, in writing, that it will not pursue march-in rights based on the information about which the contractor was notified.

(2) A march-in proceeding shall be initiated by the issuance of a written notice by the agency head or a designee to the contractor and its assignee or exclusive licensee, as applicable and if known to the agency, stating that the Government has determined to exercise march-in rights. The notice shall state the reasons for the proposed march-in, in terms sufficient to put the contractor on notice of the facts upon which the action is based, and shall specify the field or fields of use in which the Government is considering requiring licensing. The notice shall advise the contractor, assignee, or exclusive licensee of its rights as set forth in this section and in any supplemental agency regulations or procedures. The determination to exercise march-in rights shall be made by the head of the agency or designee.

(3) Within 30 days after the receipt of the written notice of march-in, the contractor, its assignee or exclusive licensee, may submit in person, in writing, or through a representative information or argument in opposition to the proposed march-in, including any additional specific information which raises a genuine dispute over the material facts upon which the march-in is based. If the information presented raises a genuine dispute over the material facts, the head of the agency or designee shall undertake or refer the matter to another official for fact-finding.

(4) Fact-finding shall be conducted in accordance with the procedures established by the agency. Such procedures shall be as informal as practicable and be consistent with principles of fundamental fairness. The procedures should afford the contractor the opportunity to appear with counsel, submit documentary evidence, present witnesses, and confront such persons as the agency may present. A transcribed record shall be made and shall be available at cost to the contractor upon request. The requirement for a transcribed record may be waived by mutual agreement of the contractor and the agency. Any portion of the march-in proceeding, including a fact-finding hearing that involves testimony or evidence relating to the utilization or efforts at obtaining utilization that are being made by the contractor, its assignee, or licensees shall be closed to the public, including potential licensees. In accordance with 35 U.S.C. 202(c)(5), agencies shall not disclose any such information obtained during a march-in proceeding to persons outside the Government except when such release is authorized by the contractor, its assignee, or licensee.

(5) The official conducting the fact-finding shall prepare or adopt written findings of fact and transmit them to the head of the agency or designee promptly after the conclusion of the fact-finding proceeding along with a recommended determination. A copy of the findings of fact shall be sent to the contractor, its assignee, or exclusive licensee by registered or certified mail. The contractor, its assignee or exclusive licensee, and agency representatives

will be given 30 days to submit written arguments to the head of the agency or designee; and, upon request by the contractor, oral arguments will be held before the agency head or designee that will make the final determination.

(6) In case in which fact-finding has been conducted, the head of the agency or designee shall base his or her determination on the facts found, together with any other information and written or oral arguments submitted by the contractor, its assignee or exclusive licensee and agency representatives, and any other information in the administrative record. The consistency of the exercise of march-in rights with the policy and objectives of 35 U.S.C. 200 shall also be considered. In cases referred for fact-finding, the head of the agency or designee may reject only those facts that have been found to be clearly erroneous, but must explicitly state the rejection and indicate the basis for the contrary finding. Written notice of the determination whether march-in rights will be exercised shall be made by the head of the agency or designee and sent to the contractor, its assignee, or exclusive licensee, by certified or registered mail within 90 days after the completion of fact-finding or 90 days after oral arguments, whichever is later, or the proceedings will be deemed to have been terminated and thereafter no march-in based on the facts and reasons upon which the proceeding was initiated may be exercised.

(7) An agency may, at any time, terminate a march-in proceeding if it is satisfied that it does not wish to exercise march-in rights.

(8) These procedures shall also apply to the exercise of march-in rights against inventors receiving title to subject inventions under 35 U.S.C. 202(d) and, for that purpose, the term "contractor," as used herein, shall be deemed to include the inventory and the term "exclusive licensee" shall be deemed to include partially exclusive licensee.

(9) An agency determination unfavorable to the contractor, its assignee, or exclusive licensee shall be held in abeyance pending the exhaustion of appeals or petitions filed under 35 U.S.C. 203(2).

(h) *Licenses and assignments under contracts with nonprofit organizations.* If the contractor is a nonprofit organization, the clause at 52.227-11 provides that certain contractor actions require agency approval, as specified below. Agencies shall provide procedures for obtaining such approval. Rights to a subject invention in the United States may not be assigned without the approval of the contracting agency, except where such assignment is made to an organization which has as one of its primary functions the management of inventions (provided that such assignee will be subject to the same provisions as the contractor).

FAR 27.304-2 Contracts placed by or for other Government agencies.

The following procedures apply unless agency agreements provide otherwise:

(a) When a Government agency requests another Government agency to award a contract on its behalf, the request should explain any special circumstances surrounding the contract and specify and furnish the patent rights clause to be used. Normally, the clause will be in accordance with the policies and procedures of this subpart. If, however, the request states that a clause of the requesting agency is required (*e.g.*, because of statutory requirements, a deviation, or exceptional circumstances) that clause shall be used rather than those of this subpart.

(1) If the request states that an agency clause is required and the work to be performed under the contract is not severable and is funded wholly or in part by the agency, then that agency clause and no other patent rights clause shall be included in the contract.

(2) If the request states that an agency clause is required, and the work to be performed under the contract is severable and is only in part for the requesting agency, then the work which is on behalf of the requesting agency shall be identified in the contract, and the agency clause shall be made applicable to that portion. In such situations, the remaining portion of the work (for the agency awarding the contract) shall likewise be identified and the appropriate patent rights clause (if required) shall be made applicable to that remaining portion.

(3) If the request states that an agency clause is not required in any resulting contract, then the appropriate patent rights clause shall be used, if a patent rights clause is required.

(b) Where use of the specified clause, or any modification, waiver, or omission of the Government's rights under any provisions therein, requires a written determination, the reporting of such determination, or a deviation, if any such acts are required in accordance with 27.303(d)(2), it shall be the responsibility of the requesting agency to make such determination, submit the required reports, and obtain such deviations, in consultation with the contracting agency, unless otherwise agreed between the contracting and requesting agencies. However, deviation to a specified clause of the requesting agency shall not be made without prior approval of that agency.

(c) The requesting agency may require, and provide instructions regarding, the forwarding or handling of any invention disclosures or other reporting requirements of the specified clauses. Normally the requesting agency shall be responsible for the handling of any disclosed inventions, including the filing of patent applications where the Government receives title, and the custody, control, and licensing thereof, unless provided otherwise in the instructions or other agreements with the contracting agency.

FAR 27.304-3 Contracts for construction work or architect-engineer services.

(a) If a solicitation or contract for construction work or architect-engineer services has as a purpose the performance of experimental, developmental, or research work or test and evaluation studies involving such work and calls for, or can be expected to involve, the design of a Government facility or of novel structures, machines, products, materials, processes, or equipment (including construction equipment), it shall include a patent rights clause selected in accordance with the policies and procedures of this Subpart 27.3.

(b) A solicitation or contract for construction work or architect-engineer services that calls for or can be expected to involve only "standard types of construction" to be built by previously developed equipment, methods, and processes shall not include a patent rights clause. The term "standard types of construction" means construction in which the distinctive features, if any, in all likelihood will amount to no more than—

(1) Variations in size, shape, or capacity of otherwise structurally orthodox and conventionally acting structures or structural groupings; or

(2) Purely artistic or esthetic (as distinguished from functionally significant) architectural configurations and designs of both structural and nonstructural members or groupings, which may or may not be sufficiently novel or meritorious to qualify for design protection under the design patent or copyright laws.

FAR 27.304-4 Subcontracts.

(a) The policies and procedures covered by this subpart apply to all contracts at any tier. Hence, a contractor awarding a subcontract and a subcontractor awarding a lower-tier subcontract that has a purpose the conduct of experimental, developmental, or research work is required to determine the appropriate patent rights clause to be included that is consistent with these policies and procedures. Generally, the clause at either 52.227-11, 52.227-12, or 52.227-13 is to be used and will be so specified in the patent rights clause contained in the higher-tier contract, but the contracting officer may direct the use of a particular patent rights clause in any lower-tier contract in accordance with the policies and procedures of this subpart. For instance, when the clause at 52.227-13 is in the prime contract because the work is to be performed overseas, any subcontract with a nonprofit organization would contain the clause at 52.227-11.

(b) Whenever a prime contractor or a subcontractor considers the inclusion of a particular clause in a subcontract to be inappropriate or a subcontractor refuses to accept the proffered clause, the matter shall be resolved by the agency contracting officer in consultation with counsel.

(c) It is government policy that contractors shall not use their ability to award subcontracts as economic leverage to acquire rights for themselves in inventions resulting from subcontracts.

FAR 27.304-5 Appeals.

(a) The agency official initially authorized to take any of the following actions shall provide the contractor with a written statement of the basis for the action at the time the action is taken, including any relevant facts that were relied upon in taking the action:

(1) A refusal to grant an extension to the invention disclosure period under subparagraph (c)(4) of the clauses at 52.227-11 and 52.227-12.

(2) A request for a conveyance of title to the Government under 27.302(d)(1)(i) through (v).

(3) A refusal to grant a waiver under 27.302(g), Preference for U.S. Industry.

(4) A refusal to approve an assignment under 27.304-1(h)(1).

(5) A refusal to approve an extension of the exclusive license period under 27.304-1(h)(2).

(b) Each agency shall establish and publish procedures under which any of the agency actions listed in paragraph (a) above may be appealed to the head of the agency or designee. Review at this level shall consider both the factual and legal basis for the action and its consistency with the policy and objectives of 35 U.S.C. 200-206 and this subpart.

(c) Appeals procedures established under paragraph (b) of this subsection shall include administrative due process procedures and standards for fact-finding at least comparable to those set forth in 37 CFR Part 401.6(e)-(g) whenever there is a dispute as to the factual basis for an agency request for a conveyance of title under 27.302(d)(1)(i) through (v) including any dispute as to whether or not an invention is a subject invention.

(d) To the extent that any of the actions described in paragraph (a) above are subject to appeal under the Contract Disputes Act, the procedures under that Act will satisfy the requirements of paragraphs (b) and (c) above.

FAR 27.305 Administration of patent rights clauses.

FAR 27.305-1 Patent rights follow-up.

(a) It is important that the Government and the contractor know and exercise their rights in inventions conceived or first actually reduced to practice in the course of or under Government contracts in order to ensure their expeditious availability to the public and to enable the Government, the contractor, and the public to avoid unnecessary payment of royalties and to defend themselves against claims and suits for patent infringement. To attain these ends, contracts having a patent rights clause should be so administered that—

(1) Inventions are identified, disclosed, and reported as required by the contract, and elections are made;

(2) The rights of the Government in such inventions are established;

(3) Where patent protection is appropriate, patent applications are timely filed and prosecuted by contractors or by the Government;

(4) The rights of the government in filed patent applications are documented by formal instruments such as licenses or assignments; and

(5) Expeditious commercial utilization of such inventions is achieved.

(b) If a subject invention is made under funding agreements of more than one agency, at the request of the contractor or on their own initiative, the agencies shall designate one agency as responsible for administration of the rights of the Government in the invention.

FAR 27.305-2 Follow-up by contractor.

(a) *Contractor procedures.* If required by the applicable clause, the contractor shall establish and maintain effective procedures to ensure its patent rights obligations are met and that subject inventions are timely identified and disclosed, and when appropriate, patent applications are filed.

(b) *Contractor reports.* Contractors shall submit all reports required by the patent rights clause to the contracting officer or other representative designated for such purpose in the contract. Agencies may, in their implementing instructions, provide specific forms for use on an optional basis for such reporting.

FAR 27.305-3 Follow-up by Government.

(a) Agencies shall maintain appropriate follow-up procedures to protect the Government's interest and to check that subject inventions are identified and disclosed, and when appropriate, patent applications are filed, and that the Government's rights therein are established and protected. Follow-up activities for contracts that include a clause referenced in 27.304-2 shall be coordinated with the appropriate agency.

(b) The contracting officer administering the contract (or other representative specifically designated in the contract for such purpose) is responsible for receiving invention disclosures, reports, confirmatory instruments, notices, requests, and other documents and information submitted by the contractor pursuant to a patent rights clause. If the contractor fails to furnish documents or information as called for by the clause within the time required, the contracting officer shall promptly request the contractor to supply the required documents or information and, if the failure persists, shall take appropriate action to secure compliance. Invention disclosures, reports, confirmatory instruments, notices, requests, and other documents and information relating to patent rights clauses shall be promptly furnished by the contracting officer administering the contract (or other designee) to the procuring agency or contracting activity for which the procurement was made for appropriate action.

(c) Contracting activities shall establish appropriate procedures to detect and correct failures by the contractor to comply with its obligations under the patent rights clauses, such as failures to disclose and report subject inventions, both during and after contract performance. Ordinarily a contractor should have written instructions for its employees covering compliance with these contract obligations. Government effort to review and correct contractor compliance with its patent rights obligations should be directed primarily towards contracts that, because of the nature of the research, development, or experimental work or the large dollar amount spent on such work, are more likely to result in subject inventions significant in number or quality, and towards contracts when there is reason to believe the contractors may not be complying with their contractual obligations. Other contracts may be reviewed using a spot-check method, as feasible. Appropriate follow-up procedures and activities may include the investigation or review of selected contracts or contractors by those qualified in patent and technical matters to detect failures to comply with contract obligations.

(d) Follow-up activities should include, where appropriate, use of Government patent personnel—

(1) To interview agency technical personnel to identify novel developments made in contracts;

(2) To review technical reports submitted by contractors with cognizant agency technical personnel;

(3) To check the Official Gazette of the United States Patent and Trademark Office and other sources for patents issued to the contractor in fields related to its Government contracts; and

(4) If additional information is required, to have cognizant Government personnel interview contractor personnel regarding work under the contract involved, observe the work on site, and inspect laboratory notebooks and other records of the contractor related to work under the contract.

(e) If it is determined that a contractor or subcontractor does not have a clear understanding of the rights and obligations of the parties under a patent rights clause, or that its procedures for complying with the clause are deficient, a post-award orientation conference or letter should ordinarily be used to explain these rights and obligations (see Subpart 42.5). When a contractor fails to establish, maintain, or follow effective procedures for identifying, disclosing, and, when appropriate, filing patent applications on inventions (if such procedures are required by the patent rights clause), or after appropriate notice fails to correct any deficiency, the contracting officer may require the contractor to make available for examination books, records, and documents relating to the contractor's inventions in the same field of technology as the contract effort to enable a determination of whether there are such inventions and may invoke the withholding of payments provision (if any) of the clause. The withholding of payments provision (if any) of the patent rights clause or of any other contract clause may also be invoked if the contractor fails to disclose a subject invention. Significant or repeated failures by a contractor to comply with the patent rights obligation in its contracts shall be documented and made a part of the general file (see 4.801(c)(3)).

FAR 27.305-4 Conveyance of invention rights acquired by the Government.

(a) Agencies are responsible for those procedures necessary to protect the Government's interest in subject inventions. When the Government acquires the entire right, title, and interest in an invention by contract, this is normally accomplished by an assignment either from each inventor to the contractor and from the contractor to the Government, or from the inventor to the Government with the consent of the contractor, so that the chain of title from the inventor to the Government is clearly established. When the Government's rights are limited to a license, there should be a confirmatory instrument to that effect.

(b) The form of conveyance of title from the inventor to the contractor must be legally sufficient to convey the rights the contractor is required to convey to the Government. Agencies may, by supplemental instructions, develop suitable assignments, licenses, and other papers evidencing any rights of the Government in patents or patent applications, including such instruments as may be required to be recorded in the Statutory Register or documented in the Government Register maintained by the U.S. Patent and Trademark Office pursuant to Executive Order 9424, February 18, 1944.

FAR 27.305-5 Publication or release of invention disclosures.

(a) In accordance with the policy at 27.302(i), to protect their mutual interest, contractors and the Government should cooperate in deferring the publication or release of invention disclosures until the filing of the first patent application, and use their best efforts to achieve prompt filing when publication or release may be imminent. The Government will, on its part and to the extent authorized by 35 U.S.C. 205, withhold from disclosure to the public any invention disclosures reported under the patent rights clauses of 52.227-11, 52.227-12, or 52.227-13 for a reasonable time in order for patent applications to be filed. The policy in 27.302(i) regarding protection of confidentiality shall be followed.

(b) The Government will also use reasonable efforts to withhold from disclosure to the public for a reasonable time other information disclosing a reported invention included in any data delivered pursuant to contract requirements; provided, that the contractor notifies the agency as to the identity of the data and the invention to which it relates at the time of delivery of the data. Such notification must be to both the contracting officer and any patent representative to which the invention is reported, if other than the contracting officer.

(c) As an additional protection for small business firms and nonprofit organizations 37 CFR Part 401 prescribes that agencies shall not disclose or release, in accordance with 35 U.S.C. 205, for a period of 18 months from the filing date of the application to third parties pursuant to request under the Freedom of Information Act or otherwise copies of any document which the agency obtained under contract which is part of an application for patent with the U.S. Patent and Trademark Office or any foreign patent office filed by the contractor (or its assignees, licensees, or employees) on a subject invention to which the contractor has elected to retain title. This prohibition does not extend to disclosure to other Government agencies or contractors of Government agencies under an obligation to maintain such information in confidence.

FAR 27.306 Licensing background patent rights to third parties.

(a) A contact with a small business firm or nonprofit organization will not contain a provision allowing the Government to require the licensing to third parties of inventions owned by the contractor that are not subject inventions unless such provision has been approved by the agency head and written justification has been signed by the agency head. Any such provision will clearly state whether the licensing may be required in connection with the practice of a subject invention, a specifically identified work object, or both. The agency head may not delegate the authority to approve such provisions or to sign justifications required for such provisions.

(b) The Government will not require the licensing of third parties under any such provision unless the agency head determines that the use of the invention by others is necessary for the practice of a subject invention or for the use of a work object of the contract and that such action is necessary to achieve the practical application of the subject invention or work object. Any such determination will be on the record after an opportunity for a hearing, and the contractor shall be given notification of the determination by certified or registered mail. The notification shall include a statement that any action commenced for judicial review of such determination must be brought by the contractor within 60 days after the notification.

FAR 52.227-1 Authorization and Consent.

As prescribed at 27.201-2(a), insert the following clause:

AUTHORIZATION AND CONSENT (JUL 1995)

(a) The Government authorizes and consents to all use and manufacture, in performing this contract or any subcontract at any tier, of any invention described in and covered by a United States patent (1) embodied in the structure or composition of any article the delivery of which is accepted by the Government under this contract or (2) used in machinery, tools, or methods whose use necessarily results from compliance by the Contractor or a subcontractor with (i) specifications or written provisions forming a part of this contract or (ii) specific written instructions given by the Contracting Officer directing the manner of performance. The entire liability to the Government for infringement of a patent of the United States shall be determined solely by the provisions of the indemnity clause, if any, included in this contract or any subcontract hereunder (including any lower-tier subcontract), and the Government assumes liability for all other infringement to the extent of the authorization and consent hereinabove granted.

(b) The Contractor agrees to include, and require inclusion of, this clause, suitably modified to identify the parties, in all subcontracts at any tier for supplies or services (including construction, architect-engineer services, and materials, supplies, models, samples, and design or testing services expected to exceed the simplified acquisition threshold); however, omission of this clause from any subcontract, including those at or below the simplified acquisition threshold, does not affect this authorization and consent.

(End of clause)

Alternate I (APR 1984). The following is substituted for paragraph (a) of the clause:

(a) The Government authorizes and consents to all use and manufacture of any invention described in and covered by a United States patent in the performance of this contract or any subcontract at any tier.

Alternate II (APR 1984). The following is substituted for paragraph (a) of the clause:

(a) The Government authorizes and consents to all use and manufacture in the performance of any order at any tier or subcontract at any tier placed under this contract for communication services and facilities for which rates, charges, and tariffs are *not* established by a government regulatory body, of any invention described in and covered by a United States patent—

(1) Embodied in the structure or composition of any article the delivery of which is accepted by the Government under this contract; or

(2) Used in machinery, tools, or methods whose use necessarily results from compliance by the Contractor or a subcontractor with specifications or written provisions forming a part of this contract or with specific written instructions given by the Contracting Officer directing the manner of performance.

FAR 52.227-2 Notice and Assistance Regarding Patent and Copyright Infringement.

As prescribed at 27.202-2, insert the following clause:

NOTICE AND ASSISTANCE REGARDING
PATENT AND COPYRIGHT INFRINGEMENT (AUG 1996)

(a) The Contractor shall report to the Contracting Officer, promptly and in reasonable written detail, each notice or claim of patent or copyright infringement based on the performance of this contract of which the Contractor has knowledge.

(b) In the event of any claim or suit against the Government on account of any alleged patent or copyright infringement arising out of the performance of this contract or out of the use of any supplies furnished or work or services performed under this contract, the Contractor shall furnish to the Government, when requested by the Contracting Officer, all evidence and information in possession of the Contractor pertaining to such suit or claim. Such evidence and information shall be furnished at the expense of the Government except where the Contractor has agreed to indemnify the Government.

(c) The Contractor agrees to include, and require inclusion of, this clause in all subcontracts at any tier for supplies or services (including construction and architect-engineer subcontracts and those for material, supplies, models, samples, or design or testing services) expected to exceed the simplified acquisition threshold at FAR 2.101.

(End of clause)

FAR 52.227-3 Patent Indemnity.

Insert the following clause as prescribed at 27.203-1(b), 27.203-2(a), or 27.203-4(a)(2) as applicable:

PATENT INDEMNITY (APR 1984)

(a) The Contractor shall indemnify the Government and its officers, agents, and employees against liability, including costs, for infringement of any United States patent (except a patent issued upon an application that is now or may hereafter be withheld from issue pursuant to a Secrecy Order under 35 U.S.C. 181) arising out of the manufacture or delivery of supplies, the performance of services, or the construction, alteration, modification, or repair of real property (hereinafter referred to as "construction work") under this contract, or out of the use or disposal by or for the account of the Government of such supplies or construction work.

(b) This indemnity shall not apply unless the Contractor shall have been informed as soon as practicable by the Government of the suit or action alleging such infringement and shall have been given such opportunity as is afforded by applicable laws, rules, or regulations to participate in its defense. Further, this indemnity shall not apply to

(1) An infringement resulting from compliance with specific written instructions of the Contracting Officer directing a change in the supplies to be delivered or in the materials or equipment to be used, or directing a manner of performance of the contract not normally used by the Contractor;

(2) An infringement resulting from addition to or change in supplies or components furnished or construction work performed that was made subsequent to delivery or performance; or

(3) A claimed infringement that is unreasonably settled without the consent of the Contractor, unless required by final decree of a court of competent jurisdiction.

(End of clause)

Alternate I (APR 1984). The following paragraph (c) is added to the clause:

(c) This patent indemnification shall not apply to the following items: _____

[*Contracting Officer list and/or identify the items to be excluded from this indemnity*]

Alternate II (APR 1984). The following paragraph (c) is added to the clause:

(c) This patent indemnification shall cover the following items: _____

[*List and/or identify the items to be included under this indemnity*]

Alternate III (JUL 1995). The following paragraph is added to the clause:

( ) As to subcontracts at any tier for communication service, this clause shall apply only to individual communication service authorizations over the simplified acquisition threshold issued under this contract and covering those communications services and facilities;

(1) That are or have been sold or offered for sale by the Contractor to the public;

(2) that can be provided over commercially available equipment; or

(3) that involve relatively minor modifications.

FAR 52.227-4 Patent Indemnity—Construction Contracts.

As prescribed at 27.203-5, insert the following clause:

PATENT INDEMNITY—CONSTRUCTION CONTRACTS (APR 1984)

Except as otherwise provided, the Contractor agrees to indemnify the Government and its officers, agents, and employees against liability, including costs and expenses, for infringement upon any United States patent (except a patent issued upon an application that is now or may hereafter be withheld from issue pursuant to a Secrecy Order under 35 U.S.C. 181) arising out of performing this contract or out of the use or disposal by or for the account of the Government of supplies furnished or work performed under this contract.

(End of clause)

Alternate I (APR 1984) Designate the first paragraph as paragraph (a) and add the following to the basic clause as paragraph (b):

(b) This patent indemnification shall not apply to the following items: _____

Contracting Officer specifically identify the item to be excluded.]

NOTE: Exclusion from indemnity of specified, identified patents, as distinguished from items, is the exclusive prerogative of the agency head or designee (see 27.203-6).

FAR 52.227-5 Waiver of Indemnity.

As prescribed at 27.203-6, insert the following clause:

WAIVER OF INDEMNITY (APR 1984)

Any provision or clause of this contract to the contrary notwithstanding, the Government hereby authorizes and consents to the use and manufacture, solely in performing this contract, of any invention covered by the United States patents identified below and waives indemnification by the Contractor with respect to such patents: _____

[Contracting Officer identify the patents by number or by other means if more appropriate.]

(End of clause)

FAR 52.227-6 Royalty Information.

As prescribed at 27.204-2, insert the following provision:

ROYALTY INFORMATION (APR 1984)

(a) *Cost or charges for royalties.* When the response to this solicitation contains costs or charges for royalties totaling more than $250, the following information shall be included in the response relating to each separate item of royalty or license fee:

(1) Name and address of licensor.

(2) Date of license agreement.

(3) Patent numbers, patent application serial numbers, or other basis on which the royalty is payable.

(4) Brief description, including any part or model numbers of each contract item or component on which the royalty is payable.

(5) Percentage or dollar rate of royalty per unit.

(6) Unit price of contract item.

(7) Number of units.

(8) Total dollar amount of royalties.

(b) *Copies of current licenses.* In addition, if specifically requested by the Contracting Officer before execution of the contract, the offeror shall furnish a copy of the current license agreement and an identification of applicable claims of specific patents.

(End of provision)

Alternate I. (APR 1984) Substitute the following for the introductory portion of paragraph (a) of the basic clause:

When the response to this solicitation covers charges for special construction or special assembly that contain costs or charges for royalties totaling more than $250, the following information shall be included in the response relating to each separate item of royalty or license fee:

FAR 52.227-7 Patents—Notice of Government Licensee.

As prescribed at 27.204-3(c), insert the following provision:

PATENTS—NOTICE OF GOVERNMENT LICENSEE (APR 1984)

The Government is obligated to pay a royalty applicable to the proposed acquisition because of a license agreement between the Government and the patent owner. The patent number is _____ [*Contracting Officer fill in*], and the royalty rate is _____ [*Contracting Officer fill in*]. If the offeror is the owner of, or a licensee under, the patent, indicate below:

[Owner] [Licensee]

If an offeror does not indicate that it is the owner or a licensee of the patent, its offer will be evaluated by adding thereto an amount equal to the royalty.

(End of provision)

FAR 52.227-8 [Reserved]

FAR 52.227-9 Refund of Royalties.

As prescribed at 27.206-2, insert the following clause. In solicitations and contracts with an incentive fee arrangement, change "price" to "target cost and target profit" wherever it appears.

REFUND OF ROYALTIES (APR 1984)

(a) The contract price includes certain amounts for royalties payable by the Contractor or subcontractors or both, which amounts have been reported to the Contracting Officer.

(b) The term "royalties" as used in this clause refers to any costs or charges in the nature of royalties, license fees, patent or license amortization costs, or the like, for the use of or for rights in patents and patent applications in connection with performing this contract or any subcontract hereunder.

(c) The Contractor shall furnish to the Contracting Officer, before final payment under this contract, a statement of royalties paid or required to be paid in connection with performing this contract and subcontracts hereunder together with the reasons.

(d) The Contractor will be compensated for royalties reported under paragraph (c) of this clause, only to the extent that such royalties were included in the contract price and are determined by the Contracting Officer to be properly chargeable to the Government and allocable to the contract. To the extent that any royalties that are included in the contract price are not in fact paid by the Contractor or are determined by the Contracting Officer not to be properly chargeable to the Government and allocable to the contract, the contract price shall be reduced. Repayment or credit to the Government shall be made as the Contracting Officer directs.

(e) If, at any time within 3 years after final payment under this contract, the Contractor for any reason is relieved in whole or in part from the payment of the royalties included in the final contract price as adjusted pursuant to paragraph (d) of this clause, the Contractor shall promptly notify the Contracting Officer of that fact and shall reimburse the Government in a corresponding amount.

(f) The substance of this clause, including this paragraph (f), shall be included in any subcontract in which the amount of royalties reported during negotiation of the subcontract exceeds $250.

(End of clause)

FAR 52.227-10 Filing of Patent Applications—Classified Subject Matter.

As prescribed at 27.207-2, insert the following clause:

FILING OF PATENT APPLICATIONS—
CLASSIFIED SUBJECT MATTER (APR 1984)

(a) Before filing or causing to be filed a patent application in the United States disclosing any subject matter of this contract classified "Secret" or higher, the Contractor shall, citing the 30-day provision below, transmit the proposed application to the Contracting Officer. The government shall determine whether, for reasons of national security, the application should be placed under an order of secrecy, sealed in accordance with the provision of 35 U.S.C. 181-188, or the issuance of a patent otherwise delayed under pertinent United States statutes or regulations. The Contractor shall observe any instructions of the Contracting Officer regarding the manner of delivery of the patent application to the United States Patent Office, but the Contractor shall not be denied the right to file the application. If the Contracting Officer shall not have given any such instructions within 30 days from the date of mailing or other transmittal of the proposed application, the Contractor may file the application.

(b) Before filing a patent application in the United States disclosing any subject matter of this contract classified "Confidential," the Contractor shall furnish to the Contracting Officer a copy of the application for Government determination whether, for reasons of national security, the application should be placed under an order of secrecy or the issuance of a patent should be otherwise delayed under pertinent United States statutes or regulations.

(c) Where the subject matter of this contract is classified for reasons of security, the Contractor shall not file, or cause to be filed, in any country other than in the United States as provided in paragraphs (a) and (b) of this clause, an application or registration for a patent containing any of the subject matter of this contract without first obtaining written approval of the Contracting Officer.

(d) When filing any patent application coming within the scope of this clause, the Contractor shall observe all applicable security regulations covering the transmission of classified subject matter and shall promptly furnish to the Contracting Officer the serial number, filing date, and name of the country of any such application. When transmitting the application to the United States Patent Office, the Contractor shall by separate letter identify by agency and number the contract or contracts that require security classification markings to be placed on the application.

(e) The Contractor agrees to include, and require the inclusion of, this clause in all subcontracts at any tier that cover or are likely to cover classified subject matter.

(End of clause)

FAR 52.227-11 Patent Rights—Retention by the Contractor (Short Form).

As prescribed in 27.303(a), insert the following clause:

PATENT RIGHTS—RETENTION BY THE CONTRACTOR
(SHORT FORM) (JUN 1997)

(a) *Definitions.* (1) "Invention" means any invention or discovery which is or may be patentable or otherwise protectable under title 35 of the United States Code, or any novel variety of plant which is or may be protected under the Plant Variety Protection Act (7 U.S.C. 2321, *et seq.*).

(2) "Made" when used in relation to any invention means the conception or first actual reduction to practice of such invention.

(3) "Nonprofit organization" means a university or other institution of higher education or an organization of the type described in section 501(c)(3) of the Internal Revenue Code of 1954 (26 U.S.C. 501(c)) and exempt from taxation under section 501(a) of the Internal Revenue Code (26 U.S.C. 501(a)) or any nonprofit scientific or educational organization qualified under a state nonprofit organization statute.

(4) "Practical application" means to manufacture, in the case of a composition or product; to practice, in the case of a process or method, or to operate, in the case of a machine or system; and, in each case, under such conditions as to establish that the invention is being utilized and that its benefits are, to the extent permitted by law or Government regulations, available to the public on reasonable terms.

(5) "Small business firm" means a small business concern as defined at section 2 of Pub. L. 85-536 (15 U.S.C. 632) and implementing regulations of the Administrator of the Small Business Administration. For the purpose of this clause, the size standards for small business concerns involved in Government procurement and subcontracting at 13 CFR 121.3-8 and 13 CFR 121.3-12, respectively, will be used.

(6) "Subject invention" means any invention of the contractor conceived or first actually reduced to practice in the performance of work under this contract, provided that in

the case of a variety of plant, the date of determination (as defined in section 41(d) of the Plant Variety Protection Act, 7 U.S.C. 2401(d)) must also occur during the period of contract performance.

(b) *Allocation of principal rights.* The Contractor may retain the entire right, title, and interest throughout the world to each subject invention subject to the provisions of this clause and 35 U.S.C. 203. With respect to any subject invention in which the Contractor retains title, the Federal Government shall have a nonexclusive, nontransferable, irrevocable, paid-up license to practice or have practiced for or on behalf of the United States the subject invention throughout the world.

(c) *Invention disclosure, election of title, and filing of patent application by contractor.* (1) The Contractor will disclose each subject invention to the Federal agency within 2 months after the inventor discloses it in writing to Contractor personnel responsible for patent matters. The disclosure to the agency shall be in the form of a written report and shall identify the contract under which the invention was made and the inventor(s). It shall be sufficiently complete in technical detail to convey a clear understanding to the extent known at the time of the disclosure, of the nature, purpose, operation, and the physical, chemical, biological or electrical characteristics of the invention. The disclosure shall also identify any publication, on sale or public use of the invention and whether a manuscript describing the invention has been submitted for publication and, if so, whether it has been accepted for publication at the time of disclosure. In addition, after disclosure to the agency, the contractor will promptly notify the agency of the acceptance of any manuscript describing the invention for publication or of any on sale or public use planned by the Contractor.

(2) The Contractor will elect in writing whether or not to retain title to any such invention by notifying the Federal agency within 2 years of disclosure to the Federal agency. However, in any case where publication, on sale or public use has initiated the 1-year statutory period wherein valid patent protection can still be obtained in the United States, the period for election of title may be shortened by the agency to a date that is no more than 60 days prior to the end of the statutory period.

(3) The Contractor will file its initial patent application on a subject invention to which it elects to retain title within 1 year after election of title, or, if earlier, prior to the end of any statutory period wherein valid patent protection can be obtained in the United States after a publication, on sale, or public use. The Contractor will file patent applications in additional countries or international patent offices within either 10 months of the corresponding initial patent application or 6 months from the date permission is granted by the Commissioner of Patents and Trademarks to file foreign patent applications where such filing has been prohibited by a Secrecy Order.

(4) Requests for extension of the time for disclosure election, and filing under subparagraph (c)(1), (2), and (3) of this clause may, at the discretion of the agency, be granted.

(d) *Conditions when the government may obtain title.* The Contractor will convey to the Federal agency, upon written request, title to any subject invention—

(1) If the Contractor fails to disclose or elect title to the subject invention within the times specified in paragraph (c) of this clause, or elects not to retain title; provided, that the agency may only request title within 60 days after learning of the failure of the Contractor to disclose or elect within the specified times.

(2) In those countries in which the Contractor fails to file patent applications within the times specified in paragraph (c) of this clause; *provided, however,* that if the Contractor has filed a patent application in a country after the times specified in paragraph (c) of this clause, but prior to its receipt of the written request of the Federal agency, the Contractor shall continue to retain title in that country.

(3) In any country in which the Contractor decides not to continue the prosecution of any application for, to pay the maintenance fees on, or defend in reexamination or opposition proceeding on, a patent on a subject invention.

(e) *Minimum rights to Contractor and protection of the Contractor right to file.* (1) The Contractor will retain a nonexclusive royalty-free license throughout the world in each subject invention to which the Government obtains title, except if the Contractor fails to disclose the invention within the times specified in paragraph (c) of this clause. The Contractor's license extends to its domestic subsidiary and affiliates, if any, within the corporate structure of which the Contractor is a party and includes the right to grant sublicenses of the same scope to the extent the Contractor was legally obligated to do so at the time the contract was awarded. The license is transferable only with the approval of the Federal Agency, except when transferred to the successor of that part of the Contractor's business to which the invention pertains.

(2) The Contractor's domestic license may be revoked or modified by the funding Federal agency to the extent necessary to achieve expeditious practical application of subject invention pursuant to an application for an exclusive license submitted in accordance with applicable provisions at 37 CFR Part 404 and agency licensing regulations (if any). This license will not be revoked in that field of use or the geographical areas in which the Contractor has achieved practical application and continues to make the benefits of the invention reasonably accessible to the public. The license in any foreign country may be revoked or modified at the discretion of the funding Federal agency to the extent the Contractor, its licensees, or the domestic subsidiaries or affiliates have failed to achieve practical application in that foreign country.

(3) Before revocation or modification of the license, the funding Federal agency will furnish the Contractor a written notice of its intention to revoke or modify the license, and the Contractor will be allowed 30 days (or such other time as may be authorized by the funding Federal agency for good cause shown by the Contractor) after the notice to show cause why the license should not be revoked or modified. The Contractor has the right to appeal, in accordance with applicable regulations in 37 CFR Part 404 and agency regulations, if any, concerning the licensing Government-owned inventions, any decision concerning their revocation or modification of the license.

(f) *Contractor action to protect the Government's interest.* (1) The Contractor agrees to execute or to have executed and promptly deliver to the Federal agency all instruments necessary to

          (i) Establish or confirm the rights the Government has throughout the world in those subject inventions to which the Contractor elects to retain title; and

          (ii) Convey title to the Federal agency when requested under paragraph (d) of this clause and to enable the Government to obtain patent protection throughout the world in that subject invention.

          (2) The Contractor agrees to require, by written agreement, its employees, other than clerical and nontechnical employees, to disclose promptly in writing to personnel identified as responsible for the administration of patent matters and in a format suggested by the Contractor each subject invention made under contract in order that the Contractor can comply with the disclosure provisions of paragraph (c) of this clause, and to execute all papers necessary to file patent applications on subject inventions and to establish the Government's rights in the subject inventions. This disclosure format should require, as a minimum, the information required by subparagraph (c)(1) of this clause. The Contractor shall instruct such employees, through employee agreements or other suitable educational programs, on the importance of reporting inventions in sufficient time to permit the filing of patent applications prior to U.S. or foreign statutory bars.

          (3) The Contractor will notify the Federal agency of any decisions not to continue the prosecution of a patent application, pay maintenance fees, or defend in a reexamination or opposition proceeding on a patent, in any country, not less than 30 days before the expiration of the response period required by the relevant patent office.

          (4) The Contractor agrees to include, within the specification of any United States patent application and any patent issuing thereon covering a subject invention, the following statement, "This invention was made with Government support under (identify the contract) awarded by (identify the Federal agency). The Government has certain rights in the invention."

          (g) *Subcontracts.* (1) The Contractor will include this clause, suitably modified to identify the parties, in all subcontracts, regardless of tier, for experimental, developmental, or research work to be performed by a small business firm or domestic nonprofit organization. The subcontractor will retain all rights provided for the Contractor in this clause, and the Contractor will not, as part of the consideration for awarding the subcontract, obtain rights in the subcontractor's subject inventions.

          (2) The Contractor will include in all other subcontracts, regardless of tier, for experimental, developmental, or research work the patent rights clause required by Subpart 27.3.

          (3) In the case of subcontracts, at any tier, the agency, subcontractor, and the Contractor agree that the mutual obligations of the parties created by this clause constitute a contract between the subcontractor and the Federal agency with respect to the matters covered

by the clause; *provided, however,* that nothing in this paragraph is intended to confer any jurisdiction under the Contract Disputes Act in connection with proceedings under paragraph (j) of this clause.

(h) *Reporting on utilization of subject inventions.* The Contractor agrees to submit, on request, periodic reports no more frequently than annually on the utilization of a subject invention or on efforts at obtaining such utilization that are being made by the Contractor or its licensees or assignees. Such reports shall include information regarding the status of development, date of first commercial sale or use, gross royalties received by the Contractor, and such other data and information as the agency may reasonably specify. The Contractor also agrees to provide additional reports as may be requested by the agency in connection with any march-in proceeding undertaken by the agency in accordance with paragraph (j) of this clause. As required by 35 U.S.C. 202(c)(5), the agency agrees it will not disclose such information to persons outside the Government without permission of the Contractor.

(i) *Preference for United States industry.* Notwithstanding any other provision of this clause, the Contractor agrees that neither it nor any assignee will grant to any person the exclusive right to use or sell any subject invention in the United States unless such person agrees that any product embodying the subject invention or produced through the use of the subject invention will be manufactured substantially in the United States. However, in individual cases, the requirement for such an agreement may be waived by the Federal agency upon a showing by the Contractor or its assignee that reasonable but unsuccessful efforts have been made to grant licenses on similar terms to potential licensees that would be likely to manufacture substantially in the United States or that under the circumstances domestic manufacture is not commercially feasible.

(j) *March-in rights.* The Contractor agrees that, with respect to any subject invention in which it has acquired title, the Federal agency has the right in accordance with the procedures in 37 CFR 401.6 and any supplemental regulations of the agency to require the Contractor, an assignee or exclusive licensee of a subject invention to grant a nonexclusive, partially exclusive, or exclusive license in any field of use to a responsible applicant or applicants, upon terms that are reasonable under the circumstances, and if the Contractor, assignee, or exclusive licensee refuses such a request the Federal agency has the right to grant such a license itself if the Federal agency determines that—

(1) Such action is necessary because the Contractor or assignee has not taken, or is not expected to take within a reasonable time, effective steps to achieve practical application of the subject invention in such field of use;

(2) Such action is necessary to alleviate health or safety needs which are not reasonably satisfied by the Contractor, assignee, or their licensees;

(3) Such action is necessary to meet requirements for public use specified by Federal regulations and such requirements are not reasonably satisfied by the Contractor, assignee, or licensees; or

(4) Such action is necessary because the agreement required by paragraph (i) of this clause has not been obtained or waived or because a licensee of the exclusive right to use or sell any subject invention in the United States is in breach of such agreement.

(k) *Special provisions for contracts with nonprofit organizations.* If the Contractor is a nonprofit organization, it agrees that—

(1) Rights to a subject invention in the United States may not be assigned without the approval of the Federal agency, except where such assignment is made to an organization which has as one of its primary functions the management of inventions; *provided,* that such assignee will be subject to the same provisions as the Contractor;

(2) The Contractor will share royalties collected on a subject invention with the inventor, including Federal employee co-inventors (when the agency deems it appropriate) when the subject invention is assigned in accordance with 35 U.S.C. 202(e) and 37 CFR 401.10;

(3) The balance of any royalties or income earned by the Contractor with respect to subject inventions, after payment of expenses (including payments to inventors) incidental to the administration of subject inventions will be utilized for the support of scientific research or education; and

(4) It will make efforts that are reasonable under the circumstances to attract licensees of subject inventions that are small business firms, and that it will give a preference to a small business firm when licensing a subject invention if the Contractor determines that the small business firm has a plan or proposal for marketing the invention which, if executed, is equally as likely to bring the invention to practical application as any plans or proposals from applicants that are not small business firms; *provided,* that the Contractor is also satisfied that the small business firm has the capability and resources to carry out its plan or proposal. The decision whether to give a preference in any specific case will be at the discretion of the contractor. However, the Contractor agrees that the Secretary of Commerce may review the Contractor's licensing program and decisions regarding small business applicants, and the Contractor will negotiate changes to its licensing policies, procedures, or practices with the Secretary of Commerce when the Secretary's review discloses that the Contractor could take reasonable steps to more effectively implement the requirements of this subparagrah (k)(4).

(1) *Communications.* (Complete according to agency instructions.)

(End of clause)

Alternate I (JUN 1989). As prescribed in 27.303(a)(3), add the following sentence at the end of paragraph (b) of the basic clause:

The license shall include the right of the Government to sublicense foreign governments, their nationals and international organizations pursuant to the following treaties or international agreements: _____ *

[* Contracting Officer complete with the names of applicable existing treaties or international agreements. The above language is not intended to apply to treaties or agreements that are in effect on the date of the award but are not listed.]

Alternate II (JUN 1989). As prescribed in 27.303(a)(3), add the following sentence at the end of paragraph (b) of the basic clause:

The agency reserves the right to unilaterally amend this contract to identify specific treaties or international agreements entered into or to be entered into by the Government after the effective date of the contract and effectuate those license or other rights which are necessary for the Government to meet its obligations to foreign governments, their nationals and international organizations under such treaties or international agreements with respect to subject inventions made after the date of the amendment.

Alternate III (JUN 1989). As prescribed in 27.303(a)(4), substitute the following in place of subparagraph (k)(3) of the basic clause:

(3) After payment of patenting costs, licensing costs, payments to inventors, and other expenses incidental to the administration of subject inventions, the balance of any royalties or income earned and retained by the Contractor during any fiscal year on subject inventions under this or any successor contract containing the same requirement, up to any amount equal to 5 percent of the budget of the facility for that fiscal year, shall be used by the Contractor for the scientific research, development, and education consistent with the research and development mission and objectives of the facility, including activities that increase the licensing potential of other inventions of the facility. If the balance exceeds 5 percent, 75 percent of the excess above 5 percent shall be paid by the Contractor to the Treasury of the United States and the remaining 25 percent shall be used by the Contractor only for the same purposes as described above. To the extent it provides the most effective technology transfer, the licensing of subject inventions shall be administered by Contractor employees on location at the facility.

Alternate IV (JUN 1989). As prescribed in 27.303(a)(5), include the following subparagraph in paragraph (f) of the basic clause:

(5) The Contractor shall establish and maintain active and effective procedures to ensure that subject inventions are promptly identified and timely disclosed, and shall submit a description of the procedures to the Contracting Officer so that the Contracting Officer may evaluate and determine their effectiveness.

DEPARTMENT OF DEFENSE

DFARS SUBPART 227.3

PATENT RIGHTS UNDER GOVERNMENT CONTRACTS

DFARS 227.303 Contract clauses.

(a) Pursuant to FAR 27.304-1(e), the contracting officer shall insert the clause at 252.227-7039, Patents—Reporting of Subject Inventions, in solicitations and contracts containing the clause at FAR 52.227-11, Patent Rights—Retention by the Contractor (Short Form).

DFARS 227.304 Procedures.

DFARS 227.304-1 General.

Interim and final invention reports and notification of all subcontracts for experimental, developmental, or research work (FAR 27.304-1(e)(2)(ii)) may be submitted on DD Form 882, Report of Inventions and Subcontracts.

DFARS 227.304-4 Subcontracts.

The contracting officer shall insert the clause at 252.227-7034, Patents-Subcontracts, in solicitations and contracts containing the clause at FAR 52.227-11, Patent Rights--Retention by the Contractor (Short Form).

DFARS 252.227-7039 Patents—Reporting of subject inventions.

As prescribed at 227.303(a), insert the following clause:

PATENTS—REPORTING OF SUBJECT INVENTIONS (APR 1990)

The Contractor shall furnish the Contracting Officer the following:

(a) Interim reports every twelve (12) months (or such longer period as may be specified by the Contracting Officer) from the date of the contract, listing subject inventions during that period and stating that all subject inventions have been disclosed or that there are no such inventions.

(b) A final report, within three (3) months after completion of the contracted work, listing all subject inventions or stating that there were no such inventions.

(c) Upon request, the filing date, serial number and title, a copy of the patent application and patent number, and issue data for any subject invention for which the Contractor has retained title.

(d) Upon request, the Contractor shall furnish the Government an irrevocable power to inspect and make copies of the patent application file.

(End of clause)

DFARS 227.7000 Scope.

This subpart prescribes policy, procedures, and instructions for use of clauses with respect to processing licenses, assignments, and infringement claims.

DFARS 227.7001 Policy.

Whenever a claim of infringement of privately owned rights in patented inventions or copyrighted works is asserted against any Department or Agency of the Department of Defense, all necessary steps shall be taken to investigate, and to settle administratively, deny, or otherwise dispose of such claim prior to suit against the United States. This subpart 227.70 does not apply to licenses or assignments acquired by the Department of Defense under the Patent Rights clauses.

DFARS 227.7002 Statutes pertaining to administrative claims of infringement.

Statutes pertaining to administrative claims of infringement in the Department of Defense include the following: the Foreign Assistance Act of 1961, 22 U.S.C. 2356 (formerly the Mutual Security Acts of 1951 and 1954); the Invention Secrecy Act, 35 U.S.C. 181-188; 10 U.S.C. 2386; 28 U.S.C. 1498; and 35 U.S.C. 286.

DFARS 227.7003 Claims for copyright infringement.

The procedures set forth herein will be followed, where applicable, in copyright infringement claims.

DFARS 227.7004 Requirements for filing an administrative claim for patent infringement.

(a) A patent infringement claim for compensation, asserted against the United States under any of the applicable statutes cited in 227.7002, must be actually communicated to and received by a Department, agency, organization, office, or field establishment within the Department of Defense. Claims must be in writing and should include the following:

(1) An allegation of infringement;

(2) A request for compensation, either expressed or implied;

(3) A citation of the patent or patents alleged to be infringed;

(4) A sufficient designation of the alleged infringing item or process to permit identification, giving the military or commercial designation, if known, to the claimant;

(5) A designation of at least one claim of each patent alleged to be infringed; or

(6) As an alternative to (a) (4) and (5) of this section, a declaration that the claimant has made a bona fide attempt to determine the item or process which is alleged to infringe, but was unable to do so, giving reasons, and stating a reasonable basis for his belief that his patent or patents are being infringed.

(b) In addition to the information listed in (a) of this section, the following material and information is generally necessary in the course of processing a claim of patent infringement. Claimants are encouraged to furnish this information at the time of filing a claim to permit the most expeditious processing and settlement of the claim.

(1) A copy of the asserted patent(s) and identification of all claims of the patent alleged to be infringed.

(2) Identification of all procurements known to claimant which involve the alleged infringing item or process, including the identity of the vendor or contractor and the Government procuring activity.

(3) A detailed identification of the accused article or process, particularly where the article or process relates to a component or subcomponent of the item procured, an element by element comparison of the representative claims with the accused article or process. If available, this identification should include documentation and drawings to illustrate the accused article or process in suitable detail to enable verification of the infringement comparison.

(4) Names and addresses of all past and present licenses under the patent(s), and copies of all license agreements and releases involving the patent(s).

(5) A brief description of all litigation in which the patent(s) has been or is now involved, and the present status thereof.

(6) A list of all persons to whom notices of infringement have been sent, including all departments and agencies of the Government, and a statement of the ultimate disposition of each.

(7) A description of Government employment or military service, if any, by the inventor and/or patent owner.

(8) A list of all Government contracts under which the inventor, patent owner, or anyone in privity with him performed work relating to the patented subject matter.

(9) Evidence of title to the patent(s) alleged to be infringed or other right to make the claim.

(10) A copy of the Patent Office file of each patent if available to claimant.

(11) Pertinent prior art known to claimant, not contained in the Patent Office file, particularly publications and foreign art.

In addition in the foregoing, if claimant can provide a statement that the investigation may be limited to the specifically identified accused articles or processes, or to a specific procurement, it may materially expedite determination of the claim.

(c) Any Department receiving an allegation of patent infringement which meets the requirements of this paragraph shall acknowledge the same and supply the other Departments which may have an interest therein with a copy of such communication and the acknowledgement thereof.

(1) For the Department of the Army—Chief, Patents, Copyrights, and Trademarks Division, U.S. Army Legal Services Agency;

(2) For the Department of the Navy—The Patent Counsel for Navy, Office of Naval Research;

(3) For the Department of the Air Force—Chief, Patents Division, Office of The Judge Advocate General;

(4) For the Defense Logistics Agency—The Office of Counsel; for the National Security Agency, the General Counsel;

(5) For the Defense Information Systems Agency—the Counsel;

(6) For the Defense Threat Reduction Agency—The General Counsel; and

(7) For the National Imagery and Mapping Agency—The Counsel.

(d) If a communication alleging patent infringement is received which does not meet the requirements set forth in paragraph (c) of this section, the sender shall be advised in writing—

(1) That his claim for infringement has not been satisfactorily presented, and

(2) Of the elements considered necessary to establish a claim.

(e) A communication making a proffer of a license in which no infringement is alleged shall not be considered as a claim for infringement.

DFARS 227.7005 Indirect notice of patent infringement claims.

(a) A communication by a patent owner to a Department of Defense contractor alleging that the contractor has committed acts of infringement in performance of a Government contract shall not be considered a claim within the meaning of 227.7004 until it meets the requirements specified therein.

(b) Any Department receiving an allegation of patent infringement which meets the requirements of 227.7004 shall acknowledge the same and supply the other Departments (see

227.7004(c)) which may have an interest therein with a copy of such communication and the acknowledgement thereof.

(c) If a communication covering an infringement claim or notice which does not meet the requirements of 227.7004(a) is received from a contractor, the patent owner shall be advised in writing as covered by the instructions of 227.7004(d).

DFARS 227.7006 Investigation and administrative disposition of claims.

An investigation and administrative determination (denial or settlement) of each claim shall be made in accordance with instructions and procedures established by each Department, subject to the following:

(a) When the procurement responsibility for the alleged infringing item or process is assigned to a single Department or only one Department is the purchaser of the alleged infringing item or process, and the funds of that Department only are to be charged in the settlement of the claim, that Department shall have the sole responsibility for the investigation and administrative determination of the claim and for the execution of any agreement in settlement of the claim. Where, however, funds of another Department are to be charged, in whole or in part, the approval of such Department shall be obtained as required by 208.7002. Any agreement in settlement of the claim, approved pursuant to 208.7002 shall be executed by each of the Departments concerned.

(b) When two or more Departments are the respective purchasers of alleged infringing items or processes and the funds of those Departments are to be charged in the settlement of the claim, the investigation and administrative determination shall be the responsibility of the Department having the predominant financial interest in the claim or of the Department or Departments as jointly agreed upon by the Departments concerned. The Department responsible for negotiation shall, throughout the negotiation, coordinate with the other Departments concerned and keep them advised of the status of the negotiation. Any agreement in the settlement of the claim shall be executed by each Department concerned.

DFARS 227.7007 Notification and disclosure to claimants.

When a claim is denied, the Department responsible for the administrative determination of the claim shall so notify the claimant or his authorized representative and provide the claimant a reasonable rationale of the basis for denying the claim. Disclosure of information or the rationale referred to above shall be subject to applicable statutes, regulations, and directives pertaining to security, access to official records, and the rights of others.

DFARS 227.7008 Settlement of indemnified claims.

Settlement of claims involving payment for past infringement shall not be made without the consent of, and equitable contribution by, each indemnifying contractor involved, unless such settlement is determined to be in the best interests of the Government and is coordinated with the Department of Justice with a view to preserving any rights of the Government against the contractors involved. If consent of and equitable contribution by the contractors are obtained, the settlement need not be coordinated with the Department of Justice.

DFARS 227.7009 Patent releases, license agreements, and assignments.

This section contains clauses for use in patent release and settlement agreements, license agreements, and assignments, executed by the Government, under which the Government acquires rights. Minor modifications of language (e.g., pluralization of "Secretary" or "Contracting Officer") in multi-departmental agreements may be made if necessary.

DFARS 227.7009-1 Required clauses.

(a) Covenant Against Contingent Fees. Insert the clause at FAR 52.203-5.

(b) Gratuities. Insert the clause at FAR 52.203-3.

(c) Assignment of Claims. Insert the clause at FAR 52.232-23.

(d) Disputes. Pursuant to FAR Subpart 33.2, insert the clause at FAR 52.233-1.

(e) Non-Estoppel. Insert the clause at 252.227-7000.

DFARS 227.7009-2 Clauses to be used when applicable.

(a) *Release of past infringement.* The clause at 252.227-7001, Release of Past Infringement, is an example which may be modified or omitted as appropriate for particular circumstances, but only upon the advice of cognizant patent or legal counsel. (See footnotes at end of clause.)

(b) *Readjustment of payments.* The clause at 252.227-7002, Readjustment of Payments, shall be inserted in contracts providing for payment of a running royalty.

(c) *Termination.* The clause at 252.227-7003, Termination, is an example for use in contracts providing for the payment of a running royalty. This clause may be modified or omitted as appropriate for particular circumstances, but only upon the advice of cognizant patent or legal counsel (see 227.7004(c)).

DFARS 227.7009-3 Additional clauses—contracts except running royalty contracts.

The following clauses are examples for use in patent release and settlement agreements, and license agreements not providing for payment by the Government of a running royalty.

(a) License Grant. Insert the clause at 252.227-7004.

(b) License Term. Insert one of the clauses at 252.227-7005 Alternate I or Alternate II, as appropriate.

DFARS 227.7009-4 Additional clauses—contracts providing for payment of a running royalty.

The clauses set forth below are examples which may be used in patent release and settlement agreements, and license agreements, when it is desired to cover the subject matter thereof and the contract provides for payment of a running royalty.

(a) *License grant—running royalty.* No Department shall be obligated to pay royalties unless the contract is signed on behalf of such Department. Accordingly, the License Grant clause at 252.227-7006 should be limited to the practice of the invention by or for the signatory Department or Departments.

(b) *License term—running royalty.* The clause at 252.227-7007 is a sample form for expressing the license term.

(c) *Computation of royalties.* The clause at 252.227-7008 providing for the computation of royalties, may be of varying scope depending upon the nature of the royalty bearing article, the volume of procurement, and the type of contract pursuant to which the procurement is to be accomplished.

(d) *Reporting and payment of royalties.* (1) The contract should contain a provision specifying the office designated within the specific Department involved to make any necessary reports to the contractor of the extent of use of the licensed subject matter by the entire Department, and such office shall be charged with the responsibility of obtaining from all procuring offices of that Department the information necessary to make the required reports and corresponding vouchers necessary to make the required payments. The clause at 252.227-7009 is a sample for expressing reporting and payment of royalties requirements.

(2) Where more than one Department or Government Agency is licensed and there is a ceiling on the royalties payable in any reporting period, the licensing Departments or Agencies shall coordinate with respect to the pro rata share of royalties to be paid by each.

(e) *License to other government agencies.* When it is intended that a license on the same terms and conditions be available to other departments and agencies of the Government, the clause at 252.227-7010 is an example which may be used.

DFARS 227.7010 Assignments.

(a) The clause at 252.227-7011 is an example which may be used in contracts of assignment of patent rights to the Government.

(b) To facilitate proof of contracts of assignments, the acknowledgement of the contractor should be executed before a notary public or other officer authorized to administer oaths (35 U.S.C. 261).

DFARS 227.7011 Procurement of rights in inventions, patents, and copyrights.

Even though no infringement has occurred or been alleged, it is the policy of the Department of Defense to procure rights under patents, patent applications, and copyrights whenever it is in the Government's interest to do so and the desired rights can be obtained at a fair price. The required and suggested clauses at 252.227-7004 and 252.227-7010 shall be required and suggested clauses, respectively, for license agreements and assignments made under this paragraph. The instructions at 227.7009-3 and 227.7010 concerning the applicability and use of those clauses shall be followed insofar as they are pertinent.

DFARS 227.7012 Contract format.

The format at 252.227-7012 appropriately modified where necessary, may be used for contracts of release, license, or assignment.

DFARS 227.7013 Recordation.

Executive Order No. 9424 of 18 February 1944 requires all executive Departments and agencies of the Government to forward through appropriate channels to the Commissioner of Patents and Trademarks, for recording, all Government interests in patents or applications for patents.

NASA SUBPART 1827.3

PATENT RIGHTS UNDER GOVERNMENT CONTRACTS

NFS 1827.301 Definitions.

Administrator, as used in this subpart, means the Administrator of NASA or a duly authorized representative.

Contract, as used in this subpart, means any actual or proposed contract, agreement, understanding, or other arrangement, and includes any assignment, substitution of parties, or subcontract executed or entered into thereunder.

Made, in lieu of the definition in FAR 27.301, as used in this subpart, means conceived or first actually reduced to practice; provided that in the case of a variety of plant, the date of determination (as defined in Section 41(d) of the Plant Variety Protection Act, 7 U.S.C. 2401(d)) must also occur during the period of contract performance.

Reportable item, as used in this subpart, means any invention, discovery, improvement, or innovation of the contractor, whether or not patentable or otherwise protectible under Title 35 of the United States Code, made in the performance of any work under any NASA contract or in the performance of any work that is reimbursable under any clause in any NASA contract providing for reimbursement of costs incurred before the effective date of the contract. Reportable items include, but are not limited to, new processes, machines, manufactures, and compositions of matter, and improvements to, or new applications of, existing processes, machines, manufactures, and compositions of matter. Reportable items also include new computer programs, and improvements to, or new applications of, existing computer programs, whether or not copyrightable or otherwise protectible under Title 17 of the United States Code.

Subject invention, in lieu of the definition in FAR 27.301, as used in this subpart, means any reportable item that is or may be patentable or otherwise protectible under Title 35 of the United States Code, or any novel variety of plant that is or may be protectible under the Plant Variety Protection Act (7 U.S.C. 2321 et seq.).

NFS 1827.302 Policy. (NASA supplements paragraphs (a), (b), (c), (d), (e), (f), (g), and (i)).

(a) *Introduction.*

(i) NASA policy with respect to any invention, discovery, improvement, or innovation made in the performance of work under any NASA contract or subcontract with other than a small business firm or a nonprofit organization and the allocation to related property rights is based upon Section 305 of the National Aeronautics and Space Act of 1958, as amended (42 U.S.C. 2457) (the Act); and, to the extent consistent with this statute, the Presidential Memorandum or Government Patent Policy to the Heads of Executive Departments and Agencies, dated February 18, 1983, and Section 1(d)(4) of Executive Order 12591.

NASA policy with respect to any invention made in the performance of experimental, developmental, or research work with a small business firm or a nonprofit organization is based on 35 U.S.C. Chapter 18, as amended.

(ii) NASA contracts subject to Section 305 of the Act shall ensure the prompt reporting of reportable items in other to protect the Government's interest and to provide widest practicable and appropriate dissemination, early utilization, expeditious development, and continued availability for the benefit of the scientific, industrial, and commercial communities and the general public.

(b) *Contractor right to elect title.*

(i) For NASA contracts, the contractor right to elect title only applies to contracts with small businesses and non-profit organizations. For other business entities, see subdivision (ii) of this paragraph.

(ii) Contractor right to request a waiver of title. For NASA contracts with other than a small business firm or a nonprofit organization (contracts subject to Section 305 of the Act), it is the policy of NASA to waive the rights (to acquire title) of the United States (with the reservation of a Government license set forth in FAR 27.302(c) and the march-in rights of FAR 27.302(f) and 1827.302(f)) in and to any subject invention if the Administrator determines that the interests of the United States will be served. This policy, as well as the procedures and instructions for such waiver of rights, is stated in the NASA Patent Waiver Regulations, 14 CFR Section 1245, Subpart 1. Waiver may be requested in advance of contract award for any or all of the subject inventions, or for individually identified subject inventions reported under the contract. When waiver of rights is granted, the contractor's right to title, the rights reserved by the Government, and other conditions and obligations of the waiver shall be included in an Instrument of Waiver executed by NASA and the party receiving the waiver.

(iii) It is also a policy of NASA to consider for a monetary award, when referred to the NASA Inventions and Contributions Board, any subject invention reported to NASA in accordance with this subpart, and for which an application for patent has been filed.

(c) *Government license.* For each subject invention made in the performance of work under a NASA contract with other than a small business firm or nonprofit organization and for which waiver of rights has been granted in accordance with 14 CFR Section 1245, Subpart 1, the Administrator shall reserve an irrevocable, nonexclusive, nontransferable, royalty-free license for the practice of such invention throughout the world by or on behalf of the United States or any foreign Government in accordance with any treaty or agreement of the United States.

(d) *Government right to receive title.* Under any NASA contract with other than a small business or nonprofit organization (i.e., those contracts subject to Section 305(a) of the Act), title to subject inventions vests in NASA when the determinations of Section 305(a)(1) or 305(a)(2) have been made. The Administrator may grant a waiver of title in accordance with 14 CFR Section 1245.

(e) *Utilization reports.* For any NASA contract with other than a small business firm or a nonprofit organization, the requirements for utilization reports shall be as set forth in the NASA Patent Waiver Regulations, 14 CFR Section 1245, Subpart 1, and any Instrument of Waiver executed under those Regulations.

(f) *March-in rights.* For any NASA contract with other than a small business firm or a nonprofit organization, the march-in rights shall be as set forth in the NASA Patent Waiver Regulations, 14 CFR Section 1245, Subpart 1, and any Instrument of Waiver executed under those Regulations.

(g) *Preference for United States industry.* Waiver of the requirement for the agreement for any NASA contract with other than a small business firm or a nonprofit organization shall be in accordance with the NASA Patent Waiver Regulations, 14 CFR Section 1245, Subpart 1.

(i) *Minimum rights to contractor.*

(1) For NASA contracts with other than a small business firm or a nonprofit organization (i.e., those contracts subject to Section 305(a) of the Act), where title to any subject inventions vests in NASA, the contractor is normally granted, in accordance with 14 CFR 1245, a revocable, nonexclusive, royalty-free license in each patent application filed in any country and in any resulting patent. The license extends to any of the contractor's domestic subsidiaries and affiliates within the corporate structure, and includes the right to grant sublicenses of the same scope to the extent the contractor was legally obligated to do so at the time the contract was awarded. The license and right are transferable only with the approval of the Administrator, except when transferred to the successor of that part of the contractor's business to which the invention pertains.

(2) The Administrator is the approval authority for revoking or modifying a license. The procedures for revocation or modification are described in 37 CFR 404.10 and 14 CFR 1245.108.

NFS 1827.303 Contract clauses. (NASA supplements paragraphs (a), (b), (c) and (d))

(a)(1)(A) See 1827.303-70(a).

(B) To qualify for the clause at FAR 52.227-11, a prospective contractor may be required to represent itself as either a small business firm or a nonprofit organization. If there is reason to question the status of the prospective contractor, the contracting officer may file a protest in accordance with FAR 19.302 if small business firm status is questioned, or require the prospective contractor to furnish evidence of its status as nonprofit organization.

(5) Alternate IV to 52.227-11 is not used in NASA contracts. See instead 1827.303-70(a).

(b)(1)(ii) FAR 52.227-12 is not used in NASA contracts. See instead 1827.303-70(b).

(c)(1)(ii) When work is to be performed outside the United States, its possessions, and Puerto Rico by contractors that are not domestic firms, see 1827.303-70(f).

(2) See 1827.303-70 (b) and (f).

(d)(1) When one of the conditions in FAR 27.303(d)(1) (i) through (iv) is met, the contracting officer shall consult with the installation intellectual property counsel to determine the appropriate clause.

NFS 1827.303-70 NASA solicitation provisions and contract clauses.

(a) When the clause at FAR 52.227-11 is included in a solicitation or contract, it shall be modified as set forth at 1852.227-11.

(b) The contracting officer shall insert the clause at 1852.227-70, New Technology, in all NASA solicitations and contracts with other than a small business firm or a nonprofit organization (i.e., those subject to section 305(a) of the Act), if the contract is to be performed in the United States, its possessions, or Puerto Rico and has as a purpose the performance of experimental, developmental, research, design, or engineering work. Contracts for any of the following purposes may be considered to involve the performance of work of the type described above (these examples are illustrative and not limiting):

(1) Conduct of basic or applied research.

(2) Development, design, or manufacture for the first time of any machine, article of manufacture, or composition of matter to satisfy NASA's specifications or special requirements.

(3) Development of any process or technique for attaining a NASA objective not readily attainable through the practice of a previously developed process or technique.

(4) Testing of, evaluation of, or experimentation with a machine, process, concept, or technique to determine whether it is suitable or could be made suitable for a NASA objective.

(5) Construction work or architect-engineer services having as a purpose the performance of experimental, developmental, or research work or test and evaluation studies involving such work.

(6) The operation of facilities or the coordination and direction of the work of others, if these activities involve performing work of any of the types described in paragraphs (b)(1) through (5) of this section.

(c) The contracting officer shall insert the provision at 1852.227-71, Requests for Waiver of Rights to Inventions, in all solicitations that include the clause at 1852.227-70, New Technology (see paragraph (b) of this section).

(d) The contracting officer shall insert the clause at 1852.227-72, Designation of New Technology Representative and Patent Representative, in all solicitations and contracts containing either of the clauses at FAR 52.227-11, Patent Rights—Retention by the Contractor (Short Form) or 1852.227-70, New Technology (see paragraph (c) of this section). It may also be inserted, upon consultation with the installation intellectual property counsel, in solicitations and contracts using another patent rights clause. The New Technology Representative shall be the Technology Utilization Officer or the Staff member (by titled position) having cognizance of technology utilization matters for the installation concerned. The Patent Representative shall be the intellectual property counsel (by titled position) having cognizance of patent matters for the installation concerned.

(e) The contracting officer shall insert the provision at 1852.227-84, Patent Rights Clauses, in solicitations for experimental, developmental, or research work to be performed in the United States, its possessions, or Puerto Rico when the eventual awardee may be a small business or a nonprofit organization.

(f) As authorized in FAR 27.303(c)(2), when work is to be performed outside the United States, its possessions, and Puerto Rico by contractors that are not domestic firms, the clause at 1852.227-85, Invention Reporting and Rights—Foreign, shall be used unless the contracting officer determines, with concurrence of the installation intellectual property counsel, that the objectives of the contract would be better served by use of the clause at FAR 52.227-13, Patent Rights—Acquisition by the Government. For this purpose, the contracting officer may presume that a contractor is not a domestic firm unless it is known that the firm is not foreign owned, controlled, or influenced. (See FAR 27.304-4(a) regarding subcontracts with U.S. firms.)

NFS 1827.304 Procedures.

NFS 1827.304-1 General. (NASA supplements paragraphs (a), (b), (c), (f), (g), and (h))

(a) Contractor appeals of exceptions. In any contract with other than a small business firm or nonprofit organization, the NASA Patent Waiver Regulations, 14 CFR Section 1245, Subpart 1, shall apply.

(b) *Greater rights determinations.* In any contract with other than a small business firm or a nonprofit organization and with respect to which advance waiver of rights has not been granted (see 1827.302(b)), the contractor (or an employee-inventor of the contractor after consultation with the contractor) may request waiver of title to an individual identified subject invention pursuant to the NASA Patent Waiver Regulations, 14 CFR Section 1245, Subpart 1.

(c) *Retention of rights by inventor.* The NASA Patent Waiver Regulations, 14 CFR Section 1245, Subpart 1, apply for any invention made in the performance of work under any contract with other than a small business firm or a nonprofit organization.

(f) *Revocation or modification of contractor's minimum rights.* Revocation or modification of the contractor's license rights (see 1827.302-(i)(2)) shall be in accordance with 37

CFR 404.10, for subject inventions made and reported under any contract with other than a small business firm or a nonprofit organization.

(g) *Exercise of march-in rights.* For contracts with other than a small business firm or a nonprofit organization, the procedures for the exercise of march-in rights shall be as set forth in the NASA Patent Waiver Regulations, 14 CFR Section 1245, Subpart 1.

(h) *Licenses and assignments under contracts with nonprofit organizations.* The Headquarters Associate General Counsel (Intellectual Property) (Code GP) is the approval authority for assignments. Contractor requests should be made to the Patent Representative designated in the clause at 1852.227-72 and forwarded, with recommendation, to Code GP for approval.

NFS 1827.304-2 Contracts placed by or for other Government agencies. (NASA supplements paragraph (a))

(a)(3) When a contract is placed for another agency and the agency does not request the use of a specific patent rights clause, the contracting officer, upon consultation with the installation intellectual property counsel, may use the clause at FAR 52.227-11, Patent Rights—Retention by the Contractor (Short Form) as modified by 1852.227-11 (see 1827.303-70(a)) or 1852.227-70, New Technology (see 1827.303-70(b)).

NFS 1827.304-3 Contracts for construction work or architect-engineer services. (NASA supplements paragraph (a))

(a) For construction or architect-engineer services contracts with other than a small business or nonprofit organization, see 1827.303-70(b).

NFS 1827.304-4 Subcontracts. (NASA supplements paragraph (a))

(a)(i) Unless the contracting officer otherwise authorizes or directs, contractors awarding subcontracts and subcontractors awarding lower-tier subcontracts shall select and include one of the following clauses, suitably modified to identify the parties, in the indicated subcontracts:

(A) The clause at 1852.227-70, New Technology, in any subcontract with other than a small business firm or a nonprofit organization if a purpose of the subcontract is the performance of experimental, developmental, research, design, or engineering work of any of the types described in 1827.303-70(b) (1)-(6).

(B) The clause at FAR 52.227-11, Patent Rights—Retention by the Contractor (Short Form), modified by 1852.227-11 (see 1827.303-70(a)), in any subcontract with a small business firm or a nonprofit organization if a purpose of the subcontract is the performance of experimental, developmental, or research work.

(ii) Whenever a prime contractor or a subcontractor considers it inappropriate to include one of the clauses discussed in paragraph (a) of this section in a particular subcontract, or a subcontractor refuses to accept the clause, the matter shall be resolved by the contracting officer in consultation with the intellectual property counsel.

NFS 1827.304-5 Appeals.

FAR 27.304-5 shall apply unless otherwise provided in the NASA Patent Waiver Regulations, 14 CFR Section 1245, Subpart 1.

NFS 1827.305 Administration of the patent rights clauses.

NFS 1827.305-3 Follow-up by Government.

NFS 1827.305-370 NASA patent rights and new technology follow-up procedures.

(a) For each contract containing a patent rights clause or the clause at 1852.227-70, New Technology, the contracting officer shall take the following actions:

(1) Furnish, or require the contractor or furnish directly, the New Technology Representative and the Patent Representative a copy of each contract (and modifications thereto), and copies of the final technical report, interim technical progress reports, and other pertinent material provided under the contract, unless the representatives indicate otherwise; and

(2) Notify the New Technology Representative as to which installation organizational element has technical cognizance of the contract.

(b) The New Technology Representative shall take the following actions:

(1) Review the technical progress of work performed under the contract to ascertain whether the contractor and its subcontractors are complying with the clause's reporting and recordkeeping requirements;

(2) Forward to the Patent Representative copies of all contractor and subcontractor written reports of reportable items and disclosures of subject inventions, and a copy of the written statement, if any, submitted with the reports.

(3) Consult with the Patent Representative whenever a question arises as to whether a given reportable item is to be considered a subject invention and whether it was made in the performance of work under the contract.

(4) Forward to the Patent Representative all correspondence relating to inventions and waivers under the New Technology clause or election of title under the Patent Rights—Retention by the Contractor (Short Form) clause.

(5) Upon receipt of any final report required by the clause, and upon determination that the contract work is complete, determine whether the contractor has complied with the clause's reporting requirements. If so, the New Technology Representative shall certify

compliance, obtain the Patent Representative's concurrence, and forward the certification to the contracting officer.

(c) The Patent Representative shall review each reportable item to ascertain whether it is to be considered a subject invention, obtain any determinations required by paragraph (b) of the clause at 1852.227-70, New Technology, and notify the contractor. As to any subject invention, the Patent Representative shall:

(1) Ensure that the contractor has provided sufficient information to protect the Government's rights and interests in it and to permit the preparation, filing, and prosecution of patent applications;

(2) Determine inventorship;

(3) Ensure the preparation of instruments establishing the Government's rights' and

(4) Conduct selected reviews to ensure that subject inventions are identified, adequately documented, and timely reported or disclosed.

(d) Either the New Technology Representative or the Patent Representative, in consultation with the other, may prepare opinions, make determinations, and otherwise advise the contracting officer with respect to any withholding of payment under paragraph (g) of the clause at 1852.227-70, New Technology. Either the New Technology Representative or the Patent Representative may represent the contracting officer for the purpose of examining the contractor's books, records, and other documents in accordance with paragraph (f) of the clause and take corrective action as appropriate. However, no action may be taken by either the New Technology Representative or the Patent Representative that would constitute a final decision under the Disputes clause, involve any change or increase in the work required to be performed under the contact that is inconsistent with any right of appeal provided in FAR 27.304-5 or 14 CFR 1245, Subpart 1, or otherwise be outside the scope of the contract.

(e) The contracting officer shall not approve release of final payment under the contract and, if applicable, any reserve set aside under the withholding provisions of the clause for deficiencies and delinquent reporting not corrected as of the time of the submission of the final report by the contractor until receipt of the New Technology Representative's certification of compliance, and the Patent Representative's concurrence.

NFS 1827.305-371 New technology reporting plan.

In contracts with an estimated cost in excess of $2,500,000 (or less when appropriate) that contain the clause at 1852.227-70, New Technology, the contracting officer may require the contractor to submit for post-award Government approval a detailed plan for new technology reporting that demonstrates an adequate understanding of and commitment to the reporting requirements of the clause.

NFS 1827.305-4 Conveyance of invention rights acquired by the Government. (NASA supplements paragraph (a))

(a) When the Government acquires the entire right to, title to, and interest in an invention under the clause at 1852.227-70, New Technology, a determination of title is to be made in accordance with Section 305(a) of the National Aeronautics and Space Act of 1958, as amended (42 U.S.C. 2457(a)), and reflected in appropriate instruments executed by NASA and forwarded to the contractor.

NFS 1852.227-11 Patent Rights—Retention by the Contractor (Short Form).

As prescribed at 1827.303-70(a) modify the clause at FAR 52.227-11 by adding the following subparagraph (5) to paragraph (f) of the basic clause. In addition, use the following subparagraph (2) in lieu of subparagraph (g)(2) of the basic clause:

(5) The contractor shall provide the contracting officer the following:

(i) A listing every 12 months (or such longer period as the contracting officer may specify) from the date of the contract, of all subject inventions required to be disclosed during the period.

(ii) A final report prior to closeout of the contract listing all subject inventions or certifying that there were none.

(iii) Upon request, the filing date, serial number and title, a copy of the patent application, and patent number and issue date for any subject invention in any country in which the contractor has applied for patents.

(iv) An irrevocable power to inspect and make copies of the patent application file, by the Government, when a Federal Government employee is a coinventor.

(End of addition)

(2) The contractor shall include this clause in the NASA FAR Supplement at 1852.227-70, New Technology, suitably modified to identify the parties, in all subcontracts, regardless of tier, for experimental, developmental, research, design, or engineering work to be performed by other than a small business firm or nonprofit organization.

(End of substitution)

NFS 1852.227-14 Rights In Data—General.

As prescribed in 1827.409(a), add the following subparagraph (3) to paragraph (d) of the basic clause at FAR 52.227-14:

(3)(i) The Contractor agrees not to establish claims to copyright, publish or release to others any computer software first produced in the performance of this contract without the Contracting Officer's prior written permission.

(ii) If the Government desires to obtain copyright in computer software first produced in the performance of this contract and permission has not been granted as set forth in paragraph (d)(3)(i) of this clause, the Contracting Officer may direct the contractor to assert, or authorize the assertion of, claim to copyright in such data and to assign, or obtain the assignment of, such copyright to the Government or its designated assignee.

(iii) Whenever the word "establish" is used in this clause, with reference to a claim to copyright, it shall be construed to mean "assert".

(End of addition)

NFS 1852.227-17 Rights in Data—Special Works

As prescribed in 1827.409(i), add the following paragraph (f) to the basic clause at FAR 52.227-17:

(f) Whenever the words "establish" and "establishment" are used in this clause, with reference to a claim to copyright, they shall be construed to mean "assert" and "assertion", respectively.

(End of addition)

NFS 1852.227-19 Commercial Computer Software—Restricted Rights.

(a) As prescribed in 1827.409(k)(i), add the following paragraph (e) to the basic clause at FAR 52.227-19:

(e) For the purposes of receiving updates, correction notices, consultation information, or other similar information regarding any computer software delivered under this contract/purchase order, the NASA Contracting Officer or the NASA Contracting Officer's Technical Representative/User may sign any vendor supplied agreements, registration forms, or cards and return them directly to the vendor; however, such signing shall not alter any of the rights or obligations of either NASA or the vendor set forth in this clause or elsewhere in this contract/purchase order.

(End of addition)

(b) As prescribed in 1827.409(k)(ii), add the following paragraph (f) to the basic clause at FAR 52.227-19:

(f) Subject to paragraphs (a) through (e) above, those applicable portions of the Contractor's standard commercial license or lease agreement pertaining to any computer software delivered under this purchase order/contract that are consistent with Federal laws, standard industry practices, and the Federal Acquisition Regulation (FAR) shall be incorporated into and made part of this purchase order/contract.

(End of addition)

NFS 1852.227-70 New technology.

As prescribed in 1827.303-70(b), insert the following clause:

NEW TECHNOLOGY (NOVEMBER 1998)

(a) *Definitions.*

"Administrator," as used in this clause, means the Administrator of the National Aeronautics and Space Administration (NASA) or duly authorized representative.

"Contract," as used in this clause, means any actual or proposed contract, agreement, understanding, or other arrangement, and includes any assignment, substitution of parties, or subcontract executed or entered into thereunder.

"Made," as used in this clause, means conception or first actual reduction to practice; *provided,* that in the case of a variety of plant, the date of determination (as defined in section 41(d) of the Plant Variety Protection Act, 7 U.S.C. 2401(d)) must also occur during the period of contract performance.

"Nonprofit organization," as used in this clause, means a domestic university or other institution of higher education or an organization of the type described in section 501(c)(3) of the Internal Revenue Code of 1954 (26 U.S.C. 501(c)) and exempt from taxation under section 501(a) of the Internal Revenue Code (26 U.S.C. 501(a)), or any domestic nonprofit scientific or educational organization qualified under a State nonprofit organization statute.

"Practical application," as used in this clause, means to manufacture, in the case of a composition or product; to practice, in the case of a process or method; or to operate, in case of a machine or system; and, in each case, under such conditions as to establish that the invention is being utilized and that its benefits are, to the extent permitted by law or Government regulations, available to the public on reasonable terms.

"Reportable item," as used in this clause, means any invention, discovery, improvement, or innovation of the contractor, whether or not patentable or otherwise protectible under Title 35 of the United States Code, made in the performance of any work under any NASA contract or in the performance of any work that is reimbursable under any clause in any NASA contract providing for reimbursement of costs incurred before the effective date of the contract. Reportable items include, but are not limited to, new processes, machines, manufactures, and compositions of matter, and improvements to, or new applications of, existing processes, machines, manufactures, and compositions of matter. Reportable items also include new computer programs, and improvements to, or new applications of, existing computer programs, whether or not copyrightable or otherwise protectible under Title 17 of the United States Code.

"Small business firm," as used in this clause, means a domestic small business concern as defined at 15 U.S.C. 632 and implementing regulations of the Administrator of the Small Business Administration. (For the purpose of this definition, the size standard contained in 13 CFR 121.3-8 for small business contractors and in 13 CFR 121.3-12 for small business subcontractors will be used.)

"Subject invention," as used in this clause, means any reportable item which is or may be patentable or otherwise protectible under Title 35 of the United States Code, or any novel variety of plant that is or may be protectible under the Plant Variety Protection Act (7 U.S.C. 2321, *et seq.*).

(b) *Allocation of principal rights*—(1) *Presumption of title.* (i) Any reportable item that the Administrator considers to be a subject invention shall be presumed to have been made in the manner specified in paragraph (1) or (2) of section 305(a) of the National Aeronautics and Space Act of 1958 (42 U.S.C. 2457(a)) (hereinafter called "the Act"), and the above presumption shall be conclusive unless at the time of reporting the reportable item the Contractor submits to the Contracting Officer a written statement, containing supporting details, demonstrating that the reportable item was not made in the manner specified in paragraph (1) or (2) of section 305(a) of the Act.

(ii) Regardless of whether title to a given subject invention would otherwise be subject to an advance waiver or is the subject of a petition for waiver, the Contractor may nevertheless file the statement described in subdivision (b)(1)(i) of thisclause. The Administrator will review the information furnished by the Contractor in any such statement and any other available information relating to the circumstances surrounding the making of the subject invention and will notify the Contractor whether the Administrator has determined that the subject invention was made in the manner specified in paragraph (1) or (2) of section 305(a) of the Act.

(2) *Property rights in subject inventions.* Each subject invention for which the presumption of subdivision (b)(1)(i) of this clause is conclusive or for which there has been a determination that it was made in the manner specified in paragraph (1) or (2) of section 305(a) of the Act shall be the exclusive property of the United States as represented by NASA unless the Administrator waives all or any part of the rights of the United States, as provided in subparagraph (b)(3) of this clause.

(3) *Waiver of rights.* (i) Section 305(f) of the Act provides for the promulgation of regulations by which the Administrator may waive the rights of the United States with respect to any invention or class of inventions made or that may be made under conditions specified in paragraph (1) or (2) of section 305(a) of the Act. The promulgated NASA Patent Waiver Regulations, 14 CFR Section 1245, Subpart 1, have adopted the Presidential Memorandum on Government Patent Policy of February 18, 1983, as a guide in acting on petitions (requests) for such waiver of rights.

(ii) As provided in 14 CFR Part 1245, Subpart 1, Contractors may petition, either prior to execution of the contract or within 30 days after execution of the contract, for advance waiver of rights to any or all of the inventions that may be made under a contract. If such a petition is not submitted, or if after submission it is denied, the Contractor (or an employee inventor of the Contractor) may petition for waiver of rights to an identified subject invention within eight months of first disclosure of invention in accordance with subparagraph (e)(2) of this clause, or within such longer period as may be authorized in accordance with 14 CFR 1245.105.

(c) *Minimum rights reserved by the Government.* (1) With respect to each subject invention for which a waiver of rights is applicable in accordance with 14 CFR 1245, Subpart 1, the Government reserves—

(i) An irrevocable, nonexclusive, nontransferable, royalty-free license for the practice of such invention throughout the world by or on behalf of the United States or any foreign government in accordance with any treaty or agreement with the United States; and

(ii) Such other rights as stated in 14 CFR 1245.107.

(2) Nothing contained in this paragraph (c) shall be considered to grant to the Government any rights with respect to any invention other than a subject invention.

(d) *Minimum rights to the Contractor.* (1) The Contractor is hereby granted a revocable, nonexclusive, royalty-free license in each patent application filed in any country on a subject invention and any resulting patent in which the Government acquires title, unless the Contractor fails to disclose the subject invention within the times specified in subparagraph (e)(2) of this clause. The Contractor's license extends to its domestic subsidiaries and affiliates, if any, within the corporate structure of which the Contractor is a party and includes the right to grant sublicenses of the same scope to the extent the Contractor was legally obligated to do so at the time the contract was awarded. The license is transferable only with the approval of the Administrator except when transferred to the successor of that part of the Contractor's business to which the invention pertains.

(2) The Contractor's domestic license may be revoked or modified by the Administrator to the extent necessary to achieve expeditious practical application of the subject invention pursuant to an application for an exclusive license submitted in accordance with 37 CFR Part 404, Licensing of Government Owned Inventions. This license will not be revoked in that field of use or the geographical areas in which the Contractor has achieved practical application and continues to make the benefits of the invention reasonably accessible to the public. The license in any foreign country may be revoked or modified at the discretion of the Administrator to the extent the Contractor, its licensees, or its domestic subsidiaries or affiliates have failed to achieve practical application in that foreign country.

(3) Before revocation or modification of the license, the Contractor will be provided a written notice of the Administrator's intention to revoke or modify the license, and the Contractor will be allowed 30 days (or such other time as may be authorized by the Administrator for good cause shown by the Contractor) after the notice to show cause why the license should not be revoked or modified. The Contractor has the right to appeal to the Administrator any decision concerning the revocation or modification of its license.

(e) *Invention identification, disclosures, and reports.* (1) The Contractor shall establish and maintain active and effective procedures to assure that reportable items are promptly identified and disclosed to Contractor personnel responsible for the administration of this New Technology clause within six months of conception and/or first actual reduction to practice, whichever occurs first in the performance of work under this contract. These procedures shall include the maintenance of laboratory notebooks or equivalent records and other records as are reasonably necessary to document the conception and/or the first actual reduction to practice of the reportable items, and records that show that the procedures for identifying and disclosing reportable items are followed. Upon request, the Contractor shall furnish the Contracting Officer a description of such procedures for evaluation and for determination as to their effectiveness.

(2) The Contractor will disclose each reportable item to the Contracting Officer within two months after the inventor discloses it in writing to Contractor personnel responsible for the administration of this New Technology clause or, if earlier, within six months after the Contractor becomes aware that a reportable item has been made, but in any event for subject inventions before any on sale, public use, or publication of such invention known to the Contractor. The disclosure to the agency shall be in the form of a written report and shall identify the contract under which the reportable item was made and the inventor(s) or innovator(s). It shall be sufficiently complete in technical detail to convey a clear understanding, to the extent known at the time of the disclosure, of the nature, purpose, operation, and physical, chemical, biological, or electrical characteristics of the reportable item. The disclosure shall also identify any publication, on sale, or public use of any subject invention and whether a manuscript describing such invention has been submitted for publication and, if so, whether it has been accepted for publication at the time of disclosure. In addition, after disclosure to the agency, the Contractor will promptly notify the agency of the acceptance of any manuscript describing a subject invention for publication or of any on sale or public use planned by the Contractor for such invention.

(3) The Contractor shall furnish the Contracting Officer the following:

(i) Interim reports every 12 months (or such longer period as may be specified by the Contracting Officer) from the date of the contract, listing reportable items during that period, and certifying that all reportable items have been disclosed (or that there are no such inventions) and that the procedures required by subparagraph (e)(1) of this clause have been followed.

(ii) A final report, within 3 months after completion of the contracted work, listing all reportable items or certifying that there were no such reportable items, and listing all subcontracts at any tier containing a patent rights clause or certifying that there were no such subcontracts.

(4) The Contractor agrees, upon written request of the Contracting Officer, to furnish additional technical and other information available to the Contractor as is necessary for the preparation of a patent application on a subject invention and for the prosecution of the patent application, and to execute all papers necessary to file patent applications on subject inventions and to establish the Government's rights in the subject inventions.

(5) The Contractor agrees, subject to paragraph 27.302(i), of the Federal Acquisition Regulation (FAR), that the Government may duplicate and disclose subject invention

disclosures and all other reports and papers furnished or required to be furnished pursuant to this clause.

(f) Examination of records relating to inventions. (1) The Contracting Officer or any authorized representative shall, until 3 years after final payment under this contract, have the right to examine any books (including laboratory notebooks), records, and documents of the Contractor relating to the conception or first actual reduction to practice of inventions in the same field of technology as the work under this contract to determine whether—

(i) Any such inventions are subject inventions;

(ii) The Contractor has established and maintained the procedures required by subparagraph (e)(1) of this clause; and

(iii) The Contractor and its inventors have complied with the procedures.

(2) If the Contracting Officer learns of an unreported Contractor invention that the Contracting Officer believes may be a subject invention, the Contractor may be required to disclose the invention to the agency for a determination of ownership rights.

(3) Any examination of records under this paragraph will be subject to appropriate conditions to protect the confidentiality of the information involved.

(g) Withholding of payment (this paragraph does not apply to subcontracts). (1) Any time before final payment under this contract, the Contracting Officer may, in the Government's interest, withhold payment until a reserve not exceeding $50,000 or 5 percent of the amount of this contract, whichever is less, shall have been set aside if, in the Contracting Officer's opinion, the Contractor fails to—

(i) Establish, maintain, and follow effective procedures for identifying and disclosing reportable items pursuant to subparagraph (e)(1) of this clause;

(ii) Disclose any reportable items pursuant to subparagraph (e)(2) of this clause;

(iii) Deliver acceptable interim reports pursuant to subdivision (e)(3)(i) of this clause; or

(iv) Provide the information regarding subcontracts pursuant to subparagraph (h)(4) of this clause.

(2) Such reserve or balance shall be withheld until the Contracting Officer has determined that the Contractor has rectified whatever deficiencies exist and has delivered all reports, disclosures, and other information required by this clause.

(3) Final payment under this contract shall not be made before the Contractor delivers to the Contracting Officer all disclosures of reportable items required by subparagraph (e)(2) of this clause, and an acceptable final report pursuant to subdivision

(e)(2) of this clause, and an acceptable final report pursuant to subdivision (e)(3)(ii) of this clause.

(4) The Contracting Officer may decrease or increase the sums withheld up to the maximum authorized above. No amount shall be withheld under this paragraph while the amount specified by this paragraph is being withheld under other provisions of the contract. The withholding of any amount or the subsequent payment thereof shall not be construed as a waiver of any Government rights.

(h) *Subcontracts.*(1) Unless otherwise authorized or directed by the Contracting Officer, the Contractor shall—

(i) Include this clause (suitably modified to identify the parties) in any subcontract hereunder (regardless of tier) with other than a small business firm or nonprofit organization for the performance of experimental, developmental, or research work; and

(ii) Include the clause at FAR 52.227-11 (suitably modified to identify the parties) in any subcontract hereunder (regardless of tier) with a small business firm or nonprofit organization for the performance of experimental, developmental, or research work.

(2) In the event of a refusal by a prospective subcontractor to accept such a clause the Contractor—

(i) Shall promptly submit a written notice to the Contracting Officer setting forth the subcontractor's reasons for such refusal and other pertinent information that may expedite disposition of the matter; and

(ii) Shall not proceed with such subcontract without the written authorization of the Contracting Officer.

(3) In the case of subcontracts at any tier, the agency, subcontractor, and Contractor agree that the mutual obligations of the parties created by this clause constitute a contract between the subcontractor and NASA with respect to those matters covered by this clause.

(4) The Contractor shall promptly notify the Contracting Officer in writing upon the award of any subcontract at any tier containing a patent rights clause by identifying the subcontractor, the applicable patent rights clause, the work to be performed under the subcontract, and the dates of award and estimated completion. Upon request of the Contracting Officer, the Contractor shall furnish a copy of such subcontract, and, no more frequently than annually, a listing of the subcontracts that have been awarded.

(5) The subcontractor will retain all rights provided for the Contractor in the clause of subdivision (h)(1)(i) or (ii) of this clause, whichever is included in the subcontract, and the Contractor will not, as part of the consideration for awarding the subcontract, obtain rights in the subcontractor's subject inventions.

(i) *Preference for United States industry.* Unless provided otherwise, no Contractor that receives title to any subject invention and no assignee of any such Contractor shall grant to any person the exclusive right to use or sell any subject invention in the United States unless such person agrees that any products embodying the subject invention will be manufactured substantially in the United States. However, in individual cases, the requirement may be waived by the Administrator upon a showing by the Contractor or assignee that reasonable but unsuccessful efforts have been made to grant licenses on similar terms to potential licensees that would be likely to manufacture substantially in the United States or that under the circumstances domestic manufacture is not commercially feasible.

(End of clause)

NFS 1852.227-71 Requests for waiver of rights to inventions.

As prescribed in 1827.303-70(c), insert the following provision in all solicitations that include the clause at 1852.227-70, New Technology:

REQUESTS FOR WAIVER OF RIGHTS TO INVENTIONS (APRIL 1984)

(a) In accordance with the NASA Patent Waiver Regulations, 14 CFR Part 1245, Subpart 1, waiver of rights to any or all inventions made or that may be made under a NASA contract or subcontract with other than a small business firm or a domestic nonprofit organization may be requested at different time periods. Advance waiver of rights to any or all inventions that may be made under a contract or subcontract may be requested prior to the execution of the contract or subcontract, or within 30 days after execution by the selected contractor. In addition, waiver of rights to an identified invention made and reported under a contract or subcontract may be requested, even though a request for an advance waiver was not made or, if made, was not granted.

(b) Each request for waiver of rights shall be by petition to the Administrator and shall include an identification of the petitioner; place of business and address; if petitioner is represented by counsel, the name, address and telephone number of the counsel; the signature of the petitioner or authorized representative; and the date of signature. No specific forms need be used, but the request should contain a positive statement that waiver of rights is being requested under the NASA Patent Waiver Regulations; a clear indication of whether the request is for an advance waiver or for a waiver of rights for an individual identified invention; whether foreign rights are also requested and, if so, the countries, and a citation of the specific section or sections of the regulations under which such rights are requested; and the name, address, and telephone number of the party with whom to communicate when the request is acted upon. Requests for advance waiver of rights should, preferably, be included with the proposal, but in any event in advance of negotiations.

(c) Petitions for advance waiver, prior to contract execution, must be submitted to the Contracting Officer. All other petitions will be submitted to the Patent Representative designated in the contract.

(d) Petitions submitted with proposals selected for negotiation of a contract will be forwarded by the Contracting Officer to the installation Patent Counsel for processing and then to the Inventions and Contributions Board. The Board will consider these petitions and where the Board makes the findings to support the waiver, the Board will recommend to the

Administrator that waiver be granted, and will notify the petitioner and the Contracting Officer of the Administrator's determination. The Contracting Officer will be informed by the Board whenever there is insufficient time or information or other reasons to permit a decision to be made without unduly delaying the execution of the contract. In the latter event, the petitioner will be so notified by the Contracting Officer. All other petitions will be processed by installation Patent Counsel and forwarded to the Board. The Board shall notify the petitioner of its action and if waiver is granted, the conditions, reservations, and obligations thereof will be included in the Instrument of Waiver. Whenever the Board notifies a petitioner of a recommendation adverse to, or different from, the waiver requested, the petitioner may request reconsideration under procedures set forth in the Regulations.

(End of provision)

NFS 1852.227-72 Designation of new technology representative and patent representative.

As prescribed in 1827.303-70(d), insert the following clause:

DESIGNATION OF NEW TECHNOLOGY REPRESENTATIVE AND PATENT REPRESENTATIVE (JUL 1997)

(a) For purposes of administration of the clause of this contract entitled "New Technology" or "Patent Rights—Retention by the Contractor (Short Form)," whichever is included, the following named representatives are hereby designated by the Contracting Officer to administer such clause:

Title

Office code

Address (including zip code)

New Technology Representative

Patent Representative

(b) Reports of reportable items, and disclosure of subject inventions, interim reports, final reports, utilization reports, and other reports required by the clause, as well as any correspondence with respect to such matters, should be directed to the New Technology Representative unless transmitted in response to correspondence or request from the Patent Representative. Inquiries or requests regarding disposition of rights, election of rights, or related matters should be directed to the Patent Representative. This clause shall be included in any subcontract hereunder requiring a "New Technology" clause or "Patent Rights—Retention by the Contractor (Short Form)" clause, unless otherwise authorized or directed by the Contracting Officer. The respective responsibilities and authorities of the above-named representatives are set forth in 1827.305-370 of the NASA FAR Supplement.

NFS 1852.227-84 Patent rights clauses.

The contracting officer shall insert the following provision as prescribed in 1827.303-70(e).

Patent Rights Clauses (December 1989)

This solicitation contains the patent rights clauses of FAR 52.227-11 (as modified by the NFS) and NFS 1852.227-70. If the contract resulting from this solicitation is awarded to a small business or nonprofit organization, the clause at NFS 1852.227-70 shall not apply. If the award is to other than a small business or nonprofit organization, the clause at FAR 52.227-11 shall not apply.

(End of Provision)

NFS 1852.227-85 Invention reporting and rights—foreign.

As prescribed in 1827.303-70(f), insert the following clause:

INVENTION REPORTING AND RIGHTS—FOREIGN (APRIL 1986)

(a) As used in this clause, the term "invention" means any invention, discovery or improvement, and "made" means the conception or first actual demonstration that the invention is useful and operable.

(b) The Contractor shall report promptly to the Contracting Officer each invention made in the performance of work under this contract. The report of each such invention shall:

(1) Identify the inventor(s) by full name; and

(2) Include such full and complete technical information concerning the invention as is necessary to enable an understanding of the nature and operation thereof.

(c) The Contractor hereby grants to the Government of the United States of America as represented by the Administrator of the National Aeronautics and Space Administration the full right, title and interest in and to each such invention throughout the world, except for the State in which this contract is to be performed. As to such State, Contractor hereby grants to the Government of the United States of America as represented by the Administrator of the National Aeronautics and Space Administration only an irrevocable, nontransferable, nonexclusive, royalty-free license to practice each such invention by or on behalf of the United States of America or any foreign government pursuant to any treaty or agreement with the United States of America, provided that Contractor within a reasonable time files a patent application in that State for each such invention. Where Contractor does not elect to file such patent application for any such invention in that State, full right, title and interest in and to such invention in that State shall reside in the Government of the United States of America as represented by the Administrator of the National Aeronautics and Space Administration.

(d) The Contractor agrees to execute or to secure the execution of such legal instruments as may be necessary to confirm and to protect the rights granted by paragraph (c) of this clause, including papers incident to the filing and prosecution of patent applications.

(e) Upon completion of the contract work, and prior to final payment, Contractor shall submit to the Contracting Officer a final report listing all inventions reportable under this contract or certifying that no such inventions have been made.

(f) In each subcontract, the Contractor awards under this contract where the performance of research, experimental design, engineering, or developmental work is contemplated, the Contractor shall include this clause and the name and address of the Contracting Officer.

(End of Clause)

NFS 1852.227-86 Commercial computer software—licensing.

As prescribed in 1827.409-70, insert the following clause:

COMMERCIAL COMPUTER SOFTWARE—LICENSING
(DECEMBER 1987)

(a) Any delivered commercial computer software (including documentation thereof) developed at private expense and claimed as proprietary shall be subject to the restricted rights in paragraph (d) of this clause. Where the vendor/contractor proposes its standard commercial software license, those applicable portions thereof consistent with Federal laws, standard industry practices, the Federal Acquisition Regulations (FAR) and the NASA FAR Supplement, including the restricted rights in paragraph (d) of this clause, are incorporated into and made a part of this purchase order/contract.

(b) Although the vendor/contractor may not propose its standard commercial software license until after this purchase order/contract has been issued, or at or after the time the computer software is delivered, such license shall nevertheless be deemed incorporated into and made a part of this purchase order/contract under the same terms and conditions as in paragraph (a) of this clause. For purposes of receiving updates, correction notices, consultation, and similar activities on the computer software, the NASA Contracting Officer or the NASA Contracting Officer's Technical Representative/User may sign any agreement, license, or registration form or card and return it directly to the vendor/contractor; however, such signing shall not alter any of the terms and conditions of this clause.

(c) The vendor's/contractor's acceptance is expressly limited to the terms and conditions of this purchase order/contract. If the specified computer software is shipped or delivered to NASA, it shall be understood that the vendor/contractor has unconditionally accepted the terms and conditions set forth in this clause, and that such terms and conditions (including the incorporated license) constitute the entire agreement between the parties concerning rights in the computer software.

(d) The following restricted rights shall apply:

(1) The commercial computer software may not be used, reproduced, or disclosed by the Government except as provided below or otherwise expressly stated in the purchase order/contract.

(2) The commercial computer software may be—

(i) Used, or copied for use, in or with any computer owned or leased by, or on behalf of, the Government; provided, the software is not used, nor copied for use, in or with more than one computer simultaneously, unless otherwise permitted by the license incorporated under paragraphs (a) or (b) of this clause;

(ii) Reproduced for safekeeping (archives) or backup purposes;

(iii) Modified, adapted, or combined with other computer software, provided that the modified, combined, or adapted portions of the derivative software incorporating restricted computer software shall be subject to the same restricted rights; and

(iv) Disclosed and reproduced for use by Government contractors or their subcontractors in accordance with the restricted rights in subdivisions (d)(2) (i), (ii), and (iii) of this clause; provided they have the Government's permission to use the computer software and have also agreed to protect the computer software from unauthorized use and disclosure.

(3) If the incorporated vendor's/contractor's software license contains provisions or rights that are less restrictive than the restricted rights in subparagraph (d)(2) of this clause, then the less restrictive provisions or rights shall prevail.

(4) If the computer software is published, copyrighted computer software, it is licensed to the Government, without disclosure prohibitions, with the rights in subparagraphs (d) (2) and (3) of this clause.

(5) The computer software may be marked with any appropriate proprietary notice that is consistent with the rights in subparagraphs (d) (2), (3), and (4) of this clause.

(End of clause)

NFS 1852.227-87 Transfer of Technical Data Under Space Station International Agreements.

As prescribed at 1827.670-2, insert the following clause:

TRANSFER OF TECHNICAL DATA UNDER
SPACE STATION INTERNATIONAL AGREEMENT (APRIL 1989)

1. In the cooperative Space Station Freedom program, NASA has the authority to provide to the international partners all information necessary to implement the multilateral Space Station Intergovernmental Agreement and the Space Station Memoranda of Understanding. NASA is committed under these Space Station agreements to provide its interna-

tional Space Station partners with certain technical data which are subject to the U.S. export control laws and regulations. NASA will have obtained any necessary approvals from the Department of State for the transfer of any such technical data. Space Station contractors, acting as agents of NASA under the specific written direction of the Contracting Officer, or designated representative, require no other separate approval under the International Traffic in Arms Regulations (ITAR) to transfer such data.

2. The Contractor agrees, when specifically directed in writing by the Contracting Officer, or designated representative, to transfer identified technical data to a named foreign recipient, in the manner directed. No export control marking should be affixed to the data unless so directed. If directed, the text of the marking to be affixed will be furnished by the Contracting Officer or designated representative.

3. It should be emphasized that the transfer is limited solely to those technical data which NASA specifically identifies and directs the Contractor to transfer in accordance with 2, above, and that all other transfers of technical data to foreign entities are subject to the requirements of the U.S. export control laws and regulations.

4. Nothing contained in this clause affects the allocation of technical data rights between NASA and the Contractor or any subcontractors as set forth in the Rights in Data clause of this Contract, nor the protection of any proprietary technical data which may be available to the Contractor or any subcontractor under that clause.

5. The Contractor agrees to include this clause, including this paragraph 5, in all subcontracts hereunder, appropriately modified to reflect the relationship of the parties.

(End of clause)

DEPARTMENT OF ENERGY

SUBPART 927.3

DEAR 927.300 General.

(a) One of the primary missions of the Department of Energy is the use of its procurement process to ensure the conduct of research, development, and demonstration leading to the ultimate commercialization of efficient sources of energy. To accomplish its mission, DOE must work in cooperation with industry in the development of new energy sources and in achieving the ultimate goal of widespread commercial use of those energy sources. To this end, Congress has provided DOE with the authority to invoke an array of incentives to secure the commercialization of new technologies developed for DOE. One such important incentive is provided by the patent system.

(b) Pursuant to 42 U.S.C. 2182 and 42 U.S.C. 5908, DOE takes title to all inventions conceived or first actually reduced to practice in the course of or under contracts with large, for-profit companies, foreign organizations, and others not beneficiaries of Pub. L. 96-517. Regulations dealing with Department's authority to waive its title to subject inventions, including the relevant statutory objectives, exist at 10 CFR part 784. Pursuant to that section, DOE may waive the Government's patent rights in appropriate situations at the time of contracting to encourage industrial participation, foster commercial utilization and competition, and make the benefits of DOE activities widely available to the public. In addition to considering the waiver of patent rights at the time of contracting, DOE will also consider the incentive of a waiver of patent rights upon the reporting of an identified invention when requested by such entities or by the employee-inventor with the permission of the contractor. These requests can be made whether or not a waiver request was made at the time of contracting. Waivers for identified inventions will be granted where it is determined that the patent waiver will be a meaningful incentive to achieving the development and ultimate commercial utilization of inventions. Where DOE grants a waiver of the Government's patent rights, either at the time of contracting or after an invention is made, certain minimum rights and obligations will be required by DOE to protect the public interest.

(c) Another major DOE mission is to manage the nation's nuclear weapons and other classified programs, where research and development procurements are directed toward processes and equipment not available to the public. To accomplish DOE programs for bringing private industry into these and other special programs to the maximum extent permitted by national security and policy considerations, it is desirable that the technology developed in these programs be made available on a selected basis for use in the particular fields of interest and under controlled conditions by properly cleared industrial and scientific research institutions. To ensure such availability and control, the grant of waivers in these programs may necessarily be more limited, either by the imposition of field of use restrictions or national security measures, than in other DOE programs.

DEAR 927.302 Policy.

(a) Except for contracts with organizations that are beneficiaries of Public Law 96-517, the United States, as represented by DOE, shall normally acquire title in and to any invention or discovery conceived or first actually reduced to practice in the course of or under the contract, allowing the contractor to retain a nonexclusive, revocable, paid-up license in the invention and the right to request permission to file an application for a patent and retain title to any ensuing patent in any foreign country in which DOE does not elect to secure patent rights. DOE may approve the request if it determines that such approval would be in the national interest. The contractor's nonexclusive license may be revoked or modified by DOE only to the extent necessary to achieve expeditious practical application of the invention pursuant to any application for and the grant of an exclusive license in the invention to another party.

(b) In contracts having as a purpose the conduct of research, development, or demonstration work and in certain other contracts, DOE may need to require those contractors that are not the beneficiaries of Public Law 96-517 to license background patents to ensure reasonable public availability and accessibility necessary to practice the subject of the contract in the fields of technology specifically contemplated in the contract effort. That need may arise where the contractor is not attempting to take the technology resulting from the contract to the commercial marketplace, or is not meeting market demands. The need for background patent rights and the particular rights that should be obtained for either the Government or the public will depend upon the type, purpose, and scope of the contract effort, impact on the DOE program, and the cost to the Government of obtaining such rights.

(c) Provisions to deal specifically with DOE background patent rights are contained in paragraph (k) of the clause at 952.227-13. That paragraph may be modified with the concurrence of Patent Counsel in order to reflect the equities of the parties in particular contracting situations. Paragraph (k) should normally be deleted for contracts with an estimated cost and fee or price of $250,000 or less and may not be appropriate for certain types of study contracts; for planning contracts; for contracts with educational institutions; for contracts for specialized equipment for in-house Government use, not involving use by the public; and for contracts the work products of which will not be the subject of future procurements by the Government or its contractors.

(d) The Assistant General Counsel for Technology Transfer and Intellectual Property shall:

(1) Make the determination that whether reported inventions are subject inventions under the patent rights clause of the contract;

(2) Determine whether and where patent protection will be obtained on inventions;

(3) Represent DOE before domestic and foreign patent offices;

(4) Accept assignments and instruments confirmatory of the Government's rights to inventions; and

(5) Represent DOE in patent, technical data, and copyright matters not specifically reserved to the Head of the Agency or designee.

DEAR 927.303 Contract clauses.

(a) In solicitations and contracts for experimental, research, developmental, or demonstration work (but see (FAR) 48 CFR 27.304-3 regarding contracts for construction work or architect-engineer services), the contracting officer shall include the clause:

(1) At 952.227-13, Patent Rights Acquisition by the Government, in all such contracts other than those described in paragraphs (a)(2) and (a)(3) of this section;

(2) At 952.227-11, Patent Rights by the Contractor (Short Form), in contracts in which the contractor is a domestic small business or nonprofit organization as defined at (FAR) 48 CFR 27.301, except where the work of the contract is subject to an Exceptional Circumstances Determination by DOE; and

(3) At 970.5227-10, 970.5227-11, or 970.5227-12, as discussed in 970.27, Patent, Data, and Copyrights, in contracts for the management and operation of DOE laboratories and production facilities.

(b) DOE shall not use the clause at (FAR) 48 CFR 52.227-12 except in situations where patent counsel grants a request for advance waiver pursuant to 10 CFR 784 and supplies the contracting officer with that clause with appropriate modifications. Otherwise, in instances in which DOE grants an advance waiver or waives its rights in an identified invention pursuant to CFR part 784, contracting officers shall consult with patent counsel for the appropriate clause.

(c) Any contract that has as a purpose the design, construction, operation, or management integration of a collection of contracts for the same purpose, of a Government-owned research, development, demonstration or production facility must accord the Government certain rights with respect to further use of the facility by or on behalf of the Government upon termination of the contract. The patent rights clause in such contracts must include the following facilities license paragraph:

[Insert appropriate paragraph no.] Facilities License. In addition to the rights of the parties with respect to inventions or discoveries conceived or first actually reduced to practice in the course of or under this contract, the Contractor agrees to and does hereby grant to the Government an irrevocable, nonexclusive, paid-up license in and to any inventions or discoveries regardless of when conceived or actually reduced to practice or acquired by the Contractor at any time through completion of this contract and which are incorporated or embodied in the construction of the facility or which are utilized in the operation of the facility or which cover articles, materials, or products manufactured at the facility (1) to practice or have practiced by or for the Government at the facility, and (2) to transfer such license with the transfer of that facility. Notwithstanding the acceptance or exercise by the Government of these rights, the Government may contest at any time the enforceability, validity or scope of, title to, any rights or patents herein licensed.

DEAR 927.370 [Reserved]

[Removed and reserved]

DEAR 927.304 Procedures.

Where the contract contains the clause at 952.227-11 and the contractor does not elect to retain title to a subject invention, DOE may consider and, after consultation with the contractor, grant requests for retention of rights by the inventor subject to the provisions of 35 U.S.C. 200 et seq. This statement is in lieu of (FAR) 48 CFR 27.304-1(c).

POSTAL REGULATIONS

CHAPTER 9

SECTION 1   GENERAL POLICIES

9.1.1 Acquiring Intellectual Property Rights

a. General. Patents, copyrights, and other rights in data are valuable intellectual property. The Postal Service acquires patents, copyrights, and other rights in data as necessary to:

1. Enhance the competitive purchasing process;

2. Ensure the ability to use, maintain, repair, and modify equipment or products procured under Postal Service contracts;

3. Recoup development costs of, and fund improvements in, Postal products and equipment;

4. Develop products and equipment for Postal Service and public use; and

5. Protects its position in the competitive marketplace.

b. Nonimpairment of Private Rights. The Postal Service's efforts directed toward competition (4.1) must not improperly demand or use data relating to privately developed intellectual property rights. The Postal Service complies with applicable laws regarding intellectual property rights. The Postal Service, however, will not refuse to award a contract on the grounds that the prospective contractor might infringe a patent. See 9.2.3.

c. Commercial Application. The Postal Service encourages commercial application of inventions made under its contracts consistent with its expressed policies for acquisition of data rights and inventions.

d. Indemnification for Use of Private Patents for Commercial Items. The Postal Service seeks indemnification for a contractor's use of private patents when the supplies or services procured are sold in the commercial open market.

e. Claims Against USPS. Contractors must protect the Postal Service against claims resulting from contractors' use of data not supplied by the Postal Service.

SECTION 2   ACQUISITION OF RIGHTS

9.2.1 General

a. The Postal Service acquires patent rights, rights in data, and rights in software to the degree necessary to protect the Postal Service's interest. Those rights can include:

1. Postal Service title to patents.

2. Less than Postal Service title to patents, such as nonexclusive licenses.

3. Unlimited rights or title to technical data and software.

4. Limited rights to technical data and restricted rights in software. These rights may be exclusive or nonexclusive.

b. Because the Postal Service is charged with behaving in a businesslike way, it is appropriate for it to consider acquiring these rights in manners consistent with its business purpose. Determinations in this regard are to be made by the contracting officer, with the advice of the requiring activity and counsel, giving full consideration to the costs and benefits of the chosen approach. Thus, for example, decisions to acquire Postal Service title to patents or unlimited rights to technical data developed by the contractor at private expense must take into account the impact of the decision on the cost of the contract and the extent to which prospective offerors may not wish to part with such rights. Conversely, determinations to take only lesser rights must consider the effect on the Postal Service of the exploitation of those rights by the contractor or others.

9.2.2 Acquisition of Patent Rights

a. Covered Contracts. This part 9.2.2 applies to all contracts and subcontracts for research, experimental, developmental, or engineering work or for initial production of products or equipment developed under a Postal Service contract.

b. Postal Service Title. Postal Service title must be acquired to subject inventions under a covered contract unless the contracting officer, after consultation with the requiring activity and the patent counsel, determines that an alternate arrangement is in the best interest of the Postal Service. The determination concerning alternate arrangements may be made at the time of solicitation (see c., or d. and e., below).

c. Less than Postal Service Title. When appropriate, the Postal Service may acquire less that title to subject inventions under covered contracts. However, in no case may the Postal Service acquire less than a nonexclusive royalty-free license to make, use, and sell each subject invention throughout the world on behalf of the Postal Service. If the Postal Service takes less than title, it may allow the contractor to retain title to all subject inventions, or may allow the contractor to elect whether to retain title on an invention-by-invention basis. When contractors are allowed to retain title, the contract must provide adequate provisions allowing the Postal Service to control the contractor's sale of the invention to competitors of the Postal Service. As an alternative, the contracting officer may consider providing for a sharing of revenue for all commercial sales of the invention, subject to a requirement that any sale of a subject invention to an organization which provides postal or parcel delivery services in competition with the Postal Service requires the advance written approval of the contracting officer. Any such alternative must be coordinated with the patent counsel.

d. Alternate Proposals

1. The contracting officer may consider any alternative proposal giving a contractor greater rights in an invention made in the performance of a contract than the solicitation contemplates if it will yield a net benefit to the Postal Service.

2. Provision 9-1, *Alternate Intellectual Property Rights Proposals*, may be included in all solicitations for covered contracts, and alternate proposals may be considered as part of the evaluation process.

e. Alternate Agreements after Award. An alternate agreement on patent rights for inventions developed at contractor expense but intended for delivery under a covered contract may be negotiated after award when in the interest of the Postal Service. Before initiating negotiations, the contracting officer must seek the advice of patent counsel.

f. Other Contracts. The contracting officer may provide for Postal Service acquisition of patent rights or may solicit alternate agreements for contracts not covered by this part with the concurrence of patent counsel. Particular consideration should be given to including such provision in noncovered contracts if it appears likely that the contractor will make an invention in performing the contract.

g. Clauses. Clause 9-1, *Patent Rights*, must be included in contracts in which the Postal Service will take title to inventions. Clause 9-15, *Patent Rights—Contractor Retention*, must be included in contracts providing for the contractor' election to retain invention rights. If an alternate patent proposal is accepted, the clause must be appropriately modified, with the concurrence of counsel, to reflect the specific right sin subject inventions that will be acquired by the Postal Service. The modified clause must clearly state that all other Postal Service rights in subject inventions remain in effect with full force. When Clause 9-15 is included in contracts, Clause 9-16, *Postal Service Title in Technical Data and Computer Software*, must also be included.

9.2.3 Use of Private Patents

a. Authorization and Consent

1. When the Government has authorized or consented to the manufacture or use of an invention described in and covered by a U.S. Patent, suit for recovery of the reasonable and entire compensation for the manufacture or use of the invention by or for the United States by a contractor (including a subcontractor at any tier) can be maintained only against the Government in the United State Court of Federal Claims and not against the contractor oar subcontractor (28 U.S.C. § 1498). To ensure that work by a contractor or subcontractor under a Postal Service contract may not be enjoined by reason of patent infringement, the Postal Service provides its authorization and consent to the use of private patents by its

contractors and subcontractors in certain situations. Broad authorization and consent is provided in the conduct of research and development activities so that the contractor or subcontractor need not avoid or invent around particular technology areas. In contracts for supplies or construction, a more limited authorization and consent is provided.

2. The liability of the Postal Service for damages in a suit of the nature described in Subparagraph a.1. above against it may ultimately be borne by the contractor or subcontractor in accordance with the terms of any patent indemnity clause included in the contract, and an authorization and consent clause does not detract from any patent indemnification commitment by the contractor or subcontractor. Therefore, both a patent indemnity clause and an authorization and consent clause may be included in the same contract.

3. Clause 9-2, *Authorization and Consent*, must be included in all covered contracts except those awarded using simplified procedures (see 4.2) or performed outside the United States.

b. Notice and Assistance

1. Clause 9-3, *Notice and Assistance Regarding Patent and Copyright Infringement*, must be included in all covered contracts except those awarded using simplified procedures (see 4.2) or performed outside the United States.

2. If the contracting officer receives notice of an infringement claim, patent counsel must be notified immediately.

9.2.4 Patent Indemnification

a. Indemnification by Postal Service. The contracting officer may not use any contract clause providing for indemnification by the Postal Service for patent infringement by a contract or subcontractor.

b. Indemnification by Contractor

1. The Postal Service's policy is to acquire indemnification for the use, by or on behalf of the Postal Service, of private patents without the authorization or consent of the patentee, when the use relates to supplies or services that the contractor offers or provides to the commercial open market.

2. Except as provided in Paragraph c. below, Clause 9-4, *Patent Indemnity*, must be included in all contracts not awarded using simplified procedures. The clause may be used in other contracts if patent infringement is likely.

c. Waiver or Modification of Patent Indemnity

1. If it is in the interest of the Postal Service to do so, the contracting officer may waive or modify the right to patent indemnification, with the prior approval of patent counsel. If the waiver or modification to the right to patent indemnification is for research or

development, Clause 9-5, *Waiver of Indemnity*, must be used, and the contract must be modified as applicable patents are identified.

2. If patent indemnification will be waived completely, Clause 9-4 may not be used.

3. Clause 9-5, *Waiver of Indemnity*, must be used if the waiver applies only to specific patents. Those patents to which the waiver applies must be listed in the clause.

Clause 9-1   Patent Rights (October 1987)

a. Definitions Used in This Clause

1. "Subject invention." Any invention or discovery, whether or not patentable, conceived or first actually reduced to practice in the course of or under this contract. The term includes, but is not limited to, any art, method, process, machine, manufacture, design, or composition of matter, or any new and useful improvement thereof, or any variety of plant, that is or may be patentable under the patent laws of the United States of America or any foreign country.

2. "Postal Service purposes." The right of the Postal Service to practice and have practiced (make or have made, use or have used, sell or have sold) any subject invention throughout the world by or on behalf o the U.S. Postal Service.

3. "Contract." Any contract, agreement, or other agreement or subcontract entered into, with, or for the benefit of the Postal Service.

4. "Subcontract and subcontractor." Any subcontract or subcontractor of the contractor under this contract and any lower-tier subcontract or subcontractor under the contract.

5. "To bring the invention to the point of practical application." To manufacture (in the case of a composition or product), practice (in the case of a process), or operate (in the case of a machine or system) under such conditions as to establish that the invention works and that its benefits are reasonably accessible to the public.

b. Rights Granted to the Postal Service. The contractor agrees to grant the Postal Service title in and to each subject invention. Nothing contained in this *Patent Rights* clause grants any rights with respect to any invention other than a subject invention.

c. Subject Invention Disclosure and Reports

1. With respect to subject inventions, the contractor must furnish the contracting officer the items described in (a) through (e) below:

(a) A written disclosure of each invention promptly after conception or first actual reduction to practice, whichever occurs first under this contract, sufficiently complete in technical detail to convey to one skilled in the art to which the invention pertains a clear understanding of the nature, purpose, operation, and (to the extent known) the physical, chemical, or electrical characteristics of the invention. When unable to submit a complete disclosure, the contractor must, within three months, submit a disclosure that includes all such technical detail then known; and unless the contracting officer authorizes a different period, submit all other technical detail necessary to complete the disclosure within three additional months.

(b) Before final settlement of this contract, a final report listing each invention, including all those previously listed, or certifying that there are no unreported inventions. (This final report and any interim report under (a) above must be submitted on Form 7398, *Report of Inventions and Subcontracts*, or other format acceptable to the contracting officer.)

(c) Information in writing, as soon as practicable, of the date and identity of any (1) public use, sale, or publication of the invention made by or known to the contractor or (2) contemplated publication by the contractor.

(d) Upon request, any duly executed instruments and other papers (prepared by the Postal Service) necessary to (1) vest in the Postal Service the rights granted it under this clause and (2) enable the Postal Service to apply for and prosecute any patent application, in any country covering the invention, where the Postal Service has the right under this clause to file such an application.

(e) Upon request, an irrevocable power of attorney to inspect and make copies of each United States patent application filed by, or on behalf of, the contractor covering the invention.

2. With respect to each subject invention in which the contractor has been granted rights, under license or otherwise, the contractor agrees to provide written reports at reasonable intervals, when requested by the Postal Service, as to:

(a) The commercial use being or intended to be made of the invention;

(b) Royalties payable to the Postal Service; and

(c) The steps taken by the contractor to bring the invention to the point of practical application, or to make the invention available for licensing.

d. Subcontracts

1. The contractor must, unless otherwise authorized or directed by the contracting officer, include a patent rights clause containing all the provisions of this *Patent Rights* clause except Paragraph g. below in any subcontract where a purpose of the subcontract is the conduct of experimental, developmental, research, or engineering work. If a subcontractor refused to accept this clause, the contractor:

(a) Must promptly submit a written report to the contracting officer setting forth the subcontractor's reasons for the refusal and any other pertinent information that may expedite disposition of the matter; and

(b) May not proceed with the subcontract without the written authorization of the contracting officer. The contractor may not, in any subcontract, or by using subcontract as consideration thereof, acquire any rights to subject inventions for its own use (as distinguished from rights required to fulfill its contract obligations to the Postal Service in the performance of this contract). Reports, instruments, and other information required to be furnished by a subcontractor to the contracting officer under a patent rights clause in a subcontract may, upon mutual consent of the contractor and the subcontractor (or by direction of the contracting officer), be furnished to the contractor for transmission to the contracting officer.

2. The contractor, at the earliest practicable date, must notify the contracting officer in writing of any subcontract containing a patent rights clause, furnish to the contracting officer a copy of the subcontract, and notify the contracting officer when the subcontract is completed. The Postal Service is a third-party beneficiary of any subcontract granting rights to the Postal Service in subject inventions, and the contractor hereby assigns to the Postal Service all the rights that the contractor would have to enforce the subcontractor's obligations for the benefit of the Postal Service with respect to subject inventions, the contractor is not obligated to enforce the agreements of any subcontractor relating to the obligation of the subcontractor to the Postal Service regarding subject inventions.

e. Domestic Filing of Patent Applications by Contractor

1. If, pursuant to Paragraph h. below, greater rights are granted in a subject invention to the extent that the contractor may claim the invention, the contractor must file in due form and within six months of the granting of these rights a United States patent application claiming the invention and furnish, as soon as practicable, the serial number and filing date of the application and the patent number of any resulting patent. As to each invention in which the contractor has been given greater rights, the contractor must notify the contracting officer at the end of the six-month period if it has failed to file or cause to be filed a patent application covering the invention. If the contractor has field or caused to be filed such an application within the six-month period, but elects not to continue prosecution of the application, it must notify the contracting officer not less than 60 days before the expiration of the response period. In either of these situations, the contractor forfeits all rights previously granted.

2. The following statement must be included in the first paragraph of any patent application filed or patent issued on an invention made under a Postal Service contract or a subcontract under Postal Service contract: "The invention herein described was made in the course of or under a contract or subcontract thereunder with the United States Postal Service."

f. Foreign Filing of Patent Applications

1. If the contractor acquires greater rights in a subject invention and has filed a United States patent application claiming the invention, the contractor, or any party other than the Postal Service deriving rights from the contractor, has the exclusive rights, subject to the rights of the Postal Service, to file applications on the inventions in each foreign country within:

(a) Six months from the date a corresponding United State patent application is filed; or

(b) Such longer period as the contracting officer may approve.

2. The contractor must notify the contracting officer of each foreign application filed and, upon written request of the contracting officer, furnish an English translation of the application and convey to the Postal Service the entire right title and interest in the invention in each foreign country in which an application has not been filed within the time specified in Subparagraph f.1. preceding.

g. Withholding Payment

1. Final payment under this contact will not be made until the contractor delivers to the contracting officer the reports required by Paragraph c. above and all information as to subcontract required by Paragraph d. above.

2. If action is deemed warranted because of the contractor's performance under the *Patent Rights* clause of this contract or of other Postal Service contracts, the contracting officer may withhold from payments such sums as considered appropriate, not exceeding $50,000, or 10 percent of the amount of this contract, whichever is less, to be held as a reserve until the contractor delivers all the reports, disclosures, and information specified in Paragraph c. above.

h. Contractor's Request for Greater Rights. The contractor, at the time of first disclosing a subject invention pursuant to Paragraph c.1.(a) above, but not later than three months thereafter, may submit in writing to the contracting officer a request for rights by license or otherwise in any invention. The contracting officer will review the contractor's request for rights and will notify the contractor whether it is granted in whole or in part. Any rights granted the contractor will be subject to, but not necessarily limited to, the provisions of Paragraph i. following.

i. Reservation of Rights to the Postal Service

1. If rights in any subject invention are vested in or granted to the contractor, such rights will, as a minimum, be subject to an irrevocable, nonexclusive, and royalty-free license to practice and have practiced the invention throughout the world for Postal Service purposes, including its practice:

(a) In the manufacture, use, and disposition of any article or material;

(b) In the use of any method; or

(c) In the performance of any service, acquired by or for the Postal Service or with funds otherwise derived through the Postal Service.

2. If rights are vested in the contractor, the contractor agrees to, and grants to the Postal Service the rights to, require the granting of a license to an applicant under any such invention:

(a) On a nonexclusive basis, unless the contractor, a licensee, or an assignee demonstrates to the Postal Service, at its request, that (1) effective steps have been taken within three years after a patent issues on the invention to bring the invention to the point of practical application or (2) the invention has been made available for licensing on terms that are reasonable in the circumstances, or can show cause why the title should be retained for a further period of time; or

(b) On terms that are reasonable in the circumstances to the extent that the invention is required for public use by the Postal Service regulations or as may be necessary to fulfill health needs, or for other public purposes stipulated in the Schedule of this contract.

j. Right to Disclose Subject Inventions. The Postal Service may duplicate and disclose reports and disclosures of subject inventions required to be furnished by the contractor pursuant to this *Patent Rights* clause.

k. Forfeiture of Rights in Unreported Subject Inventions. The contractor forfeits to the Postal Service all rights in any subject invention that it fails to report to the contracting officer where or before it:

1. Files or causes to be filed a United States or foreign application thereon; or

2. Submits the final report required by c1(b) above, whichever occurs later, provided, that the contractor will not forfeit rights in a subject invention if:

(a) Contending that the invention is not a subject invention, it nevertheless reports the invention and the facts pertinent to its contention to the contracting officer within the time specified in k1 or k2 above; or

(b) It establishes that failure to report was due entirely to causes beyond its control and without its fault or negligence. The contractor is deemed to hold any such forfeited subject invention, and the patent applications and patents pertaining to it, in trust for the Postal Service pending written assignment of the invention. The rights accruing to the Postal Service under this Paragraph k. are in addition to, and do not supersede, any other rights the Postal Service may have in relation to unreported subject inventions. Nothing contained in this clause may be construed to required the contractor to report any invention that is not in fact a subject invention.

l. Examination of Records Relating to Inventions. The contracting officer, or an authorized representative, until the expiration of three years after final payment under this contract, has the right to examine any books, records, documents, and other supporting data of the contractor that the contracting officer or authorized representative reasonably deems directly pertinent to the discovery or identification of subject inventions or to compliance by the contractor with the requirements of this clause.

Clause 9-2   Authorization and Consent (October 1987)

a. Research and Development Work. The Postal Service authorizes and consents to all use and manufacture of any invention covered by a U.S. patent in the performance of research, development, or experimental work called for, or performed as a necessary activity, in the performance of this contract or any subcontract, at any tier.

b. Supplies and Construction. The Postal Service authorizes and consents to all use and manufacture of any invention covered by a U.S. patent in performing this contract or subcontract, at any tier, that is:

1. Embodied in the structure or composition of any article, the delivery of which is accepted by the Postal Service under this contract; or

2. Used in machinery, tools, or methods whose use necessarily results from compliance by the contractor or subcontractor with (a) specifications or written provisions forming a part of this contract or (b) specific written instructions given by the contracting officer directing the manner of performance.

c. Determination of Liability. The liability of the Postal Service for patent infringement or for the unauthorized use of any patent will be determined by the provisions of any patent indemnity clause included in this contract or in any subcontract under this contract (at any tier) and by an indemnification or warranty (express or implied) otherwise provided by the contractor or subcontractor for similar products or services when supplied to commercial buyers.

d. Flowdown. The contractor must include, and require inclusion of, this clause, suitably modified to identify the parties, in all subcontracts under this contract at any tier that are expected to exceed $50,000.

Clause 9-3   Notice and Assistance Regarding Patent and Copyright Infringement (October 1987)

a. The contractor must report to the contracting officer, in writing, promptly and in reasonable detail, any notice, claim, or suit regarding patent or copyright infringement (or unauthorized use of a patent or copyright) based on performance on this contract.

b. At the contracting officer's request, the contractor must furnish all evidence and information in its possession pertaining to the suit or claim. The evidence and information will be furnished at the expense of the Postal Service except when the contractor has agreed to indemnify the Postal Service.

c. This clause must be included in all subcontracts under this contract, at any tier, over $50,000.

Clause 9-4   Patent Indemnity (October 1987)

a. Except as provided in Paragraph d. below, the contractor indemnifies the Postal Service, its employees, and its agents against liability, including costs and fees, for patent infringement (or unauthorized use) arising from the manufacture, use, or delivery of supplies, the performance of service, the construction or alteration of real property, or the disposal of property by or for the Postal Service, if the supplies, service, or property (with or without relatively minor modifications) have been or are being offered for sale or use in the commercial marketplace by the contractor.

b. The Postal Service must promptly notify the contractor of any claim or suit subject to the indemnity of Paragraph a. above alleging patent infringement or unauthorized use of a patent.

c. To the extent allowable by law, the contractor may participate in the defense of any suit to which this clause applies.

d. This indemnification does not apply to:

1. Infringements for the unauthorized use of a private patent covered by this indemnity resulting form the contracting officer's specific written direction, compliance with which requires an infringement; or

2. Infringement or unauthorized use claims that are unreasonably settled without the contractor's consent before litigation.

e. This clause must be included in all subcontracts under this contract, at any tier, over $50,000.

Clause 9-5   Waiver of Indemnity (October 1987)

a. The Postal Service authorized the making and use, solely in performing the contract, of any invention covered by the below-listed patents and waives indemnification by the contractor solely with respect to these patents.

b. The specific patents to which this waiver applies are as follows:

(*Contracting officer list each patent*)

Clause 9-15   Patent Rights—Contractor Retention (December 1992)

a. Definitions

1. "Subject invention" means any invention or discovery of the contractor conceived or first actually reduced to practice in the course of or under this contract, and

includes any art, method, process, machine, manufacture, design, or composition of matter, or any new and useful improvement thereof, or any variety of plant, which is or may be patentably under the Patent Laws of the United States of America or any foreign country.

2. "Contract" means any contract, agreement, grant, or other arrangement or subcontract entered into with or for the benefit of the Postal Service where a purpose of the contract is the conduct of experimental, developmental, or research work.

3. "States and domestic municipal governments" means the States of the United States, the District of Columbia, Puerto Rico, the Virgin Islands, American Samoa, Guam, the Trust Territory of the Pacific Islands, and any political subdivision and agencies thereof.

4. "To bring to the point of practical application" means to manufacture in the case of a composition or product, to practice in the case of a process, or to operate in the case of a machine and under such conditions as to establish that the invention is being worked and that its benefits are reasonably accessible to the public.

b. Allocation of Principal Rights

1. The contractor may retain the entire right, title, and interest throughout the world or any country thereof in and to each subject invention disclosed pursuant to Paragraph e.2.(a) of this clause, subject to the rights obtained by the Postal Service in Paragraph c. of this clause. The contractor must include with each subject invention disclosure an election as to whether he will retain the entire right, title, and interest in the invention throughout the world or any country thereof.

2. Subject to the license specified in Paragraph d. of this clause, the contractor agrees to convey to the Postal Service, upon request, the entire domestic right, title, and interest in any subject invention when the contractor:

(a) Does not elect under Paragraph b.1. of this clause to retain such rights; or

(b) Fails to have a United States patent application filed on the invention in accordance with Paragraph j. of this clause, or decides not to continue prosecution of such application; or

(c) At any time, no longer desire to retain title.

3. Subject to the license specified in Paragraph d. of this clause, the contractor agrees to convey to the Postal Service, upon request, the entire right, title, and interest in any subject invention in any foreign country when the contractor:

(a) Does not elect under Paragraph b.1. of this clause to retain such rights in the country; or

(b) Fails to have a patent application filed in the country on the invention in accordance with Paragraph k. of this clause, or decides not to continue prosecution or to pay any maintenance fees covering the invention. To avoid forfeiture of the patent application or patent, the contractor must notify the contracting officer not less than 60 days before the expiration period for any action required by the foreign patent office.

4. A conveyance, requested pursuant to Paragraph b.2. or b.3. of this clause, must be made by delivering to the contracting officer duly executed instruments (prepared by the Postal Service) and such other papers as are deemed necessary to vest in the Postal Service the entire right, title, and interest to enable the Postal Service to apply for and prosecute patent applications covering the invention in this of the foreign country, respectively, or otherwise establish its ownership of such invention.

c. Minimum Rights Acquired by the Postal Service. With respect to each subject invention to which the contractor retains principal or exclusive rights, the contractor:

1. Hereby grants to the Postal Service a nonexclusive, nontransferable, paid-up license to make, use, and sell each subject invention throughout the world by or on behalf of the Postal Service;

2. Agrees to grant to responsible applicants, upon request of the Postal Service, a license on terms that are reasonable under the circumstances;

(a) Unless the contractor, his licensee, or his assignee, demonstrates to the Postal Service that effective steps have been taken within three years after a patent issues on such invention to bring the invention to the point of practical application or that the invention has been made available for licensing royalty-free or on terms that are reasonable in the circumstances, or can show cause why the principal or exclusive rights should be retained for a further period of time, or

(b) To the extent that the invention is required for public use by governmental regulations or for other public purposes stipulated in this contract.

3. Must submit written reports at reasonable intervals, upon request of the Postal Service during the term of the patent on the subject invention regarding:

(a) The commercial use that is being made or is intended to be made of such invention; and

(b) The steps taken by the contractor or his transferee to bring the invention to the point of practical application, or to make the invention available for licensing.

4. Agrees to arrange, when licensing any subject inventions, to avoid royalty charges on procurements involving the Postal Service and to refund any amounts received as royalty charges on any subject invention in procurements for, or on behalf of, the Postal Service and to provide for such refund in any instrument transferring rights in such invention to any party; and

5. Agrees to provide for the Postal Service's paid-up license pursuant to Paragraph c.1. of this clause in any instrument transferring rights in a subject invention and to provide for the granting of licenses as required by Paragraph c.2. of this clause, and for reporting of utilization information as required by Paragraph c.3. of this clause whenever the instrument transfers principal or exclusive rights in any subject invention.

Nothing contained in this Paragraph c. will be deemed to grant to the Postal Service any rights with respect to any invention other than a subject invention.

d. Minimum Rights to the Contractor

1. The contractor reserves a revocable, nonexclusive, royalty-free license in each patent application filed in any country on a subject invention and any resulting patent in which the Postal Service acquires title. The license must extend to the contractor's domestic subsidiaries and affiliates, if any, within the corporate structure of which the contractor is a part and must include the right to grant sublicense of the same scope to the extent the contractor was legally obligated to do so at the time the contract was awarded. The license must be transferable only with approval of the contracting officer, except when transferred to the successor of that part of the contractor's business to which the invention pertains.

2. The contractor's domestic nonexclusive license retained pursuant to Paragraph d.1. of this clause may be revoked or modified to the extent necessary to achieve expeditious practical application of the subject invention. The license will not be revoked in that field of use and/or the geographical areas in which the contractor has brought the invention to the point of practical application and continues to make the benefits of the invention reasonably accessible to the public. The contractor's nonexclusive license in any foreign country reserved pursuant to Paragraph d.1. of this clause may be revoked or modified at the discretion of the contracting officer to the extent the contractor or his domestic subsidiaries or affiliates have failed to achieve the practical application of the invention in such foreign country.

3. Before modification or revocation of the license, pursuant to Paragraph d.2. of this clause, the contractor will be given written notice of the intent to modify or revoke the license and will be allowed 30 days or such longer period as may be authorized by the contracting officer for good cause shown in writing by the contractor after such notice to show cause why the license should not be modified or revoked. The contractor will have the right to contest any decision concerning the modification or revocation of the license in accordance with the Claims and Disputes clause of this contract.

e. Invention Identification, Disclosures, and Reports

1. The contractor must establish and maintain active and effective procedures to assure that subject inventions are promptly identified and timely disclosed. These procedures must include the maintenance of laboratory notebooks or equivalent records and other records as are reasonably necessary to document the conception and/or the first actual reduction to practice of subject inventions, and records which show that the procedures for identifying and disclosing the inventions are followed. Upon request, contractors must furnish

contracting officers a description of such procedures so that they may evaluate and determine their effectiveness.

2. The contractor must furnish the contracting officer:

(a) A complete technical disclosure for each subject invention, within six months after conception or first actual reduction to practice, whichever occurs first in the course of or under the contract, but in any event prior to any sale, public use, or publication of such invention known to the contractor. The disclosure must identify the contract and inventor(s) and be sufficiently complete in technical detail and appropriately illustrated by sketch or diagram to convey to one skilled in the art to which the invention pertains a clear understanding of the nature, purpose, operation, and to the extent known, the physical, chemical, biological, or electrical characteristics of the invention;

(b) Interim reports, preferably on PD Form 882, at least every 12 months from the date of the contract listing subject inventions during that period and certifying that:

(1) The contractor's procedures for identifying and disclosing subject inventions as required by this Paragraph e. have been followed throughout the reporting period; and

(2) All subject inventions have been disclosed or that there are no such inventions; and

(c) A final report, preferably on PS Form 882, within three months after completion of the contract work, listing all subject inventions or certifying that there were no such inventions.

3. The contractor must obtain patent agreements to effectuate the provisions of this clause from all persons in his employ who perform any part of the work under this contract except nontechnical personnel, such as clerical and manual labor personnel.

4. The contractor agrees that the Postal Service may duplicated and disclose subject invention disclosures and all other reports and papers furnished or required to be furnished pursuant to this clause.

f. Forfeiture of Rights in Unreported Subject Inventions

1. The contractor must forfeit to the Postal Service all rights in any subject invention which he fails to disclose to the contracting officer within six months after the time he:

(a) Files or causes to be filed a United States or foreign application thereon, or

(b) Submits the final report required by Paragraph e.2.(c) of this clause.

2. However, the contractor must not forfeit rights in a subject invention if, within the time specified in 1.(a) or 1.(b) of this Paragraph f., the contractor:

(a) Prepares a written decision based upon a review of the record that the invention was neither conceived nor first actually reduced to practice in the course of or under the contract; or

(b) Contending that the invention is not a subject invention, he nevertheless discloses the invention and all facts pertinent to his contention to the contracting officer; or

(c) Establishes that the failure to disclose did not result from his fault or negligence.

3. Pending written assignment of the patent applications and patents on a subject invention determined by the contracting officer to be forfeited (such determination to be a final decision under the Claims and Disputes clause), the contractor will be deemed to hold the invention and the patent applications and patents pertaining thereto in trust for the Postal Service. The forfeiture provision of this Paragraph f. will be in addition to and must not superseded other rights ad remedies which the Postal Service may have with respect to subject inventions.

g. Examination of Records Relating to Inventions

1. The contracting officer or his authorized representative will, until the expiration of three years after final payment under this contract, have the right to examine any books (including laboratory notebooks), records, documents, and other supporting data of the contractor which the contracting officer reasonably deems pertinent to the discovery or identification of subject inventions or to determine compliance with the requirements of this clause.

2. The contracting officer or his authorized representative will have the right to examine all books (including laboratory notebooks), records, and documents of the contractor relating to the conception or first actual reduction to practice of inventions in the same field of technology as the work under this contract, to determine whether any such inventions are subject inventions if the contractor refuses or fails to:

(a) Establish the procedures of Paragraph e.1. of this clause; or

(b) Maintain and follow such procedures; or

(c) Correct or eliminate any material deficiency in the procedures within 30 days after the contracting officer notifies the contractor of such a deficiency.

h. Withholding of Payment (Not Applicable to Subcontracts)

1. Any time before final payment of the amount of this contract, the contracting officer may, if he deems such action warranted, withhold payment until a reserve not

exceeding $50,000 or 5 percent of the amount of this contract, whichever is less, will have been set aside if in his opinion the contractor fails to:

(a) Establish, maintain, and follow effective procedures for identifying and disclosing subject inventions pursuant to Paragraph e.1. of this clause; or

(b) Disclose any subject invention pursuant to Paragraph e.2.(a) of this clause; or

(c) Deliver acceptable interim reports pursuant to Paragraph e.2.(b) of this clause; or

(d) Provide the information regarding subcontract pursuant to Paragraph i.5. of this clause.

Such reserve balance will be withheld until the contracting officer has determined that the contractor has rectified whatever deficiencies exist and has delivered all reports, disclosures, and other information required by this clause.

2. Final payment under this contract will not be made before the contractor delivers to the contracting officer all disclosures of subject inventions required by Paragraph e.2.(a) of this clause, an acceptable final report pursuant to e.2.(c) of this clause, and all past due confirmatory instruments.

3. The contracting officer may, in his discretion, decrease or increase the sums withheld up to the maximum authorized above. If the contractor is a nonprofit organization, the maximum amount that may be withheld under this paragraph will not exceed $50,0000 or 1 percent of the amount of this contract, whichever is less. No amount will be withheld under this paragraph while the amount specified by this paragraph is being withheld under other provisions of the contract. The withholding of any amount or subsequent payment thereof will not be construed as a waiver of any rights accruing to the Government under this contract.

i. Subcontracts

1. For the purpose of this paragraph, the term "contractor" means the party awarding a subcontract, and the term "subcontractor" means the party being awarded a subcontract, regardless of tier.

2. The contractor must include this patent rights clause in every subcontract hereunder having as a purpose the conduct of experimental, developmental, or research work, unless directed by the contracting officer to include another particular clause. In the event of a refusal by a subcontractor to accept such clause, the contractor:

(a) Must promptly submit a written notice to the contracting officer setting forth the subcontractor's reasons for such refusal and other pertinent information which may expedite disposition of the matter; and

(b) Must not proceed with the subcontract without the written authorization of the contracting officer.

3. The contractor must not, in any subcontract or by using a subcontract as consideration therefor, acquire any rights in his subcontractor's subject invention for his own use (as distinguished from such rights as may be required solely to fulfill his contract obligations to the Postal Service in the performance of this contract).

4. All invention disclosures, reports, instruments, and other information required to be furnished by the subcontractor to the contracting officer under the provisions of a patent rights clause in any subcontract hereunder may, at the discretion of the contracting officer, be furnished to the contractor for transmission to the contracting officer.

5. The contractor must promptly notify the contracting officer in writing upon the award of any subcontract containing a patent rights clause by identifying the subcontractor, the applicable patent rights clause, the work to be performed under the subcontract, and the dates of award and estimated completion. Upon request of the contracting officer, the contractor must furnish a copy of the subcontract. If there are no subcontracts containing patent rights clauses, a negative report must be included in the final report submitted pursuant to Paragraph e.2.(c) of this clause.

6. The contractor must identify all subject inventions of the subcontractor of which he acquires knowledge in the performance of this contract and must notify the contracting officer promptly upon the identification of the inventions.

7. It is understood that the Postal Service is a third party beneficiary of any subcontract clause granting rights to the Postal Service subject inventions, and the contractor hereby assigns to the Postal Service all rights that he would have to enforce the subcontractor's obligations for the benefit of the Postal Service with respect to subject inventions. The contractor will not be obligated to enforce the agreements of any subcontractor hereunder relating to the obligations of the subcontractor to the Postal Service in regard to subject inventions.

j. Filing of Domestic Patent Applications

1. With respect to each subject invention in which the contractor elects to retain domestic rights pursuant to Paragraph b. of this clause, the contractor must have a domestic patent application filed within six months after submission of the invention disclosure pursuant to Paragraph e.2.(a) of this clause, or such longer period as may be approved in writing by the contracting officer for good cause shown in writing by the contractor. With respect to such invention, the contractor must promptly notify the contracting officer of any decision not to file an application.

2. For each subject invention on which a patent application is filed by or on behalf of the contractor, the contractor must:

(a) Within two months after such filing, or within two months after submission of the invention disclosure if the patent application previously has been filed, deliver to the contracting officer a copy of the application as filed, including the filing date and serial number;

(b) Include the following statement in the second paragraph of the specification of the application and any patents issued on the subject invention.

"The U.S. Postal Service has rights in this invention pursuant to Contract No. _____."

(c) Within six months after filing the application, or within six months after submitting the invention disclosure if the application has been filed previously, deliver to the contracting officer a duly executed and approved instrument on a form specified by the contracting officer fully confirmatory of all rights to which the Postal Service is entitled, and provide the Postal Service an irrevocable power to inspect and make copies of the patent application file;

(d) Provide the contracting officer with a copy of the patent within two months after a patent issues on the application; and

(e) Not less than 30 days before the expiration of the response period for any action required by the Patent and Trademark Office, notify the contracting officer or any decision not to continue prosecution of the application and deliver to the contracting officer executed instruments granting the Government a power of attorney.

3. For each subject invention in which the contractor initially elects not to retain principal domestic rights, the contractor must inform the contracting officer promptly in writing of the date and identity of any sale, public use, or publication of such invention which may constitute a statutory bar under 35 U.S.C. § 102, which was authorized by or known to the contractor, or any contemplated action of this nature.

k. Filing of Foreign Patent Applications

1. With respect to each subject invention in which the contractor elects to retain principal rights in a foreign country pursuant to Paragraph b.1. of this clause, the contractor must have a patent application filed on the invention in such country, in accordance with applicable statutes and regulations, and within one of the following periods:

(a) Eight months from the date of a corresponding United States application filed by or on behalf of the contractor, or if such an application is not filed, six months from the date the invention is submitted in a disclosure pursuant to Paragraph e.2.(a) of this clause;

(b) Six months from the date a license is granted by the Commissioner of Patents and Trademarks to file foreign applications when such filing has been prohibited by security reasons; or

(c) Such longer period as may be approved in writing by the contracting officer.

2. The contractor must notify the contracting officer promptly of each foreign application filed and, upon written request, must furnish an English version of such foreign application without additional compensation.

NASA PART 1260

GRANTS AND COOPERATIVE AGREEMENTS

---

14 C.F.R. § 1260.28 Patent rights.

Patent Rights

October 2000

As stated at § 1260.136, this award is subject to the provisions of 37 CFR 401.3(a) which requires use of the standard clause set out at 37 CFR 401.14 "Patent Rights (Small Business Firms and Nonprofit Organizations)" and the following:

(a) Where the term "contract" or "Contractor" is used in the "Patent Rights" clause, the term shall be replaced by the term "grant" or "Recipient," respectively.

(a) Where the term "contract" or "Contractor" is used in the "Patent Rights" clause, the term shall be replaced by the term "grant" or "Recipient," respectively.

(b) In each instance where the term "Federal Agency," "agency," or "funding Federal agency" is used in the "Patent Rights" clause, the term shall be replaced by the term "NASA."

(c) The following item is added to the end of paragraph (f) of the "Patent Rights" clause: "(5) The Recipient shall include a list of any Subject Inventions required to be disclosed during the preceding year in the performance report, technical report, or renewal proposal. A complete list (or a negative statement) for the entire award period shall be included in the summary of research."

(d) The term "subcontract" in paragraph (g) of the "Patent Rights" clause shall include purchase orders.

(e) The NASA implementing regulation for paragraph (g)(2) of the "Patent Rights" clause is at 48 CFR 1827.304-4(a)(i)(B).

(f) The following requirement constitutes paragraph (l) of the "Patent Rights" clause:

"(l) Communications. A copy of all submissions or requests required by this clause, plus a copy of any reports, manuscripts, publications or similar material bearing on patent matters, shall be sent to the Center Patent Counsel and the NASA Grant Officer in addition to any other submission requirements in the grant provisions. If any reports contain information describing a "subject invention" for which the recipient has elected or may elect to retain title, NASA will use reasonable efforts to delay public release by NASA or publication by NASA in a NASA technical series until an application filing date has been established, provided that the Recipient identify the information and the "subject invention" to which it relates at the time of submittal. If required by the NASA Grant Officer, the Recipient shall provide the filing date, serial number and title, a copy of the patent application, and a patent number and issue date for any "subject invention" in any country in which the Recipient has applied for patents.

(g) NASA Inventions. NASA will use reasonable efforts to report inventions made by NASA employees as a consequence of, or which bear a direct relation to, the performance of specified NASA activities under this agreement and, upon timely request, will use reasonable efforts to grant the Recipient an exclusive, or partially exclusive, revocable, royalty-bearing license, subject to the retention of a royalty-free right of the Government to practice or have practiced the invention by or on behalf of the Government.

(h) In the event NASA contractors are tasked to perform work in support of specified activities under a cooperative agreement and inventions are made by Contractor employees, the Recipient will normally retain title to its employee inventions in accordance with 35 U.S.C. 202, 14 CFR Part 1245, and Executive Order 12591. In the event the Recipient decides not to pursue rights to title in any such invention and NASA obtains title to such inventions, NASA will use reasonable efforts to report such inventions and, upon timely request, will use reasonable efforts to grant the Recipient an exclusive, or partially exclusive, revocable, royalty-bearing license, subject to the retention of a royalty-free right of the Government to practice or have practiced the invention by or on behalf of the Government.

14 C.F.R. § 1260.29 [Reserved].

14 C.F.R. § 1260.30 Rights in data.

(The grant officer may revise the language under this provision to modify each party's rights based on the particular circumstances of the program and/or the recipient's need to protect specific proprietary information. Any modification to the standard language set forth under the provision requires the concurrence of the Center's Patent Counsel and that the provision be printed in full text.)

Rights in Data

October 2000

(a) Fully Funded Efforts.

(1) "Data" means recorded information, regardless of form, the media on which it may be recorded, or the method of recording. The term includes, but is not limited to, data of a scientific or technical nature, computer software and documentation thereof, and data comprising commercial and financial information.

(2) The Recipient grants to the Federal Government, a royalty-free, nonexclusive and irrevocable license to use, reproduce, distribute (including distribution by transmission) to the public, perform publicly, prepare derivative works, and display publicly, data in whole or in part and in any manner for Federal purposes and to have or permit others to do so for Federal purposes only.

(3) In order that the Federal Government may exercise its license rights in data, the Federal Government, upon request to the Recipient, shall have the right to review and/or obtain delivery of data resulting from the performance of work under this grant, and authorize others to receive data to use for Federal purposes.

(b) Cost Sharing and/or Matching Efforts. When the Recipient cost shares with the Government on the effort, the following paragraph applies:

"(1) In the event data first produced by Recipient in carrying out Recipient's responsibilities under an agreement is furnished to NASA, and Recipient considers such data to embody trade secrets or to comprise commercial or financial information which is privileged or confidential, and such data is so identified with a suitable notice or legend, the data will be maintained in confidence and disclosed and used by the Government and its Contractors (under suitable protective conditions) only for experimental, evaluation, research and development purposes, by or on behalf of the Government for an agreed to period of time, and thereafter for Federal purposes as defined in § 1260.30(a)(2)."

(c) For Cooperative Agreements the following paragraph applies:

"(1) As to data first produced by NASA in carrying out NASA's responsibilities under a cooperative agreement and which data would embody trade secrets or would comprise commercial or financial information that is privileged or confidential if it has been obtained from the Recipient, such data will be marked with an appropriate legend and maintained in confidence for 5 years (unless a shorter period has been agreed to between the Government and Recipient) after development of the information, with the express understanding that during the aforesaid period such data may be disclosed and used (under suitable protective conditions) by or on behalf of the Government for Government purposes only, and thereafter for any purpose whatsoever without restriction on disclosure and use. Recipient agrees not to disclose such data to any third party without NASA's written approval until the aforementioned restricted period expires."

14 C.F.R. § 1260.51 Cooperative agreement special condition.

Cooperative Agreement Special Condition

October 2000

(a) This award is a cooperative agreement as it is anticipated there will be substantial NASA involvement during performance of the effort. NASA and the Recipient mutually agree to the following statement of anticipated cooperative interactions which may occur during the performance of this effort:

(Reference the approved proposal that contains a detailed description of the work and insert a concise statement of the exact nature of the cooperative interactions that deals with existing facts and not contingencies.)

(b) The terms "grant" and "Recipient" mean "cooperative agreement" and "Recipient of cooperative agreement," respectively, wherever the terms appear in provisions and special conditions included in this agreement.

(c) NASA's ability to participate and perform its collaborative effort under this cooperative agreement is subject to the availability of appropriated funds and nothing in this cooperative agreement commits the United States Congress to appropriate funds therefor.

14 C.F.R. § 1260.52 Multiple year grant or cooperative agreement.

Multiple Year Grant or Cooperative Agreement

October 2000

This is a multiple year grant or cooperative agreement. Contingent on the availability of funds, scientific progress of the project, and continued relevance to NASA programs, NASA anticipates continuing support at approximately the following levels:

Second year $- - -, Anticipated funding date- - - .

Third year $- - -, Anticipated funding date- - - .

(Periods may be added or omitted, as applicable)

14 C.F.R. § 1260.59A Invention reporting and rights.

Invention Reporting and Rights

October 2000

(a) As used in this provision:

(1) The term "invention" means any invention or discovery which is or may be patentable or otherwise protectable under Title 35 of the United States Code, or any novel variety of plant which is or may be protected under the Plant Variety Protection Act (7 U.S.C. 2321 et seq.).

(2) The term "made" when used in relation to any invention means the conception or first actual reduction to practice of such invention.

(b) The Recipient shall report promptly to the grant officer each invention made in the performance of work under this grant. The report of such invention shall—

(1) Identify the inventor(s) by full name; and

(2) Include such full and complete technical information concerning the invention as is necessary to enable an understanding of the nature and operation thereof.

(c) Reporting shall be made on NASA Form 1679 Disclosure of Invention and New Technology (Including Software).

(d) The Recipient hereby grants to the Government of the United States of America, as represented by the Administrator of the National Aeronautics and Space Administration, the full rights, title, and interest in and to each such invention throughout the world.

TITLE 28 JUDICIARY AND JUDICIAL PROCEDURE

PART IV. JURISDICTION AND VENUE

28 U.S.C. § 1498 (2001)

---

§ 1498. Patent and copyright cases

(a) Whenever an invention described in and covered by a patent of the United States is used or manufactured by or for the United States without license of the owner thereof or lawful right to use or manufacture the same, the owner's remedy shall be by action against the United States in the United States Court of Federal Claims for the recovery of his reasonable and entire compensation for such use and manufacture. Reasonable and entire compensation shall include the owner's reasonable costs, including reasonable fees for expert witnesses and attorneys, in pursuing the action if the owner is an independent inventor, a nonprofit organization, or an entity that had no more than 500 employees at any time during the 5-year period preceding the use or manufacture of the patented invention by or for the United States. Notwithstanding the preceding sentences, unless the action has been pending for more than 10 years from the time of filing to the time that the owner applies for such costs and fees, reasonable and entire compensation shall not include such costs and fees if the court finds that the position of the United States was substantially justified or that special circumstances make an award unjust.

For the purposes of this section, the use or manufacture of an invention described in and covered by a patent of the United States by a contractor, a subcontractor, or any person, firm, or corporation for the Government and with the authorization or consent of the Government, shall be construed as use or manufacture for the United States.

The court shall not award compensation under this section if the claim is based on the use or manufacture by or for the United States of any article owned, leased, used by, or in the possession of the United States prior to July 1, 1918.

A Government employee shall have the right to bring suit against the Government under this section except where he was in a position to order, influence, or induce use of the invention by the Government. This section shall not confer a right of action on any patentee or any assignee of such patentee with respect to any invention discovered or invented by a person while in the employment or service of the United States, where the invention was related to the official functions of the employee, in cases in which such functions included research and development, or in the making of which Government time, materials or facilities were used.

(b) Hereafter, whenever the copyright in any work protected under the copyright laws of the United States shall be infringed by the United States, by a corporation owned or controlled by the United States, or by a contractor, subcontractor, or any person, firm, or corporation acting for the Government and with the authorization or consent of the Government, the exclusive action which may be brought for such infringement shall be an action by the copyright owner against the United States in the Court of Federal Claims for the recovery of his reasonable and entire compensation as damages for such infringement, including the minimum statutory damages as set forth in section 504(b) of title 17, United States Code: Provided, That a Government employee shall have a right of action against the Government under this subsection except where he was in a position to order, influence, or induce use of the copyrighted work by the Government: Provided, however, That this subsection shall not confer a right of action on any copyright owner or any assignee of such owner with respect to any copyrighted work prepared by a person while in the employment or service of the United States, where the copyrighted work was prepared as a part of the official functions of the employee, or in the preparation of which Government time, material, or facilities were used: And provided further, That before such action against the United States has been instituted the appropriate corporation owned or controlled by the United States or the head of the appropriate department or agency of the Government, as the case may be, is authorized to enter into an agreement with the copyright owner in full settlement and compromise for the damages accruing to him by reason of such infringement and to settle the claim administratively out of available appropriations.

Except as otherwise provided by law, no recovery shall be had for any infringement of a copyright covered by this subsection committed more than three years prior to the filing of the complaint or counterclaim for infringement in the action, except that the period between the date of receipt of a written claim for compensation by the Department or agency of the Government or corporation owned or controlled by the United States, as the case may be, having authority to settle such claim and the date of mailing by the Government of a notice to the claimant that his claim has been denied shall not be counted as a part of the three years, unless suit is brought before the last-mentioned date.

(c) The provisions of this section shall not apply to any claim arising in a foreign country.

(d) Hereafter, whenever a plant variety protected by a certificate of plant variety protection under the laws of the United States shall be infringed by the United States, by a corporation owned or controlled by the United States, or by a contractor, subcontractor, or any person, firm, or corporation acting for the Government and with the authorization and consent of the Government, the exclusive remedy of the owner of such certificate shall be by action against the United States in the Court of Federal Claims for the recovery of his reasonable and entire compensation as damages for such infringement: Provided, That a Government employee shall have a right of action against the Government under this subsection except where he was in a position to order, influence, or induce use of the protected plant variety by the Government: Provided, however, That this subsection shall not confer a right of action on any certificate owner or any assignee of such owner with respect to any protected plant variety made by a person while in the employment or service of the United States, where such variety was prepared as a part of the official functions of the employee, or in the preparation of which Government time, material, or facilities were used: And provided further, That before such action against the United States has been instituted, the appropriate corporation owned or controlled by the United States or the head of the appropriate agency of the Government, as the case may be, is authorized to enter into an agreement with the certificate owner in full settlement and compromise, for the damages accrued to him by reason of such infringement and to settle the claim administratively out of available appropriations.

(e) Subsections (b) and (c) of this section apply to exclusive rights in mask works under chapter 9 of title 17 [17 USCS §§ 901 et seq.], and to exclusive rights in designs under chapter 13 of title 17 [17 USCS §§ 1301 et seq.], to the same extent as such subsections apply to copyrights.